BRIEF CONTENTS

iiviii Brief Contents

12 **The Supreme Court and the African American Quest for Universal Freedom   296**

13 **State and Local Politics and the African American Quest for Universal Freedom   326**

PART V   PUBLIC POLICY   349

14 **Domestic Policy and the African American Quest for Social and Economic Justice   351**

15 **The African American Quest for Universal Freedom and U.S. Foreign Policy   372**

CONTENTS

9 Voting Behavior and Elections 194

PART IV INSTITUTIONS 221

10 The Congress and the African American Quest for Universal Freedom 223

PREFACE

Overview of the Text

The eighth edition of this long-standing text arrives at a momentous point in the nation's race relations: The end of the first African American presidency and the beginning of what seems to be a pitched battle between African American citizens and the police. The policing problem in America is, of course, nothing new. What is new is the persistence and prevalence of police involved shootings attracting not just media and popular attention, but spawning new movements against it, notably Black Lives Matter, featured prominently in the revised edition of the text.

This book examines the institutions and processes of American government and politics from the perspective of the African American presence and influence. We want to show how the presence of Africans in the United States affected the founding of the Republic and its political institutions and processes from the colonial era to the present. Blacks, for example, took no part in the drafting of the Declaration of Independence or the design of the Constitution; however, their presence exerted a profound influence on the shaping of both these seminal documents. So it has been throughout American history.

The structure follows standard works in political science on American government and politics. It is unique, however, in two respects:

First, it is organized around *two interrelated themes* pursued throughout much of the textbook: the *idea of universal freedom* and the *concept of minority–majority coalitions*. We argue, in their quest for their own freedom in the United States, blacks have sought to universalize the idea of freedom. In their attack on slavery and racial subordination, African Americans and their leaders have embraced doctrines of universal freedom and equality. In doing so, they have had an important influence on the shaping of democratic, constitutional government and on expanding or universalizing the idea of freedom not only for themselves but also for all Americans.

Blacks have not acted alone. Indeed, given their status as a subordinate racial minority they could not act alone. Rather, in their quest for freedom blacks have sought to forge coalitions with whites via *minority–majority coalitions* (or, more precisely, *minority-inspired majority coalitions*). Historically, however, because of the nation's ambivalence about race, these coalitions tend to be unstable and temporary; requiring that they be constantly rebuilt in what is an ongoing quest.

The second distinctive aspect of this study is that it is historically informed. In each chapter, we trace developments over a period of time. Relevant historical background is critical to understanding the evolution of race and the American democracy. Such material also brings contemporary events into a sharper focus.

Our principal rationale for writing this book is that we saw a void in the available literature. More importantly, we believe that race is the most important cleavage in American life, with enormous impact on the nation's society, culture, and politics. Indeed, as we show throughout this book, race has always been the enduring fault line in American society and politics—thus the need for a volume that treats this important topic with the seriousness it deserves. We seek to accomplish this in a study that has historical sweep and depth and is comprehensive in its coverage; a book that is readable and interesting to undergraduate students while maintaining the highest intellectual standards. We believe the study of the rich, varied, and critical presence of African Americans in *all* areas of the political system demands nothing less.

The intellectual tradition of this text emerges out of the African American Politics subfield. The scholars who are the founders and innovators in the study of Black Politics created this scholarly subfield out of nothing. Principally, working in Historically Black Colleges and Universities (HBCUs), without major financial support or grants and with large numbers of classes and students, these scholars decades ago launched in small steps and limited ways a new area of academic study. They published in obscure and poorly diffused journals and little-known presses, which resulted, in many instances, in their work being overlooked and undervalued due to racism's manifestations in academia; allowing much valuable work to remain unseen. Not only was the result of their research made invisible, but these scholars themselves became invisible in the profession. Of this unseen tradition it has been written:

> The second research tradition in America's life is the unheralded, the unsung, unrecorded but not unnoticed one. Scholars belonging to this tradition literally make something out of nothing and typically produce scholarship at the less recognized institutions of higher learning. These are the places, to use Professor Aaron Wildavsky's apt phrase, where the schools "habitually run out of stamps" and where other sources of support are nonexistent. . . . [Yet] here . . . scholars . . . nevertheless scaled the heights, and produced stellar scholarship.[1]

They persisted and persevered. It is out of this tradition that the National Conference of Black Political Scientists (NCOBPS) was founded in 1969 by some of these scholars who created their own academic journal, the *National Political Science Review* (NPSR). And while their work is scattered and sometimes difficult to locate, it formed the basis for a new vision and perspective in political science. Beginning in 1885, the discipline of political science emerged during an era of concern about race relations and developed its study of race politics from this perspective.

The race relations perspective became the major consensus in the discipline on the study of race until the 1960s. In essence, this framework on the study of African American politics focused on the concern of whites about stability and social peace rather than the concerns of blacks about freedom and social justice.[2]

Challenging the dominant consensus in the mid- to late 1960s, black political scientists offered a different, more empowering perspective on political reality, which became known as the African American Politics (or Black Politics) view or perspective.[3] Instead of focusing on how the African American quest for freedom might distress whites and disrupt stability and social peace, this new perspective focused on how an oppressed group might achieve power so as to provide solutions to long-standing social and economic problems. This perspective deals with freedom and power rather than stability and social peace as articulated by Mack Jones's "Dominant-Subordinate Group" theoretical framework (see Chapter 1 for full explanation). Our approach is part of this intellectual tradition.

The purveyors of this tradition include Professor Robert Brisbane and Tobe Johnson of Morehouse College, the ever-erudite Samuel DuBois Cook at Atlanta University, Professors Emmett Dorsey, Bernard Fall, Harold Gosnell, Ronald Walters, Robert Martin, Vincent Browne, Nathaniel Tillman, Brian Weinstein, Morris Levitt, and Charles Harris at Howard University, and Jewel Prestage at Southern and Prairie View A&M University. Their insightful ideas, cogent theories, and brilliant teaching made this book possible. When we, the original authors—the late Hanes Walton, Jr. (1941–2013) and Robert C. Smith—sat down at the Holiday Inn in Jackson, Mississippi, in March 1991 (at the annual meeting of the National Conference of Black Political Scientists), to develop the book theme and lay out its goals and structure, we were standing on the shoulders of these pioneering political scientists. They built the intellectual foundation. We hope this work makes them proud. We hope it will do the same for our children.

Finally, a note on the terms used. We use the terms *black* (lowercase—the typical standard use) and *African American* interchangeably, having no preference for either and viewing each as a legitimate and accurate name for persons of African descent in the United States.[4] We recognize given that there are significant populations of people of African descent that have recently immigrated, often described as "pan-ethnicity," to the United States from a myriad of countries across the African diaspora for which such terms can be contentious; however, our use aligns with our historical focus. For instructors, it might be a good idea to discuss the history of the different uses of or provide links to materials that trace the use of the terms used to describe African

Americans and the terms African Americans use to describe themselves as active political agents in their struggle for freedom and acts of "self-determination."

New to This Edition

This new eighth edition includes two core additions. The first is an assessment of the 2016 presidential and congressional elections in relationship to the themes of the text. We pay particular attention to the gender–race interactions in the Hillary Clinton defeat, and explore the extent to which she was unable to maintain the Obama "rainbow coalition" in the general election. We also look at the candidacy of Ben Carson for the Republican nomination, comparing him to previous black Republican candidates.

While we focus on the 2016 election in Chapters 8 and 9, given the significance historically of the election of the first black president, we have retained for purposes of history the fundamentals of Obama's campaigns and elections in 2008 and 2012.

The second core addition in this new edition is an overall, general assessment of the record of the first African American president in domestic and foreign policies generally, and with respect to race specifically.

All chapters have been updated with new content and the latest data available, specifically:

- **Revisions to Chapter 3 "Political Culture and Socialization."** The chapter has been completely rewritten with more discussion on "Elements on Black Culture" and updated material on the political significance of African American music and the African American Church.
- **Revisions to Chapter 4 "Public Opinion."** The chapter discussion on the "Impact of Barack Obama on Symbolic Racism" has been expanded. The various strands of African American ideology now include discussion on conservatism, and feminism and intersectionality.
- **New addition in Chapter 5 "African Americans and the Media."** The chapter includes a new section on the African American celebrity impact on politics.
- **New addition to Chapter 6 "Social Movements and a Theory of African American Coalition Politics."** The chapter includes a full discussion of the political significance of the increasing ethnic diversity of the black community as a result of immigration from Africa and the Caribbean. Also, it provides extensive coverage of "Black Lives Matter," including an intersectionality analysis of the movement.
- **Revisions to Chapter 7 "Interest Groups."** This chapter now includes full discussion on African American women interest group activities from an intersectional approach. The discussion on the "State of Black Nationalist Movements" has been revised substantially.

- **Revisions to Chapter 8 "Political Parties."** This chapter has been rewritten to refine the discussion on the role of race in the polarization of American politics, a full overview of the election of the first African American president, the significance of the Jesse Jackson campaigns on Barack Obama's first campaign including the 2008 primaries and caucuses, full overview of the 2008 and 2012 general elections, and more inclusion of race and gender challenges to identities and loyalties when it comes to supporting and voting for presidential candidates.
- **New addition to Chapter 9 "Voting Behavior and Elections."** This chapter includes full coverage of the 2016 presidential and congressional elections, focusing on the role of race in the Clinton–Sanders contest; an interpretation of the Trump "phenomenon" as a manifestation of white nationalism; an analysis of the limitations of the Obama "rainbow" coalition; and the results of the congressional elections with respect to partisan control of Congress and the size of the black congressional delegation.
- **Revisions to Chapter 10 on "Congress."** In this chapter, the section on substantive representation has been expanded for a more detailed discussion.
- **Combined discussion in Chapter 11 on the "Presidency" and the "Bureaucracy."** This chapter combines previous separate chapters on the presidency and bureaucracy. It also includes a full assessment of the race policies of President Obama, reclassifying him from "race neutral" to "anti-racist." The bureaucracy focus has been reduced and revised as a reflection of presidential power.
- **Revisions to Chapter 12 on the "Supreme Court."** This chapter includes new material on the Voting Rights Act and the latest Supreme Court case testing institutional racism.
- **New chapter, Chapter 13, on "State and Local Politics."** This chapter includes a historical overview of state and local governments during the brief era of universal freedom during Reconstruction; a discussion of constitutionalism and federalism in the states and the significance of the period of devolution; the descriptive and substantive representation of blacks in state legislatures and executive offices, highlighting intersectionality and black women in state politics; the impact of Republican control of state governments on rights- and material-based freedoms; and ends with challenges for black majority-rule in "black regime" cities and "black-belt" counties with concentrated, racialized poverty.
- **Revision to Chapter 14 on "Domestic Policy."** This chapter has been substantially revised, focusing on the race–class intersection and measures of economic well-being in the African American community to examine income inequality and levels of unemployment, underemployment, poverty, incarceration, education, median net worth, affluence resulting in the black/white wealth gap.

Features of This Innovative Text

- Structured to accord with American Government texts and courses, featuring content in all major subfields specifically relevant to African American politics.
- Each chapter opens with an updated Learning Objective keyed to chapter content.
- Each chapter concludes with a Chapter Summary and Critical Thinking Questions.
- Selected Bibliographies for each chapter include new suggested readings for students.
- An Appendix at the end of the text excerpts the U.S. Constitution specifically in relation to African American people and politics.
- Boxes throughout the text focus on "Faces and Voices in the Struggle for Universal Freedom" as well as key issues and actors like the African American Church, Black Political Scientists in the Media, and the Joint Center for Political and Economic Studies.
- Figures, tables, and photos have been updated (where possible) through the 2016 elections throughout.
- A new Instructor's Guide with Lecture PowerPoints for professors offers links to a wide variety of additional resources. This is available at www.routledge.com/9781138658141.

Acknowledgments

In early editions, Margaret Mitchell Ilugbo typed several of the draft chapters for Hanes Walton, and Greta Blake designed the tables and figures. We appreciate their years of fine work.

Robert Smith's wife, Scottie, has been indispensable in the preparation of each edition. Her discerning and untiring work is deeply appreciated.

On the eighth edition, Sherri Wallace received assistance from her colleague, Kristopher Grady, and research assistant, Maria Delane. In addition to the colleagues selected by the publishers, we are pleased to acknowledge the colleagues who had an active role in criticism and preparation of this work, over all editions. Our thanks to:

Walton Brown-Foster, Central Connecticut State University; Nancy Burns, University of Michigan; Michael L. Clemons, Old Dominion University; Samuel Craig, Wayne County Community College; Donald Culverson, Governors State University; Marilyn A. Davis, Spelman College; Yomi Durotoye, Wake Forest University; Sekou Franklin, Middle Tennessee State University; Jose Angel Gutierrez, University of Texas–Arlington; Charles Henry, University of California, Berkeley; Theophilus Herrington, Texas Southern University; Jerome R. Hunt, University of the District of Columbia; Mack Jones, Clark–Atlanta

University; Mary Lou Kendrigan, East Lansing Community College; Maurice Magnam, Texas Southern University; Jeanette Mendez, University of Houston; François N. Muyumba, Indiana State University; Marion Orr, Brown University; Ravi K. Perry, Virginia Commonwealth University; Tasha Philpot, University of Michigan; Wilbur C. Rich, Wellesley College; Diarra Osei Robertson, Bowie State University; J. Clay Smith, Howard University Law School; Karin L. Stanford, California State University–Northridge; and Sharon D. Wright-Austin, University of Florida. In addition, we are very grateful to anonymous reviewers for their insightful and valuable comments. We incorporated nearly all the helpful suggestions.

About the Authors

Hanes Walton, Jr., a pioneering scholar of political science and professor at the University of Michigan, is a graduate of Morehouse College. He earned his master's degree in political science from Atlanta University and was the first person to earn the doctorate in political science from Howard University. He served on numerous editorial boards of academic journals, was a consultant to the National Academy of Sciences, the Educational Testing Service, and the National Endowment for the Humanities. He was a Ford, Rockefeller, and Guggenheim Fellow and held memberships in several honor societies, including Pi Sigma Alpha, Alpha Kappa Mu, and Phi Beta Kappa. He also worked on Capitol Hill in the office of Congressman Mervyn Dymally (D, CA). He was the recipient of the 1993 Howard University Distinguished Ph.D. Alumni Award. Shortly after the revisions for the seventh edition, Dr. Walton died, on January 7, 2013. He was the architect of this text, and its two interrelated themes—the idea of universal freedom and the concept of minority–majority coalitions—are the product of his fertile mind. Hanes was also an architect of the modern study of African American politics. Over four decades of prodigious research (including 25 books) and conceptual refinement, he helped to make the subfield of African American politics a major area of study in political science. His death leaves a large void in the field, and in our personal and intellectual life, but his friendship and intellectual legacy are abiding sources of comfort and inspiration.[5] In 2013, the American Political Science Association established the Hanes Walton, Jr. Award to recognize a political scientist whose lifetime of scholarship "made a significant contribution to our understanding of racial and ethnic politics and illuminates the conditions under which diversity and intergroup tolerance thrive in democratic societies."

Robert C. Smith is professor of political science at San Francisco State University. An honors graduate of the University of California, Berkeley, he holds a master's degree from UCLA and a doctorate from Howard University. He is the author or coauthor of dozens of articles and 12 books, most recently *Conservatism and Racism and Why in America They Are the Same, John F.*

Kennedy and Barack Obama: The Politics of Ethnic Incorporation and Avoidance and *Polarization and the Presidency: From FDR to Barack Obama.* He was associate editor of the *National Political Science Review,* and is general editor of the State University of New York (SUNY) Press African American Studies series. He has taught African American politics and American government for more than 40 years. In 1998, he was the recipient of the 1998 Howard University Distinguished Ph.D. Alumni Award. His *Encyclopedia of African American Politics* was published in 2003.

Sherri L. Wallace is professor of political science at the University of Louisville. By participating in the American Political Science Association's Ralph Bunche Summer Institute in 1988, she discovered her love for the discipline. She earned her master's and doctorate degrees from Cornell University, where she also received a President's Council for Cornell Women Fellowship for her dissertation research. She has published numerous peer-reviewed articles on college textbook diversity, women of color in academe, and community economic development. She teaches African American politics, American politics, public policy, state politics, and urban politics. She is the recipient of 2014 Anna Julia Cooper Teacher of the Year Award from the National Conference of Black Political Scientists. She actively engages in service in the discipline serving as an officer or member of standing (executive) committees, organized sections, and program and award committees for the National Conference of Black Political Scientists, American Political Science Association, Midwest Political Science Association, Southern Political Science Association, Southwestern Political Science Association, and Western Political Science Association.

Notes

1   Hanes Walton, Jr., "The Preeminent African American Legal Scholar: J. Clay Smith," *National Political Science Review* 6 (1997): 289.
2   Hanes Walton, Jr., Cheryl Miller, and Joseph P. McCormick, "Race and Political Science: The Dual Traditions of Race Relations Politics and African American Politics," in J. Dryzek, et al., eds., *Political Science and Its History: Research Programs and Political Traditions* (New York: Cambridge University Press, 1994): 145–74; and Hanes Walton, Jr., and Joseph P. McCormick, "The Study of African American Politics as Social Danger: Clues from the Disciplinary Journals," *National Political Science Review* 6 (1997): 229–44.
3   For an intellectually critical collection of essays by African American political scientists on race and the study of politics in the United States, see Wilbur Rich, ed., *African American Perspectives on Political Science* (Philadelphia: Temple University Press, 2007), and for a useful collection of papers by an influential political scientist whose writings contributed to the development of the scientific study of black politics see Mack H. Jones, *Knowledge, Power and Black Politics: Collected Essays* (Albany: SUNY Press, 2010).
4   For discussion of the various controversies about names in African American history— that is, what persons of African origins in the United States should call themselves—see W. E. B. Du Bois, "The Name Negro," *The Crisis* 35 (March 1928): 96–101; Lerone

Bennett, "What's in a Name?" *Ebony,* 23 (November 1967): 46–48, 50–52, 54; Ben L. Martin, "From Negro to Black to African-American: The Power of Names and Naming," *Political Science Quarterly* 106 (1991): 83–107; Robert C. Smith, "Remaining Old Realities," *San Francisco Review of Books* 25 (Summer 1990): 16–19; Ruth Grant and Marion Orr, "Language, Race and Politics: From 'Black' to 'African American,'" *Politics & Society* 24 (1996): 137–52; James F. Davis, "Who is Black? One Nation's Definition," from *Who is Black?* (Philadelphia: Pennsylvania State Press, 1991); "The Journey from 'Colored' to 'Minorities' to 'People of Color,'" *CodeSwitch*, National Public Radio (March 31, 2014) (Accessed at: www.npr.org/blogs/codeswitch/2014/03/30/295931070/the-journey-from-colored-to-minorities-to-people-of-color); Sterling Stuckey, *Slave Culture: Foundations of Nationalist Theory* (New York: Oxford University Press, 1987): chap. 4, "Identity and Ideology: The Names Controversy"; Erika V. Hall et al. "A Rose by Any Other Name? The Consequences of Subtyping 'African-Americans' from 'Blacks,'" *Journal of Experimental Social Psychology* 56 (2015): 183–90; Jennifer Schuessler, "Use of 'African-American' Dates to Nation's Early Days," *The New York Times*, April 20 (Accessed at http://nyti.ms/1G0zmc0), on *Lawrence O'Donnell Show* (Accessed at www.msnbc.com/the-last-word/watch/the-origin-of-the-term-african-american-4318 44419894) or HULU (www.hulu.com/watch/781555).

5 On Hanes's career and intellectual legacy, see Marion Orr, Pearl Ford Dove, Tyson King-Meadows, Joseph McCormick, and Robert C. Smith, "Hanes Walton, Jr.," *PS: Political Science & Politics* 44 (July 2013): 674–75; and "Hanes Walton, Jr." in Robert C. Smith, *Encyclopedia of African American Politics* (New York: Facts on File, 2003).

PART I

Foundations

CHAPTER 1

Universal Freedom Declared, Universal Freedom Denied

Racism, Slavery, and the Ideology of White Supremacy in the Founding of the Republic

---

LEARNING OBJECTIVE

Explain the idea of universal freedom and describe how it was compromised in the Constitution by racism and the ideology of white supremacy.

So, what is this thing called freedom? In 1865, General Oliver O. Howard, commissioner of the Freedmen's Bureau, asked an audience of newly freed slaves, "But what did freedom mean? It is necessary to define it for it is apt to be misunderstood."[1] William Riker writes, "The word 'freedom' must be defined. And volumes have been written on this subject without conspicuous success on reaching agreement."[2] Orlando Patterson begins his book *Freedom in the Making of Western Culture* with the observation that "Freedom, like love and beauty, is one of those values better experienced than defined."[3] Finally, John Hope Franklin, in *From Slavery to Freedom: A History of Negro Americans*, writes,

> It must never be overlooked that the concept of freedom that emerged in the modern world bordered on licentiousness and created a situation that

3

approached anarchy. As W. E. B. Du Bois has pointed out, it was the freedom to destroy freedom, the freedom of some to exploit the rights of others. It was, indeed, a concept of freedom with little or no social responsibility. If, then, a man was determined to be free, who was there to tell him that he was not entitled to enslave others.[4]

The idea of freedom is therefore a contested idea, with many often conflicting and contradictory meanings. Since the idea of freedom—universal freedom—is central to this book, in this first chapter we must attempt to define it because, as General Howard said, it is apt to be misunderstood.

In the last several decades, an important body of scholarship has emerged on how the idea and practice of freedom began in Europe and the United States. These historical and philosophical studies suggest that the idea of freedom— paradoxically—is inextricably linked to the idea and institution of slavery.[5] With respect to Europe, "it now can be said with some confidence," according to Patterson, "that the idea and value of freedom was the direct product of the institution of slavery. Where there has been no slavery there has never been any trace of freedom even as a minor value."[6] And in the United States, "without the institution of slavery America in all likelihood would have had no democratic tradition and would not have come to enshrine freedom at the very top of the pantheon of values."[7] In other words, the very idea of freedom in the Western world has its origins in the struggles of the slave to become free.[8]

While there is much of value in Patterson's studies, we are not persuaded by his argument that freedom in its origins is a uniquely Western value. On the contrary, we believe freedom is a fundamental driving force of the human condition. And while slavery was undoubtedly important in the genesis of the idea of freedom in the Western world, it is also likely that the idea in the West stems from other sources such as the desire of people to be free of harsh rule, treatment, or prohibitions that fall short of slavery (freedom of religion, for example).

Freedom: A Typological Analysis

The word *freedom* is difficult to define. Indeed, a number of writers on the subject have concluded that the effort to construct an objective or universal definition may be futile. Increasingly, therefore, students of the subject have sought not to define the term in one all-encompassing definition but rather, given the rich, varied, and conflicting meanings of the word, have sought instead to develop typologies of freedom that are broad and varied enough to cover the diverse shades of meaning held by scholars as well as ordinary women and men.

Table 1.1 displays three typologies of freedom. These typologies are drawn from the most recent scholarship on the subject. Again, these writers do not attempt to develop one universal definition of the term but see *freedom* as having

TABLE 1.1 Typologies of Freedom		
Orlando Patterson	**Eric Foner**	**Richard King**
Personal	Natural Rights[a]	Liberal
Sovereignal[b]	Civil Rights	Autonomy
Civic	Political Rights	Participatory
	Social Rights	Collective Deliverance

[a] Foner uses the term *rights* rather than *freedoms*.
[b] In his article Patterson uses the term *organic* instead of *sovereignal* to refer to this type of freedom.

Sources: Orlando Patterson, *Freedom in the Making of Western Culture* (New York: Basic Books, 1991): 3–5; Orlando Patterson, "The Unholy Trinity: Freedom, Slavery and the American Constitution," *Social Research* 54 (Autumn 1987): 556–59; Eric Foner, *Reconstruction: America's Unfinished Revolution, 1863–1877* (New York: Harper & Row, 1988): 231; Richard King, *Civil Rights and the Idea of Freedom* (New York: Oxford University Press, 1992): 26–28.

multiple shades of meaning. Patterson identifies three types of freedom. *Personal freedom* is defined as giving a person the sense that, on the one hand, he or she is not coerced or restrained by another person in doing something desired, and, on the other hand, that one can do as one pleases within the limits of that other person's desire to do the same. *Sovereignal* or *organic* freedom is simply the power to act as one pleases, without regard for others, or simply the ability to impose one's will on another. *Civic freedom* is defined as the capacity of adult members of a community to participate in its life and governance.[9]

Eric Foner discusses four notions of freedom—he prefers the term *rights*— that were part of the political vocabulary of the nation's leaders on the eve of the Civil War. *Natural rights*, those rights or freedoms inherent in one's humanity, are what Jefferson in the Declaration of Independence referred to as life, liberty, and the pursuit of happiness. *Civil rights* can be defined as equality of treatment under law, which is seen as essential to the protection of natural rights. *Political rights* involve the right to vote and participate fully in governing the community. *Social rights* involve the right to freely choose personal and business associates.[10]

King identifies "four meanings of freedom within American/western thought that link up with the language of freedom and the goals of the civil rights movement."[11] *Liberal freedom* is the absence of arbitrary legal or institutional restrictions on the individual, including the idea that all citizens are to be treated equally. *Freedom as autonomy* involves an internalized individual state of autonomy, self-determination, pride, and self-respect. *Participatory freedom* involves the right of the individual to participate fully in the political process.

Collective deliverance is understood as the liberation of a group from external control—from captivity, slavery, or oppression.[12]

Clearly, there is considerable overlap among the types of freedom addressed by Patterson, Foner, and King, especially in the realm of politics or the right of citizens to equal treatment under law and the right to vote and participate in the governance of the community. However, two of the types identified have special relevance to the African American experience and to this book's theme of universal freedom. First, throughout their history in the United States, African Americans have consistently rejected the idea of organic or sovereignal freedom, the notion that one person or group should have the freedom to impose their will on another without regard to the rights of others. This is the freedom of might makes right, of the strong to oppress the weak, of the powerful to dominate the powerless, and of the slave master to enslave. From its beginning, African American political thought and behavior has been centrally concerned with the abolition of this type of freedom, and in doing so African Americans developed the idea of universal freedom—a freedom that encompasses natural rights, civil rights, and social rights. In rejecting the Patterson notion of sovereignal freedom, blacks in the United States fully embraced King's idea of freedom as collective deliverance. As part of a captive, oppressed, enslaved people, one could expect nothing less. However, in fighting for their own liberation, for their freedom, blacks have had to fight for universal freedom, for the freedom of all people. As Aptheker puts it, "The Negro people have fought like tigers for their freedom, and in doing so have enhanced the freedom struggles of all people."[13]

Freedom, Power, and Politics

All the typologies of freedom listed in Table 1.1 are related in one way or another to power or the lack of power, and power is central to politics and political science. As Lasswell and Kaplan write in their classic study *Power and Society*, "The concept of power is perhaps the most fundamental in the whole of political science: The political process is the shaping, distribution and exercise of power."[14] The definition of power, like freedom, however, also has an ambiguous, elusive quality.[15] At a minimum, scholars agree that A has power over B to the extent that A can affect B's behavior or get B to do something B otherwise would not do. Max Weber, one of the founders of modern sociology and political science, writes, "In general, we understand by 'power' the chance of a man or a number of men to realize their own will in a communal action against the resistance of others who are participating in the action."[16] Political scientists generally analyze power in terms of (1) its bases, (2) its exercise, and (3) the skill of its exercise in particular circumstances, situations, or contexts. With respect to African American politics, Mack Jones postulates that whites occupy a "superordinate" or dominant position in relationship to blacks.[17] That is, historically whites have had a near monopoly on the critical or "hard" power bases (wealth, size, status, technology, and violence) and used it to subordinate blacks and maintain control over them. Blacks, on the other hand, have attempted to acquire power, often the "soft" power bases of morality, religion, and appeals to democratic principles, to alter their subordinate status in a quest for universal freedom. In this sense black politics, Jones writes, "is essentially a power struggle between blacks and whites" characterized by an asymmetrical power relationship between the groups.[18] However, in order to fully understand black politics and distinguish it from other group conflicts in the United States, Jones contends that it is necessary to specify that the subordination of blacks is justified on the basis of the ideology of white supremacy.[19] We discuss the ideology of white supremacy later in this chapter, but in sum in analyzing African American politics as a quest for universal freedom we need to think in terms of blacks seeking to alter their subordinate status vis-à-vis whites and the asymmetrical power between the groups in the context of the ideology of white supremacy.

Thomas Jefferson and the Writing of the Declaration

After voting to declare independence, the Continental Congress appointed a committee to draft a document setting forth the reasons for the revolution. The committee was composed of Robert Livingston, Roger Sherman, Benjamin Franklin, John Adams, and Thomas Jefferson. The other members turned the task of drafting to Adams and Jefferson, and according to Adams, Jefferson was asked to actually write the document because his writings were characterized by a "peculiar felicitousness of expression."[20] The Declaration, however, is not the creation of one man. Rather, "eighty-six substantive revisions were made in Jefferson's draft, most of them by members of the Continental Congress who also excised about one fourth of the original text."[21] Jefferson was said to be extremely displeased by the changes in his draft and for the remaining 50 years of his life was angry, arguing that the Congress had "mangled" his manuscript.[22]

The majority of the substantive changes or deletions in Jefferson's draft—including the most famous—focused on the long list of charges against King George III. Most historians say that the charges against the King as listed in the Declaration are exaggerated, and in any event they are misplaced, since many of the actions complained of were decisions of the Parliament rather than the King. The King, however, made a more convenient target than the anonymous, amorphous Parliament.

The most famous of the changes deleted from Jefferson's draft was the condemnation of the King for engaging in the African slave trade. Jefferson had written the following:

> He has waged cruel war against human nature itself, violating the most sacred rights of life and liberty in the persons of a distant people who never offended him, captivating and carrying them into slavery in another

hemisphere, or to incur miserable death in their transportation thither. This piratical warfare, the opprobrium of infidel powers, is the warfare of the Christian King of Great Britain. Determined to keep open a market when MEN should be bought and sold, he has prostituted his negative for suppressing every legislative attempt to prohibit or restrain this execrable commerce; and this assemblage of horrors might want no fact of distinguished die, he is now exciting these very people to rise among us, and to purchase that liberty of which he deprived them, by murdering the people upon whom he also obtruded them, thus paying off former crimes committed against the liberties of one people, with crimes which he urges them to commit against the lives of others.[23]

This passage, which was to be the climax of the charges against the King, was obviously an exaggeration and an especially disingenuous one; the colonists themselves (including Jefferson) had enthusiastically engaged in slave trading and, as was made clear to Jefferson, had no intention of abandoning it after independence. Jefferson recalls that "the clause too, reprobating the enslaving of the inhabitants of Africa, was struck out in compliance to South Carolina and Georgia, who had never attempted to restrain the importation of slaves and who still wished to continue it."[24] Not only was there opposition to the passage from the southern slave owners, but more tellingly, as Jefferson went on to say, "our northern brethren also I believe felt a little tender under these censures; for tho' their people have few slaves themselves yet they have been pretty considerable carriers of them."[25] In other words, virtually all the leading white men in America, Northerner and Southerner, slave owner and non-slave owner, had economic interests in the perpetuation of slavery. A good part of the new nation's wealth and prosperity was based on the plantation economy. To be consistent, one might have thought that the Continental Congress would also have deleted the phrase on the equality of men and their inherent right to liberty. They did not, apparently seeing no inconsistency since the words did not mean what they said (see Box 1.1).

The magnificent words of the Declaration of Independence declaring freedom and equality as universal rights of all "men" were, however, fatally flawed, compromised in that the men who wrote them denied freedom to almost one-fourth of the men in America. To understand how the idea of universal freedom was fundamentally compromised, one needs to see Thomas Jefferson as the paradigmatic figure: author of the Declaration, preeminent intellectual—acquaintance through correspondence of eminent African American intellectual Benjamin Banneker—and also a racist, a white supremacist, and a slave owner.[26]

Racism and White Supremacy Defined

We have described Jefferson—one of the great men of American history and one of the most enlightened men of his day—as a racist and white supremacist;

BOX 1.1

Like Humpty Dumpty Told Alice, "When I Use a Word It Means What I Say It Means"

Before the ink was dry on Jefferson's Declaration, there was controversy about what was meant by the words "all men are created equal." Rufus Choate, speaking in 1776 for Southerners embarrassed by Jefferson's words, said Jefferson did not mean what he said. Rather, the word *men* referred only to nobles and Englishmen who were no better than ordinary American freemen. "If he meant more," Choate said, it was because Jefferson was "unduly influenced by the French school of thought."[a] (Jefferson was frequently accused of being influenced by Jean Jacques Rousseau's writings, a charge that he denied.) On the eve of the Civil War, Chief Justice Roger B. Taney, in his opinion in the *Dred Scott* (1857) case, said that on the surface the words "all men are created equal" applied to blacks. Yet he concluded, "It is too clear for dispute that the enslaved African race were not intended to be included, and formed no part of the people who framed and adopted the Declaration." Similarly, during his famous debates with Abraham Lincoln, Stephen Douglas argued that the phrase simply meant that Americans were not inferior to Englishmen as citizens. It was Lincoln's genius at Gettysburg in his famous address to fundamentally repudiate Choate, Taney, and Douglas in what Garry Wills calls an "audacious" and "clever assault." Lincoln accomplished this by claiming that the Civil War had given

rise to a "new birth of freedom" that had been conceived by Jefferson "four score and seven years ago" when he wrote the Declaration.[b] Conservative scholars have long attacked Lincoln's "radical" redefinition of the meaning of the Declaration. Wilmore Kendal, writing a century after Gettysburg, argued that the word *men* in the Declaration referred to property holders or to the nations of the world but not men as such, writing blatantly that "the Declaration of Independence does not commit us to equality as a national goal."[c] As Daniel Boorstin, the former librarian of Congress and author of the celebrated *The Americans: The Democratic Experience* (New York: Vintage Books, 1974), writes, "We have repeated that 'all men are created equal' without daring to discover what it meant and without realizing that probably to none of the men who spoke it did it mean what we would like it to mean."[d]

[a] Quoted in Carl Becker, *The Declaration of Independence: A Study in the History of an Idea* (New York: Vintage Books, 1922, 1970): 27.
[b] Garry Wills, *Lincoln at Gettysburg: The Words That Remade America* (New York: Touchstone, 1992).
[c] Wilmore Kendal, *Basic Symbols of the American Political Tradition* (Baton Rouge: Louisiana State University Press, 1970), as cited in M. E. Bradford, "How to Read the Declaration of Independence: Reconsidering the Kendal Thesis," *Intercollegiate Review* (Fall 1992): 47.
[d] Ibid., p. 46.

therefore, we should define these terms since they are key distinguishing features of the African American experience in the United States.[27] They are also central to the analysis presented throughout this book. Racism and the ideology of white supremacy are fundamental to an understanding of certain crucial features in the development of the American democracy as well as the different treatment of black and white Americans.

Racism as a scientific concept is not an easy one for the social scientist. It is difficult to define with precision and objectivity; also, the word is often used indiscriminately and in an inflammatory way. We start by distinguishing between racism and the set of ideas used in the United States to justify it. The latter we refer to as the ideology of white supremacy or black inferiority. In the United States, racism was and to some extent still is justified on the basis of the institutionalized belief that Africans are inherently inferior people. We refer to an individual who holds such beliefs as a *white supremacist*.

By racism we mean, following the definition of Carmichael and Hamilton in *Black Power*, "the predication of decisions and policies on considerations of race for the purpose of subordinating a racial group and maintaining control over it."[28] The definition says nothing about why this is done, about racism's purposes or rationales; thus it does not imply anything about superiority or inferiority of the groups involved. It does not say, as many definitions and concepts of racism do, that racism involves the belief in the superiority, inherent or otherwise, of a particular group and that on this basis policies are implemented to subordinate and control the group. Rather, the definition simply indicates that whenever one observes policies that have the intent or effect of subordinating a racial group, the phenomenon is properly identified as *racism*, whatever, if any, the justificatory ideology may be.

Carmichael and Hamilton's definition is particularly useful to political scientists because it focuses on power as an integral aspect of the phenomenon. For racism to exist, one racial group (or individual) must have the relative power—the capacity to impose its will in terms of policies—over another relatively less powerful group or individual. Without this relative power relationship, racism is a mere sentiment: Although group A may wish to subordinate group B, if it lacks the effective power to do so, the desire remains simply a wish.

Carmichael and Hamilton also write that racism may take two forms: individual and institutional.[29] Individual racism occurs when one person takes into consideration the race of another to subordinate, control, or otherwise discriminate against an individual; institutional racism exists when the normal and accepted patterns and practices of a society's institutions have the *effect* or *consequence* of subordinating or discriminating against an individual or group on the basis of race.[30]

It is in this sense that we refer to Thomas Jefferson as a white supremacist and a racist. He believed that blacks were inherently inferior to whites, stating in his *Notes on Virginia* that they were "inferior by nature, not condition" (see Box 1.2). He was also a racist, individually and institutionally, in that he took the race of individual blacks into consideration so as to discriminate against them, and he supported, although ambivalently, the institution of slavery that subordinated blacks as a group.

Just in case readers may infer that white supremacy is a phenomenon of the nation's distant past, one need look only as far back as February 2016 to former Ku Klux Klan Grand Wizard David Duke's endorsement of Republican presidential candidate Donald Trump, Trump's subsequent appointment of

BOX 1.2

Thomas Jefferson's *Notes on Virginia* and the Idea of the Inferiority of the African People

In the Declaration of Independence, Jefferson engaged in a kind of moral reasoning to reach his conclusions as to the self-evident equality of men. In his *Notes on Virginia*, written several years later, he engaged in a more scientific approach to the analysis of the problem of racial inequality.[a] In doing so, Jefferson the slaveholder made an eloquent condemnation of slavery, proposing his view of a just and equitable way to end slavery in the United States while simultaneously offering what he took to be scientific proof of the inferiority of the African people. Understanding Jefferson's views on race is therefore critical to an appreciation of how racism fundamentally compromised the idea of universal freedom at the very creation of the American Republic.[b]

In 1780 Francois Barbe-Marbois, the secretary of the French delegation in Philadelphia, sent a letter to each of the state governors requesting that they answer questions on particular customs and conditions in their states. Jefferson delayed his response until after he left the governor's office. Although Jefferson offered a general assessment of conditions in the state, his *Notes* are best known for what he said about slavery, the African people, and Virginia society.

While defending the institution of slavery Jefferson nevertheless saw it as evil and unjust, writing, "There must doubtless be an unhappy influence on the manners of our people produced by the existence of slavery among us. The whole commerce between master and slave is perpetual exercise of the most boisterous passions, the most unremitting despotism on the one part, and degrading submission on the other."[c] In a famous passage that would be echoed by Abraham Lincoln during the Civil War, Jefferson suggested that God would surely punish America: "Indeed, I tremble for my country when I reflect that God is just; that his justice cannot sleep forever. . . . The almighty has no attribute which can take side with us in such a contest."[d]

Since slavery was an evil, but a necessary one given the need for labor in the plantation economy, Jefferson proposed a revision in Virginia law that would gradually free the slaves; train them; provide tools, seeds, and animals; and then transport them to a new land as a "free and independent people" while simultaneously sending ships "to other parts of the world for an equal number of white inhabitants" to replace them.[e]

Jefferson anticipated that the inevitable question would be why not simply free the slaves and integrate them into Virginia society, thereby saving the money involved in colonialization of the slaves and the transportation of the whites. His response was first that "deep rooted prejudices entertained by whites, ten thousand recollections by the blacks of injuries they have sustained, the real distinctions which nature has made and many other circumstances" made impossible the integration of the black and white populations on the basis of freedom and equality.[f] Indeed, Jefferson believed that if the races were not separated, "convulsions" would occur, probably ending in the "extermination of one or the other race."[g]

Jefferson was not satisfied to base his argument for racial separation on these essentially practical arguments. Rather, he wanted to be "scientific," to base his conclusions on the "facts," on his "empirical observations." Thus, in the *Notes* he advocated what was one of the first of many "scientific proofs" of black inferiority as justification for black subordination. First, he argued that blacks compared to whites were less beautiful, had a "strong and disagreeable odor," and were more "ardent after their female." Ultimately, however, for Jefferson the basis of black inferiority was his "suspicion" that blacks were "inferior in faculties of reason and imagination."[h]

Noting that the differences he observed between blacks and whites might be explained by the different conditions under which they lived, Jefferson rejected this explanation, concluding it was not their "condition" but their "nature" that produced the difference.[i]

[a] This distinction between Jefferson's moral reasoning in the Declaration and his scientific approach in the *Notes* is the central theme of Jean Yarbrough, "Race and the Moral Foundation of the American Republic: Another Look at the Declaration and the Notes on Virginia," *Journal of Politics* 53 (February 1991): 90–105. Yarbrough argues that "the self-evident truths of the Declaration rest on a kind of moral reasoning which is morally superior to and incompatible with the so called scientific approach Jefferson adopts in the *Notes*" (p. 90).

[b] A comprehensive treatment of Jefferson's views on race is in Winthrop Jordan, *White over Black: American Attitudes Toward the Negro, 1550–1812* (Baltimore, MA: Penguin Books, 1969): chap. 12, "Thomas Jefferson: Self and Society."

[c] Thomas Jefferson, *Notes on the State of Virginia*, edited by William Peden (Chapel Hill: University of North Carolina Press, 1954): 162–63.

[d] Ibid.

[e] Ibid., pp. 138–39.

[f] Ibid., p. 138. This was also the view of Abraham Lincoln (see chap. 14). In *Democracy in America* (New York: Knopf, 1945)—probably the single most important and influential book ever written on the subject—Alexis de Tocqueville also reached the same pessimistic conclusion that blacks and whites could not live

Thomas Jefferson is the embodiment of the contradiction in the American democracy between its declaration of universal freedom and equality and its practice of slavery.

Source: The White House Historical Association

together on the basis of freedom and equality. Tocqueville thought that whites would either subjugate the blacks or exterminate them. See *Democracy in America*, vol. 1, edited by Phillips Bradley (New York: Vintage Books, 1945): chap. 18.

[g] *Notes on the State of Virginia*, pp. 138–39.

[h] Ibid.

[i] Ibid.

---

alt-right Breitbart News head Steve Bannon as campaign CEO, or former Nixon advisor Pat Buchanan's declaration upon the 2012 election results that "White America died last night. Obama's reelection killed it." Buchanan went on to say in clear white supremacist language that it was "obvious" that whites were superior to non-whites: "Anything worth doing on this earth was done first by white people."[31]

Philosophy, Politics, and Interest in Constitution Formation

The framers of the Constitution were influenced in their work by their readings in philosophy and history. But the framers were also practical politicians and men of affairs, and, as in all politics, they were men with distinct interests. In what is generally a sympathetic portrayal of the framers, historian William Freehling writes, "If the Founding Fathers unquestionably dreamed of universal freedom, their ideological posture was weighed down equally with conceptions of priorities, profits, and prejudices that would long make the dream utopian."[32] The first or principal priority of the framers was the formation and preservation of the union of the United States. This priority was thought indispensable to the priority of profit—that is, to the economic and commercial success of the nation. And as Freehling notes, their concern with profits grew out of their preoccupation with property, and slaves as property were crucial; thus, "it made the slaves' right to freedom no more 'natural' than the master's right to property."[33] It was this crucial nexus between profits, property, and slavery that led the men at Philadelphia to turn the idea of universal freedom into a utopian dream.

African Americans in the Constitution

As far as we can tell from the records of the federal convention, slavery was not the subject of much debate at that gathering. Certainly its morality was never at issue, although there were several passionate opponents of slavery present, including the venerable Benjamin Franklin, president of the Pennsylvania Society for Promoting the Abolition of Slavery. But neither Franklin nor any other delegate proposed abolition at Philadelphia, knowing that to do so would destroy any possibility of union. Hence, slavery was simply just another of the issues (such as how the small and large states were to be represented in the Congress) that had to be compromised to accomplish the objective of forming the union.

Slavery is dealt with explicitly in four places in the Constitution, although the words *slave* and *slavery* are never used. It was James Madison, generally considered the "Father of the Constitution," who insisted that all explicit references to slavery be excluded.[34] It is worth noting, as Joe R. Feagin does, that while the Constitution's racist provisions relating to slavery have been overridden by amendments, they have not been deleted. This is because, as Feagin writes, "At no point has a new Constitutional Convention been held to replace this document with one created by representatives of all the people, including the great majority of the population not represented at the 1787 Convention."[35]

The Three-Fifths Clause, the Slave Power, and the Degradation of the American Democracy

Before the Sixteenth Amendment was adopted (permitting Congress to tax income directly), Congress could impose and collect taxes only on the basis of a state's population. The larger a state's population, the greater its tax burden. For this reason, the southern states insisted that the slaves not be counted, as, like horses and cows, they were property. However, for purposes of representation in the House (where each state is allocated seats on the basis of the size of its population), the South wished to count the slaves as persons, although they, of course, could not vote. This would enhance the South's power not only in the House but also in choosing the president, since the number of votes a state may cast for president in the electoral college is equal to the total of its representation in the House and Senate. The northern states, on the other hand, wished to count the slaves for purposes of taxation but not representation. Hence, the great compromise—the Three-Fifths Clause. In Article I, Section 2, paragraph 3:

> Representatives and direct taxes shall be apportioned among the several states that may be included within this union, according to their respective numbers which shall be determined by adding to the whole number of free persons, including those bound to service for a Term of years and excluding Indians not taxed, three fifths of all other persons.

In attempting to justify or explain this compromise, Madison (in *The Federalist Papers No. 54*) disingenuously puts his words in the mouth of a fictional Southerner:

> The Federal Constitution, therefore, decides with great propriety on the case of our slaves, when it views them in the mixed character of persons and property. . . . Let the slaves be considered, as it is in truth a peculiar one. Let the compromising expedient of the Constitution be mutually adopted which regards them as inhabitants, but as debased by servitude below the equal level of free inhabitants; which regards the slave as divested as of two fifths of the man.[36]

But as Professor Donald Robinson so astutely observes,

> It bears repeating . . . that Madison's formula did not make blacks three-fifths of a human being. It was much worse than that. It gave slave owners a bonus in representation for their human property, while doing nothing for the status of blacks as nonpersons under the law.[37]

For the first time in this textbook we are able to precisely and comprehensively document the extent of this bonus over time with the specific number and percentage of House seats provided by the Three-Fifths Clause to the slaveholding states. In Figure 1.1 and Figure 1.2, we see the number and percentage of additional House seats gained by southern and border states as a consequence of the clause. In the first congressional election in 1788, five states (Georgia, Maryland, North Carolina, South Carolina, and Virginia) gained 14 seats or a bonus of 48 percent, allowing them to reach near parity in the number of House

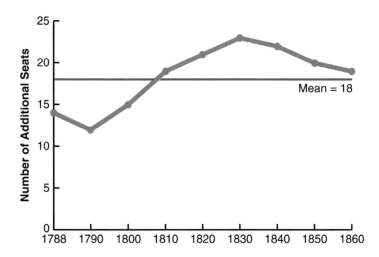

FIGURE 1.1

The Number of Additional Seats Given by the Three-Fifths Clause to the Slave States in the House of Representatives

Sources: The population estimates used by the 1787 Constitutional Convention to apportion the first House of Representatives were taken from Merrill Jensen and Robert Becker, eds., *The Documentary History of the First Federal Elections 1788–1790* (Madison: University of Wisconsin Press, 1976): xxiv. The apportionment ratio and seats for each decade from 1790 to 1860 were taken from Department of Commerce, *Congressional District Data Book* 93rd Congress (Washington, DC: Government Printing Office, 1973): Appendix A, 548. Data on the African American slave and free population for 1790–1915 were taken from Department of Commerce, *Negro Population 1790–1915* (Washington, DC: Government Printing Office, 1918): 57. Data on the African American and white populations in each state from 1790 to 1860 were taken from Department of Commerce, *Negroes in the United States 1920–1932* (Washington, DC: Government Printing Office, 1935): 10–11. Calculations for each seat or fraction of a seat for each decade were done by the authors.

seats (47–53) with the eight larger northern states. This bonus in numbers increased until 1830 and in percentages until 1860, when the numbers began to decline somewhat. Over the nine censuses and reapportionments of House seats from 1778 until 1860 (the Clause was abolished during the 1860s as a result of the Civil War), the mean or average bonus percentage of seats was 25.

Similarly, Figure 1.3 shows the percentage of additional electoral votes going to the slave states as a result of the Three-Fifths Clause, ranging from a low of 8 percent in 1792 to a high of 19 percent in most presidential elections between 1788 and 1860 (the mean over these 19 elections was a 17 percent bonus). This helped the southern states to elect four of the first five presidents.

This is the essence of the slave power and how it degraded the American democracy even among white men. It gave, for example, a white man in Virginia who owned a hundred slaves the equivalent of 60 votes compared to a Pennsylvania white man who owned no slaves having 1 vote.

The slave power was so pervasive and corrupting that Timothy Pickering, George Washington, and John Adams's secretary of state coined the terms

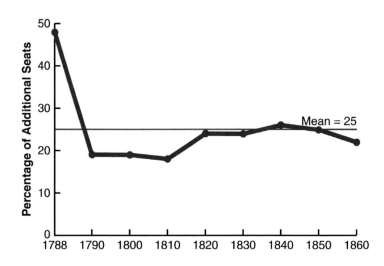

FIGURE 1.2

The Percentage of Additional Seats Given by the Three-Fifths Clause to the Slave
States in the House of Representatives

Sources: The population estimates used by the 1787 Constitutional Convention to apportion the first
House of Representatives were taken from Merrill Jensen and Robert Becker, eds., *The
Documentary History of the First Federal Elections 1788–1790* (Madison: University of Wisconsin
Press, 1976): xxiv. The apportionment ratio and seats for each decade from 1790 to 1860 were
taken from Department of Commerce, *Congressional District Data Book: 93rd Congress*
(Washington, DC: Government Printing Office, 1973): Appendix A, 548. Data on the African
American slave and free population for 1790–1915 were taken from Department of Commerce,
Negro Population 1790–1915 (Washington, DC: Government Printing Office, 1918): 57. Data on the
African American and white populations in each state from 1790 to 1860 were taken from
Department of Commerce, *Negroes in the United States 1920–1932* (Washington, DC: Government
Printing Office, 1935): 10–11. Calculations for each seat or fraction of a seat for each decade were
done by the authors.

"Negro President" and "Negro Congressmen" to refer to those presidents and
members of Congress elected on the basis of the three-fifths bonus.[38] Not only
did this slave power elect "Negro Presidents" and "Negro Congressmen," but
it also resulted in "Negros" serving as speakers of the House and chairs of the
Ways and Means Committee (79 and 92 percent of the time, respectively, until
1824), then and now the most powerful House committee.[39]

The Three-Fifths Clause was effectively repealed with the adoption of the
Thirteenth Amendment. Ironically, however, this resulted in an increase in the
power of southern racists and white supremacists. This is because the
emancipated slaves were now counted as whole persons, but from the 1870s to
the 1970s, most of these whole black persons were denied the right to vote. The
authors of the Fourteenth Amendment had anticipated that the former slave
owners would attempt to deny the vote to blacks. Therefore, they included in
it a provision (Section 2) providing that those states that deprived blacks
(actually black men) of the right to vote would be deprived of the proportionate

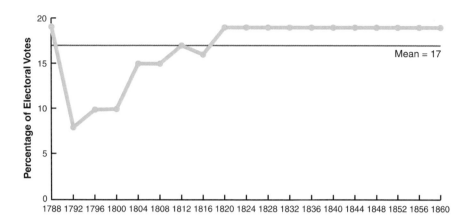

FIGURE 1.3

The Percentage of Additional Electoral Votes Given by the Three-Fifths Clause to the Slave States in Presidential Elections

Sources: The total number of additional House of Representatives seats for each state in the slave bloc was taken from the analyses derived to develop the summary for Figure 1.1 and treated as additional electoral votes for that state. The total number of electoral votes for each state that were advantaged by the Three-Fifths Clause was taken from *Congressional Quarterly's Guide to U.S. Elections*, 4th ed., vol. 1 (Washington, DC: Congressional Quarterly, 2001): 817–36. Calculations were prepared by the authors.

number of seats in the House. But this provision was never enforced.[40] So, in effect the slave power of the seventeenth and eighteenth centuries became the segregation power of the nineteenth and twentieth centuries. Whether slave power or segregation, however, it continued to degrade the democracy and deny African Americans universal freedom (see Box 1.3).

The other clauses dealing explicitly with slavery include Article I, Section 9, paragraph 1, prohibiting Congress from stopping the slave trade before 1808 and limiting any tax on imported slaves to $10; Article V, prohibiting any amendment to the Constitution that would alter the 1808 date or rate of taxation on imported slaves; and Article IV, Section 2, paragraph 2, requiring the northern states to return slaves who escaped to freedom back to their bondage in the South. As far as we know, none of these provisions caused much controversy at the convention, although the fugitive slave clause in Article IV initially would have required that escaped slaves be "delivered up as criminals"; this, however, was modified to relieve states of the obligation.[41]

The framers, while committed to freedom, had a limited, non-universal vision of it. Freedom was for some—the some who were white men with property, including property in other men, women, and children. Professor Robinson cautions us, "One wants to be fair to the framers, and above all to avoid blaming them as individuals for the sins of the culture, in which we all share. We must be careful not to imply that they should have done better unless

BOX 1.3

Slavery and the Electoral College

The electoral college is the mechanism used to elect the president of the United States. In the American democracy, a person is elected president not on the basis of winning a majority of the votes of the people but rather on the basis of winning a majority of votes in the electoral college. The electoral college is actually 51 electoral colleges representing the states and the District of Columbia. Each state is granted as many electoral college votes as it has members of Congress, which means that each state and the District of Columbia has at least three electors (based on two senators and a minimum of one member of the House). In all states except Maine and Nebraska, the electoral college votes are based on the principle of winner takes all. The candidate who wins most of the votes of the people (even if this is less than a majority in a multicandidate race) receives all the state's electoral votes. Thus, a hypothetical candidate running in California who receives 39 percent of the vote in a four-person race would receive 100 percent of the state's 55 electoral votes. This system of choosing the president means that a loser can become the winner. That is—as in the 2000 election of George W. Bush and the 2016 election of Donald Trump—a person can lose a majority of the votes of the people but nevertheless become president by winning a majority of the electoral votes. This undemocratic system of choosing the president is rooted partly in slavery and was part of several compromises the framers of the Constitution made to accommodate the interests of slaveholders, which undermined the interests of blacks and compromised the principle of democracy.

The framers of the Constitution confronted three alternatives in considering how the president might be elected. The first was election by the Congress. This alternative was rejected because it violates the principle of the separation of powers. The second alternative was election by the legislatures of the states. It was rejected because it would have violated the principle of an independent federal government. The last—and most obvious and most democratic—method was election by the people. This alternative was rejected because some of the framers said the people would not be educated or informed enough to make a good choice. However, election by the people would also have disadvantaged the slaveholding southern states. James Madison, who at first favored election by the people, changed his mind in favor of the electoral college because he said election by the people would disadvantage the South since their slaves could not vote. The electoral college compromise did not disadvantage the southern states; it gave them a bonus by allowing them to count their slaves in determining electoral votes on the basis of the Three-Fifths Clause used to allocate seats in the House of Representatives. In its earliest years of operation, the electoral college did work to the advantage of the South, as four of the first five presidents elected in the first 30 years were slave owners from Virginia.

The electoral college also represented other compromises that undermined democratic principles. While it gave the states with the largest population the larger share of electoral votes, it gave the smaller states a two-seat bonus based on their senators. It left the manner of choosing the electors up to the states except that they were prohibited from holding any federal office (including being members of Congress) and from meeting together as a group (the electors meet separately on the same day in each state's capital). The electors may be chosen in any manner a state's legislature determines—by the legislature itself, by appointment of the governor, or by the voters. (It was not until the 1840s that all states allowed the people to choose the electors in direct elections.) Once selected, the electors are free to vote for anyone they wish (as long as the person meets the constitutional qualifications of age, native-born citizenship, and residency), even if the person did not run in the first place. The states are also free to determine the allocation of the electoral votes—whether winner-take-all on a statewide basis or proportionally.

Five times the electoral college has resulted in a loser becoming the winner, including in 2016 when Hillary Clinton won more than 2.5 million votes than Donald Trump. In 1828, Andrew Jackson won most of the votes of the people and most (but not a majority) of the electoral college votes in a four-man race but lost the presidency to John Q. Adams. In 1876, Samuel J. Tilden won the popular vote majority but in the so-called "Compromise of 1877" Rutherford B. Hayes won by a one-vote margin in the electoral college. In 1888, Grover Cleveland narrowly won the popular vote, but Benjamin Harrison won the electoral college by a large margin. In 2000, Albert

Gore won the election by a margin of a half million votes but lost the electoral college by a one-vote margin to George W. Bush. As three ironies of history, the elections of 1876, 1888, and 2000 all involved allegations of suppression of the black vote in Florida and other southern states.

Although the electoral college is partly rooted in slavery, it is unclear whether its abolition in favor of choice by direct vote of the people would advantage or disadvantage African Americans in presidential elections. Although the small states where few blacks live have a bonus in the electoral college, it is the large states of the Northeast and Midwest that decide presidential elections. African Americans are disproportionately represented in these states. Therefore, in close elections, African Americans can sometimes constitute the balance of power in determining the winner.

---

we are prepared to show how better provisions might have been achieved politically." Fair enough. But Robinson continues, "At the same time, we must be lucid in recognizing the terrible mistakes made at the founding. In the end the framers failed on their own terms."[42] Or as Thurgood Marshall, the first African American justice of the Supreme Court, said in a speech in 1987 marking the 200th anniversary of the Constitution,

> nor do I find the wisdom, foresight, and sense of justice exhibited by the framers particularly profound. To the contrary, the government they devised was defective from the start, requiring several amendments, a civil war, and momentous social transformations to attain the system of constitutional government, and its respect for the individual freedoms and human rights, we hold as fundamental today. When contemporary Americans cite "The Constitution," they invoke a concept that is vastly different from what the framers began to construct two centuries ago.[43]

Constitutional Principles and Design

In designing the Constitution, the framers were guided by two overarching and interrelated principles. First, the primary object of government was the protection of private property, and second, the power of government had to be limited to avoid tyranny. These two principles are interrelated because a government of unlimited powers could itself become a threat to private property, thereby undermining one of its core purposes. These two principles gave rise to what are the two most important contributions of the framers to the art and practice of government: the idea of the separation of powers of the government into distinct parts or branches and federalism.

In *The Federalist Papers No. 10*, James Madison, a man of little property himself, wrote, "The diversities in the faculties of men from which the rights of property originates is not less an insuperable obstacle to uniformity of interests. *The protection of these faculties is the first object of government*" (emphasis added).[44] How does government carry out its first object in a democratic society? The problem confronting the framers, stated simply, was this: In a democratic, capitalist society where only a minority has property but a majority has the right to vote, it is likely the majority will use its voting rights to threaten the property rights of the minority. To avoid this danger while preserving what Madison called the "spirit and form" of democracy was the principal objective of the framers in designing the Constitution.

How is this objective attained? The principal means is through the separation of powers. Again, we quote Madison. Writing in *The Federalist Papers No. 47* he argued, "No political truth is certainly of greater intrinsic value or stamped with the authority of more enlightened patrons of liberty than that ... the accumulation of all powers, legislative, executive and judiciary, in the same hands ... may justly be pronounced the very definition of tyranny."[45] It was not, however, the mere separation of powers of the government into four distinct parts (including the two parts of the Congress); in addition, the Constitution allowed the people—the voters—to elect directly only one of the four parts: the House of Representatives, arguably the least powerful of the four.

The second major principle of constitutional design was federalism, a system of government in which powers are shared between a national (federal) government and the governments of the several states. The last of the Bill of Rights, the Tenth Amendment, establishes this federal system by *delegating* some powers to the federal government, *prohibiting* both the states and the federal government from exercising certain powers, and *reserving* all others to the states. The major powers of the federal government were limited to regulating commerce and the currency, conducting diplomacy, and waging war. Everything else done by the government was to be done by the states.

As Robinson writes, when this system of government was being devised, "tensions about slavery were prominent among the forces that maintained the resolve to develop the country without strong direction from Washington."[46] In limiting the power of the federal government in Washington, the framers simultaneously limited the possibility of universal freedom. Again, to quote from Robinson's *Slavery in the Structure of American Politics*:

> Therefore, in the United States a political system "exquisitely" sensitive to
> elements of which it was composed and whose structure, both formal and

informal, was geared to frustrate and facilitate public action at the national level could not be expected to produce action to end slavery, particularly when the group with the most immediate interest in overthrowing slavery was itself completely unrepresented.[47]

African Americans, however, given their status first as slaves and subsequently as a poor, oppressed minority, have always found the status quo unacceptable. They favored—and favor today—rapid, indeed radical, change in the status quo. They have also favored action by the federal government rather than by the states. Historically, African Americans and their allies have made an important contribution to universalizing freedom through their support for a powerful federal government. The power of the federal government has increased markedly during three periods in American history: the Reconstruction Era in the 1860s, the New Deal Era in the 1930s, and the civil rights–Great Society Era of the 1960s. In two of these periods, the black quest for freedom was central to the expansion of federal power (see Chapter 2 for more detailed discussion of these three periods of expanding federal power). As we show in the chapter on public opinion, Chapter 4, African Americans remain the most distinctively and persistently liberal of all the various groups of the American population, strongly supporting an activist, interventionist federal government.

Faces and Voices in the Struggle for Universal Freedom
JAMES FORTEN (1766–1842)

James Forten contributed to universal freedom by working to make the principles of equality expressed by Jefferson in the Declaration of Independence real for all persons. Forten was part of the founding generation of Americans. Born in Philadelphia to a family of free black persons, as a boy he fought in the American Revolution, and by the time of his death in 1842, he was among the wealthiest men in the United States. A master sailmaker, Forten employed an integrated workforce and used his wealth to organize and finance the abolitionist movement. In 1813, he published *A Series of Letters by a Man of Color*. In this pamphlet, Forten argued that freedom was universal. Anticipating Frederick Douglass's famous 1852 "Fourth of July Address" and Martin Luther King, Jr.'s famous 1963 "I Have a Dream" speech, Forten wrote,

> We hold these truths to be self-evident, that God creates all men equal, is one of the most prominent features in the Declaration of Independence, and in the glorious fabric of collected wisdom, our noble Constitution. This idea embraces the Indian and the European, the savage and the saint, the Peruvian

James Forten.

Source: "Black Patriots During the Revolution," Varsity Tutors. Retrieved October 4, 2016 from https://www.google.com/search?q=jame+fort en&source=lnms&tbm=isch&sa=X&ved=0ahU KEwi3plqbysHPAhXq7YMKHRfyDGsQ_AUICC gB&biw=1280&bih=900#tbm=isch&q=jame+f orten%2C+black+and+white%2C+image&img rc=W9KJUBu0nsFW9M%3A

and the Laplander, the white man and the African, and whatever measures are adopted subversive of this inestimable privilege, are in direct violation of the letter and spirit of our Constitution, and become subject to the animadversion of all.

Forten defied the odds, and his life, work, and writings demonstrated that African Americans were equal to the white men of his generation who founded the Republic.[a]

[a] Julie Winch, *A Gentleman of Color: The Life of James Forten* (New York: Oxford University Press, 2002).

Summary

Freedom is a major value in Western and American culture. Yet freedom as a value in the West and in the United States has its origins partly in the struggles of slaves for freedom. While espousing the value of freedom, many Western philosophers and many of the founders of the American republic embraced racism and the ideology of white supremacy, which gave them the freedom to deprive others of their freedom. Thus, in writing the social contract—the Constitution—that established the United States, African Americans were left out, thereby setting in motion the centuries-long African American freedom struggle. Power—the central concept in politics and political science—is intimately related to freedom. Whites with power used it to fashion a notion of their freedom that allowed them to destroy freedom for Africans and African

Americans. African Americans, on the other hand, with relatively little power, developed the idea of universal freedom as part of their ongoing struggles to reclaim their own freedom.

The American Constitution is a remarkable document, widely admired around the world as one of freedom's great charters. However, from the outset it was a terribly flawed document that compromised the Declaration of Independence's promise of universal freedom and equality. From Thomas Jefferson's Declaration to the writing of the Constitution at Philadelphia, the founders of America compromised the idea of universal freedom in pursuit of a union based on property, profits, slavery, and the ideology of white supremacy. As a result, they created a government of limited powers, one that would act cautiously and slowly. The African American freedom struggle, however, has always required a government that could act decisively—whether to abolish slavery and segregation or to secure social and economic justice. The Constitution itself therefore is one of the factors that has limited and continues to limit their quest for universal freedom.

Critical Thinking Questions

1. James Baldwin, a notable black author, wrote, "Words like 'freedom,' 'justice,' and 'democracy' are not common concepts; on the contrary, they are rare. People are not born knowing what these are. It takes enormous and, above all, individual effort to arrive at the respect for other people that these words imply." Given this context, what do words like freedom, justice, and democracy mean to you?
2. Given the types of freedom defined in this chapter, which are most relevant to the African American experience and universal freedom?
3. Define "power" and discuss the relationship between freedom and power.
4. Trace the social construction of race and white supremacy in relation to the development of democracy in the United States.
5. How has the Constitution limited and continues to limit the African American quest for universal freedom?

Selected Bibliography

Beard, Charles. *An Economic Interpretation of the Constitution*. New York: Free Press, 1913, 1965. The classic, controversial book suggesting that the framers of the Constitution wrote an undemocratic document in order to protect their economic interests.

Becker, Carl. *The Declaration of Independence: A Study in the History of an Idea*. New York: Vintage Books, 1922, 1970. The classic study of the writing of the Declaration.

Brown, Robert. *Charles Beard and the Constitution: A Critical Analysis of an Economic Interpretation of the Constitution*. New York: Norton, 1965. A comprehensive critique of Beard's controversial book.

Davis, David Brion. *The Problem of Slavery in Western Culture.* Ithaca, NY: Cornell University Press, 1966. An early, groundbreaking study of the interrelationship between slavery and the emergence of freedom as a value in the Western world.

Farrand, Max. *The Framing of the Constitution of the United States.* New Haven, CT: Yale University Press, 1913. A short, readable account of the writing of the Constitution by the scholar who prepared the four-volume documentary record of the proceedings of the Philadelphia convention.

Fehrenbacher, Don, and Ward McAfree. *The Slaveholding Republic: An Account of the United States Government's Relations to Slavery.* New York: Oxford University Press, 2001. The most recent and the most detailed study of the subject.

Freehling, William. "The Founding Fathers and Slavery." *American Historical Review* 77 (1972): 81–93. A generally sympathetic account of how slavery influenced the framers' work on the Constitution.

Harding, Vincent. *There Is a River: The Black Struggle for Freedom in America.* New York: Harcourt Brace Jovanovich, 1981. A lyrical, poetic, inspiring narrative.

Jordan, Winthrop. *White over Black: American Attitudes toward the Negro, 1550–1812.* Baltimore, MA: Penguin, 1968. A monumental study tracing the origin and development of white attitudes toward Africans and African Americans from the sixteenth century through the early history of the United States.

Patterson, Orlando. *Freedom in the Making of Western Culture.* New York: Basic Books, 1991. The most recent study of how freedom in the West emerges out of the experience of slavery.

Robinson, Donald. *Slavery in the Structure of American Politics.* New York: Harcourt Brace Jovanovich, 1971. The best book on the role slavery played in the debates and compromises that shaped the writing of the Constitution.

The Federalist Papers. Introduction by Clinton Rossiter. New York: New American Library, 1961. The authoritative interpretation of the Constitution written during the debate on ratification by James Madison, Alexander Hamilton, and John Jay. It is also a classic in American political thought.

Notes

1 Eric Foner, Reconstruction: America's Unfinished Revolution, 1863–1877 (New York: Harper & Row, 1988): 77.

2 William Riker, *Federalism: Origins, Operation and Significance* (Boston, MA: Little, Brown, 1964): 140.

3 Orlando Patterson, *Freedom in the Making of Western Culture* (New York: Basic Books, 1991): 1.

4 John Hope Franklin, *From Slavery to Freedom: A History of Negro Americans* (New York: Knopf, 1980): 31.

5 See Patterson, *Freedom in the Making of Western Culture* and his "The Unholy Trinity: Freedom, Slavery and the American Constitution," *Social Problems* 54 (Autumn 1987): 543–77. See also Edmund Morgan, *American Slavery, American Freedom: The Ordeal of Colonial Virginia* (New York: Norton, 1975); David Brion Davis, *The Problem of Slavery in Western Culture* (Ithaca, NY: Cornell University Press, 1966), and his *The Problem of Slavery in the Age of Revolution* (Ithaca, NY: Cornell University Press, 1975).

6 Patterson, "The Unholy Trinity," pp. 559–60. Patterson, in *Freedom in the Making of Western Culture*, contends that freedom is a uniquely Western value and that "almost never outside the context of western culture and its influence, has it [non-

Western culture] included freedom. Indeed, non-Western peoples have thought so little about freedom that most human languages did not even possess a word for the concept until contact with the West" (p. x).

7 Patterson, "The Unholy Trinity," p. 545.

8 W. E. B. Du Bois, *The Gift of Black Folk: The Negroes in the Making of America* (New York: Square One Publishers, 2009): 57.

9 Patterson, *Freedom in the Making of Western Culture*, pp. 3–5.

10 Foner, *Reconstruction*, p. 231.

11 Richard King, *Civil Rights and the Idea of Freedom* (New York: Oxford University Press, 1992): 26.

12 Ibid., pp. 26–28.

13 Herbert Aptheker, *A Documentary History of the Negro People in the United States*, vol. 1 (New York: Citadel Press, 1967): 1.

14 Harold Lasswell and Abraham Kaplan, *Power and Society: A Framework for Political Inquiry* (New Haven, CT: Yale University Press, 1950): 26.

15 Robert Dahl, "The Concept of Power," *Behavioral Science* 2 (July 1957): 201–15.

16 Max Weber, "Class, Status and Party," in H. H. Gerth and C. Wright Mills, eds., *From Max Weber* (New York: Oxford, 1958): 180.

17 Mack H. Jones, "A Frame of Reference for Black Politics" in Jones, *Knowledge, Power and Black Politics* (Albany: SUNY Press, 2014): 5.

18 Ibid.

19 Ibid.

20 Carl Becker, *The Declaration of Independence: A Study in the History of an Idea* (New York: Vintage Books, 1922, 1970): 320.

21 Joseph Ellis, "Editing the Declaration," *Civilization* (July/August 1995): 60. See Becker's *The Declaration of Independence* for a detailed analysis of the various changes made in Jefferson's original draft.

22 Ellis, "Editing the Declaration."

23 Becker, *The Declaration of Independence*, pp. 212–13.

24 From *The Writings of Thomas Jefferson*, p. 324, as cited in Becker, *The Declaration of Independence*, p. 25.

25 Ibid.

26 A comprehensive treatment of Jefferson's views on race is in Winthrop Jordan, *White over Black: American Attitudes Toward the Negro, 1550–1812* (Baltimore, MA: Penguin Books, 1969): chap. 12, "Thomas Jefferson: Self and Society."

27 Jones, "A Frame of Reference for Black Politics," pp. 3–15.

28 Stokely Carmichael and Charles Hamilton, *Black Power: The Politics of Black Liberation* (New York: Vintage Books, 1967): 3–4.

29 Ibid.

30 Jenny Williams, "Redefining Institutional Racism," *Ethnic and Racial Studies* 8 (1985): 323–75; Louis Knowles and Kenneth Prewitt, *Institutional Racism in America* (New York: Prentice Hall, 1969); Robert C. Smith, *Racism in the Post–Civil Rights Era: Now You See It, Now You Don't* (Albany: SUNY Press, 1995): 54–75.

31 Daily Currant, *Buchanan: 'White America' Died Last Night*, November 7, 2012. www.dailycurrant.com/2012/11/07/buchanan-white-america-dead/.

32 William Freehling, "The Founding Fathers and Slavery," *American Historical Review* 77 (1972): 83.

33 Ibid.

34 Ibid.

35 See Joe R. Feagin, *Racist America: Roots, Current Realities and Future Reparations* (New York: Routledge, 2000): 16.

36 *The Federalist Papers*, Introduction by Clinton Rossiter (New York: New American Library, 1961): 337.

37 Donald Robinson, "The Constitutional Legacy of Slavery," *National Political Science Review* 4 (1994): 11.

38 For a provocative discussion of Thomas Jefferson as the first "Negro President," see Garry Wills, *Negro President: Jefferson and Slave Power* (Boston, MA: Houghton Mifflin, 2003).

39 See Leonard Richards, *Slave Power* (Baton Rouge: Louisiana State University Press, 2000): 42.

40 For discussion of the last effort to enforce Section 2 organized by the Student Nonviolent Coordinating Committee (SNCC), see Carmichael and Hamilton, *Black Power*, chap. 4.

41 Robinson, "The Constitutional Legacy of Slavery," p. 12.

42 Ibid.

43 Address by Justice Thurgood Marshall at the Annual Seminar of the San Francisco Patent and Trademark Association, May 6, 1987. Reprinted as "Racial Justice and the Constitution: A View from the Bench," in J. H. Franklin and G. R. MacNeil, eds., *African Americans and the Living Constitution* (Washington, DC: Smithsonian Institution Press, 1995): 315.

44 *The Federalist Papers*, p. 78. In a way, whether Madison or any of the other framers were themselves men of property is irrelevant since, as Donald Robinson writes, "Every one of them had made a pile of money, married a wealthy woman or committed his professional life to the service of wealthy clients." Donald Robinson, *To the Best of My Ability: The Presidency and the Constitution* (New York: Norton, 1987): 65.

45 Ibid., p. 301.

46 Donald Robinson, *Slavery in the Structure of American Politics* (New York: Harcourt Brace Jovanovich, 1971): 435.

47 Ibid. In his more recent book on the American political system, Robinson calls for major modifications in the separation of powers so that the federal government may act more coherently and rapidly. See his *To the Best of My Ability*, chap. 12.

CHAPTER 2

Federalism and the Limits of Universal Freedom

LEARNING OBJECTIVE

Explain the principles of federalism, and how they advantage and disadvantage African Americans in their quest for freedom.

Robert Bork, nominated in 1987 by President Reagan for a seat on the Supreme Court, argues that federalism is an important means to protect individual liberty and freedom. Bork argues that indeed federalism is the Constitution's most important protector of an individual's freedom and that it has been of special value to African Americans in their quest for freedom. With respect to African Americans, Bork writes,

> People who found state regulations oppressive could vote with their feet and in massive numbers they did. Blacks engaged in the great migration at a time when southern states blatantly discriminated. . . . [O]f course this freedom to escape came at a price. But if another state allows you the liberty you value, you can move there and the choice is yours alone, not dependent on those who made the Constitution.[1]

In his classic study *Federalism: Origins, Operation and Significance*, William Riker rejects Bork's arguments about the relationship between federalism and freedom, stating flatly that "federalism may have more to do with destroying freedom than encouraging it."[2] With respect to federalism and the African American quest for freedom, Riker is equally harsh in his condemnation: "The main beneficiaries throughout American history have been southern whites, who have been given the freedom to oppress Negroes, first as slaves and later as a depressed caste."[3] Thus, for Riker, "if in the United States one disapproves of racism, one should disapprove of federalism."[4]

For African Americans, at least until the 1960s civil rights revolution, federalism has had an ambivalent, contradictory effect on their quest for universal freedom. The Civil Rights Act of 1964 universalized freedom throughout the United States with respect to race discrimination. Prior to the 1960s, however, federalism operated in an ambivalent way with respect to race, since each state was free to make any laws it wished regarding the oppression of blacks. So, for example, in 1640 Virginia was the first state to pass laws legally enslaving blacks, but in the 1780s Massachusetts was the first state to legally abolish slavery. In the Antebellum Era, antislavery abolitionists used the power of northern state governments to undermine slavery in the South by refusing to return escaped slaves as required by the Constitution and the Fugitive Slave Act—thus, the idea of north to freedom, of following the North Star, and

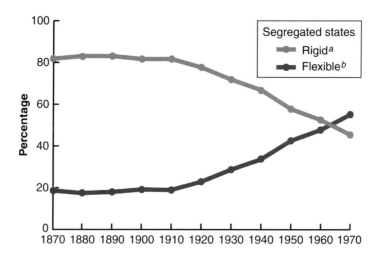

FIGURE 2.1

The Percentage of the African American Population in the Rigid (South) and Flexible (Non-South) Segregated States: 1870–1970

[a] Rigid segregated states are the 11 states of the Old Confederacy.
[b] Flexible segregated states are the other states of the Union.

Sources: Adapted from U.S. Bureau of Census, *Negro Population in the United States: 1790–1915* (Washington, DC: Government Printing Office, 1918): 43–44, for the data from 1870 to 1910. U.S. Bureau of Census, *Negro Population in the United States: 1920–1932* (Washington, DC: Government Printing Office, 1935): 9–11, for the data from 1920 to 1930. U.S. Bureau of Census, *Census for Population: 1950 Vol. II: Characteristics of the Population: Part I United States Summary* (Washington, DC: Government Printing Office, 1951): Table 59, 1–106, for the 1950 data. U.S. Bureau of Census, *Historical Statistics of the United States: Colonial Times to 1970* (Washington, DC: Government Printing Office, 1975): 24–37, for data for 1940, 1960, and 1970. All calculations were prepared by the authors.

of north to freedom's "Promised Land." In this sense, until the abolition of slavery in the 1860s, federalism allowed some space, although limited, for African American freedom in the United States.

Similarly, once a system of rigid segregation was imposed in the South beginning in the 1870s, blacks, as the Bork quote points out, began once again to look to the North for freedom, to vote with their feet in the mass exodus from the South. In Figure 2.1, data are displayed on the percentage of African Americans living in the "rigidly segregated" southern states (see Box 2.1), compared to the more "flexibly segregated" northern states. In 1870, 81 percent of the African American population lived in the rigidly segregated South. Then, starting as early as 1915, a slow, steady migration—commonly known as the "Great Migration"—of African Americans began to the more flexibly segregated North so that by 1970 only 55 percent of African Americans still lived in the South.[5] The Civil Rights Act of 1964, the Voting Rights Act of 1965, and the Fair Housing Act of 1968 universalized freedom insofar as they made racial discrimination illegal throughout the United States, North and South. Therefore, one should probably qualify Riker's blanket condemnation of federalism because during the eras of slavery and segregation, it did provide some opportunity in the North for the exercise of limited forms of freedom.

Federalism: Origins and Operations in the United States

Federalism—the sharing of the powers of government between the national (federal) government and the governments of the states—along with the separation of powers, is one of the major contributions of the framers of the Constitution to the art and practice of government. In Western political thought, the *sovereign power* of the government (its supreme, absolute, unrestrained authority over its citizens) could not be divided. Jean Bodin, the leading Western philosopher on the idea of sovereignty, argued that sovereignty could not be divided, that it was indivisible and must reside in a single person (a monarch) or institution (parliament).[6] The framers of the American Constitution rejected Bodin's idea of the indivisibility of the sovereign power of government on the theory that since the people of the United States were sovereign, they, if they wished, could divide sovereignty in order to create a well-ordered government that would secure their liberties.

The idea that ultimate sovereignty or power of the government rests with the people is the underlying philosophical principle of the American government that shapes both federalism and the separation of powers. However, there is a practical reason that the framers felt compelled to adopt the federal system: Without federalism, it is unlikely that there could have been a union of all the 13 states. Some of the framers favored a unitary rather than a federal

BOX 2.1

The "Absurd" Career of Jim Crow[a]

As most Americans are aware, with the end of Reconstruction and the adoption of the doctrine of "separate but equal" by the Supreme Court in *Plessy* v. *Ferguson*, the southern states required or permitted the separation of blacks and whites in virtually all areas of life, public and private. Schools, playgrounds, swimming pools, beaches, parks, hotels, hospitals, libraries, restaurants, cemeteries, water fountains, toilets, and buses and streetcars were all segregated. Interracial sex, marriage, and love were also outlawed. Jim Crow's strange career, however, in some places bordered on the absurd. Alabama prohibited blacks and whites from playing checkers together; in some states, schoolchildren of different races could not use the same books; Louisiana established separate districts for black and white

prostitutes; in Oklahoma, blacks and whites could not use the same public telephone. In North Carolina, young children could be arrested for interracial kissing. Finally, in Georgia and several other states, blacks were required to use separate polling places, separate courthouse doors, separate record rooms, separate record books, separate pens and ink, and separate color-coded tax receipts—white for white taxpayers and pink for blacks.

[a] C. Vann Woodward, *The Strange Career of Jim Crow* (New York: Oxford University Press, 1966). Woodward writes that the origin of the term *Jim Crow* to refer to racial segregation is "lost in obscurity"; however, it is probably related to minstrel songs done by whites in blackface.

Segregated Water Fountains.
Source: Elliot Erwitt/Magnum Photos

government. The Virginia delegation at Philadelphia proposed in its Virginia Plan essentially a unitary government. The people as a whole would elect the House, and the House in turn would elect the Senate, the president, and the judiciary. Under the plan, the Congress would have unlimited powers to "legislate in all cases to which the separate states are incompetent . . . [and]

to negative all laws passed by the several states, contravening in the opinion of the national legislature under the Articles of the union."[7] In other words, the Congress was to have unlimited powers, including the power to "negative" or veto acts of the state legislatures.

The Virginia Plan was rejected by the convention on several grounds. However, a major reason was that the southern slaveholding states feared that a unitary government with the power to "negative all laws passed by the states" might interfere with their wish to maintain slavery. Thus, philosophical principles aside, federalism was necessary in the United States for wholly practical reasons: to establish the Union.[8]

Who Is Sovereign: The People or the States? An Old Debate Renewed

It is generally accepted today that the whole people of the United States are sovereign and that acting collectively created the U.S. government. This, however, was not always the accepted view. Thomas Jefferson, for example, apparently believed that the United States was created by the states rather than the people, and consequently each state had the right to act independently of the federal government by nullifying (vetoing) federal laws with which it disagreed.[9] This view was firmly rejected by Lincoln and in a sense was settled by the Civil War. However, in a 1995 case, Supreme Court justice Clarence Thomas in a dissenting opinion (joined by the Chief Justice, Justice O'Connor, and Justice Scalia) renewed this 200-year-old debate.

The case is *U.S. Term Limits Inc. et al.* v. *Thornton et al.*, a case dealing with whether a state (in this case Arkansas) could on its own authority impose term limits on its members of Congress.[10] The Court, in a five-to-four decision, said no, holding that only all the people of the United States by amending the Constitution could limit the terms of members of Congress. In a long dissenting opinion, Justice Thomas, again writing for himself and three of his colleagues, argued that each state could limit congressional terms because *"the ultimate source of the Constitution's authority is the consent of the people of each state, not the consent of the undifferentiated people of the nation as a whole"* (emphasis added).[11] Noting that the "United States" is consistently a plural noun and that the original preamble to the Constitution reads "We the People of the States of New Hampshire, Massachusetts, etc.," Justice Thomas concluded, "The Constitution simply does not recognize any mechanism for action by the undifferentiated people of the nation."[12]

In his opinion for the majority, Justice John Paul Stevens rejected Thomas's analysis. He argued that the states under the Articles of Confederation retained their sovereignty as independent states, but with the adoption of the Constitution, *"the framers envisioned a uniform national system, rejecting the notion that the nation was a collection of states and instead creating a direct link between the national government and the people"* (emphasis added).[13] In a separate concurring opinion, Justice Anthony Kennedy wrote, "In my view, however, it is well settled that the whole people of the United States asserted their political identity and unity of purpose when they created the federal system."[14]

This debate between Justice Thomas and his colleagues on whether the people of the United States or the people of the various states established the Constitution may seem like an arcane, theoretical, academic debate with no practical consequences. It is not. Rather, it is a debate central to the thesis of this book: whether the United States is a nation of uniform, universal rights and freedom or whether it is one of freedom limited by states' rights. It is also part of an ongoing effort by conservatives on the Court and in the Congress to radically reshape the federal system, by taking power from the federal government and returning it to the states (see the section, "The Rehnquist Court and Roberts Courts, and the Revival of State-Centered Federalism," later in this chapter, and Chapter 13).

Federalism: Advantages and Disadvantages

Perhaps the most frequently stated advantage of the federal system is that it allows the states to serve as "laboratories" for public policy innovation and experimentation. In other words, each of the 50 states is free to "experiment" with the best ways to deliver education, health, and welfare services and to provide for the punishment of crime (see Box 2.2). Through the "diffusion of innovation," each state can learn from the successes and failures of the others and change its policies according to what works best.[15] Related to this, federalism grants to citizens "choice," the freedom to move from one state to another in search of a better life.

Another advantage of federalism is that it provides opportunities for minority groups in the country as a whole to be majorities (the Mormons in Utah) or larger, more politically significant minorities (Jews in New York, Latinos in California, or blacks in Louisiana) at the state and local levels. This provision enhances the opportunities for minority groups to participate in politics and to be elected to office, again a situation that would not be possible in a unitary system. This is especially true in the United States with roughly 89,527 units of government including the national, states, counties, municipalities, towns, school districts, and special districts. This enormous diversity of governments is particularly important for African Americans; although they are a national minority, they can become a local majority and control the governments in localities, including many of the nation's larger and more important cities.

There are clear advantages to a federal system, but there are clear disadvantages as well, especially to blacks in their quest for universal rights and freedoms. First, in its essence, federalism is an impediment to universal freedom because it allows the different states to define rights and freedoms for their

BOX 2.2

Federalism, Felonies, and the Right to Vote[a]

Under federalism, each state is free to set its own qualifications for voting, except the vote may not be denied on account of race, religion, gender, age (18), or the person's failure to pay a poll tax. But under what conditions might citizens lose and then regain the right to vote? As part of the voter registration efforts of the 1995 Million Man March, the National Coalition on Black Voter Participation surveyed each of the states in order to learn whether citizens lost their right to vote as a consequence of conviction for a felony and if so, how they could have the right restored. Thirty-five of the 50 states responded to the survey. Three states (Maine, Utah, and Vermont) with small black populations do not deprive convicted felons of the right to vote. Arkansas and West Virginia have no clearly stated procedures for restoration, three states require action by the governor, and most of the rest require action of the state pardon and parole boards or local election commissions. Mississippi (which at 37 percent has the largest percentage black population of any state) is different. Its constitution states, "The legislature, *may* by a two-thirds vote of both houses, of all members elected, restore the right of suffrage to any person disqualified by reason of crime, but the reason therefore shall be spread upon the journal and the vote shall be by yeas and nays." Thus, in Mississippi it is more difficult for a citizen who has committed a crime to regain the right to vote than it is to impeach the president of the United States. In Mississippi, African Americans are more than three times as likely to be convicted of felonies as whites. Thus, they are three times as likely to lose the right to vote, and once lost, it is very difficult to regain. Perhaps these are mere coincidences, but it is striking that in Mississippi—the state with the worst history of race oppression and the largest black population—citizens find it more difficult than in any other of the 35 responding states to regain their voting rights once lost. It is striking because the effect of the Mississippi procedure is to deny the vote to a large number of its black citizens.

In the 2004 election, 4,686,539 Americans were denied the right to vote because they had been convicted of a crime. A study using data from the U.S. Census's Current Population Survey estimates the net effect of felony disenfranchisement laws on the probability of voting by blacks and whites. It found that overall voter turnout is lower in states with the most restrictive felony disenfranchisement laws.[b] In terms of blacks, specifically, the probability of blacks in those states voting in the 1996 presidential election declined by 10 percent and in 2000 by 7 percent.[c] The authors also looked specifically at Florida, the site of the closely contested Bush–Gore 2000 presidential race. They found that "in 1996 an estimated 204,600 African American men were disenfranchised because of criminal convictions in the state. If disenfranchisement figures were similar (or greater) in 2000 it is possible that the election results might have been different if Florida had a less restrictive criminal disenfranchisement law."[d] In 2007, Florida's newly elected Republican governor, Charlie Crist, persuaded the state's Executive Clemency Board to immediately restore voting rights to most felons who have served their sentences. However, in 2011 the legislature in Florida reversed the governor and adopted measures to permanently ban convicted felons from voting.

Congressman John Conyers, the senior African American member of Congress, introduced legislation in 2000 that would restore voting rights in federal elections to former prisoners nationwide (although their right to vote in state and local elections would still be left to the states). This legislation, however, has been blocked in committee as critics contend it is unconstitutional because it extends the power of the federal government into an area reserved to the states. However, in 2005 two states took actions to restore voting rights to felons. In Iowa, Governor Tom Vilsack issued an executive order restoring voting rights to all felons who had completed their sentences, and in Nebraska, the legislature overrode the governor's veto and voted to overturn its ban on felony voting and automatically restore voting rights to felons after they complete their sentences and a two-year waiting period.[e] (In 2011 the Iowa legislature reversed the governor's order.)

In 2007, the Maryland General Assembly adopted legislation that allowed all felons to vote immediately after they complete their sentences, including parole or probation, and Rhode Island adopted an even more liberal law allowing felons on parole or probation to vote. In 2016 Maryland's Democratic legislature overturned Republican Governor Larry Hogan's veto of a bill allowing felons to vote as soon as they are released and in Virginia, Democratic Governor Terry McAuliffe issued an executive order allowing felons to vote. After the Virginia Supreme Court ruled the governor's executive order violated the state constitution, McAuliffe decided to get around the court's decision by personally signing individual clemency grants to ensure felon voting rights.

Kentucky's newly elected Republican Governor Matt Bevin revoked the executive order of his Democratic predecessor, Steve Beshear, restoring voting rights to felons. Meanwhile, in *Farrakhan* v. *Gregoire* (2010) the full Ninth Circuit Court of Appeals reversed a three-judge panel decision overturning Washington State's felon disenfranchisement law. The full court ruled that while the state's law had a racially discriminatory effect or result, in order to violate the Voting Rights Act or the Fifteenth Amendment, one had to show a racially discriminatory intent or purpose.

In addition to their impact on voting and elections, felon disenfranchisement laws may have direct public policy consequences. Comparing low and high disenfranchisement states, Professor Richard Brice found that disenfranchisement may have reduced social expenditures by as much as 18 percent, reducing by $1.8 billion services and programs that might otherwise have gone to areas of concentrated poverty with large black populations.[f]

[a] Hanes Walton Jr. and Simone Green, "Voting Rights and the Million Man March: The Problem of Restoration of Voting Rights for Ex-Convicts/Felons," *African American Research Perspectives* 3 (Winter 1997): 68–74. It is estimated that 13 percent of black men compared to less than 2 percent of white men have lost the right to vote as a result of felony convictions, including 32 percent of the African American men in Alabama, 31 percent in Florida, and 29 percent in Mississippi.
[b] Aman McLeod, Ismail White, and Amelia Gavin, "The Locked Ballot Box: The Impact of State Criminal Disenfranchisement Laws on African American Voting Behavior and Implications for Reform," *Virginia Journal of Social Policy and Law* 11 (2003): 66–88.
[c] Ibid., p. 79.
[d] Ibid., p. 83. On the impact of felon disenfranchisement on the 2000 election, as well as numerous U.S. Senate races see Christopher Uggen and Jeff Manza "Democratic Contraction: The Consequences of Felon Disenfranchisement," *American Sociological Review* 67 (2002): 477–803.
[e] The most comprehensive study of the history, nature, and social and political implications of denying ex-felons the right to vote is Elizabeth Hull, *The Disenfranchisement of Ex-Felons* (Philadelphia, PA: Temple University Press, 2006).
[f] See Sean McElwee, "How the Prison–Industrial Complex is Corrupting Elections," *Salon*, May 26, 2015.

citizens. Historically, this power has allowed a minority of southern whites to limit the freedom of African Americans, even against the wishes of a majority of the American people. Second, federalism, as a number of political scientists have shown, tends to lead to irresponsible government.[16] Woodrow Wilson, political scientist and 28th president of the United States, eloquently stated the case for the irresponsibility of divided power in his 1898 book *Congressional Government.* Wilson observed that "the more power is divided the more irresponsible it becomes. A mighty baron who can call half the country to arms is watched with great jealousy, and, therefore restrained with more vigilant care than is ever vouchsafed the feeble master of a single and solitary castle."[17] In other words, citizens are more likely to be aware of and exercise restraint on or greater control of one powerful central government than they are of scores of state and local governments. This situation is even more the case today than when Wilson was writing in 1898, given the development of a national news media (particularly television) that focuses its attention on events in Washington. Average citizens living in Detroit or San Francisco are more likely to be aware of what the president and the Congress are doing in Washington than they are of what the governor and legislature are doing in Lansing and Sacramento.

E. E. Schattsneider has argued that widening or nationalizing the scope of government decision making tends to enhance the power of minority groups.[18] That is, a minority such as African Americans is more likely to be able to influence decision makers in Washington than in any of the 50 state capitals. This is because decisions at the national level tend to be more visible, and minority interest groups tend to be better organized in national than state politics. For this reason, for example, African American leaders opposed "Devolution," the efforts of the Republican congressional majority in 1995 to transfer responsibility for social welfare programs (welfare, Medicaid, food stamps, etc.) to the states. Another reason African Americans oppose the transfer of social programs to the states is that instead of one uniform, universal standard for welfare or Medicaid, there would be 51. Again, this is part of the essence of federalism. As Riker writes, "The grant of autonomy to local majorities to create confused policies has resulted in a cost to the whole society that is probably greater than the cost of uniformity."[19] To relate Riker's point to the theme of this book, uniformity in national policies, as opposed to multiple state policies, is more likely to result in universal rights and freedoms.

Reconstruction, the New Deal, and the Civil Rights Movement: The Triumph of National-Centered Power

Throughout American history there has been debate and conflict between those who favor *national-centered power* and those who favor *state-centered power.* Generally, the American political tradition tends to favor state-centered power, and advocates of national-centered power have tended to prevail only in times of national crisis. Even then, the advocates of state-centered power reassert themselves in calls for a return of power to the states. Frederick Douglass during Reconstruction—the first triumph of national-centered power—observed that "no political idea is more deeply rooted in the minds of the country [than] the right of each state to control its own affairs."[20] Thus, it is not surprising that after each period of expanding national power, there were subsequent calls for a return of power to the states.

Reconstruction

National-centered power—greater authority and responsibility to the federal government—has triumphed only during periods of crisis. The first such crisis, the gravest in the nation's history, was the Civil War and the effort to reconstruct the South in its aftermath. As Reconstruction historian Eric Foner shows, an activist federal government as an instrument of reform emerges in the Reconstruction Era of the Civil War.[21]

During this period, the power of the president—particularly his commander-in-chief powers—expanded enormously under Lincoln. Then under President Andrew Johnson, the powers of Congress also expanded as that body passed several civil rights laws requiring the states to accord the newly freed slaves universal freedom and equal rights. For a time during this period, the U.S. Army was maintained in the southern states to enforce these rights. The federal government also established its first social welfare agency—the Freedmen's Bureau—to provide assistance first to the newly freed slaves and subsequently to poor whites displaced by the war. Finally, three amendments were added to the Constitution: the Thirteenth abolishing slavery, the Fourteenth establishing universal citizenship and equality and fairness under law for all persons, and the Fifteenth guaranteeing voting rights to all men regardless of race. The Fourteenth Amendment eventually was to become one of the most important mechanisms for expanding the power of the federal government in relationship to the states. (On the pro-universal freedom, progressive policies of state and local governments during Reconstruction, see Chapter 13.)

The New Deal

National-centered power expanded for a second time during Franklin Roosevelt's New Deal.[22] In the midst of the Great Depression, the federal government took on a wide array of responsibilities previously left to the states or market forces, including universal access of the elderly to retirement income, welfare for fatherless children, and government-supported public works jobs for the unemployed. In addition to the beginnings of the modern welfare state, the New Deal also expanded the power of the regulatory state with respect to banking, agriculture, the stock market, and the relationship between workers and their employers. The Supreme Court initially declared many of the New Deal programs unconstitutional because the Court said they exceeded the federal government's Article 1, Section 8, powers. Eventually, however, under pressure from the popular Roosevelt, the Court changed its mind and approved virtually all aspects of the New Deal. Thus, for the first time in American history, Congress established a series of universal programs designed to assure the employment and social security of *all* its citizens.

During the New Deal, the federal government also established a series of grants in aid to the states and localities—funds to assist them in carrying out their responsibilities in such areas as public works, housing, and health. These grants in aid were vastly expanded in the 1960s as part of Lyndon Johnson's Great Society (by the 1970s there were more than 600 such specific grants covering everything from alcohol and drug abuse to youth training programs). These grants usually come with strings attached; that is, they carry uniform or universal conditions that states and localities must comply with.

The Civil Rights Revolution and the Great Society

The civil rights reforms of the 1960s ushered in the last great expansion of federal power. In a sense, these reforms were a second reconstruction or a completion of the first. As in the original Reconstruction, Congress passed three new civil rights laws guaranteeing universal access to the ballot, public education, employment, restaurants, hotels and other public places, and the sale and rental of housing. Two new amendments were added to the Constitution granting the right to vote for president to the largely black city of Washington, DC, and abolishing the poll tax. The Supreme Court, then the president, and finally the Congress began to enforce the Fourteenth and Fifteenth Amendments for the first time in 100 years. And on two occasions (Little Rock in 1957 and the University of Mississippi in 1962), the U.S. Army, again for the first time in a century, was deployed in the South to enforce African American civil rights.

Federal social welfare programs also expanded during this period as a part of Lyndon Johnson's Great Society and "war on poverty." Universal access to health care for the elderly and to nursing homes for the poor elderly was guaranteed, as was health care for the poor. The Great Society also provided federal support for elementary and secondary education and loans and grants for college and postgraduate education. Again, these were universal programs, providing support to persons no matter where they lived in the country.

Yet, as always in American history, there was reaction to this expanding power of the federal government from those favoring state-centered power. During Reconstruction, Foner writes, "A more powerful national state and a growing sense that blacks were entitled to some measure of civil equality produced their own countervailing tendencies as localism, laissez-faire and racism, persistent forces in the nineteenth century American life, reasserted themselves."[23] One hundred years later these same persistent, countervailing tendencies emerged in reaction to the Great Society and civil rights reforms of the 1960s. Beginning in 1968 with the election of Richard Nixon, again in 1980 with the election of Ronald Reagan, and again in 1994 with the election of Republican congressional majorities, these forces of localism, laissez-faire, and racism were reasserted, continuing the historic tension and conflict between advocates of national-centered and state-centered power.

The Fourteenth Amendment: The American Charter of Universal Freedom

Of the Fourteenth Amendment, Fred Friendly and Martha Elliot write, "It was as if Congress had held a second constitutional convention and created a federal government of vastly expanded proportions."[24] And of the three Civil War amendments, including the Fourteenth, Justice Samuel Miller in the *Slaughterhouse Cases* wrote,

> No one can fail to be impressed with the one prevailing purpose found in them all, lying at the foundation of each, and without which none of them would have been suggested; we mean the freedom of the slave race, the security and firm establishment of that freedom and the protection of the newly made freeman and citizen from the oppression of those who had formerly exercised dominion over him.[25]

Of the Fourteenth specifically, Justice Miller wrote, "*It is so clearly a provision for that race ... that a strong case would be necessary for its application to any other*" (emphasis added).[26]

Although the Fourteenth Amendment did vastly expand the power of the federal government in relation to the states and establish a basis for the protection of the freedom of African Americans, it took 100 years for this to happen. In the meantime, contrary to Justice Miller's view, the amendment has been applied to persons of other races, including those fictitious persons called corporations. *Indeed, until the 1960s the amendment was more frequently used to protect the freedom of corporations than it was the freedom of blacks.* Thus, to fully appreciate how the amendment became the great charter of universal freedom for all Americans, we need to trace the history of its adoption and implementation from the 1860s to the 1960s.

The Fourteenth Amendment: Origins and Development

The Fourteenth Amendment was approved by the House and Senate in 1866 and ratified by the necessary three-fourths of the states two years later. William Nelson noted that much of the opposition to the amendment, North and South, was "deeply racist" as opponents argued that equality should not be granted to the "inferior races," specifically not just blacks but also Indians and the Chinese on the West Coast.[27] Although racism was the principal basis of opposition, opponents also argued that the amendment violated the principles of federalism as it gave the federal government unprecedented authority to interfere in the affairs of the states.

The Fourteenth Amendment, with five sections, is one of the longest amendments to the Constitution. The most important and controversial part is Section 1, which establishes universal citizenship and declares freedom and equality throughout the United States. As Friendly and Elliot wrote in *The Constitution: That Delicate Balance*, the following 17 words brought about a "quiet revolution" in American government and politics: *No state shall make or enforce any law which shall abridge the privileges or immunities of citizens of the United States, nor shall any state deprive any person of life, liberty or property without due process of law; nor deny to any person within its jurisdiction the equal protection of the law.*[28] The controversy about this important language is whether its authors intended it to "incorporate" the Bill of Rights—that is, whether the "privileges and immunities" of citizens of the United States are those rights spelled out in the first nine amendments to the Constitution.[29]

Although the principal sponsors of the amendment in both the House and the Senate (Representative Jonathan Bingham of New York and Senator Jacob Howard of Michigan) declared during the debates that it would require the states to abide by the Bill of Rights, there is still no agreement even today among scholars who have studied the amendment's history. Some argue that the intent of the Fourteenth Amendment was clearly to incorporate the Bill of Rights.[30] Others are just as certain from their research that this was not the amendment's intent.[31] There is, as Professor William Nelson notes, voluminous research to support both sides of the argument; thus, he concludes there is an "impasse in scholarship."[32] That is, we do not know for sure—and perhaps never will—the intent of the framers of the amendment.

The Supreme Court and the Fourteenth Amendment, 1865–1925: Universal Freedom Denied

The Supreme Court historically has also been divided on the intent of the amendment. Immediately after its adoption, the Court took the view that it did not make the Bill of Rights applicable to the states. The *Slaughterhouse Cases* were the first heard by the Court under the Fourteenth Amendment. In his opinion for the court's majority, Justice Miller rejected the argument that the amendment's privileges and immunities clause incorporated the Bill of Rights, holding that the only rights protected were access to Washington, DC, and coastal seaports; the right to protection on the high seas; the right to use the navigable waters of the United States; the right of assembly and petition; and the privilege of *habeas corpus*. Three justices dissented in this case; however, what modern legal scholars call Justice Miller's "pernicious" opinion remained the law of the land until the beginning of the twentieth century.[33]

The Supreme Court took a similar view in its reading of the amendment's equal protection clause when it declared the Civil Rights Act of 1875 unconstitutional. This act prohibited racial discrimination in public accommodations such as hotels, theaters, and streetcars. In the *Civil Rights Cases of 1883*, Justice Joseph Bradley declared that the Fourteenth Amendment's equal protection clause only prohibited discrimination by the states, not private businesses or persons. In language reminiscent of that used today by conservative judges and others who oppose affirmative action, Justice Bradley declared,

> When a man has emerged from slavery, and by the aid of beneficent legislation has shaken off the inseparable concomitants of that state, there must be some stage in the progress of his elevation when he takes the rank of a mere citizen, and ceases to be the special favorite of the laws, and when his rights as a citizen, or a man, are to be protected in the ordinary modes by which other men's rights are protected.[34]

In his dissent, Justice John Marshall Harlan argued that the civil rights law did not make blacks "special favorites of the law" and that the clear purpose of both the Thirteenth and the Fourteenth Amendments was to establish and decree "universal freedom throughout the United States." In 1896 in *Plessy* v. *Ferguson*, the Court continued its narrow reading of the amendment when it declared that racial segregation did not violate the equal protection clause. Again Justice Harlan dissented, declaring that the Fourteenth Amendment made the Constitution "color blind"; but his view was not to prevail until the Supreme Court's 1954 *Brown* v. *Board of Education* decision.

Ironically, until the 1960s, the Fourteenth Amendment's great charter of universal freedom was used to protect the freedom of corporations rather than that of African Americans or any other real persons. William Blackstone, in his *Commentaries on the Laws of England* published in 1765, defines corporations as "artificial persons who may maintain a perpetual succession and enjoy a kind of legal immortality."[35] In 1905 in *Lochner* v. *New York*, the Supreme Court struck down a New York state law that limited the hours of bakery workers to 10 hours a day and 60 hours a week. The Court held that New York's minimum hours law violated "the general rights to make a contract in relation to his business which is part of the liberty of the individual protected by the Fourteenth Amendment of the federal Constitution."[36] New York had passed the law in the exercise of its *police powers*—that is, to protect the health and safety of the workers; however, the Court held that the "liberty of contract" guaranteed by the Fourteenth Amendment's due process of law clause meant that if a business wanted to require its workers to work more than 60 hours a week, the states could not interfere. Using similar reasoning, the Court subsequently invalidated other government regulations of business, including child labor laws.[37] The Court's decision in *Lochner* was controversial, but it remained the law until the

Court changed its mind during the Depression, when government regulation of corporations and the economy became more imperative, not to mention popular.

The Supreme Court and the Fourteenth Amendment, 1925–2015: The Universalization of Freedom

Today the Fourteenth Amendment is largely used to protect civil liberties and civil rights. *Civil liberties* are generally understood as the rights of individuals that are protected from government abridgement. *Civil rights* are generally understood as the right of minorities (blacks, women, and homosexuals) to freedom and equality under the law. The Court first began to interpret the Fourteenth Amendment as protecting civil liberties embodied in the Bill of Rights in 1925, and it began to seriously enforce the amendment's guarantee of equality for blacks and other minorities in the 1950s and 1960s.

In 1925 in *Gitlow* v. *New York*, the Supreme Court began the gradual process of incorporating or universalizing the Bill of Rights. In this case, the Court for the first time held that "freedom of speech and of the press . . . are among the fundamental personal rights and 'liberties' protected by the due process clause of the Fourteenth Amendment from impairment by the states."[38] In *Gitlow* the Court overturned more than 50 years of prior decisions on the Fourteenth Amendment. Then, as Table 2.1 shows, the Court began a gradual, year-by-year, amendment-by-amendment process, sometimes called *selective incorporation of the Bill of Rights*. In this process, the Court applied the rest of the First Amendment to the states, and then, in the 1960s, it applied those provisions of the Bill of Rights dealing with the rights of persons accused of crimes (the Fourth, Fifth, Sixth, and Eighth Amendments). And in 1973 in *Roe* v. *Wade*, the Court interpreted the Fourteenth Amendment as creating a right to privacy (either in the Fourteenth's guarantee of liberty or as a Ninth Amendment unmentioned right) that is broad enough to cover a woman's right to choose an abortion. In 2003 in *Texas et al.* v. *Lawrence*, the Court extended this right of privacy to gays and lesbians, prohibiting the states from making homosexual relations a crime. And in 2015 in *Oberfeld* v. *Hodges*, the Court held that denial of the right to marry to same sex couples violated both the Equal Protection and Due Process Clauses of the Fourteenth Amendment. Thus, an amendment once described as only for the "Colored race" is now used to secure rights and freedoms for all Americans.

With respect to the "Colored's," in 1954 the Supreme Court declared in *Brown* v. *Board of Education* that, at least in terms of the public schools, racial segregation was a violation of the Fourteenth Amendment's equal protection clause, reversing the half-century precedent set in *Plessy* v. *Ferguson*. Then in the 1960s, Congress, responding to the protests and demonstrations led by Dr. Martin Luther King Jr., passed a series of laws designed to enforce the

TABLE 2.1 Dates of U.S. Supreme Court Decisions Ensuring Bill of Rights Protections Nationwide

Freedom: Selected Provisions and Amendments (1–10) *(Key Cases are Italicized)*	Year of Incorporation/ Universalization
Eminent Domain (5)[a] *Key case: Chicago, Burlington, and Quincy R.R. v. Chicago*	1897
Free speech (1) *Key case: Gitlow v. New York*	1925
Free press (1) *Key case: Near v. Minnesota*	1931
Free exercise of religion (1) *Key case: Hamilton v. Regents of the University of California*	1934
Freedom of assembly (1) and freedom to petition the government for the redress of grievances (1) *Key case: DeJonge v. Oregon*	1937
No establishment of state religion (1) *Key case: Everson v. Board of Education*	1947
Freedom from unreasonable search and seizure (4) *Key case: Mapp v. Ohio ("exclusionary rule")*	1961
Freedom from cruel and unusual punishment (8) *Key case: Robinson v. California*	1962
Right to counsel in any criminal trial (6) *Key case: Gideon v. Wainwright*	1963
Right against self-incrimination and forced confessions (5) *Key cases: Malloy v. Hogan and Escobedo v. Illinois*	1964
Right to counsel and to remain silent when questioned by police (6) *Key case: Miranda v. Arizona*	1966
Right against double jeopardy (5) *Key case: Benton v. Maryland*	1969
Right to keep and bear arms (2) *Key case: McDonald v. Chicago*	2010

[a] Number in parentheses refers to the Amendment to the Constitution addressing that right or freedom. The Court first incorporated the right to privacy in *Griswold* v. *Connecticut* (381 U.S. 479, 85. S.Ct., 1678), a 1965 case involving the right of married couples to use contraceptives.

Source: Craig Ducat and Harold Chase, *Constitutional Interpretation*, 4th ed. (St. Paul, MN: West, 1988): 845–46.

Fourteenth's guarantee of universal freedom and equality. But in passing the public accommodations section of the 1964 Civil Rights Act (which prohibited discrimination in hotels, motels, and restaurants), Congress relied not on the Fourteenth Amendment but instead on its power to regulate interstate commerce (because hotels and motels received products or served customers who crossed state lines). Since the Supreme Court in 1883 had invalidated a similar civil rights law based on the Fourteenth's Section 5 enforcement power, the Congress, by using the commerce clause, avoided the problem of having the Court overrule yet another of its precedents. (In general, the Court is reluctant to overturn its prior decisions, relying on the principle of *stare decisis*—let the previous decision stand.)[39] This led Justice William O. Douglas in his concurring opinion in the case, *Heart of Atlanta Motel* v. *the United States*, upholding the 1964 law to write,

> I am reluctant to . . . rest solely on the commerce clause. My reluctance is not due to any conviction that Congress lacks the power to regulate commerce in the interests of human rights. It is rather my belief that the right of the people to be free of state action that discriminates against them because of race . . . occupies a more protected place in our constitutional system than does the movement of cattle, fruit, steel and coal across state lines. Hence, I would prefer to rest on the assertion of legislative power contained in section 5 of the Fourteenth Amendment which states "The Congress shall have the power to enforce, by appropriate legislation, the provisions of this article"— a power which the Court concedes was exercised at least in part.[40]

One hundred years after the adoption of the Fourteenth Amendment, it became the Constitution's great charter of freedom in fact as well as theory, establishing a new vision of universal freedom, equality, and liberty under law for all Americans. It is a vision of freedom that Abraham Lincoln invoked in 1863 at Gettysburg and that Martin Luther King Jr. invoked a hundred years later at the Lincoln Memorial in Washington (see Box 2.3).

To achieve Lincoln's vision and King's dream required a fundamental transformation in federalism as well as reversal by the Supreme Court of more than 50 years of its decisions on the relationship between federalism and freedom. Unfortunately, for African Americans and others interested in universal freedom, the Supreme Court once more appears to be reversing itself. This time, however, the Court is seeking to limit freedom by reviving old principles of federalism and states' rights.

The Rehnquist and Roberts Courts, and the Revival of State-Centered Federalism

The "states are not mere political subdivisions of the United States," so said Justice Sandra Day O'Connor in *New York* v. *United States*, a case invalidating

BOX 2.3

Abraham Lincoln at Gettysburg and Martin Luther King Jr. at Lincoln Memorial: Two Speeches in the Quest for Universal Freedom

In 1863, Abraham Lincoln was asked to deliver "a few appropriate remarks" at the dedication of the cemetery at the Gettysburg battlefield. One hundred years later, Martin Luther King Jr. was asked to deliver the closing remarks at the Lincoln Memorial after the March on Washington. Lincoln spoke for three minutes before a crowd of 20,000. King spoke for 17 minutes before a crowd of 250,000. Lincoln spoke on the bloody battlefield at Gettysburg to give meaning to the Civil War. King spoke at the Lincoln Memorial to give meaning to the civil rights movement's bloody battles then taking place in the South. Of all the American presidents, Abraham Lincoln was the most gifted in the rhetoric of freedom, and of all the leaders of the African American people, Martin Luther King Jr. was the most gifted in the rhetoric of freedom. Each man in his own time and his own way sought to universalize the idea.

Lincoln at Gettysburg invoked the words of Thomas Jefferson written "four score and seven years ago" in order to declare that *all* men are created equal and that the Civil War that would free the slaves had ushered in "a new birth of freedom." At Lincoln's Memorial, King invoked the words of Lincoln's Emancipation Proclamation written, as King said, "five score years ago" to declare that he had a dream of universal freedom, a dream that one day "*all* of God's children, black men and white men, Jews and Gentiles, Protestants and Catholics, will be able to join hands and sing in the words of the old Negro spiritual 'Free at last! Free at last! Thank God Almighty, we are free at last!'"

Abraham Lincoln was murdered on April 15, 1865. Martin Luther King Jr. was murdered on April 4, 1968. Neither man died in vain because by their words and

Dr. Martin Luther King Jr. delivers the "I Have A Dream" speech from the Lincoln Memorial, August 28, 1963.

Source: AP Images

deeds they helped to remake the idea of freedom for America and the world.[a]

[a] On Lincoln's address, see Garry Wills, *Lincoln at Gettysburg: The Words That Remade America* (New York: Touchstone, 1992), and on King's "I Have a Dream Speech," see Drew Hansen, *The Dream: Martin Luther King Jr. and the Speech That Inspired a Nation* (New York: Ecco, 2003). A panel of experts on the history of American political rhetoric ranked "I Have a Dream" as the greatest speech of the twentieth century. See Thurston Clarke, *Ask Not: The Inauguration of John F. Kennedy and the Speech That Changed America* (New York: Henry Holt, 2004): 218.

a federal law that required the states either to regulate low-level radioactive waste within their boundaries or to assume legal liability for it.[41] Justice O'Connor's observation in this case and the decision of the Court seem to represent an attempt by the Court's conservative majority to radically alter the existing relationship between the federal government and the states. In doing so, the Court reopened the 200-year-old debate between advocates of national-centered versus state-centered power in American politics.

The late Chief Justice Rehnquist—appointed by President Nixon in 1972 and elevated to the Chief Justice by President Reagan in 1986—was an advocate of state-centered federalism, arguing that much of the Court's federalism jurisprudence since the New Deal was wrong and not supported by a fair reading of the Constitution. Until the 1980s, Rehnquist was a lonely dissenter, as his views on federalism (and civil liberties and civil rights) were not shared by his colleagues on the nine-member Court. However, with the appointments of Justices Sandra Day O'Connor, Antonin Scalia, and Anthony Kennedy by President Reagan, and Justice Clarence Thomas by President Bush, the Rehnquist Court (1972–1986) frequently commanded a narrow five-person majority on many federalism and Fourteenth Amendment cases that continues, with some inconsistency, under the Roberts Court (Chief Justice John Roberts was appointed by President G. W. Bush in 2005).

Several important cases decided by the Court suggest that it may be returning to its Reconstruction Era jurisprudence. Earlier in this chapter we discussed Justice Thomas's extraordinary dissent in the term limits case, in which he argued that the federal government has only those powers expressly granted or necessarily implied in the Constitution. In his opinion for the Court's narrow majority in the term limits case, Justice John Paul Stevens said this of Thomas's dissent:

> It would seem to suggest that if the Constitution is silent about the exercise of a particular power—that is, where the Constitution does not speak either expressly or by necessary implications—the federal government lacks the power and the states enjoy it. . . . Under the dissent's unyielding approach, it would seem *McCulloch* was wrongly decided. Similarly, the dissent's approach would invalidate our dormant commerce clause jurisprudence.[42]

Although Thomas and his colleagues did not prevail in the term limits case (Justice Kennedy, as he occasionally does, voted with the Court's more centrist or liberal justices in this case), in several cases involving the powers of Congress and federal–state relations, the conservatives have been in the majority. In *United States* v. *Lopez*, the five-person conservative majority declared unconstitutional a federal law that prohibited the possession of guns near a school.[43] This was the first time since the New Deal that the Court invalidated an act of Congress based on its exercise of its commerce clause powers. Similarly, in *Seminole Tribe* v. *Florida*, the Court held (again five to four) that individuals could not sue a state to enforce federal laws or rights passed by Congress pursuant to its authority under the commerce clause because such cases were an "unconstitutional intrusion on state sovereignty," thereby overturning its own decision in *Pennsylvania* v. *Union Gas*, in which it explicitly held that Congress could use its commerce clause authority to grant rights to citizens enforceable in the federal courts against the states.[44] In his dissent in *Seminole Tribe*, Justice Stevens used unusually strong language, describing the majority's decision as "a sharp break with the past," "shocking," and "profoundly misguided."[45]

By the mid- to late 1990s, the Court continued its "sharp break with the past" in the area of federalism. The Court's conservative majority invalidated three federal laws, including the Religious Freedom Restoration Act, a provision of the "Brady" gun control law, and the Communications Decency Act. In addition, the Court also decided a series of cases that increased the power of the states at the expense of Congress and private citizens. Summing up these cases, the *New York Times* legal correspondent concluded that they represented "the most powerful indication yet of a narrow majority's determination to reconfigure the balance between state and Federal authority in favor of the states."[46]

By the early 2000s, the Court continued its attack on the idea of universal or national rights by declaring several acts of Congress unconstitutional, including parts of the 1994 Violence against Women Act. In doing so, the Court's five-person majority declared that violence against women did not significantly impact interstate commerce.[47] In *Kimel* v. *Florida Board of Regents*, the Court ruled that Congress exceeded its authority when it allowed federal lawsuits by state employees alleging discrimination on the basis of age. Writing for the majority, Justice O'Connor concluded, "States may discriminate on the basis of age without offending the Fourteenth Amendment if the age classification in question is rationally related to a legitimate state interest."[48] Finally, in *Board of Trustees of the University of Alabama et al.* v. *Garrett et al.*, the Court ruled that states were immune from suits under the 1991 Americans with Disabilities Act if the state's discrimination had a "rational basis." Writing for the majority, Chief Justice Rehnquist said, "The Fourteenth Amendment does not require states to make special accommodations for the disabled, so long as their actions toward individuals are rational. They could quite hardheadedly—and perhaps hardheartedly—hold to job requirements which do not make allowance for the disabled."[49] In each of these cases, the four more liberal justices who dissented declared that the majority's decisions were a radical curtailment of Congress's authority to regulate the economy and protect civil rights.

The Court's relentless attack on the idea of universal freedom or federally guaranteed rights came to somewhat of a halt in its 2002–2004 terms. Although its decisions since the mid-1990s returning power to the states on the basis of the Tenth and Eleventh Amendments have not been noticed by the public at large, they have excited concern in academic and legal circles and among those concerned with civil liberties and civil rights. A good example of this concern was raised by John T. Noonan, a judge on the Ninth Circuit Court of Appeals. Noonan was so alarmed by the Rehnquist Court's state-centered federalism that he wrote *Narrowing the Nation's Power: The Supreme Court Sides with the States* (2002) to call the matter to broad public attention.[50] Noonan essentially takes the view of the dissenting justices in the federalism cases since the 1990s, a stance somewhat unusual for a lower court judge who is supposed to follow and implement the decisions of the Supreme Court majority. But Noonan believes so strongly that the Rehnquist majority is wrong (particularly in the way it has interpreted the Eleventh Amendment to deprive individuals of the right to sue the states) that he argues he is obligated as an informed citizen to speak out. And speak out he does, arguing that the Court's recent federalism decisions are hypocritical; are without foundation in the history or text of the Constitution; and threaten, if not halted and reversed, to undermine principles of universal freedom and democratic government.

Although it is doubtful that Noonan's book or the many critical articles in the law reviews about the Court's federalism cases have affected its decisions, in 2003 and 2004 it did appear in two important cases to back away, if only slightly, from its state-centered federalism. The two cases involved the Family Leave Act and the Americans with Disabilities Act. However, in one case the Court continued to narrow the power of the federal government in relationship to the states. In a 5–4 decision, the Court ruled that the Eleventh Amendment prohibited the federal government from suing the states to enforce its regulations. In this case, the Federal Maritime Commission sued the Port of Charleston, South Carolina, in order to enforce provisions of the Federal Shipping Act. Justice Thomas, writing for the majority, said the Eleventh Amendment precluded the suit because the amendment's preeminent purpose was to "accord the states the dignity that is consistent with their status as sovereign entities."[51] Justice Stephen Breyer, writing for the dissenters, rejected the idea that the states were "sovereign" and went on to argue that the majority decision lacked "any firm anchor in the Constitution's text."[52]

This, however, was a rather minor, technical administrative case without great impact on the rights and freedoms of the people (it involved a dispute about a ship that claimed it had been wrongfully denied berth at the Charleston port), although the principle underlying the decision has potential far-reaching implications. In two cases with broad and immediate impact on the lives of ordinary people, the Court backed away from its rigid adherence to state-centered federalism. In 2003 in *Nevada Department of Human Resources* v. *Hibbs*, the Court upheld the right of persons to sue the states to enforce provisions of the Family Leave Act. In 1993 Congress, using the Fourteenth Amendment's equal protection clause, enacted the Family Leave Act in order to remedy what it viewed as widespread gender discrimination in the workplace (the act allows men and women to take up to 12 weeks of unpaid leave to care for a sick relative). William Hibbs, an employee of Nevada's Department of Human Resources, was fired when he took leave to care for his sick wife. He then sued the state, and in a 6–3 decision, the Court rejected Nevada's claim of sovereign immunity under the Eleventh Amendment. The Chief Justice wrote that the act was "narrowly targeted" to "protect the right to be free from gender-based discrimination in the workforce by addressing the pervasive sex-role stereotype that caring for family members is women's work."[53]

In 2004, the Court upheld provisions of the Americans with Disabilities Act, allowing individuals to sue states that fail to provide access (ramps or elevators) to their courthouses. Although the Court had previously rejected the right of the disabled to sue states for employment discrimination, in *Tennessee v. Lane* a 5–4 majority said access to the courts was such a fundamental right that the states' Eleventh Amendment immunity had to give way to Congress's authority to enforce the equal protection clause of the Fourteenth Amendment.[54] Justice Stevens's opinion was limited, however, to access to courthouses, and a particularly egregious case of discrimination in which George Lane, a paraplegic, was literally forced to crawl up the stairs of the courthouse in Benton, Tennessee. (When his case was not heard in the morning session and he refused to crawl up a second time, he was arrested and jailed for failing to appear.)[55] That is, Justice Stevens specifically refused to rule that states could be sued if they denied access to the disabled to other public places such as classrooms, swimming pools, or libraries. It is generally believed that Justice Stevens refused to extend his opinion to cover all public places because Justice O'Connor (who joined his opinion) would have dissented. Thus, while the Court has retreated a bit from state-centered federalism, it still does not have a majority that embraces the Fourteenth Amendment as the great charter of universal freedom for all Americans in all cases. With some inconsistencies in cases affecting federal–state relations, the Roberts Court continued the pattern established by the Rehnquist Court. For example, in 2012 in *Coleman* v. *Court of Appeals of Maryland et al.*, the court used the Eleventh Amendment to declare that states were immune from suits by citizens for violating the Family Medical Leave Act (see also the 2013 decision of the Court on the Voting Rights Act discussed in Chapter 13).

Faces and Voices in the Struggle for Universal Freedom
ELEANOR ROOSEVELT (1884–1962)

Eleanor Roosevelt, wife of President Franklin D. Roosevelt, contributed to universal freedom and equality through a passionate commitment to racial equality in the 1930s and 1940s and her work in the drafting and enacting of

Former U.S. First Lady Eleanor Roosevelt.

Source: "AP Photo #693150408695." *AP Images.* 9 December 2014. Associate Press. Web 4 October 2016.

the United Nations (UN) Declaration of Human Rights. Mrs. Roosevelt, with little success, constantly prodded her husband to take a forthright position in opposition to lynchings and in support of African American freedom and equality. Although she could not "educate" her husband on universal freedom and equality, she did educate the public through her speeches and her "My Day" column, which she wrote daily from 1936 to 1962. Mrs. Roosevelt also championed the cause of women, workers, and the poor and dispossessed.

After her husband's death, President Truman in 1945 appointed her to head the UN Human Rights Commission. Three years later, she was the major figure in securing adoption by the international community of the Declaration of Human Rights. The UN Declaration declares that all persons are equal and human rights are universal. In addition to civil rights, the Declaration also declares that all persons are entitled to social and economic rights, including the "right to a standard of living adequate for the health and well-being of his family including food, clothing, housing, medical care and social services."[a]

[a] Shelia K. Hershan, *The Candles She Lit: The Legacy of Eleanor Roosevelt* (Westport, CT: Praeger, 1993).

Summary

Federalism is an integral part of the American system of government. But from the beginning of the country's history, there has been tension and debate between those who favor state-centered power and those who favor national-centered power. For most of American history, advocates of state-centered power have been dominant. However, in three periods of national crisis—two of which were directly related to the African American freedom struggle—advocates of national-centered power triumphed. During the Civil War and Reconstruction, the

Depression and the New Deal, and the 1960s civil rights revolution, the powers of the federal government in relationship to the states were enormously expanded. In each of these periods, the federal government began to play a more active role in protecting civil liberties and civil rights and in regulating the market economy. The Fourteenth Amendment, adopted after the Civil War to secure the freedom and equality of African Americans, has been central to the expansion of national-centered power, serving as the great charter of universal freedom for all Americans.

Yet after each period of expanding federal power, the forces of states' rights and localism reasserted themselves. In the earliest days of the Republic, these forces were generally liberal, progressive, antifederalist Democrats, but since the Civil War and especially since the New Deal, conservative Republicans have generally been hostile to expanding the power of the federal government. Since the election of Richard Nixon in 1968, Republican presidents have consistently called for a return of power to the states. The idea of states' rights appears to be the direction of the current conservative majority on the Supreme Court. Thus, the tide in American politics may once again be shifting toward state-centered power and limited rather than universal freedom.

Critical Thinking Questions

1. Explain federalism, and discuss how it may advantage and disadvantage racial or ethnic groups in their quest for freedom and equality.
2. Explain the relationships between federalism, race, felonies, and the right to vote.
3. Explain the difference between national-centered power and state-centered power.
4. What was the role of the Freedmen's Bureau and how did it facilitate the freedom and citizenship for formerly enslaved Africans and poor whites?
5. Why is the Fourteenth Amendment referred to as the American charter of universal freedom?

Selected Bibliography

Curtis, Michael. *No State Shall Abridge: The Fourteenth Amendment and the Bill of Rights*. Durham, NC: Duke University Press, 1988. A strong argument for the case that the Fourteenth Amendment was intended to incorporate the Bill of Rights.

Dye, Thomas. *American Federalism*. Lexington, MA: Lexington Books, 1990. One of the better studies of the operations of the federal system.

Foner, Eric. *Reconstruction: America's Unfinished Revolution, 1863–1877*. New York: Harper & Row, 1988. The definitive study of the Reconstruction Era and the first major expansion of the power of the federal government.

Grodzins, Morton. *The American System*. Chicago, IL: Rand McNally, 1966. A standard study of the operations of the federal system.

Nelson, William. *The Fourteenth Amendment: From Political Principle to Judicial Doctrine*. Cambridge, MA: Harvard University Press, 1988. A balanced analysis of the debate on the intent of the framers of the Fourteenth Amendment and the Bill of Rights and the relationship of their intent to federalism.

Noonan, John, T. *Narrowing the Nation's Power: The Supreme Court Sides with the States*. Berkeley: University of California Press, 2002. A federal appeals court judge's critique of the Rehnquist Court's state-centered federalism.

Riker, William. *Federalism, Origin, Operation and Significance*. Boston, MA: Little, Brown, 1964. An important study whose thesis is that federalism in the United States operates to limit freedom and benefit southern racists.

Wilkerson, Isabel. *The Warmth of Other Suns: The Epic Story of America's Great Migration*. New York: Vintage, 2011. An extensive, in-depth analysis of the migration from 1915 to 1970 of the six million or so Southern blacks who moved to northern and western cities.

Notes

1 Robert Bork, *The Tempting of America: The Seduction of the Law* (New York: Free Press, 1990): 52–53. Bork's nomination to the Court was defeated 58 to 42.

2 William Riker, *Federalism: Origins, Operation and Significance* (Boston, MA: Little, Brown, 1964): 140.

3 Ibid., pp. 132–33.

4 Ibid., p. 155.

5 On the great black migration from the South to the North between the 1920s and the 1960s, see Neil Flingstein, *Going North: Migration of Blacks and Whites from the South 1900–1950* (New York: Academic Press, 1981); and James Grossman, *Land of Hope: Chicago, Black Southerners and the Great Migration* (Chicago, IL: University of Chicago Press, 1989). For an extensive, in-depth analysis from 1915 to 1970, see also Isabel Wilkerson, *The Warmth of Other Suns: The Epic Story of America's Great Migration* (New York: Vintage, 2011).

6 Jean Bodin's political theory and idea of sovereignty are discussed in George Sabine, *A History of Political Theory*, 4th ed. (Hinsdale, IL: Dryden Press, 1973): 377–84.

7 Max Farand, *The Records of the Federal Constitutional Convention* (New Haven, CT: Yale University Press, 1937), vol. 1, cited in Riker, *Federalism*, p. 22.

8 Of the 190-plus governments in the world, about 17 are federal—mostly in large nations such as Australia, Canada, India, and Nigeria.

9 The most famous proponent of this view in American history is South Carolina's senator John C. Calhoun in his doctrine of "concurrent majorities," which argues that on legislation affecting the interests of the states, both congressional and state legislative majorities should be required. In other words, the states should have a veto over federal laws affecting the state's vital interests. See Calhoun's *A Disquisition on Government*, edited by C. G. Post (New York: Liberal Arts Press, 1963).

10 *U.S. Term Limits, Inc. et al.* v. *Thornton et al.* (slip opinion) #93-1456 (1995). A slip opinion is a preliminary draft of a decision issued prior to formal publication.

11 Ibid.

12 Ibid. Justice Thomas contends that the framers deleted the reference to the states in the Preamble because they were not certain that all the states would ratify the Constitution.

13 Ibid.

14 Ibid.

15 See Jack L. Walker's classic article on this topic, "The Diffusion of Innovation among the American States," *American Political Science Review* 63 (September 1969): 880–99.

16 See E. E. Schattsneider, *The Semi-Sovereign People* (New York: Holt, Rinehart and Winston, 1960); Grant McConnell, *Private Power and American Democracy* (New York: Vintage Books, 1966); and Woodrow Wilson, *Congressional Government: A Study in American Politics* (Gloucester, MA: Peter Smith, 1885, 1973).

17 Wilson, Congressional Government, p. 77.

18 Schattsneider, *The Semi-Sovereign People.*

19 Riker, *Federalism*, p. 144.

20 Eric Foner, *Reconstruction: America's Unfinished Revolution, 1863–1877* (New York: Harper & Row, 1988): 251.

21 Ibid.; see especially chaps. 6–10.

22 On the New Deal, see William Leuchtenburg, *Franklin D. Roosevelt and the New Deal* (New York: Crowell, 1967); and Otis Graham, *An Encore for Reform: The Old Progressives and the New Deal* (New York: Oxford, 1967).

23 Foner, *Reconstruction*, p. 34.

24 Fred Friendly and Martha Elliot, *The Constitution: That Delicate Balance* (New York: McGraw-Hill, 1984): 18.

25 *The Slaughterhouse Cases*, 16 Wall (83 U.S.) 26 (1873) as reprinted in Kermit Hall, William Wiecek, and Paul Finkelman, eds., *American Legal History: Cases and Materials* (New York: Oxford University Press, 1991): 240.

26 Ibid., p. 240. In its 2000–2001 term, the Supreme Court provided striking examples of how the Fourteenth Amendment is applied to protect the rights and freedoms of persons who are not of the black "race." In *Troxel et vir* v. *Granville* (#99-138, 2000), the Court declared unconstitutional a Washington state law that granted grandparents visitation rights to the daughter of their deceased son, over the objections of the girl's mother. In declaring the law unconstitutional, the Court held that the Fourteenth Amendment's due process clause provides protection against government interference with certain fundamental rights and liberties of all persons, and that one of those rights is the right of parents to make decisions about rearing their children without government intrusion. In an ironic decision—given the origins and purposes of the amendment—in *Bush* v. *Gore* (#00-949, 2000), the Court used the amendment's equal protection clause to in effect award the presidency to Bush, the candidate opposed by more than 90 percent of the blacks for whom the amendment was originally adopted.

27 William Nelson, *The Fourteenth Amendment: From Political Principle to Judicial Doctrine* (Cambridge, MA: Harvard University Press, 1988): 96.

28 Friendly and Elliot, *That Delicate Balance*, p. 18.

29 In 1833 the Supreme Court in *Barron* v. *Baltimore* held that the Bill of Rights applied only to the federal government.

30 See, for example, Michael Curtis, *No State Shall Abridge: The Fourteenth Amendment and the Bill of Rights* (Durham, NC: Duke University Press, 1988). This is also Foner's view in *Reconstruction*, pp. 251–61.

31 Charles Fairman, "Does the Fourteenth Amendment Incorporate the Bill of Rights? The Original Understanding," *Stanford Law Review* 2 (1949): 5–139.

32 Nelson, *The Fourteenth Amendment*, chap. 1.

33 The term *pernicious* is used by Hall, Wiecek, and Finkelman in *American Legal History* to describe the opinion, p. 241.

34 *The Civil Rights Cases*, 109 U.S. 3 (1883) as reprinted in Hall, Wiecek, and Finkelman, p. 241.

35 Ibid., p. 140.

36 *Lochner* v. *New York*, 198 U.S. 45 (1905).

37 Traditionally, the idea of due process of law as it is found in the Fifth and Fourteenth Amendments was *procedural*—that a person would have a fair trial and hearing. *Lochner* and similar decisions introduced the notion of *substantive* due process—the idea that the substance of a legislative act in and of itself could be unfair and thus a violation of due process.

38 *Gitlow* v. *New York*, 268 U.S. 652 (1952). Benjamin Gitlow was a communist who advocated violent revolution. He was convicted under New York's criminal anarchy law. In deciding the case, however, the Court did not overturn his conviction but simply made the theoretical point that the free speech clause applied to the states.

39 Another reason that the commerce clause rather than the Fourteenth Amendment was used is that it permitted the leaders of the Senate to refer the bill to the Commerce Committee (which was chaired by Senator Warren Magnuson, a pro-civil rights liberal from Washington) rather than the Judiciary Committee, which was chaired by James Eastland, a racist, white supremacist from Mississippi. See Robert Loevy, *Hubert Humphrey and the Civil Rights Act of 1964: First Person Accounts of Congressional Enactment of the Law That Ended Racial Segregation* (Albany, NY: SUNY Press, 1996).

40 *Heart of Atlanta Motel, Inc.* v. *United States*, 379 U.S. 241 85 S.CT., 348 (1964).

41 *New York* v. *United States*, 505 U.S. 144 (1995).

42 Justice Stevens's reference to McCulloch is to *McCulloch* v. *Maryland* (4 Wheaton, 316), decided in 1819. This case, along with *Marbury* v. *Madison* (1 Cranch, 137, 1813), in which the Court first asserted its power of judicial review, is one of the landmark cases in the development of constitutional jurisprudence in the United States. In *McCulloch* the Court established two fundamental principles that Thomas's dissent appears to challenge. The first is the doctrine of implied powers, which asserts that Congress has powers beyond those expressly listed in Article 1, Section 8; second is the doctrine of the supremacy of federal laws over those enacted by the states. Justice Stevens's reference to commerce clause jurisprudence refers to Article I's interstate commerce clause, which since the New Deal has been the major constitutional basis for Congress's authority to pass laws regulating the economy as well as social welfare and civil rights legislation.

43 *United States* v. *Lopez* (slip opinion) #93-1260 (1995).

44 *Pennsylvania* v. *Union Gas*, 491 U.S. 1, 24 (1989).

45 Seminole Tribe of Florida v. Florida et al. (slip opinion) #94-12 (1996).

46 Linda Greenhouse, "States Are Given New Legal Shield by Supreme Court," *New York Times on the Web* (June 24, 1999).

47 *United States* v. *Morrison et al.*, 529, U.S. (2001). In this case a female student at Virginia Polytechnic Institute sued three male students she alleged raped her.

48 In this case several Florida State University professors sued the state board of regents, contending that younger faculty members were treated more favorably when it came to salaries and promotions. In this case, the Court also ruled that the Eleventh Amendment gave the states immunity from most suits by individuals in federal court.

49 In this case, Alabama in one instance demoted an employee after she was treated for breast cancer, and in another refused to make accommodations for an employee who said his health required that he work in an environment free of carbon monoxide and cigarette smoke.

50 John T. Noonan, *Narrowing the Nation's Power: The Supreme Court Sides with the States* (Berkeley: University of California Press, 2002).

51 Linda Greenhouse, "Supreme Court Expands Rights of States in Maritime Suit," *New York Times* (May 28, 2002).

52 Ibid.

53 Nevada Department of Human Resources v. Hibbs (slip opinion) #01-1368 (2003).

54 *Tennessee* v. *Lane* (slip opinion) #02-1667 (2004).

55 Adam Cohen, "Can Disabled People Be Forced to Crawl up the Courthouse Steps?" *New York Times* (January 11, 2004).

PART II

Political Behaviorism

CHAPTER 3

Political Culture and Socialization

LEARNING OBJECTIVE

Identify the distinctive elements of African American political culture, and the distinctive roles played by the church, informal groups, and events in the political socialization process.

In political science, *political culture* is generally understood in terms of "psychological or subjective orientations towards politics."[1] Specifically, political culture refers to political orientations—attitudes toward the political system and toward the role of the individual in the system. Simply put, the concept refers to the individual's long-lasting, relatively fixed attitudes, beliefs, and values about politics and the political system.

Political culture refers to attitudes, values, and beliefs about politics and the political system. *Political socialization* refers to the ongoing process by which individuals acquire these attitudes, values, and beliefs.[2] In simple terms, political socialization refers to the processes of political learning. For purposes of studying this process, political scientists usually center their attention on what are called *agents of socialization*—those mechanisms by which individuals acquire their attitudes, beliefs, and values.[3] The agents include *family, church, school, peer groups*, the *media*, and *political events*.

Political Culture

In countries as large and diverse as the United States, there is not a single, homogeneous political culture.[4] Most Americans share common or core values of the culture (individualism, constitutionalism, democracy, patriotism), and often tend to think and behave politically in similar ways. Yet various groups in the country distinguished by race, ethnicity, religion, language, or region may be regulated by different patterns of thought and behavior, and these are regarded as political subcultures.[5] Thus, a *subculture* or a *political subculture* refers to variations among groups in political attitudes and behavior within the context of the larger shared culture. In the United States we may refer to a Jewish subculture, a southern subculture, and an evangelical subculture. Given their distinctive history in America and their subordinate location in the social structure, African Americans possess perhaps the most distinctive political culture or subculture in the United States. The political culture of the oppressed is likely to be different from that of the oppressor. And "Insofar as systems of ethnic relations are largely determined by structural asymmetries in wealth, prestige and power between groups, an inventory of cultural differences are frequently symptoms rather than determinants of intergroup behavior, even in systems where the distinguishing criterion of group membership is cultural."[6] And as Holden writes "Since culture is behavior learned in cohorts, it follows when two groups are separated by legal or behavioral frontiers over any significant time, some tendency toward cultural difference must develop."[7] And Holden continues "The obverse is also true, at the same time, if they coexist within the same linguistic, economic or political system they must develop significant commonalities."[8] Holden's formulation is useful in calling attention to the fact that blacks in the United States share cultural commonalities with whites but also certain "partially distinctive" attributes that "constitute a black culture. The problem, then, is to identify those attributes that constitute black culture and shape long lasting or relatively fixed black political attitudes and behavior."[9] Again, when we refer to political culture we distinguish it from public opinion (discussed in the next chapter) which tends to change rather rapidly depending on issues, events, personalities, and the nature of the times. Political culture, on the other hand, is relatively fixed, stable, long-lasting beliefs, values, and patterns of behavior. To be cultural these attributes have to cut across lines of class, region, place of residence (i.e., urban, suburban, or rural spaces), or other divisions to encompass the community as a whole.

Elements of Black Culture

The first attribute of the black culture is the idea of the black community itself; a black community, based on shared history and memory, and includes persons of African descent of all classes, ethnicities, and regions. This element of the culture is displayed empirically in evidence from survey data on racial group consciousness and identity; for example surveys show that more than 90 percent of blacks say they "feel close to black people in this country," 69 percent say they share a common or "linked" fate with other blacks and that "what happens generally to blacks in this country will have something to do with what happens in their life."[10]

A second element of black culture, widely acknowledged, is religiosity—an Africanized Christianity—which, in the view of some scholars, is the "foundation" of the culture. Measured in survey data in questions about belief in God, frequency of church attendance, and prayer and biblical literalism, African Americans are among the most religious people in the United States.[11]

V. P. Franklin in *Black Self-Determination: A Cultural History of the Faith of Our Fathers* identifies self-determination, resistance, education, and freedom as "core values" of black culture. However, he avers that these values are not unique to African Americans but are found among other subordinated or oppressed groups such as the Irish and Palestinians.[12] Unique to African American culture, Holden writes, is the value of the "wish for resistance" or "defiance" of whites and white domination. Of this attribute, Holden writes that it is used "to compensate for the pervasive insults and humiliations of the past and present by telling 'the white man' where to go and what to do. . . . Defiant heroism is represented by the plantation folklore of the 'bad Nigger' or the 'crazy Nigger' who, pushed beyond his tolerance limits, retaliated with the simple self-help of personal violence, even if doing this guaranteed his death."[13]

Houston Baker writes of the "collectivist ethos" and an "ethos of repudiation," which help to distinguish African American culture from white American culture. This collectivist ethos, Baker suggests, rejects the "fantasies" of individual advancement in favor of collective advancement of the race as a whole based on changes in societal rather than individual behavior. Related to this ethos, there is an egalitarian value in African American culture, reflected, for example, in survey data showing that blacks are much more likely to agree with the statement "The government should reduce income inequality between rich and poor; 73 percent of blacks compared to 44 percent of whites."[14] Klugel and Smith, after close examination of American attitudes on inequality, wrote "Judged by the black–white gap in beliefs potentially challenging the dominant ideology, blacks are the group closest to being 'class conscious' in the Marxian definition."[15]

Finally, on general attributes or elements of the culture Smith and Seltzer used survey data to document interpersonal alienation or what Hannerz describes as a "relative suspiciousness of the motives of others" as a characteristic of black culture.[16] They concluded that stability on this attribute, cutting across all categories of blacks including education, income, age, gender, region, and residence, "is remarkable, indicating a high degree of cohesiveness on this cultural trait."[17] This trait undoubtedly has an impact on black politics at both elite and mass levels (on its impact at the mass level on many contemporary issues see the opinion data on alienation in the next chapter). Walters, who traces the trait back to slavery, which he writes created the "cultural damage done to the black community that inhibits the trust necessary to pool their resources for economic and social development."[18]

The specifically "civic culture" element of the political culture includes attitudes toward the political system and the role of the individual in the system, including such things as knowledge of politics, interest in politics, political efficacy (the sense that one thinks one can influence the system), and trust in government. These civic attributes, except for trust in government, tend to be shaped more by class than race. That is, middle-class persons, whatever their race or ethnicity, tend to have more knowledge, interest, and efficacy in politics then poor and working-class individuals.[19] The middle class also tend to vote and participate in politics generally more than the poor and working class, again regardless of race or ethnicity. Thus, the civic culture in the United States is largely a product of class, not ethnic cultures. In other words, middle-class blacks and whites and lower-class blacks and whites generally tend to resemble each other in civic attitudes more than they resemble persons in their racially defined communities or cultures.

There is, however, one exception to these generalizations about race and the civic culture. Among whites lower-class persons have tended to score lower on trust in government than middle-class respondents.[20] But among blacks there is little relationship between class and trust in government. Blacks at all class levels tend to display a relatively low level of political trust.[21] This suggests that relatively low levels of political trust may go hand in hand with low levels of interpersonal trust as a characteristic specific to African American culture.

Political Socialization

Political socialization refers to the process by which individuals acquire political attitudes, values, beliefs, and opinions, with the process of learning and adapting to political culture.

In 1959, political scientist Herbert Hyman published *Political Socialization*. This book was the first scientific study of political socialization in the field of political science. Hyman's work focused on socialization as a process that begins in childhood and is generally completed by adolescence or certainly by early adulthood. The early socialization studies by Hyman and others focused on agents or transmitters of socialization, especially the family and schools but also the church and the media. The work of Hyman established the agenda for socialization research for several decades, but by the 1980s, scholars were departing from the view that socialization was complete by adolescence and questioning the centrality of the role of family and schools. The new socialization research suggested that the process is a lifelong one. The process of acquiring political attitudes and values (indeed, all attitudes and values) does not end at adolescence as it is rarely, if ever, fixed at a given age; rather, it is a developmental process that covers the entire life span. And while not downplaying the significance of family and school as agents of socialization, the more recent research tends to place greater emphasis on the media and on events and the environment as socialization agents. This new approach, while promising as an area of inquiry, has not stimulated a great deal of empirical work, unlike Hyman's seminal book, which resulted in a massive outpouring of socialization studies in the 1960s and 1970s. Rather, socialization studies since the 1980s— whether using Hyman's approach focusing on children and adolescents or the new approach focusing on the entire life span—have been in short supply. Thus, we know relatively little about the political socialization process as it unfolded in the late twentieth century among Americans generally and even less as it has unfolded among African Americans, since there have been even fewer studies of the socialization process in the black community.

One thing is clear about the political socialization process in black America: It is more complicated than what takes place in white America, since it requires socialization into the dominant mainstream political culture and simultaneous socialization into the political subculture of the black community. This dual process of political socialization may involve resocialization and counter-socialization.[22] That is, black children and adults may be first socialized in the general political culture and then later resocialized to hold different attitudes and values as a result of exposure to changing environments and events, or these processes may be reversed, with initial subcultural socialization being dominant and then mainstream resocialization. With the present state of the research, these processes of socialization and resocialization are not completely clear. Also, while the same basic agents or transmitters of socialization—family, church, school, and media—are present in the black community, they may function differently because of differences in the structures of these agents. Finally, there is a clear and discernable process of deliberate countersocialization as a result of movements of social change.

The family undoubtedly is the major transmitter of attitudes and values in both white and black America, but some scholars have seen a decline or attenuation in the role of the family as an agent of socialization, the result of the changing structure and role of the family in the United States. While noting a decline in the role of the family, other scholars have observed a simultaneous increase in the role of the media, which has grown in size, diversity, and pervasiveness. Since the first socialization studies in the 1960s, there has been interest in the role of the black family because of the disproportionately large number of female-headed households. This difference in structure between black and white families raises the question of whether children, especially boys, develop different attitudes and values as a result of being reared in households where no father figures are present. Some of the earliest studies suggested that male children from fatherless homes exhibited less interest in politics and were less politically efficacious.[23] However, these findings were tentative at the time, and since the 1980s there have been few systematic empirical studies, although the proportion of female-headed black families has increased dramatically since the 1970s.

Research on the school as an agent of socialization is also limited in terms of the impact of the civics curriculum and the physical environment and atmosphere of many ghetto schools, where conditions of neglect may operate as independent agents of socialization. We do know from extensive research that the black church and religiosity are important agents of lifelong socialization, transmitting civic attitudes and participatory norms.

The media's role in political socialization is unclear. Historically, the African American media was an important agent of socialization and resocialization, working against the negative stereotypes and negative portrayals of blacks in the mass media and inculcating a heritage of race pride and ethos of protest. More recent research is ambiguous on the role of the African American media. Studies on the impact of the mainstream media's role in transmitting political attitudes and values are also ambiguous in their findings.

Music has been shown to be an important component of the overall culture of African Americans, with possibly both positive and negative consequences. Concern about the role of music in the socialization process was heightened in the late twentieth century, with the emergence of rap music (see Box 3.1).

The roles of the physical environment and events have also been shown to be powerful socialization agents, especially when the process is understood to be a lifelong one. From the earliest to the most recent studies, it has been shown that the conditions of poverty and danger in many ghetto neighborhoods are powerful socializing agents, providing independent learning about the negative attitudes of white society and the government toward blacks. Thus blacks, wherever they live, tend to be cynical about the government, but these attitudes are much more pronounced in high-poverty neighborhoods. Adults in these neighborhoods also tend to express more antiwhite attitudes and are somewhat more likely to embrace elements of the philosophy of Black Nationalism.[24]

Events as Agents of Socialization

Events may also be important agents of socialization. The civil rights and black power movements were enormously influential agents of socialization and resocialization as were the 1960s periods of civil unrest and rebellion.

In the 1960s and 1970s, black artists—visual, literary, and performing—began to focus on political issues and to develop new images of blacks and the black community, stemming from the black power movement.[25]

When the black power movement peaked, a new African American socializing agent appeared—African American Democratic presidential candidates. First, the 1972 presidential campaign of African American congresswoman Shirley Chisholm.[26] Her effort galvanized thousands of women and African American Democrats.[27] Although the electoral dimension of the Chisholm campaign failed, its socializing influence was unique and important. (See Faces and Voices, Chapter 8.)

BOX 3.1

African American Music As An Agent of Political Socialization

Many observers of African American culture have pointed to the important role played by music in the socialization process. African Americans have often been heard to say, "You can tell where black people are at any given moment by our music." Novelist James Baldwin once said, "It is only in his music that the Negro in America has been able to tell his story." Political scientist Charles Henry argues that music, especially the blues, is an important socialization agent in African American politics; historian Frank Kofsky has demonstrated a relationship between the revolution in jazz symbolized in the work of John Coltrane and the militant nationalism of Malcolm X; poet and musicologist Leroi Jones points historically to a relationship between black music and black politics; and music critic Nelson George argues that in the 1960s and 1970s rhythm and blues was inspired by and gave inspiration to the civil rights and black power movements.[a]

In a comprehensive study of black music as a political agent during the 1960s, Robert Walker carried out a content analysis of all 1,100 songs that appeared on *Billboard's* cumulative annual best-selling black (soul) listings from 1946 to 1972. Walker's hypothesis was that the events of the 1960s produced a distinctive race group consciousness and solidarity that was manifested in an increase in songs with a political message. His data show a steady increase in "message songs" beginning after 1957 and that a sustained increase of "inordinate proportions" occurred between 1966 and 1969, the peak years of the black movement. By comparing black to white music in this same period, Walker was able to show that this increase in message music was peculiar to black music.[b] Among the popular songs with a political message during this period were James Brown's "I'm Black and I'm Proud," the Temptations' "Message to the Black Man," Marvin Gaye's "Inner City Blues,"

Entertainer Curtis Mayfield. From "Keep on Pushing" in the 1960s to "A New World Order" in the 1990s, Mayfield's music consistently involved political messages or "sermons," often dealing with themes of freedom.

Source: Bettmann/Corbis

B. B. King's "Why I Sing the Blues," and Curtis Mayfield's "We're a Winner." Mayfield's "We're a Winner" was thought to be so politically inflammatory that some black radio stations were urged not to play it for fear it might cause uprisings in the summer of 1968.

In some ways, rap artists embraced the Obama presidential campaign in the same fashion rhythm and blues artists embraced the civil rights and black power movements. Obama rap songs and lyrics and online videos appeared throughout the campaign by such artists as Ludacris, Nas, and Jay-Z. (Will.I.AM.'s "Yes We Can" YouTube music video was viewed by nearly 10 million people prior to the Democratic convention.) The "Hip Hop Caucus" launched an eighteen-city-swing-state-targeted tour featuring numerous artists who supported Obama. In fact, on November 3, 2008, Jay-Z stood on a North Philadelphia stage—flanked by Sean Combs, Mary J. Blige, Beyoncé, and Philadelphia mayor Michael Nutter—and told a crowd of roughly 10,000: "Rosa Parks sat so Martin Luther King could walk. Martin Luther King walked so Obama could run. Obama's running so all the children can fly." [c] Obama even used Jay-Z's "dirt-off—my shoulder" gesture to dismiss his critics. A hip-hop fan, Obama, however, at times criticized artists for misogynist lyrics, use of the "N" word, and materialism.[d]

[a] Charles Henry, *Culture and African American Politics* (Bloomington: Indiana University Press, 1990); Frank Kofsky, *Black Nationalism and the Revolution in Music* (New York: Pathfinder Press, 1970); Leroi Jones, *Blues People* (New York: Morrow, 1963); Nelson George, *The Death*

of Rhythm and Blues (New York: Dutton, 1989). For a history of black music and its relationship to politics, hear the six-CD collection (108 recordings ranging from gospel to rap), *Say It Loud: A Celebration of Black Music in America*, produced by Patrick Milligan, Shawn Amos, and Quincy Newell (Los Angeles, CA: Rhino Entertainment, 2001); and Harry Belafonte's five-CD collection, *The Long Road to Freedom: An Anthology of Black Music* (New York: Buddha Records, 2001).
[b] Robert Walker, "Soul and Society," Ph.D. dissertation, Stanford University, 1976.
[c] Dewey Clayton, *The Presidential Campaign of Barack Obama: A Critical Analysis of a Racially Transcendent Strategy* (New York: Routledge, 2010): 151. Originally quoted in Zach Baron, "Rappers for Obama, and Vice Versa," *Black Power*, Entertainment, Politics, January 23, 2009, www.blackpower.com/entertainment/rappers-for-obama-and-vice-versa/.
[d] Shaun Ossei-Owusu, "Barack Obama's Anomalous Relationship with the Hip-Hop Community," in Charles Henry, Robert Allen, and Robert Chrisman, eds., *The Obama Phenomenon: Toward a Multiracial Democracy* (Urbana: University of Illinois Press, 2011).

In 1984 and 1988, civil rights activist Reverend Jesse Jackson took a page from Chisholm and entered the Democratic presidential primaries. It was a sensation in the African American community,[28] and at the level of political socialization, it generated significant grassroots political activities and local candidacies for office.[29] It also enlarged the number of registered voters. Thus, it socialized both masses and elites in the community. As shown in Chapter 8, the Obama campaigns in 2008 and 2012 had similar effects.

In the aftermath of these presidential candidacies, a different socializing agent came in the form of the dramatic Million Man March in October 1995.[30] Led by the controversial black nationalist religious figure Louis Farrakhan, the march brought more African Americans to Washington, DC, than did King's 1963 March on Washington, and it sent numerous individuals back to their local communities committed and reinvigorated toward developing grassroots self-help organizations and programs.

African American Political Socialization: The Church and Informal Institutions

Professor Ronald Brown took the theories about the church and religion as African American socializing agents, reduced them to a psychological dimension, and placed them as testable propositions in questionnaire form in two National Black Election Studies and the National Black Politics Survey. Brown undertook these studies with a variety of different colleagues, but he has been the most consistent and persistent analyst of the religious attribute. In his first work, with colleagues Richard Allen and Michael Dawson, Brown stressed that an African American racial belief system existed and that religiosity influenced and socialized that belief system. Writing about this approach, Brown and his colleagues told "how belief systems in general and this belief system in particular help process, constrain, and bias one's interpretations of reality and influence social and political behavior"; the article then shows how "religiosity . . . influences the content of individual African American belief systems."[31] Other studies have documented a strong relationship between religiosity, voting, and other forms of political participation as well as a sense of racial identification, consciousness, and political obligation to the black community.[32] (See Box 3.2.)

Informal Institutions in the Processes of Political Socialization

Melissa Harris-Lacewell has explored how "everyday talk" among African Americans in autonomous "black spaces" may contribute to processes of political socialization and the development and sustaining of black ideological thought.[33] These "safe" spaces such as barber and beauty shops, black fraternities and sororities, and to some extent historically black colleges and universities (HBCUs)[34] operate beyond the presence and control of whites and therefore are likely spaces for storytelling and shared experiences in everyday talk that help to define and shape the historical, cultural, social, and political meanings and boundaries of blackness. African Americans interacting in these places are likely to be especially important agents in the lifelong processes of resocialization and countersocialization. However, like political socialization in general we have very few empirical studies of these informal institutions as socialization agents. As Harris-Lacewell writes, these are "largely unstudied space(s),"[35] and more research is necessary before we can prove the hypothesized role of these informal institutions in the socialization process.

Collective Memory: The Transmission Belt of African American Political Socialization

In 2004, the fourth wave of the University of Michigan's longitudinal political socialization project (running from 1965 to 1997) was completed. It demonstrates that the dominant political socialization model, which focuses on the transmission process between generations from parents to children, does not completely explain the process.[36] Although our discussion in this chapter is focused on the similar and the unique agents of political socialization within

BOX 3.2

The African American Church

Faith in God, the belief that "God will deliver us some day," has been described as the single most common theme in African American culture.[a] Given the central role of religion in black life, the church becomes the central political institution in the black community. Freedom is also central in the African American religious tradition. Lincoln and Mamiya write,

> A major aspect of black Christian belief is found in the importance given to the word "freedom." Throughout black history the term "freedom" has found deep religious resonance in the lives and hopes of African Americans. . . . In song, word and deed freedom has always been the superlative value of the black cosmos.[b]

African Americans are more religious than whites (measured by frequency of church attendance and prayer, and subjective identification with God), and religiously inclined blacks are more likely to vote and engage in other forms of political participation, such as lobbying.[c]

"The church historically has always been the central arena of the political activities of blacks, the place where the 'struggle for power and the thirst for power could be satisfied.'"[d] In the United States today, there are approximately 60,000 black churches, 50,000 clergy, and a membership of more than 17 million. These churches are organized into seven denominations. Although in recent years white evangelical Christians have used the church as a political base (forming the Christian Coalition led by Reverend Pat Robertson, a 1988 Republican candidate for president), the black church has always been politically conscious and active. During the 1960s, the largest black church denomination—the National Baptist Convention—was led by a conservative, anti-civil rights clergyman, Reverend J. H. Jackson. Jackson's leadership was challenged by Dr. Martin Luther King Jr.

President Obama Delivers Eulogy in Charleston, SC

Source: "Obama Calls for Racial Understanding, Unity as Thousands Mourn S. C. Pastor," *Washington Post*. 26 June 2015. Retrieved 4 October 2016 from https://www.washingtonpost.com/politics/thousands-gather-to-mourn-the-rev-clementa-pinckney-in-charleston/2015/06/26/af01aaae-1c0c-11e5-ab92-c75ae6ab94b5_story.html

and other progressive ministers, and the black church became the principal base of the civil rights movement. Today, it is a principal base of political organizing and electoral campaigning. It served as an important source of organizing and fundraising for Jesse Jackson's two presidential campaigns and functions as a platform for white politicians seeking the support and votes of African Americans.

Empirical studies reveal that church attendance and the overall religious experience in the black community remains higher than any other racial or ethnic group in the United States given its historical position stemming from black culture where the African American spiritual experience was necessary for survival;[e] however, like church attendance generally in America, attendance by blacks has been declining, and the mainstream black denominations have been losing members to nondenominational "charismatic" churches. Many of these churches are "mega churches" with thousands of members. This has led some scholars to surmise that they tend to be less politically and socially conscious, focusing instead on "Prosperity Gospel" which tends to use religion as a means less to pursue race group interests and social change and more as a means for individuals to personally become wealthy, healthy, and fulfilled.[f] Yet, the latest empirical study by Coleman found that when variables for religious preferences were measured against data on human capital, labor market, demographic,

political, and ideological equality with whites, spiritual differences for African Americans actually increased rather than decreased when compared to other racial or ethnic groups, providing evidence that the black religious experience seems to stem from African American culture and is not related simply to the politicoeconomic and sociocultural conditions that African Americans face; it is "part and parcel of the historic and continuing politico-economic and socio-cultural conditions of racial inequality in which Black Americans find themselves."[g]

[a] Matthew Holden, Jr., *The Politics of the Black Nation* (New York: Chandler, 1973): 17.
[b] C. Eric Lincoln and Lawrence Mamiya, *The Black Church in the African American Experience* (Durham, NC: Duke University Press, 1990): 3–4.
[c] Robert C. Smith and Richard Seltzer, *Race, Class and Culture: A Study in Afro-American Mass Opinion* (Albany, NY: SUNY Press, 1992): 29–30, 126–28. For a thorough study of the impact of religion on black political participation, see Fredrick Harris, *Something Within: Religion and African American Political Activism* (New York: Oxford University Press, 1999).
[d] E. Franklin Frazier, *The Negro Church in America* (New York: Schocken Books, 1964): 43.
[e] Major Coleman, "Holier than Thou: The Impact of Politico-Economic Equality on Black Spirituality," *National Political Science Review* 17(2) (2016): 57–94.
[f] Stephanie Mitchum, *Name It and Claim It: Prosperity Gospel and the Black Church* (Columbus, OH: Pilgrim Press, 2007).
[g] Ibid., Coleman, pp. 61 and 93.

the African American experience, with this completed research we can address in another way the question of how the black community transmits values and beliefs from generation to generation. This research indicates that it is done through a process called "collective memory." This collective memory within the black community allows the agents of socialization to not only transmit recent events such as black presidential campaigns or other contemporary political events but to integrate them with the past (slavery, the civil rights movement, etc.) in order to transmit enduring beliefs and values. This collective memory is the intergenerational transmission belt that helps to maintain the value of universal freedom in African American politics.

Research on this collective memory has been based on multiple methodologies that have been invaluable in bringing depth to the understanding of this vital but underexplored process. In addition to surveys by political scientists, this process has been examined using historical and sociological methods.[37] The work of political scientist Fredrick Harris, centering on religion and the church, shows that they are among the main repositories of this memory and principal agents of its intergenerational transmission.[38] And African American psychologists, who use the concept of collective identity, have also done important theoretical and empirical work on collective memory.[39]

Faces and Voices in the Struggle for Universal Freedom
HARRY BELAFONTE (1927–)

Harry Belafonte, the singer and actor, used his status as a cultural icon to advance the cause of universal freedom through his support of the civil rights movement, the anti-apartheid movement, and the cause of international human rights. In 1965, Belafonte's "The Banana Boat Song (Day-O)" became an instant classic and made him an international celebrity. In this same year, he met Martin Luther King Jr. and became his abiding friend, advisor, and financial supporter. He rallied celebrities to support the movement, financed the freedom rides, and raised funds to bail protesters (including Dr. King) out of jail. After Dr. King's

Harry Belafonte.

Source: "Harry Belafonte #ZZZ003917-PP-RC1" Wolfgang's Vault. Retrieved 4 October 2016 from http://images.wolfgangsvault.com/images/catalog/detail/ZZZ003917-PP.jpg

death, Belafonte became active in the anti-apartheid movement and close friend and advisor to Nelson Mandela. In 1987, the United Nations Children Fund named him a general goodwill ambassador.

Conscious of the role that music and art can play in freedom movements, Belafonte was instrumental in bringing to American attention the South African musicians Hugh Masekela and Miriam Makeba. In 1985, he organized an all-star cast to produce "We Are the World," a multicultural recording that raised millions of dollars for famine relief in Africa. And in 2001, he finally released *A Long Road to Freedom*, a historical album on the African American musical tradition.

The son of Jamaican immigrants, Belafonte's music and his music history represent a systematic effort to show that African, African American, and Caribbean music are part of an integral tradition related to the freedom struggles of African people.

Summary

The political culture or subculture of African Americans is characterized by a relatively high degree of racial group consciousness and relatively low levels of trust in the government, although this level of trust varies with the responsiveness of the system. The political culture is also characterized by a mix of oppositional and supportive attitudes with respect to the political system. It also displays a relatively high degree of alienation and ideological liberalism, attitudes considered in greater detail in Chapter 5.

The political socialization process of black Americans is shaped by the same agents that shape the process in the United States generally—family, church, school, peers, the media, and political events. However, due to their "closeness" or "linked" fate based on shared history and memory, and to the extent that these institutions are different in the black community, then the outcome of the process—political culture and public opinion—will also be different. The church—because of the religiosity of blacks and the historical role of the black church as a political institution—is a particularly powerful agent of political socialization, and some scholars see music as an important agent. Finally, events from the civil rights movement of the 1960s to the presidential campaigns of Barack Obama also shape political attitudes, opinion, and behavior and contribute to the development of a collective identity or "collective memory."

Critical Thinking Questions

1. Explain the concept of political subcultures.
2. Identify several distinctive attributes of the African American political culture.

3. How are the elements of African American political culture unique in terms of attitudes about race and civic culture?

4. What is meant by a "dual process of political socialization"? How do the "agents" or "transmitters of socialization" function in the African American community?

5. Discuss the role of the black church and music in the political socialization of African Americans.

Selected Bibliography

Abramson, Paul. *The Political Socialization of Black Americans: A Critical Evaluation of Research on Efficacy and Trust*. New York: Free Press, 1977. A solid review and assessment of the early literature on black political socialization.

Almond, Gabriel, and Sidney Verba. *The Civic Culture*. Princeton, NJ: Princeton University Press, 1963. This classic behavioral study compares the political cultures of five nations.

Almond, Gabriel, and Sidney Verba, eds. *The Civic Culture Revisited*. Boston, MA: Little, Brown, 1980. A conceptual and methodological reexamination of the concept by an international group of scholars.

Brown, Ronald, and Monica Wolford. "Religious Resources and African American Political Action." *National Political Science Review* 4 (1994): 30–48. A pathbreaking empirical article charting the effects of religion and the church as agents of political socialization.

Conover, Pamela. "Political Socialization: Where's the Politics?" In W. Crotty, ed., *Political Science: Looking to the Future, Political Behavior*, vol. 3. Evanston, IL: Northwestern University Press, 1991. An overview of the origins and evolution of the concept.

Divine, Donald. *The Political Culture of the United States*. Boston, MA: Little, Brown, 1972. A pioneering behavioralist effort to locate the component parts of the nation's political culture.

Fendrich, James Max. *Ideal Citizens: The Legacy of the Civil Rights Movement*. Albany, NY: SUNY Press, 1993. A study of the long-term socializing effects of the civil rights movement.

George, Nelson. *The Death of Rhythm and Blues*. New York: Dutton, 1989. An analysis of the relationship between black music and the black movements of the 1960s and 1970s.

Harris, Fredrick. *Something Within: Religion in African American Political Activism*. New York: Oxford University Press, 1999. The most comprehensive study of the subject.

Henry, Charles. *Culture and African American Politics*. Bloomington: Indiana University Press, 1990. An examination of the roots and nature of African American culture, focusing on religion and music.

Jones, Leroi. *Blues People: The Negro Experience in White America and the Music That Developed from It*. New York: William Morrow, 1963. An influential study of the centrality of music in African American culture.

Lincoln, Eric C., and Lawrence Mamiya. *The Black Church and the African American Experience*. Durham, NC: Duke University Press, 1990. A comprehensive historical study of the role of the black church.

Morris, Aldon, Shirley Hatchett, and Ronald Brown. "The Civil Rights Movement and Black Political Socialization." In R. Siegel, ed., *Political Learning in Adulthood*. Chicago, IL: University of Chicago Press, 1989. An excellent article demonstrating the impact and influence of ad hoc and transitory socializing agents in the African American community.

Smith, Robert C., and Richard Seltzer. *Race, Class and Culture: A Study in Afro-American Mass Opinion*. Albany, NY: SUNY Press, 1992. An effort to identify empirically certain components of African American political culture.

Walton, Hanes, Jr. "African American Political Culture: The Moral Voice and Perspective in the Recent Urban Riots." In Hanes Walton, Jr., ed., *African American Power and Politics: The Political Context Variable*. New York: Columbia University Press, 1997. Explores and delineates the existence of the African American political culture in non-conventional political behavior.

Notes

1 Glenda Patrick, "Political Culture," in G. Sartori, ed., *Social Science Concepts: A Systematic Analysis* (Beverly Hills, CA: Sage, 1984): 266.

2 Pamela Johnston Conover, "Political Socialization: Where's the Politics?" in William Crotty, ed., *Political Science: Looking to the Future. Political Behavior*, vol. 3 (Evanston, IL: Northwestern University Press, 1991): 126.

3 Ibid., pp. 273–85.

4 Gabriel Almond and Sidney Verba, *The Civic Culture: Political Attitudes in Five Nations* (Princeton, NJ: Princeton University Press, 1963). The five nations were the United States, the United Kingdom, West Germany, Mexico, and Italy. For some of the more interesting studies of political culture in the United States, see Donald Devine, *The Political Culture of the United States* (Boston, MA: Little, Brown, 1972); and Daniel Elazar, *American Federalism: A View from the States* (New York: Crowell, 1972); Gabriel Almond, "The Intellectual History of the Civic Culture Concept," in G. Almond and S. Verba, eds., *The Civic Culture Revisited* (Boston, MA: Little, Brown, 1980): 23.

5 William Reisinger, "The Renaissance of a Rubric: Political Culture as Concept and Theory," *International Journal of Public Opinion Research* 7 (Winter 1995): 348.

6 Pierre van der Berghe, *Race and Racism* (New York: John Wiley, 1967): 141.

7 Matthew Holden, Jr., *The Politics of the Black "Nation"* (New York: Chandler, 1973): 17.

8 Ibid.

9 Ibid.

10 These and related data are analyzed in detail in Michael Dawson, *Behind the Mule: Race and Class in African American Politics* (Princeton, NJ: Princeton University Press, 1994).

11 Fredrick Harris, *Something Within: Religion in African American Political Activism* (New York: Oxford University Press, 1999): 8.

12 V. P. Franklin, *Black Self-Determination: A Cultural History of the Faith of Our Fathers* (Westport, CT: Lawrence Hall, 1984).

13 Holden, *The Politics of the Black "Nation,"* p. 18.

14 Houston Baker, "Completely Well: One View of Black American Culture," in Nathan Huggins, Martin Kilson, and Daniel Fox, eds., *Key Issues in the Afro-American Experience* (New York: Harcourt Brace Jovanovich, 1971): 21. The survey data are

from the 1996 General Social Survey, National Opinion Research Center, University of Chicago.

15 James Klugel and Eliot Smith, *Beliefs About Inequality: American Views of What Is and What Ought to Be* (New York: Aldine de Gruyter, 1986): 289.

16 Robert C. Smith and Richard Seltzer, *Race, Class and Culture: A Study in Afro-American Mass Opinion* (Albany, NY: SUNY Press, 1992): 89–92, and Ulf Hannerz, *Soulside: Studies in Ghetto Culture and Community* (New York: Columbia, 1969).

17 Smith and Seltzer, *Race, Class and Culture*, p. 92.

18 Ronald Walters, *The Price of Racial Reconciliation* (Ann Arbor: University of Michigan Press, 2008): 211.

19 Sidney Verba and Norman Nie, *Participation in America: Political Democracy and Social Equality* (New York: Harper & Row, 1972).

20 Smith and Seltzer, *Race, Class and Culture*, pp. 54–57.

21 Ibid., p. 57. See also J. M. Avery, "The Sources and Consequences of Political Mistrust Among African Americans," *American Politics Research* 30 (2006): 653–82.

22 Hanes Walton, Jr., *Invisible Politics: Black Political Behavior* (Albany, NY: SUNY Press, 1985): 45–48.

23 Paul Abramson, *The Political Socialization of Black Americans* (New York: Free Press, 1977). More recently see Vonnie McLoyd et al., "Marital Processes and Parental Socialization in Families of Color: A Decade Review of Research," *Journal of Marriage and Family* 62 (2000): 1070–93.

24 Cathy Cohen and Michael Dawson, "Neighborhood Poverty and African American Politics," *American Political Science Review* 87 (1993): 288–99.

25 Morris, Hatchett, and Brown, "The Civil Rights Movement," p. 293. See also Michael Schwarz, *Visions of a Liberated Future: Black Arts Movement Writings* (New York: Thunder Mouth Press, 1989).

26 Shirley Chisholm, *The Good Fight* (New York: Harper & Row, 1973).

27 Hanes Walton, Jr., "Black Female Presidential Candidates: Bass, Mitchell, Chisholm, Wright, Reid, Vans and Fulani," in Hanes Walton, Jr., ed., *Black Politics and Black Political Behavior: A Linkage Analysis* (Westport, CT: Praeger, 1994): 251–74.

28 On the Jackson campaigns, see Joseph McCormick and Robert C. Smith, "Through the Prism of Afro-American Culture: An Interpretation of the Jackson Campaign Style," in L. Barker and R. Walters, eds., *Jesse Jackson's Presidential Campaign: Challenge and Change in American Politics* (Urbana: University of Illinois Press, 1988): 96–107; Robert C. Smith, "From Insurgency toward Inclusion: The Jackson Campaigns of 1984 and 1988," in Lorenzo Morris, ed., *The Social and Political Implications of the 1984 Jesse Jackson Presidential Campaign* (Westport, CT: Praeger, 1990): 215–31; Ronald Walters, *Black Presidential Politics in America: A Strategic Approach* (Albany, NY: SUNY Press, 1988); Lucius Barber, *Our Time Has Come* (Urbana: University of Illinois Press, 1989); Charles P. Henry, *Jesse Jackson: The Search for Common Ground* (Oakland, CA: Black Scholar Press, 1991); Thomas Cavanaugh and Lorin Foster, *Jesse Jackson's Campaign: The Primaries and Caucuses* (Washington, DC: Joint Center for Political Studies, 1984).

29 Leslie McLemore and Mary Coleman, "The Jesse Jackson Campaign and the Institutionalization of Grass-Roots Politics: A Comparative Perspective," in Walton, Jr., ed., *Black Politics and Black Political Behavior: A Linkage Analysis*, pp. 49–60.

30 Hanes Walton, Jr., "Public Policy Responses to the Million Man March," *The Black Scholar* 25 (Fall 1995): 17–23; Hanes Walton, Jr., and Simone Green, "Voting Rights and the Million Man March: The Problem of Restoration of Voting Rights for Ex-Convicts," *African American Perspectives* (Winter 1997): 68–74.

31 Richard Allen, Michael Dawson, and Ronald Brown, "A Schema-Based Approach to Modeling an African American Racial Belief System," *American Political Science Review* 83 (June 1989): 421.

32 Ronald Brown and Monica Wolford, "Religious Resources and African American Political Action," *National Political Science Review* 2 (1990): 25–37; Laura Reese and Ronald Brown, "The Effects of Religious Messages on Racial Identity and System Blame Among African Americans," *Journal of Politics* 57 (1995): 23–35.

33 Melissa Harris-Lacewell (aka Harris-Perry), *Barbershops, Bibles and BET: Everyday Talk and Black Political Thought* (Princeton, NJ: Princeton University Press, 2004).

34 A study by Gallup reported that African American graduates of HBCUs are more than twice as likely as African American graduates of non-HBCUs to recall experiencing support measures like experiential learning opportunities, long-term projects and extracurricular activities that prepared them to be engaged in their professional workplaces and communities, and to thrive financially (see "Gallup-USA Funds Minority College Graduates Report, pp. 5–6). These findings are supported by the work of Ebony O. McGee and David Stovall, "Reimagining Critical Race Theory in Education: Mental Health, Healing, and the Pathway to Liberatory Praxis," *Educational Theory* 65 (2015): 491–511. McGee and Stovall argue that " 'Weathering,' . . . is a phenomenon [that is observable among African American students at predominantly white colleges] characterized by the long-term physical, mental, emotional, and psychological effects of racism and of living in a society characterized by white dominance and privilege. [It] severely challenges and threatens a person's health and ability to respond in a healthy manner to their environment. This can cause wear and tear, both corporeal and mental, and lead to a host of psychological and physical ailments, including heart disease, diabetes, and accelerated aging" (p. 491).

35 Harris-Lacewell (aka Harris-Perry), *Barbershops, Bibles and BET: Everyday Talk and Black Political Thought*, p. 170.

36 M. Kent Jennings, "Survey Research and Political Socialization," in J. House et al., eds., *A Telescope on Society: Survey Research and Social Science at the University of Michigan and Beyond* (Ann Arbor: University of Michigan Press, 2004): 101–2. Jennings, the principal investigator of this four-wave study who has followed the same members of a 1965 senior class over 32 years, summarizes the latest research on the model from the study's vantage point.

37 See Genevieve Fabre and Robert O'Meally, *History and Memory in African-American Culture* (New York: Oxford University Press, 1994); Howard Shuman and Jacqueline Scott, "Generations and Collective Memories," *American Sociological Review* 54 (1989): 359–81; Maurice Halbwachs, *The Collective Memory* (New York: Harper & Row, 1951); Mary Francis Berry and John Blassingame, *Long Memory: The Black Experience in America* (New York: Oxford University Press, 1982).

38 See Fredrick C. Harris, *Something Within: Religion in African American Political Activism* (New York: Oxford University Press, 1999); and his recent work " 'They Kept the Story Before Them': Collective Memory, Micromobilization, and Black Political Activism in the 1960s" (Rochester, NY: University of Rochester, unpublished paper): 1–39.

39 For the best theoretical psychological work, see William E. Cross, Jr., *Shades of Black: Diversity in African American Identity* (Philadelphia, PA: Temple University Press, 1991). For the best empirical work, see Richard Allen, *The Concept of Self: A Study of Black Identity and Self-Esteem* (Detroit, MI: Wayne State University Press, 2001).

CHAPTER 4

Public Opinion

LEARNING OBJECTIVE

Identify three distinctive components of African American mass opinion.

Like many of the terms used by social scientists, *public opinion* has no precise, universally agreed-on definition.[1] Lord Bryce said of public opinion, it is the "aggregate of views men hold . . . that affect the community," whereas V. O. Key in *Public Opinion and American Democracy* specifically links the term to government, writing that public opinion is those "opinions held by private persons which governments find it prudent to heed."[2] Bernard Hennessy, on the other hand, writes that it is simply "the complex of preferences expressed by a significant number of persons on an issue of general importance."[3] Lane and Sears avoid the problem of definition altogether, assuming (presumably) that its meaning is obvious. So they write that "opinions have to be *about* something,"[4] and the "something" they say *public* opinion is about is (1) the political system, (2) the choice of group loyalties and identifications (race, religion, region, and social class), (3) the choice of leaders, and (4) public policy preferences.[5]

White Public Opinion on Race and Racism

From the inception of the scientific study of American public opinion more than 60 years ago, countless surveys have found that the American public is in general indifferent and uninformed about politics, political leaders, ideologies, and issues.[6] Very few Americans structure their opinions on politics in ideological terms, and their views on issues tend to be ad hoc, inconsistent, transitory, and often contradictory. These generalizations hold for virtually all issues—foreign and domestic—except for race.

74

In one of the classic studies documenting the lack of ideological or issue content in white American mass opinion, Phillip Converse wrote, "For the bulk of the mass public the object with the highest centrality is the visible, familiar population grouping (Negroes) rather than abstract relations among parts of government and the like."[7] More than 30 years later Kinder and Sanders concluded, "Compared with opinion on other matters, opinions on race are coherent, more tenaciously held and more difficult to alter. . . . [White] Americans know what they think on matters of race."[8] Thus, *the first thing to note about the race opinion of whites is that it tends to be one of the few consistent anchors in the thinking of white Americans.*

Second, in the last 50 years, surveys have shown a steady and generally consistent decline in overt expressions of racist and white supremacist attitudes among white Americans.[9] For example, in 1963, 31 percent of whites agreed with the statement that blacks were an inferior people; in 1978, 15 percent agreed.[10] Studies also show significant progress in that white Americans by large margins now embrace the *principle* of racial equality.[11]

However, while white Americans in general are less openly racist in their attitudes toward blacks, hostility toward the race has by no means disappeared or withered away. Instead, it has become less obvious, more subtle, and more difficult to document. This new, more subtle form of racism has been labeled "symbolic racism," "modern racism," "racial resentment," or "laissez-faire racism."[12] What this research purports to show is that white Americans are not racist in the old-fashioned way; instead, they resent or are hostile to blacks because of the whites' commitment to basic or core American values, particularly individualism.[13] White Americans prize self-sufficiency and individualism, and they believe that black Americans lack these values. Sniderman summarizes the research this way: "White Americans resist equality in the name of self-reliance, achievement, individual initiative, and they do so not merely because the value of individualism provides a socially acceptable pretext but because it provides an integral component of the new racism."[14]

In this modern racism, blacks, according to whites, are not inferior and could get ahead in society except that they lack the initiative or drive to succeed. As a function of individualism, modern racism is a product of the "finest and proudest of American values."[15] It is as American as the flag, baseball, the Fourth of July, and apple pie. Now that racism is expressed in the language of American individualism, many white's opposition to race-conscious policy is based on "the conjunction of racism and a belief in the principle of hard work . . . self-reliance [and] opposition to big government or limited-government values."[16] White Americans' disapproval of broad-based race-conscious policy provides more cover than one based on individualist claims,[17] which allows many white Americans to "protect their [own] institutional privileges without admitting racial privilege."[18]

This symbolic racism empirically is based on the embrace by large percentages of whites of negative racial stereotypes. For example, in its General Social Surveys between 1990 and 1996, the University of Chicago found that 47 percent of whites agreed that blacks tend to be lazy, 59 percent that they prefer welfare to work, 54 percent that blacks were prone to violence, 65 percent rated blacks as less hardworking, and 60 percent that they were less intelligent.[19] Although the negative stereotyping subsequently falls for the latter two traits, in particular, it will remain relatively stable over the ensuing decade.[20] During the 2008 presidential campaign, major news organizations reported similar results.[21] An important question to consider on white race opinion is what impact, if any, has the campaigns, election, and presidency of Barack Obama had on white stereotypes about blacks.

The Impact of Barack Obama on Symbolic Racism

There is disagreement in the literature on whether Obama's presence and prominence on the national scene has had a negative, positive, or no effect on white race opinion insofar as racial stereotypes are concerned. Pasek, Krasnick, and Tompson found a statistically significant increase between 2008 and 2012 in "explicit anti-black attitudes or negative stereotyping, from 47.6 percent to 50.9 percent."[22] This increase in antiblack attitudes among whites was particularly pronounced among Republicans, increasing from 71 to 79 percent; however, it also increased slightly among Democrats from 31 to 32 percent.[23] Pasek, Krasnick, and Tompson conclude, "According to both explicit and implicit measures of racial attitudes, it appears that the Obama administration has not been a time of decline in anti-black attitudes in America. Indeed, these data suggest that anti-black attitudes have become slightly more prevalent over those years, especially during the last two years."[24]

Separate studies by Seth Goldman, and Susan Welch and Lee Sigelman found contrary results. Goldman found that exposure in the mass media of Obama and his family presented a "counter–stereotypical image" of blacks and produced a "significant and substantive decline in white race prejudice," even among McCain supporters, Republicans, and conservatives. Indeed, because Republicans and conservatives have more preexisting negative stereotypes about blacks, exposure to Obama reduced their antiblack attitudes more than among Democrats and liberals, who had more positive views to begin with.[25] Welch and Sigelman write, "Obama's emergence, candidacy and election appear to have had modest effects on whites' assessment of blacks' work ethic and intelligence."[26] According to Welch and Sigelman, the largest shifts toward more positive attitudes toward blacks occurred among both the young and the old. Among the young, they suggest this is because they had fewer deeply held negative stereotypes to begin with and thus were more open to Obama's appeal. Among older whites, they write, the change occurred in part "because Obama so clearly defied the racial stereotypes that had prevailed when older whites were growing up, he directly challenged their prejudices and caused many of them to rethink their image of blacks in general."[27] Welch and Sigelman conclude that Obama's election was one of those historical events such as the civil rights movement that moved "mass public opinion in a more equalitarian direction."[28] It helped, they write, that in his image "Obama is the type of political leader who has historically been popular among whites—one who was not part of the Civil Rights Movement, who accommodates rather than confronts, and who maintains close personal and political ties with whites."[29]

Another study by Vincent Hutchings compares antiblack stereotypes in the 2008 election with the 1988 election when Jesse Jackson last ran for president. He found "scant evidence" that white antiblack stereotypes have "undergone a fundamental transformation" during this period. On the contrary, he writes, it is "more of the same."[30]

David Wilson concurs in his study measuring "racialized political anger" arguing that "racial sentiments are tied to Obama and beliefs about race serve as a stronger predictor of anger toward Obama than one's subjective evaluation of the economy, media exposure, or other situational factors."[31] Moving beyond the traditional measures of racial resentment to measure the effects across the ideological spectrum of white conservatives and liberals, he found evidence that

> beliefs about race are more enduring and more strongly tied to emotions because racial predispositions rarely change. These more enduring sentiments become a more consistent part of the appraisal system, and individuals tend to look at race as a relevant feature of one's social position even when it is not. This reasoning leads to the expectations that anger toward Obama and anything he does, and by extension anything the federal government does, is largely driven by racial attitudes.[32]

At this point, the available research on the Obama effect on symbolic racism is early, ambiguous, and inconclusive, partly due to differences in methods, modeling, and data. However, the most recent comprehensive study, using time series data from the National Election Study and the General Social Survey from 1988 to 2014, found Obama's presidency had no effects on white racial resentment; on traditional racial stereotypes; or attitudes about biological racism. The authors conclude "Taking all these results into account, what comes through is the tenacity of prejudice."[33]

African American Public Opinion: Alienation

A key component of contemporary African American public opinion is a pervasive and deep sense of alienation from or distrust of the government. Black trust in the government in general tends to fluctuate with system responsiveness to black concerns. For example, trust in the federal government was very high during the 1960s era of liberal Democratic reforms when Lyndon Johnson was president and very low during the 1980s era of conservative Republican reaction when Ronald Reagan was president. However, surveys conducted since the 1990s show a level of distrust or alienation from the government that is apparently independent of the perception of the responsiveness of government to black concerns or whether Democrats or Republicans occupy the presidency.

For example, multiple surveys conducted throughout the 1990s show 64 percent of African Americans, compared to 6 percent of whites, were far more likely to believe that the "government deliberately makes sure that drugs are easily available in poor black neighborhoods in order to harm black people."[34] A comparable racial gap also occurs when respondents were asked whether they believed the statement that the Central Intelligence Agency (CIA) was involved in importing cocaine into the black community—78 percent of blacks agreed compared to 16 percent of whites. By a margin of 59–15 percent, blacks are more likely to agree that "the government does not make a strong effort to combat AIDS in the black community because the government cares less about black people than whites," and were less likely at 79 percent compared to 38 percent whites to deny the possibility that HIV and AIDS were being used as a plot to deliberately kill African Americans.[35] This profound sense of alienation from and distrust of the American government coupled with the deep racial divide between blacks and whites were reflected in 2005–2006 public opinion polls conducted to measure black and white opinion about the government's response to Hurricane Katrina, the nation's largest and costliest natural disaster that devastated the overwhelmingly black, low-income Lower Ninth Ward in New Orleans. For example, a *CNN/USA Today* poll found that 60 percent of blacks believed that race caused the delayed government response, a view shared by only 12 percent of whites.[36] Similarly, a Pew poll found that 66 percent of blacks thought the government's response would have been faster if most of the victims had been white, a view shared by only 17 percent of whites.[37] The Pew poll also found that 71 percent of blacks thought the hurricane showed that racial inequality was still a major problem in the United States, compared to 32 percent of whites. A poll by Michael Dawson found similar results, with 84 percent of blacks believing the response of the government would have been faster if the victims had been white (20 percent of whites) and 90 percent agreeing that Katrina showed there was a problem of continued racial inequality in the United States, compared to 38 percent of whites.[38]

Recent studies continue to reflect this pervasive sense of alienation and large racial cleavages on issues regarding black attitudes about policing, criminal justice, and opportunities for black advancement. After the release of the 2014 Ferguson Commission Report,[39] a series of polls conducted between 1968 and 2015 and archived by the Roper Center for Public Opinion at Cornell University, revealed the same persistent pattern of views between black and white attitudes on policing,[40] the Roper issue brief surmised, many of the same concerns and recommendations raised in the 1967 Kerner Commission Report[41] appeared again in the Ferguson Report, such as issues on police accountability, appropriate use of force, training, and inadequate protection of citizens; and, "in almost all of these areas, blacks perceived greater problems than whites, [yet] there is significant agreement on many proposed solutions."[42] (For more discussion, see Chapter 14.)

African American Ideology: Liberalism

In one of the earliest scientific studies of the political beliefs of the American people, Free and Cantril wrote, "The Negroes were phenomenally liberal."[43] In his historical tracing of the roots of African American political ideologies, Dawson identified six unique visions asserting that these ideologies, "and the discourses around them, form the core of black political thought, which historically has not only captured the range of political debate within the black community, but has also produced one of the most trenchant critiques of the theory and practice of American 'democracy.'"[44] Of the six historical black political ideologies identified, only the four most prevalent and persistent are discussed here: liberalism, conservatism, nationalism, and the intersection of race with gender via black feminism. All of the distinctive ideologies, developed out of the historical experiences and collective memory of African Americans, are similar in that each vision "tend[s] to 'reinterpret' western ideologies to 'better fit the realities of black life by each new generation of activists and intellectuals in the black community."[45] The shared components found among the distinctions that characterize African American political thought are: (1) each vision is explicitly expressed via the point of view of African American or a segment of the African American community;[46] (2) each vision embraces a communal or holistic approach to politics over individualistic;[47] (3) each vision embeds a spiritual component, expressed in the "values, hopes, and fears" for "liberation" unique only to black philosophies; and (4) each vision will view theory and practice as interdependent or symbiotic, yet all variants of African American political thought envision futures which differ from the dominant culture's understanding of the American Dream as a result of their collective, unique experiences in America.[48]

In the United States, African American liberalism, the oldest and most dominant tradition, is understood as the rejection of the "negative" policeman state (where the government would maintain law and order, provide for the national defense, and do little else) in favor of a "positive" welfare state where the federal government intervenes in the economy, society, and the states in order to secure the rights of individuals and provide them with some degree of social security in the form of education, health, housing, and retirement income.[49]

As a long oppressed and economically exploited people, "Negroes," Free and Cantril wrote, "tend to see government action, particularly action by the federal government, as the most efficacious way—indeed perhaps the only way—to remedy problems besetting them."[50]

Although strands of black liberalism are characterized differently based on historical periods, African Americans have been consistently and increasingly identified as liberal. Nie, Verba, and Petrocik aver,

> even with this predominantly liberal profile in the 1950s, the degree of change in political attitudes is greater for blacks than for any other group in the population. The extreme and homogeneous liberal opinion profile of blacks in the early 1970s is striking. Where we once found 25 percent in the most liberal decile, we now find 62 percent of all blacks at this point. What is more, 85 percent of black Americans now respond to the issues in a way which places them in the three most liberal deciles. . . . That over 60 percent of a group should be found to have such a uniform pattern of response is an unusual phenomenon.[51]

Blacks have tended to be liberal not only on the welfare state and race-related issues such as school integration and affirmative action but also on issues of national defense (favoring less spending on the military) and foreign policy, where they tend to be skeptical or hostile to U.S. military interventions abroad (see Chapter 15). However, if African Americans have tended to be phenomenally liberal on the role of the federal government, the welfare state, and civil rights or race-related issues and defense and foreign policy, on social or moral issues, such as abortion and gay rights, blacks have tended to be as conservative as white Republicans.[52] These conservative attitudes in black America appear to be shaped significantly by religion.[53]

African American Ideology: Conservatism

Black conservatism is described as the "most marginal tendency" or tradition in African American political thought during most historical periods.[54] Mostly associated with the views expressed by Booker T. Washington (discussed in the next chapter), the tenets expressed by adherents to this philosophy, regardless of the historical period, and often shared with conservative white Republicans, include a belief in "self-reliance" or "self-help" approaches, "an attack on the welfare state as a set of institutions that retard societal progress in general and black progress in particular, and [the] belief in the anti-discriminatory aspects of markets, all in the name of service to the black community."[55] Generally, black conservatives tend to embrace economic development approaches over political strategies given their belief that "any strategy or policy which diminishes the 'honor' of African Americans" in favor of the perception of "undeserved benefits" is considered both immoral and counterproductive.[56] Also, black conservatives tend to "view themselves as the fiercest defenders of the poor and disadvantaged of the black community—warriors who attack middle-class complacency, smugness, and abandonment of the black poor."[57] In an in-depth analysis of contemporary black conservatism, using the 2008 National Election Study and the 2004 National Politics Study, Angela Lewis found four ideological distinctions—the black right, Afrocentric conservatives, neoconservatives, and individualist conservatives—largely based on the differences by which each cluster critiques the black community, the extent to which each believes whites bear responsibility for the conditions in the black community, and whether economic empowerment should be purely market driven, government subsidized, a combination of both, or strictly within the black community.[58] Lewis highlights the uniqueness found among these ideological camps:

> The Black Right is similar to the mainstream Religious Right. They focus on the moral values of blacks and see the lack of these values as the cause of the black condition. Afrocentric conservatives also have a religious dimension similar to the Black Right and they support self-help and the patriarchic family. Nonetheless, they depart from other groups of conservatives because they have a strong racial identity and they see racism as practiced by whites as the primary cause of the black condition. And because these conservatives have a strong racial identity, they are often misunderstood because they do not fit very well with other camps of black conservatives. There is no white equivalent to Afrocentric conservatives. Individualist and neoconservatives are similar in that they support a limited government, a free market, and the black condition is largely a result of the inability of blacks to compete. The major difference between these two groups is that neoconservatives were former liberals and individualist conservatives have low levels of linked fate, they do not have feelings of closeness to other Blacks.[59]

However, despite some evidence of support in black America for their views on socially conservative positions, such as school prayer, attitudes about abortion and civil rights for lesbian, gay, bisexual, and transgendered (LGBT) citizens, this ideological tradition has little grassroots support.

In fact, black opinion on LGBT rights appears to be becoming more liberal. For example, an October 2009 Gallup Poll found 38 percent of blacks supported same-sex marriage. By February 2010, Gallup reported that support had increased to 55 percent. The endorsement in 2012 of same-sex marriage by President Obama and the National Association for the Advancement of Colored People (NAACP) likely contributed to this liberal trend.

Also, while blacks may have conservative opinions on social and moral issues, they tend, unlike whites, not to vote on the basis of those opinions. Rather, the black vote is largely liberal because blacks prioritize issues of the welfare state, civil rights, and foreign policy, which explains why support for black conservative candidates remains low.

Although blacks continue to constitute the most homogeneous and consistently liberal voting bloc in the electorate, Michael Dawson finds among some blacks increasing disillusionment with liberalism and Katherine Tate argues that there is a trend toward the center among blacks on welfare and race-related issues.[60]

African American Ideology: Black Nationalism

The ideology of black nationalism is as old as the African American experience in the United States. While African Americans embrace most tenets of the liberal ideology, the 1993 National Black Politics Survey—although more than 20 years old, offers the most comprehensive set of questions about Black political ideology[61]—suggests blacks also embrace elements of black nationalism, which emphasizes racial solidarity, self-definition, self-reliance, self-determination and various degrees of cultural, social, economic, and political separation from white America.[62] This view is "partly a function of the perception that America has yet to live up to its promise of racial fairness."[63] Table 4.1 clearly demonstrates strong attitudinal support for African American autonomy or nationalism.

Most previous studies have largely treated black nationalism as a singular, uniform ideology. But recent, careful, innovative empirical research has found that like all ideologies, black nationalism is complex, fluid, and hence multidimensional, having at least two dimensions that can be characterized as "community nationalism" and "separatist nationalism." The former category

TABLE 4.1 Percentage of Support for African American Autonomy in Mass Public Opinion

Statements from Survey	Percentage Agreeing
Blacks should rely on themselves and not others.	68
Blacks should control the government in black communities.	89
Blacks should participate in black-only organizations whenever possible.	67
Blacks should shop in black stores whenever possible.	84
Black children should study an African language.	70

Source: Michael Dawson and Ronald Brown, "Black Discontent: The Preliminary Report of the 1993–1994 National Black Politics Study," Report 1, University of Chicago. The results are based on a representative, randomly selected sample of the national black population. Percentages are of respondents agreeing with the statement.

can be said to exist when African Americans "control and support communities and institutions where they predominate," while the latter category "rejects inclusion within the white-dominated American state and seeks the creation of a new homeland."[64] The research also reveals that better educated, middle-class African Americans support community nationalism, while younger, poorer, less educated African Americans tend to favor separatist nationalism. However, despite these differences, supporters of both dimensions of black nationalism converge around the belief that "whites want to keep blacks down" and that "Africa is a special homeland for blacks." But they diverge around the issue of whether other racial and ethnic groups should be used as allies and coalition partners. Those African Americans who support separatist nationalism see no benefits in forming coalitions and joining alliances with whites, while community nationalists have no problem with such allies and coalitions. The groups are also divided on the outlook for the future. Ironically, separatists see themselves as achieving their goals and objectives, and for them the future is bright and promising. The community nationalists doubt that they will be able to achieve their goals and therefore have a tendency to be pessimistic about the future, much like black liberals, who can become "disillusioned with racial progress."[65]

Contrary to the view of many scholars, black nationalism—one of the least understood black ideologies—is not associated with a general mistrust, hatred, or intolerance of white America, but arguably is an attempt to affirm black culture, promote racial progress through racially collective action while adapting to evolving challenges of race relations.[66] Debates continue to ensue over lasting causes of African American support for the ideology. Yet, recent evidence suggests the intersection between perceived linked fate and one's level of disillusionment impacts the varying degrees of African American attitudes and commitment to a range of political attitudes, practices, and support of nationalistic political strategies to advance their political interests.[67] Those unfamiliar with African American perspectives and dialogue, and their unique experiences, often misunderstand that African Americans are attuned to the nation's contradictory legacies on racial justice, and their opinions and attitudes about America reveal both affection and disaffection.[68] Polls show that a very strong adherence to the nationalist ideology is associated with disaffection from whites, particularly white supremacist ideology, but not, as is often alleged, gays, lesbians, feminists, or middle-class blacks.[69]

African American Ideology: Feminism and Intersectionality

African American women have played a continual role in the struggle for universal freedom and social justice. By the last half of the nineteenth century, black women were collectively asserting their rights as women in the "women club movements" and as African Americans. By the 1970s, feminism emerged as an important ideology in African American politics. Feminism is the ideology of gender equality and freedom. Black feminism investigates the intersection of race, class, gender, and sexuality. Strikingly similar to the research approaches used by W. E. B. Du Bois in his works in the mid-1890s,[70] "Intersectionality"[71] research, as employed by black feminism, utilizes a range of theoretical, methodological, and policy approaches, to focus on the simultaneous and interactive effects of race, gender, class, sexual orientation, and other social categories of difference in the United States and beyond.[72] Black feminist thought "offers a different understanding of how power, via discourse, is organized, maintained, and perpetuated."[73] Primarily, black feminist thought recognizes that analytic categories like race or ethnicity, class, gender, and other social descriptors are not separate and additive, but are rather interactive and multiplicative[74] dimensions that intersect and overlap, resulting in different social and lived experiences, particularly for black women. Dawson writes that "adherents of black feminism exhibit more agreement on what constitutes the political core of their ideology than the adherents of any other ideology" in the black community.[75] However, he also notes that feminism is often in conflict with other ideologies in the black community, especially black nationalism.[76] Harris-Lacewell also notes that feminism, like conservatism, is unpopular among many segments of the black community, partly because it is critical of black sexism and patriarchy.[77] Yet, Nikol Alexander-Floyd asserts,

> Some might regard attention to Black women as a key point of emphasis to be misguided, either because it centers on identity or because it should be replaced by considerations of gender as a sole analytic category. But, a priority on research centering on Black women as political, social, historical, and economic subjects, especially from a specifically Black feminist frame of reference, is of central importance in countering the paradox of invisibility and hyper-invisibility. . . . in terms of the dominant cultural systems by which [black women] are defined, a fact that accounts for the impact of stereotypes, . . . [and] in the development of social welfare and family-related policy.[78]

For most black women, race trumps gender. That is, "race remains the dominant screen through which black women view politics, not only because most consider racism a greater evil than sexism, but because gender is simply a weak vehicle for political identification,"[79] which suggests for black women, race is a more salient category of identification than gender. Recent studies show promise that black feminism and black women's experiences and politics are "*central* to how we know and understand space and place [and politics]; [particularly] black women [politics] and workable and lived subaltern [realities]," tell a different story about women and racial progress.[80]

Black feminism, however, is not monolithic. There are divisions among black feminist ideologies—ranging from liberal to radical—and differences based on class, sexual orientation, age, and marital status. Yet, the unifying distinguishing characteristics include "a tendency to see the struggle of African American women as being more holistic and universalist than that of most white feminists," placing greater emphasis on the concern for the entire community.[81] Thus, issues like abortion rights (since *Roe v. Wade* the right to an abortion has become widely accepted in the black community, generally supported by the public, and supported by virtually all black organizations and leaders except black nationalists), equal employment and pay, health and child care, violence against women, and the full inclusion of women in the political process are necessary to racial advancement and ending multiple forms of oppression for black women. In 2015, in a public opinion poll of black women voters, conducted by *Essence* magazine and the Black Women's Roundtable, 78% would strongly support 2016 presidential candidates who "want to improve law enforcement/community relations," in addition to other communal issues most important to them such as affordable healthcare (49%), living wage jobs (43%), college affordability (38%), and access to a quality public education (38%).[82]

African American Opinion: Monolithic and Diverse

African American opinion compared to the opinion of whites is near monolithically liberal; however, there is also considerable diversity. While liberalism is the dominant ideology, there is some degree of support in black opinion for a variety of ideologies, including conservatism. Since the Reagan administration, black conservative spokespersons (largely in the media, think tanks, and universities) have argued that liberal black politicians and civil rights leaders have imposed the liberal ideology on the masses of blacks, and, acting as a kind of thought police, have suppressed and marginalized conservative ideas.[83] The available social science research, however, indicates that while African Americans were not immune to the conservative political climate ushered in by the Reagan presidency, there was little increase in black support for the Republican Party and its conservative ideology. While there is a great deal of ideological diversity in black America—liberalism, conservatism, feminism, black nationalism, and Marxism—conservatism is the weakest of the ideologies among African Americans.

Evidence reveals that liberal ideology is not imposed on the black community by politicians and civil rights leaders. Rather, studies show that black opinion— as perceived by views on linked fate and levels of disillusionment—is shaped at the mass level by a variety of community institutions, such as churches, barbershops, beauty salons, and the black media.[84] These institutions contribute to the diversity of black opinion by airing multiple ideologies and complex belief systems.

Faces and Voices in the Struggle for Universal Freedom
RONALD W. WALTERS (1938–2011)

At his death, Ronald Walters was the nation's foremost scholar of the politics of race. Like W. E. B. Du Bois, he was an activist scholar or what the *Washington Post* called a "participatory pundit," committed to synthesizing theory and practice in service to what he often called "the liberation of black people."[a] Walters's activism in the struggle for universal freedom began in the early years of the protest phase of the civil rights movement, when at the age of 20 in 1958 he organized and led the first modern lunch counter sit-in.[b]

After graduating from Fisk University, Walters earned a Ph.D. from American University. In the late 1960s, he established and became the founding chair of the first African American Studies program at Brandeis University. In the early 1970s, he chaired Howard University's political science department, helping to turn it into one of the two leading academic centers for the study of African American politics. He was later named distinguished leadership professor at the University of Maryland and director of its Academy of African American Leadership.

In addition to his academic work, Walters was the leading interpreter of African American politics in the national media, writing articles for most of the leading newspapers and appearing on virtually all of the national television and radio news and commentary programs. His column on black politics was syndicated by the National Newspaper Association.

Dr. Ronald Walters.

Source: Edney, Hazel Trice. "Dr. Ron Walters: 'Scholarly Giant,'" *Los Angeles Sentinel.* 17 September 2010. Retrieved 4 October 2016 from https://lasentinel.net/dr-ron-walters-scholarly-grant.html

From these vantage points, Walters contributed to the development and maturation of black participation in electoral politics, serving as an advisor to the Congressional Black Caucus and multiple organizations of black elected officials. His 1988 book *Black Presidential Politics: A Strategic Approach* developed the theory of "leverage politics" to explain how blacks could use their vote in presidential elections to extract policy benefits from the political system. As the principal strategist in the Jesse Jackson presidential campaigns, they in effect became laboratories for the testing of his leverage theory. At the time of his death, he was pressing black leaders to leverage President Obama to develop race-specific policies to address the double-digit unemployment rate in the black community.[c]

[a] Jacqueline Trescott, "Ronald Walters: Howard University's Participatory Pundit," *Washington Post*, November 8, 1980.

[b] Matt Schudel, "Scholar Ronald W. Walters Led What Is Considered the First Lunch Counter Sit-in," *Washington Post*, September 12, 2011. See also Gretchen Cassel Eick, *Dissent in Wichita: The Civil Rights Movement in the Midwest, 1954–1972* (Urbana: University of Illinois Press, 2001): 1–17.

[c] For an assessment of Walters's contributions see Robert C. Smith, Cedric Johnson, and Robert Newby, eds., *What Has This Got to Do with the Liberation of Black People?: The Impact and Influence of Ronald W. Walters on African American Thought and Leadership* (Albany, NY: SUNY Press, 2014), and Smith's *Ronald W. Walters and the Promises and Paradoxes of Black Power: A Political and Intellectual Biography* (Albany, NY: SUNY Press, Forthcoming).

Summary

Since the 1960s, there has been a major decline in racist and white supremacist opinion among white Americans. However, scholars of race opinion have identified what they call modern racism, where whites today do not say blacks are inferior but rather they say blacks lack the initiative or drive to succeed. Meanwhile, African American opinion tends to blame racism for the failure of blacks to get ahead in the United States. African American public opinion also has a strong degree of racial group identification and consciousness, alienation from or distrust of the government, and ideological liberalism. There is also a tendency for strong support of elements of black nationalism.

Critical Thinking Questions

1. What is symbolic or modern racism?
2. Discuss how African American political opinion differs from white public opinion on certain issues.
3. Discuss the historical components of black ideologies. What are distinctive elements?
4. Discuss the differences between liberalism, conservatism, and nationalism among African Americans. Why is liberalism the dominant ideology among African Americans?

5. In the quest of universal freedom, discuss how the concept of "inter-sectionality" explains the lived unique experiences of African Americans generally and black women specifically.

Selected Bibliography

Converse, Phillip. "The Nature of Belief Systems in Mass Publics." In D. Apter, ed., *Ideology and Its Discontent*. New York: Free Press, 1964. A seminal work on the methodology of studying public opinion.

Dawson, Michael. *Behind the Mule: Race and Class in African-American Politics*. Princeton, NJ: Princeton University Press, 1994. A study that analyzes the relationship between racial and class attitudes and their different influences on individual political behavior.

Dawson, Michael. *Black Visions: The Roots of Contemporary African-American Political Ideologies*. Chicago, IL: University of Chicago Press, 2001. A comprehensive study of the subject.

Harris-Lacewell, Melissa. *Barbershops, Bibles and BET: Everyday Talk and Black Political Thought*. Princeton, NJ: Princeton University Press, 2004. An interesting study of opinion formation in black America.

Key, V. O. *Public Opinion and American Democracy*. New York: Alfred Knopf, 1961. The classic study of public opinion and its relationship to government leaders and the policy process.

Kinder, Donald, and Lynn Sanders. *Divided by Color: Racial Politics and Democratic Ideals*. Chicago, IL: University of Chicago Press, 1996. A comprehensive study of black–white opinion differences in the United States.

Rosenstone, Steven J., and John Mark Hensen. *Mobilization, Participation and Democracy in America*. New York: Macmillan, 1993. Covers African American attitudes about political mobilization and participation in America.

Sigelman, Lee, and Susan Welch. *Black Americans' Views of Racial Inequality: The Dream Deferred*. Cambridge, MA: Cambridge University Press, 1994. A pathbreaking analysis of black opinion about the sources of blacks' inequality in American society and the appropriate means for achieving equality.

Smith, Robert C., and Richard Seltzer. *Contemporary Controversies and the American Racial Divide*. Lanham, MD: Rowman & Littlefield, 2000. A study of the huge differences between blacks and whites on recent controversial issues, such as O. J. Simpson, Rodney King, AIDS-HIV, the Iraq War, and crack cocaine.

Tate, Gayle and Lewis Randolph, *Dimensions of Black Conservatism* (New York: Palgrave Macmillan, 2002). A collection of essays by black scholars assessing the origins and substantive policy content and consequences of contemporary black conservatism.

Tate, Katherine. *From Protest to Politics: The New Black Voters in American Elections*. Enlarged edition. Cambridge, MA: Harvard University Press, 1994. Analyzes the attitudes of African American voters in the 1984, 1988, and 1992 presidential elections.

Notes

1 Bernard Hennessy, *Public Opinion*, 5th ed. (Belmont, CA: Brooks/Cole, 1985).
2 V. O. Key, *Public Opinion and American Democracy* (New York: Knopf, 1961): 14.

3 Hennessy, *Public Opinion*, p. 8.

4 Robert Lane and David Sears, *Public Opinion* (Englewood Cliffs, NJ: Prentice Hall, 1964): 2.

5 Ibid., pp. 2–3.

6 Donald Kinder, "Diversity and Complexity in Public Opinion," in A. Finifter, ed., *The State of the Discipline, I* (Washington, DC: American Political Science Association, 1983); and Paul Sniderman, "The New Look in Public Opinion Research," in A. Finifter, ed., *The State of the Discipline, II* (Washington, DC: American Political Science Association, 1993).

7 Phillip Converse, "The Nature of Belief Systems in Mass Publics," in D. Apter, ed., *Ideology and Its Discontent* (New York: Free Press, 1964): 238.

8 Donald Kinder and Lynn Sanders, *Divided by Color: Racial Politics and American Democracy* (Chicago, IL: University of Chicago Press, 1996): 14.

9 Howard Schuman, Charlotte Steeth, and Lawrence Bobo, *Racial Attitudes in America: Trends and Interpretations* (Cambridge, MA: Harvard University Press, 1985).

10 Louis Harris, *A Study of Attitudes Toward Racial and Religious Minorities and Women* (New York: National Conference of Christians and Jews, 1978): 16. By the late 1990s, only 10 percent of whites agreed with the statement that blacks were an inferior people.

11 Schuman, Steeth, and Bobo, *Racial Attitudes in America*. See also Paul Sniderman and Michael Hagan, *Race and Inequality: A Study in American Values* (Chatham, NJ: Chatham House, 1985).

12 David Sears, "Symbolic Racism," in P. Katz and D. Taylor, eds., *Eliminating Racism* (New York: Plenum, 1988); Kinder and Sanders, *Divided by Color*, pp. 272–76; and Lawrence Bobo, James Klugel, and Ryan Smith, "Laissez-Faire Racism: The Crystallization of a 'Kinder, Gentler' Anti-Black Ideology," in S. Tuch and J. Martin, eds., *Racial Attitudes in the 1990s: Continuity and Change* (Westport, CT: Praeger, 1997).

13 Sniderman and Hagan, *Race and Inequality*.

14 Sniderman, "The New Look in Public Opinion Research," p. 232.

15 Sears, "Symbolic Racism," p. 54.

16 J. Gainous, "The New 'New Racism' Thesis: Limited Government Values and Race-Conscious Policy Attitudes," *Journal of Black Studies* 43(3) (2012): 252.

17 Ibid., p. 253.

18 M. Beeman, M. Chowdhry, and K. Todd, "Educating Students about Affirmative Action: An Analysis of University Sociology Texts," *Teaching Sociology* 28(2) (2000): 101.

19 Cited in Robert C. Smith, *Racism in the Post Civil Rights Era: Now You See It, Now You Don't* (Albany, NY: SUNY Press, 1995): 39.

20 See Lawrence Bobo, Camille Z. Charles, Maria Krysan, and Alicia D. Simmons, "The *Real* Record on Racial Attitudes," in Peter V. Masden, ed., *Social Trends in American Life: Findings from the General Social Survey since 1972* (Princeton, NJ: Princeton University Press, 2012): 59.

21 See, for example, Jon Cohen, "3 in 10 Americans Admit to Race Bias," *Washington Post*, June 22, 2008.

22 Josh Pasek, Jon Krasnick, and Trevor Tompson, "The Impact of Anti-Black Racism on Approval of Barack Obama's Job Performance and Voting in the 2012 Presidential Election," Unpublished Manuscript, Stanford University, 2012.

23 Ibid.

24 Ibid., p. 18.

25 Seth Goldman, "Effects of the 2008 Presidential Campaign on White Prejudice," *Public Opinion Quarterly* 76 (2012): 663–87.

26 Susan Welch and Lee Sigelman, "The Obama Effect and White Attitudes," *Annals of the American Academy of Political and Social Science* 634 (2011): 207.

27 Ibid., p. 218.

28 Ibid.

29 Ibid., pp. 219–20.

30 Vincent Hutchings, "Change or More of the Same: Evaluating Racial Attitudes in the Obama Era," *Public Opinion Quarterly* 73 (2009): 917.

31 David Wilson, "Racialized Political Anger: Affective Reactions to Barack Obama and the Federal Government," *National Political Science Review* 17 (2016): 22.

32 Ibid., p. 23.

33 Donald Kinder and Jennifer Chudy, "After Obama," *Forum* 14 (2016): 6.

34 These and related data are analyzed in detail in Robert C. Smith and Richard Seltzer, *Contemporary Controversies and the American Racial Divide* (Boulder, CO: Rowman & Littlefield, 2000): chap. 5, "Rumors and Conspiracies: Justified Paranoia."

35 Ibid.

36 "Reaction to Katrina Split on Racial Lines," *USA Today*, September 13, 2005.

37 Pew Poll for the People and the Press, September 13, 2005.

38 Glen Ford and Peter Gamble, "Katrina: A Study, Black Consensus, White Dispute," *The Black Commentator*, January 5, 2006.

39 See the report, "Forward through Ferguson: A Path to Racial Equality" (2014), published by the Ferguson Commission. Accessed online on January 23, 2016 at http://forwardthroughferguson.org/.

40 See the Issue Brief, "Black, White, and Blue: Americans' Attitudes on Race and Police," published by the Roper Center (Ithaca, NY: Cornell University), September 22, 2015. Accessed online on January 21, 2016 at http://ropercenter.cornell.edu/black-white-blue-americans-attitudes-race-police/.

41 See digital report, "National Advisory Commission on Civil Disorders (The Kerner Report), 1967." Accessed online on January 21, 2016 at http://staff.washington.edu/qtaylor/documents_us/Kerner%20Report.htm.

42 Ibid., "Black, White, and Blue: Americans' Attitudes on Race and Police."

43 Lloyd Free and Hadley Cantril, *The Political Beliefs of Americans: A Study in Public Opinion* (New Brunswick, NJ: Rutgers University Press, 1967): 17.

44 See Michael Dawson, *Black Visions: The Roots of Contemporary African-American Political Ideologies* (Chicago, IL: University of Chicago Press, 2001): 2.

45 Ibid., p. 5.

46 Ibid., p. 22. See also Mack Jones, "A Frame of Reference for Black Politics," in Jones, *Knowledge, Power and Black Politics* (Buffalo, NY: SUNY Press, 2014).

47 Ibid. See also Fred Lee Hord and Jonathan Scott Lee, *I Am Because We Are: Readings in Black Philosophy* (Amherst: University of Massachusetts Press, 1995).

48 Ibid.

49 The concepts of the "negative" and "positive" are derived from Isaiah Berlin, "'Two Concepts of Liberty' in Berlin," *Two Essays on Liberty* (New York: Oxford, 1970): 118–72.

50 Free and Cantril, *The Political Beliefs of Americans*, p. 36.

51 Norman Nie, Sidney Verba, and John Petrocik, *The Changing American Voter* (Cambridge, MA: Harvard, 1976): 253–54.

52 Frank Newport, "Blacks as Conservative as Republicans on Some Moral Issues," www.gallup.com/poll12807/blacks-conservative-republicans-some-moral. See also Robert C. Smith and Richard Seltzer, *Race, Class and Culture: A Study in Afro-*

American Mass Opinion (Albany, NY: SUNY Press, 1992): 41; and Katherine Tate, *What's Going On?: Political Incorporation and the Transformation of Black Public Opinion* (Washington, DC: Georgetown University Press, 2010): 15.

53 Ibid.

54 Dawson, *Black Visions*, p. 19.

55 Ibid., p. 20.

56 Ibid.

57 Ibid.

58 See Angela K. Lewis, *Conservatism in the Black Community: To the Right and Misunderstood* (New York: Routledge, 2013): 30.

59 Ibid., p. 30.

60 Dawson, *Black Visions*, pp. 273–80; and Tate, *What's Going On?*

61 See Ray Block, Jr., "What About Disillusionment? Exploring the Pathways to Black Nationalism," *Political Behavior* 33 (2011): 27–51. Online version, published June 25, 2010, doi:10.1007/s11109-010-9126-9, http://link.springer.com/article/10.1007%2Fs11109-010-9126-9.

62 Ibid., p. 30. See Dawson, *Black Visions*, p. 21.

63 Ibid., p. 27.

64 Robert Brown and Todd Shaw, "Separate Nations: Two Attitudinal Dimensions of Black Nationalism," *Journal of Politics* 64 (2002): 20–44.

65 See Block, Jr., "What About Disillusionment? Exploring the Pathways to Black Nationalism," p. 28.

66 Ibid., p. 30.

67 See ibid., pp. 27–51.

68 Ibid., p. 28.

69 See Mary Herring, Thomas Jankowski, and Ronald Brown, "Pro-Black Doesn't Mean Anti-White: The Structure of African American Group Identity," *Journal of Politics* 61 (1999): 363–86, and Darren Davis and Robert Brown, "The Antipathy of Black Nationalism: Behavioral and Attitudinal Implications of African American Ideology," *American Journal of Political Science* 46 (2000): 717–32.

70 See Aldon Morris, *The Scholar Denied: W. E. B. Du Bois and the Birth of Modern Sociology* (Oakland: University of California Press, 2015): 220.

71 See Kimberle Crenshaw, "Demarginalizing the Intersection of Race and Sex: A Black Feminist Critique of Antidiscrimination Doctrine, Feminist Theory and Antiracist Politics," *University of Chicago Legal Forum* (1989): 139–67. See also, Julia S. Jordan-Zachery, " 'Talking' about Gender While Ignoring Race and Class: A Discourse Analysis of Pay Equity Debates," *National Political Science Review* 16 (2014): 49–66; and Nikol Alexander-Floyd, "Why Political Scientists Don't Study Black Women, But Historians and Sociologists Do: On Intersectionality and the Remapping of the Study of Black Political Women," *National Political Science Review* 16 (2014): 3–17.

72 Evelyn M. Simien and Ange-Marie Hancock, "Mini-Symposium: Intersectionality Research," *Political Science Quarterly* 64 (2011): 185–86.

73 See Jordan-Zachery, " 'Talking' about Gender While Ignoring Race and Class: A Discourse Analysis of Pay Equity Debates," p. 52.

74 See Prudence Carter, Sherrill L. Sellers, and Catherine Squires, "Reflections on Race/Ethnicity, Class and Gender Inclusive Research," *Perspectives* 5 (2007): 111–24.

75 Dawson, *Black Visions,* p. 153.

76 Ibid., p. 140. See also Alexander-Floyd, "Why Political Scientists Don't Study Black Women, But Historians and Sociologists Do," pp. 3–17.

77 Melissa Victoria Harris-Lacewell (aka Harris-Perry), *Barbershops, Bibles and BET: Everyday Talk and Black Political Thought* (Princeton, NJ: Princeton University Press, 2004): 115.
78 Alexander-Floyd, "Why Political Scientists Don't Study Black Women, But Historians and Sociologists Do," p. 10.
79 Claudine Gay and Katherine Tate, "Doubly Bound: The Impact of Gender and Race on the Politics of Black Women," *Political Psychology* 19 (1998): 12.
80 Alexander-Floyd, "Why Political Scientists Don't Study Black Women, But Historians and Sociologists Do," p. 15.
81 Dawson, *Black Visions*, p. 20.
82 See the discussion of the poll results of black women voters in the report, "The Power of the Sister Vote," conducted by *Essence* magazine and the Black Women's Roundtable, published in *Essence* magazine (November 2015): 96–99. http://ncbcp. org/news/releases/Essence.BWR.Power_of_the_Sister_Vote_Poll_Results.9.15.15.FIN AL.pdf.
83 Shelby Steele, *The Content of Our Character: A New Vision of Race in America* (New York: St. Martin's Press, 1990).
84 See Taeku Lee, *Mobilizing Public Opinion: Black Insurgency and Racial Attitudes in the Civil Rights Era* (Chicago, IL: University of Chicago Press, 2002); and Harris-Lacewell, *Barbershops, Bibles and BET*.

CHAPTER 5

African Americans and the Media

LEARNING OBJECTIVE

Contrast the coverage of the black community by the mainstream and African American media.

"We wish to plead our own cause. Too long have others spoken for us."[1] So said the editorial in the first edition of the first black newspaper, appropriately called *Freedom's Journal*, founded in 1827 by Samuel Cornish and John B. Russwurm. Since 1827, the black press and the black church have been central institutions in the African American freedom struggle. Historically, the African American media has played three distinct roles in black society and politics. First, it has served as a crucial socialization agent, fostering race group consciousness and solidarity. Second, it has been a vehicle of protest against racism and the ideology of white supremacy. Third, it has portrayed positive images of blacks and the black community as an antidote to the negative stereotypes and characterizations in the white press.

The African American Media and African Americans in the Mass Media

The African American Media

Like the media in general, the African American media are quite diverse. They include about 200 weekly newspapers, approximately 450 black-oriented radio stations, seven black-owned full power television stations, and several national circulation news and special interest magazines. BET (now owned by Viacom),

TVONE, and OWN are black-owned or oriented cable entertainment and information networks and blacks also own and operate Bounce. The broadcast Radio One, "The Power" (now owned by SiriusXM, "Urban View"), is an all-African American talk channel on satellite radio (as of 2013 blacks owned 11 percent of AM radio stations, 6 percent of FM stations, and 6 percent of broadcast television stations).[2] In general, the black weeklies serve as the voice for the local African American communities, focusing on local rather than national news.[3] Their focus tends to be on the internal black community's civic, cultural, and religious affairs. The mainstream or white-dominated media tend to ignore the internal life of the black community, thus the black media serve as a vehicle for intragroup communication and solidarity. Many, although not all, of the black weeklies serve as watchdogs on local government and continue the tradition of a fighting press. For example, in 1995 during the time of the famous O. J. Simpson case, research revealed while the *Los Angeles Times* tended to present the O. J. Simpson arrest and trial in an unsympathetic way, the black *Los Angeles Sentinel* in effect became Simpson's champion in the media, apparently reflecting the views of the city's black community as the *Los Angeles Times* reflected the views of the city's whites.[4]

At the national level, in 2014 *Jet* ceased publication—but relaunched as an online weekly—leaving *Ebony* (a monthly) as the only general circulation news and information African American magazine. Earlier, *Emerge*, the only serious national black news magazine, was shut down in 2000. There are specialized magazines such as *Essence* (focusing on women), *The Source* (the hard-news hip-hop magazine), and *Black Enterprise* (focusing on business). Although these magazines occasionally provide critical coverage on race issues and internal black society, culture, and politics,[5] they generally tend to focus on celebrities and consumerism showcasing the black middle class. Thus, with the loss of print outlets like *Emerge* (see Box 5.1) and *Jet*, there is not a national circulation magazine providing hard news and critical commentary on issues important to the black community. Broadcast radio retains high levels of connectivity for black America, with 92 percent of African Americans tuning in to various formats each week.[6] One powerful black voice on radio is Tom Joyner, the host of the *Tom Joyner Morning Show*, whose nationally syndicated show is heard by over 10 million listeners in more than 100 cities, giving him an audience size equivalent to Howard Stern and Rush Limbaugh. (During the 2008 election, Joyner's program was a major forum for the mobilization of the black vote.) Joyner also operates a website—Black America Web—that logs millions of page views daily, and manages the Tom Joyner Foundation that, through its annual "Fantastic Voyage" cruise and "Family Reunion," has raised millions to help keep students in HBCUs.[7] With the expansion of digital platforms, other black-oriented simulcasts have the potential to reach a national audience dealing with social, economic, cultural, and political issues from African American perspectives.

BOX 5.1

Media Conglomerates and the African American Media

The mass media in the United States are business corporations that provide news, information, and entertainment in order to make a profit. In recent years in pursuit of profits, many media companies have been purchased by large multinational corporations. For example, NBCUniversal, is a subsidiary of Comcast, CBS of Viacom, ABC of Walt Disney, and Time-Warner is an enormous media conglomerate that owns *Time* and CNN, and is also the largest magazine publisher, the largest record company, the second largest cable company, and one of the largest book publishers in the world. This trend toward media conglomeration in 2001 affected the African American media when BET, the black cable company, was purchased by Viacom for $3 billion. Earlier Time-Warner had purchased *Essence*, the black women's magazine, and later Africana.com, a major black online news site. By 2014, iHeartMedia, Inc. (formerly Clear Channel Communications) effectively wiped out many small and black-owned radio stations with its purchase of more than 850 AM/FM stations nationwide. While the acquisition of these black media outlets by large white-owned conglomerates may provide more resources for news gathering, programming, marketing, and distribution, it may also result in less competition and the loss of independent African American voices in the media. It also may result in undue focus on the corporate bottom line at the expense of independent, critical, and controversial reporting of the news from African American perspectives.

The $20 billion lawsuit filed by the African American Byron Allen's Entertainment Studios Networks, Inc., against Comcast and Time-Warner raised

this concern.[a] In the lawsuit filed initially against Comcast, Time-Warner Cable, Al Sharpton's National Action Network, the NAACP, and the Urban League (Comcast later became the only defendant), Allen alleged Comcast conspired with the civil rights organizations and federal officials to systematically discriminate against black-owned media companies and deny them carriage placement. On the basis of evidence showing these mega-companies decreased ownership opportunities for African Americans as well as opportunities for business relationships, the proposed merger of Comcast and Time-Warner was struck down by the Federal Communications Commission (FCC); however, the AT&T merger with DirectTV was approved. While the Allen case against Comcast was dismissed, a separate $10 billion lawsuit was filed in 2016 against the FCC and Charter Communications by Allen and the National Association of African American Owned Media (NAAAOM) for "racial discrimination in contracting for television channel carriage." In a statement, Allen asserted, "Everyone talks about diversity, but diversity in Hollywood and the media starts with ownership. African Americans don't need handouts and donations; we can hire ourselves if white corporate America does business with us in a fair and equitable way."[b]

[a] See press release, "Statement," March 10, 2015, http://nabob.org/wp-content/uploads/2015/05/press_031015.pdf.
[b] See Janell Hazelwood, "FCC and Charter Face $10 Billion Racial Discrimination Lawsuit," January 31, 2016, www.blackenterprise.com/lifestyle/fcc-and-charter-face-10-billion-racial-discrimination-lawsuit/.

African Americans and Digital Media

Traditional media is on the decline. Innovations in technology have substantially increased the number of digital platforms that provide much more critical news and analysis of issues from African American perspectives. The choices available through content online, accessible across an array of devices, has made the journey to content discovery virtually endless.[8] Popular websites in the African American media digital footprint (e.g. The Root, NewsOne, The Grio, the Huffington Post "Black Voices," and NBCBLK.com—NBC's site targeted at African Americans) mirror the content and format as traditional venues.[9] The hard news and critical commentary are found on other verticals like The Black Commentator and Black Politics on the Web. The major civil rights organizations, black members of Congress, and the Congressional Black Caucus (CBC) also maintain sites, as do the National Newspaper Publishers Association (NNPA), the trade association of the black newspapers that distributes news exclusively from the black media; and Reach Media, Inc., the digital affiliation pool of national black radio shows and websites.[10] In 2000, at the outset of systematic data collection of digital usage, it was estimated that only 36 percent of black households were online compared to 50 percent of whites, 41 percent of English-speaking Latinos, and 69 percent of Asian Americans.[11] However, the racial "digital divide" has significantly narrowed. One recent study found that African Americans "fully engage and connect through various mainstream and niche media outlets and platforms, and they consume more content than other groups on all fronts."[12]

In fact, a digital-based study found African American voters overwhelmingly rely on a mix of mainstream and digital platforms to receive content and information on candidates and political issues.[13] Although most black Americans still prefer television, print, and the radio broadcasts that are "culture-rich," they have become avid users of social media and blogging channels via their mobile devices. In fact, smartphone penetration for African Americans is 81 percent compared to 71 percent of whites, 81 percent of Latinos, and 84 percent of Asian Americans.[14] Engaging politics and political action via the power of the Internet has been led by young black online activists and bloggers, who have demonstrated remarkable intellectual sophistication with the use of social media (e.g. Facebook, Twitter, Instagram, etc.),[15] successfully mobilizing thousands of citizens and activists across the nation to action, from the "Jena 6" protest against race-based mistreatment of black school children in Jena, Louisiana, in 2007, to the propagation of the #BlackLivesMatter movement, spurred by the murder of Trayvon Martin in 2012.

African Americans in the Mass Media

Until the 1960s, relatively few blacks were employed in the mass media. In the aftermath of the rebellions in the 1960s, many newspapers and radio and television stations for the first time began to hire black reporters, editors, and producers.[16] Yet, even today, their numbers in the mainstream mass media are relatively small. And, according to the National Association of Black Journalists, the ranks of black journalists (between 2002 and 2012) employed by newspapers were cut by nearly a thousand, the largest decline for any ethnic group. During this period, overall employment of journalists dropped by 2.4 percent, but for blacks it was 5.2 percent.[17]

Table 5.1 displays data for 2014. Blacks constitute 4.4 percent of newspaper, 10.8 percent of television, and 4.4 percent of radio workforces; black news directors comprise 1.7 percent in radio and 4.3 percent in television. Blacks and other minorities in the mass media tend to be concentrated in larger cities. Approximately, one-fourth of minority television journalists work in the 25 largest cities compared to 10 percent in the nation's smallest cities.[18] The same phenomenon is observed with respect to newspapers. Indeed, 44 percent of the nation's daily newspapers (mostly in smaller cities) have no black reporters.[19] More recently, however, African Americans assumed two of the most powerful and influential positions in the American media. In 2014, Dean Baquet was named executive editor of the *New York Times,* the nation's most influential newspaper, and in 2015, Lester Holt became anchor and managing editor of NBC Nightly News.

The mainstream or mass media is just that: "mass" media; this designation means that it gathers and reports news of interest to the mass public—in general, middle-class whites. For this reason, news in the newspapers and on radio and

TABLE 5.1   African Americans in the Mass Media: Television, Radio, and Major Newspapers, 2014

Media	Percentage of African Americans
Radio	
News Workforce	4.4
News Directors	1.7
Television	
News Workforce	10.8
News Directors	4.3
Newspapers	
News Workforce	4.4

Source: Data on radio and television personnel are based on a survey of all 1,659 operating, nonsatellite television stations in the United States and a sample of 3,263 radio stations. The survey was conducted in the fourth quarter of 2013 by the Radio-Television News Directors Association and Hofstra University. Data on newspaper personnel are based on a 2014 survey of the 1,446 daily newspapers conducted by the American Society of Newspaper Editors.

television tends to be essentially the same, whether one watches NBC, CBS, or ABC, or reads the *New York Times*, the *Detroit Free Press*, the *Washington Post*, the *San Francisco Chronicle*, *Time*, or *Newsweek*, although the *Washington Post* and the *New York Times* do provide more detailed stories on national and international affairs.

In an important study, sociologist Herbert Gans argues that the primary motive guiding the mass media is the preservation of "social order," the prevailing values and power relationships in the society.[20] The African American community, however, are often dissatisfied with the prevailing values and power relationships given the routine, day-to-day coverage in mass media. This dissatisfaction tends to place in a difficult position the African American journalist who wishes to reflect the perspective of her community. She must simultaneously seek to balance the "black perspective" on the news with the mass media's social control perspective. A former *Washington Post* reporter describes this as a "creative tension" between "Uncle Tomming and mau mauing."[21] (See Box 5.2.)

Mass Media Coverage of African Americans

Content analysis of the mass media has consistently shown that routine, day-to-day coverage of African Americans is predominantly negative and stereotypical; blacks are portrayed as poor or criminal, or they were shown as athletes and entertainers.[22] Although this kind of coverage is on the decline in mass media, due to diversity in employment, today media still fails to display the full diversity of black humanity. There remains a kind of "split image" in the portrayal of African Americans, as the old stereotypes persist especially in the coverage of crime and poverty.[23]

Examples of this continuing stereotypical coverage were on display in 2005 in coverage of Hurricane Katrina. A widely cited example, in numerous studies, was two Associated Press photos showing a person taking food from an abandoned grocery story. The caption under the photo of a black man described his behavior as "looting" while a photo of two whites described the same behavior as "finding" food. Television newscasts repeatedly broadcast photos (often the same ones) showing blacks allegedly looting, reinforcing the stereotype of African Americans as criminals. During the hurricane disaster the media also reported unsubstantiated allegations and rumors—later proven false—of violent and sadistic behavior by black men in the Superdome and other shelters, including robberies, sniper attacks, rape, and murder. Although many of these rumors were given credence by the city's black mayor and police chief, as Dyson writes: "It is safe to say that the media's framework was ready to receive and recycle rumors of vicious black behavior because such rumors seemed to confirm a widely held view about poor blacks."[24]

BOX 5.2

Political Scientists on Television

On cable television, most of the talk is about politics, but very few of the hosts or their regular contributors are political scientists. Indeed of the multiple shows on FOX, CNN, and MSNBC, the only two regularly featured African American political scientists are Melissa Harris-Perry and Dorian Warren on MSNBC. Harris-Perry was, until she left the network in 2016 in a dispute over election year coverage,[a] the host of a morning program—*The Melissa Harris-Perry Show*—on the weekends, and Warren is an MSNBC contributor and host of *Nerding Out* on the networks' digital platform, shift.msnbc.com. Both remain active in academia and the profession. Harris-Perry is the Presidential Chair Professor of Politics and International Affairs at Wake Forest University, and the author of two important works in black politics: *Barbershops, Bibles, and BET: Everyday Talk and Black Political Thought* (Harris-Lacewell, 2004) and *Sister Citizen: Shame, Stereotypes, and Black Women in America* (Harris-Perry, 2011). Warren is an associate professor in the Department of Political Science, the School of International and Public Affairs, and the Institute for Research in African-American Studies at Columbia University; and is Co-Director of the Program on Labor Law & Policy, specializing in labor studies, and a Fellow at the Roosevelt Institute.

MSNBC, the most liberal of the cable news channels, has the smallest audience of the three major outlets (Fox has an average 1.8 million daily viewers, CNN 730,000, and MSNBC about 600,000). However, it is the network of choice for African Americans, who make up 30 percent of the network's audience.[b] The network features more black hosts and contributors (in addition to Harris-Perry and Warren, civil rights leader Al Sharpton for a time hosted a daily show and now hosts a Sunday morning program, Tamron Hall is a daily news anchor, and Joy Reid, Michael Eric Dyson, and former Republican National Committee chair, Michael Steele,

Dr. Melissa Harris-Perry.

Source: "Melissa Harris-Perry on MSNBC" Retrieved 4 October 2016 from www.msnbc.com/sites/msnbc/files/styles/headshot—260tall/public/field_headshot_small/melissaharris-perry_s.png?itok=EBYtvLMu

Dr. Dorian Warren.

Source: "Dorian Warren at the Roosevelt Institute" Retrieved 4 October 2016 from http://rooseveltinstitute.org/dorian-warren/

are regular contributors) and focuses more on issues of concern to the black community.

All of the cable news talk programs in format and content tend to be characterized by their overwhelming sameness. Harris-Perry's program (which began in 2012), was somewhat distinctive. Although no one would confuse it with a political science seminar, it frequently displayed more intellectual content than the typical cable talk show, tended to feature more professors as contributors, to focus more on popular culture, and to feature more diverse guests and

contributors. The program also tended to focus more on issues of race and gender than the typical cable program.

a Paul Farhi, "MSNBC Severs Ties with Melissa Harris-Perry after Host's Critical Email," *The Washington Post*, February 28, 2016, accessed at https://www.washingtonpost.com/lifestyle/style/msnbc-will-cut-ties-with-show-host-who-wrote-critical-email-to-colleagues/2016/02/27/bce30c8e-dd82-11e5-891a-4ed04f4213e8_story.html.
b Kelefa Sanneh, "Twenty Four Hour Party People: MSNBC Tries to Figure Out What Liberals Really Want," *New Yorker*, September 2, 2013.

African American Celebrity Impact on Politics

Throughout black history, entertainment was not only a form of cultural expression for black America, but also a form of resistance to oppression. Each period from the "New Negro" Movement (also known as the Harlem Renaissance) to the Jim Crow era, the Civil Rights and Black Power Movements witnessed the emergence of black art, music, literature, and other creative impressions that "tasked blacks with instilling dignity and uplifting the race" by using their talent to encourage the black community, affirm black pride, and counter prevailing stereotypes in a white-dominated society.[25] Celebrities and athletes, during these periods, often used their "star power" as a platform to raise consciousness about the struggle in the black community. Many risked their careers due to their social and political activism: Paul Robeson, Harry Belafonte, Eartha Kitt, Nina Simone, Sam Cooke, Dick Gregory, Bill Russell, James Brown, Stevie Wonder, Muhammad Ali, and Kareem Abdul Jabar, to name a few. In the post–civil rights era, with the integration of black entertainment into the mainstream, the millennial generation of black celebrities has been criticized for their silence,[26] lack of cultural awareness, and accountability to the black community to vocalize issues of social injustice, racial oppression, and white privilege. In fact, evidence shows that the visibility of famed African Americans can influence the attitudes of black America. In a study by the Pew Research Center,[27] black respondents rated two celebrities—Oprah Winfrey (at 87 percent) and Bill Cosby (at 85 percent)—as the most influential black newsmakers edging out prominent political actors (this study was conducted before the widespread allegations of Cosby's sexual abuse of women).

A related study by University of Maryland economists,[28] testing the effects of celebrity endorsements during the 2008 presidential primary (see Chapter 8), found evidence that Oprah Winfrey's public endorsement of Obama during the Democratic caucuses and primaries had a positive effect on the political outcomes of Barack Obama's candidacy. Winfrey's visibility and involvement increased the share of the vote and number of contributions received by the Obama campaign. This was the first time the immensely popular Winfrey had ever endorsed a presidential candidate. With her proven track record of influencing the consumerism choices of her millions of fans—composed disproportionately of white suburban women—via her daytime talk show, the O! *Oprah magazine*, Oprah's Book Club, the study estimated that Winfrey's endorsement gave Obama as much as a million votes in the democratic primaries.[29] This became known as the "Oprah Effect."

Political scientists usually discount the effects of celebrity endorsements on how citizens vote. In fact, research is mixed on the validity of "The Oprah Effect"—defined as the influence of consuming soft news political content on vote choice and action.[30] Although not all celebrity endorsements have the level of influence of Oprah Winfrey, the research suggests given the increasing emphasis on celebrated personal images and audiences' preference for personality over policy dimensions, one's fame "can be politically advantageous," and one's associated media enterprises "can be a serious channel of communication in the fast-moving, complex, political landscapes of the present day."[31]

The Transformation of the Black Press in the Post–Civil Rights Era

In the post–civil rights era, as a result of integration, the black press has to continually transform as both an instrument of protest and of group solidarity and direction. It has to adapt as an instrument of protest because the withering away of overt white supremacism and racism removes the direct targets of protest that had given purpose to black press since the founding of the first newspaper. It has to acclimate as an instrument of group solidarity and direction as a result of the integration of blacks, in various ways, into the mainstream of American society. With the decline of "culture-rich" traditional media outlets, still preferred by the majority of black Americans, African American media has reemerged on myriad digital platform choices, accessible across an array of devices, and heavily utilized by African Americans. Few studies exist to measure the impact of African American digital media on black community solidarity and direction, but one thing is certain, this medium has proven successful in mobilizing thousands of citizens and activists across the nation to action.

Faces and Voices in the Struggle for Universal Freedom

Ida B. Wells-Barnett (1862–1931)

Ida B. Wells-Barnett used her pen to pursue the cause of universal freedom. Perhaps the most famous black journalist of her time, she was sometimes referred to as the "princess of the black press." Born during slavery, at age 16 she assumed responsibility for raising her five siblings after her parents died of yellow fever. After attending Fisk University, she edited two newspapers and then began writing a weekly column under the pen name "Iola." This column, which was published in black newspapers throughout the country, made her one of the most prominent African American leaders in the United States.

Wells-Barnett is best known for her campaign against lynching. After three of her friends were lynched, at great personal risk she became the nation's leading crusader against lynching. She conducted detailed investigations and wrote articles and pamphlets and lectured throughout the United States and Europe. Her 1895 *Red Record: Tabulated Statistics and Alleged Causes of Lynching in the United States* is a classic study of the subject. In addition to work in the media, Wells-Barnett was a founding member of the National Association for the Advancement of Colored People (NAACP), a leader of the National Association of Colored Women, and was active in several women's suffrage organizations. She also ran unsuccessfully for the Illinois state senate.[a]

Ida B. Wells-Barnett.

Source: "Legend: Ida B. Wells-Barnett, Journalist and Anti-Lynching Crusader" National Women's History Museum. Retrieved 4 October 2016 from https://www.nwhm.org/html/support/events/depizan/ida.html

[a] Linda O. Murray, *To Keep the Waters Troubled: The Life of Ida B. Wells* (New York: Oxford University Press, 1998).

Summary

Since the 1827 founding of *Freedom's Journal*, the first black newspaper, the media have been a central institution in the African American struggle for freedom and equality and a major agent of political socialization. As a result of the integration of blacks into the mainstream media and the expanded coverage of the black community, the influence of the black media has broadened beyond traditional mainstream outlets to a multiplicity of digital platforms. Yet the black media are still important institutions in black America. This is partly because African American employment is not fully or proportionately integrated into the mainstream media, and there is still a tendency toward racial and gender stereotyping in mainstream media coverage of the African American community.

Critical Thinking Questions

1. Discuss the role of the black media as socialization agent in fostering group consciousness and solidarity and as a vehicle of protest in the black community.
2. Discuss the use of social media among African Americans. How do young African Americans use social media? Are there links between the use of social media and major events affecting the black community? Discuss and provide specific examples.
3. Discuss the representation of African Americans in the mainstream media.
4. Is there a difference in the coverage of major events in the African American community by African American journalists? Discuss and provide examples.
5. How do stereotypes in the mass media reinforce blacks' subordinate status and work against universal freedom for African Americans? Discuss and provide examples.

Selected Bibliography

Behnken, Brian, and Gregory Smithers, *Racism in American Popular Media: From Aunt Jemima to the Frito Bandito.* Santa Barbara, CA: ABC-Clio, 2015. A history of the racist stereotyping of blacks and other minorities in the media.

Dates, Jannette, and William Barlow, eds. *Split Images: African Americans in the Mass Media*, 2nd ed. Washington, DC: Howard University Press, 1993. The leading work on the macrolevel dimension of the media and African Americans.

Gans, Herbert. *Deciding What's News: A Study of the CBS Evening News, NBC Nightly News, Newsweek and Time.* New York: Pantheon, 1979. An important sociological analysis of the relationship between social order and conflict in determining what is news.

Graber, Doris. *Mass Media and American Politics*, 4th ed. Washington, DC: Congressional Quarterly, 1992. The standard political science analysis of the role of the media in American politics.

Nelson, Jill. *Volunteer Slavery: My Authentic Negro Experience.* Chicago, IL: Nobel Press, 1993. A humorous and passionate account of the travails of the *Washington Post*

Magazine's first black and first woman reporter, a post from which she resigned because she says she was unable to tolerate the *Post*'s "paternalistic culture."
Wolseley, Roland. *The Black Press, U.S.A.*, 2nd ed. Ames: Iowa State University Press, 1990. A general survey of the black press, covering newspapers and magazines.

Notes

1 See "The First Negro Newspaper's Opening Editorial, 1827," in H. Aptheker, ed., *A Documentary History of the Negro People in the United States* (New York: Citadel, 1967): 82.
2 See Kristol Brent Zook, "Blacks Own Just 10 U.S. Television Stations, Here is Why," *Washington Post*, August 17, 2015.
3 Roland Wolseley, *The Black Press, U.S.A.* (Ames: Iowa State University Press, 1990).
4 Ronald Jacobs, "Civil Society and Crisis: Culture, Discourse and the Rodney King Beating," *American Journal of Sociology* 101 (1996): 1238–72.
5 For example, in 2015 *Essence* magazine partnered with Black Women's Roundtable, a program of the National Coalition on Black Civic Participation, Inc., to conduct surveys on black women's political behavior (www.essence.com/2015/09/16/essence-and-black-womens-roundtable-release-survey-power-sister-vote). Also, in 2014, *Essence* partnered with the Nielsen Company on a custom survey of African American consumer choices (http://sites.nielsen.com/africanamericans/).
6 Black Radio Today 2013: How America Listens to Radio, Radio's Enduring Relationship with Black Listeners, www.arbitron.com/downloads/Black_Radio_Today_2013_execsum.pdf.
7 Summary statistics were taken from Reach Media, Inc., accessed online on January 27, 2016, www.reachmediainc.com/
8 Data from two studies conducted by the Nielsen and *Essence* magazine were used, "Powerful. Growing. Influential. The African-American Consumer 2014 Report" and "The Total Audience Report December 2014." Both can be accessed at http://sites.nielsen.com/africanamericans/.
9 The Pew Research Center, State of the News Media, African-American Media Fact Sheet, April 29, 2015, www.journalism.org/2015/04/29/african-american-media-fact-sheet/.
10 Reach Media, Inc., www.reachmediainc.com/.
11 See reports, "Wire Internet Use," Pew Internet & American Life Project, July 2009, pp. 3–6; and "African-Americans and Technology Use: A Demographic Portrait," Pew Research Center, January 6, 2014.
12 Quoted from Nielsen report summary released on the website on February 3, 2015, www.nielsen.com/us/en/insights/news/2015/multifaceted-connections-african-american-media-usage-outpaces-across-platforms.html.
13 See "The Race for the White House 2016: Registered Voters and Media and Information during the Primaries," released January 2016, www.iab.com/insights/the-race-for-the-white-house-2016-registered-voters-and-media-and-information-during-the-primaries/.
14 See "The Total Audience Report December 2014," p. 20.
15 Ibid., and "African-Americans and Technology Use: A Demographic Portrait" report.
16 The National Advisory Commission on Civil Disorders (popularly known as the Kerner Commission) was appointed by President Johnson to investigate the causes of the civil unrest. The commission's findings pointed to the absence of black reporters and scant coverage of the black community as factors contributing to the discontent

that led to the uprisings. Also, many newspapers and television stations found that without black reporters they could not adequately cover the rebellions, since white reporters were reluctant to go into the black community or did not understand what they saw and heard.

17 "Black Journalists' Ranks Cut By Nearly 1,000 in Past Decade," *NABJ News*, April 4, 2012, www.nabj.org/news/88558/.

18 See Vernon Johnson, "Minorities and Women in Television News" and "Minorities and Women in Radio News" (University of Missouri, School of Journalism, 1996).

19 American Society of Newspaper Editors, press release on the 1996 Annual Survey on Diversity in the Newsroom, April 16, 1996.

20 Herbert Gans, *Deciding What's News: A Study of the CBS Evening News, NBC Nightly News, Newsweek and Time* (New York: Pantheon, 1979).

21 Jill Nelson, *Volunteer Slavery: My Authentic Negro Experience* (Chicago, IL: Noble Press, 1993).

22 Brian Behnken and Gregory Smithers, *Racism in American Popular Media* (Santa Barbara, CA: ABC-Clio, 2015).

23 Jannette Dates and William Barlow, eds., *Split Images: African Americans in the Mass Media*, 2nd ed. (Washington, DC: Howard University Press, 1993) and Martin Gilens, "Race and Poverty in America: Public Perceptions and the American News Media," *Public Opinion Quarterly* 50 (1996): 515–41.

24 Michael Eric Dyson, *Come Hell or High Water: Hurricane Katrina and the Color of Disaster* (New York: Basic Civitas, 2006): 72.

25 Cierra Lockett, "Ending Apathy from African-American Entertainers," July 28, 2015, www.huffingtonpost.com/cierra-lockett/ending-apathy-in-entertai_b_7861846.html.

26 Ibid.

27 See "Optimism about Black Progress Declines: Blacks See Growing Values Gap Between Poor and Middle Class," Pew Research Center, November 2007, p. 45.

28 Craig Garthwaite and Tim Moore, "The Role of Celebrity Endorsements in Politics: Oprah, Obama, and the 2008 Democratic Primary," August 2008, p. 39, www.stat.columbia.edu/~gelman/stuff_for_blog/celebrityendorsements_garthwaitemoore.pdf.

29 Ibid., see also Brian Stetler, "Endorsement from Oprah Quantified: A Million Votes," *New York Times,* August 11, 2008.

30 Matthew A. Baum and Angela Jamison, "Soft News and the Four Oprah Effects," in Robert Y. Shapiro and Lawrence R. Jacobs, eds., *The Oxford Handbook of American Public Opinion and the Media* (Oxford: Oxford University Press, 2011): 123.

31 Ibid., pp. 134–35.

PART III

Coalitions, Movements, Interest Groups, Parties, and Elections

CHAPTER 6

Social Movements and a Theory of African American Coalition Politics

LEARNING OBJECTIVE

Define minority–majority coalitions in the context of social movements that have been important in African American history.

For much of their history in the United States, African Americans have been excluded from the normal, routine processes of political participation such as lobbying, voting, elections, and political parties. Indeed, in the Republic's more than 200-year history, African Americans have been included as nearly full participants for barely 60 years—the 10-year Reconstruction period from 1867 to 1877 plus the years since the adoption of the Voting Rights Act in 1965. As for much of their history, African Americans have been excluded from the interest group, electoral, and party systems, they have had to resort to social movements to challenge the exclusionary system. William Gamson makes this point when he observes that in the United States certain groups have been systematically denied entry into the political process and gain entry only through protest or system crisis—what he calls "the breakdown of the normal operation of the system or through demonstration on the part of challenging groups of a willingness to violate 'rules of the game' by resorting to illegitimate means of carrying on political conflict."[1]

Therefore, before we examine the African American interest group, voting, and party behavior, we need to look first at African American participation in social movements. A *social movement* may be understood as a group of persons organized in a sustained, self-conscious challenge to an existing system and its values or power relationships. An *interest group* is typically defined as a group of persons who share a common interest and seek to influence the government to adopt policies favorable to that interest. In other words, movements challenge systems, whereas interest groups accept and work within systems. In this rather long chapter we examine the history, development, and contemporary manifestations of African American social movement behavior. Before doing this, however, we develop a theory of African American minority–majority coalition politics.

A Theory of African American Coalition Politics

This book has two major themes. The first is that African Americans in their quest for freedom in the United States have sought to universalize the idea of freedom. The second theme is that African Americans—given their status first as slaves and then as an oppressed racial minority—have had to form coalitions with whites to achieve their freedom. Historically, however, these black–white coalitions have been tenuous and unstable, requiring constant rebuilding in an ongoing quest. To understand the dynamic instability of African American coalition politics, we must know some basic concepts and theoretical propositions.

There are various concepts and definitions of coalitions, including complicated, technical–mathematical ones and social–psychological and economic cost/benefit analyses.[2] But simply, a *coalition* involves two or more persons or groups bringing their resources together to achieve a common objective. When a group can achieve its objectives alone, it is less likely to join a coalition. Historically, as blacks have sought freedom in the United States, this has rarely been the case for them. They have always needed coalition partners to achieve many, if not all, of their objectives. However, blacks frequently have not been able to find coalition partners among whites for their objectives; thus, they have been forced to act alone. Black nationalists in the United States reject in principle the possibility of whites as reliable coalition partners and therefore always embrace the strategy of *intraracial* coalitions among blacks rather than *interracial* coalitions with whites. But even those blacks (the overwhelming majority) who in principle accept the idea of interracial coalitions have also embraced the go-it-alone strategy, when suitable white coalition partners were not available or when independent race group organizations were thought to be preferable or complementary to coalition politics. A final theoretical point is that a coalition, to be viable, must have sufficient resources—money, status, size—to achieve its objectives vis-à-vis opposing groups and coalitions. In summary, a theory of African American coalition politics suggests that blacks will seek to pool their resources with whites, when possible, in order to achieve their objectives. When suitable white partners are not available, they will seek to pool their resources among themselves to achieve these objectives.[3]

Historically, as Figure 6.1 shows, African Americans have sought to form or participate in two categories of coalitions. The first type is a *rights-based coalition*, one that seeks to achieve fundamental universal freedom in terms of basic human, constitutional, and legal rights; examples are the abolitionist and civil rights movements. The second is a *material-based coalition*, which seeks access to economic benefits such as land, education, employment, and social security; examples are the populist movement, Franklin Roosevelt's New Deal Coalition, and Jesse Jackson's Rainbow Coalition.[4] Historically, also, the rights-based coalitions have had priority over the material-based ones. For example, before the black slaves could fight for land and education, their first objective had to be the abolition of slavery. Similarly, a major objective of black leaders and organizations during the 1970s was to form a material-based coalition to secure passage of legislation guaranteeing full employment (see the discussion of the Humphrey-Hawkins Act in Chapter 10). Before this material-based issue

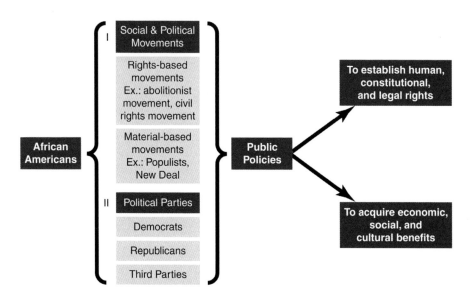

FIGURE 6.1

The Dual Categories for Coalition Formation of African Americans: Rights- and Material-Based

Sources: Adapted from Hanes Walton, Jr., *Black Politics: A Theoretical and Structural Analysis* (Philadelphia, PA: J. B. Lippincott, 1972); and Robert Allen, *The Reluctant Reformers: Reform Movements in the United States* (Washington, DC: Howard University Press, 1993).

could become the priority, however, the rights-based objectives of the civil rights movement had to be achieved.

African American minority–majority coalitions tend to be tenuous and unstable because of racism, white supremacist thinking, and the ambivalence of white Americans toward race and universal freedom and equality. Figure 6.2

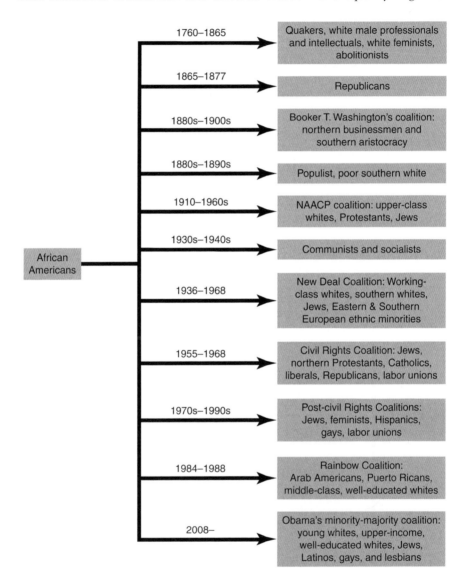

FIGURE 6.2

African American Coalition Partners, 1700s–Forward

Sources: Robert Allen, *The Reluctant Reformers: Reform Movements in the United States* (Washington, DC: Howard University Press, 1973); and Robert Smith, *We Have No Leaders: African Americans in the Post–Civil Rights Era* (Albany, NY: SUNY Press, 1996).

displays the white and other coalition partners of blacks from the founding of the Republic in the 1770s to the present. It shows that in both rights- and material-based coalitions, blacks have over time formed coalitions with all elements of the white population (and since the 1960s, other racial minority groups)—Quakers and Jews, middle-class professionals and poor white farmers, white liberals and white conservatives, rural whites and urban whites, and white men and white women. Yet, as we show in this chapter and in those following on electoral and party coalitions, these varied coalitions have frequently been weak and unstable because of the forces of racism and white supremacy.

In summary, here are the basic elements of this theory of African American coalitions, as we use them to analyze black social movements in this chapter and to examine interest groups, elections, and party behavior in Chapters 7, 8, and 9:

- Black–white coalitions tend to shift from rights-based to material-based, depending on historical conditions.
- Viable coalitions with whites are sometimes not possible, forcing blacks to act alone in black nationalist or other forms of intragroup coalitions.
- Because of racism and white supremacist thinking, when coalitions with whites are formed they tend to be tenuous, unstable, and frequently short-lived, requiring constant rebuilding.

Given these basic theoretical points, we begin by analyzing the first significant African American coalition: the rights-based abolitionist movement.

The First Rights-Based Movement: The Abolitionist Coalition

The movement that emerged in the 1830s to abolish slavery was the first rights-based coalition in the United States. It, like the early twentieth-century civil rights movement, was organized and led by well-educated, middle- to upper-class blacks and whites, many of whom (especially among the blacks) were ministers.[5] The abolitionist movement anticipates the conflicts and tensions that have characterized all subsequent reform coalitions involving African Americans and whites, whether rights-based or material-based.

In *The Reluctant Reformers: Racism and Social Reform Movements in the United States*, Robert Allen analyzes six major social reform movements, beginning with the abolitionist movement and including populism, the progressive movement, feminism, the labor movement, and the socialist and communist movements. African Americans were involved in each of these reform movements in coalitions with whites. These alliances span 100 years, from the 1830s to the 1930s, and as Allen points out, they cover the whole span of social classes from middle- and upper-class whites in the abolitionist movement to poor and working-class whites in the populist and labor movements. Some of these movements were based in the North; some, like the populist movements, were rural; and others, like the progressive and labor movements, were predominantly urban. White men led most of these movements, but white women in the 1860s developed a movement of their own. However, as Allen observed, none of these differences among whites—middle class or poor, urban or rural, North or South, and male or female—resulted in the absence of some degree of racism.[6] That is, beginning with the abolitionist movement, racism and the ideology of white supremacy have operated to effectively undermine all reform coalitions in the United States.

The principal white leader of the abolitionist movement was William Lloyd Garrison, who in 1833 founded the American Anti-Slavery Society. The leading black abolitionist was Frederick Douglass. Although both Douglass and Garrison were "militant abolitionists," favoring the immediate abolition of slavery, they differed over strategy and tactics. Eventually, these differences led to the breakup of the coalition.

Garrison was an uncompromising critic of slavery and the Constitution that ordained it, as may be seen in the following famous quote from the first issue of his newspaper *The Liberator:*

> Let southern oppressors tremble . . . let northern apologists tremble, let all the enemies of the persecuted blacks tremble. . . . Urge me not to use moderation in a cause like the present. I am in earnest—I will not equivocate—I will not excuse—and I will be heard![7]

Despite this militancy, Garrison was committed to "moral suasion," nonviolence, and white leadership of the abolitionist movement. Garrison and his followers were also opposed to the formation of the all black National Negro Congress. These positions eventually led Douglass and other black abolitionists to break with Garrison and seek their way alone. One hundred years later, similar differences between blacks and whites would lead to a breakup of the civil rights coalition and the emergence of the separatist black power movement.

Although the middle-class whites who led the abolitionist movement were not racists, many were white supremacists and based their opposition to slavery not on a belief in the equality of the races but on moral and religious grounds. That is, although blacks might not be the equal of whites, for one man to enslave another was nevertheless a violation of the principles of the Declaration of Independence and Jesus's doctrine of universal brotherhood.[8] This moral and religious basis of the movement led many whites to insist that nonviolent resistance was the only acceptable way to oppose slavery.

Douglass initially embraced Garrison's moralism and nonviolence, but as time went on and these approaches did not prove successful, he and many other black abolitionists abandoned a sole reliance on moral suasion and embraced political action (support for the antislavery Liberty Party) and violent resistance and revolt. The final reason for the collapse of the abolitionist coalition was the issue of who should lead it—in Douglass's words, who should be part of "the generalship of the movement." Douglass argued that whites in the movement ignored blacks, refusing to recognize or respect their leadership. In words that sound like Stokely Carmichael and the 1960s black power advocates, Douglass said,

> The man who has *suffered* the wrong is the man to demand the redress—the man struck is the man to CRY OUT and he who has endured *the cruel pangs of slavery* is the man to *advocate liberty*. It is evident that we must be our own representatives and advocates, but peculiarly—not distinct from—but in connection with our white friends.[9]

This first rights-based coalition did not directly result in the abolition of slavery but it did, along with the slave revolts and John Brown's raid at Harpers Ferry, contribute to the climate that resulted in the crisis leading up to the Civil War.[10]

Abolitionism and Feminism

Early black and some white feminists—advocates of equality of rights for women—supported the abolition of slavery as part of a general moral stance in favor of universal freedom for all persons. Black women abolitionists Harriet Tubman, Sarah Forten, Lucy Stanton, Frances Ellen Watkins Harper, Isabella Baumfree (aka "Sojourner Truth"), and Sarah Parker Redmond blatantly criticized the institution of slavery and its violent attempts at dehumanization for enslaved Africans.[11] Frederick Douglass, viewed as the prominent voice and leader of the black race, and many black male abolitionists were strong supporters of women's rights, again as part of a general moral stance in favor of universal freedom.[12] Thus, these two rights-based movements formed a coalition on the basis of equality and universal freedom for all persons without regard for race or gender. Yet this coalition, like the abolitionist coalition, was tenuous and unstable; in the end, it collapsed.

First, unlike Douglass, many male abolitionists—black and white—discriminated against women, refusing, for example, to allow women to sign the Anti-Slavery Society's Declaration of Principles, hold leadership positions in the group, or serve as antislavery lecturers. As a result, a group of "women of color" organized America's first women's antislavery organization, the Salem Female Anti-Slavery Society, to champion their cause for supporting secular and Sabbath schools for free blacks, and it assisted blacks in bondage who were newly freed or runaway via the Freedmen's Bureau, and opposed racial segregation and discrimination in the northern free states. Two years after its founding, the society expanded its membership to include white women.[13] Although most white female abolitionists and early feminists were also middle class, men nevertheless argued that they, too, were inferior in status and therefore should not be allowed to exercise freedom on the same basis as men. White feminists were also white supremacists who embraced the antislavery coalition only as a means to advance the cause of women's rights for whites, which would ultimately become the key issue, leading to the collapse of the black–feminist coalition. The crucial issue was black suffrage—whether black men should be granted the right to vote before white women. This issue first emerged with the adoption of the Fourteenth Amendment, which for the first time included the word *male* in the Constitution. Foner contends that feminist leaders felt a "deep sense of betrayal" by this action and "consequently embarked on a course that severed their historic alliance with abolitionism and created an independent feminist movement, seeking a new constituency outside of the reform milieu."[14]

The decisive break came with the adoption of the Fifteenth Amendment, which granted black men the right to vote but denied it to women. Leading white feminists opposed the amendment unless women were included because they said it would permit black men, their "inferiors," more rights than white women. Although most black women feminists viewed the amendment as necessary for racial advancement, some like Sojourner Truth argued that without voting rights for black women, the race could not progress at all. Truth argued that "Men have got their rights, and women has [*sic*] not got their rights. That is the trouble. When woman gets her rights man will be right. . . . The great fight was to keep the rights of the poor colored people."[15] Frederick Douglass, a supporter of women's suffrage and vice-president of the National Equal Rights League, made an eloquent rebuttal to these arguments:

> I must say that I do not see how anyone can pretend that there is the same urgency in giving the ballot to the woman as the Negro. With us the matter is a question of life and death, at least in fifteen states of the union. When women are dragged from their houses and hung up on lamp posts; when their children are torn from their arms and their brains dashed on the pavement; when they are the object of insult and outrage at every turn; when they are in danger of having their homes burnt down over their heads; when their children are not allowed to enter schools; then they will have an urgency to the ballot equal to our own.[16]

Douglass's arguments were not persuasive, and by the end of Reconstruction, the feminist movement had become largely a movement of mostly whites, with white women advocating for inclusion on an equal basis in racist America.[17] This again illustrates our theoretical point about the tenuousness and instability of black–white coalitions. These tensions and conflicts between the women's-based rights movement and the black-based rights movement continue 100 years later, as reflected in the debate about the inclusion of gender in the Civil Rights Act of 1964 and the debate about affirmative action in the 1990s which fail to recognize the intersectionality of black women's struggles and experiences.

Booker T. Washington's Coalition for Limited Freedom

In many ways the strangest and most paradoxical coalition in African American politics is the one fashioned by Booker T. Washington in the aftermath of Reconstruction. It can be considered strange and paradoxical because it was a coalition for limited rather than universal freedom. For a brief period of time during Reconstruction, African Americans had the freedom to exercise their basic civil rights, including the right to vote, hold office, and have access along with whites to places of public accommodation such as inns, theaters, and restaurants. However, as a result of the so-called Compromise of 1877 that led to the disputed election of President Rutherford B. Hayes, these freedoms were taken away. The essence of the 1877 Compromise was Hayes's promise to withdraw the army from the southern states in exchange for the electoral votes that would allow him to become president. The withdrawal of these soldiers was critical to the end of Reconstruction since they had protected the newly freed slaves in the exercise of their newly won freedoms. Once the soldiers left, white southerners engaged in a campaign of open terror, torture, massacres, and lynchings in order to deprive African Americans of their freedoms. In spite of the Fourteenth and Fifteenth Amendments, blacks were denied the right to vote and were denied access to public office, public places, and quality education. Finally, in the 1896 case of *Plessy* v. *Ferguson*, the Supreme Court codified this denial of freedom by declaring that the Fourteenth Amendment's guarantee of equality did not prevent the states from segregating the races in all public places, from streetcars to schoolrooms.

Frederick Douglass and other African American leaders bitterly protested this denial of freedom as a betrayal not only of the Negro but also of the very idea of freedom for which the war had been fought. While Frederick Douglass and others continued their fight for universal freedom, Booker T. Washington, the head of Tuskegee University in Alabama and probably the single most powerful African American leader in the history of the United States, formed a coalition with the former southern slave owners and northern businessmen that embraced the idea of limited freedom. That is, he argued that the newly freed slaves were not at the time ready for universal freedom because he said they lacked the necessary education, property, and character. Thus, he argued that Reconstruction was a mistake and blacks, at least temporarily, should give up their quest for universal freedom in terms of social and political rights. In return for giving up social and political freedoms, Washington asked the former slave owners to grant blacks personal autonomy or freedom, the freedom to work, and the freedom to develop their own economic, social, and cultural institutions on a separate but equal basis.[18]

Booker Washington's thought is ambivalent and controversial. He is viewed by many African Americans as the quintessential "Uncle Tom"—a man who sold out the interests of the race to rich and powerful whites. Yet, for others, he was a pragmatic politician who made the best deal for his people he could, given the concrete conditions and circumstances of the time—circumstances of overwhelming white hostility and antiblack violence. There was also in Washington's thought a powerful strain of black nationalism in terms of racial separatism in economics, education, and community autonomy. (Marcus Garvey, the 1920s black nationalist leader, originally came to the United States to visit Washington, whose thought had tremendously impressed him as a young man in Jamaica.) In any event, Washington's thought is unique in the African American experience since it embraced limited, not universal, freedom. However, it should be clear that for Washington this was a temporary accommodation to the conditions of the time. That is, he thought—wrongly as it turned out—that through education, work, and property, African Americans would eventually "earn" universal freedom or what he called "full citizenship rights."

Material-Based Coalitions: From Populism to Communism

Populism

The populist movement of the 1890s set the pattern of all future material-based coalitions between whites and African Americans. C. Vann Woodward, historian of the populist movement, writes, "It is altogether probable that during the brief populist upheaval of the nineties Negroes and Native whites achieved a greater comity of mind and harmony of political purpose [than] ever before or since in the south."[19] A reexamination of Woodward's research on the populist movement shows, as one historian says, that he was "much too generous"— that rather than being a grand coalition of poor whites and blacks, populism from the outset was undermined by the racism and white supremacist thinking of its white leaders who sought to manipulate their black coalition partners for their own interests.[20]

The populist movement emerged out of the economic depression of the 1890s as black sharecroppers and poor white farmers were faced with falling wages and prices, high taxes, and heavy debt. As a result of this crisis, there was a material basis for a coalition between these two groups, who by pooling their resources (including their votes) could effectively challenge the power of the dominant economic and political elites. Led by Tom Watson of Georgia, the populists formed the Southern Alliance and later the Populist Party, both of which advocated such progressive reforms as debt relief, government ownership or regulation of the railroads, and a graduated income tax. Although some white populists for a time sincerely tried to build a biracial, class-oriented movement, from the outset racism was a major stumbling block. For example, blacks were not allowed to join the Southern Alliance; rather, they were segregated in a separate white-led Colored Farmers Alliance. And while the Populist Party appealed for black voter support and allowed blacks to serve as leaders (although in small numbers), it too was eventually undermined as poor whites were convinced by Democratic Party leaders that a vote for the interracial Populist Party was racial treason.[21] As a result, white populists eventually succumbed to what Richard Hofstadter called the "Negro bogey," and within a decade, this first material-based coalition of African Americans and whites had collapsed.[22] Eventually, Tom Watson, the movement's leader, turned from preaching interracial unity and solidarity to an extreme form of racism and white supremacy, supporting lynching and the disenfranchisement of blacks.[23] Thus, within the short span of a decade, populism went from "colored and white in the ditch unite" to "lynch the Negro."[24]

The Progressives

The populist movement was, as Hofstadter writes, "the first modern political movement of practical importance in the United States to insist that the federal government has some responsibility for the common weal; indeed it was the first such movement to attack seriously the problems created by industrialism."[25] It was succeeded a generation later by the progressive movement. The progressives, unlike the populists, were largely urban, middle-class professional whites who sought, like the populists, federal regulation of the economy and reforms in the political process, such as the initiative and referendum. It too, however, was affected by the "Negro bogey."[26] The Progressive Party, for example, refused to condemn racial discrimination, lynching, or the denial of black voting rights. One of its principal leaders, President Theodore Roosevelt, was one of the most racist presidents of the twentieth century (see Chapter 11).

The Labor Movement

The African American people are largely a working-class people; therefore, their natural coalition partners should be working-class whites and their trade union organizations. As Carmichael and Hamilton said in their chapter "The Myth of Coalitions" in the book *Black Power*, "It is hoped eventually that there will be a coalition of poor whites and blacks. This is the only coalition which seems acceptable to us and we see such a coalition as the major instrument of change in American society."[27] For much of American history, Carmichael and Hamilton's hope for a coalition with the white working class has been just that, a hope, because for much of its history the American labor movement was committed to white supremacy and racism. With a few exceptions—the Knights of Labor during Reconstruction and the International Workers of the World early in the twentieth century—American trade unions have either excluded blacks or forced them into segregated unions.[28] Even today, although organized labor has abolished racial segregation and was a major partner in the 1960s civil rights coalition, the white working class continues to exhibit more racist, white supremacist thinking than do middle-class, professional whites.

As is shown in Chapters 8 and 9, blacks and working-class whites were partners, although uneasy ones, in the New Deal coalition (which enacted many of the reform proposals of the populists and progressives), but this was because President Franklin D. Roosevelt scrupulously avoided taking any stand on race issues, even refusing to support antilynching legislation. Once the Democratic Party in the 1960s embraced the cause of civil rights, the New Deal coalition of blacks and working-class whites began to collapse. Despite eloquent pleas and constant campaigning on working-class concerns, Jesse Jackson in his two campaigns for president received more support from middle-class white professionals than from poor and working-class whites, as did Barack Obama in 2008.

Socialists and Communists

Even socialists and communists have not been able to avoid the "Negro bogey" of racism and white supremacy. The Socialist Party was organized in 1901, and although it was ostensibly devoted to a broad-based coalition of workers, it initially embraced racism and white supremacy. Jack London, one of the party's founders, said, "I am first a white man and only then socialist," and the party's newspaper, *Appeal to Reason*, declared, "Socialists believe in justice to the Negro, not social equality. Socialism will separate the races."[29] Only when the socialists began to face competition from the Communist Party did they change their racist position, begin to recruit blacks (such as A. Phillip Randolph, the labor leader), and, under the leadership of Norman Thomas in the 1930s, take forthright stands against racial segregation and discrimination.[30] The Communist Party probably was more sympathetic to universal freedom than any other organized group of white Americans.

However, as the African American novelist Richard Wright argued in his eloquent essay in *The God That Failed*, although the Communist Party supported the cause of universal freedom sincerely, it was also a part of a strategy dictated from Russia to manipulate African Americans in order to further the objectives of the Soviet Union.[31]

Historically, blacks have been willing to join as partners in material-based reform coalitions with whites; however, whites have been reluctant, unreliable partners, forcing blacks to act alone or seek white partners in rights-based coalitions.

A "Rainbow" Coalition?

In 1984 and 1988, Jesse Jackson ran for the Democratic Party's presidential nomination. In both the campaigns, he sought to build what he called a "Rainbow Coalition" of blacks and other "peoples of color"—Latinos and Arab and Asian Americans—as well as progressive or liberal whites. The idea of a multiracial coalition of peoples of color is attractive to African American leaders because since the 1960s the United States has become increasingly racially diverse as a result of immigration from Asia, Latin America, and, to a somewhat less extent, Africa. Until the 1960s, the immigration laws of the United States were based on principles of racism. Enacted in the 1920s, these laws generally excluded persons from eastern and southern Europe and the so-called Third World. Partly as a result of the antiracism reform climate brought about by the civil rights movement, the immigration laws were changed in 1965 to permit immigration from all parts of the world. These changes in the law, the globalization of the economy, and the creation of refugees as a result of wars in Asia, Africa, and Latin America have resulted in a massive influx of immigrants, documented and undocumented, since the 1970s. The 2010 U.S. Census indicated that persons from Latin America or "Hispanics" accounted for 16 percent of the U.S. population of 309 million, Asian Americans 5 percent, African Americans 13 percent, and non-Hispanic whites 63 percent—about half the Hispanics identified themselves as white. (This represents a dramatic change from the 1960s when blacks and whites accounted for approximately 90 percent of the population.) Although it is common for social scientists and journalists to refer to Hispanics and Asian Americans as if they are single, discrete ethnic groups, they obviously are not, and to treat them as single, discrete groups conceals the extent of ethnic diversity in the United States. While Latinos share a common language, they do not necessarily share a common culture, and Asian Americans do not share a common language, let alone a culture. Thus, it is important to break down these artificially created groups because they may hold different racial and political attitudes and engage in different political behavior. Among Hispanics, the largest ethnic group is Mexican Americans at 58.5 percent, Puerto Ricans are 28.4 percent, Cubans 3.5 percent, and persons from other Latin American countries 21 percent. Among Asian Americans the breakdown is Chinese at 23.7 percent, Filipinos (classified as Asian although many speak Spanish) 18 percent, Korean 9.5 percent, Japanese 7 percent, Asian Indians 16 percent, Vietnamese 11 percent, and persons from other Asian countries 12.5 percent.

Given this ethnic diversity, the idea of a rainbow coalition of people of color is based on the assumption that the new immigrants tend to be poor and may face discrimination or racism from the white majority, and therefore there is an objective basis for a coalition with blacks in terms of support for civil rights and social welfare legislation. Blacks and the leaders of Asian American and

Latino communities are part of a broad leadership coalition for civil rights, but it has been marked by tensions and conflicts (see Box 7.2). At the mass level, while majorities of both Latinos and Asian Americans feel they face discrimination from the white majority, they feel they have more in common with whites than they do with blacks.[32] Latinos and Asian Americans in general tend to embrace the same negative stereotypes about blacks. For example, a major report shows that 51 percent of Latinos, 53 percent of Asian Americans, and 45 percent of whites said they believed blacks were prone to crime and violence; and 40 percent of whites, 33 percent of Latinos, and 48 percent of Asian Americans said they believed blacks "care less about family." As the authors of the report write, these negative stereotypes regarding blacks constitute a "serious barrier" to cooperation and coalitions between blacks and other people of color.[33] Thus, Jesse Jackson in his two campaigns for president received relatively little support from other groups of color except Puerto Ricans in New York. There is also competition for political offices and resources between blacks and Mexican Americans in California and Texas, between blacks and Cuban Americans in Florida, between blacks and Puerto Ricans in New York and Illinois, and even between blacks and African Americans of West Indian origins in New York. Thus, whether in the twenty-first century the relationship between blacks and the new immigrants will be characterized by cooperation and coalition or competition and conflict is unclear.[34]

African Americans, Immigration, and the Prospects for a New Majority Coalition

Historically, African Americans have been skeptical or hostile to immigration, fearing competition for jobs.[35] As Frederick Douglass said in the 1880s referring to the waves of immigrants from Europe, "The old employment by which we have heretofore gained our livelihood, are gradually and it may seem inevitably, passing into other hands. Every hour sees the black man elbowed out of employment by some newly arrived immigrant whose hunger and color are thought to give him a better title to the place."[36] Yet, the reforms that ended racial discrimination in the nation's immigration laws in 1965 and opened the doors to immigrants from all over the world were partly an outgrowth of the civil rights movement. As Vernon Briggs writes, "It was the passage of the Civil Rights Act of 1964 . . . that created the national climate needed to legislatively end the discriminatory national origin system the following year with the adoption of the Immigration Act of 1965."[37] However, in 1977 it was Barbara Jordan, the nationally renowned African American congresswoman from Texas, who chaired a commission that recommended, among other things, substantial reductions in the annual level of legal immigration, limits on the admission of unskilled adults, and a concerted effort to stop illegal immigration.[38]

Although the econometrics literature is mixed on the impact of immigration on the employment and wages of low-income workers in general and African Americans particularly,[39] it is clear that immigration has increased the supply of low-wage labor, which tends to reduce wages and employment opportunities for low-wage American citizens and legal immigrants.[40] Employers may also prefer to hire undocumented immigrants, who are viewed as harder working and less complaining than native-born Americans. Yet, immigrants also likely contribute to growth in the overall economy and may do certain kinds of work that native-born Americans are unwilling to do, at least at the prevailing wages.[41] Finally, the new immigrants from Latin America, Asia, and, to a lesser extent, Africa may provide a long-term basis for the expansion of a multicultural rainbow coalition that could increase support for affirmative action, unionization, living wages, and national health insurance.

By 2050, the U.S. Census Bureau estimates that nonwhites will constitute half the U.S. population, bringing an end to the majority status of white or European Americans. (Latinos are projected to constitute 24 percent of the population, blacks 14 percent, Asians 8 percent, and 4 percent Native American, Hawaiian and Pacific Islanders, and mixed race.)[42] This suggests the possibility or prospect in the future that a rainbow coalition could become the electoral majority in the United States. In other words, immigrants could become the basis for a new coalition in the quest for universal freedom. (See Chapter 9, which discusses the growth of the rainbow coalition in the 2012 presidential election.)

Black Ethnicity and Immigration: The Impact on Race and Group Consciousness

In the reporting in the media and in scholarship on immigration, much of the attention focuses on immigrants from Latin America and to a lesser from Asia, with little reporting or research on immigrants from Africa and the Caribbean. Similarly, in the reporting and research on black Americans, relatively little attention is devoted to the increasing ethnic diversity of the group as a result of the immigration which has led to an increasingly diverse group of blacks in the United States. However, just as it is necessary to disaggregate Hispanic and Asian Americans into discrete ethnic groups, it is also imperative to disaggregate blacks into discrete ethnicities, distinguishing the historical and common experiences between those descendants from the "native born" (i.e., those whose roots emanate from the transatlantic slave trade) and those from the multiple nations of Africa and the Caribbean who have voluntarily migrated to the United States.

For generations in American history, there has been a significant West Indian or Caribbean part of the African American community;[43] with the West Indian community having produced such notable black figures as Marcus

Garvey, Stokely Carmichael, Shirley Chisholm, and Colin Powell. (President Barack Obama is the biracial son of a Kenyan immigrant father and white American mother.) Until recently the African immigrant population was small and concentrated heavily along the east coast. But in the last decade—due to changes in immigration law, particularly the Refugee Act of 1980—immigration from Africa has increased rapidly and has become dispersed widely across the country.[44] In 2013, an estimated 1.8 million African-origin immigrants resided in the United States, up from 800,000 in 2000.[45] Overall, according to the 2010 census there were 1.5 million immigrants from Africa and 3.5 million from the Caribbean. Together they constitute close to 10 percent of the all-inclusive black population of the United States.

While the census tends to lump persons from Africa and the Caribbean into single groups, disaggregation here is also needed as there are distinct differences in languages and cultures among and between the influx of documented and undocumented immigrants from Nigeria, Ghana, Ethiopia, Somalia, Kenya, and South Africa as well as those from Jamaica, Haiti, the Dominican Republic, and other Caribbean nations.[46] Diversity among African-descended communities "remains a black box and a mystery to most Americans,"[47] given the dearth of available research and the link to the ethnic diversity within black America generally.

Most of the research on ethnic diversity focuses on educational attainment. For example, the 2000 census reported among all immigrants, 43.8 percent of African immigrants had earned a college degree, compared to 42.5 percent of Asian Americans, 28.9 percent for immigrants from Europe, Russia, and Canada, and 23.1 percent of the U.S. population as a whole.[48] Similar findings, highlighting aspects of ethnic diversity within black America, were reported in the census bureau's 2012 *American Community Survey* that found 30 percent of African-born blacks residing in New York City had a college degree, compared with 22 percent of native-born blacks, 18 percent of Caribbean-born blacks, and 19 percent of the non-black foreign.[49] In fact, the media tend to laud the achievements of first- or second-generation African immigrants' offspring—particularly those who have been accepted to multiple Ivy League schools—sparking new debates about affirmative action (black immigrants now comprise the overwhelming majority of black students at these elite institutions),[50] as the "invisible model minority."[51] However, more studies are needed to investigate black immigrants' feelings about racial identity, group consciousness, and solidarity with native-born African Americans and their levels of political participation.

A recent study is Cristina Greer's *Black Ethnics: Race, Immigration and the Pursuit of the American Dream.* Greer uses the concept of "elevated minorities" to analyze the interrelationships between black immigrants, whites, and native African Americans. Akin to the idea of Asian Americans as "model minorities," whites tend to view foreign-born blacks as "different," "special," as harder working and more productive than native blacks.[52] Some Caribbean and African immigrants tend to play into this idea by maintaining their immigrant status so as not to be linked with the negative attitudes many whites have toward native blacks. Meanwhile native black opinion tends to vary between feelings of racial solidarity and feelings of threat "as competitors for jobs, resources and overall political advancement."[53]

More specifically, Greer found that Caribbean ethnic groups are more likely to support black racial identity and solidarity than the African groups, and the African groups are more likely to express positive attitudes toward the possibility of success in the U.S.[54] On issues native and foreign born tend to share the liberal ideology, favoring, for example, increased spending on domestic education, health and welfare programs while opposing increases in defense spending.[55]

Overall, Greer concludes that while ethnic differences are present, "a significant overreaching black racial solidarity is present among native born and foreign born populations."[56] This, she theorizes, is because "It is impossible to remove the black phenotype that serves as the fundamental distinction between black immigrants from Africa and the Caribbean and assimilationist narratives of Irish, Italian or Jewish immigrants or even current immigrants from Latin America or Asia."[57] Further, events like the police killing of Amadou Diallo (an unarmed African immigrant), the torture and sodomizing of Abner Louima (a Haitian immigrant) "socialize the effects of race in the minds of blacks in the United States, regardless of their origin."[58] In other words, "where public safety is concerned, black is all that matters."[59]

As of this writing, there are no major studies that disaggregate the political participation of black immigrants. However, Sharon Wright Austin, Director of African American Studies at the University of Florida, will serve as the editor of a special issue of the *National Political Science Review*, the journal of the national conference of black political scientists (NCOBPS), entitled *The Caribbeanization of Black Politics: Race, Group Consciousness and Political Participation*,[60] based on her forthcoming book.

The Second Rights-Based Coalition: The Civil Rights Movement

The NAACP Coalition

The civil rights movement has its origins in the Niagara Conference, comprised of 29 leading black men and women business owners, teachers, and clergy[61] called by W. E. B. Du Bois and William Monroe Trotter in 1905 (see Box 6.1). Four years after the conference, the National Association for the Advancement of Colored People (NAACP) was founded; until the 1960s it was the principal civil rights protest organization. Until the late 1960s, the NAACP was the classic

▬▬▬▬▬▬▬ **BOX 6.1** ▬▬▬▬▬▬▬

We Face a Condition, Not a Theory:
W. E. B. Du Bois and the Changing African
American Quest for Universal Freedom

It is often suggested that political philosophy and ideas are the products of the concrete conditions and circumstances of a people. Nowhere is this better demonstrated than in the long life and career of Dr. W. E. B. Du Bois, the greatest scholar and thinker in the history of African American thought. Du Bois was born on February 23, 1868, in Great Barrington, Massachusetts. He died 95 years later in the West African country of Ghana on the eve of the 1963 March on Washington. In these 95 years, Du Bois's life was one of extraordinary scholarship and political leadership, a life that at one point or another embraced every tendency in African American thought—integration, black nationalism, and finally socialism and communism.

Du Bois graduated from Fisk University, a black institution in Nashville, Tennessee, in 1888. In 1895, he became the first African American to receive a Ph.D. from Harvard (he came within a couple of months of earning a second Ph.D. from

the University of Berlin). His doctoral dissertation, *The Suppression of the African Slave Trade to the United States, 1638–1870*, was the first volume published in Harvard's Historical Studies series. He later went on to publish 15 other books on politics and race, three historical novels, two autobiographies, and numerous essays and works of fiction and poetry. While a professor at Atlanta University, Du Bois directed the first large-scale social science research project on the problem of race in the United States. Among his more important books are *Black Reconstruction in America*, a massive study showing that Reconstruction was one of the first efforts in American history to achieve democracy for working people; *The Philadelphia Negro: A Social Study*, the first sociological analysis of an urban community; and *The Souls of Black Folk*, his classic analysis of the psychological, cultural, and sociopolitical underpinnings of the African American experience. Probably no other

Dr. W. E. B. Du Bois, preeminent African American intellectual, a leader of the civil rights and Pan-African movements, embraced communism in the last years of his life.

Source: Schomburg Center/Art Resource, NY

book has had a greater impact on African American thinking than *The Souls of Black Folk*. In it Du Bois states for the first time the enduring tension in African American thought between integration and nationalism:

> One ever feels his twoness—an American, a Negro, two souls, two thoughts, two unreconciled strivings, two warring ideals in one dark body, whose dogged strength alone keeps it from being torn asunder. . . . He simply wishes to make it possible for a man to be both a Negro and American, without being cursed and spit upon by his fellows, without having the doors of opportunity closed roughly in his face.

In addition to his life of the mind and scholarship, Du Bois was an extraordinary political leader (from the death of Booker T. Washington in 1915 until the mid-1930s, Du Bois was probably the most influential African American leader). Early in his career, Du Bois remarked, "We face a condition, not a theory." Therefore, any philosophy, ideology, or strategy that gave promise of altering the oppressed conditions of the race should be embraced. As the conditions of African Americans changed, so did the thought of Du Bois. Early in his career in his famous "Conservation of Races" essay, Du Bois appears to embrace black nationalism and separate development as a means to conserve the distinctive culture of the group. Later, in the face of Booker Washington's accommodation of the segregation and racial oppression that emerged after the end of Reconstruction, Du Bois embraced integration, organizing in 1905 the Niagara Conference as a forum for militant protest for civil rights and universal freedom in the United States. In organizing the Niagara Conference and authoring its manifesto, Du Bois became the "Father of the Civil Rights Movement." Four years later in 1909, Du Bois was the major black among the founders of the NAACP. Until the 1930s he edited *The Crisis*, the NAACP's magazine, using it as a forum to attack white supremacy and racism and to espouse the cause of equality and universal freedom. Watching the deteriorating conditions of blacks during the Depression, Du Bois once again embraced black nationalism, arguing that blacks should develop a separate "group economy" of producers and cooperative consumers. Charging that the NAACP had become too identified with the concerns of middle-class blacks, in 1934 Du Bois resigned from the association and his editorship of *The Crisis*. Du Bois also expressed his interest in nationalism in terms of Pan-Africanism—the idea that the African people everywhere share a common culture and interest. In 1900, he organized the first Pan-African Conference in London, which brought together African leaders and intellectuals from Africa, the United States, and the Caribbean. He was a principal leader of the four other Pan-African Conferences held between 1912 and 1927. At the end of World War I and again at the end of World War II, Du Bois attended the peace conferences, urging that the European powers should develop plans to free their African colonies. Du Bois briefly joined the Socialist Party in 1912 and continued to flirt with socialist ideas thereafter; however, during the 1950s he apparently came to the conclusion that universal freedom for blacks and working people could not be achieved under capitalism, and so in 1956 he joined the Communist Party and shortly thereafter moved to Ghana. The last years of his life were spent editing the *Encyclopedia Africana*, a project funded and supported by the Ghana Academy of Sciences.

In his autobiography, Du Bois wrote,

> I think I may say without boasting that in the period 1910–1930 I was a main factor in revolutionizing the attitude of the American Negro toward caste. My stinging hammer blows made Negroes aware of themselves, confident of their possibilities and determined self-assertion. So much so that today common slogans among Negro people are taken bodily from the words of my mouth.

Du Bois was not an immodest man; in fact, he was often referred to as an arrogant elitist, but in regard to the preceding observation, he was not exaggerating.[a]

[a] There are several good book-length studies of Du Bois's life and career. See Francis Broderick, *W. E. B. Du Bois: New Leader in Time of Crisis* (Palo Alto, CA: Stanford University Press, 1959); Elliot Rudwick, *W. E. B. Du Bois: Propagandist of the Negro Protest* (New York:

Athenaeum, 1968); Gerald Horne, *Black and Red: W. E. B. Du Bois and the Afro-American Response to the Cold War, 1944–1963* (Albany, NY: SUNY Press, 1986); David L. Lewis, *W. E. B. Du Bois: Autobiography of a Race, 1868–1919* (New York: Henry Holt, 1973); and Lewis, *W. E. B. Du Bois: The Fight for Equality and the American Century, 1919–1963* (New York: Henry Holt, 2000).

interracial (mostly black–white) rights-based coalition. It was founded by upper-middle-class white Protestants and Jews, including Mary White Ovington, Oswald Garrison Villard, William English Walling, and Dr. Henry Moscowitz. Appalled at the continuing violence committed against blacks, these white liberals, socialists, and descendants of abolitionists issued a call for a meeting to discuss racial justice. Some 60 people—seven of whom were prominent African American leaders like Du Bois, Ida B. Wells-Barnett, and Mary Church Terrell—signed the call that became its founding charter, released on the 100th anniversary of the birth of Abraham Lincoln.[62]

From the beginning, there was tension between blacks and whites in the organization over its leadership and strategy. William Monroe Trotter and a number of other blacks who were involved in the Niagara Conference refused to join the group, arguing that whites could not be trusted to advance the cause of blacks. These tensions over white leadership continued until the 1960s (the association did not get its first black executive director until James Weldon Johnson was appointed in 1920) when blacks took over all the top leadership positions and the overwhelming majority of seats on the executive board.

The Strategy of the NAACP, 1910–1954: Persuasion, Lobbying, and Litigation

The civil rights movement may be divided into three phases, based on the dominant strategy employed to pursue its goals.[63] From roughly 1910 to the 1930s, the dominant forms of activity were persuasion and lobbying. During these years, the NAACP developed a campaign of public education and propaganda under the direction of Du Bois, editor of the NAACP magazine, *The Crisis*.[64] This campaign was designed to combat white supremacist propaganda and shape a favorable climate of public opinion on civil rights for African Americans.

The NAACP also engaged in an unsuccessful lobbying effort to convince Congress to pass a law making lynching a federal crime. Under the federal system, lynching—the ritual murder of blacks by southern racists—was a state crime, but southern states refused to arrest and punish the perpetrators. Thus, there was need for a federal law. Although the antilynching legislation twice passed the House, it was defeated in the Senate as a result of southern filibusters.[65] The NAACP was more successful in other lobbying efforts. It succeeded in blocking passage of immigration legislation that would have prohibited the legal entry into the United States of persons of African descent. And in a coalition with organized labor, it was successful in lobbying the Senate to defeat President Herbert Hoover's nomination of John C. Parker to the Supreme Court because of his alleged antilabor and antiblack views.[66]

From the 1930s to the 1950s, litigation was the dominant strategy of the NAACP. In 1939, the NAACP created a separate organization—the NAACP Legal Defense Fund—and this organization under the leadership of Charles Hamilton Houston and later Thurgood Marshall filed a series of cases in the Supreme Court seeking enforcement of the Fourteenth and Fifteenth Amendments. Several important cases were won during this period, including *Smith* v. *Allwright*, which invalidated the Texas Democratic Party's whites-only primary, and the famous *Brown* v. *Board of Education* decision, which reversed the doctrine of separate but equal established in 1896 in *Plessy* v. *Ferguson*[67] (see Chapter 12).

The Southern Christian Leadership Conference and the Strategy of Protest, 1955–1965

The final phase of the civil rights movement involved mass protests and demonstrations.[68] From the 1900s until the 1950s, the civil rights movement was dominated by the middle-class, northern-based NAACP coalition. From 1955 to 1965, the movement was dominated by Dr. Martin Luther King Jr. and the Southern Christian Leadership Conference (SCLC). Unlike the NAACP, the SCLC was an intraracial coalition of black ministers and churches filled with active men and women parishioners based in the South.[69] Beginning with the Montgomery bus boycott (a city-wide boycott spurred by the heralded act of Rosa Parks, a civil rights activist who refused to surrender her bus seat to a white passenger on December 1, 1955), King and the SCLC led a series of demonstrations in the South protesting segregation in public places and the denial of black voting rights. King and the SCLC were later joined in the southern protest movement by the Student Nonviolent Coordinating Committee (SNCC), an interracial coalition of black and white college students, and the Congress of Racial Equality (CORE), also an interracial coalition of black and white activists.[70]

Although the strategy of King and his colleagues was to hold peaceful, nonviolent demonstrations, these actions were met with widespread violence by racist southern whites (including the police). This violence, televised around the world, forced a reluctant President Kennedy (and later President Lyndon

Johnson) to propose comprehensive civil rights and voting rights legislation. After the violent demonstrations in 1963 at Birmingham, Alabama, President Kennedy proposed the Civil Rights Act, which Congress enacted in 1964. After the violent demonstrations in Selma, Alabama, in 1965, President Johnson proposed and Congress passed the Voting Rights Act.

Two points should be emphasized about the passage of these laws in 1964 and 1965. First, the president and Congress responded to the demands of the movement only after the violence at Selma and Birmingham was televised. Second, the strategy of protest developed by Dr. King and his associates was deliberately designed to bring pressure on the president and Congress by activating a broad lobbying coalition: liberals, labor, and northern religious groups.[71] It was this broad coalition—not blacks acting alone—that brought about the ultimate passage of the first comprehensive civil rights legislation since Reconstruction.[72] However—as our theory of African American coalition politics predicts—almost immediately after the passage of the Voting Rights Act, this coalition of blacks and whites began to fall apart, as blacks shifted from a rights-based movement politics to a material-based interest group politics.

The Black Power Movement and the Transformation from Movement to Interest Group Politics

The Origins of the Black Power Movement

The political scientist Sidney Tarrow writes,

> Protest cycles can either end suddenly, through repression, or more slowly, through a combination of features: the institutionalization of the most successful movements, factionalization within them and new groups which rise on the crest of the wave, and the exhaustion of mass political involvement. The combination of institutionalization and factionalization often produce determined minorities, who respond to the decline of popular involvement by turning upon themselves and—in some cases—using organized violence.[73]

This combination of features characterized the end of the civil rights movement.[74]

Two weeks after the signing of the Voting Rights Act, Watts, the black section of Los Angeles, exploded in three days of civil unrest. The 1965 Watts rebellion was followed by a series of revolts in most of the large cities of the North. In 1966, Stokely Carmichael, the newly elected chairman of the SNCC, started the black power movement. The urban rebellions and black power led to a fundamental transformation of the civil rights movement and the emergence of a new structure of black interest organizations.

The SNCC—the most radical of the civil rights organizations—sparked this transformation by introducing the rhetoric and symbol of black power during the 1966 Meredith March in Mississippi.[75] For several years, the more nationalistic SNCC workers had attempted to bring a greater number of nationalist themes into the civil rights movement, themes drawn from Malcolm X and Algerian writer Frantz Fanon.[76] In 1966, they prepared a position paper that set forth the fundamental themes of black power, including a call for the exclusion of whites from the organization. Although Stokely Carmichael initially joined the majority of the SNCC staff in rejecting these nationalist themes, after he defeated the incumbent SNCC chairman John Lewis (now a revered congressman from Georgia) in a bitter and divisive election, he changed his position and embraced the principles of black power. He then persuaded the SNCC to join the Meredith March and use it as a forum to articulate and build support for black power. For a week, television coverage of the Meredith March highlighted the divisions within the civil rights movement. In his speeches, Dr. King continued to espouse the philosophy of black–white coalitions, integration, and nonviolence, while Carmichael shouted black power and called for racial separatism and violent resistance to attacks by southern racists. Although the national media presented black power as a radical, revolutionary movement, it actually had a dual impact on African American politics: one radical, one reform.

The Dual Impact of Black Power: Radicalism and Reform

As Figure 6.3 illustrates, the black power movement sparked two separate, distinct, and contradictory developments in black politics. First, it stimulated the development of a wide variety of radical, nationalistic, and revolutionary organizations and leaders, including Huey Newton and the Black Panther Party (see Box 6.2), Ron Karenga and US (a radical cultural nationalist organization), and Imari Obadele and the Republic of New Africa. For a decade the African American freedom struggle took a sharp turn toward radicalism. However, by 1980, as a result of factionalism and infighting within and among the groups, and political repression by the Federal Bureau of Investigation (FBI), the army, and the police, the radical wing of the movement had collapsed.[77]

The second development sparked by black power was the beginning of the integration or incorporation of blacks into the routine interest group structure of conventional American politics. Although radicalism and nationalism characterized the early years of black power, ultimately it came to represent, as Figure 6.3 shows, a mild form of reformist black nationalism appealing to race

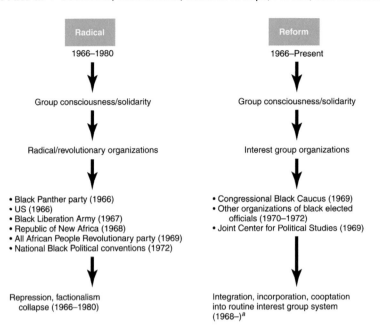

FIGURE 6.3

The Dual Impact of the Black Power Movement on African American Politics, 1960–1990.

ª Integration, incorporation, and cooptation are used interchangeably to mean the absorption of previously unrepresented groups into the routine operation of the political system.

Source: Robert C. Smith, *We Have No Leaders: African Americans in the Post–Civil Rights Era* (Albany, NY: SUNY Press, 1996).

BOX 6.2

The Black Panther Party

The Black Panther Party for Self-Defense was founded in 1966, one year after the Watts rebellion, by Huey P. Newton and Bobby Seale, student activists at Oakland's Merritt College in efforts to combat police brutality. Two years later, FBI director J. Edgar Hoover declared that the Black Panthers were "the greatest threat to the internal security of the United States" and targeted the group for elimination.ª By 1970, the party was in disarray and on the verge of collapse as a result of the FBI's systematic campaign of repression and of the group's own factional infighting and corruption.

The Black Panthers adopted the name and symbol, black panther, from the

Lowndes County, Alabama, Freedom Democratic Party, which used a black panther as its symbol. (The Lowndes County party was founded in the early 1960s by southern civil rights workers to encourage blacks to register to vote and run for office.) The Panthers, as the full name of the party implies, was originally founded as a "self-defense" organization. Newton and Seale were aware that the police in the nation's big cities frequently harassed and brutalized blacks. To try to stop this kind of police misconduct, the Panthers (dressed in black leather jackets and berets) organized armed patrols and dispatched them to the scene of any police incident involving blacks. Their purpose was to observe the behavior of the officers. Their slogan, to "Observe and protect," was derived from the Los Angeles Police Department's motto, "To serve and protect." In addition, Newton found a loophole in California law that allowed the open carry of loaded weapons. Thus, the Panthers were the first political group to fiercely defend the Second Amendment right to bear arms—as a means to monitor police patrols in African American neighborhoods—prior to the National Rights Association (NRA) open-carry movement.[b] Although the Panthers did not intervene in the police incidents, the mere presence of armed black men observing their behavior alarmed the police. Soon a series of deadly gun battles occurred between the Panthers and the police in Oakland and San Francisco. Shortly thereafter the California legislature began consideration of legislation to ban carrying loaded weapons in public. To protest this legislation, 30 armed Panthers marched into the state capitol at Sacramento on May 2, 1967. This demonstration received widespread attention and brought the heretofore obscure group to the attention of the nation. The image of armed black men dressed in black captured the imagination of young blacks across the country, and Panther party membership and chapters grew rapidly. By late 1968, the group had a membership estimated at 3,000–5,000 and more than 30 chapters throughout the United States. Accompanying this rapid growth in membership, the Panthers adopted the ideology of revolutionary black nationalism and Marxist–Leninism, calling for violent revolution to overthrow the government of the United States.

Many of the Black Panthers were brave young men and women, willing to sacrifice their lives for freedom. Despite the paranoia and corruption of some of its top leaders, in the early years the party did good works, including forcefully challenging police brutality and providing a variety of community services such as free medical clinics, breakfast programs for poor kids, and food cooperatives. However, once the party turned from a

Huey P. Newton and Bobby Seale, founders of the Black Panther Party.

Source: S.F. Examiner/AP Images

primarily self-defense and self-help group to violent revolution, its destruction was inevitable, since no government that has the power will long tolerate a violent challenge to its authority.[c]

[a] U.S. Congress, Senate, *Select Committee to Study Government Operations with Respect to Intelligence Activities and the Rights of Americans, Book III, Final Report* (Washington, DC: Government Printing Office, 1976): 187. Additionally, as mentioned in Box 11.5, the government's program of political repression known as "COINTELPRO" also targeted mainstream leaders such as Martin Luther King Jr. and the Southern Christian Leadership Conference. See Nelson Blackstock, *COINTELPRO: The FBI's Secret War on Political Freedom* (New York: Pathfinder, 1975).
[b] See John Blake, "The Black Panthers are Back—and Never Really Went Away," accessed at www.cnn.com/2016/02/16/us/balck-panthers/index.html, February 17, 2016.
[c] For an overview of the rise and decline of the Panthers, see Charles E. Jones, ed., *The Black Panther Party Reconsidered* (Baltimore, MD: Black Classics Press, 1998); and Joshua Bloom and Waldo Martin, *Black Against Empire: The History and Politics of the Black Panther Party* (Berkeley: University of California Press, 2013).

group consciousness, solidarity, and independent, all-black interest group organizations.[78]

Black Power and Race Group Solidarity

Black power contributed to an increase in black group identification and solidarity. Political scientist Warren Miller observed that, as a result of black power,

> the appropriate dimension for understanding the political behavior of black citizens may have changed. Contemporary black leaders may have helped shape the political meaning of being black in ways black leaders two decades before could not. Certainly, racial identity is now the most useful prescriptive measure of the political choice of many citizens.[79]

Table 6.1 displays data on the immediate impact of black power in historical context. The data show the progression of black political conceptualization in terms of racial group interest during the 20-year period 1960–1980—from 26 percent in 1960 to 54 percent in 1980; comparable figures for whites are 31 percent in 1960 and 28 percent in 1980. Although the highest level of group benefit responses among blacks is observed in 1968 at the high point of the black power movement, even after black power declined in salience, the group benefit percentages did not return to their earlier low levels. This rise in group-based identification and solidarity is true of all categories of blacks, irrespective of gender, education, age, or partisan affiliation.[80]

Black Power, Black Groups, and System Incorporation

Related to this increase in race group consciousness and solidarity, the black power movement also sparked the creation of a large number of new, racially

TABLE 6.1 Racial Differences in "Group Benefit" Level of Political Conceptualization: 1960–1980

	1960	1964	1968	1972	1976	1980
Whites	31%	25%	20%	24%	23%	28%
Blacks	26%	47%	60%	51%	48%	54%

Source: Paul R. Hagner and John C. Pierce, "Racial Differences in Political Conceptualization," *Western Political Quarterly* 37 (June 1984): 222. Employing data from the Interuniversity Consortium for Political Research at the University of Michigan, Hagner and Pierce identified four major levels of political conceptualization: ideological, group benefit, nature of the times, and no political content. The "group benefit" category measures the extent to which individuals evaluate political issues in terms of their negative or positive impact on the group or group interests.

exclusive (all-black) interest group organizations, including for a time an intraracial black coalition—the National Black Political Convention.[81] From 1966 to 1969—the peak years of black power activism—more than 70 new black interest organizations were formed.[82] These organizations covered a broad range of interests—business and economic, educational and cultural, and professional and political. Also during this period, the growing number of black elected officials began to form racially separate caucuses, including the Congressional Black Caucus and caucuses of black mayors, school board members, and state legislators.[83]

At the beginning of this chapter, we discussed the argument of William Gamson that some groups are excluded from the routine system of American interest group politics and gain entry only as a result of a crisis in the system or if the excluded group shows a willingness to violate the "rules of the game" by resorting to illegitimate means for carrying on political conflict. The radical, revolutionary rhetoric of black power, the summers of urban civil unrest from 1965 to 1968, and the revolutionary politics of the Black Panthers and other groups created a perception of crisis and showed that some blacks were indeed willing to engage in illegitimate forms of political conflict. Thus, the most enduring consequence of black power was reform, not radicalism—the Congressional Black Caucus rather than the Black Panther Party.

Yet another consequence of the black power and civil rights movements was their impact on other American citizens who felt excluded from the system. These black movements of the 1960s served as models for a wave of social movements and interest groups in the late 1960s to date. Among the groups that patterned their activities after the civil rights and black power movements are women, Indians, Mexican Americans, Puerto Ricans, gays, Chinese Americans, the elderly, and, to an extent, the youth and antiwar protesters.[84] In fact, over 50-years after the educational comic book *Martin Luther King and the Montgomery Story* was released in 1958, the executive director of the American Islamic Congress said it was translated into Arabic and Farsi and used to bring a message of nonviolent resistance to the Middle East. That message was especially important in Egypt, where protesters gathered in February 2011 in Cairo's Tahrir Square to call for an end to the 30-year rule of Hosni Mubarak in what would later become known as the "Arab Spring."[85] As recently as 2016, the civil rights protest anthem, "We Shall Overcome," was sung in defiance by citizens and survivors of recent terrorist attacks in Paris and Brussels as well.

New Movements in African American Politics: Values and Beliefs in the Post–Civil Rights Era

By the late 1970s, many black–white civil rights coalitions dissipated; even while the majority of black Americans showed favor for interest group politics and inclusion over radicalism as the more effective means of securing rights- and material-based outcomes. Some scholars had pronounced the civil rights movement as dead because of the tendency to view it as a national rather than a series of local movements. Within the scholarship on the civil rights movement, as Professor Clayborne Carson observes, is "the assumption that the black struggle can be understood as a protest movement orchestrated by national leaders in order to achieve national legislation."[86] However, this creates a problem in understanding the movement because it ignores the role that a wide range of local movements played during the civil rights era. A careful review of social movements will reveal that, often, local movements and leaders laid the groundwork that resulted in the success of national leaders and legislation. And, because universal freedom values and beliefs are embedded in black culture, this collective memory is transmitted generationally through grassroots activism. A similar process can be seen occurring in the post–civil rights struggles calling for socioeconomic justice as well as racial and gender inclusion throughout American society. These localized campaigns have coalesced around the lowering of the confederate flag on state buildings in the south,[87] environmental racism,[88] racial profiling and policing, and the restoration of voting rights while challenging state efforts to limit access to the ballot. However, some scholars have tended to ignore or downplay local movements that do not have national leaders or dimensions as witnessed in the grassroots demonstrations like Occupy Wall Street, raising the national minimum wage, the fight for "living wages," marriage equality, and climate change. Yet, these movements have proved successful at focusing public attention on the issue, placing the issues on the public agenda, and winning favorable legislation without centralized leadership. One can argue that this process is uniquely unfolding via diverse, allied coalitions emanating from the "Black Lives Matter" movement. Emerging out of mounting anger over the killing of unarmed citizens by the police,[89] this movement may be pivotal in a resurgent national discussion on race in the "post–racial era," and as part of the centuries-long struggle for universal freedom.

The "#BlackLivesMatter" Movement

Black Lives Matter (BLM) originated in the summer of 2013 as a conversation among friends. What began as a Facebook post[90] by Alicia Garza then "retweeted" on Twitter as a hashtag (#BlackLivesMatter) by Patrisse Cullors and Opal Tometia, grew into an online slogan and became an Internet-driven contemporary human rights movement.[91] These self-identified queer activists— born of native-born African American and African immigrants—were outraged not only by the acquittal of George Zimmerman, a white security officer who fatally shot Trayvon Martin, an unarmed black teenager as he walked in his gated community; but, more so, by the way Martin was in a sense posthumously placed on trial for his own murder in raising suspicion about his "character" while not holding Zimmerman accountable for the racial bias that led to the killing.[92] Using their professional backgrounds[93] in community organizing and drawing inspiration from the long tradition of African American activism in historical movements, including the civil rights, black power, black feminists, Pan-African, anti-apartheid, political hip-hop, LGBT rights, and Occupy Wall Street,[94] Garza writes that their hashtag/call to action is "an ideological and political intervention in a world where Black lives are systematically and intentionally targeted for demise. It is an affirmation of Black folks' contributions to this society, our humanity, and our resilience in the face of deadly oppression."[95] Their collective effort is to raise awareness about the "anti-Black racism that permeates our society" through a neoteric digital campaign against antiblack, state-sanctioned violence and violation.[96] The movement was propelled forward by the availability of video—captured mostly on personal smartphones—gone viral on the Internet that showed out-of-control and sometimes lethal actions by the police against blacks.[97] The ability to connect instantly across multiple digital platforms (e.g. Facebook, Twitter, Tumblr, and Instagram) to showcase high-profile, racially charged incidents as they occurred led to "moving the hashtag from social media to the streets."[98]

In August 2014, Garza, Cullors, and Tometi, and their allies, organized their first national protest in the form of a "Black Lives Matter Ride," (modeled after "Freedom Rides") to Ferguson, Missouri, after Darren Wilson, a white police officer, fatally shot Michael Brown, another unarmed black teenager whose body was then left untended for four and a half hours in the street.[99] Reminiscent of the 1960s civil rights movement, the series of events[100] leading up to the protests in Ferguson, Missouri, were historically rooted in the pernicious effects of decades of racial and socioeconomic segregation, due to discriminatory housing practices and unregulated suburban development.[101] In addition, the complicated structure of municipal government, black political disenfranchisement because of low voter turnout and voter ineligibility, and the "arrogance" of white elected officials, created a sense of "empowerment" among the predominantly white and working-class police force that may have contributed to the killing of Brown,[102] which by now had the full attention of the black public that became more outraged each time videos surfaced of police killings involving black victims. In the wake of the events and protests organized to focus public attention on police killings, the BLM social media network[103] became the organizing project linking other online movements, including "This is the Movement" (#Ferguson) and "Campaign Zero," in support of policies to end police brutality and mass incarceration.

With its role in shaping the public agenda, mainstream media coverage focused heavily on the random outbreaks of retaliation such as glass smashed along routes leading to panic and retreat, the destruction of black-owned businesses, and burning of police cars in Ferguson;[104] the disruption "from a week-long sit-in" that led to the "deadly scuffle between Minneapolis police" and BLM demonstrators in Minneapolis;[105] the confrontations of 2016 democratic presidential candidates, Bernie Sanders and Hillary Clinton, at their respective rallies.[106] However, coverage in black media portrayed the incidents, more positively, from the perspective of the black community. As a black reporter wrote, "[T]he people have been blocking highways, shutting down shopping malls, lying in the streets, and walking out of classrooms around the world," with the rallying cry, "Hands up; don't shoot."[107] In an in-depth analysis of the movement, Professor Jerome Karabel, a sociologist at the University of California, Berkeley, concluded, "The videos—and the outrage that followed—helped to ignite the most powerful civil rights movement since the 1960s."[108]

The BLM is not without its critics in the media. Leaders of the Republican Party, including most of its 2016 presidential candidates and the conservative media (particularly Fox News), have demonized it "as an inflammatory or even hateful anti-white expression that has no legitimate place in a civil rights campaign."[109] Veterans of the 1960s civil rights movement have also been critical of the movement. For example Barbara Reynolds, the former African American columnist for *USA Today* wrote, "This ain't your grandparents' civil rights movement."[110] Describing BLM activists as "boorish in language and dress" and as a "motley-looking group . . . [lacking] dignity and decorum," she wrote, "It is difficult to distinguish BLM legitimate activists from mob actors who burn and loot . . . demonstrations are peppered with hate speech, profanity, and guys with sagging pants that show their underwear."[111] And Harvard law professor Randall Kennedy wrote,

> a marginalized group should be attentive to how it is perceived. The politics
> of respectability is a tactic of public relations that is, per se, neither
> necessarily good nor necessarily bad. A sound assessment of its deployment
> in a given instance depends on its goals, the manner in which it is practiced,
> and the context within which a given struggle is being waged. Its association
> with esteemed figures and episodes in African American history suggests that
> the politics of respectability warrants a more respectful hearing [from BLM]
> than it has recently received.[112]

Yet, despite the critiques about their style of protests, the BLM made the issues of police killings and mass incarceration politically salient for the public agenda.

The BLM is therefore another movement in the struggle for universal freedom, that deploys the civil rights activism styles of Bayard Rustin and Ella Baker ("a gay guy and a woman"[113]); meaning, this movement is about radical inclusivity—the essence of intersectionality—that seeks to frame contemporary racial justice movements in a digitized society as something beyond the black masculine-centered narratives to include the voices of women, queer and trans people.[114] As the BLM movement progresses, cofounder Alicia Garza has written a reminder to those who wish to co-opt their work, but exclude or erase their contributions as queer black women:

> Black Lives Matter is a unique contribution that goes beyond extrajudicial killings of Black people by police and vigilantes. It goes beyond the narrow nationalism that can be prevalent within some Black communities, which merely call on Black people to love Black, live Black and buy Black, keeping straight cis Black men in the front of the movement while our sisters, queer and trans and disabled folk take up roles in the background or not at all. Black Lives Matter affirms the lives of Black queer and trans folk, disabled folks, Black-undocumented folks with records, women and all Black lives along the gender spectrum. It centers those that have been marginalized within Black liberation movements. It is a tactic to (re)build the Black liberation movement. When we say Black Lives Matter, we are talking about the ways in which [ALL] Black people are deprived of our basic human rights and dignity.[115]

Black Lives Matter has made a unique and important contribution to the debate about state-sanctioned violence against African Americans, affecting the policy debate and the 2016 presidential election. What is not clear is whether it is an enduring movement or a transitory moment in the long African American protest tradition.

Faces and Voices in the Struggle for Universal Freedom
John Brown (1800–1859)

John Brown, a deeply religious white man, was so committed to African American freedom and equality that he was willing to do what few black Americans have been willing to do—use revolutionary violence to fight for freedom. In 1859, Brown and an interracial group of 22 men attacked the federal arsenal at Harpers Ferry, Virginia. Their plan was to seize weapons, flee into the mountains, and establish a base of operations to wage guerrilla war. Prior to Harpers Ferry, Brown and his men had killed pro-slavery settlers in Kansas, pledging to "purge this land with blood" in order to end slavery and establish democracy for all. Completely free of white supremacist thinking, Brown interacted with African Americans on the basis of complete equality.

Brown's raid at Harpers Ferry failed. He and most of his men were killed or captured and quickly executed. At his sentencing, Brown made an eloquent speech in favor of universal freedom. The day of his execution was declared "martyr's day" by black leaders; businesses were closed and churches held

John Brown.

Source: "John Brown, 1800–1859" The West, *PBS*. Retrieved 4 October 2016 from www.pbs.org/weta/thewest/people/a_c/brown.htm

memorial services. The song "John Brown's Body" became a Union marching song during the Civil War and is an enduring part of the African American folk tradition.

Although Brown's raid failed, historians agree that it contributed to the intensification of the crisis that resulted in the bloody Civil War that emancipated the slaves.[a]

[a] David Reynolds, *John Brown: The Man Who Killed Slavery, Sparked the Civil War and Seeded Civil Rights* (New York: Knopf, 2005).

Summary

When a group is excluded from participation in the political system, it will often resort to social movements as a means to challenge the system in order to gain entry and inclusion. From the abolitionist movement of the 1830s to the civil rights and black power movements of the 1960s, African Americans engaged in movement politics. Throughout, however, as an oppressed, relatively powerless minority they have had to form coalitions with whites—male and female—and all ideologies, regions, and social classes. Because of racism and white supremacy, these coalitions have tended to be tenuous, unstable, and short-lived, and they have been more effective on rights-based than material-based issues. The black movements of the 1960s served as models and inspiration for similar movements among other Americans and spurred protests in other nations that followed thereafter.

Critical Thinking Questions

1. What is the fundamental difference between a social movement and an interest group?
2. What is a minority–majority coalition? Explain why they have been indispensable in the African American quest for freedom.
3. Distinguish between rights- and material-based coalitions in African American politics, providing examples of each.
4. Explain the idea of a rainbow coalition.
5. Given what you have learned about what constitutes a social movement, would you characterize #BlackLivesMatter as a social movement or historical moment? Explain your answer using examples.

Selected Bibliography

Alex-Assensoh, Yvette, and Lawrence Hanks, eds. *Black and Multiracial Politics in America*. New York: New York University Press, 2000. A useful collection of papers exploring the relationship between black and multiracial politics.

Allen, Robert. *The Reluctant Reformers: Racism and Social Reform Movements in the United States*. Washington, DC: Howard University Press, 1983. A study of how racism historically has undermined liberal and progressive reform movements in the United States.

Browning, Rufus, D. Marshall, and D. Tabb. *Protest Is Not Enough: The Struggle of Blacks and Hispanics in Urban Politics*. Berkeley: University of California Press, 1984. An influential study of the conditions and policy consequences of multiethnic coalitions in post–civil rights era urban politics.

Carmichael, Stokely, and Charles Hamilton. *Black Power: The Politics of Liberation in America*. New York: Vintage Books, 1967. The influential manifesto of the rationale and strategy for the transformation from civil rights movement politics to black interest group politics.

Freeman, Jo, ed. *Social Movements of the Sixties and Seventies*. New York: Longman, 1983. A collection of papers showing how the African American civil rights and black power movements served as a model for social movement activism of many other groups in American society.

Gomes, Ralph, and Linda Faye Williams. "Coalition Politics: Past, Present and Future." In R. Gomes and L. Williams, eds. *From Exclusion to Inclusion: The Long Struggle for African American Political Power*. Westport, CT: Praeger, 1992. A historical analysis of African American coalition politics and a discussion of future prospects.

Greer, Christina, *Black Ethnics: Race, Immigration and the Pursuit of the American Dream* (New York: Oxford, 2013). The most comprehensive study of the growing ethnic diversity of the U.S. black community, and its political consequences.

Kluger, Richard. *Simple Justice: The History of* Brown *v.* Board of Education *and Black America's Struggle for Racial Equality*. New York: Vintage Books, 1977. A long but interesting account of the NAACP's litigation strategy from the 1930s to the 1950s, focusing on a detailed study of the famous *Brown* school desegregation case.

Morris, Aldon. *Origins of the Civil Rights Movement*. New York: Free Press, 1984. A study of the development of the final protest phase of the civil rights movement, focusing on the role of indigenous institutions such as black churches and colleges.

Nelson, William, and Jessica Lavariega Moniforti, eds. *Black and Latino/a Politics: Issues in Political Development in the United States*. Miami, FL: Barnhardt & Ashe Publishing, 2005. A wide-ranging collection of essays on black and Latino politics and their interrelationships.

Payne, Charles. *I've Got the Light of Freedom: The Organizing Tradition in Mississippi*. Berkeley: University of California Press, 1995. An alluringly written account of the role of local movements during the civil rights era.

Piven, Frances Fox, and Richard Cloward. *Poor People's Movements: Why They Succeed, Why They Fail*. New York: Vintage Books, 1977. A detailed study of how various reform movements of poor people have been transformed into interest groups and thereby rendered largely ineffective.

Shulman, Steven, ed. *The Impact of Immigration on African Americans*. New Brunswick, NJ: Transaction, 2004. This volume presents research and analysis that reflects and advances the debate about the economic and political consequences of immigration for African Americans.

Smith, Robert C. "Black Power and the Transformation from Protest to Politics." *Political Science Quarterly* 96 (Fall 1981): 431–44. A theoretical and empirical analysis of the important role of the black power movement in shaping contemporary black politics.

Walters, Ronald, and Robert C. Smith. *African American Leadership*. Albany, NY: SUNY Press, 1999. A treatment of the topic historically, theoretically, and in relationship to its practice.

Wilke, H. A. M. *Coalition Politics*. New York: Harcourt, 1985. Although somewhat technical, a useful collection of papers on theory and research on coalition formations in politics.

Zackodnik, Teresa C. *"We Must Be Up and Doing": A Reader in Early African American Feminisms*. Ontario, Canada: Broadview Press, 2010. A comprehensive collection of writings by African American women in the early nineteenth century.

Zangrando, Robert. *The NAACP Struggle against Lynching, 1909–1965*. Philadelphia, PA: Temple University Press, 1980. A study of the NAACP's lobbying strategy, focusing on the unsuccessful effort to secure passage of federal antilynching legislation.

Notes

1   William Gamson, "Stable Unrepresentation in American Society," *American Behavioral Scientist* 12 (November–December 1968): 18.

2   See Aldon Morris and Cedric Herring, "Theory and Research on Social Movements," in S. Long, ed., *Annual Review of Political Science*, vol. 2 (Norwood, NJ: Ablex, 1987): 137–98; and H. A. M. Wilkie, ed., *Coalition Formation* (New York: Harcourt, 1985).

3   Ralph Gomes and Linda Williams, "Coalition Politics: Past, Present and Future," in Gomes and Williams, eds., *From Exclusion to Inclusion: The Long Struggle for African American Political Power* (New York: Greenwood Press, 1992): 129–60.

4   In drawing a distinction between material- and rights-based issues and coalitions, we do not mean to imply that the right to health care or a job might not be appropriately viewed as a civil or citizenship right. Rather, the point is that in the United States a sharp line is usually drawn between economic and political or civil rights, a distinction African Americans and their leaders, willingly or not, have embraced. See Dana Hamilton and Charles Hamilton, *The Dual Agenda: Social*

Policies of Civil Rights Organizations, New Deal to Present (New York: Columbia University Press, 1996).

5 On the abolitionist movement, see Leronne Bennett, *Before the Mayflower* (Baltimore, MD: Penguin Books, 1966): chap. 6; John Hope Franklin, *From Slavery to Freedom* (New York: Knopf, 1980): 180–89; and Robert Allen, *The Reluctant Reformers: Racism and Social Reform Movements in the United States* (Washington, DC: Howard University Press, 1983): chap. 2.

6 Allen, *The Reluctant Reformers*, p. 248.

7 Quoted in Allen, *The Reluctant Reformers*, p. 24.

8 Franklin, *From Slavery to Freedom*, p. 182.

9 Quoted in Bennett, *Before the Mayflower*, p. 149.

10 On the slave revolts, see Herbert Aptheker, *American Negro Slave Revolts* (New York: Columbia University Press, 1948); and Eugene Genovese, *From Rebellion to Revolution: Afro-American Slave Revolts in the Making of the New World* (New York: Vintage Books, 1981).

11 Teresa C. Zackodnik, *"We Must Be Up and Doing": A Reader in Early African American Feminisms* (Ontario, Canada: Broadview Press, 2010): xiii–xv.

12 Benjamin Quarles, "Frederick Douglass and the Women's Rights Movement," *Journal of Negro History* 25 (1940); and Phillip Foner, *Frederick Douglass on Women's Rights* (Westport, CT: Greenwood Press, 1976).

13 July Roy Jeffrey, *The Great Silent Army of Abolitionism: Ordinary Women in the Antislavery Movement* (Chapel Hill: University of North Carolina Press, 1998) and Shirley J. Yee, *Black Women Abolitionists: A Study in Activism, 1828–1860* (Knoxville: University of Tennessee Press, 1992), and the Phillips Library of the Peabody Essex Museum, Salem, Massachusetts, see more at www.blackpast.org/aah/female-anti-slavery-society-salem-massachusetts-1832-1866#sthash.GUI7Iz8s.dpuf.

14 Eric Foner, *Reconstruction: America's Unfinished Revolution, 1863–1877* (New York: Harper & Row, 1988): 253–54.

15 Beverly Guy-Sheftall, *Words of Fire: An Anthology of African-American Feminist Thought* (New York: New Press, 1995): p. 36.

16 Quoted in Allen, *The Reluctant Reformers*, p. 143.

17 Ibid., p. 128.

18 Washington stated his ideas most succinctly in his famous Atlanta Exposition Address delivered in September 1895 at Atlanta's Cotton States Exposition. The address is reprinted in the 2nd edition of August Meier, Elliott Rudwick, and Francis Broderick, eds., *Black Protest Thought in the Twentieth Century* (New York: Bobbs-Merrill, 1971): 3–8. On Washington's leadership of black America, see Louis Harlan, *Booker T. Washington: The Making of a Black Leader* (New York: Oxford University Press, 1972) and his *Booker T. Washington: The Wizard of Tuskegee* (New York: Oxford University Press, 1983).

19 C. Vann Woodward, *The Strange Career of Jim Crow* (New York: Oxford University Press, 1966): 64. See also Woodward's detailed study of populism, *Tom Watson: Agrarian Rebel* (New York: Oxford, 1938, 1963).

20 John Herbert Roper, *C. Vann Woodward, Southerner* (Athens: University of Georgia Press, 1987): 114.

21 On blacks and the populist movement, see Charles Crowe, "Tom Watson, Populists and Blacks Reconsidered," *Journal of Negro History* 40 (April 1970): 99–116; and Gerald Gaither, *Blacks and the Populist Revolt: Ballots and Bigotry* (Tuscaloosa: University of Alabama Press, 1977).

22 Richard Hofstadter, *The Age of Reform* (New York: Vintage Books, 1955): 61.

23 Historians disagree as to whether Watson was always a racist or whether his attitudes changed over time with changing circumstances.

24 This quote is from Roper, *C. Vann Woodward*, p. 121.

25 Hofstadter, *The Age of Reform*, p. 61.

26 On the progressives, see Hofstadter, *The Age of Reform*, chaps. 4–7.

27 Stokely Carmichael and Charles Hamilton, *Black Power* (New York: Vintage Books, 1967): 82.

28 On the racist, exclusionary history of organized labor, see Phillip Foner, *Organized Labor and the Black Worker, 1619–1981* (New York: Praeger, 1974).

29 Allen, *The Reluctant Reformers*, p. 213.

30 Ibid., p. 215.

31 Richard Crossman, ed., *The God That Failed* (New York: Harper & Row, 1949). On this point, see also Harold Cruse, *The Crisis of the Negro Intellectual* (New York: William Morrow, 1967): 147–71.

32 National Conference of Christians and Jews, *Taking America's Pulse: The Full Report of the National Conference Survey on Inter-Group Relations* (New York: National Conference of Christians and Jews, 1994): 7. See also Paula McClain et al., "Racial Distancing in a Southern City: Immigrant Views of Black Americans," *Journal of Politics* 68 (2006): 541–84.

33 Ibid.

34 See Paula McClain and Albert Karnig, "Black and Hispanic Socioeconomic and Political Competition," *American Political Science Review* 84 (1990): 535–45; and Yvette Alex-Assensoh and Lawrence Hanks, eds., *Black and Multiracial Politics in America* (New York: New York University Press, 2000).

35 Roger Daniels, *Coming to America: A History of Immigration and Ethnicity* (New York: HarperCollins, 1990): 76, 323.

36 Quoted in Steven Shulman and Robert C. Smith, "Immigration and African Americans," in C. Conrad et al., eds., *African Americans in the U.S. Economy* (Boulder, CO: Rowman & Littlefield, 2005): 199.

37 Vernon Briggs, "The Economic Well-Being of Black Americans: The Overarching Influence of U.S. Immigration Policies," in S. Shulman, ed., *The Impact of Immigration on African Americans* (New Brunswick, NJ: Transaction, 2004): 12.

38 U.S. Commission on Immigration, *Reform, Legal Immigration: Setting Priorities* (Washington, DC, 1994), cited in ibid., p. 19.

39 See Shulman, *The Impact of Immigration on African Americans*.

40 Ibid.

41 Ibid.

42 Projected Population Change in the United States, by Race and Hispanic Origin: 2000–2050 (Washington, DC: U.S. Bureau of the Census, 2001).

43 Mary Waters, *Black Identities: West Indian Immigrants Dreams and American Realities* (Cambridge, MA: Harvard, 2000).

44 "African Immigrant Population in the U.S. Steadily Climbs," Pew Research Center Fact Sheet, November 2, 2015, http://pewrsr.ch/2oo5CTT. See also, "Influx of African Immigrants Shifting National and New York Demographics," *New York Times*, September 1, 2014, http://nyti.ms/1x3rTds.

45 "African Immigrant Population in the U.S. Steadily Climbs," Pew Research Center.

46 "Influx of African Immigrants Shifting National and New York Demographics," *New York Times*.

47 Ibid., "African Immigrant Population in the U.S. Steadily Climbs," Pew Research Center.

48 Clarence Page, "Black Immigrants, An Invisible 'Model Minority'," *Real Clear Politics*, March 19, 2007, www.realclearpolitics.com/articles/2007/03/black_immigrants_an_invisible.html.
49 Ibid., "Influx of African Immigrants Shifting National and New York Demographics," *New York Times*.
50 Page, "Black Immigrants, An Invisible 'Model Minority'"; see also Douglas S. Massey, Margarita Mooney, Kimberly C. Torres, and Camille Z. Charles, "Black Immigrants and Black Natives Attending Selective Colleges and Universities in the United States," *American Journal of Education* 113 (November 2006): 243–271, published electronically, https://www.soe.vt.edu/highered/files/Perspectives_Policy News/02-07/BlackImmigrants.pdf.
51 Page, "Black Immigrants, An Invisible 'Model Minority'."
52 Christina Greer, *Black Ethnics: Race, Immigration and the Pursuit of the American Dream* (New York: Oxford, 2013): 7.
53 Ibid., p. 83.
54 Ibid.
55 Ibid., p. 6.
56 Ibid., p. 39.
57 Ibid., p. 17.
58 Ibid., p. 17.
59 Quoted in "Influx of African Immigrants Shifting National and New York Demographics," *New York Times*.
60 Sharon Austin, *The Caribbeanization of Black Politics: Race, Group Consciousness and Political Participation* (Albany, NY: SUNY Press, Forthcoming).
61 Kate Tuttle, "Niagara Movement," *Africana: The Encyclopedia of the African and African American Experience* (New York: Oxford University Press, 2005); Susan Altman, "Niagara Movement," *The Encyclopedia of African American Heritage* (New York: Facts On File, 1997); Scott Kirkwood, "And Justice for All," National Parks (Washington, DC: Summer 2006), see more at: www.blackpast.org/aah/niagara-movement-1905-1909#sthash.E5GB79MK.dpuf.
62 Taken from NAACP.org history, www.naacp.org/pages/naacp-history.
63 See Robert C. Smith, "Politics Is Not Enough: On the Institutionalization of the Afro-American Freedom Struggle," in Gomes and Williams, eds., *From Exclusion to Inclusion*, pp. 97–126; and Robert C. Smith, *We Have No Leaders: African Americans in the Post–Civil Rights Era* (Albany, NY: SUNY Press, 1996): chap. 1.
64 David Lewis, *W. E. B. Du Bois: Biography of a Race, 1868–1919* (New York: Henry Holt, 1993): chap. 15.
65 Robert Zangrando, *The NAACP Crusade Against Lynching, 1909–1950* (Philadelphia, PA: Temple University Press, 1980).
66 Gilbert Ware, "Lobbying as a Means of Protest: The NAACP as an Agent of Equality," *Journal of Negro Education* 33 (Spring 1964): 103–7. On the NAACP's lobbying strategy, see the biography of its long-time chief Washington lobbyist by Denton Watson, *Lion in the Lobby: Clarence Mitchell and the Black Struggle* (New York: William Morrow, 1990).
67 Richard Kluger, *Simple Justice: History of* Brown *v.* Board of Education *and Black America's Struggle for Racial Equality* (New York: Vintage Books, 1975).
68 Aldon Morris, *The Origins of the Civil Rights Movement* (New York: Free Press, 1984).
69 David Garrow, *Bearing the Cross: Martin Luther King, Jr., and the Southern Christian Leadership Conference* (New York: William Morrow, 1986).

70 Clayborne Carson, *In Struggle: SNCC and the Black Awakening of the 1960s* (Cambridge, MA: Harvard University Press, 1981); and August Meier and Elliot Rudwick, *CORE: A Study in the Civil Rights Movement* (New York: Oxford University Press, 1973). For excellent studies of the heroic role of ordinary people in the civil rights movement, see John Dittmer, *Local People: The Struggle for Civil Rights in Mississippi* (Urbana: University of Illinois Press, 1995); and Charles Payne, *I've Got the Light of Freedom: The Organizing Tradition and the Mississippi Freedom Struggle* (Berkeley: University of California Press, 1995).

71 Michael Lipsky, "Protest as a Political Resource," *American Political Science Review* 62 (1968): 1144–58; and David Garrow, *Protest at Selma* (New Haven, CT: Yale University Press, 1978): chap. 7.

72 The last of the 1960s civil rights acts—the Fair Housing Act of 1968—was enacted shortly after Dr. King's murder, in part as a kind of final memorial tribute to him. Prior to his death the bill appeared to be stalled in Congress.

73 Sidney Tarrow, "Aiming at a Moving Target: Social Science and the Recent Rebellions in Eastern Europe," *Political Science and Politics* 24 (1991): 15.

74 Smith, *We Have No Leaders*, chaps. 1–2.

75 The Meredith March was initially organized by James Meredith, the first known African American to be graduated from the University of Mississippi, as a "march against fear." It was designed to demonstrate to blacks in the state that they need not fear to exercise their newly gained civil rights. On the second day of the march, Meredith was shot and wounded. The civil rights leadership then decided to continue the march in Meredith's honor and as a means to demonstrate to the nation the continuing climate of fear and violence in the state.

76 Carson, *In Struggle*, chap. 14.

77 By political repression, we mean "a process by which those in power try to keep themselves in power by attempting to destroy or render harmless organizations and ideologies that threaten their power"; see Robert Goldstein, *Political Repression in Modern America* (Cambridge, MA: Schenkman Press, 1979): xvi. The FBI's program of political repression was called COINTELPRO (for counterintelligence program). The black groups targeted by the program included the SNCC, the SCLC, the Nation of Islam, and the Black Panther Party. See Nelson Blackstock, *COINTELPRO: The FBI's Secret War on Political Freedom* (New York: Vintage Books, 1975); and Stephen Tompkins, "Army Feared King, Secretly Watched Him, Spying on Blacks Started 75 Years Ago," *Memphis Commercial Appeal*, March 21, 1993, p. A1.

78 See Robert C. Smith, "Black Power and the Transformation from Protest to Politics," *Political Science Quarterly* 96 (Fall 1981): 431–44; and Smith, *We Have No Leaders*, chap. 1.

79 Quoted in Paul Hagner and John Pierce, "Racial Differences in Political Conceptualization," *Western Political Quarterly* 37 (June 1984): 215.

80 Ibid., p. 215.

81 Smith, *We Have No Leaders*, chap. 2.

82 Smith, "Black Power and the Transformation from Protest to Politics," pp. 436–37.

83 Ibid.

84 See Jo Freeman, ed., *Social Movements of the Sixties and Seventies* (New York: Longman, 1983).

85 Elliott Francis, "MLK Comic Book Helped Inspire Arab Spring," August 24, 2011 http://wamu.org/news/11/08/24/mlk_comic_book_helped_inspire_arab_spring.php.

86 Carson, *In Struggle*, p. 13.

87 Although the goals were somewhat different in each state, in all three there was a consensus set of values and beliefs that the confederate flag was a symbol of slavery,

white supremacy, inequality, and injustice. Each of these flag protests were local with the Mississippi and Georgia movements emanating out of efforts in South Carolina. Each also had embedded within them a generalized American quest for freedom from this symbol of slavery and segregation. South Carolina lowered its flag only after the fatal massacre of nine parishioners gunned down in the historical Emanuel AME Church in Charleston in 2015.

88 Robert Bullard, *Dumping in Dixie: Race, Class and Environmental Quality*, (Boulder, CO: Westview Press, 1994): 35. Bullard's empirical research—upheld by a 1983 U.S. Government Accountability Office (GAO) study—documents that toxic waste dumps, garbage incinerators, and other environmentally hazardous sites are much more likely to be located in mostly black neighborhoods and communities, particularly in the south (regardless of class), than either affluent or poor white neighborhoods.

89 Jerome Karabel, "Police Killings Surpass the Worst Years of Lynching, Capital Punishment, and a Movement Responds," *Huffington Post*, November 4, 2015, www.huffingtonpost.com/jerome-karabel/police-killings-lynchings-capital-punishment_b_8462778.html.

90 The title of the Facebook post was "A Love Note to Black People" that ended with "Our Lives Matter, Black Lives Matter."

91 John Eligon, "One Slogan, Many Methods: Black Lives Matter Enters Politics," *New York Times*, November 18, 2015, http://nyti.ms/1SFUnQY. See also Herbert Ruffin, "Black Lives Matter: The Growth of a New Social Justice Movement," blackpast.org. Retrieved 10 November 2015, www.blackpast.org/perspectives/black-lives-matter-growth-new-social-justice-movement.

92 Alicia Garza, "A Herstory of the #BlackLivesMatter Movement," *thefeministwire. org*, see www.thefeministwire.com/2014/10/blacklivesmatter-2/.

93 Alicia Garza is a special projects director for the National Domestic Workers Alliance (Los Angeles, CA), Patrisse Cullors is a reinvestment director at the Ella Baker Center for Human Rights (Oakland, CA), and Opal Tometi is an executive director of the Black Alliance for Just Immigration (Brooklyn, NY), as told to *Cosmopolitan Magazine*, "Meet the Women Who Created #BlackLivesMatter," October 17, 2015, www.cosmopolitan.com/entertainment/a47842/the-women-behind-blacklivesmatter/.

94 Elizabeth Day, "#BlackLivesMatter: The Birth of a New Civil Rights Movement," *The Guardian*. Retrieved November 19, 2015, www.theguardian.com/world/2015/jul/19/blacklivesmatter-birth-civil-rights-movement; see also, "Black Lives Matter: How the Events in Ferguson Sparked a Movement in America," cbsnews.com. August 7, 2015. Retrieved November 19, 2015, www.cbsnews.com/news/how-the-black-lives-matter-movement-changed-america-one-year-later/.

95 Garza, "A Herstory of #BlackLivesMatter."

96 Treva B. Lindsey, "Post–Ferguson: A 'Herstorical' Approach to Black Violability," *Feminist Studies* 41 (1) (2015): 232.

97 Karabel, "Police Killings Surpass the Worst Years of Lynching, Capital Punishment, and a Movement Responds."

98 Garza, "A Herstory of #BlackLivesMatter."

99 Darryl Pinckney, "In Ferguson," *New York Review of Books*, January 8, 2015, www.nybooks.com/articles/2015/01/08/in-ferguson/.

100 Pinckney, "In Ferguson," see this report for a comprehensive review of the history of Ferguson.

101 Daniel Marans and Mariah Stewart, "Why Missouri Has Become the Heart of Racial Tension in America," *HuffPost Black Voices*, November 16, 2015,

www.huffingtonpost.com/entry/ferguson-mizzou-missouri-racial-tension_us_5647
36e2e4b08cda3488f34d.

102 Pinckney, "In Ferguson."

103 As of this writing, the Black Lives Matter network consists of 26 local chapters, including Toronto and Ghana.

104 Pinckney, "In Ferguson."

105 Jessica Mendoza, "How Black Lives Matter Operates When Spotlight Is Trained Elsewhere," CSMonitor, November 25, 2015, www.csmonitor.com/USA/Society/2015/1125/How-Black-Lives-Matter-operates-when-spotlight-is-trained-elsewhere.

106 John Eligon, "One Slogan, Many Methods: Black Lives Matter Enters Politics."

107 Pinckney, "In Ferguson."

108 Karabel, "Police Killings Surpass the Worst Years of Lynching, Capital Punishment, and a Movement Responds."

109 "The Truth of Black Lives Matter," New York Times, September 3, 2015.

110 Barbara Reynolds, "I was a Civil Rights Activist in the 1960s, But It's Hard for Me to Get Behind Black Lives Matter," Washington Post, August 24, 2015.

111 Ibid.

112 Randall Kennedy, "Lifting as We Climb: A Progressive Defense of Respectability," Harper's Magazine, harpers.org/archive/2015/10/lifting-as-we-climb/2.

113 Pinckney, "In Ferguson." The author mentioned Bayard Rustin, the architect of the March on Washington for Jobs and Freedom, who put emphasis on building coalitions among black groups, white liberals, labor unions, and religious progressives; and Ella Baker's activist career as an organizer for tenants' rights (1930s), voter registration for the NAACP (1940s), field organizer for SCLC (1950s), and youth organizer for SNCC (1960s), who favored broad coalitions and decentralization in activism.

114 Lindsey, "Post–Ferguson: A 'Herstorical' Approach to Black Violability."

115 Garza, "A Herstory of #BlackLivesMatter."

CHAPTER 7

Interest Groups

LEARNING OBJECTIVE

Identify major black interest groups and explain how they differ from major and majority-white interest groups in the United States.

As late as the late 1960s, with the exception of the NAACP, the Urban League, and, to a lesser extent, the SCLC and the National Council of Negro Women, there was little organized black interest group influence on the Washington policy-making process. Even the NAACP and Urban League were engaged mainly in rights-based civil rights lobbying rather than in broader, material-based public policy concerns.[1] However, since the 1970s blacks have developed a significant presence in the Washington policy-making process, one that focuses on both rights-based and broader, material-based policy interests.

Table 7.1 displays the contemporary structure of black interest groups, illustrating the range of interest and policy concerns of the organized black community. Many of these groups (such as the National Medical Association and the National Association of Black Manufacturers), like their white counterparts, are special interest organizations, generally pursuing their own narrow professional or economic interests. Others, like Trans Africa, have a single policy focus—in its case, American foreign policy toward Africa and the Caribbean. (On Trans Africa's influence on policy in these regions, see Chapter 15.) Still others have broad, multiple-policy agendas (the NAACP, the Congressional Black Caucus), lobbying on the full range of domestic and foreign policy issues.

TABLE 7.1	The Structure of African American Interest Organizations—Selected Groups	

Civil Rights	Economic/Professional
NAACP (1909)[a]	National Medical Association (1885)
Urban League (1910)	National Bar Association (1925)
Southern Christian Leadership Conference (1957)	National Business League (1900)
NAACP Legal Defense Fund (1939)	National Conference of Black Lawyers (1969)
National Council of Negro Women (1937)	National Association of Black Manufacturers (1970)
	Coalition of Black Trade Unionists (1972)
PUBLIC POLICY	CAUCUSES OF BLACK ELECTED OFFICIALS
Trans Africa (1977)	Congressional Black Caucus (1969)
Children's Defense Fund (1973)[b]	National Caucus of Black Elected Officials (1970)
National Association of Black Social Workers (1969)	Southern Conference of Black Mayors (1972) National Black Caucus of State Legislators (1977) National Caucus of Black School Board Members (1971)
RELIGIOUS	
National Baptist Convention (1882)	
Nation of Islam (1930)	

[a] Year in parentheses refers to the year the group was organized. For a fairly comprehensive list of black organizations, their purposes, and their memberships, see *A Guide to Black Organizations* (New York: Philip Morris, 1984).

[b] Strictly speaking, the Children's Defense Fund is an interracial advocacy organization; however, it was founded and is led by a black woman—Marian Wright Edelman—and much of its advocacy is for poor and disadvantaged minority children.

Black Groups, the "Black Agenda," and the Problem of Resource Constraint

The broad-based policy agenda encompassing both rights- and material-based issues is one of the major problems confronting the African American lobby in Washington. It is agenda-rich but resource-poor. Political scientist Dianne Pinderhughes writes,

> The subordinate, dependent status of the black population limits the capacity of black interests to create well-funded and supported groups capable of the

consistent monitoring required in administration and implementation of law. This same status multiplies the number of potential issue areas of importance to black constituencies, but their resource difficulties limit the number of issues they can address, and weaken their likelihood of being taken seriously within any of those areas.[2]

The problem identified by Pinderhughes may be seen by comparing the post–civil rights era black agenda of African Americans and the resources of the three major Washington black interest organizations compared with the resources of selected nonblack Washington-based interest groups.

The Joint Center for Political and Economic Studies is a Washington-based think tank devoted to research on African American affairs (Box 7.1). In 1976, it called a bipartisan (Democrats and Republicans) conference of more than 1,000 black elected officials as well as appointed officials then serving in the Carter administration. At the conference's conclusion, the group issued a document, the "Seven Point Mandate," that it said represented a leadership consensus on the post–civil rights era black agenda.

The agenda includes *rights-based items* (busing for purposes of school desegregation and contract set-asides for minority businesses), but its main items are *material-based, nonracial issues*, such as universal health insurance and full employment. In this sense, the "black" agenda is not really black but is rather a broad-based liberal reform agenda. It is also a consensus agenda. With minor changes in emphasis and specifics, the original items remain the principal issues on the black agenda today. This agenda has been periodically revised and extended at various black agenda-setting conventions since 1976, for example, at the 2004 "Black Agenda Convention" in Boston. The focus of most of these more recent agendas has involved the criminal justice system and material-based issues such as employment, home ownership, black wealth, poverty, the media, and entrepreneurship.[3]

Blacks therefore have a broad-based material and rights agenda; yet when compared to other lobby groups in Washington—many with narrow, single-issue agendas—black groups have relatively few resources. Table 7.2 displays data on the membership and financial resources of selected Washington interest groups, including the three most important black groups. Although the African American groups are not competitive in membership or budgets with such giants of the lobbying world as the American Association of Retired Persons, known today as simply the AARP (with its 38 million members and $1.4 billion annual budget, no group can be competitive with this association that seeks membership from and claims to represent everybody over the age of 50), or even the National Rifle Association (NRA). The NRA has 4.5 million members and a budget of almost $250 million, compared to the NAACP's 200,000 or so members and $33 million budget. The budgets of the three black groups are somewhat competitive in resources with groups such as Mothers Against Drunk

BOX 7.1

The Joint Center for Political and Economic Studies

Think tanks—organizations of scholars and former government officials who do research and planning on domestic and foreign policy issues—are an important part of the policy-making process in the United States.[a] They develop ideas that shape the public policy debate and, unlike university-based scholars, they tend to be directly linked to Washington policy makers, frequently serving in the government for periods of time and then returning to the think tank to do research on policy-related issues. For example, many of the ideas that shaped the Reagan administration's early policy agenda came directly from the Heritage Foundation, a conservative think tank. Other important Washington think tanks include the Brookings Institution, the American Enterprise Institute, and the Urban Institute.

As the civil rights era drew to a close and black politics began its shift from movement-style protests to routine interest group policies, it was recognized early that African Americans needed their own think tank. The Joint Center for Political and Economic Studies was founded to meet this need for policy research and analysis.

In 1972, Eddie Williams became president of the Joint Center. Williams set about to broaden the center's work beyond its heretofore educational, technical assistance, and research support for black elected officials. The result was an announcement that the center would become a "national research organization in the tradition of Brookings and the American Enterprise Institute," rather than simply a "technical and institutional support resource for black elected officials."[b]

Although its budget was modest compared to the budgets of other Washington think tanks, the center did a remarkable job in facilitating the institutionalization of black politics. Its studies of the growth and development of black elected officials, its work on the implementation of the Voting Rights Act, its work on the development of a consensus black agenda, and its monthly newsletter *Focus* made the Joint Center the recognized, authoritative source on black politics in the post–civil rights era.[c]

Unfortunately for research and data collection on black politics, in 2014 the Center virtually ceased operations. This came about as a result of a steady decline in corporate, foundation, and government financial support. Although it maintained a small research unit on health policy, its political and economic staff and programs were terminated. Black elected officials and others pledged to try to raise funds to reestablish these programs; it is unlikely, however, that the Center will ever be able to reestablish itself as the preeminent think tank on black politics and public policy.[d]

[a] For an analysis of the increasingly important roles played by think tanks in policy making, see James Smith, *Think Tanks and the Rise of the New Policy Elites* (New York: Free Press, 1991).
[b] Joint Center for Political Studies, *Annual Report*, 1991, p. 3.
[c] For a more detailed analysis of the history and development of the Joint Center, see Robert C. Smith, *We Have No Leaders: African Americans in the Post–Civil Rights Era* (Albany, NY: SUNY Press, 1996): 113–20.
[d] Hazel Trice Edney, "Joint Center, Once Bastion of Black Political Research Now Pressing to Survive", *Trice Edney News Service*, May 25, 2014.

TABLE 7.2 A Comparison of the Resources of the Three Major African American Interest Organizations with Selected National Interest Organizations

African American Organization	Estimated Membership	Annual Budget[a]
NAACP	150–250,000; 2,000 local chapters	$33
Urban League	95 local affiliates	$58
Congressional Black Caucus[b]	43 members of Congress	$11
Selected National Organizations		
AARP	38 million	$1.4 billion
Mothers Against Drunk Driving	86 local chapters	$37
National Rifle Association	4.5 million	$250
Sierra Club	2.4 million	$98
Anti-Defamation League	27 Affiliate Offices	$57
Human Rights Campaign	1.5 million	$38

[a] Unless otherwise noted, the budget figure is rounded in millions of dollars.
[b] The budget for the Congressional Black Caucus is for the Congressional Black Caucus Foundation, a separate, tax-exempt organization formed in 1982 to raise funds to support the group. Until 1995, the Caucus itself raised $4,000 from each of its members to support its operations. The Republican congressional majority under speaker Newt Gingrich discontinued this form of member support.

Sources: Annual reports or tax returns for each organization, accessed online. The data are for 2013 or 2014.

Driving and the Sierra Club, the Jewish Anti-Defamation League, and the Human Rights Campaign, the principal lobby for gay and lesbian rights. The black groups, however, have a multiple-issue agenda that focuses on rights- and material-based issues in both domestic and foreign affairs.

The size of an interest group's membership and budget are important resources. A large membership permits grassroots mobilization by letters and phone calls to the media and members of Congress as well as voter mobilization on election day. Money is, as former California House Speaker Jesse Unruh once said, "the mother's milk of politics." It can be employed in a wide range of activities, such as grassroots organizing, voter mobilization, polling, radio and television ads, and litigation. A large financial base is critically important because it permits interest groups to form PACs—political action committees—to raise and give campaign contributions to candidates for office. Since the 1970s, PACs have become very important in the lobbying-election process, contributing nearly half the money raised by incumbent congressional candidates. Many nonblack groups (e.g., the NRA, the trial lawyers, the AFL-CIO) have large PACs that contribute millions of dollars to congressional candidates. None of the black interest groups have PACs, although several unsuccessful efforts to form one were made in the 1970s by a number of black groups.[4]

Given their multiple rights- and material-issue agendas and their relative lack of resources compared to other interest groups, black groups are at a considerable disadvantage unless they can form coalitions with other groups. On most rights-based issues, civil rights lobbying is done through a broad,

BOX 7.2

The Leadership Conference on Civil and Human Rights

The theory of African American coalitions we have developed in this book suggests that such coalitions, whether rights-based or material-based, tend to be unstable and frequently short-lived. While this is generally true, there is one coalition—the LCCR (originally the Leadership Conference on Civil Rights)—that has lasted more than a half-century; although in recent years it too has experienced tensions and conflicts.

The LCCR is a rights-based coalition. It was founded in 1949 by A. Phillip Randolph, the African American labor leader; Roy Wilkins, assistant director of the NAACP; and Arnold Aronson, a Jewish labor activist. Initially it was a coalition of about 40 black, labor, and Jewish and other religious groups whose principal objective was to secure legislation ensuring the civil rights of African Americans, especially those in the South. This coalition, along with the NAACP, was the principal lobby group for the 1964 Civil Rights Act (at that time, Clarence Mitchell, head of the NAACP's Washington office, also was head of the LCCR).

The African American civil rights movement of the 1960s and its successes served as a model for other groups facing various forms of discrimination. These groups (women, gays, and other minorities) joined the LCCR, expanding its memberships from about 40 groups in 1949 to more than 150 today. In 1949, most of the organizations in the LCCR were black, and it was widely viewed as an African American coalition. Today, this is no longer the case, as black organizations constitute little more than a third of the LCCR's membership.[a] The expansion of the coalition has inevitably led to tensions and conflicts along racial, ethnic, and gender lines.

From the beginning there were gender conflicts within the civil rights coalition. African Americans, labor leaders, and spokespersons for working-class women opposed the inclusion of a ban on sex discrimination in employment in the 1964 Civil Rights Act. Labor opposed gender equality in favor of preferential treatment for women: laws limiting working hours and the physical burden of work for women and providing such special benefits as rest and maternity leave. African American leaders (mainly men) opposed the inclusion of gender because they argued that it would take jobs from black men—the putative family breadwinner—and give them to white women. By contrast, support for the inclusion of gender came from conservatives (the amendment on sex was introduced by Howard Smith of Virginia, an opponent of civil rights, who thought the inclusion of sex would kill the entire bill) and white upper-class women's groups such as the National Federation of Business and Professional Women. Although African Americans and labor leaders now support gender equality in employment, sex–race tensions continue over affirmative action, with some African Americans arguing that white women are the principal beneficiaries of a program originally set up for blacks. Affirmative action has also caused conflict with some Jewish groups in the LCCR; these groups tend to object to racial quotas and preferences (especially in higher education) because quotas historically were used to exclude Jews and because some Jewish leaders see them as a violation of merit and the principle of equality for all persons. Jewish–black tensions in the coalition were also exacerbated by conflicts over black support for the Palestinians in the Middle East conflict, Israeli support for the apartheid regime in South Africa, and the anti-Semitic remarks of the Nation of Islam's Louis Farrakhan.

Another source of tension in the LCCR is between African Americans and Mexican Americans. When the 1965 Voting Rights Act was renewed in 1975, the NAACP opposed the inclusion of an amendment to prohibit discrimination against language minorities. Decisions of the LCCR require a unanimous vote of its executive committee, thus the NAACP's opposition effectively killed coalition support, forcing Latino groups in the coalition to act alone in a successful effort to get language groups covered by the Voting Rights Act.[b] Although this issue is now settled, it for a time left a residue of bad feeling between blacks and Latinos. In addition, some African Americans have expressed concerns about the impact of illegal immigration on the employment opportunities of low-income urban blacks, a position that upsets the Asian American and Hispanic American groups in the coalition.

The LCCR is a rights-based coalition that has endured for 50 years, but its successes in the 1960s, the development of new rights groups in the 1970s and 1980s, and the expansion of the coalition have inevitably created some instability. However, as a broad-based coalition that embraces universal rights for all Americans, it is likely to endure, although not without continuing conflicts and tensions.[c] In 2010 to reflect its broader universal freedom constituency and concerns, the group modified its name to Leadership Conference on Civil and Human Rights.

[a] Dianne Pinderhughes, "Black Interest Groups and the 1982 Extension of the Voting Rights Act," in Huey Perry and Wayne Parent, eds., *Blacks and the American Political System* (Gainesville: University Press of Florida, 1995): 206.
[b] Ibid., p. 211.
[c] Dianne Pinderhughes, "Divisions in the Civil Rights Community," *Political Science and Politics* 25 (1992): 485–87.

Wade Henderson, President and CEO of LCCHR.

Source: Malet, Jeff. "Inside the D.C. Statehood Senate Hearings," *The Georgetowner.* 17 September 2014. Retrieved 4 October 2016 from www.georgetowner.com/articles/2014/sep/17/inside-dc-statehood-senate-hearing-photos/

multiethnic coalition: the Leadership Conference on Civil and Human Rights (LCCHR). (There are, however, tensions within this group; see Box 7.2.) On welfare and poverty issues, the Center for Budget Priorities (a white group) is an effective lobby and advocacy group, and on national health insurance and full employment, the AFL-CIO and the Conference of Catholic Bishops are, with blacks, part of a broad labor–liberal reform coalition.

African American Women and the Quest for Universal Freedom

Although some black male leaders were ardent feminists—supporters of universal freedom for women—most were not and even those who were always were more concerned with ending racism and white supremacism than sexism and male dominance (see Chapter 6). Thus, African American women in politics have tended to embrace a more universal version of freedom than African American men, a version encompassing the elimination of race, gender, and other barriers to equality. We know that feminism—the ideology of gender equality and freedom—has historically been an ambivalent phenomenon in the black community and in African American politics. Black feminism promotes an intersectional approach to understanding the complex ways in which race, gender, class, sexual orientation, and other social categories of difference have simultaneously and inextricably been interwoven in black women's lives (see Chapter 4). In this context, African American women historically have faced oppression and discrimination not only as a result of racism and sexism, but also in relation to how their multiple social statuses intersect and overlap, which result in different social and lived experiences. This creates dilemmas. On one hand, the challenge is to decide whether the elimination of racism or sexism—often viewed as mutually exclusive—is to be the main focus of the struggles of black women committed to racial justice. On the other hand, in their fight for gender equality, black women must consider to what extent should they identify and form coalitions with white women, some of whom can be as racist in their thinking as some white men. Also, historically in the United States the struggle for women's rights and the struggle for the rights of blacks have been symbiotic and conflictual. Mainstream history records that the earliest movement for women's rights originated from the activism of largely middle- to upper-class white women in the abolitionist movement, who tended to view sexism as equal as or more important than racism. Although the modern feminist movement that originated in the late 1960s and early 1970s also has its roots in black social movements for freedom, it specifically emphasized the activism of middle-class white women in the protest phase of the civil rights movement during the 1960s.[5] In addition, the modern movement for women's liberation also drew on the black power movement for parts of its militancy in rhetoric, strategies, and organizing principles. But, as during the abolitionist movement, tensions emerged with black allies or intergroup coalitions as these middle-class white women also tended to see sexism as equal as or more important than racism.

The roots of black feminism predates white feminism early in the Antebellum Era in the writings and activism of women like Maria B. Stewart, Frances Ellen Watkins Harper, and Sojourner Truth, and in the late nineteenth-century writings of women like Ida B. Wells-Barnett, Mary Church Terrell, Nannie Helen Burroughs, and Anna Julia Cooper, whose 1892 book *A Voice from the South* is an important early work in the development of a distinctive black feminist thought. Black feminism is also rooted in the activities of black women abolitionists and the club movement among women (see Chapter 6). These activities led to America's first women's and nonwhite abolitionist organization, the Salem Female Anti-Slavery Society in 1832,[6] the formation of the National Association of Colored Women in 1896, and later the National Council of Negro Women in 1935. The National Association of Colored Women, organized a decade before the NAACP, was the first national black organization to deal with race issues, and the National Council of Negro Women, founded by Mary McLeod Bethune and for years led by Dorothy Height, dealt with women's issues as well as broader issues of civil rights during the 1950s and 1960s. The success of the civil rights movement in removing the obvious barriers to racial equality allowed for a renewed focus on gender equality among black women.

In the 1970s, black women's issues became marginalized in the black nationalist movements and isolated from the middle-class dominated white feminist movement. In fact, black feminists during this period spent much time "deconstructing" the racial/sexual politics dichotomy, captured eloquently in the book title "all the women are white, all the blacks are men, but some of us are brave,"[7] that often excluded women of color. In the political arena, Shirley Chisholm's election as the first black woman in Congress in 1968 and her 1972 campaign for the presidency were important symbolically in inspiring black female political activism, which historically has been concentrated in working-class, grassroots black women's activism seeking to improve the living conditions in their racially segregated communities with access to jobs, childcare, health care, environmental justice, crime, and affordable housing.[8] This prompted black women in New York City to form the National Coalition of 100 Black Women, taking its name from 100 Black Men of America, with local chapters nationwide to address these common issues. The Supreme Court's 1973 decision in *Roe* v. *Wade* to legalize abortion was a catalyst to action, particularly for working-class and low-income black women who viewed access to reproductive health as key to eradicating the concentrated, residual effects related to the feminization of poverty.[9] The decision was opposed by virtually the entire male-dominated black leadership establishment, including the NAACP and the Urban League. The National Black Political Convention in 1972 rejected a resolution supporting legal abortions; leading black nationalists denounced the decision as genocidal and Jesse Jackson equated *Roe* v. *Wade* with the *Dred Scott* decision. (Of major black organizations, only the Black Panther Party endorsed *Roe* and a woman's right to choose an abortion.)

In 1973, black women formed the National Black Feminist Organization, which advocated a specifically black agenda of gender equality. In 1974, self-identified "radical black feminists and lesbians" formed the Combahee River Collective (taking its name from a campaign led by Harriet Tubman that freed several hundred slaves), which issued a manifesto defining concepts of identity as it relates to black women "struggling against racial, sexual, heterosexual and class oppression"; an intersectional approach to women's liberation. (This group was heavily influenced by the writings of Audre Lorde, a young black lesbian feminist and political activist who saw sexuality as an important part of black feminism.)[10] In 1984, politically active black women led by convening founders, Shirley Chisholm and C. Delores Tucker, formed the National Congress of Black Women in order to pursue a distinctive agenda dedicated to African American women and their families, focusing on related political issues and the election and appointment of black women to office. In 1990, C. Delores Tucker and other black women also founded the national African-American Women for Reproductive Freedom as a way to show support for *Roe* v. *Wade*. More recently, the millennial National Coalition Black Women's Roundtable, an intergenerational civic engagement network of the National Coalition on Black Civic Participation founded in 1976, was formed to champion public policies that promote health and wellness, economic security, education, and global empowerment.

The State of Black Nationalist Movements

Black nationalism is a movement more than an interest group organization. Interest groups accept the legitimacy of the system and seek to have it accept their demands for rights and freedoms; movements challenge system legitimacy and seek fundamental system transformation. Historically, black nationalists have certainly challenged the legitimacy of the American system; in their view, it is incapable of delivering universal freedom and equality. This is shown clearly in the system-challenging rhetoric of nationalist leaders, with each new generation altering their views to better fit contemporary realities of black life. This means that over time the black nationalist continuum has moved from emigration to community separation while maintaining its focus on self-determination, entrepreneurism, and activities that emphasize and promote race group solidarity.

As early as 1901, Bishop Henry M. Turner, born a free man of color in 1834 who became a successful entrepreneur,[11] caused a national furor when he proclaimed "to the Negro in this country the American flag is a dirty and contemptuous rag. Not a star in it can the colored man claim, for it is no longer a symbol of our manhood rights and freedom."[12] In the 1890s, Turner attempted to organize the first mass effort at a "back-to-Africa" movement because in his view the choice for blacks was simple: "emigrate or perish."[13] Faced by the withdrawal of African American freedom, the terrorism of white southern racists, and Booker T. Washington's "accommodationist" strategy for black liberation, Turner drafted and delivered speeches, organized numerous conferences, and filed many petitions with Congress requesting support for his plan; he was even able to persuade several racist southern congressmen to introduce emigration legislation. Relatedly, for a time, he was also an honorary vice-president of the American Colonialization Society, an organization of racists formed in the 1770s that favored and monetarily supported emigration because, in its view, the United States was a "white man's country." By the time of Turner's death, it is estimated that perhaps a thousand blacks emigrated to Africa.[14]

In the end, Turner's overall plan was met with little success due to these enduring dilemmas for black nationalist groups: On one hand, those who advocate emigration are faced with rejection by most African Americans—especially the middle class—who do not wish to leave the United States. On the other hand, their potential white coalition partners tend to be racists and white supremacists. However, from a policy perspective, Turner was the first African American leader to petition Congress for reparations, calling for a $40 billion payment to blacks for their 200 years of slave labor (see Box 7.3).

In 1914, Marcus Garvey, a Jamaican immigrant inspired by Booker T. Washington's vision, would ignite a second major black nationalist and Pan-African movement during the Harlem Renaissance era with the formation of his Universal Negro Improvement Association (UNIA). At its peak in the 1920s, it claimed a membership of 2 million in the United States and the West Indies.[15] Like Turner, Garvey promoted race group solidarity in all facets of life from the sacred to the secular. Also, like Turner, he founded a steamship company, a newspaper, and a number of small factories and businesses—entrepreneurism is heavily valued by black nationalists. A charismatic leader and powerful orator, Garvey would draw huge crowds to his rallies and UNIA parades through Harlem. An autocratic leader, in 1921 Garvey declared himself provisional president of Africa, although he had never set foot on the continent and never would.

Similar to Turner's movement, Garvey's was opposed by the mainstream, middle-class black leadership establishment (an especially bitter critic was W. E. B. Du Bois). Also, he met with representatives of the Ku Klux Klan (KKK) and other racist groups about forming coalitions to secure emigration. Garvey's strongest base of support came from the poor and working classes in racially segregated neighborhoods, primarily in the North. Unlike Turner's movement, Garvey's attracted the attention of the federal government, since its mass following and radicalism were viewed as a threat to internal security, making

██████████ **BOX 7.3** ██████████

The African American Reparation Movement

In the Post–Reconstruction Era, Bishop Henry M. Turner was the first African American leader to demand reparation—repayment for the damages of slavery—from the American government. After the Civil War, there was talk of providing a kind of reparation to blacks in the form of "40 acres and a mule." In the 1865 Freedmen's Bureau Act, Congress included a provision granting blacks 40 acres of abandoned land in the southern states. President Andrew Johnson, however, vetoed the bill, arguing that to take land from the former slave owners was "contrary to that provision of the Constitution which declares that no person shall 'be deprived of life, liberty and property without due process of law.' "[a] The closest the U.S. government ever came to paying reparation was General William Sherman's Special Order #15 issued on January 16, 1865.[b] It provided 40 acres to black families living on the Georgia and South Carolina coasts (some of the descendants of these families still live or own property on these lands). Blacks, however, never abandoned their claim for reparations,[c] and the payment by the Congress and several American cities of reparation to Japanese Americans for their World War II incarceration contributed to the rebirth of an African American movement seeking similar remuneration.[d]

The contemporary reparation movement was led by Imari Obadele, a former professor of political science at the historically black Prairie View A & M University and the former provisional president of the Republic of New Africa. The Republic of New Africa is a black nationalist organization founded in 1968 by Obadele (who was then known as Richard Henry). The organization favors the creation of a separate, all-black nation in the southern part of the United States. In 1989, Obadele and others formed the National Coalition of Blacks for Reparations (NCOBRA), a nonprofit coalition of black religious, civic, and fraternal organizations.

Since its formation, the coalition engaged in a variety of tactics to advance the cause of reparation, including petitions to Congress and the president, lawsuits, and protest demonstrations at the White House.

Using the Japanese case as a precedent, NCOBRA made a proposal to Congress, called "An Act to Stimulate Economic Growth in the United States and Compensate, in Part, for the Grievous Wrongs of Slavery and the Unjust Enrichment Which Accrued to the United States Therefrom." The proposal indicates no dollar amount for payment (suggesting that the figure be established by an independent commission, as was done in the Japanese American case) but requires that one-third of the payment go to each individual African man, woman, and child; one-third to the Republic of New Africa; and one-third to a national congress of black church, civic, and civil rights organizations.[e]

In the Japanese case, the first step was the appointment by the Congress of a commission to study the issue. Thus, in 1995, Congressman John Conyers, an African American, and Congressman Norman Mineta, a Japanese American, introduced a bill to establish a "Commission to Study Reparations for African Americans."[f] Also, in 1995 several African Americans filed a suit in a federal court in California asking the court to direct the government to pay reparation. The Court of Appeals of the Ninth Circuit rejected the suit, holding that the United States could not be sued unless it waived its "sovereign immunity" and that the "appropriate forum for policy questions of this sort . . . is Congress rather than the courts."[g]

This new reparation movement, given the present climate of race relations in the United States, has little prospects for success in the near term.[h] However, in part because of the publication in 2000 of *The Debt: What America Owes Blacks* by Randall Robinson, the head of Trans

Africa, the issue received increased attention. In 1992, the state of Florida agreed to pay reparations to the survivors and descendants of Rosewood (a black town that was destroyed by a white mob in 1923), and the Oklahoma Commission to Study the Tulsa Race Riots of 1921 recommended that the survivors and descendants be paid reparations for the riots in which white mobs attacked a black neighborhood, destroying homes and businesses and killing hundreds of people. In June 2014 the *Atlantic* published a major cover story article making the case for reparations, which stimulated national debate. The article by Ta-Nehisi Coates, "The Case for Reparations,"[i] not only revived debate in the national media on the controversial issue but made Coates, an award-winning essayist, something of a national spokesperson on reparations. In "The Black Family in the Age of Mass Incarceration"[j] in the October 2015 *Atlantic* he argued that the ultimate solution to mass incarceration was not reform of the criminal justice system, but comprehensive reparations. When Bernie Sanders, the socialist candidate for the 2016 Democratic presidential nomination expressed opposition to reparations as impossible to pass Congress and "divisive," Coates wrote a scathing rejoinder declaring that if a "candidate of the radical left" could so casually dismiss reparations "then expect white supremacy in American Politics to endure well beyond our lifetimes and lifetimes of our children. Reparations is not *one* possible tool against white supremacy. It is *the* indispensable tool against white supremacy"[k] (*italics by authors*). Meanwhile, a 2014 HuffPost/YouGov poll found overwhelming opposition among whites to reparations in the form of "cash payments" or special job training and educational programs for "descendants" of slaves. Ninety-four percent opposed cash payments and 81 percent opposed employment and educational programs. And although Congress in 2009 formally apologized for the enslavement of Africans, the HuffPost/You Gov poll found 79 percent of whites in 2014 were opposed.[l]

In another development, in January 2016 a United Nations panel—the Working Group of Experts on People of African Descent—in a preliminary report urged the U.S. Congress to consider reparations to descendants of Africans enslaved in the U.S. A final report of the panel will be issued at the end of 2016.

[a] The text of the Freedmen's Bureau bill and President Johnson's veto message are in *The Forty Acres Documents*, Introduction by Amitcar Shabazz (Baton Rouge, LA: House of Songhay, 1994): 65, 74, 75–94.

[b] The text of Sherman's Order is also in *The Forty Acres Document*, pp. 51–58.

[c] See Boris Bittker, *The Case for Black Reparations* (New York: Random House, 1973); and Daisy Collins, "Reparations for Black Citizens," *Howard University Law Review* 82 (1979): 65–94.

[d] Tom Kenworthy, "House Votes Apology, Reparations for Japanese Americans," *Washington Post,* September 18, 1987, p. A1.

[e] Chokwe Lumumba, Imari Obadele, and Nkechi Taifa, *Reparations NOW!* (Baton Rouge, LA: House of Songhay, 1995): 67.

[f] The text of the Conyers-Mineta bill is in Lumumba, Obadele, and Taifa, *Reparations NOW!* pp. 97–107.

[g] *Cato et al.* v. *United States of America,* United States Circuit Court of Appeals, Ninth Circuit #94-17102 (1995): 151–62.

[h] An ABC News poll found that overall, 77 percent of Americans were opposed to reparation for blacks. Sixty-five percent of blacks supported the idea, while it was opposed by 88 percent of whites. See ABC News *Nightline*, July 7, 1997.

[i] Ta-Nehisi Coates, "The Case for Reparations," *The Atlantic*, June 2014, www.theatlantic.com/magazine/archive/2014/06/the-case-for-reparations/361631/.

[j] Ta-Nehisi Coates, "The Black Family in the Age of Mass Incarceration," *The Atlantic*, October 2015, www.theatlantic.com/magazine/archive/2015/10/the-black-family-in-the-age-of-mass-incarceration/403246/.

[k] Ta-Nehisi Coates, "Why Precisely Is Bernie Sanders Against Reparations?," *The Atlantic*, January 2016, www.theatlantic.com/politics/archive/2016/01/bernie-sanders-reparations/424602/.

[l] Emily Swanson "Americans Can't Stomach an Apology for Slavery, Much Less Reparations," *Huff/Post*, June 2, 2014.

him a primary target of the FBI and New York City police. In 1925, Garvey and several of his associates were indicted on federal mail fraud charges of using the mail to sell phony stock in his steamship company. His associates were found not guilty, but Garvey was convicted, sentenced to prison for several years, and then deported. With his deportation in 1927, his organization and movement split into a number of small sects and factions and lost its effectiveness. He died in London in 1940.

Garvey's movement promoted self-help and a separatist philosophy of social, political, and economic freedom for blacks. In fact, tenets of his UNIA community program would appeal to and influence a range of black nationalist groups such as the Nation of Islam, Father Divine's Universal Peace Mission, and the Rastafarian movement. Of these groups, the most influential black nationalist organization of the post–civil rights era is the Nation of Islam, under the leadership of Minister Louis Farrakhan. The Nation of Islam—popularly known as the "Nation" or the Black Muslims—was founded by W. D. Fard in 1931. After Fard's disappearance, it was led by Elijah Muhammad until his death in 1976.[16]

The Nation grew slowly until the charismatic convert Malcolm X became its national spokesman in the 1960s. Like Garvey, Malcolm helped to build a large following for the group among the urban poor and working class.[17]

Malcolm X with Elijah Muhammad, leader of the Nation of Islam.

Source: Eve Arnold/Magnum Photos

Like Garvey's movement, the Nation was based on racial chauvinism, glorifying everything black, condemning white supremacy, and characterizing whites as "racist devils," which made it a target of the FBI as well. The Nation, similar to Garvey's movement, also promoted self-help through entrepreneurism, established chapters (mosques) throughout the country, operated small businesses and farms, and published a weekly newspaper. Unlike the historic Turner and Garvey movements, the Nation did not establish a steamship line since it does not favor emigration to Africa. Instead, it desires the creation of a separate black nation within the boundaries of the United States.

When Elijah Muhammad died in 1976, the Nation of Islam split into a series of sects and factions; the main body of the group, led by Wallace Muhammad, Elijah Muhammad's son, was transformed into a mainstream, integrationist (including whites as members) orthodox Islamic group.[18] For a short time in the 1970s, the Nation of Islam disappeared until Minister Farrakhan rebuilt it on the original principles of Elijah Muhammad.[19] However, in his clearest break with the traditions of the Nation, Farrakhan in 1993 abandoned the Nation's doctrine of nonparticipation in American electoral politics. Farrakhan did this first by encouraging his followers to register and vote for Chicago mayoral candidate Harold Washington in 1983, and in 1984 he supported Jesse Jackson's campaign for president.

Unlike most African American organizations, the Nation of Islam receives no money from white-dominated corporations or businesses, but has accepted funding from leaders of Islamic nations. It has approximately 120 mosques in various cities around the country, operates a series of modest small business enterprises, and has a somewhat effective social welfare system for its members. It publishes a weekly newspaper and Farrakhan can be seen and heard on broadcast and digital media globally. The organization does not reveal the size of its membership, but it is estimated at roughly 20,000. However, the Nation and Farrakhan have millions of followers. A 1994 *Time* magazine poll found that 73 percent of blacks were familiar with Farrakhan, making him, with Jesse Jackson, one of the best-known African American leaders. Most blacks familiar with Farrakhan viewed him favorably, with 65 percent saying he was an effective leader, 63 percent that he speaks the truth, and 62 percent that he was good for black America.[20] The *Time* poll that produced these figures was taken prior to Farrakhan's success in calling the 1995 Million Man March—the largest mass demonstration in Washington in American history—which drew notable black male leaders, including Jesse Jackson, Al Sharpton, and Barack Obama. The demonstration failed to inspire a movement. By 2007, Louis Farrakhan was no longer identified by African Americans as an influential leader on any major public opinion poll. In fact, in 2013 only 3 percent of blacks indicated that he speaks for them.[21]

Faces and Voices in the Struggle for Universal Freedom
MARIA W. STEWART (1803–1879)

Maria W. Stewart contributed to universal freedom and equality by becoming the first African American woman to take a leadership role in the abolitionist movement. Born in Boston in 1803, at age 5 she was orphaned and became a servant to a white clergyman, where she received her education by attending Sunday school and reading books from the church library. A deeply religious woman, she was widowed after three years of marriage, at which time she began her brief career as an antislavery and feminist lecturer.

Historians describe Stewart as the first black woman lecturer and writer and probably the first woman, black or white, to speak before an audience of both men and women. Stewart's career as a writer and lecturer lasted only three years, during which, while living in Boston, she gave three public lectures and published a political treatise and a religious pamphlet. In addition to her antislavery work, Stewart was also an ardent feminist. Not only did she encourage the formation of black women's rights organizations, she also urged black women to pursue education and careers outside the home, writing, "How long shall the fair daughters of Africa be compelled to bury their minds and talents beneath a load of iron pots and kettles?"

Maria W. Stewart.

Source: Zeilinger, Julie. "Maria W. Stewart." *Identities.Mic.* 3 March 2015. Retrieved 4 October 2016 from https://images.mic.com/qhcestoueglge8xiosoiud9tz6weiwycnpn9no98io8f0f7xzb48wb l2ztgnybfh.jpg

After the Civil War, Stewart became a teacher in Washington, DC. She died in 1879. Shortly before her death she published a collection of her speeches and essays, *Meditations from the Pen of Mrs. Maria W. Stewart.*[a]

[a]Marilyn Richardson, *Maria Stewart: America's First Black Woman Political Writer* (Bloomington: Indiana University Press, 1987).

Summary

Once a group gains entry into the American political system, if it is to be effective it has to form interest groups. Although there is a fairly diverse structure of interest group organizations representing black interests in Washington, these interests are multifaceted, embracing both rights- and material-based interests. In addition, compared to nonblack interest groups, black groups tend to be relatively underfunded. Historically, a number of black leaders and groups have rejected participation in the system, believing it is not effective because of racism and white supremacy and/or because they desire to pursue independent, autonomous political paths. These individuals and groups have embraced black nationalism. In addition, African American women have developed separate organizations in their quest for universal freedom, utilizing an intersectional approach to combat the interactive and interlocking effects of racism, sexism, classism, heterosexism, and other social identities of difference that may impact their daily lives.

Critical Thinking Questions

1. Explain the fundamental difference between interest groups and political parties.
2. Explain the problem of resource constraint in African American interest group lobbying in Washington.
3. Discuss the differences between the rights-based and material-based issues on the "Black Agenda." What issues have received the most attention from African American elected officials?
4. Explain the symbiotic and conflictual relationships historically between the African American and women's freedom movements in the United States.
5. What is the state of the black nationalist movement in relation to interest group formation and activities? Define and discuss highlighting the black nationalist programs of Bishop Henry M. Turner, Marcus Garvey, and Louis Farrakhan.

Selected Bibliography

Garson, G. David. *Group Theories of Politics.* Beverly Hills, CA: Sage, 1978. A review and critique of the major theories and the research on the interest group basis of American politics.

Giddings, Paula. *When and Where I Enter: The Impact of Black Women on Race and Sex in America.* New York: William Morrow, 1984. One of the earliest and best studies of the subject.

Guy-Sheftall, Beverly. *Words of Fire: An Anthology of African-American Feminist Thought.* New York: New Press, 1995. A comprehensive anthology of African American feminist thought from the Antebellum Era to the late twentieth century.

Hamilton, Dana, and Charles Hamilton. *The Dual Agenda: Social Policies of Civil Rights Organizations from the New Deal to the Present.* New York: Columbia University Press, 1996. Although they do not use the terms *rights-based* and *material-based,* this book is an exhaustive study of the dual agenda of black Americans.

Johnson, Ollie, and Karen Stanford, eds. *Black Political Organizations.* New Brunswick, NJ: Rutgers University Press, 2003. A collection of 11 essays examining the activities and impact of contemporary black interest organizations, including the NAACP, Urban League, the Rainbow/PUSH Coalition, Nation of Islam, and the National Council of Negro Women.

Lowi, Theodore. *The End of Liberalism.* New York: Norton, 1979. An influential study of how interest groups manipulate public policy making in pursuit of narrow, parochial interests.

Pinderhughes, Dianne. "Collective Goods and Black Interest." *Review of Black Political Economy* 12 (Winter 1983): 219–36. A largely theoretical analysis of the role of black interest groups in pursuing the multiple policy interests of blacks in an environment of resource constraints.

Pinderhughes, Dianne. "Black Interest Groups and the 1982 Extension of the Voting Rights Act." In Huey Perry and Wayne Parent, eds., *Blacks and the American Political System,* pp. 203–24. Gainesville: University Press of Florida, 1995. A case study of African American interest group politics in the context of the contemporary civil rights coalition.

Smith, Robert C. *We Have No Leaders: African Americans in the Post–Civil Rights Era.* Albany, NY: SUNY Press, 1996. A detailed study of the transformation of the 1960s African American freedom struggle from movement to interest groups politics, focusing on African American interest groups, the Congressional Black Caucus, black presidential appointees in the executive branch, and Jesse Jackson's Rainbow Coalition.

Stuckey, Sterling. *The Ideological Origins of Black Nationalism.* Boston, MA: Beacon, 1972. A seminal study that includes some of the classic black nationalist writings.

Taylor, James. *Black Nationalism in the United States: From Malcolm X to Barack Obama.* Boulder, CO: Lynne Rienner, 2011. Focusing on the religious foundations of nationalist ideologies, this book provides an assessment of the contemporary relevance of black nationalism.

Notes

1 Harold Wolman and Norman Thomas, "Black Interests, Black Groups and Black Influence in the Federal Policy Process: The Cases of Housing and Education," *Journal of Politics* 32 (November 1970): 875–97.

2 Dianne Pinderhughes, "Racial Interest Groups and Incremental Politics" (unpublished paper, University of Illinois, Urbana, 1980): 36.

3 See the National Black Agenda, National Black Agenda Convention, Boston, 2004. www.nationalblackagenda.com_NatinalBlackAgendafinal.pdf.

4 Ibid.

5 Michelle Newman, *White Women's Right: The Racial Origins of Feminism in the United States* (New York: Oxford University Press, 1999).

6 July Roy Jeffrey, *The Great Silent Army of Abolitionism: Ordinary Women in the Antislavery Movement* (Chapel Hill: University of North Carolina Press, 1998); and Shirley J. Yee, *Black Women Abolitionists: A Study in Activism, 1828–1860* (Knoxville: University of Tennessee Press, 1992).

7 Gloria Hull, Bell Scott, and Barbara Smith, *All the Women are White, All the Blacks Are Men, But Some of Us are Brave: Black Women's Studies* (New York: Feminist Press, 1982).

8 See Andrea Y. Simpson, "Going It Alone: Black Women Activists and Black Organizational Quiesence," in Wilbur Rich, ed., *African American Perspectives on Political Science* (Philadelphia, PA: Temple University Press, 2007): p. 152.

9 Ibid., p. 153.

10 See Audre Lorde, *I Am Your Sister: Black Women Organizing Across Sexualities* (Latham, NY: Kitchen Table Women of Color Press, 1985).

11 On the historical origins of black nationalist thought, see Sterling Stuckey, *The Ideological Origins of Black Nationalism* (Boston, MA: Beacon, 1972); and Sterling Stuckey, *Slave Culture: Foundations of Nationalist Thought* (New York: Oxford, 1967). In these texts, it is noted that Turner was a bishop of the African Methodist Episcopal church. He served as a chaplain in the Union army and as a member of the Reconstruction, Georgia constitutional convention. Also, he organized the Colored Emigration League, published a monthly newsletter, and established the Afro-American Steamship Company. And, he was the first black leader to declare that God is black, a notion advanced by Marcus Garvey and some sects of the Black Muslims.

12 Edwin Redkey, "The Flowering of Black Nationalism: Henry McNeal Turner and Marcus Garvey," in Nathan Huggins, Martin Kilson, and Daniel Fox, eds., *Key Issues in the Afro-American Experience*, vol. 2 (New York: Harcourt Brace Jovanovich, 1971): 115.

13 Stuckey, *The Ideological Origins of Black Nationalism*, p. 199.

14 Ibid., p. 114.

15 See Edmund Cronon, *Black Moses: The Story of Marcus Garvey and the Universal Negro Improvement Association* (Madison: University of Wisconsin Press, 1955).

16 Claude Andrew Clegg, *An Original Man: The Life and Times of Elijah Muhammad* (New York: St. Martin's Press, 1997).

17 Bruce Perry, *Malcolm: The Life of a Man Who Changed Black America* (Barrytown, NY: Station Hill Press, 1991); and Manning Marable, *Malcolm X: A Life of Reinvention* (New York: Viking, 2011).

18 Don Terry, "Black Muslims Enter Islamic Mainstream," *New York Times*, May 3, 1993.

19 On Farrakhan's strategy to revitalize the Nation of Islam, see Robert C. Smith, *We Have No Leaders: African Americans in the Post–Civil Rights Era* (Albany, NY: SUNY Press, 1996): 99–100; Lawrence Mamiya, "From Black Muslim to Bialian: The Evolution of a Movement," *Journal for the Scientific Study of Religion* 21 (1982): 141; and Mattias Gardell, *In the Name of Elijah Muhammad: Louis Farrakhan and*

the Nation of Islam (Durham, NC: Duke University Press, 1996). Gardell's work contains a detailed analysis of the theological underpinnings of the Nation of Islam.

20 William Henry, "Pride and Prejudice," *Time*, February 28, 1994, p. 22.

21 See "Optimism about Black Progress Declines: Blacks See Growing Values Gap Between Poor and Middle Class," Pew Research Center, November 2007, p. 45. The Grio's "2011 African-American Leadership Survey," at http://thegrio.com/2011/01/17/thegrios-2011-african-american-leadership-survey/. Robert Johnson and Zogby Analytics poll 2013 at www.rljcompanies.com/phpages/wp-content/uploads/2013/03/Results-of-a-National-Opinion-Poll-Conducted-by-Zogby-Analytics-Black-Opinions-in-the-Age-of-Obama_2013.pdf.

CHAPTER 8

Political Parties

LEARNING OBJECTIVE

Explain the history of political party participation as it relates to African Americans.

In 2008 the impossible happened: An African American was elected president of the United States. To understand the extraordinary nature of Obama's capture of the Democratic nomination and the presidency and its significance in the African American quest for universal freedom, one must locate the 2008 election in the historical context of the African American relationship to the two-party system. It is also necessary to analyze what happened in 2008 in relation to the role of blacks in the Democratic Party since the pivotal 1964 election and the collapse of the New Deal coalition. Finally, to fully understand the Obama phenomenon, it is useful to compare his campaign for the nomination with previous efforts by African Americans to win major party nominations, particularly Jesse Jackson's.

African Americans and the American No-Party System

Virtually all political scientists are committed to the idea that a competitive party system is indispensable to the effective operation of any democracy. The essence of this commitment according to Leon Epstein is the theory "that voters should be able to choose between recognizable competing leadership groups" that offer alternative programs and policies addressing citizen needs and interests.[1] The two-party system in the United States has historically worked reasonably well for white Americans, offering alternative candidates, programs, and policies from which they could choose. For African Americans, this has rarely been the case.

The American two-party system, Paul Frymer argues, represents a form of institutional racism, in that it was partly designed to marginalize black interests by keeping the issue of slavery off the national political agenda.[2] Thus, for most of American history, blacks have faced a no-party system, as from 1787 until the 1860s both major parties ignored the major issue of concern to blacks—freedom.

African Americans—where they were allowed to vote—supported the antislavery Free Soil and Liberty parties from the 1840s to the 1860s. However, these parties, because of the structural characteristics of the electoral system that maintain the two-party system, were rarely able to elect their members to office[3] (see Box 8.1). It was not until the Civil War brought about the emergence of the Republican Party and the destruction of slavery that one of the two major parties began to pay some attention to the interests of blacks.

African Americans and the American One-Party System: 1868–1936

During the Civil War–Reconstruction era, when African American men first achieved the right to vote, Frederick Douglass is said to have told a group of black voters, "The Republican Party is the deck, all else the sea."[4] What Douglass meant was that only one of the two major parties—the Republican—was willing to address the concerns of blacks. The Democratic Party, on the other hand, was the party of racism and white supremacy, committed to denying universal freedom to the newly emancipated Africans. Since Douglass's days, except for the brief period of the New Deal, discussed in the following section, hardly anything has changed; one party is the deck, the other the sea—except that today the deck is the Democratic Party.

The Republican Party became the deck because beginning with the Emancipation Proclamation it adopted policies that addressed the universal freedom concerns of blacks, including three constitutional amendments and three civil rights bills. It also addressed the material-based concerns of blacks with legislation establishing the Freedmen's Bureau, the government's first social welfare agency (see Chapter 2). Although we do not have precise figures, it is probably the case that from the 1868 election (when African Americans in significant numbers were first allowed to vote) until 1936 the Republican Party averaged more than 80 percent of the black vote in presidential elections.

By the late 1870s, however, a white backlash developed, and in the "Compromise of 1877," the Republicans under the leadership of President Rutherford B. Hayes effectively abandoned the interests of blacks in favor of reconciliation with southern white racists. The African American leadership and those blacks who could still vote continued to support the Republicans because the Democratic Party was worse. Thus, as Gurin, Hatchett, and Jackson

BOX 8.1

Beyond the Two-Party System?

Polls indicate that more than half the public, black as well as white, is dissatisfied with the two-party system and would like to see another party or parties in addition to the Democrats and Republicans. In spite of this discontent, the structure of the electoral system makes the emergence of a viable third party extremely unlikely. The American electoral structure involves two distinct features that discourage the formation of third parties. The first is the *winner-take-all* method of allocating electoral college votes for president, in which the candidate with the most votes gets all of a state's electoral college votes. (For example, in 1992 Bill Clinton got 43 percent of the popular vote in California but 100 percent of that state's 55 electoral votes.) The second is the *single-member district* system used in electing members of the House, in which voters vote for only one congressperson and the winner needs only a plurality to win. By contrast, virtually every other democratic country uses some form of *proportional representation* that encourages the formation of third or minor parties, since their candidates have a chance to win. A system of proportional representation in the United States would allocate electoral college votes to a candidate according to the proportion of the popular vote that candidate won. Had such a system been in effect in 1992, Ross Perot, who received 20 percent of

the vote, would have been awarded 108 electoral votes (20 percent of 538) instead of the zero he got. Similarly, a *multimember district* system for House elections could allow a minor party to win because seats in the House would be determined by each party's percentage of the vote. For example, if in a 10-member district, the Democrats won 40 percent of the vote, they would get four seats; the Republicans, with 40 percent, would get four seats, and Ross Perot's Reform Party, with 20 percent of the vote, would get two seats.

There is discussion in academic circles about reform of the American electoral system to encourage proportional representation and a multiparty system.[a] But unless a massive grassroots movement develops, these reform ideas will probably not go very far, since the Democrats and Republicans will not easily yield their shared monopoly on political power.

[a] See Lani Guinier, *The Tyranny of the Majority: Fundamental Fairness in American Democracy* (New York: Free Press, 1994); Douglas Amy, *Real Choices/New Voices: The Case for Proportional Representation Elections in the United States* (New York: Columbia University Press, 1993); and Kay Lawson, "The Case for a Multiparty System," in P. Herrnson and J. Green, eds., *Multiparty Politics in America: Performance, Promise, Prospects and Possibilities* (Boulder, CO: Rowman, Littlefield, 1999).

conclude, "The history of the black electorate is characterized by blacks' continual commitment to the electoral system and repeated rejection by one party or the other," but "black leaders have persistently searched for strategies that would make the party system work for the black electorate."[5] Those strategies have included abandoning the Republican Party in favor of Democrats, attempting to use the black vote as the balance of power between the two parties, and running as candidates for the Democratic presidential nomination.

African Americans, Limited Party Competition, and the Balance of Power, 1936–1964

Most blacks remained loyal to the Republican Party in the Depression era 1932 presidential election, in which Franklin Delano Roosevelt defeated Herbert Hoover in a landslide. In 1936, however, a majority of blacks voted Democratic in a presidential election for the first time. Blacks did not vote for FDR because he was a Democrat or because he supported their concerns for civil rights and universal freedom. Rather he was able to win black support in 1936 and thereafter because he embraced their material-based interests in jobs, housing, and social security.

By 1945, a majority of blacks were voting Democratic in national elections, but a significant minority remained Republican, and even some black Democrats would vote Republican if the candidate and his policies were attractive. Thus, for the first time in history—and for a brief time—African American voters enjoyed the benefit of a two-party system. Thus, they could occasionally operate as the balance of power determining the winner in close elections.

On the eve of the 1948 election, Henry Lee Moon, the NAACP's public relations director, wrote *Balance of Power: The Negro Vote*. This volume summarized the strategic significance of the black vote: "The Negro's political influence in national elections derives not so much from its numerical strength as from its strategic diffusion in the balance of power and marginal states whose electoral votes are considered vital to the winning candidate."[6]

The black vote (in the swing states of the Northeast and Midwest) did tip the balance to President Truman in 1948 and to President Kennedy in 1960. But it was not a monolithic vote during this period. Truman's Republican opponent in 1948 received about 25 percent of the black vote, as did Republican Richard Nixon in 1960, and Dwight Eisenhower in the 1950s may have received as much as 35 percent. Both parties during this period attempted to appeal to black concerns. In the 1950s, Eisenhower's civil rights record was about as good as the Democratic nominee and Nixon's in 1960 was the equal of Kennedy's.

The Collapse of the New Deal Coalition and the Return of the One-Party System

With the entry of blacks into the New Deal coalition, it became inherently unstable and subject to collapse. The coalition FDR patched together included the industrial working class of the Northeast and Midwest, with such ethnic immigrants as Poles, Italians, and the Irish; it also had Jews, liberal intellectuals, white southerners, and blacks. This coalition of opposites—African Americans and southern white racists—was held together by a common interest in universal material benefits. Once the Democratic Party embraced the African American civil rights agenda—first in 1948 under President Truman and then in the 1960s under Presidents Kennedy and Johnson—the New Deal coalition began to fall apart. In 1948, southern white supremacists and racists left the coalition and formed a third "Dixiecrat" Party. With South Carolina's Strom Thurmond as its presidential candidate, the new party carried four Deep South states. In 1964, southern racists again left the coalition—this time to support the Republican presidential candidate Barry Goldwater, who had opposed the Civil Rights Act of 1964. Goldwater, like Thurmond, carried the Deep South states. In the 1968 presidential election, southern whites supported George Wallace, the racist, white supremacist governor of Alabama, and in 1972, they supported Richard Nixon. By 1972, the New Deal coalition was dead; southern whites had defected along with elements of the northern white industrial working class. By 1980, the Republican Party had consolidated itself as the conservative party of racial reaction. The New Deal coalition collapsed for many reasons, but the major one was racism. Many whites, especially in the South, were unwilling to be a part of a broad material-based coalition if that coalition also embraced the historic quest of African Americans for equality and universal freedom.

The collapse of the New Deal coalition signaled the return of one-party politics. The Democratic Party was now the deck, all else the sea. While only 10 percent of the overall electorate, blacks since the 1970s have constituted 20 percent of the Democratic Party's electorate.[7] The size and geographic distribution (in the South and Midwest) of the vote within the Democratic Party means that the black vote routinely constitutes the balance of power in determining the party's presidential nominee. This was the case with the nominations of Jimmy Carter in 1976, Bill Clinton in 1992, Barack Obama in 2008, and Hillary Clinton in 2016.

However, since the 1970s and especially since the 1980s, the Democratic Party has taken the black vote for granted, just as the Republicans did a century ago. Knowing that it can count on nearly 90 percent of the black vote, the Democrats pocket it at the outset of the elections, while offering little in the way of policies to address the main concerns of blacks—joblessness and racialized poverty (see Chapter 14). Indeed, in order to compete for the votes of "Reagan Democrats" since the 1990s, the party under Clinton has moved steadily to the right on most issues of concern to blacks.[8] Meanwhile, the Republicans ignore the black vote altogether or, as in the case of President George W. Bush, engage in patronage and symbolism.

Nevertheless, at the beginning of the twenty-first century in the American party system, black identification with the Democrats is near universal. This is because black partisanship is based on "their perceptions of each Party's responsiveness to the needs and interests of the black community."[9] That is, individual black voters hold a group-based perception of the parties. In other words, racial identification determines Democratic partisanship.

It is in this context of the historic one-party system in the United States, and the emergence of blacks since the 1960s as the core Democratic voting bloc, that Barack Obama won the Democratic nomination in 2008. Beyond these broad historical considerations, the Obama nomination emerges out of two other circumstances. First, the efforts spearheaded by blacks to democratize the Democratic Party and universalize access to its nominating process. Second, Jesse Jackson's two campaigns for president helped to universalize access to the party and laid the foundations for the kind of rainbow coalition that Obama built on in his quest for the nomination.

The Democratization of the Democratic Party and the Role of African Americans

Donald Robinson writes, "ever since the founding a determination to democratize the selection of presidents gradually cast aside every impediment."[10] In the latter half of the twentieth century, African Americans played a major role in this democratization process. The African American role in the process began with the challenge by the Mississippi Freedom Democratic Party to the seating of the all-white Mississippi delegation at the 1964 convention (see Box 8.2). The 1964 challenge was "historically important," writes Walters, because "it ultimately set the stage for other challenges and, thus, some changes in the delegate allocation process."[11] At the 1968 Democratic Convention (where antiwar protesters were beaten by police outside the convention hall), Hubert Humphrey won the nomination although he had not competed in any of the primaries and was clearly not the popular choice of most Democrats. To avoid such a situation in the future, a commission was established to reform the nominating process. Headed by Senator George McGovern, among the commission's findings was that although blacks comprised more than 20 percent of Democratic voters, they were only 5.5 percent of delegates at the 1968 convention. To remedy this inequality, the commission required the states to take "affirmative measures to encourage the representation of minority groups, young people and women in a reasonable relationship to their presence in the population of the state."[12] The commission also required each state to establish delegate-selection procedures to "assure that voters in each state, regardless of race, color, creed or national origin will have meaningful and timely opportunities to participate fully in the election or selection of such delegates and alternates."[13]

The results of these reforms were to take the selection of delegates out of the hands of party leaders and place it in the hands of the people through primaries and caucuses. (In 1968, only 17 states used primaries or caucuses to select delegates.) In 1972, the party required all states to use some form of proportional allocation of delegates, instead of the winner-take-all approach, which was used by many states.

BOX 8.2

"No Two Seats"

In 1964, a poor sharecropper from Mississippi challenged Lyndon Johnson and the Democratic Party and helped to set in motion a process that fundamentally changed the relationship of the Democratic Party and African American voters.

Fannie Lou Hamer was born in rural Mississippi in 1917, the youngest of 20 children. She spent most of her life working as a sharecropper on a plantation; in 1962 her life was changed forever when she was inspired by a civil rights rally to attempt to register to vote. For this she was fired and ordered off the plantation. From this point until her death at the age of 59 in 1977, she was a major leader of the southern civil rights movement.

In 1964, Fannie Lou Hamer cofounded the Mississippi Freedom Democratic Party, an interracial party that challenged the white supremacist, all-white regular Mississippi Democratic Party. In 1964, the Mississippi Freedom Democratic Party (MFDP) challenged the seating of the all-white Mississippi delegation at the Democratic convention. Mrs. Hamer, the party's co-chair, in a dramatic, nationally televised testimony, recounted the atrocities committed against Mississippi blacks who tried to register and vote, including a vivid description of her own brutal beating in a Mississippi jail. Despite the eloquence of her testimony, the convention, under instructions from President Johnson, rejected the MFDP challenge, voted to seat the all-white delegation, and as a compromise offered the MFDP two honorary "at large" seats. The MFDP, despite the urgings of Martin Luther King Jr. and white liberal leaders such as Hubert Humphrey, rejected the compromise because, as Mrs. Hamer said, it represented "token rights" and "we didn't come all this way for no two seats." Later, she led a demonstration on the convention floor, protesting the compromise and singing freedom songs.

Fannie Lou Hamer, speaking at the 1968 Democratic National Convention on behalf of the Mississippi Freedom Democratic Party.

Source: Bettmann/Corbis

Although Mrs. Hamer and the MFDP did not succeed in 1964, they were seated at the 1968 convention, and it was their uncompromising position at the 1964 convention that helped to spark the reforms of 1972 that eventually opened the Democratic Party to full or universal participation by all Americans. In 1977 Fannie Lou Hamer died, poor and humble despite her fame and still uncompromising in the struggle for universal freedom.[a]

[a] See Mamie Locke, "Is This America? Fannie Lou Hamer and the Mississippi Freedom Democratic Party," in Vicki Crawford et al., eds., *Women in the Civil Rights Movement: Trailblazers and Torchbearers, 1941–1965* (Brooklyn, NY: Carlson Publishing, 1990): 27–37. See also Kay Mills, *This Little Light of Mine: The Life of Fannie Lou Hamer* (New York: Dutton, 1993).

New York Congresswoman Shirley Chisholm, the first African American to seek a major-party presidential nomination, appears on "Meet the Press" in 1972, with the other candidates George McGovern, Hubert Humphrey, Edmund Muskie, and Henry Jackson.

Source: Bettmann/Corbis

When Jesse Jackson ran for president in 1984, he won 18 percent of the vote but was allocated only 8 percent of the delegates. Jackson argued that this was undemocratic and pressed for changes in the rules.[14] As a result, the 1984 Convention appointed a "Fairness Commission," which revised the delegate allocation rules so that they would more closely reflect the wishes of the voters. Without these reforms in the nominating process, Obama could not have won the Democratic nomination.

In reaction to these democratizing reforms, party leaders attempted to place some limitations on the role of the people in choosing the nominee. This led in 1980 to the creation of "super delegates" (members of Congress, governors, and national and state party leaders)—delegates who could be seated at the convention without having run in the primaries and could vote for any candidate they wished.[15] In general, as Richard Herrera shows, super delegates are more likely to support establishment candidates than outsiders. In 1988, for example, Jackson got 20 percent of the primary vote but only 9.3 percent of the super delegates' votes, but Congressman Dick Gephardt, a congressional leader, received 5 percent of the primary vote but 19 percent of the super delegates' votes.[16]

In 2008, these super delegates accounted for 20 percent of the total. Senator Hillary Clinton, as the establishment candidate, expected these super delegates to be a "reliable firewall against the Obama insurgency."[17] This was one of several strategic miscalculations on her part, since in the end most super delegates ended up supporting Obama.

Race and the Polarization of American Politics

A principal theme of this text is that the presence of African Americans has pervasively influenced American political institutions and processes. The contemporary polarized state of American politics is yet another example of this influence.

It is generally agreed that the Democratic and Republican parties are more ideologically polarized today than at any time since the late nineteenth century. It is also generally agreed that after the civil rights movement the parties realigned and polarized ideologically on the basis of race, setting in motion a process that over time resulted in a return to the historic levels of polarization observed in the late nineteenth and early twentieth centuries. Although issues like abortion, prayer in school, and other social–moral issues played important roles in the transformation, as well as changes in the economy, communications, and lifestyles, it is clear that the proximate and most consequential cause of the transformation was the issue of race.[18] The most recent study is clear and unambiguous in its conclusion "Stated succinctly, the partisan and political transformation of the South over the past half century has, most centrally, revolved around the issue of race" and "the level of polarization in the American party system is inconceivable in the absence of disintegration of the Solid South and the partisan transformation of southern politics. . . . [In fact, the] southern political dynamic enabled the development of whatever ideological polarization exists in the modern party system."[19]

It is also generally conceded that polarization in the party system is asymmetrical, with the Republican Party being much more ideologically conservative than the Democratic Party is ideologically liberal. While both parties are more ideologically cohesive than in the 1950s and 1960s, it is fair to say the Republican Party has displaced nearly all of its previously moderate faction that acted as a buffer on the party's more extreme conservative faction.[20] The emergence and influence after the 2010 election of the Tea Party movement reinforced this conservative ideological homogeneity and hegemony.[21] The Democratic Party while dominantly liberal is more a broad center–left, middle-of-the-road coalition. For example, when Barack Obama was elected only 37 percent of Democrats identified as liberals, 39 percent were moderates, and 22 percent were conservative.[22] Meanwhile, the Republican Party was 77 percent conservative, 18 percent moderate, and only 6 percent liberal.[23] The result of this asymmetrical polarization is "The Republican Party has become an insurgent outlier—ideologically extreme; contemptuous of the inherited social and economic policy regime, scornful of compromise, unpersuaded by conventional understanding of facts; and dismissive of the legitimacy of its political opposition."[24]

In general, in a separation of powers, two-party system polarizations of the parties is a recipe for incoherence, inconsistency, irresponsibility, and gridlock in policy making, often with abrupt changes in policy as party control of government alternates. Historically, this situation is only changed when one of the parties utterly defeats the other and establishes a new governing majority coalition and consensus as the Republicans did in 1896 and the Democrats in 1932. In the *long run* demographic and ideological trends suggest the Democrats may be better positioned to achieve this new majority coalition and consensus.[25] However, we emphasize in the long run. In the meantime, with the parties evenly divided the U.S. in the short term will have only a semblance of a responsible and accountable government. Yet another example of how the presence of African Americans continues to profoundly shape American government and politics.

The Election of the First African American President

Barack Hussein Obama, Jr. was born in Hawaii in 1961. His father was from Kenya studying at the University of Hawaii where he met Obama's white American mother, Stanley Ann Dunham. Obama and Dunham were married in 1961 but shortly after Obama's birth his parents divorced. Because his mother was frequently away doing anthropological research, he was raised mainly by his white grandparents. Although raised in a white household, Obama in his coming of age memoir *Dreams From My Father: A Story of Race and Inheritance* tells us his mother and grandparents socialized him to be black, and as a young boy he identified with and embraced African American culture.[26]

After graduating from an exclusive prep school in Honolulu, Obama attended Columbia University and earned a degree in political science. After graduation and a brief visit to his father's ancestral village in Kenya, he moved to Chicago where for a year he worked as a community organizer in a low-income African American community. He then entered Harvard Law School, where he was graduated Magna Cum Laude and was the first African American elected president of the *Harvard Law Review*. After law school he returned to Chicago to start a political career. In 1997 he was elected to the Illinois state senate. Three years later in 2000 he challenged Bobby Rush, the eight-term congressman and former leader of the Black Panther Party. Although easily defeated by the popular Rush, Obama was undaunted and in 2004 he ran for the U.S. Senate. After he won the Democratic nomination for the Senate, Obama was immediately seen as a "rising star" in the Democratic Party. John Kerry, the 2004 Democratic presidential nominee, invited Obama to deliver the keynote address at the Democratic convention. The speech was a sensation, and immediately political commentators began to suggest that the young, charismatic, biracial senator might become the first black president. In 2006 after only two years in the Senate Obama announced that he would indeed seek the Democratic nomination for president.

The Jesse Jackson Campaigns: Implications for the Obama Campaign

Obama was not the first African American to run for the Democratic presidential nomination. In 1972 New York Congresswoman Shirley Chisholm ran a largely symbolic campaign for the nomination (see Faces and Voices in the Struggle for Universal Freedom at end of this chapter). Despite the nature of the campaign, the 151 delegate votes cast for her were the largest for an African American and a woman until Jesse Jackson in 1984 and Hillary Clinton in 2008.

In 1984 and 1988 civil rights leader Jesse Jackson ran for the Democratic nomination. Unlike Obama, Jackson did not expect to win the nomination or the presidency. Rather, the strategic purposes of his campaigns were to exercise "leverage" on the party and its nominee.[27] The leverage Jackson wished to exercise was to use the campaigns to slow or stop the conservative drift of the party, to inject progressive perspectives on policy into the campaign debates and party platform, to mobilize the black vote by increasing registration and turnout, to serve as the "balance of power" in determining the nominee, and to lay the groundwork for the mobilization of a multiethnic "rainbow coalition" that might in the future become an electoral majority in presidential politics.

Although Jackson achieved few of these objectives, as discussed earlier the changes in the delegate allocation rules that were a result of the Jackson campaigns were indispensable to Obama winning the nomination. (Jackson's 1,219 delegates—29 percent of the total—in 1988 were the largest for a black candidate until Obama in 2008.) Jackson's campaigns also established in their demography the kind of "rainbow" Obama would assemble in his winning minority–majority coalition. First, both candidates relied on the size and solidarity of the black community, each receiving 90 percent or more of the black vote. Second, their white support was drawn disproportionately from the young, well-educated, and high income rather than the elderly, less educated, poor or working class. Although the class and age bases of the Obama and Jackson coalitions were identical, Obama's white support was larger—large enough to allow him to win the nomination.

The Obama campaign was a genuine *phenomenon*, not in the technical sense that scientists use the word but rather as a rare, exceptional, unexpected occurrence. That an African American—any African American—could win a major party nomination for the presidency is phenomenal in itself. However, that an African American of immigrant African heritage with a foreign sounding name and less than four years' experience in national politics could be nominated is even more phenomenal. In winning the nomination, Obama, 46, defeated some of the leading Democratic politicians of the era, including Hillary Clinton, the 60-year-old former first lady and two-term U.S. senator.

The 2008 Primaries and Caucuses

Obama's presidential campaign, in the primaries and caucuses of 2008 and in the general elections of 2008 and 2012, established a more sophisticated organization than his opponents. The campaign employed teams of behavioral scientists and technicians to develop detailed databases of potential Obama voters, and it was the first presidential campaign to make extensive use of social media such as Facebook, Twitter, Flickr, and YouTube.

The campaign organization first demonstrated its sophistication in fundraising.[28] It relied on the Internet and small donors (less than $100) and advertisements on Yahoo, Google, and Microsoft search engines (more than half of the online donations of less than $100 came from 1.5 million donors, the highest in history for any presidential campaign). Overall, Obama raised $240 million compared to Clinton's $195 million. Although Obama relied disproportionately on small donors, like all presidential candidates he received major contributions from wealthy, corporate-connected individuals and Hollywood celebrities. Oprah Winfrey's endorsement of Obama and campaigning with him during the early caucuses and primaries may, however, have been worth more to the campaign than all the celebrity campaign contributions combined. As we indicated previously, her endorsement of Obama was estimated to be worth as much as a million votes (see Chapter 5).

The Obama campaign organization also deployed a more sophisticated political strategy[29] during the contest with Hillary Clinton (the organization was led almost entirely by whites). The Clinton strategy was based on winning the popular vote in the big states on "Super Tuesday" when 24 states voted on the same day. Obama, by contrast, focused on winning delegates in the small, largely white caucus states, while holding down her margin in the big states so that he would get a reasonable share of their delegates. The strategy worked. On Super Tuesday, Clinton won eight states (including all of the big ones except Illinois), but Obama won in the smaller, largely white states, winning 14 states to her 8 and 847 delegates to her 834. Thereafter, he went on to win 11 consecutive states, which gave him an insurmountable delegate lead.

Obama's strategy was also based in part on winning overwhelming support in African American congressional districts. The Democratic Party awards bonus delegates to districts with a history of strong support for the party, giving them in some cases twice as many delegates as less loyal or more Republican districts. Since African Americans are the party's strongest supporters, winning their districts gave him an advantage over Clinton in the states she won, like Ohio, Texas, California, and New York. Obama, thus, won the nomination —paradoxically—by winning in the "blackest" Democratic places and in the "whitest" most Republican places—states like Alaska, Utah, Wyoming, and Nebraska.

Obama, unlike Jesse Jackson, ran a campaign based on the strategy or theory of "Deracialization."[30] The fundamentals of the theory require black candidates running for high office in majority white constituencies (governor, U.S. senator, president) to avoid references to issues of concern to blacks such as affirmative action or antipoverty policies. Instead, a deracialized campaign focuses on issues important to the white middle class, such as tax cuts, health care, and education. It also requires the candidate to project a "nonthreatening" image; for example, he or she should avoid association with black leaders such as Jesse Jackson and Al Sharpton. In other words, a black candidate should avoid any association with "blackness."

With respect to issues and ideology in general, in 2008 all the Democratic candidates were liberals, and there was widespread agreement among them on the issues of taxes, health care, education, immigration, the environment and the Iraq war. Of the major candidates, however, Obama was the only one to oppose the Iraq war from the beginning. During the campaign debates, he used his early opposition to the war to make the case that while he did not have the long Washington experience of Clinton and his other opponents, his opposition to the war showed he had better judgment. (By the time of the election more than 80 percent of Democratic voters opposed the Iraq war.)

On issues of specific concern to blacks, there were little differences between Clinton and the deracialized Obama. In early 2008, the NAACP submitted 37 questions to Clinton and Obama, asking them their position on issues ranging from affirmative action to reparations. The Obama and Clinton positions were almost identical (both opposed reparations). On welfare, Obama indicated he supported the legislation signed by President Clinton in 1996 (which ended the federal guarantee of assistance to poor women and their children), although he and virtually the entire black leadership had opposed it at the time. On the death penalty Obama also flip-flopped. When he ran for the state Senate in 1996, he opposed the death penalty, but in his 2004 U.S. Senate campaign he said he accepted it for "the most heinous crimes." On affirmative action, he implied that it should be a class- rather than race-based program, saying he did not think his daughters should be eligible, because of their class, for affirmative action in university admissions.

Since there were no ideological differences between Clinton and Obama, the campaign came down to style or symbolism. Obama emphasized change—"change we can believe in." Clinton emphasized experience—that she would be ready to be president "on day one." The media coverage and the opinions of voters matched these symbolic differences between the candidates.

Obama won a bare 50.5 percent of the Democratic primary vote, and 2,158.5 delegates to Clinton's 1,920. He won majority support among only two demographic categories, African Americans, where he had a 67-point advantage over Clinton, and among young whites (ages 18–29) where he had a 9-point advantage. Clinton won among white men and women—particularly those who were without a college education, low income, and over 65—and Latinos. Both Obama and Clinton received roughly the same proportion of the white college-educated and upper income vote. Obama narrowly won the Jewish vote, but Clinton defeated Obama by a margin of two-to-one among Asian Americans, and she won the gay and lesbian vote 60 to 25 percent.

Race and Gender: The Challenge to Identities and Loyalties

As we indicated in Chapter 6, the African American and mainstream women's freedom movements have existed in tentative, unstable coalitions for universal freedom. So, it was perhaps inevitable that tensions would emerge when the first woman with a realistic chance of winning the presidency would compete with the first African American, a man, with a chance to win. Some white feminist leaders, including the feminist icon Gloria Steinem and Geraldine Ferraro, the first female vice presidential nominee, claimed Obama was clearly less qualified than Clinton and that he was able to thwart the dream of the first woman president because of sexism.[31]

The Democratic electorate was divided, with a huge race–gender chasm in voting. African American women, as we discussed in Chapter 4, tend to prioritize race over gender because race is considered more salient for collective action to achieve universal freedom. Thus, from the earliest voting in the Iowa caucuses, there was no gender gap in black voting behavior. Black women were as likely to vote for Obama as black men; indeed black women had the highest level of turnout and support for Obama. There were, however, significant gender gaps in the white electorate: Among white men, there was only a modest 3-point gap in voting, with Clinton on 48 percent and Obama 45 percent. But among white women, the gap was 24; with 60 to 34 percent in favor of Clinton. The gap was especially pronounced among older white women, who overwhelmingly supported Clinton. Clinton's core constituency was white women, who comprised 37 percent of the primary electorate and nearly half of her total vote. Obama's core constituency of African Americans constituted 19 percent of the electorate and provided him more than a third of his vote. Put another way Clinton won the votes of almost 3 million more white women than Obama, but he won 4 million more black votes than she.

Initially, the Obama campaign divided the African American community. For example, African Americans were extraordinarily supportive of Bill Clinton, although on race he governed "In the Shadow of Ronald Reagan" with conservative policies on crime, welfare, and to an extent affirmative action[32] (see Chapter 11). In the earliest stages of the 2008 election, support for President Clinton translated into support for his wife. A late November 2007 poll, for example, found that her favorability rating among blacks (83 percent) was higher than Obama's (75 percent). Early preference polls showed her leading Obama by as much as 30 points. However, after Obama defeated Clinton in near all white Iowa—demonstrating that he could possibly defeat her and perhaps become the first black president—virtually the entire black community rallied around him.

A few blacks expressed sentiments that he was not "black" or, at least, not black enough, because of his mixed race heritage and the fact that he was raised by his white grandparents. But this was mainly chatter in the media, because there is little evidence this was ever a major concern of the black mass public. In a fall 2008 poll, 70 percent of blacks said there was a "black experience in America" and 83 percent said Obama was "in touch with it."[33] Earlier in a 2006 poll, when respondents were told about the ethnic background of Obama's parents and asked to identify his ethnicity, two-thirds of blacks labeled him black, while more than three-quarters of whites, Latinos, and Asians identified him as multiracial.[34]

Ultimately, the idea of Obama—a talented, handsome, and charismatic young black man—becoming president captivated almost the entire black community. After hundreds of years of slavery, lynching, and Jim Crow segregation, Obama's candidacy came to embody Dr. King's dream. As Valerie Grimm, chair of Indiana University's African American Studies Department said:

> I have parents who are still living who are very enthusiastic about Obama. They live in Mississippi. For a time my parents couldn't vote, and when they could vote, their only choice was a white person. This means more than just seeing a black person on the ticket. It represents things they had been denied. It is being able to see the unbelievable, that the impossible might be possible. It represents for them a new day.[35]

The 2008 and 2012 General Elections

Once Obama won the Democratic nomination in 2008, he knew the only thing that could defeat him in the general election was his race. And it almost did. Most presidential elections are "retrospective"; that is, they are referendums on the past four years.[36] This made for an ideal strategic environment for Obama or any Democratic nominee in 2008. Throughout the year the "generic" ballot (which asks voters which party they would like to see win the presidency) showed a double-digit Democratic lead. As the general election approached 90 percent of the electorate thought the country was headed in the wrong direction; the nation faced rising gasoline prices, a collapse of the housing market, a massive budget deficit, rising unemployment, an unpopular war, and an incumbent president whose popularity was in the low 30s. A month before the election the stock market dramatically declined and the credit markets collapsed, requiring a $700 billion bailout from the federal treasury. Newspaper headlines and television newscasts raised the specter of another Great Depression. Under these circumstances it hardly mattered who the Republicans or Democrats nominated; the Republican was going to lose.

Neither race or racism were nonfactors in the 2008 election but compared to prior post–civil rights era presidential elections (1968–2000),[37] appeals based on race and racism were rare and inconsequential. Senator John McCain, the Republican nominee, was encouraged by his vice presidential running mate Alaska governor Sarah Palin and others to use the controversial remarks of Obama's then pastor, Rev. Jeremiah Wright, Jr., to exploit racial fears and anxieties but he declined to do so.

Obama joined Wright's Afro-Centric church as part of his quest to reinforce his blackness. He was aware that Wright—whom *Ebony* magazine named in 1998 as one of the 15 leading black preachers in America—adhered to black liberation theology, which holds that God is committed to the liberation of his most oppressed peoples—Africans—and it requires preachers to be unapologetically committed to blackness and militant opposition to racism and white supremacy. Thus, among the black churches of Chicago, Wright's church—Trinity United Methodist—was unique, when compared to traditional black Baptist and Methodist congregations.

Rev. Wright also preached jeremiads, prophetic, sometimes apocalyptic, and always passionate outcries against racial injustices. Excerpts from one of Wright's jeremiads was broadcast in the midst of the Democratic primaries, which Obama's aides described as "the greatest threat to Obama's candidacy" that put the campaign in a "desperate fight for survival."[38] In the excerpts, Wright suggested the 9/11 attacks on the United States were God's punishment for the injustices of U.S. foreign policy and that the government purposely created AIDS to harm blacks. "America's chickens are coming home to roost" he preached and "The government gives them [African Americans] drugs, builds bigger prisons, passes a three strike law and then wants us to sing 'God Bless America'. No, no, no, God Damn America."[39]

Because of the controversy about Wright's remarks, Obama decided to give the only speech of the campaign devoted specifically to race. Titled "A More Perfect Union," the speech was delivered at Philadelphia's Constitution Hall. The speech was well received by the public and the press, with the *New York Times* comparing it to inaugural addresses by Abraham Lincoln and Franklin Roosevelt and John Kennedy's 1960 speech on religion.[40]

The speech quieted the controversy about Wright (Obama and his wife subsequently resigned from Wright's church), but Sarah Palin and some McCain advisors urged McCain to make television ads exploiting the relationship between Wright and Obama. Although McCain declined to do so, his campaign did attempt to portray Obama as a radical because of his association with Bill Ayres, the University of Illinois professor and former Weatherman—commonly known as the Weather Underground, a 1960s radical left-wing organization. Although Obama's association was longer and more substantive with Wright than his association with Ayres, the campaign nevertheless focused on Ayres, with Palin frequently accusing Obama of "palling around with terrorists." The

Associated Press and other news outlets suggested that this was a subtle appeal to racism. Palin's comments, the wire service wrote, were "tinged with racism," were "incendiary," and "whether intended or not . . . portraying Obama as 'not like us' is another potential appeal to racism. . . . Palin's words avoid repulsing voters with overt racism. But there is a subtext for creating the false image of a black presidential nominee 'palling [*sic*] around' with terrorists while assuring a predominantly white audience that he doesn't see their America."[41] The McCain campaign also attempted to "otherize" Obama by suggesting that he was a socialist, and parts of the conservative media suggested that he was a Muslim who might be associated with terrorists.[42]

Obama won the election 53 to 46 percent, winning 65 million votes to McCain's 57 million and 28 states and the District of Columbia with 364 electoral votes to McCain's 163. However, multiple political scientists suggest that if Obama had not been black he would have won in a landslide with at least 55 percent of the vote.[43] Alan Abramowitz explains the "race deficit" or the effects of "Ballot Box Racism": "Obama's twelve point deficit among white voters was identical to Gore's in 2000. However, the fact that white voters favored the Republican candidate by a double-digit margin in 2008 despite the poor conditions of the economy and the unpopularity of the incumbent Republican president suggests racial prejudice did affect the level of white support for the Democratic candidate."[44] Among whites Obama lost by 12 points, winning only 43 percent although he won a majority among young whites (ages 18–29) of 53 percent. In addition, he won among Jews (86 percent), Latinos (67 percent), and Asian Americans (66 percent).

Obama also won 94 percent of the black vote. However, it was not his margin of victory among blacks that was crucial (since 1964 Democratic presidential nominees have averaged about 88 percent of the black vote), it was the turnout. While the number of non-Hispanic white voters remained the same as in 2004, in 2008 2 million more blacks turned out, nearly equaling (at 65 percent) for the first time ever the white turnout of 66 percent. Obama's campaign mobilized its black base in other ways as well, with black participation greater than whites with respect to volunteering (14 to 7 percent) and campaign contributions (31 to 21 percent).[45] Smith refers to this mobilization of the black vote as "ballot-box blackness," writing "This relatively high turnout and participation of blacks suggest that Obama was successful because he was black; that is, among whites Obama suffered a race deficit because of ballot-box racism, but among blacks because of racial consciousness and solidarity, he benefited from ballot-box blackness."[46] In other words "Obama's race elected him and it almost defeated him."[47]

The 2012 election was not strategically conducive to Obama's reelection. The recovery from the recession of 2007–2009 was the weakest since the Great Depression, with the unemployment rate at 8 percent it was the highest ever recorded this long after a recession. GDP (gross domestic product) growth during

Obama's first term averaged 1.6 percent, the worst for any postwar recovery. Adjusted for inflation real wages grew by only 0.8 percent, also the worst for any postwar recovery.[48] Finally, unlike in 2008 when the Obama campaign had an enormous financial advantage over McCain (spending more than $750,000 compared to McCain's $350,000), in 2012 the Republican and Democratic campaigns were evenly matched (each with about $900 million), and if expenditures by outside, private groups are included, the Republicans outspent the Democrats.

In this dismal strategic environment the Obama campaign's main strategy was to make his opponent, Mitt Romney, the multimillionaire businessman, the issue. The campaign did this by portraying Romney as a "vulture capitalist," a rich, tax-avoiding, job exporting businessman who did not care about ordinary people, and who destroyed jobs in America and outsourced them to China. Romney seemingly added credibility to the idea that he did not care about ordinary voters when he was videotaped telling a group of wealthy donors that Obama supporters were the "47 percent of the population which did not pay taxes and believed the government should take care of them."[49] In other related campaign gaffes, Romney remarked that he "liked to fire people" and that "corporations were people."

The Obama strategy of demonizing his opponent apparently worked. Exit polls identified four qualities that voters said were important in a president—sharing respondents' values, strong leadership, and a vision for the future and "cares about people like me." Of the four, Obama was viewed favorably on only one, but in 2012 perhaps the most important one, whether the candidate cares "about people like me." From this group—21 percent of the electorate—Obama won an overwhelming 81 percent of the vote. For the 74 percent in the other three categories Romney averaged 57 percent.[50]

Like 2008, race was not an issue in 2012; however it is estimated Obama suffered a net loss of 3 percentage points because he was black.[51] He won by the narrowest of margins 51.1 percent, winning 26 states and the District of Columbia, and 332 electoral votes to Romney's 206. Obama won majorities among mostly racial and ethnic groups (93 percent of blacks, 71 percent Latinos, and 73 percent Asian Americans), while losing among the white majority, including—and unlike in 2008—the white youth vote by a margin of 44 to 51 percent. Also, he won a majority of the Jewish vote, although it was down from 86 percent in 2008 to 78 percent in 2012. Overall, Obama's 2012 minority–majority coalition was constituted by 80 percent of mostly racial and ethnic groups and 39 percent by whites, with the former groups constituting 26 percent of the electorate in 2012, up from 25 percent in 2008. (In 2012 for the first time ever black turnout exceeded the turnout of whites, 66 to 64 percent.)

The expansion of support for Obama among Latinos, and especially Asian Americans may be significant for the future prospects of a progressive rainbow coalition, since these multiethnic cohorts are the fastest growing segments of the electorate while the white majority is declining. Again, this is especially important in the case of Asian Americans, since this group—particularly Japanese and Asian Indians—tends to be wealthier and better educated than blacks and Latinos and historically has tended to lean Republican (as late as 1992 Bill Clinton received only 31 percent of the Asian American vote). If the 2012 vote is an indicator, this part of the rainbow is not only growing but may be trending in a left–liberal Democratic direction.

The election of the first African American to the presidency was a historical watershed in a country founded on principles of racism, white supremacy, and the enslavement and subordination of Africans. However, it perhaps should be emphasized that Obama's winning coalition in both elections was a *minority–majority* coalition, and his average white vote in both elections was well below 50 percent. Put another way, if the white majority had its way in 2008 and 2012 Obama would not have become the nation's first black president.

Faces and Voices in the Struggle for Universal Freedom
SHIRLEY CHISHOLM (1924–2005)

"I ran because somebody had to be first," said Shirley Chisholm of her 1972 campaign for the Democratic Party presidential nomination. Chisholm went on to write in her memoir of the campaign, "The next time a woman of whatever color, or a dark-skinned person of whatever sex aspires to be President, the way should be a little smoother because I helped to pave it."[a] Chisholm, the first African American woman elected to Congress, in the 1960s and 1970s, became a

Congresswoman Shirley Chisholm (D, NY).

Source: Photo retrieved 4 October 2016 from www.marketsmithinc.com/wp-content/uploads/2013/02/Chisholm.gif

national symbol of black, feminist, and liberal politics, and her 1972 campaign for the presidency helped prepare the groundwork for the historic 2008 campaigns for the Democratic nomination by Hillary Clinton and Barack Obama.

Shirley St. Hill (she married Conrad Chisholm in 1949) was born in Brooklyn, New York, in 1924 to Caribbean immigrants. As a child, she often accompanied her father, a follower of Marcus Garvey, to black nationalist rallies. After graduating from Brooklyn College and earning a Master's from Columbia, she became a teacher and activist in Democratic Party politics in the Bedford-Stuyvesant section of Brooklyn. Although Bedford Stuyvesant was more than two-thirds black, in the 1960s it was dominated politically by the white-controlled Democratic Party Machine. Chisholm and her fellow activists in the Bedford Stuyvesant Political League ousted the Machine, and in 1964 Chisholm was elected to the New York state assembly. In 1968, she was elected to the U.S. House of Representatives. Running under the slogan "unbought and unbossed," she challenged the Brooklyn establishment with a coalition of blacks, Latinos, and women. In Congress, she continued her maverick style, challenging the seniority system as "rule by a small group of old men."[b] She was an outspoken opponent of the Vietnam War, and a passionate advocate for children, racial and gender equality, and abortion rights.

Chisholm's 1972 presidential campaign was opposed by the largely male black political establishment. An early feminist, she said, "I've always faced more discrimination being a woman than being black. . . . Men are men."[c] Although the Chisholm campaign was largely symbolic, the 151 delegate votes cast for her at the convention were the largest for an African American and a woman until Jesse Jackson in 1984 and Hillary Clinton in 2008.

In addition to her pioneering roles in congressional and presidential elections, Chisholm was a founder of the Congressional Black Caucus and the National Congress of Black Women. In 1982, at the peak of her power (she was then the only woman and African American among the House Democratic Party leadership), Chisholm retired from Congress. Subsequently, she taught women's studies at Mount Holyoke and Spellman Colleges. In 1984 and 1988, she campaigned for Jesse Jackson. She was inducted into the National Women's Hall of Fame in 1991. In 2015, Chisholm was posthumously awarded the Presidential Medal of Freedom by President Obama. In addition to the memoir of the 1972 campaign, Chisholm also authored *Unbought and Unbossed*.[d]

[a] Shirley Chisholm, *The Good Fight* (New York: Harper & Row, 1973): 161–62.
[b] James Barron, "Shirley Chisholm, 'Unbossed' Pioneer in Congress, is Dead," *New York Times*, January 3, 2005.
[c] Ibid.
[d] PBS televised a documentary of Chisholm's 1972 campaign "Unbought and Unbossed," 2004. See also Hanes Walton, Jr. "Black Female Presidential Candidates," in Walton (ed.) *Black Politics and Black Political Behavior: A Linkage Analysis* (Westport, CT: Praeger, 1994); and Susan Brownmiller, *Shirley Chisholm: A Biography* (New York: Doubleday, 1970).

Summary

For most of their history, African Americans have had to deal with a no-party system or a one-party system. Until the Civil War–Reconstruction era, blacks confronted a no-party system since they were excluded from both major parties. Since Reconstruction, except for the brief period from 1936 to 1968, blacks have confronted a one-party system, with one party ignoring the black vote and the other taking it for granted. Since the 1960s, blacks have been the most loyal and reliable voters in the Democratic Party coalition, but since the 1970s, the Democrats have been reluctant to embrace black concerns, especially their material-based interests. In order to leverage their influence in the Democratic Party, blacks have sought the party's presidential nomination. None, however, came close until Barack Obama in 2008. What impact the nomination of the deracialized Obama will have on the party system and the capabilities of African Americans to use it in their continuing struggle for universal freedom cannot now be known. One thing is clear, however: It is likely for the foreseeable future that blacks will reinforce their attachment to the Democratic Party, thus reinforcing the one-party system.

Critical Thinking Questions

1. Explain why for most of African American history the U.S. party system has been a one-party system.
2. Explain the concept of the black vote as the balance of power in presidential elections.
3. Discuss the role of the Mississippi Freedom Democratic Party (MFDP) and its challenge to the all-white Mississippi delegation at the 1964 convention. How did their efforts advance universal freedom for African Americans and political party participation?
4. Describe the presidential campaign coalitions of Jesse Jackson and Barack Obama. Are there significant similarities or differences? Explain using examples.
5. Explain the concept of deracialization as the campaign strategy of African Americans running for office in majority white places. What is the implication for universal freedom?

Selected Bibliography

Abramowitz, Alan. *The Disappearing Center: Engaged Citizens, Polarization and American Democracy.* New Haven, CT: Yale University Press, 2010. An important study focusing on the role of race, and the mass base of the polarization of the party system.

Baer, Kenneth. *Reinventing the Democrats: The Politics of Liberalism from Reagan to Clinton.* Lawrence: University of Kansas Press, 2000. A study of how and why the Democratic Party moved in a more conservative direction.

Chisholm, Shirley. *The Good Fight.* New York: Harper & Row, 1973. A memoir of her run for the presidency in 1972.

Clayton, Dewey M. *The Presidential Campaign of Barack Obama: A Critical Analysis of a Racially Transcendent Strategy.* New York: Routledge, 2010. This text is a comprehensive analysis of the 2008 Barack Obama presidential campaign and unique, innovative organizational strategies used to win office.

Eldersveld, Samuel, and Hanes Walton, Jr. *Political Parties in American Society.* Boston, MA: Bedford/St. Martin's Press, 2000. A comprehensive assessment of the status of the American party system.

Frady, Marshall. *Jesse: The Life and Pilgrimage of Jesse Jackson.* New York: Random House, 1996. A comprehensive, full-length biography of the civil rights leader and presidential candidate.

Frymer, Paul. *Uneasy Alliances: Race and Party Competition in America.* Princeton, NJ: Princeton University Press, 1999. A study of the two-party system and how it operates to create a one-party system for blacks.

Gillespie, Andra, ed. *Whose Black Politics?: Cases in Post–Racial Black Leadership.* New York: Routledge, 2010. A series of papers examining the new generation of black leadership from which Obama emerges.

Henry, Charles. *Jesse Jackson: The Search for Common Ground.* Oakland, CA: Black Scholar Press, 1991. A brief, readable account of the Jackson campaigns.

Henry, Charles, and Robert Allen, eds. *The Obama Phenomena: Toward A Multiracial Democracy.* Urbana: University of Illinois Press, 2011. A group of eminent African American political scientists interpret Obama's election.

Ladd, Everett C., and Charles Hadley. *Transformation of the American Party System: Political Coalitions from the New Deal to the 1970s.* New York: Norton, 1975. An analysis of the decline of the New Deal coalition.

Lawson, Kay, ed. *Political Parties and Linkage.* New Haven, CT: Yale University Press, 1980. A collection of papers examining the decline of political parties as the linkage between citizens and government.

Marable, Manning, and Kristen Clarke, eds. *Barack Obama and African American Empowerment.* New York: Palgrave Macmillan, 2010. Another group of distinguished black scholars assess the Obama campaign.

Mills, Kay. *This Little Light of Mine: The Life of Fannie Lou Hamer.* New York: Dutton, 1993. A biography of the famous Mississippi freedom fighter.

Morris, Lorenzo. "Race and the Rise and Fall of the Two Party Systems." In L. Morris, ed., *The Social and Political Implications of the 1984 Jesse Jackson Campaign.* New York: Praeger, 1990. An important article analyzing the functional limitations of the two-party system in terms of black voter choice.

Obama, Barack. *Dreams from My Father.* New York: Crown, 1995. A memoir of his journey to adulthood and his search for community.

Obama, Barack. *The Audacity of Hope.* New York: Crown, 2006. A campaign manifesto.

Rigueur, Leah Wright. *The Loneliness of the Black Republican: Pragmatic Politics and the Pursuit of Power.* Princeton, NJ: Princeton University Press, 2014. A study of the often "lonely" struggle of blacks for acceptance and inclusion in the Republican Party, focusing on the period since the Goldwater nomination in 1964.

Walter, John C. *The Harlem Fox: J. Raymond Jones and Tammany Hall.* Albany, NY: SUNY Press, 1989. A memoir of the first African American head of Tammany Hall, the New York City Democratic Party organization.

Walters, Ronald. *Black Presidential Politics in America: A Strategic Approach.* Albany, NY: SUNY Press, 1988. An influential study of the strategic use of the black vote in presidential elections.

Walton, Hanes, Jr. *Black Political Parties: A Historical and Political Analysis.* New York: Free Press, 1972. A comprehensive analysis of African American political parties.

Walton, Hanes, Jr. "Democrats and African Americans: The American Idea." In P. Kover, ed., *Democrats and the American Idea.* Washington, DC: Center for National Policy Press, 1992. A brief history of African Americans in the Democratic Party.

Weiss, Nancy. *Farewell to the Party of Lincoln: Black Politics in the Age of FDR.* Princeton, NJ: Princeton University Press, 1983. A historical account of the shift of blacks from the Republican to the Democratic Party.

Wilson, John. *Barack Obama: This Improbable Quest.* New York: Paradigm, 2008. An examination of Obama's candidacy from liberal and conservative perspectives.

Notes

1 Leon Epstein, "The Scholarly Commitment to Parties," in A. Finifter, ed., *The State of the Discipline* (Washington, DC: American Political Science Association, 1983): 129.

2 Paul Frymer, *Uneasy Alliances: Race and Party Competition in America* (Princeton, NJ: Princeton University Press, 1999).

3 Hanes Walton, Jr., *The Negro in Third Party Politics* (Philadelphia, PA: Dorrance, 1969).

4 This section draws on Robert C. Smith and Richard Seltzer, "The Deck and the Sea: The African American Vote in the Presidential Elections of 2000 and 2004," *National Political Science Review* 22 (2008): 263–70.

5 Patricia Gurin, Shirley Hatchett, and James Jackson, *Hope and Independence: Black Response to Electoral and Party Politics* (New York: Russell Sage, 1991): 64.

6 Henry Lee Moon, *Balance of Power: The Negro Vote* (Garden City, NY: Doubleday, 1948): 198.

7 Robert Axelrod, "Where the Votes Come From: An Analysis of Electoral Coalitions," *American Political Science Review* 66 (1972): 11–20; and his "Communications," *American Political Science Review* 76 (1982): 393–96.

8 Kenneth Baer, *Reinventing the Democrats: The Politics of Liberalism from Reagan to Clinton* (Lawrence: University Press of Kansas, 2000); and Robert C. Smith, "In the Shadow of Ronald Reagan: Civil Rights Policy Making in the Clinton Administration," in Kenneth Osgood and Derrick White, eds., *Winning While Losing: Civil Rights, the Conservative Movement and the Presidency from Nixon to Obama* (Gainesville: University Press of Florida, 2014).

9 Michael Dawson, *Behind the Mule: Race, Class and African American Politics* (Princeton, NJ: Princeton University Press, 1994): 112. See also Katherine Tate, *From Protest to Politics: The New Black Vote in American Elections* (Cambridge, MA: Harvard University Press, 1994).

10 Donald Robinson, *To the Best of My Ability: The Presidency and the Constitution* (New York: Norton, 1987): 173.

11 Ronald Walters, *Black Presidential Politics: A Strategic Approach* (Albany, NY: SUNY Press, 1988): 53.

12 Quoted in ibid., p. 55.

13 Ibid.

14 E. J. Dionne, "Jackson Says Delegate Rules Have Been Unfair," *New York Times,* May 5, 1988.

15 Samuel Eldersveld and Hanes Walton, *Political Parties in American Society,* 2nd ed. (New York: Bedford/St. Martin's Press, 2000): 215, 216.

16 Richard Herrera, "Are Super Delegates Super," *Political Behavior* 16 (1994): 79–92.

17 Katherine Seelye, "For Clinton, a Key Group Didn't Hold," *New York Times*, June 5, 2008.

18 The seminal study of the impact of race on the transformation of the modern party system is Edward Carmines and James Stimson, *Issue Evolution: Race and the Transformation of the Party System* (Princeton, NJ: Princeton University Press, 1989). See also Joel Olson, "Whiteness and the Polarization of American Politics," *Political Research Quarterly* 61 (2009): 704–18.

19 M. V. Hood, III, Quentin Kidd, and Irwin Morris, *The Rational Southerner: Black Mobilization, Republican Growth and the Partisan Transformation of the South* (New York: Oxford, 2012): 180, 187.

20 Nies Gilmon, "What the Rise of the Republicans as America's First Ideological Party Means to Democrats," *The Forum* 2 (2004).

21 Alan Abromowitz, "Partisan Polarization and the Rise of the Tea Party Movement." Paper prepared for presentation at the annual meeting of the American Political Science Association, September 1–4, 2011, Seattle.

22 Robert C. Smith and Richard Seltzer, *Polarization and the Presidency: From FDR to Barack Obama* (Boulder, CO: Lynne Rienner, 2015): 247.

23 Ibid., p. 135.

24 Thomas Mann and Norman Ornstein, *It's Even Worse than It Looks: How the American Constitutional System Collided with the New Politics of Extremism* (New York: Basic Books, 2012): xiv.

25 Alan Abramowitz, *The Disappearing Center: Engaged Citizens, Polarization and American Democracy* (New Haven, CT: Yale University Press, 2010): 163–78. See also Smith and Seltzer, *Polarization and the Presidency*, pp. 284–85.

26 Barack Obama, *Dreams from My Fathers: A Story of Race and Inheritance* (New York: Crown, 1995): 46–47, 80–81.

27 Ronald Walters, *Black Presidential Politics in America: A Strategic Approach*, chap. 5. For a comparison of the 1984 and 1988 Jackson campaigns and the 2004 campaigns of Al Sharpton and Carol Mosley Braun with the 2008 Obama campaign see Katherine Tate, "Black Power and Presidential Bids from Jackson to Obama," *National Political Science Review* 13 (2012): 3–22.

28 Dewey M. Clayton, *The Presidential Campaign of Barack Obama: A Critical Analysis of a Racially Ascendant Strategy* (New York: Routledge, 2010): 136–51. See this work for a review of the pioneering and innovative technology and media used by the campaign.

29 Ibid., pp. 57–63.

30 Joseph McCormick and Charles Jones, "The Conceptualization of Deracialization," in Georgia Persons, ed., *Dilemmas of Black Politics* (New York: Harpers/Collins, 1973). See also Clayton, *The Presidential Campaign of Barack Obama*, pp. 42–45.

31 Gloria Steinem, "Women Are Never Front-Runners," *New York Times*, January 8, 2008; and Geraldine Ferraro, "Healing the Wounds of Democratic Sexism," *Boston Globe*, May 30, 2008.

32 Robert C. Smith, "Civil Rights Policymaking in the Clinton Administration: In Reagan's Shadow," in Kenneth Osgood and Derrick White, eds., *Winning While Losing: Civil Rights, the Conservative Movement and the Presidency from Nixon to Obama* (Gainesville: University Press of Florida, 2014).

33 Frederick Harris, *Survey of Race, Politics and Society* (New York: Columbia University, Center on African American Studies, 2008): 9.

34 Cited in G. Reginald Daniel, "Race, Multiculturalism and Barack Obama: Toward a More Perfect Union," *Black Scholar* 39 (2009): 51–59.

35 Darryl Fears, "Black Community Is Increasingly Protective of Obama," *Washington Post*, May 10, 2008.

36 Morris Fiorina, *Retrospective Voting in National Election* (New Haven, CT: Yale University Press, 1981).

37 On racism in post–civil rights era elections see Tali Mendelberg, *The Race Card: Campaign Strategies, Implicit Messages and the Norm of Equality* (Princeton, NJ: Princeton University Press, 2001).

38 Quoted in Robert C. Smith, *John F. Kennedy, Barack Obama and the Politics of Ethnic Incorporation and Avoidance* (Albany, NY: SUNY Press, 2013): 153.

39 "Preacher with a Penchant for Controversy," *Washington Post*, March 15, 2008.

40 "Mr. Obama's Profile in Courage," *New York Times*, March 9, 2008.

41 Douglass Daniel, "Analysis: Palin's Words Carry Racial Tinge," *West County Times*, October 5, 2008.

42 Nickolas Kristoff, "The Push to Otherize Obama," *New York Times*, September 21, 2008.

43 Michael Lewis-Beck, Charles Tien, and Richard Nadeau, "Obama's Missing Landslide: A Racial Cost?" paper prepared for presentation at the annual meeting of the Southern Political Science Association, February 7–11, 2009, New Orleans; Spencer Piston "How Explicit Racial Prejudice Hurt Obama in the 2008 Election," *Political Behavior* 32 (2010): 431–51; and Walter Hill, "Should Obama Have Won in a Landslide in 2008 as Did Roosevelt in 1936?" paper prepared for presentation at the 2011 annual meeting of the Midwest Political Science Association, March 31–April 2, Chicago.

44 Alan Abramowitz, *The Disappearing Center: Engaged Citizens, Polarization and American Democracy* (New Haven, CT: Yale University Press, 2010): 115.

45 Harris, *Survey on Race, Politics and Society*, p. 11.

46 Smith, *John F. Kennedy and Barack Obama*, p. 163.

47 Ibid.

48 Paul Wiseman, "Economic Recovery?: The Numbers Don't Say So," *West County Times*, May 16, 2012.

49 Mitt Romney, "47 Percent" comments, www.youtube.com/water?r=m2gry2wqi7m.

50 Exit Poll, 2012 Election, CNN.

51 Charles Tien, Richard Nadeeau, and Michael Lewis-Beck, "Obama and 2012: Still A Racial Cost to Pay," *PS: Political Science and Politics* 45 (2012): 591–95.

CHAPTER 9

Voting Behavior and Elections

LEARNING OBJECTIVE

Identify trends in racial or ethnic groups' voting behavior and participation in elections.

In 1984, during his campaign for the presidency, Jesse Jackson would frequently tell black audiences, "Hands that picked cotton can now pick presidents." To understand the significance of the black vote in American politics and presidential elections, we must place the phenomenon in its historical and systemic contexts.

The Historical and Systemic Dimensions of African American Voting Behavior

The first presidential election in American history in which virtually all African Americans could vote was 1968, three years after passage of the Voting Rights Act in 1965.

Between the Constitutional Convention of 1787 and the end of the Civil War in 1865, only six states permitted the "Free" Negroes to vote; enslaved persons, of course, could not vote in any state. The Revolutionary War, with all its discussion of freedom, did not change the nonvoting status of African Americans. In fact, between the Revolutionary and Civil Wars, Tennessee in 1834, North Carolina in 1835, and Pennsylvania in 1838, all withdrew the right to vote from "Free Negroes."

New York, on the other hand, did not deny the right; rather, it restricted voting by requiring that "Free Negroes" show ownership of property valued at

$200. When this rule went into effect, the number of voters dropped. New York subsequently held three statewide suffrage referenda in which the state's white voters were asked to decide whether to give "Free Negroes" full, universal voting rights. The first referendum was held in 1846, the second in 1860, and the third in 1869. All three were voted down by the state electorate.[1]

However, if the northern and Midwestern states opposed a simple aspect of universal freedom such as voting rights prior to the Civil War and thereafter, the South would become the central opponent after the Civil War until the present day. Beginning with the Compromise of 1877, which the South brought about through the fraud, corruption, and violence of the 1876 election, African Americans' newly won voting rights were once again restricted and curtailed, the Fifteenth Amendment notwithstanding. The South's drive to eliminate African Americans from the ballot box culminated in the "era of disenfranchisement" (1890–1901), when all 11 of the states of the Old Confederacy adopted new state constitutions that prevented, prohibited, or manipulated African Americans out of their voting rights. Because of a series of inventive, innovative, and amazingly effective devices like the Grandfather Clause, white primaries, preprimaries, poll taxes, reading and interpretation tests, multiple ballot boxes, single-month registration periods, party- instead of state-administered primaries, single-state party systems, evasion, economic reprisals, terror, fraud, corruption, violence, mayhem, and murder, African Americans found it exceedingly difficult to register, much less to vote.[2] In Louisiana, one of the southern states where voter registration data were kept by race, it is possible to see in empirical terms just how effective these tactics were in crippling African American voters. Figure 9.1 shows percentages for an entire century comparing the eligible African American voting age population with those who overcame the obstacles and became registered voters. African American registered voters plummeted from a high of 130,444 in 1897 to a low of 5,320 in 1910. The new state constitution in Louisiana disenfranchised, in a very short span of time, more than 95 percent of the entire African American electorate. Nearly the same reality prevailed in the other states of the Old Confederacy.

But as had happened in the antebellum period, African Americans once again organized and lobbied to regain their suffrage rights, doing so from 1895 to 1965. With the NAACP taking the lead nationally and numerous courageous individuals and groups spearheading efforts at the local and state levels, the drive to regain the ballot met with some success.[3] Although the success was uneven, painfully slow, and in numerous places quite deadly, some partial success was achieved.

Initially, victories came from Supreme Court cases, like *Guinn and Beal* v. *U.S.* (1914), which declared the Grandfather Clause unconstitutional; *Lane* v. *Wilson* (1939), which voided the single-month registration scheme; *Smith* v. *Allwright* (1949), which outlawed white primaries; *Terry* v. *Adams* (1953), which eliminated privately administered elections; and a federal district court

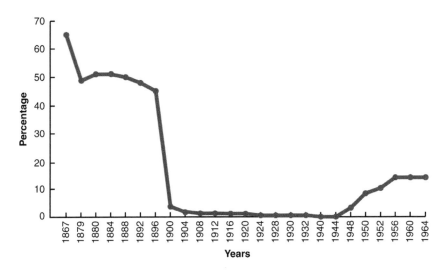

FIGURE 9.1

The Percentage of African American Registered Voters in Louisiana, 1867–1964

Sources: Adapted from *Annual Cyclopedia and Register of Important Events of the Year 1867*, vol. VII (New York: D. Appleton and Company, 1869): 461 for the year 1867; Perry H. Howard, *Political Tendencies in Louisiana*, revised and expanded (Baton Rouge: Louisiana State University Press, 1971): 421–22 for the years 1879–1964. Calculations prepared by the authors, thus some year intervals are irregular due to various data sources.

decision in 1949 that declared "understanding and explaining clauses" to be unconstitutional.[4]

Later, congressional legislation assisted the court decisions. The Civil Rights Acts of 1957 and 1960 and Title I of the 1964 Civil Rights Act added limited federal protection for African American voting rights. Then in 1965, Congress passed the Voting Rights Act, which was renewed in 1970, 1975, 1982, and 2006. This law permitted federal registrars to go into the states covered by the law and register African Americans to vote. However, by the 1960s, the African American community in the South had lost considerable political power. For example, as Table 9.1 shows, in 1900 blacks were a majority of the population in Mississippi and South Carolina, but by the 1960s, they constituted less than a third of citizens of voting age. Between 1900 and 1970, in particular, similar declines in voting power are observed in Louisiana, Georgia, Alabama, and Florida. An upward trend in African American voting power is not observed until after 2000.

African American Voting Behavior: Empirical Renderings

Data from the Bureau of the Census permit us to compare voter registration to actual voting in Table 9.2. From the mid-1960s until the present, nearly two-

TABLE 9.1 Percentage of African Americans of Voting Age in the Southern States: 1900–2010

Southern States	1900	1910	1920	1930	1940	1950	1960	1970	1980	1990	2000	2010
Alabama	43.9	41.7	37.7	35.6	33.4	29.5	26.2	21.1	22.5	23.2	20.0	25.7
Arkansas	27.8	28.2	27.4	26.6	24.6	20.5	18.5	14.8	13.9	13.6	14.3	15.0
Florida	44.2	42.0	34.0	29.0	26.0	20.1	15.2	11.9	11.6	11.9	13.6	14.2
Georgia	44.6	43.0	39.8	36.6	32.8	28.6	24.5	22.7	23.9	24.5	26.8	30.9
Louisiana	45.4	42.2	38.2	36.6	34.4	30.3	28.5	26.0	27.3	28.0	29.4	31.0
Mississippi	56.9	54.9	51.3	49.4	47.1	41.3	36.1	30.3	31.2	31.7	33.0	35.8
North Carolina	30.7	29.4	28.1	27.2	25.6	23.8	21.6	18.7	19.6	20.2	20.2	21.6
South Carolina	54.0	50.5	47.2	42.0	38.7	33.9	29.2	25.4	27.7	27.5	27.4	27.1
Tennessee	23.1	21.6	19.9	19.2	18.1	16.1	15.0	13.4	14.0	14.7	15.0	16.1
Texas	18.7	16.7	15.4	14.6	14.0	12.3	11.7	11.0	11.7	11.4	12.1	12.9
Virginia	32.7	30.5	28.8	25.3	23.1	21.1	18.9	16.2	17.4	17.8	19.1	19.3

Sources: Adapted from U.S. Bureau of the Census, *Statistical Abstract of the United States: 1910–2000* (Washington, DC: Government Printing Office, 1911–2000). The 2010 data were based on estimates tabulated using the U.S. Bureau of the Census, *2010–2014 American Community Survey 5 Year Estimates* for "Voting Age Population by Citizenship and Race (CVAP)" (Washington, DC: Census Bureau, 2014). Calculations prepared by the authors.

thirds of the African American community registered to vote. With the exception of the 1976 presidential election, more than half of all African American registered voters voted in presidential elections. There is, however, an almost 10 percent gap between African American registered voters and those who actually vote.

Table 9.3 reveals the demographic correlates of the black vote. African American voters tend to be female and over 45 years of age. The majority live in the South and Midwest, four-fifths have a high school education or better, two-thirds earn more than $25,000 per year, and over half own their own homes.

The Election of 2016

The Presidential Candidates and Identity Politics

The 2016 presidential election was one of the most extraordinary in American history, comparable in its distinctiveness, in some ways, to the historic election of the first African American president in 2008. In addition to the Election of Donald J. Trump, the 2016 election featured the first major party nomination

TABLE 9.2 Percentage of African Americans Registered and Voting, 1964–2014

Year	Percentage Registered	Percentage Voting
1964	60.0[a]	59.0
1966	60.0	42.0
1968	66.0	58.0
1970	61.0	44.0
1972	66.0	52.0
1974	55.0	34.0
1976	59.0	49.0
1978	57.0	37.0
1980	60.0	51.0
1982	59.0	43.0
1984	66.0	56.0
1986	64.0	43.0
1988	65.0	52.0
1990	39.0	39.0
1992	64.0	54.0
1994	59.0	37.0
1996	64.0	51.0
1998	60.2	39.6
2000	68.0	57.0
2002	62.4	67.5
2004	68.7	60.0
2006	60.9	41.0
2008	69.7	64.7
2010	62.8	43.8
2012	73.1	66.2
2014	64.3	42.2

[a] Estimated data.

Sources: For the presidential election data, see Jerry T. Jennings, "Voting and Registration in the Election of November 1992," *Current Population Reports, Population Characteristics, Series P20-422* (Washington, DC: Government Printing Office, 1993); for congressional election data, Jerry T. Jennings, "Voting and Registration in the Election of November 1990," *Current Population Reports, Population Characteristics, Series P10-453* (Washington, DC: Government Printing Office, 1991); U.S. Bureau of the Census, "Voting and Registration in the Election of November 1998," *Current Population Survey P20-523RV* (Washington, DC: Census Bureau, 2000); U.S. Bureau of the Census, "Voting and Registration in the Election of November 2000," *Current Population Reports, Population Characteristics, Series P20-542* (Washington, DC: Census Bureau, 2002): 5; U.S. Bureau of the Census, "Voting and Registration in the Election of November 2002," *Current Population Reports, Population Characteristics, Series P20-552* (Washington, DC: Census Bureau, 2004): 5; U.S. Bureau of the Census, "Voting and Registration in the Election of November 2004," *Current Population Reports, Population Characteristics, Series P20-556* (Washington, DC: Census Bureau, 2006): 4; U.S. Bureau of the Census, "Voting and Registration in the Election of November 2006," *Current Population Reports, Population Characteristics, Series P20-557* (Washington, DC: Census Bureau, 2008): 4; "Voting and Registration in the Election of November 2008," *Current Population Reports, Population Characteristics, Series P20-562RV* (Washington, DC: Census Bureau, 2012): 4; and "The Diversifying Electorate—Voting Rates by Race and Hispanic Origin in 2012 (and Other Recent Elections)," *Current Population Survey, Population Characteristics, Series P20-568* (Washington, DC: Census Bureau, 2013): 3.

TABLE 9.3 Demographic Correlates of African American Voters in the 2000, 2004, 2008, and 2012 Presidential Elections

Demographic Variables	Percentage of 2000 Voters	Percentage of 2004 Voters	Percentage of 2008 Voters	Percentage of 2012 Voters
TOTAL CITIZENS REPORTED VOTED	56.8	60.0	64.7	66.2
SEX				
Male	46.0	46.5	58.2	60.4
Female	54.0	53.5	64.1	66.4
AGE				
Under 45	61.0	52.4	59.7	55.6
Over 45	39.0	47.6	68.3	71.2
REGION				
Northeast	17.6	16.0	58.6	57.0
Midwest	18.8	20.5	67.3	62.9
South	54.8	53.9	66.0	56.83
West	8.9	9.6	63.0	54.75
EDUCATION				
Grade school	7.1	8.1	12.8	11.8
High school	49.7	28.6	35.0	31.3
Some college	26.8	31.0	31.9	32.4
College	16.5	21.1	20.2	24.4
LABOR				
Employed	60.8	62.7	59.5	57.9
Unemployed	5.0	6.7	6.6	7.7
Not in labor force	34.2	30.6	33.9	35.0
FAMILY INCOME				
Under $25,000	39.7	32.6	27.1	32.7
$25,000–$49,999	29.7	20.1	25.4	26.9
$50,000 and above	23.7	35.2	28.3	40.4
TENURE				
Owner occupied	47.1	62.3	60.0	57.7
Renter occupied	52.9	36.7	39.0	41.4

Sources: Adapted from U.S. Bureau of the Census, "Voting and Registration in the Election of November 2000," *Current Population Reports, Population Characteristics, Series P20-542* (Washington, DC: Census Bureau, 2002); U.S. Bureau of the Census, "Detailed Tables for Voting and Registration in the Election of November, 2004," *Current Population Reports, Population Characteristics, Series P20-556* (Washington, DC: Census Bureau, 2006); "Voting and Registration in the Election of November 2008," *Current Population Reports, Population Characteristics, Series P20-562RV* (Washington, DC: Census Bureau, 2012): 4; and "The Diversifying Electorate—Voting Rates by Race and Hispanic Origin in 2012 (and Other Recent Elections)," *Current Population Survey, Population Characteristics, Series P20-568* (Washington, DC: Census Bureau, 2013). Calculations prepared by the authors.

of a woman; the first credible candidacy of a declared socialist; the nomination for only the second time by a major party of a candidate with no prior government or military experience (the first was the Republican Wendell Willkie in 1940); and the most ethnically diverse field of candidates ever, including the first credible Jewish candidate, two persons of Hispanic origins, an Indian American, two women, and an African American.

Although the field of candidates was ethnically diverse, all of the "ethnic" candidates downplayed their ethnic identities. Florida Senator Marco Rubio and Texas Senator Ted Cruz, sons of Cuban immigrants, presented themselves as "Anglo" Cubans rather than Hispanics, while embracing positions on immigration that antagonized much of the Hispanic community. Dolores Huerta, the iconic Mexican American civil rights and labor leader, called Rubio and Cruz "sellouts" and "traitors" who "turn[ed] their backs on the Latino community."[5] Louisiana's Republican Governor Bobby Jindal, the son of immigrants from India, declared that he was "done with all the talk about hyphenated Americans"; he was "just American."[6] Many in the Indian American community said they were "disappointed" and felt "abandoned" because Jindal had changed his name from "Piyush" to Bobby and was "trying to run away from his identity and was embarrassed about being Indian."[7] Bernie Sanders, the Jewish candidate, downplayed his Jewish identity referring to himself as the son of Polish rather than Jewish immigrants and declaring he was "not very religious."[8] Sanders also took positions on the Israeli–Palestine conflict which antagonized some in the Jewish community. The African American candidate Ben Carson, the esteemed neurosurgeon, while adhering to the extreme individualism of black conservatism, nevertheless embraced his black identity, even going so far as to suggest because Obama was "raised white" that *he* would actually be the first "black" president.[9]

Notably, Carson is the third African American to seek the Republican nomination. In 1996 and 2000 Alan Keyes, the political scientist and state department official, ran for the nomination and in 2012 Herman Cain, the businessman and talk show host, was a candidate. Charles Henry avers that since the Republican Party is "not interested in changing its positions on issues to appeal to the black community. It simply seeks to find a black face to sell [its] position to that community."[10] Leah Wright Rigueur, author of *The Loneliness of the Black Republican* (2014), wrote:

> For white conservative audiences Carson is safe. . . . For Carson racism is something to be changed through individual acts rather than something to be eradicated through structural change. Conservative voters can thus look at Carson and have their personal beliefs on race validated, especially because a black man is articulating these same beliefs.[11]

Carson came to the attention of conservative elites after he made a gratuitous attack on President Obama, while the President was sitting, at the 2013 National

Prayer Breakfast. After the breakfast speech, the *Wall Street Journal* editorially urged him to run for president. Subsequently, Carson went on the conservative lecture circuit and Fox television attacking the President's health insurance program, calling it "the worst thing that has happened since slavery . . . and a new conservative folk hero was born."[12]

At several points during the primaries and caucuses polls showed the mild-mannered, religiously devout Carson running second to Trump. Carson also raised a respectable $77 million and had a plausible performance in several debates. In the end, however, he did not win a single caucus or primary, and dropped out after the second Super Tuesday and endorsed Trump. Although Carson likely never had a realistic chance to win, he is the most successful of black Republican presidential candidates, coming in fifth in a field of seventeen and winning 850,000 votes and seven pledged delegates. After endorsing Trump, Carson became an advisor and Trump surrogate on television.

The Republican Party and the Nomination of Donald J. Trump

Like the nomination of Obama, Trump's nomination was a genuine phenomenon; a rare, exceptional unexpected occurrence. When Trump announced, political scientists and political pundits dismissed his candidacy as a fantasy and a distraction from the real contest between establishment candidates like Senators Ted Cruz, Marco Rubio, and Rand Paul, and Governors Jeb Bush, Scott Walker, Chris Christie, and Rick Perry. Trump was dismissed as a possible nominee because he had no prior political experience and was viewed by many as a buffoon. Yet, he prevailed in one of the most stunning upsets in American political history.

Trump briefly considered running for the presidency in 2012 on a campaign based on "Birtherism," the discredited idea that Obama was not born in the United States. Starting in 2011, he began to appear on television questioning Obama's birth certificate. He claimed he had sent investigators to Hawaii to look into Obama's birth and repeatedly asserted, "They cannot believe what they are finding."[13] Although he probably never sent investigators to Hawaii,[14] Trump's repeated questions about the legitimacy of Obama's birth certificate increased his standing in the early 2012 preference polls for the nomination; in some polls he was tied for first place.[15] After Obama definitively settled the matter by releasing his long form birth certificate, Trump stopped talking about the issue and decided not to run in 2012. However, the issue had "served its purpose, raising Mr. Trump's profile and whether he knew it or not at the time, providing him a rudimentary foundation upon which to build the 2016 campaign."[16] This is because the idea Obama was foreign-born is a widely held belief among about 43 percent of Republicans, and roughly one in five

Americans.[17] Thus, when Trump announced his presidential candidacy in June 2016 he already had a constituency among Republican base voters.

As soon as Trump announced his campaign he began to attract large crowds and established a lead in the polls he never relinquished. Trump maintained this lead despite saying, according to the *Washington Post,* "twenty-three things that would have doomed another candidate."[18] Among the things the *Post* identified were calling Mexican immigrants rapists, alluding to a newswoman's menstruation, alluding to the size of his penis, insulting the looks of Carly Fiorina, his female opponent, claiming George Bush was involved in the 9/11 attacks, mocking a disabled reporter, falsely claiming thousands of Muslims in New Jersey celebrated the 9/11 attack, proposing to ban all Muslims from entering the United States, encouraging violence at his rallies, attacking the Pope, and declining to immediately disavow the former leader of the Ku Klux Klan. Major newspapers routinely ran stories and columns suggesting Trump was a fascist and a racist.[19] Mitt Romney, the 2012 Republican nominee, labeled Trump a "con man" and a "fraud" who practiced "trickle-down bigotry," "trickle down racism," "trickle down misogyny," and has been "vulgar time and time again."[20] His major competitor in the Republican primaries, Senator Cruz, said Trump was a "pathological liar," "utterly immoral," a "bully" a "serial philanderer," and a "narcissist."[21] The *National Review,* the leading journal of conservative opinion, labeled Trump a "philosophically unmoored political opportunist," the *New York Times*, "a shady, bombastic liar," and the *Washington Post* lamented the "utter ugliness" of Trump's "pernicious and preposterous" campaign.[22] In conclusion, George Will, the dean of the nation's conservative pundits, announced after Trump won the Republican nomination that he was leaving the Republican Party. Meanwhile, thousands of the nation's writers signed a letter "opposing as a matter of conscience, unequivocally, the Trump candidacy."[23]

Yet, in spite of, or perhaps, in some cases, because of this widespread opposition of both the liberal and conservative intellectual, political, and media establishments, Trump won—decisively—the Republican nomination. In winning, he defeated 16 opponents including four incumbent senators, three incumbent governors, and three former governors, including Jeb Bush, the former Florida governor and son and brother of a president. Trump won 13 million votes (the largest ever for a Republican primary winner), 41 states or territories, and 1,441 delegates. His nearest competitor, Senator Cruz, won almost 8 million votes, 11 states, and 551 delegates. Although Trump's 13 million votes (45 percent of the total) was a record for a Republican primary candidate, he also set a record for the most votes against a nominee (16 million), and while he received 70 percent of the delegates, the 30 percent opposed to him were also a record for a Republican nominee.[24]

Yet Trump's extraordinary achievement should not be gainsaid. His thoroughly unorthodox campaign raised and spent relatively little money

($58 million, mostly in candidate loans) compared to Jeb Bush's $138 million, Cruz's $127 million, and Rubio's $111 million. The campaign did not employ a pollster, speech-writer, or advertisement consultant, had little organization and ran few ads. Trump won, therefore, not on the basis of the traditional metrics—organization, money, polls, and television ads—but on the basis of charisma, the force of his personality and the controversial, unorthodox nature of his issue positions.

In a study of media coverage of the campaign, the *New York Times* estimated in the early months of the campaign Trump earned close to $2 billion in free media coverage, twice the amount earned by Hillary Clinton the next best in free media, while Sanders earned more free media attention than any of Trump's Republican opponents.[25] A Harvard Kennedy School study of media coverage of Trump concluded, "Trump [was] arguably the first bona fide media created nominee. ... Journalists are attracted to the new, the unusual and sensational. Trump fit that need as no other candidate in recent memory."[26] Most of the coverage of Trump was positive by a margin of 2–1, notwithstanding the media criticism of Trump discussed above.[27] This was because, as usual in presidential campaigns, the media focused on the "horserace" and since Trump was winning the race the coverage was positive (only 12 percent of coverage focused on issues).[28]

Trump's support in the primaries came disproportionately from white, low-income males with only a high school education. There are too few nonwhite voters in Republican primaries to calculate Trump's support, but exit polls conducted in 27 states show Trump did well among all categories of white voters.[29] For example, while he won 45 percent of the male vote, he also received 37 percent of the vote of women, winning a plurality of the female vote in 19 of the 27 states where exit polls were conducted. And while he won 52 percent of the votes of those with only a high school diploma, he won 45 percent among college graduates. Forty-five percent of low-income voters (making less than $50,000) supported Trump, but so did 40 percent of the higher income. Thus, in a field of multiple candidates Trump's triumph was broad-based among the virtually all-white Republican electorate in terms of class and gender.

What explains Trump's remarkable victory in the face of the overwhelming opposition of the Republican establishment? In the years ahead, hundreds of dissertations and articles and scores of books will be written to explain this phenomenon. At this early stage in the research, some view Trump's nomination as the maturing of trends since the late 1960s toward authoritarianism among Republican voters, accelerated by demographic and economic changes "which activated authoritarian tendencies, leading many Americans to seek out a strong man leader who would preserve the status-quo under threat and impose order on a world they perceive as increasingly alien."[30] Others view it as a populist revolt by those who believe the system is stacked against them.[31] While still others reject authoritarianism and populism and instead see Trump's success as rooted in white racial prejudice.[32] At this point, we do not have sufficient research to accept any single theory of "Trumpism." It likely may be explained by some combination of theories; however, we advance the theory of white nationalism as the most comprehensive explanation of Trump's success.

White nationalism as an explanation was advanced in several media assessments of the Trump campaign.[33] These media accounts are supported by a small but robust body of political science research. In his seminal book, *White Nationalism, Black Interests: Conservative Public Policy and the Black Community* (2003), Ronald Walters—the late pioneering scholar in identifying white nationalism or white identity politics as an emergent force in American politics—traced its beginnings to the election of Ronald Reagan in 1980 (see Faces and Voices in the Struggle for Universal Freedom in Chapter 6). Walters attributes the activation of white nationalist sentiments among segments of the white population to three factors: First, white resentment of perceived black social, economic and political advancement, which many whites viewed as coming unjustly at their expense through programs such as affirmative action.[34] Second, white economic stagnation and growing income inequality, which results in a third factor, "the perception of a threat to white dominance which has "produced growing anxiety among whites, especially males."[35]

In 2010, a team of political scientists prepared a proposal for the American National Election Study (ANES) entitled, "White Racial Consciousness in the U.S.," which concluded that because of two decades of mass immigration, a growing nonwhite population, and the election of a black president the "dominance of whites as a racial group seems to be in jeopardy."[36] As a result, "There is growing evidence that in response to this threat, whites are increasingly identifying with their racial group, and this group attachment has important political consequences."[37] One of these political consequences is the Election of Donald Trump.

In fact, survey data show that both white identity and nationalist beliefs are associated with voter support for Trump in the Republican primaries. For example, those whites who said their identity as whites was "extremely important" to them were 30 points more likely to vote for Trump; those who perceive a great deal of discrimination against whites, 40 points more likely; and those who thought it was "extremely likely that many whites were unable to find a job because employers were hiring minorities," 50 points more likely.[38] Moreover, Trump supporters were more likely to report they were economically struggling and that whites were "losing out" because of preferences for African Americans and Latinos.

Thus, white nationalism appears to be at least one robust explanation for the Trump triumph. White identity becomes nationalist politics "when group conflict leads to perceptions that one's group is relatively deprived and collective action is an agreed upon means by which to challenge the social order in an effort to improve the position of the group."[39] Many whites, as a result of economic stagnation, Hispanic immigration, and affirmative action perceive themselves under threat; thus, white nationalist politics may become even more pronounced as the nation trends toward a "majority–minority" status. The Trump phenomenon, even without Trump, may be an enduring feature of American politics, which undermines the quest for universal freedom for all American citizens.

Consequently, at the 2016 Republican Convention of 2,472 delegates only 18 (0.7 percent) were African American, the lowest number since 1964 when the party nominated the conservative, anti-civil rights Senator Barry Goldwater. Black delegates reportedly felt dismayed as the Convention "veered unexpectedly and unhappily toward lecturing, moralizing . . . as [it] focused on appealing to voters."[40]

The Democratic Party and the Nomination of Hillary Rodham Clinton

The black vote was central to Hillary Clinton's success in her second bid for the Democratic nomination, just as it was central when she lost to Barack Obama in 2008.

When Gallup in 1937 first asked Americans would they vote for a woman for president if she was qualified "in every other respect," 64 percent said "no." In 2016, when Clinton announced for a second time, less than 5 percent said "no." In fact, in 2016 she was considered likely to win the Democratic nomination without serious competition until Senator Bernie Sanders, the 74-year-old Vermont registered Independent, self-declared socialist, announced his candidacy as a democrat, and subsequently ran a surprisingly competitive race.

Interestingly, first, because of Sanders's socialist ideology, which has long been a "bogeyman" in American politics, according to a June 2015 Gallup poll that revealed 90 percent plus of Americans would vote for a woman, Catholic, African American, Latino, or a Jew for the presidency, 81 percent for a Muslim, 74 percent for a homosexual, 58 percent for an atheist, but only 47 percent for a socialist. Whites were particularly hostile to socialism with only 24 percent expressing a positive view compared to 55 percent of blacks and 44 percent of Latinos.[41] Forty-nine percent of young people had a positive opinion of socialism compared to 13 percent of those 65 and older, and 59 percent of liberal democrats compared to 6 percent of conservative Republicans. Thus, the "socialist" Sanders had a potential base constituency among African Americans, Latinos, young people, and liberal Democrats. We have limited data on the voting behavior of Latinos and liberal Democrats during the Democratic primaries, but we know that young people did constitute a base of Sanders's constituency while African Americans were the core Clinton constituency.

Sanders's major issue during the campaign was the struggle for equality, an issue that has consumed him for most of his career. A long-term leftist (Sanders and his first wife honeymooned in the Soviet Union), Sanders in the 1960s was a member of the Young People's Socialist League and affiliated with two of the more radical black civil rights organizations, SNCC and CORE. Sanders during the campaign did not, however, propose traditional or explicit socialist policies such as nationalization of industries or confiscatory taxes on inherited wealth. Instead, he advanced traditional liberal ideas such as universal health insurance ("Medicare for All"), a $15 minimum wage, paid family leave, free tuition at public universities, expanded social security and pensions for the elderly and increased taxes on corporations and the wealthy. Most of these ideas were advanced or accepted by Clinton. In foreign policy Sanders, unlike Clinton, opposed the Iraq war, U.S. intervention in Libya and Syria, and was critical of what he called the "one-sided" U.S. support for Israel.

Sanders and Clinton each raised more than $200 million. More than 90 percent of Sanders's contributions were from individuals in small contributions under $200 with an average contribution of $27[42]—a popular slogan during campaign speeches—while most of Clinton's were from wealthy individuals connected to lawyers, corporations, and financial institutions.

Initially Sanders's campaign was ignored by the media; however, after he started to attract large crowds and gain support in the polls press coverage increased and tended to be positive while coverage of Clinton was overwhelmingly negative.[43] Plagued by "scandals" involving her emails and Benghazi, "Clinton's negative coverage can be equated to millions of dollars in attack ads, with her on the receiving end."[44]

Nevertheless, Clinton easily prevailed, winning 55 percent of the primary votes, 34 states or territories, and 54 percent of the pledged delegates compared to Sanders's 45 percent primary vote, 23 states, and 43 percent of the pledged delegates. As the favorite of the party establishment, Clinton received 78 percent of the super delegates compared to Sanders's 3 percent.

Sanders won the white vote 49 to 47 percent; the vote among men was even at 49 percent each while Clinton decisively won the vote of women, 60 to 38.[45] Sanders's core or base constituency was young people (ages 18–29), which he won 68 to 21, while Clinton won the elderly vote by an equally decisive margin of 64 to 30. The limited data available indicates that Clinton also won the Latino vote 56 to 43. No exit poll data are available on the Jewish vote, not even from New York and Florida where it is sizeable. This is inexplicable since Sanders was the first competitive Jewish candidate for a major party nomination.

Clinton won 80 percent of the African American vote, which provided the competitive edge in states won, primary votes, and pledged delegates. To put it another way, if Clinton's margin among African Americans had been similar to her margin among whites or even among Latinos, she could have only won the nomination with the super delegates who in that case might have decided to split their votes.

How can we account for this overwhelming lack of support for the most liberal candidate by the most liberal group in the electorate, and the group most positive toward socialism? First, at the start of the campaign Sanders was nearly completely unknown to most African Americans compared to the well-known and popular Clintons. Second, Clinton was generally supportive of Obama while Sanders was often critical of Obama's failure to do more to remedy income inequality, challenge Wall Street, or pursue more comprehensive health insurance. Third, while Sanders attacked Clinton for supporting the "crime and welfare" bill—adopted as the Violent Crime Control and Law Enforcement Act—signed by her husband, former President Bill Clinton, these issues apparently had little impact on African American voters (Sanders voted for the crime bill because, he said, it included provisions related to violence against women). Fourth, while Sanders addressed the problem of income inequality generally he did not offer policies to address or target specifically racial inequality or poverty. Moreover, some economists calculated that Sanders's specific proposals for family leave, college tuition, and health insurance would disproportionately benefit the middle class rather than the poor.[46] Finally, although Sanders was endorsed by African American celebrities like Spike Lee, Danny Glover, and Harry Belafonte, no African American mayor, civil rights leader and only one of the 43 black members of Congress endorsed him.

At the Democratic National Convention, African Americans accounted for 1,182 or 25 percent of the delegates compared to the 18 delegates or 0.7 percent at the Republican National Convention.[47] And rather than moralizing lectures about their behavior, the mothers of African Americans killed by the police were spotlighted as a positive nod to the Black Lives Matter movement. Their tempered, emotional appeal for accountability was reinforced by the First Lady, Michelle Obama, during her memorable, impassioned speech about being an African American and a mother at this time in America's history. And, President Obama's celebratory speech sought to unite the Democratic Party by appealing to Sanders's "Bernie or Bust" backers in a strong endorsement of Clinton. The party platform in general and with respect to civil rights and poverty was the most liberal since 1972, promising vigorous enforcement of the former and a renewed assault on the latter. It also promised reform of the criminal justice system and development of policies to address institutional racism and the racial wealth gap.[48]

Interestingly, at the end of the national conventions, both parties (Republican and Democratic) had nominated candidates disliked and distrusted by the electorate. Indeed, Trump and Clinton had near the end of the primaries the highest "very" unfavorable ratings of any candidates in modern history: Clinton at 37 percent, Trump 53 percent (the previous highs were Obama at 24 in 2008 and Reagan at 20 in 1980 and 1984).[49] Clearly, for many voters, the contest between Trump and Clinton was a choice between two of the most disliked candidates in recent American history, setting the stage for one of the most rancorous presidential elections ever.

The Election of Donald J. Trump

By September, the Clinton-Trump campaign was vitriolic, vituperative and dispiriting, leaving many voters angry, fearful and disgusted. The American Psychological Association in a report released in mid-October reported that half the electorate was suffering from what might be called "election stress disorder," including headaches, stomachaches and loss of sleep.[50] The two campaigns began with both Clinton and Trump accusing each other of corruption, racism, misogyny, bigotry[51] and personal attacks that grew progressively worse.

In early October, the *Washington Post* published a story and accompanying video of Trump bragging in lewd and obscene language about how he interacts with women, which was analogous to sexual assault. Then, eleven women came forward alleging that Trump had sexually assaulted them. The Clinton campaign exploited the issue targeting women voters and their allies. Trump retaliated by accusing former president Bill Clinton of sexual assault, and even had four women, who were his alleged victims, as guests at the second presidential debate.

Beginning at the Republican National Convention and repeatedly thereafter, Trump said Clinton, because of her use of a private email server while Secretary of State, was a criminal—referring to her as "Crooked Hillary"—who should be jailed. His supporters at the national convention and his campaign rallies often shouted "Lock her up! Lock her up!" and referred to her in unspeakable epithets and gendered language. At their final debate, Trump derisively called Clinton a "nasty woman" and stated, if he won, that he would have a special prosecutor appointed to investigate and jail her.

Both campaigns came under scrutiny by the FBI. In July, in an unprecedented news conference, the FBI Director, James Comey, declared that while Clinton had been "extremely careless" in her use of the private email server, there was no evidence of criminal behavior. However, in October, less than two weeks before the general election, the Director released a letter sent to Congress indicating that there may be possible incriminating emails sent by Clinton that were found on the computer of former congressman, Anthony Wiener—the estranged husband of one of Clinton's top aides—discovered during an investigation of him in a sexting scandal with a minor. As a result, Comey reopened the previous investigation. Then, just two days before the general election, he indicated the FBI had once again found no criminal wrong-doing by Clinton. Meanwhile, US intelligence agencies accused Russia of hacking the emails of the Democratic National Committee and the Clinton campaign in order to help Trump, leading Clinton to accuse the Trump campaign of working with the Russians to corrupt the election. The hacked emails, released by WikiLeaks, resulted in allegations that donors to the Bill, Hillary & Chelsea Clinton

Foundation had been given special access and favors by Clinton while she was Secretary of State. The leaked emails also revealed some of the unsavory maneuvering of Clinton aides as they attempted to undermine the Sanders' campaign during the primaries. With respect to Trump's campaign, the US intelligence agencies' accusations proved to be true; it was revealed a day after the election that a senior Russian diplomat confirmed that Russian government officials conferred with members of his campaign team.[52]

As Election Day grew closer, nearly all of the media pundits and pollsters had Clinton projected as the winner, causing Trump to repeatedly imply that the entire election was "rigged" and corrupt. In fact, he even refused to say he would accept the results if he did not win, and called on his supporters to be "vigilant against widespread voter fraud"[53] and to monitor polling places for "ballot security" in "certain areas."[54] In response, in the last week before the election, the Democratic Party filed lawsuits against the Trump campaign and the Republican Party in four states charging violations of the 1871 Ku Klux Klan Act—the basis of the RNC 1982 consent decree whereby the RNC agreed to curb its vote watching tactics— and the Voting Rights Act alleging they were conspiring to intimidate and discourage nonwhites from voting in the election.[55]

It was within this venomous, vulgar atmosphere that dispirited Americans went to the polls on November 8 to elect Donald John Trump the 45th President of the United States in, perhaps, the most stunning upset in presidential election history.

Race and the 2016 Election

Race was not a major issue during the campaign. Although Trump occasionally made racially insensitive remarks, overall he did not attempt to use race as a wedge issue in the way, for example, he used immigration. To the contrary, Trump was the first Republican nominee since Richard Nixon in 1960 to make explicit appeals to the black electorate. Among Trump's white nationalist supporters, two issues are salient: immigration and affirmative action. Trump began his campaign by exploiting the immigration issue but paid no attention to affirmative action. Indeed, he never mentioned it, even though affirmative action is more unpopular among whites generally—both liberals and conservatives—than immigration.[56]

Trump's overtures to blacks were often arrogant, condescending and ill-informed. He charged that for fifty years the Democrats had taken the "black vote" for granted while doing nothing to address the problems of the community. In making this charge, Trump frequently exclaimed that the "inner cities"—his description for African American communities—had "[h]orrible education, no housing, no homes, no ownership; crime at levels that nobody has seen. . . what in the hell do you have to lose?" in voting for him.[57] Despite his crude appeal, he nevertheless was the first Republican nominee in decades to verbally raise the issue of the plight of low-income and poor African Americans. He proposed enhanced access to education, tax incentives for businesses to locate in black communities, easing access to credit, creating jobs and infrastructure rebuilding as part of what he called a "New Deal for Black America."[58] However, some of the proposed solutions (e.g., "stop and frisk" and "school choice") are controversial in the African American community.

Whatever the merits of Trump's entreaties toward the black electorate, exit polls revealed he had little appeal to African American voters perhaps because of his racially insensitive rhetoric, the well-documented "long history of racial bias" by his real estate company in New York,[59] and his refusal to renounce the endorsement days before the election by the official newspaper of the Ku Klux Klan. Perhaps, his "black outreach" was not directed to African Americans, but rather was an effort to assuage white voters concerned about voting for a person often accused of racism.[60]

Like the Democratic platform, Clinton embraced the most progressive *rhetoric* on race since 1972, even going so far as to adopt some of the language of the Black Lives Matter Movement.[61] However, the leaked emails revealed that even during the primaries Clinton and her staff were wary of talking about poor people and poverty for fear of alienating white conservative and centrist voters in the general election.[62] As one commentator wrote,

> [s]he struggled always to neatly encapsulate her vision of America. [Her slogan] 'Stronger Together' was never as snappy as [Trump's] 'Make America Great Again.' Indeed, the Clinton campaign went through dozens of possible slogans, which spoke of her difficulties in crafting a message.[63]

In order to win, she had to appeal to the diverse electorate in Obama's rainbow coalition—comprised of majority nonwhite, women, millennial, working-class, LGBT, liberal voters.

Barack Obama's Winning Rainbow Coalition: The Challenge for Hillary Clinton

In another unprecedented act in the history of presidential campaigns, both President Obama and First Lady Michelle Obama frequently and fervently campaigned for Clinton's election. The president told audiences that her election was indispensable to preservation of his legacy, declaring "everything we have done over the last eight years will be reversed with a Trump presidency."[64] If the President was correct, the outcome of the election was not just a rejection of Hillary Clinton but could be a repudiation of his legacy.

A key question from the outset of Clinton's campaign was would she be able to maintain Obama's winning minority-majority rainbow coalition. The data in Table 9.4, comparing the demographic bases of Obama's coalition in 2012 with Clinton in 2016, show she was not. While Latinos and Asians in the coalition slightly increased their share of the electorate (from 10 to 11 percent and 3 to 4 percent, respectively), their support for Clinton declined when compared to Obama in 2012 (Latino support decreased from 71 to 65 percent and Asian support from 73 to 65 percent). Although the African American share of the electorate declined from 13 to 12 percent, Clinton received 88 percent of their vote—the highest among all groups—compared to Obama's 93 percent. The white share of the electorate also declined from 72 to 70 percent; Clinton received 37 percent compared to Obama's 39 percent.

Women were a key constituent in the rainbow coalition. Interestingly, the first woman major party nominee did less well among women than the first African American male nominee at 54 to 55 percent, respectively. While Clinton did only one point better than Obama among white women generally (43 to 42 percent), due mainly to college educated white women,[65] she trailed Obama among white men 31 to 35 percent. Clinton won among nonwhite women and men voters, including 94 percent of black women.

Among the millennials, 18-to-24-year-olds, Obama won 60 percent and Clinton won 55 percent, including 83 percent of blacks, 70 percent of Latinos, but only 43 percent of whites.[66] Among the 30-to-34-year-olds, Obama won 52 percent and Clinton won 50 percent, including 87 percent of blacks, 71 percent of Latinos, but only 55 percent of whites.[67] This population comprised a significant share of Clinton's coalition, in addition to her share of LGBT (78 percent), Jewish (71 percent) and voters of secular backgrounds (68 percent), which was comparable to Obama's (76, 78, 70 percent, respectively).

Obama won voters with a high school or some college education (51 and 49 percent). Clinton received 45 and 43 percent of these voters, losing to Trump who won 51 to 52. As in the primaries, Trump won disproportionately among white men and women without a college education[68] with a majority-white coalition—comprised of conservatives, populists, racists and white nationalists—that was broad-based, including white college graduates, suburbanites and persons living in rural areas.[69]

Overall, these relatively small changes in voter turnout and margins of support—possibly due overall to lack of enthusiasm and new voter suppression laws—made the difference in Trump's election, making him the fifth president in history who became a winner while losing. That is, Clinton led in the popular vote with 65.2 million (48%) to Trump's 62.6 (46%) for more than 2.5 million votes. Yet, Trump won thirty states compared to Clinton's twenty and the District of Columbia yielding an Electoral College margin of 279 to 228. This unexpected outcome caused thousands to erupt into organic protests in cities across the country and on social media, exclaiming "Trump is not my president."[70]

TABLE 9.4 **A Comparison of the 2012 and 2016 Presidential Elections, by Selected Demographic Categories**

	2012			2016		
	Percent Electorate	Percent Obama	Percent Romney	Percent Electorate	Percent Clinton	Percent Trump
Gender						
Women	53	55	44	52	54	42
Men	47	45	52	48	41	53
Race/Ethnicity						
Black	13	93	6	12	88	8
White	72	39	61	70	37	58
Men	34	35	62	34	31	63
Women	38	42	56	37	43	53
Latino	10	71	27	11	65	29
Asian	3	73	26	4	65	29
Religion						
Protestant	53	30	69	52	39	58
Evangelical	26	21	78	26	16	81
Catholic	25	40	59	23	45	52
Jewish	2	78	21	3	71	24
None	12	70	26	15	68	26
Age						
18–29	19	60	37	19	55	37
30–34	27	52	45	25	50	42
35–64	38	47	51	40	44	53
65+	16	44	56	15	45	53
Education						
High school	21	51	48	18	45	51
Some college	29	49	48	32	43	52
College Grad.	29	47	51	32	49	45
Postgraduate	18	55	42	18	58	37
Sexual Orientation						
LGBT[a]	5	76	22	5	78	14
Heterosexual	95	49	49	95	49	48

[a] LGBT is Lesbian, Gay, Bisexual or Transgender identity.

Source: CNN Presidential Race, 2016, www.cnn.com/election/results/exit-polls. CNN, Presidential Race, 2012. www.cnn.com/election/2012/results/race/president#exitpolls. Exit poll data are only rough approximations of turn out and voting behavior.

The electorate was as politically and ideologically polarized as it was by race, age and gender. Although a number of Republican and conservative elites abandoned Trump, 90 percent of Republicans and 81 percent of conservatives voted for him while 89 percent of Democrats and 84 percent of liberals supported Clinton.[71]

Trump's surprising victory was all the more remarkable since Clinton had a clear advantage in money, outspending Trump on everything from television ads to staffing field offices to get out the vote.[72] Her campaign organizational infrastructure, modeled on Obama's winning strategy, was also viewed as more effective; and the polls indicated, by overwhelming margins, Clinton won each of the three debates. Yet in the end, as one reporter wrote, "few people personify the political establishment more than Hillary Clinton. During this campaign, for millions of angry voters, she became the face of America's broken politics . . . seen . . . as an east coast elite that looked down, sneeringly, on working people. . . . even though they happily voted for a property tycoon."[73]

The Congressional Elections

The 2016 congressional election saw more people of color elected as Democrats. In the Senate, Kamala Harris (California), the biracial daughter of an African American father and Indian American mother, became the sixth African American and first Indian American elected to the Senate, meaning for the first time in history, three blacks will serve at the same time in that body. In the House of Representatives, Democrats gained three more African Americans: Lisa Blunt Rochester (Delaware),[74] Valdez Venita "Val" Demings (Florida) and Donald McEachin (Virginia).[75] However, the election of Adriano Espaillat, the first Dominican elected to Congress, succeeding longtime, retiring Representative Charles Rangel, signaled a change in historic black Harlem, indicative of changes taking place in many urban areas, as the population transitions from majority or plurality African American to Hispanic.[76] The size of the African American House delegation in the 115th Congress will increase to forty-seven.

Although the Democrats won six House and two Senate seats, both houses remained firmly under Republican control. This could mean that the Trump administration may be able to enact much of its policy agenda, beginning with the repeal of the Affordable Care Act ("Obamacare") and other significant accomplishments[77] under President Obama. For African Americans in their quest for universal freedom, the 2016 election of Donald Trump could be the most decisive setback since the 1912 election of Woodrow Wilson, arguably the most racist President of the 20th century.[78]

Faces and Voices in the Struggle for Universal Freedom
JOHN MERCER LANGSTON (1829–1897)

John Mercer Langston was the first African American elected to office in the United States. Born free in Virginia, he was the son of a wealthy white slave holder and a woman of mixed African and Indian ancestry. When his father died, he left Langston an inheritance, which he used to get a good education and accumulate a substantial fortune. After graduating from Oberlin College in Ohio in 1850, he aspired to become a lawyer. Ohio law prohibited African Americans from practicing law, but because of his light skin color it was decided that Langston was entitled to the privileges of a white man. A successful practice led to his election to the Oberlin town council, making him not only the first black elected to office but also the first from a majority white constituency (ironically, blacks were not allowed to vote in Ohio, so a special exception had to be made in order that Langston could vote for himself). In many ways, Langston resembles Barack Obama: born to mixed-race parents, highly educated, and charismatic, he was able to appeal across racial boundaries to establish a minority–majority coalition. Langston was also mentioned as a possible Republican vice presidential candidate.

After the Civil War, Langston returned to Virginia where he was elected to Congress, where he fought for free and fair elections as the indispensable foundation for universal freedom. (Because of a long dispute about irregularities in the election, Langston was able to serve only three months of his two-year

John Mercer Langston.

Source: Brady, Mathew. "John Mercer Langston." Library of Congress Prints and Photographs Division. Brady-Handy Photograph Collection. Retrieved 4 October 2016 from http://hdl.loc.gov

term.) In addition to holding elective office, Langston organized the National Equal Rights League (a forerunner to the NAACP) and was the founding dean of Howard University law school. He was appointed by President Rutherford B. Hayes as minister to Haiti and the Dominican Republic. In 1894, three years before his death, he wrote his autobiography, *From the Virginia Plantation to the National Capital.*[a]

[a] William and Aimee Lee Cheek, *John Mercer Langston and the Fight for Black Freedom* (Urbana: University of Illinois Press, 1989).

Summary

Until the adoption of the Fifteenth Amendment in 1870, African Americans were denied the right to vote even in northern states such as New York. Even after the adoption of the amendment, it would take passage of the Voting Rights Act of 1965 before African Americans gained the universal right to vote throughout the United States. Today, blacks vote at about the same rate as whites when social class is taken into account. From time to time, the black vote has been the balance of power in presidential elections, determining the outcome when the white vote is closely divided. This process is episodic, however, because generally the black vote is a "captive vote" in national elections, ignored by the Republicans and taken for granted by the Democrats. In 2008 and 2012, however, the black vote was in a sense "liberated," playing a crucial role in the election and reelection of the first African American president. In 2016, however, the black vote while cohesive was not able to determine the outcome of the election because of the larger, more cohesive vote of the white majority.

Critical Thinking Questions

1. Discuss the various factors that prevented African Americans from voting in U.S. elections until 1968.
2. Explain the significance of the Civil Rights Act of 1957, 1960, 1964, and the subsequent Voting Rights Act of 1965 legislation on advancing universal freedom and democratic voting in the United States.
3. Describe the typical African American voter. Explain the significance in the quest for universal freedom.
4. Discuss the significance of social media integration in the Obama 2008 and 2012 campaigns. How has the use of social media impacted subsequent presidential campaigns?
5. Discuss the presidential campaigns of 2016. What were the similarities and differences with the Obama campaigns? What role did race play in these campaigns?

Selected Bibliography

Guinier, Lani. *The Tyranny of the Majority*. New York: Free Press, 1994. President Clinton's failed nominee for assistant attorney general for civil rights explains the limitations of the Voting Rights Act and blacks' use of the ballot to achieve race reform.

Jarvis, Sonia. "Historical Overview: African Americans and the Evolution of Voting Rights." In R. Gomes and L. Williams, eds., *From Exclusion to Inclusion: The Long Struggle for African American Political Power*. Westport, CT: Greenwood Press, 1992. A concise overview of the long struggle of blacks to obtain the ballot.

Leighley, Jan, and Jonathan Nagler. *Who Votes Now?: Issues, Inequality and Turnout in the United States*. Princeton, NJ: Princeton University Press, 2014. Especially useful on nonvoters, minorities, and youth, and their potential impact on election outcomes.

Pinderhughes, Dianne. "The Role of African American Political Organizations in the Mobilization of Voters." In R. Gomes and L. Williams., eds., *From Exclusion to Inclusion: The Long Struggle for African American Political Power*. Westport, CT: Greenwood Press, 1992. A study of the role that black political organizations play in registering and turning out the black vote.

Reid, John. "The Voting Behavior of Blacks." *Intercom* 9 (1981): 8–11. A brief but very useful analysis of the factors shaping the black vote.

Tate, Katherine. *From Protest to Politics: The New Black Voter*. Cambridge, MA: Harvard University Press, 1994. A sophisticated study of the black vote intention and the vote itself, focusing on their determinants.

Teixeria, Ray. *The Emerging Democratic Majority*. New York: Lisa Drew/Scribner, 2002. An analysis of how demographic changes suggest increasing support for the Democratic Party.

Walton, Hanes, Jr., ed. "Black Voting Behavior in the Segregationist Era." In Walton, *Black Politics and Black Political Behavior: A Linkage Analysis*. Westport, CT: Praeger, 1994. An examination of how blacks registered and voted in Georgia during the era of disenfranchisement.

Notes

1 Phyllis Field, *The Politics of Race in New York: The Struggle for Black Suffrage in the Civil War Era* (Ithaca, NY: Cornell University Press, 1982): 59, 124–26, 198.

2 On these various schemes used in the South to deprive blacks of the vote, see Hanes Walton, Jr., *Black Politics* (Philadelphia, PA: J. B. Lippincott, 1992): 33–54.

3 For an engaging memoir of one of these courageous individuals, see John H. Scott (with Cleo Scott), *Witness to the Truth: My Struggle for Human Rights in Louisiana* (Columbia: University of South Carolina Press, 2003).

4 For citations to and discussions of these cases, see Walton, *Black Politics*, pp. 33–40.

5 Mary Jordan, "Liberal Hispanic Activists Assail Rubio, Cruz as 'Traitors' to Their Culture," *Washington Post*, December 15, 2015.

6 Asma Khalid, "Indian-Americans Feel 'Disappointed', 'Abandoned' by Bobby Jindal," accessed at: www.npr.org/2015/11/181/4565180861unhyphenated-bobby-jindal-disappointed-indian-americans.

7 Ibid.

8 Julie Zauzmer, "Bernie Sanders is Jewish: Why Isn't that Convincing Jews to Vote for Him?" *Washington Post*, March 8, 2016.

9 Glen Thrush, "Ben Carson: Obama Was Raised White," *Politico*, February 23, 2016.

10 Charles Henry, "Herman Cain and the Rise of the Black Right," *Journal of Black Studies* 44 (2013): 71.

11 Leah Wright Rigueur, "Ben Carson? The Long Tradition of Black Conservatism," *Washington Post*, September 10, 2015.

12 Robert Samuels, "Ben Carson: From Inspiring to Polarizing," *Washington Post*, January 3, 2016.

13 Ashley Parker and Steve Elder, "Inside the Six Weeks Donald Trump was a Birther," *New York Times*, July 2, 2016.

14 Ibid.

15 Ibid.

16 Ibid.

17 Sam Frizell, "One in Five Americans Still Think Obama Is Foreign-Born, According to Poll," *Time*, September 14, 2015.

18 Phillip Bump, "23 Things Donald Trump Said that Would Have Doomed Another Candidate," *Washington Post*, June 17, 2016.

19 Ross Douthat, "Is Donald Trump a Fascist?" *New York Times,* December 3, 2015; Pam Grier, "Is Donald Trump Really A Fascist?" *Christian Science Monitor*, November 25, 2015; Dana Milibank, "Donald Trump is a Bigot and a Racist," *Washington Post*, December 1, 2015; David Hersey, "Donald Trump's Fascist Inclinations Do Not Bother His Fans," *Los Angeles Times*, December 14, 2015; "The New Fuehrer," *Philadelphia Daily News*, December 8, 2015; Timothy Egan, "Goose-Steppers in the GOP," *New York Times*, December 12, 2015; Robert Kagan, "This is How Fascism Comes to America," *Washington Post*, May 19, 2016. Also, the *New York Daily News* ran several front-page headlines calling Trump a fascist. See, for example, the issue of December 9, 2015. See also Nicholas Kristof, "Is Donald Trump a Racist?" *New York Times*, July 24, 2016.

20 Interview, CNN with Wolf Blitzer, June 10, 2016.

21 See www.cnn.com/2016/05/03/politics/donald-trump-rafael-cruz-indiana/.

22 See www.politico.com/story/20116/01/trump-nationalreview-218079; the *New York Times*, "The Party of Trump and the Path Forward for Democrats," March 3, 2016; and the *Washington Post,* "Donald Trump Is a Poison Pill for the Republican Party," December 6, 2015.

23 Susan Hinckley, "Thousands of Writers Pen Letter Denouncing Trump," *Christian Science Monitor*, May 26, 2016.

24 Phillip Bump, "Donald Trump Was Just Nominated with the Eighth-Lowest Delegate Percentage in GOP History," *Washington Post*, July 20, 2016.

25 Nicholas Confessore and Karen Yourish, "Measuring Trump's Big Advantage in Free Media," *New York Times*, March 17, 2016.

26 Thomas Patterson, *Pre-Primary News Coverage of the 2016 Presidential Race: Trump's Rise, Sanders' Emergence, Clinton's Struggle*. See http://shorensteincenter.org/pre-primary-news-coverage-2016-trump-clinton-sanders/p.5.

27 Ibid.

28 Ibid.

29 See www.cnn.com/election/primaries/polls.

30 Amanda Taub, "The Rise of American Authoritarianism," *Vox*, March 1, 2016. See www.vox.com/2016/3/1/11127424/trump-authoritarianism. On the increasing significance of authoritarian tendencies in American politics since the early 1970s, see Marc Hetherington and Jonathan Weiler, *Authoritarianism and Polarization in American Politics* (New York: Cambridge University Press, 2009).

31 Ron Fournier, "The Populist Revolt," *The Atlantic*, February 10, 2016.

32 Adam Enders and Steven Smallpage, "Racial Prejudice, Not Populism or Authoritarianism Predicts Trump's Support," *Washington Post*, May 26, 2016.
33 See, as examples, Daniel Marans, "How Trump Is Inspiring a New Generation of White Nationalists," *Huffington Post*, March 3, 2016; Michael Tesler and John Sides, "How Political Science Helps Explain the Rise of Trump: The Role of White Identity and Grievances," *Washington Post*, March 3, 2016; and Alex Altman, "The Billionaire and the Bigots: How Trump's Campaign Brought White Nationalists Out of the Shadows," *Time*, April 25, 2016.
34 Ronald W. Walters, *White Nationalism, Black Interests: Conservative Public Policy and the Black Community* (Detroit, MI: Wayne State University Press, 2003): 27.
35 Ibid., p. 155.
36 See "White Racial Consciousness in the U.S.: 2016 ANES Pilot Study Proposal," p. 1. On modern white nationalist politics see also Matthew Hughey, *White Bound: Nationalists, Antiracists and the Shared Meanings of Race* (Stanford, CA: Stanford University Press, 2012).
37 Ibid.
38 Tesler and Sides, "How Political Science Helps Explain the Rise of Trump: The Role of White Identity and Grievances."
39 See "White Racial Consciousness in the U.S.: 2016 ANES Pilot Study," p. 3. See also Nicholas Confessore, "For Whites Sensing Decline, Donald Trump Unleashes Words of Resistance," *New York Times*, July 13, 2016.
40 Yamiche Alexander and Jeremy Peters, "Black Republicans See a White Convention, Heavy on Lectures," *New York Times*, July 19, 2016.
41 See www.people-press-org/2011/12/28/little-change-in-public-response-to-capitalism-socialism/5/30/16.
42 Phillip Bump, "Bernie Sanders Keeps Saying His Average Donation is $27, but His Own Numbers Contradict That," *Washington Post*, April 18, 2016.
43 Patterson, Pre-Primary News Coverage of the 2016 Presidential Race.
44 Ibid., p. 14.
45 Calculations by the authors from the 27 states where exit polls were conducted.
46 Max Ehrenfrand, "What Didn't Happen after Sanders Slammed Clinton on Helping Poor People," *Washington Post*, May 10, 2016.
47 See "Numbers Don't Lie: So We Counted All the Women and People of Color at the DNC and RNC . . .," *Fusion*, July 27, 2016. In fact, it was reported that the DNC was more inclusive than the RNC with women accounting for 2,887 of the 4,766 delegates, while 292 delegates were Asian Americans, 747 were Latinos, 147 were Native Americans, and 633 were LGBTQ-identified persons, respectively, http://fusion.net/story/330193/dnc-rnc-women-people-of-color-numbers/.
48 See www.presidency.ucsb.edu/papers_pdf/117717.pdf.
49 Harry Enten, "Americans' Dislike of Both Trump and Clinton Is Record-Breaking," at http://fivethirtyeight.com/features/americans-distaste-for-both-trump-and-clinton-is-record-breaking/
50 American Psychological Association, "APA Survey Reveals 2016 Presidential Election Source of Significant Stress for Half of Americans," at www.apa.org/news/press/release/2016/101presidential-election-stress.aspx
51 Gabriel Debenedetti and Louis Nelson, "Trump and Clinton Hurl the R Word," *Politico*, August 25, 2016.
52 By David Filipov and Andrew Roth, "Moscow had contacts with Trump team during campaign, Russian diplomat says," *Washington Post*, November 10, 2016.
53 Trip Gabriel, "Donald Trump's Call to Monitor Polls Raises Fears of Intimidation," *New York Times*, October 18, 2016.

54 Matt Friedman, "Democrats: RNC Violating Anti-Voter Intimidation Agreement," *Politico*, October 27, 2016.

55 Ibid.

56 On the consistent and overwhelming opposition to affirmative action – when defined as racial preferences or advantages in employment or university admissions – even among white liberals see Robert C. Smith and Richard Seltzer, *Polarization and the Presidency: From FDR to Barack Obama* (Boulder, CO.: Lynne Rienner, 2015): passim, p. 278.

57 Danny Vinik, "Donald Trump's Confused Portrait of Black America," *Politico*, October 21, 2016. Many African Americans found Trump's description of their community offensive, crude and insulting, see Richard Fausset and Yamiche Alcindor, "Donald Trump's Description of Black America is Offending Those Living in It," *New York Times*, August 25, 2016.

58 Ben Kamisar, "Trump Promises New Deal for Black America," *The Hill*, October 26, 2016.

59 Jonathan Mahler and Steve Eder, "How Trump Got His Start, and Was First Accused of Bias," *New York Times*, August 28, 2016.

60 Philip Rucker, Robert Costa and Jenna Johnson, "Inside Donald Trump's New Strategy to Counter the View That He is a Racist," *Washington Post*, August 23, 2016.

61 Farah Stockman, "The Subtle Phrases Hillary Clinton Uses to Sway Black Voters," *New York Times*, September 29, 2016.

62 Benjamin Appelbaum, "The Millions of Americans Donald Trump and Hillary Clinton Barely Mention," *New York Times*, August 11, 2016.

63 Nick Bryant, "Hillary Clinton and the US election: What Went Wrong for Her?" BBC News, November 9, 2016 at http://www.bbc.com/news/election-us-2016-37922959

64 Edward Isaae Dorere, "Trump Close to Winning Obama Warns," *Politico*, November 5, 2016.

65 National President Election, 2016 Exit Polls at www.cnn.com/election/results/exit-polls.

66 Ibid.

67 Ibid.

68 Ibid.

69 Nicholas Confessore and Nate Cohn, "A Victory Built on a Unique Coalition of Whites," *New York Times*, November 10, 2016.

70 Matea Gold, Mark Berman and Renae Merle, "'Not my president': Thousands protest Trump in Rallies Across the U.S.," *Washington Post*, November 11, 2016.

71 National President Election, 2016 Exit Polls at www.cnn.com/election/results/exit-polls.

72 Kenneth Vogel and Isaac Arnsdory, "Clinton's Homestretch Advantage: $99 million," *Politico*, October 28, 2016.

73 Bryant, "Hillary Clinton and the US election: What Went Wrong for Her?"

74 Amber Phillips, "One Election Bright Spot for Democrats: Women of Color," *Washington Posts*, November 10, 2016. In fact, Lisa Blunt Rochester will also be the first woman to serve in Congress from Delaware leaving only two states that have yet to elect a woman: Mississippi and Vermont.

75 Ibid.

76 Daniel Trotta, "Hispanic claims victory in Harlem race to replace Rangel in U.S. Congress," *Reuters*, June 29, 2016.

77 Paul Glastris, Ryan Cooper, and Siyu Hu, "Obama's Top 50 Accomplishments," *Washington Monthly*, March/April 2012.
78 Zenitha Prince, "Trump Victory: The Plight of African Americans Has Suddenly and Drastically Changed," *Washington Afro*, November 9, 2016.

PART IV

Institutions

CHAPTER 10

The Congress and the African American Quest for Universal Freedom

LEARNING OBJECTIVE

Identify the two periods in history when the Congress was most responsive to the African American quest for freedom.

The framers of the Constitution intended for Congress to be the dominant branch of the government. Of the legislative power, John Locke had written, it "is not only the supreme power of the commonwealth, but sacred and unalterable in the hands where the community have once placed it."[1] Following Locke's logic, the framers made the Congress the first branch of government (Article I), preceding the presidency (Article II) and the judiciary (Article III). Article I is also by far the longest of the three articles, specifying in detail the broad powers of the U.S. government.

Legislation is understood as a general rule of broad application *enacted by a broadly representative body*.[2] We emphasize the words to make the point that in democratic societies, legislation and representation are closely connected, such that a defining property of a legislative institution is the extent to which it fairly represents the people. The English philosopher John Stuart Mill stated the case for the necessary relationship between legislation, representation, and democracy in his 1869 book *Considerations on Representative Government*.

> In a really equal democracy, every or any section would be represented, not disproportionately, but proportionately. A majority of electors would always have a majority of the representatives but a minority of electors would

always have a minority of representatives, man for man, they would be as fully represented as the majority; unless they are, there is not equal government, but government of inequality and privilege: One part of the people rule over the rest: There is a part whose fair and equal share and influence in representation is withheld from them contrary to the principle of democracy, which professes equality as its very root and foundation.[3]

The Representation of African Americans in Congress

Given that in a democracy the legislature should represent the people equally, the first question becomes: How representative of African Americans is the Congress? Political scientists usually measure the representativeness of a legislative institution on the basis of three criteria: descriptive, symbolic, and substantive.[4] *Descriptive representation* is the extent to which the legislature looks like the people in a demographic sense; *symbolic representation* concerns the extent to which people have confidence or trust in the legislature; and *substantive representation* asks whether the laws passed by the legislature correspond to the policy interests or preferences of the people. In this section, we discuss the extent to which Congress represents African Americans descriptively, symbolically, and substantively.

Historically, the Congress has not been descriptively representative of African Americans. Of more than 11,000 persons who have served in the House, only 138 have been black, including the 43 currently serving.[5] From 1787, the year of the first Congress, until 1870, no African American served in Congress. In 1870–1871, six blacks were seated in the House of Representatives. From the 1870s to 1891, blacks averaged two representatives in the House, and in the next decade, there was only one black congressman to represent the nation's population of more than 8 million blacks. In 1901, George White of South Carolina became the last Reconstruction Era African American to serve in Congress. In his farewell speech, White told his white colleagues, "This, Mr. Chairman, is perhaps the Negroes' temporary farewell to the American Congress; but let me say like the Phoenix he will rise again. These parting words are in behalf of an outraged, heart-broken, bruised and bleeding but God-fearing people, faithful, industrious loyal, rising people—full of potential force."[6]

From 1901 to 1929, no blacks served in the House. In 1929, Oscar DePriest was elected from Chicago, and in 1944, Adam Clayton Powell was elected from Harlem. Until the post–civil rights era, only five blacks served in the House. Then in 1969 and again in 1992, there was a fairly rapid rise in black representation in the House, reaching an all-time high of 43 in 2006. The growth in black representation is a function of several factors: the concentration of blacks in highly segregated urban neighborhoods, the Supreme Court's "one person, one vote" decisions in *Baker* v. *Carr* and *Wesberry* v. *Sanders*, and the implementation of the 1965 Voting Rights Act.[7]

Of the more than 2,000 U.S. senators, only nine have been black. Of these nine, two were appointed by the state legislature of Mississippi during Reconstruction, and three were appointed by governors to fill vacancies. Thus, only four blacks have been actually elected to the Senate—Edward Brooke of Massachusetts in 1966, Carol Mosley-Braun from Illinois in 1992, Barack Obama from Illinois in 2004, and Cory Booker from New Jersey in 2013. Senators are elected on a statewide basis, and since no state has a black majority, it has been very difficult for blacks to win Senate seats. Because of racist and white supremacist thinking, whites have been reluctant to vote for black candidates.

Although blacks have made substantial progress in achieving fair and equitable representation in the House, the Congress, as Table 10.1 shows, is

TABLE 10.1 Selected Demographic Characteristics of Members of the 114th Congress 2015–2017

Percentage Population	Demographic Characteristics	House (%)	Senate (%)
51.2	**Women**	19	20
	Race/Ethnicity		
69.1	White	81	93
12.5	Black	10	2
12.5	Latino	8	4
3.6	Asian American	3	1
0.7	Native American[a]	0	0
	Religion		
62	Protestant	57	55
27	Catholic	31	26
2.5	Jewish	4	9
	Other[b]	8	10
	Education		
23	College	94	100
77	Noncollege	6	0
32.8	**Average Age**	57	61

a There are two Native Americans in the House, both from Oklahoma.

b The other religious faiths are mainly Mormon and Greek Orthodox, but there also were three Buddhists (one in Senate, two in House), one Hindu, and two Muslim members. Ten members of the House did not specify a religion. There were also six openly gay and lesbian members including one member of the Senate.

Source: Membership of 114th Congress: A Profile, Congressional Research Service, 2015.

still best described as a body of middle-age, middle-class white men. In the House and Senate, Asian Americans are reasonably represented, in part because they are a voting plurality in Hawaii. However, blacks and Latinos are not equitably represented; African Americans, for example, are 12 percent of the population but 2 percent of the Senate and 10 percent in the House. Women, who constitute more than half the population, are 19 percent of the House and 20 percent of the Senate. These numbers for women are small, but they are much better than the numbers of a decade ago when there were only one or two female senators and women constituted only 5 percent of the House. The nation's major religious groups—Protestants, Catholics, and Jews—are equitably represented in both the House and the Senate. In sum, the Congress is not a representative body insofar as African American, Latino, and female citizens are concerned.

With respect to symbolic representation, African Americans, like most Americans, have relatively low levels of trust or confidence in Congress, with levels falling in 2015 to less than 10 percent.

The most comprehensive, detailed study of the substantive representation by Congress of the American people generally is Martin Gilens's 2014 book, *Affluence and Influence: Economic Inequality and Political Power in America*. Gilens used national surveys of public responses to thousands of questions about the policy preferences of Americans from 1964 to 2006. He then matched the public's policy preferences with the laws passed or not passed by Congress. He found that in most cases affluent citizens exert substantial influence over policies adopted by Congress, while poor Americans exert virtually no influence. This is so for the poor even when Democrats control Congress and the presidency. About half the policies examined during this period showed little or no differences in policy preferences between the poor, middle class, and affluent Americans (i.e., persons who fall in the 10th, 50th and 90th income percentiles, respectively, for the three groups), but on those issues where there was a difference the position of wealthy Americans are adopted about half the time, while the support or opposition of the middle class and the poor had no impact on policy adoption.[8]

The differential impact of the wealthy and nonwealthy on public policies adopted by the federal government, especially economic policy, is substantial. Gilens concludes that if the poor and middle class had equal substantive representation with the affluent, the United States would have a higher minimum wage, more generous unemployment benefits, stricter regulations of corporations, and a more progressive income tax.[9] Overall, the research indicates "the majority does not rule—at least not in the casual sense of determining policy outcomes. When a majority of citizens disagrees with economic elites or with organized interests they generally lose."[10] Before we discuss the extent to which Congress represents the substantive interests of African Americans, particularly, we examine how congressional elections can impact descriptive, symbolic, and substantive representation for majority-partisan racial or ethnic districts, generally.

Congressional Elections and African Americans

Reapportionment and Redistricting

The Constitution requires that every 10 years the government conduct a census, an "enumeration" of the population. The primary constitutional purpose of the census is to provide a basis for reapportioning seats in the House. The size of the House is fixed by law at 435. *Reapportionment* involves the allocation of these 435 seats among the 50 states on the basis of changes in population—for example, the movement of the population in the last four decades from the "snowbelt" states of the Midwest and Northeast to the "sunbelt" states of the South and West. After reapportionment, the states then engage in the process of *redistricting*, the allocation of seats within a state on the basis of populations within each congressional district, with each district containing roughly 700,000 persons. The census is, therefore, important as a basis of allocating political power among and within the states. This has particular implications for America's racial minorities since it is well known that the census regularly undercounts blacks and Latinos, thereby depriving them of a fair share of political power as well as other social and economic benefits that are allocated on the basis of population. In the 1990 census, an estimated 4.8 percent of the black population and 5.2 percent of the Latino population were not counted.[11] Although it is possible for the Census Bureau to "statistically adjust" the census count to include those left out, the Supreme Court has held that such an adjustment is not required by the Constitution.[12] However, for the 2000 census, the Census Bureau agreed to employ statistical sampling as a means to count those persons most often missed by traditional methods of counting. The Republican leadership in the House blocked this change, saying the plan violated the Constitution's requirement that there be an actual "enumeration" of the population; also, it would likely help Democrats by increasing the number of minorities and urban dwellers.

In 1999 the Supreme Court ruled that federal law bars the use of statistical sampling for apportioning seats in the House. Instead, the Court, in a 5–4 decision upholding the ruling of a special three-judge federal district court in Richmond, Virginia, said that while sampling could be used for other purposes (such as redistricting state legislatures and allocating federal money to the states), Congress had mandated that an actual enumeration or "head count" be used in congressional reapportionment. The decision split the Court on ideological lines, with the four more liberal justices dissenting, holding that while sampling could not be a substitute for an enumeration, it was a permissible "supplement" to "achieve the very accuracy that the census seeks and the Census Act itself demands."[13]

The 2000 census did include both the actual enumeration and a statistically adjusted figure based on sampling. Although statistical experts declared that the 2000 census was probably the most accurate ever, there was, nevertheless, an estimated undercount of 1.2 percent (about 3.3 million persons) of the overall population compared to 1.6 percent in 1990. It is estimated that 2.1 percent of blacks and 2.9 percent of Latinos were missed in the 2000 count. In the 2010 census, it is estimated that 2.1 percent of blacks and 1.5 percent of Latinos were missed.

In 2016, in *Evenwel* v. *Abbot,* the Court in a unanimous decision reaffirmed the principle of one person, one vote, rejecting a claim by Texas eligible voters that legislative districts should be based on only the population of eligible or registered voters rather than total population, which includes non-eligible voters such as children and undocumented immigrants. If the Court had not rejected the claim, a disproportionate percentage of African American, Latino, and Asian American persons would not be counted for purposes of legislative reapportionment and redistricting. While the decision was unanimous, Justices Thomas and Alito wrote separate concurring opinions suggesting while states were not required to draw legislative districts based only on eligible voters if they wished to do so they perhaps could without violating the Constitution.

Black Congressional Districts, Campaigns, and Elections

Of the 43 congressional districts represented by blacks in the House (not including the District of Columbia and the Virgin Islands), 24 are majority black, 10 are majority white, and the rest are majority–minority (African Americans and Latinos).[14] The average black population of the districts is 44 percent, ranging from 1.8 percent in Congresswoman Mia Love's Utah district to 65 percent in the Mississippi district of Congressman Bennie Thompson. (One white congressman represents a majority black district, Steven Cohen of Memphis, Tennessee.) All of the blacks in the House are Democrats except Congresswoman Love of Utah and Congressman Will Hurd of Texas. Until 1992, virtually all the black majority districts were urban, northern, and disproportionately poor.[15] As a result of the 1992 redistricting, the large southern (52 percent of the total) and rural (25 percent) black population is now represented in the House (all the southern states except Arkansas send at least one black to the House).

The black districts—often regarded as "safe seats" for their representatives—are overwhelmingly Democratic in party registration and invariably elect Democrats. Like most members of the House, once elected, blacks are routinely reelected. The *advantages of incumbency* make it virtually impossible to defeat an incumbent congressperson; more than 90 percent who seek reelection are reelected.

Finally, except for their race and the greater representation of women, blacks in Congress are quite similar to whites: well-educated, mostly middle-class men. Black women, however, are better represented, constituting 45 percent of the black congressional delegation compared to about 20 percent among white women.

The Color of Representation: Does Race Matter?

In 1993, Carol Swain in a controversial book *Black Faces, Black Interests: The Representation of African Americans in Congress* argued that white members of Congress could represent the interests of blacks as well as and, in some cases, perhaps, better than blacks.[16] That is, she argued that taking into account a representative's party and region, whites in the House represented the black community as well as blacks. Swain's study, however, was limited, based on the roll-call votes of a limited number of congresspeople (nine blacks and four whites) during a two-year time frame. More comprehensive and detailed studies have disproven Swain's argument. Kenny Whitby in *The Color of Representation: Congressional Behavior and Black Interests* found that racial differences in congressional voting are more likely to show up when bills are amended than on the final roll-call votes studied by Swain. Studying congressional voting behavior from 1973 to 1992, Whitby found that race matters even after controlling for party and region.[17] In general, he found that the policy payoffs in the form of more effective antidiscrimination policies in education, employment, and housing are more likely to come from black than white representatives. David Canon in *Race, Redistricting and Representation: The Unintended Consequences of Black Majority Districts* found that race matters in Congress, not just in terms of substantive voting but also in various forms of symbolic representation. For example, black members of the House are more likely than whites to make speeches concerning race (50.8 percent of the speeches by blacks compared to 12.8 percent of whites); more likely to sponsor and introduce bills dealing with race (42 percent for blacks, 5 percent whites); more likely to hire blacks for top staff positions (72.3 percent, 6.7 percent); and more likely to raise race issues in their press releases and newsletters (24.6 percent compared to 12.6 percent).[18] Finally, Katherine Tate in *Black Faces in the Mirror: African Americans in the U.S. Congress* substantiates the work of Whitby and Canon, finding that black members are the most reliable and consistent supporters of substantive black interests in Congress. She also found an important symbolic dimension to this representation in that in general black constituents feel they are better represented in Congress when their representatives are black.[19] In her most recent work, *Concordance: Black Lawmaking in the US Congress from Carter to Obama,* Tate suggests that, partly, as a result of the increasing incorporation of black representatives into House Democratic leadership and committee power structures, they have become less representative of substantive black interests.[20]

African American Power in the House

Power or influence in the House of Representatives is best gauged by committee and subcommittee assignments, seniority, and party leadership positions.[21] In addition, in the last several decades House members have increasingly attempted to exercise power outside the formal committee and party leadership positions by forming caucuses of like-minded members.

The Congressional Black Caucus: Increasing Size, Declining Solidarity

There are now more than 100 legislative caucuses in the House. These groups are organized by members with a common interest or policy agenda so that they can exchange research and information, develop legislative strategies, and act as a unified voting bloc to bargain in support of or against particular bills and amendments.[22]

The Congressional Black Caucus (CBC) is one of the oldest House caucuses, formed in 1969 as an outgrowth of the black power movement's call for racial solidarity and independent black organization. In addition to its role as an internal House legislative caucus, the CBC also plays an external role by forming coalitions with interest groups outside the Congress and operating as one of the two or three major African American interest organizations in Washington.[23] The work of the caucus includes such activities as lobbying the president, presenting various black legislative agendas and alternative budgets in floor debates, and holding its annual legislative weekends. The legislative weekends, held in the fall of each year, usually bring several thousand African American scholars, elected officials, and civil rights leaders to Washington to participate in panels and workshops on issues affecting African Americans.

Power in the House is allocated first on the basis of party. The majority party (the party with one more seat than the other) leads the House and its committees and establishes its agenda, deciding which bills and which, if any, amendments will be allowed to come to a vote. Thus, blacks exercise relatively little power in the House when the Republicans are the majority party. In addition, with Democrats in the majority, African Americans chair committees and subcommittees.

However, even with the Democratic majority in the House, the power of the CBC will depend on its being a *unified* minority. Although the CBC is still a relatively cohesive, liberal voting bloc, its unity or solidarity has declined as it has grown in size. When it was first organized in 1969, it had 13 members, all of whom represented urban areas generally in the North or West. It operated during its early history as a small, highly unified group that was a reliable source of voting cues for its members.[24] Today the CBC has 43 members, and they represent diverse districts, with many in the rural South and others with substantial Latino and white populations.

Inevitably, this growth in size results in declining solidarity. Five members of the CBC (Ford of Tennessee, Davis of Alabama, Scott and Bishop of Georgia, and Wynn of Maryland) were also members of the conservative Democratic Leadership Council, or the so-called House "Blue Dogs," the coalition of moderate–conservative southern Democrats. On several issues including the Iraq War, the bankruptcy bill (the credit card industry supported legislation that makes it virtually impossible for persons to completely liquidate their debts), and legislation lowering the estate tax, several CBC members voted with the conservative Republican majority.

The decline in CBC solidarity is not surprising since it is axiomatic in politics that the larger a group, the greater the likelihood of internal conflicts and divisions. For a minority group like the CBC, however, any decline in solidarity represents a potential loss of power.

In the 2006 Democratic congressional primaries, one of the longest serving of these black "blue dogs"—Albert Wynn of Maryland—was defeated for renomination. Wynn, who had served in the House for 15 years, was defeated by Donna Edwards, an African American attorney. National liberal and labor organizations targeted Wynn and supported Edwards in an effort to send a message that moderate–conservative Democrats would be held accountable by their liberal constituents. In 2008 the second Muslim was elected to the Congress. Andre Carson, an African American, was elected from Indianapolis to complete the unexpired term of his grandmother, Representative Julia Carson. The Carson district is 63 percent white, 29 percent black. (The first Muslim elected, Keith Ellison in 2006, is also an African American, representing a largely white Minnesota district.)

African Americans in the Congressional Power Structure

Party Leadership

The principal members of the Democratic Party power structure in the House are the speaker, majority leader, the majority whip, the deputy whips, the members of the Steering and Policy Committee (which makes committee assignments and establishes broad party policy), and the officers of the Democratic Caucus. From 1989 to 1991, when he resigned to become president of the United Negro College Fund, Pennsylvania congressman Bill Gray served as majority whip, the number three leadership position. In 2004, Congressman James Clyburn was elected majority whip. After the Democrats lost their majority in 2010, a new position of assistant democratic leader was created so that Clyburn could maintain his position as the only African American in the party leadership.

In 1999, third-term congressman J. C. Watts of Oklahoma was elected chairperson of the Republican Party Conference, the fourth-ranking position in the Republican leadership structure in the House. This was widely interpreted as a move by the party to reach out to black and other minority voters. Watts's selection marked the first time an African American had held a leadership position in the House Republican Party.

In 2002, however, Congressman Watts decided to retire from the Congress. Watts cited personal reasons for retirement (wanting to spend more time with family and to pursue business interests), but reportedly he privately complained that he was not adequately respected by some of his colleagues in the Republican leadership.[25]

Committees and Committee Leadership

In the 111th Congress, blacks served on every standing committee of the House. In Table 10.2, data are displayed on black membership and seniority on the major or "power" committees of Congress and on those committees that are especially important to black interests. The major or power committees are the ones dealing with money: the Budget Committee, the Committees on Ways and Means (taxes) and Appropriations (spending), the Rules Committee, the Energy and Commerce Committee (because of its broad jurisdiction under the commerce clause), and the Armed Services Committee (because of the importance of military policy and the size of the military budget). The Judiciary Committee is important to black interests because of its jurisdiction over civil rights legislation; the Financial Services Committee because of its jurisdiction over urban and housing policy; and the Education and Workforce Committee because of its jurisdiction over education, labor, and parts of welfare and health policy.

Table 10.2 shows that African Americans are represented on each of the major or power committees, and they are heavily represented on those committees of special relevance to black interests—Judiciary, Financial Services, and Education and Workforce. In the 114th Congress, African Americans were "Ranking Member" (in line to become chair when the Democrats hold the majority) of seven of 20 House committees, including such important ones as Judiciary, Financial Services, and Homeland Security. They also served as ranking member of 17 subcommittees. Because of the operation of the seniority system and the ability of African Americans to be routinely reelected to the Congress, black members have gained considerable power in the House (and see Box 10.1).

TABLE 10.2 **African American Members of the House, Assignments on Major/Power Committees and Committees of Special Interest to Blacks, 114th Congress, 2015–2017**

Major/Power Committees	Democratic Members	Black Members and Ranks[a]
Appropriations	21	Fattah (9) Bishop (10) Lee (11)
Armed Services	21	Johnson (11)
Budget[b]	14	Moore (5) Lee (8)
Energy and Commerce	23	Rush (2) Butterfield (10) Clark (19)
Rules	4	Hastings (3)
Ways and Means[c]	10	Rangel (2) Lewis (6) Davis (14)

COMMITTEES OF SPECIAL INTEREST TO BLACKS

Financial Services	26	Waters (1) Meeks (5) Clay (8) Scott (10) Green (11) Cleaver (12) Moore (13) Ellison (14) Carson (19) Beatty (24)
Education and Workforce	16	Payne (1) Wilson (9) Fudge (6) Jeffries (13)
Judiciary	16	Conyers (1) Jackson-Lee (4) Johnson (6) Bass (11) Richmond (12) Jeffries (14)

a The number in parentheses represents the member's rank or seniority among Democratic members of the committee.
b The Budget Committee prepares the annual congressional budget, setting targets for taxation, spending, and borrowing.
c In addition to its power to impose taxes on personal, corporate, and other income, the Ways and Means Committee also has responsibility for Social Security, Medicare, Medicaid, welfare, and international trade. Congressman Charles Rangel, former chair and ranking Democrat on Ways and Means, was forced to give up the position in 2010 because of allegations of violating House ethics rules.

BOX 10.1

The Diversifying Black Representative: A Look at Congresswoman Mia Love of Utah

Reflecting the increasing ethnic diversity of the African American population, and the Republican Party's efforts to demonstrate racial, ethnic, and gender diversity in its leadership, Ludmya "Mia" Bourdeau Love is the first African American from Utah and first black female Republican elected to the Congress. Self-described as a conservative, a Mormon, and a Tea Party Republican, Love was born in Brooklyn, New York, in 1975 to Haitian immigrants. In 1998, after converting to the Church of Jesus Christ of Latter Day Saints (Mormons), she moved with her husband to Utah where she became active in community affairs and local politics. In 2009, she was elected mayor of the small town of Saratoga Springs. After losing her first bid for Congress in 2012, in 2014 she was narrowly elected in a district less than 2 percent black.

Given her descriptive characteristics as a conservative, black, immigrant woman, Love's candidacy was enthusiastically embraced by the national Republican Party establishment, including Speaker of the House John Boehner, and Mitt Romney and Paul Ryan, the 2012 Republican presidential and vice presidential nominees. As a young, combative, charismatic black woman conservative, Love is poised to symbolically become a new face and voice of the Republican Party and the Conservative Movement.

As an indicator of her aggressiveness, unlike her black Republican colleague from

Congresswoman Mia Love (R, UT).

Source: Getty Images/CQ Roll Call/Meredith Dake

Texas Will Hurd who declined to join the Congressional Black Caucus, Love indicated she intended to join the group. Describing the Black Caucus as "demagogic" and "racist," Love said she intended to join the group to "try to take the thing apart from the inside out."[a]

[a] Dennis Pomby, "'Love Would Take Apart' Congressional Black Caucus if Elected in Utah's 4th District," *Deseret News*, May 11, 2014.

Congressional Responsiveness to the African American Quest for Universal Rights and Freedom

Rights-Based Issues: From Arguing about Slavery to the Civil Rights Act of 1991

Like each of the major institutions of the American government, the Congress's response to the black demand for universal freedom and equality has been hesitant, tentative, and unstable. Interestingly, the first congressional response to the African American demand for universal freedom was a debate over whether the Congress should listen—simply hear—let alone respond to the demand for African freedom. From 1835 to 1844, Congress debated whether it should even receive African American petitions for freedom. Until 1836, black petitions to end slavery were received, printed in the record, and referred to committee. But in 1836, Congressman James Hammond of South Carolina demanded that these petitions not even be received by Congress because to do so was an unconstitutional infringement on slavery. For nine years, the House debated this "gag rule," with the opponents (led by former president John Quincy Adams, by then a House member) arguing that to ban slave petitions was a violation of the First Amendment right of petition, which, they claimed, should be accorded even to slaves. In 1844, the House finally defeated the gag rule on slave petitions.[26]

Before Congress enacted the first wave of civil rights legislation during Reconstruction, it took three other actions dealing with the issue of slavery. First, in 1787 in the Northwest Ordinance Act, Congress banned slavery in the new territories of the upper Midwest, which prevented the spread of slavery into places like Illinois and Indiana.[27] Second, in 1808 Congress abolished the slave trade. Although this was an important law, the illegal importation of additional slaves actually continued until the Civil War.[28] Finally, in 1862 in the middle of the Civil War, Congress abolished slavery in the District of Columbia.

Congressional responsiveness to the African American agenda of universal rights and freedom occurred in two periods: the 1860s during Reconstruction and the 1960s during the civil rights movement. As Table 10.3 shows, from 1866 to 1875 Congress passed six civil rights bills including three civil rights enforcement acts. Between 1957 and 1968 the Congress passed five civil rights bills, including the crucially important Civil Rights Act of 1964, the Voting Rights Act of 1965, and the Fair Housing Act of 1968.

In many ways, the civil rights laws of the 1960s simply duplicate those passed in the 1860s. The Supreme Court invalidated the 1860s laws as unconstitutional or declined to require their enforcement; thus, the Congress in the 1960s had

TABLE 10.3 **List of Civil Rights Laws Enacted by Congress: Reconstruction Era, Civil Rights Era, and Post–Civil Rights Era**

Reconstruction Era	Civil Rights Era	Post–Civil Rights Era
Civil Rights Act, 1866	Civil Rights Act, 1957	Equal Employment Opportunity Act, 1972
Civil Rights Act, 1870	Civil Rights Act, 1960	
Civil Rights Act, 1875	Civil Rights Act, 1964	Civil Rights Restoration Act, 1988
Enforcement Act, 1870	Voting Rights Act, 1965	
Enforcement Act, 1871	Fair Housing Act, 1968	Civil Rights Act, 1991
Enforcement Act, 1875		

to repass them, which again shows the tenuousness and instability of rights-based coalitions. Similarly, the Civil Rights Restoration Act of 1988 and the Civil Rights Act of 1991 were passed to overturn Supreme Court decisions that made parts of the 1964 act difficult to enforce (see Chapter 12). In addition to these major civil rights laws, Congress in the 1970s passed a series of amendments to the 1964 act allowing the government to engage in affirmative action to achieve equality in employment for African Americans, other minorities, and women.[29]

The Renewal of the 1965 Voting Rights Act

The Voting Rights Act of 1965 and the Civil Rights Act of 1964 are the major legislative achievements of the 1960s civil rights movement. Unlike the 1964 act, provisions of the Voting Rights Act are temporary, requiring periodic renewals by the Congress. These provisions were last renewed for 25 years in 1982 and expired in 2007. Of the provisions requiring renewal or "reauthorization," two are controversial. The first is Section 5, which requires states with a history of racial discrimination to apply to the U.S. Justice Department or the U.S. District Court in Washington before making any change in their election laws or procedures. The second controversial provision is Section 203 (added when the act was renewed in 1975), requiring jurisdictions with large numbers of foreign-language-speaking persons to provide multilingual ballots. The so-called "preclearance" requirements of Section 5 cover most of the southern states and parts of several northern states, including California and New York.

President George W. Bush and the leaders of both parties in the House and Senate in 2006 enthusiastically endorsed renewal of the act for 25 more years. (The House bill to renew the act was "HR9," indicating it was among the Republican leaders' top 10 priorities.) However, some southern conservative Republicans in the House and Senate objected to the renewal of Section 5, claiming preclearance is unnecessary because their states no longer engage in racial discrimination. They also allege that Section 5 is unconstitutional because it results in the creation of legislative districts based on race and is discriminatory against the South. Conservative Republicans also objected to Section 203, arguing, in the words of Iowa congressman Steven King, that use of multilingual ballots "encourages the linguistic division of the nation."[30] African American and Latino leaders strongly supported renewal of the act, contending that there is still evidence of racial discrimination at the polls and that the act is responsible for the steady increase in the number of black and Latino elected officials.

In the summer of 2006, the House approved renewal of the act by 309 to 33 (all negative votes cast by Republicans). An amendment to delete Section 5 was defeated 302 to 18 and an amendment to drop Section 203 was defeated 238 to 185. Two weeks after the House approved the bill, the Senate passed it 98–0. In spite of the enthusiastic support of the President and the overwhelming congressional vote, the Supreme Court in 2013 effectively gutted the preclearance requirement of the Act (see Chapter 12).

Restoring Civil Rights

Twice before (in 1988 and 1991), Congress passed civil rights laws designed to overturn unfavorable Supreme Court decisions: decisions that made it difficult to enforce the Civil Rights Act of 1964. In 2008, two similar bills were proposed. Both were introduced by Senator Edward Kennedy (see Box 10.2).

The first was the Fair Pay Restoration Act. In 2007, in *Ledbetter* v. *Goodyear Tire* the Court in a 5–4 decision ruled that employees complaining of pay discrimination had to file the charges within 180 days of the initial act of discrimination. But as Justice Ruth Bader Ginsberg noted in her dissent, often an employee would not know it when the initial act of discrimination takes place, because salaries and raises of employees are often confidential. (Lilly Ledbetter, the plaintiff in the case, did not learn that she was given smaller raises than her male counterparts until years later.) The Fair Pay Restoration Act overturned the Court's decision by establishing that the 180-day deadline starts when the employee receives the unequal pay, not when the employer made the decision to discriminate. The act also requires that the 180 days begin anew with each discriminatory paycheck. President Bush threatened to veto the bill and Republicans in the Senate used a filibuster to keep it from coming to a vote. The bill was quickly passed in 2009 and became the first act signed by President Obama.

The second bill, the Civil Rights Act of 2008, was introduced in the House by Congressman John Lewis. It would reverse the Court's decision in *Alexander* v. *Sandoval* and restore to individuals the right to sue in cases of institutional racism as well as individual discrimination, whether it involves race, age, gender, ethnicity, or disability. The House easily passed the bill but, like the fair pay bill, it was blocked in the Senate; no action was taken on this bill during Obama's

BOX 10.2

Two Massachusetts Senators and the African American Quest for Universal Freedom

Massachusetts is often referred to as "freedom's birthplace" and as the "citadel of American liberalism." Whether this reputation is deserved or not, in Senator Charles Sumner and in Senator Edward "Ted" Kennedy,[a] Massachusetts has sent to the Senate two men who have distinguished themselves in the African American quest for universal freedom.

Frederick Douglass described Senator Sumner as the greatest friend the Negro people ever had in public life. Born in 1811, Sumner served in the Senate from 1852 until his death in 1874. During his career in the Senate, he was that body's most outspoken champion of the freedom of the enslaved African. In an 1856 Senate speech, he bitterly attacked two of his colleagues for their support of slavery. Two days later, Congressman Preston Brooks entered the Senate chamber and nearly beat Sumner to death, arguing that his remarks were a libel on the South. After a three-year recovery period, Sumner returned to the Senate to continue his struggle for black freedom, both rights-based and material-based.

Sumner made his greatest contribution to the African American freedom struggle after the Civil War. With Congressman Thaddeus Stevens, he led the fight in Congress for civil rights legislation and passage of the Fourteenth and Fifteenth Amendments. Stevens and Sumner were also responsible for the idea of "40 acres and a mule," introducing legislation to confiscate the slaveholders' plantations, divide them up, and give them to the slaves as compensation or reparation and as a means to punish the slaveholders for treason.

At the time of his death, Sumner was fighting for a civil rights bill that would have banned discrimination and segregation in every public place in the United States—from schools to churches, from cemeteries to hospitals. On his deathbed, surrounded by Frederick Douglass and other African American leaders, Sumner's last words were said to have been, "Take care of my civil rights bill—take care of it—you must do it."

One hundred years later, another senator from Massachusetts took up Sumner's cause. Senator Edward Kennedy was elected to the Senate in 1962 to take the seat vacated by his brother when he became president. Throughout his more than four decades in the Senate, Kennedy was a leader in the passage of every civil rights bill, from the Civil Rights Act of 1964 to the Civil Rights Act of 1991. Especially after the murder of his brother Robert in 1968, Kennedy made the cause of the poor and racially oppressed his cause. As the senior Democrat on both the Labor and Public Welfare Committee and the Judiciary Committee, he led the fight for minimum wage legislation, national health insurance, immigration reform, and education and employment legislation. In 1993, his Labor and Public Welfare Committee was the only committee to report and send to the floor national health insurance legislation, largely due to his leadership as chair. In 1996, he was the floor leader of the fight to increase the minimum wage, to provide health coverage for laid-off workers, and to ban discrimination against homosexuals in employment.

Perhaps the Senate's most famous member, Kennedy was regarded as one of the body's most passionate and skilled legislators on issues of civil rights and social justice. In 1980, he challenged President Jimmy Carter for renomination, charging that the president had abandoned the liberal cause. After his loss to Carter, Kennedy returned to the Senate, where he became a leading opponent of the Reagan administration's civil rights and social welfare policies. Although his goal of succeeding his brother as president was not to be, he left his mark, as there is no major piece of civil rights or liberal reform legislation of the last four decades that was not influenced by the senator from Massachusetts. In 2008, Senator Kennedy endorsed Barack Obama for the Democratic nomination, hailing him as a new generation of leadership that recalled his brother. In 2010, he died of complications from brain cancer.

a On Sumner, see Frederick Blue, *Charles Sumner and the Conscience of the North* (New York: Norton, 1976); and on Kennedy, see Adam Clymer, *Edward M. Kennedy: A Biography* (New York: Morrow, 1999). See also Senator Kennedy's memoir completed shortly before his death, *True Compass: A Memoir* (New York: Twelve, 2011).

presidency. However, both the House and Senate did take actions dealing with the disparity in sentencing for crack and powdered cocaine. The House Judiciary Committee approved a measure, completely eliminating the disparity; while the Senate unanimously passed a bill reducing the disparity from 100 to 1 to 18 to 1 (five years mandatory for 28 grams of crack instead of the 5 grams in current law, while the amount for five years for powdered would remain 500 grams). The Senate also joined the House in 2009 in unanimously passing a resolution apologizing for slavery.

Material-Based Rights: From 40 Acres and a Mule to the Humphrey–Hawkins Full Employment Act

If Congress has been reluctant and tentative in terms of responsiveness to the rights-based black agenda, it has been even less responsive to the material-based agenda. The Constitution, after adoption of the Fourteenth Amendment, may be interpreted to guarantee universal civil and political freedoms; however, many, perhaps most, Americans tend to think that access to material benefits (land, health care, jobs) should not be universal but rather individual. That is, in a free enterprise, capitalist system, it is up to each individual to get his or her own land, health care, and employment. This view was expressed very clearly by President Andrew Johnson when he vetoed the Freedmen's Bureau Act, which, in addition to granting blacks land, provided other welfare and educational benefits to the former slaves. In his veto message, the president wrote, "The idea on which the slaves were assisted to freedom was that on becoming free they would be a self-sustaining population. Any legislation that shall imply they are not expected to attain a self-sustaining condition must have a tendency injurious alike to their character and their prospects."[31] The ideas of President Andrew Johnson were echoed by Newt Gingrich and Bill Clinton, who argued that welfare is injurious to the character, individual responsibility, and sense of self-reliance of the African American community.

The Humphrey–Hawkins Act

The 1963 March on Washington during which Dr. King gave his famous "I Have a Dream" speech was a march for "jobs and freedom." However, as we pointed out in Chapter 6, rights-based demands usually take precedence over material-based ones. Thus, the demand for jobs had to wait for the gaining of freedom in the form of the 1960s civil rights laws. But the problem of joblessness was clearly a major problem in the African American community, especially in the cities of the North, where blacks already had basic civil and political rights. Since the end of the Depression, African Americans have never experienced full employment (see Chapter 14). In general, in the post–World War II era, black unemployment has been twice that of whites, generally at about 10 percent of the adult labor force. Thus, at the end of the civil rights era, the material-based demand for jobs— full employment guaranteed by the federal government—became the principal African American demand, the priority item on the black agenda.

At the time of his death in 1968, Dr. King was planning to lead a multiracial coalition of poor people to march on Washington, the principal demand of which was a guaranteed job or income. After Dr. King's death, this demand for jobs became the principal priority of African American interest groups. In the late 1960s, the Congressional Black Caucus, under the leadership of California congressman Augustus Hawkins, developed a broad coalition of blacks, liberal, labor, and religious groups to try to persuade Congress to pass legislation "guaranteeing a job to all willing and able to work." Once before, in 1946, a broad liberal–labor coalition had sought similar legislation. By the time the bill was passed as the Employment Act of 1946, however, the job guarantee provision had been deleted and the act was little more than a policy-planning mechanism, creating the President's Council of Economic Advisors and a Joint Economic Committee in the Congress.[32]

Critics of the Employment Act of 1946, including business leaders, academic economists, the mainstream media, and conservative politicians, argued that the idea of full employment guaranteed by the federal government was "socialistic," "anti-free enterprise," "utopian," and "un-American" and would result in "runaway inflation." Similar criticisms were made of the 1978 legislation intro-duced by Congressman Hawkins and former vice president and then senator Hubert Humphrey. The bill, "The Full Employment and Balanced Growth Act," as originally introduced provided each American citizen with a legal right or entitlement to a job and required the Congress, if necessary, to create public-sector jobs if an individual could not find a job in the private economy. By the time the bill was passed and signed by President Carter, these provisions, as was the case in 1946, had been deleted, making the bill little more than a symbolic statement of principles.[33]

In the years since the passage of the Humphrey–Hawkins Act, neither the president nor the Congress nor the Federal Reserve has sought to use the planning process established by the act to move toward a 4 percent unemployment rate. As Congressman Hawkins woefully wrote in a 1986 article, "Since the passage of the Act, we have yet to see an economic report from the President, a Federal Reserve report or a Joint Economic Committee report that constructs the actual programmatic means for achieving full employment."[34] To the contrary, economic policy makers today generally consider 5–5.5 percent unemployment as the so-called natural rate of unemployment. This natural rate of unemployment, which translates into 10–12 percent for blacks, is accepted by Democrats and Republicans and liberals and conservatives—what one writer calls "a bipartisan fear of full employment."[35]

Faces and Voices in the Struggle for Universal Freedom
JOHN LEWIS (1940–)

John Lewis's contribution to universal freedom and equality derives from his leadership of the SNCC (the Student Nonviolent Coordinating Committee) during the civil rights movement and his work in Congress. Born in Troy, Alabama, Lewis was inspired to join the civil rights movement in 1958 after meeting Dr. Martin Luther King Jr. In 1961, Lewis was among the founding

John Lewis.

Source: AP Photo/Ric Feld

members of the SNCC, a minority–majority coalition of black and white college students. In 1963, he was elected chairman of the SNCC. SNCC was the most radical of the civil rights organizations, and the young women and men in the group displayed extraordinary courage in confronting vicious racists throughout the South. But of all the brave people in the SNCC, perhaps none was more courageous than Lewis. In 1961, he was beaten unconscious in Montgomery, Alabama, on one of the first freedom rides. In 1965, he suffered a similar fate as he led a march from Selma to Montgomery. Arrested more than 40 times, Lewis always responded nonviolently and with expressions of Christian love. Decades later, reflecting on Lewis's work in the civil rights movement, *Time* magazine referred to him as a "living saint."

In 1986, Lewis was elected to Congress from Atlanta, forging a minority-majority coalition composed of 90 percent of the white vote and 40 percent of the black vote. In the House, he continued to emphasize coalition building. His status as a genuine American hero facilitated his capacity to build multiracial coalitions. A member of the powerful Ways and Means Committee, Lewis has devoted much of his time to persuading the Congress to recognize the contributions of African Americans and the civil rights movement to American history. Among his achievements are the establishment of a Washington memorial to Dr. King and a national museum of African American history. In 1999, he wrote a memoir, *Walking with the Wind: A Memoir of the Movement.*

Summary

Congress as a legislative body in theory should represent all the people of the United States. Historically, the American Congress has not represented its black citizens in a fair and equitable way. Although some progress has been made in enhancing the representation of blacks in Congress in the last two decades, blacks are still not equitably represented, especially in the Senate, where two blacks serve and only seven have been elected in the more than 200-year history of that body. Although African Americans are not equitably represented in Congress, because they are routinely reelected through the operation of the seniority system, blacks in the House have accumulated considerable power in terms of positions of committee leadership. In two periods—the 1860s and 1960s—Congress has responded to the black quest for universal freedom by passing several major civil rights bills. However, Congress has been less responsive to the African American quest for material rights and benefits such as land in the 1860s and jobs in the 1970s.

Critical Thinking Questions

1. Discuss the representation of African Americans in Congress descriptively and substantively.
2. Why has the solidarity of the Congressional Black Caucus declined in recent years?
3. Explain the impact of race with respect to descriptive, substantive, and symbolic representation in Congress. Which type of representation is most impacted by the race of the congressional member?
4. Why do African Americans have more power in Congress when the Democrats are the majority party?
5. Discuss the two periods in history when the Congress has been most representative of African American interests.

Selected Bibliography

Baker, Ross. *House and Senate*, 2nd ed. New York: Norton, 1995. A comparative analysis of the two houses focusing on how the differences in their sizes affect their operations.

Barone, Michael, and Grant Ujifusa. *The Almanac of American Politics 2016*. Washington, DC: National Journal, 2015. The biannual compilation of data on the districts and members of the House and Senate.

Berg, John. *Unequal Struggle: Class, Gender and Race in the U.S. Congress*. Boulder, CO: Westview Press, 1994. A perceptive analysis of how the structure of the capitalist economy constrains progressive action that would benefit minorities, workers, and women.

Canon, David. *Race, Redistricting and Representation*. Chicago, IL: University of Chicago Press, 1999. A comprehensive analysis of how blacks in Congress more effectively represent black interests than whites.

Champagne, Richard, and Leroy Rieselbach. "The Evolving Congressional Black Caucus: The Reagan–Bush Years." In H. Perry and W. Parant, eds., *Blacks and the American Political System*. Gainesville: University Press of Florida, 1995. A historical survey of the Caucus from its founding in 1969 to the last years of the Bush administration.

Congressional Quarterly. *Origins and Development of Congress*. Washington, DC: Congressional Quarterly, 1976. A concise account of the history of Congress.

Congressional Quarterly. *Powers of Congress*. Washington, DC: Congressional Quarterly, 1976. A concise overview of the powers of Congress.

Graham, Hugh Davis. *The Civil Rights Era: Origins and Development of National Policy*. New York: Oxford University Press, 1990. A comprehensive study of the passage and implementation of the 1960s civil rights laws.

Jones, Charles E. "An Overview of the Congressional Black Caucus, 1970–1985." In F. Jones et al., eds., *Readings in American Political Issues*. Dubuque, IA: Kendall/Hunt, 1987. An overview of the Caucus's operations from its founding through the middle Reagan years.

Loevy, Robert, ed. *The Civil Rights Act of 1964: The Passage of the Law that Ended Racial Segregation*. New York: SUNY Press, 1996. Firsthand, behind-the-scenes accounts of how the Civil Rights Act was passed.

Singh, Robert. *The Congressional Black Caucus: Racial Politics in the U.S. Congress*. Thousand Oaks, CA: Sage, 1998. An analysis of the limited effectiveness of the Caucus as a lobby for black interests in Congress.

Smith, Robert C. "Financing Black Politics: A Study of Congressional Elections." *Review of Black Political Economy* 17 (1988): 5–30. A study of the role of money in the election of blacks to Congress.

Swain, Carol. *Black Faces, Black Interests: The Representation of African American Interests in Congress.* Cambridge, MA: Harvard University Press, 1993. A controversial analysis suggesting that whites in Congress represent the interests of blacks as well as blacks do.

Tate, Katherine. *Black Faces in the Mirror: African Americans and Their Representatives in Congress.* Princeton, NJ: Princeton University Press, 2003. A study of black House members and the symbolic and substantive impact of their representation.

Tate, Katherine. *Concordance: Black Lawmaking in the U.S. Congress from Carter to Obama.* Ann Arbor: University of Michigan Press, 2014. A detailed statistical examination of the increasing centrism of the Congressional Black Caucus as a result of the incorporation of its members into the Congressional Democratic Party.

Wilson, Woodrow. *Congressional Government: A Study in American Politics.* Gloucester, MA: Peter Smith, 1956. The 28th president's still-insightful study of how the organization and procedures of Congress make it an inefficient, irresponsible, and ineffective legislative institution.

Notes

1 John Locke, *The Second Treatise of Government*, edited by Thomas Peardon (Indianapolis, IN: Bobbs-Merrill, 1952): 75.

2 Benjamin Akzin, "Legislation: Nature and Function," *International Encyclopedia of the Social Sciences* (New York: Free Press, 1972): 223.

3 John Stuart Mill, *Considerations on Representative Government* (Indianapolis, IN: Bobbs-Merrill, 1869, 1952): 146.

4 Hanna Pitkin, *The Concept of Representation* (Berkeley: University of California Press, 1972): 5

5 For a list and biographical and related information on each person who has served in the Congress, see *Biographical Directory of the American Congress, 1774–1996* (Washington, DC: Congressional Quarterly, 1998). See also U.S. House, Office of the Historian, "Members of Congress," 2015.

6 Quoted in Rayford Logan, *The Betrayal of the Negro* (New York: Collier Books, 1965): 98.

7 In *Baker* v. *Carr* (369 U.S. 186, 1962), the Supreme Court held that the Fourteenth Amendment's equal protection clause required that state legislative districts be equal in population, and that each legislator represent roughly the same number of people. In *Wesberry* v. *Sanders* (376 U.S. 1, 1964), the Court applied this equality in representation principle to congressional districts.

8 Martin Gilens, *Affluence and Influence: Economic Inequality and Political Power in America* (Princeton, NJ: Princeton University Press, 2012).

9 Ibid., p. 6, chap. 3.

10 Martin Gilens and Benjamin Page "Testing Theories of American Politics: Elites, Interest Groups and Average Citizens," *Perspectives on Politics* 12 (2014): 876. See also Jacob Hacker and Paul Pierson, *Winner Take All Politics: How Washington Made the Rich Richer and Turned Its Back on the Middle Class* (New York: Simon & Schuster, 2011).

11 Linda Greenhouse, "Supreme Court Agrees to Hear Case on Government's Refusal to Adjust Census," *New York Times*, September 28, 1995, p. A14.

12 *Wisconsin* v. *City of New York* #94-1614, 1996 (slip opinion).

13 Linda Greenhouse, "In Blow to Democrats, Court Says Census Must Be by Actual Count," *New York Times on the Web* (January 26, 1999).

14 Congresswoman Eleanor Holmes Norton, who is black, represents the District of Columbia. Each of the U.S. territories—Puerto Rico, Guam, the Virgin Islands, and American Samoa—are allowed to send delegates to the House. These delegates are allowed to vote in committees and participate in floor debates, but they are not allowed to vote on the floor. The delegate from the Virgin Islands is also black.

15 Robert C. Smith, "The Black Congressional Delegation," *Western Political Quarterly* 34 (June 1981): 204–5.

16 Carol Swain, *Black Faces, Black Interests: The Representation of African Americans in Congress* (Cambridge, MA: Harvard University Press, 1993).

17 Kenny Whitby, *The Color of Representation: Congressional Behavior and Black Interests* (Ann Arbor: University of Michigan Press, 1998): 110–11.

18 David Canon, *Race, Redistricting and Representation: The Unintended Consequences of Black Majority Districts* (Chicago, IL: University of Chicago Press, 1999): 189, 191, 209, and 219.

19 Katherine Tate, *Black Faces in the Mirror: African Americans and Their Representatives in the US Congress* (Princeton, NJ: Princeton University Press, 2003). Research also shows that black voters attach less significance to descriptive representation but are more likely than whites to contact black members of Congress. See Claudine Gay, "Spirals of Trust: The Effect of Descriptive Representation on Relationships between Citizens and Their Government," *American Journal of Political Science* 46 (2000): 714–32.

20 Katherine Tate, *Concordance: Black Lawmaking in the U.S. Congress from Carter to Obama* (Ann Arbor: University of Michigan Press, 2014).

21 Richard Fenno, "The Internal Distribution of Influence: The House," in D. Truman, ed., *The Congress and America's Future* (Englewood Cliffs, NJ: Prentice Hall, 1965): 52.

22 Susan Webb Hammond, Daniel Mulhollan, and Arthur Stevens, "Informal Congressional Caucuses and Agenda Setting," *Western Political Quarterly* 38 (1985): 583–605; and Burdett Loomis, "Congressional Caucuses and the Politics of Representation," in L. Dodd and B. Oppenheimer, eds., *Congress Reconsidered* (Washington, DC: Congressional Quarterly, 1981): 204–20.

23 On the Congressional Black Caucus's origins and evolution, see Charles Jones, "An Overview of the Congressional Black Caucus," in F. Jones et al., eds., *American Political Issues* (Dubuque, IA: Kendall/Hunt 1987): 219–40; Richard Champagne and Leroy Rieselbach, "The Evolving Congressional Black Caucus," in H. Perry and W. Parant, eds., *Blacks and the American Political System* (Gainesville: University Press of Florida, 1995): 130–61; and Robert Singh, *The Congressional Black Caucus: Racial Politics in the U.S. Congress* (Thousand Oaks, CA: Sage, 1998).

24 Arthur B. Levy and Susan Stoudinger, "Sources of Voting Cues for the Congressional Black Caucus," *Journal of Black Studies* 7 (1976): 29–46.

25 Juliet Eilperin, "GOP's J. C. Watts Will Leave Congress," *West County Times*, July 2, 2002.

26 The story of the battle to lift the gag rule on slave petitions is told in William Lee Miller, *Arguing about Slavery: The Great Battle in the United States Congress* (New York: Knopf, 1995).

27 William Freehling, "The Founding Fathers and Slavery," *American Historical Review* 77 (1972): 87. To get around the law, Illinois and Indiana passed black indentured servant laws; these, although not law, in effect legalized African slavery.

28 Ibid.
29 Robert C. Smith, *We Have No Leaders: African Americans in the Post–Civil Rights Era* (Albany, NY: SUNY Press, 1996): chap. 6. The Senate during the 1970s also killed in close votes or blocked through filibusters House-passed bills that would have banned school busing for purposes of school desegregation.
30 Charles Babington, "GOP Rebellion Stops Voting Rights Act," *Washington Post,* June 22, 2007.
31 Veto message of President Andrew Johnson, the Freedmen's Bureau Act, February 19, 1966, as reprinted in Amilcar Shabazz, ed., *The Forty Acres Documents* (Baton Rouge, LA: House of Songhay, 1994): 84.
32 Stephen K. Bailey, *Congress Makes a Law: The Story Behind the Employment Act of 1946* (New York: Vintage Books, 1964).
33 For a detailed case study of the Humphrey–Hawkins Act, see Smith, *We Have No Leaders,* chap. 7.
34 Augustus Hawkins, "Whatever Happened to Full Employment?" *Urban League Review* 10 (1986): 11.
35 F. Thayer, "A Bipartisan Fear of Full Employment," *New York Times*, October 12, 1988.

CHAPTER 11

The Presidency, Bureaucracy, and the African American Quest for Universal Freedom

---

LEARNING OBJECTIVE

Identify the classifications used to explain racial attitudes of American presidents, and how presidential discretion influences the capacity of the bureaucracy to advance universal freedom.

My paramount object in this struggle is to save the union, and is not either to save or destroy slavery—If I could save the union without freeing any slave I would do it, and if I could save it by freeing all the slaves I would do it; and if I could save it by freeing some and leaving others alone I would also do that—what I do about slavery and the colored race, I do because I believe it helps to save the union—I shall do less whenever I shall believe what I am doing hurts the cause, and I shall do more whenever I shall believe doing more will help the cause—I shall try to correct errors when shown to be errors; and I shall adopt new views so fast as they shall appear to be true views—I have here stated my purpose according to my view of official duty; and I intend no modification of my oft-expressed personal wish that all men everywhere could be free.[1]

—*Abraham Lincoln (1862)*

We begin this chapter with the famous quotation from Abraham Lincoln's letter to newspaper editor Horace Greeley. We do so initially because Lincoln was the first American president to deal in a positive, antiracist way with the African American quest for universal freedom. Second, in his timid, cautious, moderate approach to dealing with the freedom of African Americans, Abraham Lincoln is the paradigmatic president, setting an example—a pattern or model— for the handful of other American presidents who have dealt in a positive way with the African American freedom quest.

Abraham Lincoln: The Paradigmatic President

Horace Greeley, a former congressman and liberal reform leader (best known for his famous saying, "Go West, young man"), urged President Lincoln to turn the Civil War into a moral crusade against slavery. Lincoln refused. Writing to Greeley that while he personally opposed slavery and supported universal freedom for all men everywhere, his principal objective in the war, according to his view of "official duty" as president, was to save the Union and that what he did about slavery was secondary to this "paramount objective." What President Lincoln was saying and what all other American presidents from George Washington to Barack Obama have said is that the problem of African American freedom must take second place to what is good for the nation—the Union—as a whole.

Lincoln was a skilled politician, despite his reputation as a backcountry lawyer from Illinois.[2] Thus, he might also have said that what he did about slavery was also secondary to what was good for him as a politician in terms of public opinion (white public opinion) and his chances for reelection. While American presidents perhaps should attempt to lead public opinion on issues important to the nation's well-being—and occasionally some have done so— most have not, choosing instead to follow rather than lead. This may be an enduring dilemma of the American democracy on all kinds of issues but especially on issues of race and racism, where Bryce's description of presidential leadership is apt: "timid in advocacy . . . infertile in suggestion . . . always listening for the popular voice, always afraid to commit himself to a point of view which may turn out unpopular."[3] Alexis de Tocqueville's *Democracy in America*, published in 1835, is generally considered the most perceptive and prophetic book ever written on the subject of America's democracy. In it, he argued that universal freedom and equality for blacks and whites were unlikely to occur in any country, but it was especially unlikely in the United States precisely because of its democracy. Tocqueville wrote,

> I do not imagine that the white and black races will ever live in any country upon an equal footing. But I believe the difficulty to be still greater in the United States than elsewhere. . . . A despot who should subject the Americans and their former slaves to the same yoke, might perhaps succeed in commingling the races, but as long as the American democracy remains at

the head of affairs, no one will undertake so difficult a task; and it may be foreseen that the freer the white population of the United States becomes, the more isolated it will remain.[4]

Nearly 200 years after Tocqueville's pessimistic assessment, political scientist Richard Riley writes of the history of the presidency and the African American struggle for freedom (and see Box 11.1):

> These incentive structures made it extremely unlikely that someone fervently committed to racial equality would rise through the popularly based electoral process to the presidency in the first place, or that, once there he or she would feel free (or compelled) to invest presidential power in the controversial enterprise. . . . At bottom, on the question of African American rights, the presidency became an agency of change only when movements for equality had successfully reoriented the incumbent's perception of those role requirements, by preparing public opinion and illuminating the risks of inequality in periods of heightened danger to the nation's peace and security.[5]

BOX 11.1

Executive Power, Executive Orders, and Race[a]

Executive orders have been frequently employed by American presidents in the development of civil rights policy. Although the legislative power is vested exclusively in the Congress, presidents since Lincoln have claimed the right to issue directives of broad and general application that have the same legal effect as a law passed by Congress. Presidents trace their authority to engage in this kind of quasi-legislative activity to the general grant of the "executive power" to the president and to the command of Article II: "He shall take care that the laws be faithfully executed." The Supreme Court has upheld this broad interpretation of presidential power by holding that executive orders have the full force of law unless they conflict with a specific provision of the Constitution or of the law. Presidents use executive orders to establish policies when Congress refuses to do so. For example, when Congress refused to pass legislation prohibiting businesses from firing workers who go on strike, President Clinton issued an executive order prohibiting businesses with government contracts from doing so (most large corporations and many small

companies have contracts with the federal government to deliver products or services).[b]

Until the 1960s, Congress refused to legislate in the area of civil rights; thus, presidents, beginning with Franklin D. Roosevelt (FDR), began to use executive orders as a way to get around congressional inaction on civil rights policy. Here are the most important executive orders (E.O.s) dealing with civil rights:

- Establishes policy of nondiscrimination in employment by companies with defense contracts and creates the Committee on Fair Employment Practices—Franklin D. Roosevelt
- E.O. 9980 (1948): Establishes policy of nondiscrimination in government employment and creates a Fair Employment Board within the Civil Service Commission—Harry Truman
- E.O. 9981 (1948): Establishes policy of nondiscrimination in the armed forces and creates the President's Committee on Equality of Treatment and Opportunity in Armed Services—Harry Truman[c]

- E.O. 10479 (1953): Establishes Government Contract Committee to ensure that government contractors and subcontractors comply with nondiscrimination provisions in employment—Dwight Eisenhower
- E.O. 10925 (1961): Establishes President's Committee on Equal Employment Opportunity and requires government contractors to take "affirmative action to ensure that applicants are treated equally during employment, without regard to their race, creed, color or national origin"—John Kennedy
- E.O. 11063 (1962): Prohibits discrimination in federally assisted housing and creates President's Committee on Equal Housing—John Kennedy
- E.O. 11246 (1965): Requires government contractors to take affirmative action as a prerequisite to the award of a contract and requires the Labor Department to enforce the order—Lyndon Johnson
- E.O. 11246 Revised (1971): Requires government contractors to develop affirmative action plans with goals and timetables for hiring, training, and promoting African Americans and other minorities—Richard Nixon[d]

- E.O. 13583 (2011): Establishes a coordinated government-wide initiative to promote diversity in the federal workforce—Barack Obama.

Executive orders are an easy way for a president to establish public policy; however, Congress, if it wishes, may vote to overturn such orders. Since they are the policy decisions of a single individual, what one president gives, another may take away by a simple "stroke of his pen."

[a] On the use of executive orders to make civil rights policy from the Roosevelt to the Johnson administration, see Ruth Morgan, *The President and Civil Rights: Policy Making by Executive Order* (New York: St. Martin's Press, 1970).
[b] A three-judge federal appeals court in Washington ruled that President Clinton's striker replacement order was illegal because it conflicted with federal labor law. The administration declined to appeal this ruling to the Supreme Court, fearing the conservative court might issue a sweeping ruling undermining the president's power to issue executive orders. See "Clinton Accepts Defeat on Strikers' Protection," *San Francisco Chronicle*, September 10, 1996, p. A9.
[c] President Truman based this order on his authority as commander in chief as well as the executive power and the "take care" clause.
[d] This order is the basis and model for the affirmative action programs and policies discussed in Box 11.3.

Lincoln, Emancipation, and Colonialization

Historian George Fredrickson describes President Lincoln as a "pragmatic white supremacist."[6] Throughout his public career, Lincoln opposed slavery—because he thought it was morally wrong but also because he thought it was economically unwise, favoring instead "free labor on free soil."[7] But Lincoln also was a white supremacist, holding that the African people were "inferior in color and perhaps moral and intellectual endowment."[8] While Lincoln was antiracist in his attitudes toward slavery, he was racist in the sense that he, like the overwhelming majority of northern whites, opposed social and political equality for blacks. Whether Lincoln's views on racial equality were sincere or simply politically expedient is not known. However, as Frederick Douglass said, "Clearly, if opposition to black equality constituted a strong and general conviction of the white community, Lincoln would be prepared to accept it as a fact of life, not readily altered even if morally wrong."[9] (See Box 11.2.)

BOX 11.2

The First Thirteenth Amendment[a]

As the prospects of secession and civil war increased, the House and Senate appointed special committees to investigate the situation and make recommendations that might avoid war. Among the recommendations proposed by the House committee was an amendment to the Constitution that would have prohibited any amendment to the Constitution granting the Congress the power to interfere in any way with slavery in any state. The text of the amendment read as follows:

> No amendment shall be made to the Constitution which will authorize or give to Congress the Power to abolish or interfere, within any state, with the domestic institutions thereof, including that of persons held to labor or service by the laws of said state.

This extraordinary amendment, intended to freeze slavery into the Constitution forever, was adopted on March 2, 1861, by a Congress that was overwhelmingly northern, since by that time the senators and representatives from seven southern states that had already seceded were not present. President Lincoln took the extraordinary and completely unnecessary step of personally signing the amendment, the first time a president has signed a constitutional amendment. Three states—Ohio, Illinois, and Maryland—quickly ratified the amendment. However, the attack one month later on Fort Sumter that brought on the Civil War ended any prospect of preserving the Union by preserving slavery, and no other state ratified this first Thirteenth Amendment. Ironically, the second Thirteenth Amendment, adopted four years later, abolished slavery throughout the United States. (Lincoln signed this amendment also.)

[a] For a history of the first Thirteenth Amendment and an analysis of whether it would have been constitutional if it had been ratified, see Mark Brandon, "The 'Original' Thirteenth Amendment and the Limits to Formal Constitutional Change," in Sanford Levinson, ed., *Responding to Imperfection: The Theory and Practice of Constitutional Amendment* (Princeton, NJ: Princeton University Press, 1995).

As Lincoln told Greeley in his letter, if he could save the Union without freeing any slave, he would do it; if he could do it by freeing some, he would do it; and if he could do it by freeing some and leaving others alone, he would do that. As the war progressed, Lincoln eventually concluded that to save the Union, he must *promise* freedom to *some* of the slaves. Thus, on January 1, 1863, the president, using his authority as commander in chief of the army and navy, issued the Emancipation Proclamation. The Proclamation was issued as a war measure, a measure necessary to win the war. Lincoln called it a "fit and necessary war measure for suppressing said rebellion."[10] The Emancipation Proclamation applied only to those parts of the country under Confederate control—"the states and parts of states . . . wherein the people are this day in rebellion."[11] It specifically exempted Union border slave states such as Maryland and those parts of the South controlled by the Union army (e.g., New Orleans). Thus, at the time the Emancipation Proclamation was issued, it freed very few slaves.[12] Rather, it was important as a war measure to encourage blacks in the

South to rise and join the struggle because once the war was won; the Proclamation promised that they "henceforward shall be free." In addition to being a war measure, the Proclamation had a diplomatic purpose, which was to encourage European support for the Union cause by transforming the war into a moral crusade against slavery.

Lincoln's use of the commander-in-chief clause to promise freedom to the slaves was unprecedented and of questionable constitutionality, since it may have violated the Fifth Amendment provision against the "taking of private property without just compensation."[13] The Thirteenth Amendment, however, settled the question of the constitutionality of the Proclamation. What should be done with the African Americans, once they were free, became the central question before the president and the country.

Lincoln's position was similar to that of Thomas Jefferson, and it was clear and long-standing: colonialization. Once freed, the Africans should be deported out of the country. In his first message to Congress, Lincoln urged recognition of Liberia and Haiti and colonialization of blacks there or in some other places where the climate was "congenial to them."[14] Why colonialization? Why not instead integration and universal freedom? Lincoln's response was public opinion, telling a delegation of black leaders at the White House that "insurmountable white prejudice made racial equality impossible in the United States."[15] And "on this broad continent, not a single man of your race is made the equal of a single man of ours. Go where you are treated the best and the ban is still on you."[16] Colonialization was an impractical scheme, costly and complex. Thus, nothing ever came of it although Lincoln supported it until the day of his death.

Lincoln was the first president to act decisively in favor of African American freedom, but his actions were partial (promising limited rather than universal freedom), limited by his own prejudices, by public opinion, and by the exigencies of winning the war. Lincoln is near universally considered the nation's greatest president. Yet, in his approach to the problem of race, he was timid and cautious, "always listening for the popular voice, always afraid to commit himself to a point of view that may turn out unpopular." This is how it has always been with American presidents and race—and perhaps, as Tocqueville said, must be. Frederick Douglass summed up the paradigmatic Lincoln in a speech unveiling a monument to the president on April 14, 1876. He told the whites in the audience, "You are the children of Lincoln, we are at best his step-children," but Douglass said:

> Viewed from the genuine abolition ground, Mr. Lincoln seemed tardy, cold, dull and indifferent, but measuring him by the sentiment of his country, a sentiment he was bound as a statesman to consult, he was swift, zealous, radical and determined.[17]

Lincoln himself could not have summed it up better.

The Racial Attitudes and Policies of American Presidents from George Washington to Barack Obama

The American presidency is an office of great power and majesty, and there are a variety of theories, typologies, and apologies in the literature on presidential leadership.[18] Few studies have addressed presidential accountability in the context of race relations. Yet, it is important to understand how the racial attitudes and policies of American presidents have been a crucial factor in the African American quest for universal freedom.

Of the 44 men who have served as president, very few have been allies in the African American freedom struggle. On the contrary, most have been hostile or at best neutral or ambivalent. Table 11.1 lists the American presidents in terms of their racial attitudes and policies. Twenty-three (more than half) were white supremacists, including, as we have said, Abraham Lincoln. Eighteen have also been racists, supporting either slavery (including eight slave owners) or segregation and racial inequality. Thirteen have been neutral or ambivalent in their attitudes toward African American freedom. Nine—Lincoln, Grant, Benjamin Harrison, Truman, Kennedy, Johnson, Nixon, Carter, and Obama—have pursued antiracist policies in terms of emancipation of the slaves and their freedom and equality in the United States. Although we classify Lincoln as an antiracist president on the basis of the Emancipation Proclamation, as we indicated, he was ambivalent, favoring freedom for the slaves but not racial equality and universal rights. Table 11.1 also shows that with the exception of Lincoln, Grant, and Harrison, all the antiracist presidents served in the mid-twentieth century, most since the 1960s.[19] Of the 10 greatest American presidents, according to the most recent poll of American historians—Lincoln, Washington, Franklin D. Roosevelt, Jefferson, Jackson, Theodore Roosevelt, Wilson, Truman, Polk, and Eisenhower—eight were white supremacists, six were racists, and only two—Lincoln and Truman—were antiracists.[20]

The Presidency and the African American Quest for Universal Freedom: From the Revolutionary Era to the Post–Civil Rights Era

This section is necessarily brief since, as we indicated in the previous section, most American presidents have been unresponsive to the African American quest for universal freedom.

Historical Period	White Supremacist[b]	Racist	Racially Neutral	Racially Ambivalent	Antiracist
Revolutionary (1789–1829)	George Washington **(1)** (1789–1797)	George Washington[c]			
		John Adams **(2)** (1798–1801)			
	Thomas Jefferson **(3)** (1801–1809)	Thomas Jefferson[c]			
	James Madison **(4)** (1809–1817)	James Madison[c]			
	James Monroe **(5)** (1817–1825)	James Monroe[c]			
		John Q. Adams **(6)** (1825–1829)			
Antebellum (1830–1860)	Andrew Jackson **(7)** (1829–1837)	Andrew Jackson[c]			
	Martin Van Buren **(8)** (1837–1841)	Martin Van Buren			
	William H. Harrison **(9)** (1841)	William H. Harrison			
	John Tyler **(10)** (1841–1845)	John Tyler			
	James Polk **(11)** (1845–1849)	James Polk[c]			
	Zachary Taylor **(12)** (1849–1850)	Zachary Taylor[c]			
	Millard Fillmore **(13)** (1850–1853)	Millard Fillmore			
	Franklin Pierce **(14)** (1853–1857)	Franklin Pierce			
	James Buchanan **(15)** (1857–1861)	James Buchanan			

Reconstruction (1863–1877)

Abraham Lincoln (16) (1861–1865)
Andrew Johnson (17) (1865–1869)

Abraham Lincoln
Andrew Johnson^c

Ulysses S. Grant (18) (1869–1877)

Rutherford B. Hayes (19) (1877–1881)

James Garfield (20) (1881)

Benjamin Harrison (23) (1889–1893)

Post-Reconstruction (1880–1930)

Grover Cleveland (22 & 24) (1885–1889, 1893–1897)

Chester Arthur (21) (1881–1885)
Grover Cleveland

William McKinley (25) (1897–1901)

William McKinley

Theodore Roosevelt (26) (1901–1909)   Theodore Roosevelt

William H. Taft (27) (1909–1913)

Woodrow Wilson (28) (1913–1921)   Woodrow Wilson

Warren G. Harding (29) (1921–1923)

Warren G. Harding
Calvin Coolidge (30) (1923–1929)
Herbert Hoover (31) (1929–1933)
Franklin D. Roosevelt (32) (1933–1945)

Civil Rights (1930–1970)

Harry S. Truman (33) (1945–1953)
Dwight Eisenhower (34) (1953–1961)

Harry S. Truman

Dwight Eisenhower

John F. Kennedy (35) (1961–1963)
Lyndon B. Johnson (36) (1963–1969)

TABLE 11.1 Typology of the Racial Attitudes and Policy Perspectives of American Presidents from George Washington to Barack Obama (1st–44th)[a] *continued*

Historical Period	White Supremacist[b]	Racist	Racially Neutral	Racially Ambivalent	Antiracist
Post–Civil Rights (1970–forward)	Richard Nixon **(37)** (1969–1974)			Gerald Ford **(38)** (1974–1977)	Richard Nixon
					Jimmy Carter **(39)** (1977–1981)
				Ronald Reagan **(40)** (1981–1989)	
				George H. W. Bush **(41)** (1989–1993)	
				William Clinton **(42)** (1993–2000)	
				George W. Bush **(43)** (2001–2009)	
					Barack Obama **(44)** (2009–2017)

[a] We classify a president as follows: (1) a white supremacist, if the historical record indicates that he held a belief in the inferiority of the African people; (2) a racist is one who supported the institutions of slavery and segregation; (3) a racial neutral is a president whose record shows no positions on racial issues; (4) while a racial ambivalent is a president whose actions on race issues vary from antiracist to racial neutral; and (5) an antiracist president is one whose record is characterized by actions to dismantle at least parts of the system of racial subordination. All presidents until Lincoln were racist since they defended the institution of slavery, as sanctioned by the Constitution. After Lincoln, we do not classify presidents as racists or white supremacists unless there is evidence in the historical record that they believed blacks were an inferior people or they supported racial segregation and inequality. There is unavoidably some ambiguity in these classifications. For example, as president, John Q. Adams took no antiracist or antislavery actions, but he was not personally racist; after leaving the presidency, Adams, as a congressman, was a vigorous opponent of slavery and the slave trade. And Jefferson—clearly a white supremacist and a racist—acted as soon as the Constitution permitted to abolish the slave trade.

[b] Information on the attitudes and racial policies of the presidents were obtained from various biographical sources including the entire University Press of Kansas American Presidency series and the summary works of George Sinkler, *Racial Attitudes of American Presidents: From Abraham Lincoln to Theodore Roosevelt* (Garden City, NY: Doubleday, 1971); Kenneth O'Reilly, *Nixon's Piano: Presidents and Racial Politics from Washington to Clinton* (New York: Free Press, 1995); and Richard Riley, *The Presidency and the Politics of Racial Inequality: Nation-Keeping from 1831 to 1965* (New York: Columbia University Press, 1999). Years in parentheses indicate tenure in office.

[c] Indicates slave owners.

The Revolutionary Era

Perhaps all the early American presidents supported the institution of slavery because they thought it was economically necessary or because doing so was politically expedient. O'Reilly in his book on the racial attitudes of American presidents indicates that several Revolutionary Era presidents (Washington, Jefferson, Madison, and John Q. Adams) saw slavery as morally wrong and hoped that it would wither away.[21] Yet, none of these early presidents favored universal freedom for blacks; rather, they, like Lincoln, tended to favor colonialization.[22] The only action against slavery by an American president during this period was Jefferson's decision to stop the slave trade as soon as the Constitution permitted. In fact, he proposed to end slavery in 1807, one year before the constitutionally permissible year of 1808. In his annual message to Congress on December 2, 1806, Jefferson wrote,

> I congratulate you fellow citizens on the approach of the period when you may interpose your authority constitutionally [to stop Americans] from further participation in those violations of natural rights which have been so long continued on the unoffending inhabitants of Africa, and which the morality, reputation and best interests of our country have long been eager to proscribe.[23]

The Antebellum Era

None of the nine presidents who served during the Antebellum Era (1830–1860) took any action in response to the African American quest for universal freedom, ignoring or attempting to repress the increasingly militant demands for freedom coming from the abolitionist movement.

The Reconstruction Era

Andrew Johnson, who succeeded Lincoln after his murder, was one of the more racist of American presidents in his attitudes and policies. A white supremacist and racist slave owner from Tennessee, Johnson vetoed civil rights legislation and the Freedmen's Bureau Act. When Congress overrode his vetoes, he refused to faithfully carry out the law as required by the Constitution—one of the factors that led to his impeachment by the House (he came within one vote of being convicted in the Senate and removed from office). By contrast, Ulysses S. Grant, Johnson's successor, was one of the most antiracist presidents in American history. Although he owned one slave, Grant freed him early, and once Grant became president, he attempted to enforce the civil rights laws vigorously, urging his white countrymen to grant African Americans universal suffrage and equality under the law. Grant also appointed blacks to federal office for the first time. Frederick Douglass said of Grant that he never exhibited "vulgar prejudices of any color."[24] Even so, when Grant left office, most of the southern states were under the control of white racists and the tide of public opinion in the North was shifting against his policies.

Grant was followed in office by Rutherford B. Hayes. While antiracist in his personal convictions, Hayes, to win the presidency, agreed in the famous "Compromise of 1877" to withdraw federal troops from the South, effectively bringing the brief era of Reconstruction to an end.[25]

The Post–Reconstruction Era

Most presidents after Hayes ignored the problems of race and racism. White public opinion was indifferent or hostile to the African American quest for freedom, and American presidents, whatever their personal attitudes, followed rather than led during this period: 1880s–1930s. Presidents Grover Cleveland and Theodore Roosevelt were attacked because they had eaten dinner with blacks. Cleveland denied it and Roosevelt, who invited Booker T. Washington to the White House for dinner, promised never to do it again. Woodrow Wilson, the first Democratic candidate for president to receive significant black support, nevertheless once in office immediately sought to impose racial segregation throughout the federal workplace in Washington.

Benjamin Harrison was the first antiracist president since Grant and the last before Truman. Among his antiracist policies was a proposed constitutional amendment to overturn the Supreme Court decision invalidating the Civil Rights Act of 1875, legislation to allow the federal government to enforce African American voting rights in the South, and antilynching legislation.[26] Harrison also responded to the material-based interests of blacks by supporting legislation—the Blair Act—that would have provided large sums of federal money to improve southern schools.

From Benjamin Harrison to Franklin D. Roosevelt, American presidents were largely silent on the issues of race and racism. Roosevelt, the first Democratic president to receive a majority of the black vote, is typical of the political expediency of American presidents on issues of race and racism. In more than 13 years in office, Roosevelt never took any stand on issues of racial discrimination, refusing, despite the urging of his wife Eleanor, even to speak out against lynchings. Like President Kennedy a generation later, Roosevelt's response was always, "I can't take the risk."[27] That is, the president argued that he could not risk losing the support of the powerful white supremacist southern Democrats for his New Deal economic program. Thus, he was willing to sacrifice or trade off the civil rights of blacks to obtain material benefits for all Americans. Blacks benefited from Roosevelt's material-based reforms—public works, housing, and agricultural programs—although the programs were administered on a racially discriminatory basis.

Roosevelt was also concerned that support for civil rights would jeopardize his renomination and reelection, since southern whites controlled an important bloc of votes at the Democratic convention and in the Electoral College.

Roosevelt did respond to one black demand during his term in office. This was the material-based demand for jobs in the war industries, but he did so only after the threat of a massive march on Washington by African American workers. Charging that there was widespread discrimination in the growing war industries, A. Phillip Randolph, the African American head of the Brotherhood of Sleeping Car Porters, threatened to bring hundreds of thousands of blacks to Washington in a massive protest demonstration. To convince Randolph to call off the march, Roosevelt in June 1941 issued Executive Order 8802 that prohibited discrimination in employment of workers in industries with government contracts. The order also created a committee on Fair Employment Practices; however, it was poorly funded and staffed and was not very effective in ending employment discrimination.[28]

The Civil Rights Era

Although President Truman shared the same white supremacist views of his native Missouri, as president he took a strong antiracist position. He did so for two reasons. First, faced with a third-party challenge from the liberal, progressive Henry Wallace, Truman judged that a strong civil rights program would help him rally the black vote in the big cities of the electoral-vote-rich northeastern and Midwestern states. Second, Truman judged that support for civil rights was a cold war imperative. That is, as the leader of the "free world," the United States would be embarrassed and ridiculed by the Soviet Union if it continued to adhere to racism as a national policy.[29]

Thus, President Truman became the first Democratic president in history to propose a civil rights reform agenda to the Congress, including a ban on employment discrimination, antilynching legislation, and a proposal to end the poll tax. President Truman also issued Executive Order 9981 banning discrimination in the armed services, ordered an end to discrimination in federal employment, was the first president to address an NAACP convention, and directed the Justice Department to file a brief in support of school desegregation cases then pending before the Supreme Court. Although the Congress did not pass Truman's civil rights proposals, his administration was the first in 50 years to place the issue of civil rights on the national agenda.[30]

Two minor civil rights bills were passed during the administration of President Eisenhower (the first since Reconstruction); however, his support for them was reluctant. Eisenhower was a white supremacist and a race ambivalent, preferring to avoid taking any action on civil rights or race-related issues if at all possible. He did issue executive orders prohibiting discrimination in government employment and by companies with government contracts, and he appointed a few blacks to minor positions in his administration. The major civil rights issue during the Eisenhower administration was the Supreme Court's *Brown* desegregation decision. Eisenhower opposed the Court's decision and was reluctant to enforce it. However, when Arkansas governor Orval Faubus used the state's National Guard to block the admission of nine black schoolchildren to Little Rock's Central High School, Eisenhower felt he had no choice as president but to "take care that the laws be faithfully executed." Thus, he reluctantly dispatched the U.S. Army to enforce the Court's order that the children be admitted.

John F. Kennedy would not have won one of the closest elections in American history without the support of black voters. But, like Franklin D. Roosevelt, he was reluctant to risk losing the support of white southerners by introducing civil rights legislation. Only after the civil rights demonstrations led by Dr. King created a national crisis did Kennedy finally propose civil rights legislation. In his 1963 speech proposing what was to become the Civil Rights Act of 1964, Kennedy became the first American president to declare that racism was morally wrong.

President Kennedy also appointed a number of blacks to high-level posts in his administration and was the first president to openly entertain blacks at the White House. He also reluctantly issued Executive Order 11063 banning discrimination in federally assisted housing. During the 1960 campaign, Kennedy had promised with a "stroke of the pen" to end discrimination in the sale and rental of housing. Yet, he delayed, and blacks sent hundreds of pens to the president in case he had misplaced his. Finally, in late 1962, he signed the order, but it was limited, excluding all existing housing and covering only housing

President Johnson signing the Civil Rights Act of 1964.

Source: Cecil Stoughton/LBJ Library Collection

owned or directly financed by the federal government. Also, President Kennedy, like President Eisenhower, reluctantly sent the army into Mississippi to enforce a court order desegregating the state's university.

Unlike Presidents Kennedy and Roosevelt, President Johnson was willing "to take the risk" of losing the support of white southern Democrats by enthusiastically and unequivocally supporting civil rights legislation (when he signed the 1964 Act, he told his aides, "We have just lost the South for a generation"). In addition to signing three major civil rights bills, Johnson also initiated the Great Society and the "war on poverty" designed to deal with the material-based needs of urban and rural poor people, many of whom were African Americans. Johnson also made a number of historic appointments, placing the first black in the cabinet and the first black on the Supreme Court.

The Post–Civil Rights Era

Although Richard Nixon was a white supremacist and his 1968 campaign was based on a strategy of attracting the white racist vote in the South,[31] as the first post–civil rights era president he presided over the successful desegregation of southern schools, the renewal of the Voting Rights Act in 1970, implementation of Executive Order 11246 establishing affirmative action, and the appointment of scores of blacks to high-level positions in the government. In addition, Nixon proposed a far-reaching material-based reform—the Family Assistance Plan—that would have guaranteed an income to all families with children. Although this reform was defeated by an odd coalition of blacks and liberals (who thought the income guarantee was too low) and conservatives (who wanted no guarantee at all), if it had passed, it would have substantially raised the income of poor families, many of whom were black.[32] (Nixon also proposed a comprehensive national health insurance program.) Historians are unclear as to why Nixon took such a strong civil rights policy stance (especially on affirmative action),[33] but the political climate in the late 1960s probably made such positions seem politically expedient.

In his nearly two and a half years in office, President Gerald Ford distinguished himself on race by appointing the second black to the cabinet and by waging a year-long campaign to get the courts and the Congress to end busing for purposes of school desegregation.

Jimmy Carter appointed a number of blacks to high-level positions in his administration and to the federal courts,[34] supported affirmative action in the form of the *Bakke* case (see Box 11.3), and reorganized the civil rights enforcement bureaucracy.[35] However, he rejected an ambitious proposal by his African American housing secretary Patricia Roberts Harris for a new urban antipoverty program[36] and supported only a watered-down version of the Humphrey–Hawkins full employment bill.

Ronald Reagan's two terms in office were characterized by ambivalence on race. He came into office determined to dismantle the Great Society and

BOX 11.3

African Americans and Presidential Policy Making: A History of the Role African Americans Played in Affirmative Action Policy Making

Affirmative action—a variety of programs and policies designed to enhance the access of historically marginalized racial and ethnic groups and women to education, employment, and government contracts—is one of the most controversial civil rights policies of the day, as it has been since it was created by African American policy makers in the Johnson and Nixon administrations. Although affirmative action as national policy was developed by African Americans and is widely supported by African Americans and their leaders, in the Carter administration African American policy makers sought to abolish such programs.

Late in the Johnson administration, Edward Sylvester, an African American who headed the Labor Department's Office of Federal Contract Compliance, developed the "Cleveland Plan" designed to assure equal employment opportunity for blacks in the Cleveland, Ohio, construction industry. The Cleveland Plan required that construction companies with government contracts develop detailed plans specifying the precise number of blacks they planned to hire in all phases of their work. This plan brought protests from labor unions, business groups, conservatives, and liberals who argued that it established racial hiring quotas. Eventually, the comptroller general (head of the General Accounting Office, the congressional watchdog agency) ruled that the plan was illegal, not because it required quotas but because it violated standard contract bidding procedures. Sylvester's plan was dropped; however, to the surprise of most observers, it was resurrected in the conservative, business-oriented Nixon administration, again under the policy leadership of African Americans. President Nixon appointed Arthur Fletcher as an assistant secretary of labor and John Wilks as director of the Office of Federal Contract Compliance. Immediately these

two African Americans set about to revive Sylvester's plan. Using Philadelphia as the model city, the "Philadelphia Plan" required government contractors to set specific numerical goals for the employment of workers from historically marginalized backgrounds. Unlike Sylvester's Cleveland Plan, the Philadelphia Plan complied with standard contracting procedures, but the comptroller general again ruled it was illegal, this time because it used race as a factor in determining employment. President Nixon, however, rejected the comptroller general's ruling, arguing that as president he had the inherent "executive power" to implement the Philadelphia Plan by executive order (E.O. 11246). The Senate later passed an amendment upholding the comptroller general's decision, but after intense lobbying by President Nixon and his secretary of labor, George Shultz, the House by a vote of 208 to 156 rejected the Senate's amendment, and affirmative action effectively became the law of the land. Ironically, given Democratic support for affirmative action and Republican opposition to it today, in 1971, a majority of Democrats in Congress voted against affirmative action while it was supported by a majority of Republicans.

The Philadelphia Plan became the model for affirmative action throughout American society, including admission to colleges and universities. In the late 1970s, the University of California at Davis established an affirmative action program at its medical school in order to increase the number of historically marginalized racial and ethnic students enrolled there. Under its plan, 16 of its 100 openings were set aside for minorities only. Allan Bakke, a white applicant who was rejected for admission, sued the university, arguing that for a university to consider race in making its admission decisions was a violation of the Civil Rights Act of 1964 and the Fourteenth Amendment's equal protection clause. The California Supreme Court in the case of *Regents of the University of California* v. *Bakke* (1978) declared the Davis plan unconstitutional. The university appealed this decision to the U.S. Supreme Court.

A sharply divided Supreme Court upheld the university's right to use race in making admission decisions but agreed that setting a quota of 16 slots for minorities only was unconstitutional. We discuss the details of the Court's opinion in *Bakke* and other affirmative action cases in Chapter 12; here we focus on the role of African American policy makers. In important cases, the Supreme Court will "invite" the administration to submit an *amicus curiae* ("friend of the court") brief explaining how it thinks the case should be decided. In the Carter administration, the two policy makers responsible for preparing the administration brief were Wade McCree, who was solicitor general, and Drew Days, III, assistant attorney general for civil rights (and later solicitor general in the Clinton administration). In the first draft of the brief prepared by the solicitor general, the very principle of affirmative action—that race could be considered in admissions or employment decisions—was rejected as a violation of the equal protection clause. It read, "we doubt that it is *ever* proper to use race to close any portion of the class for competition by members of all races" and that "racial classifications favorable to minority groups are presumptively unconstitutional."[a] If this position had been adopted by the Court, affirmative action would have been eliminated, not just in university admissions but in employment and government contracting. McCree's brief, however, was leaked to the press, and after intense lobbying by the NAACP, the Congressional Black Caucus, and others, President Carter instructed the attorney general to request the solicitor general to rewrite the brief. Although McCree was reportedly outraged by what he considered unseemly political pressure, the brief was rewritten to uphold the right of the university to use race in its admissions decisions. Again, the irony here is that affirmative action created by black men serving in a conservative

Republican administration was almost eliminated by black men serving in a liberal Democratic administration.

Several decades after the Philadelphia Plan and after *Bakke,* affirmative action is still under attack. President Reagan implied during the 1980 campaign that he would abolish affirmative action in the federal government by revoking Nixon's 1971 order. But he backed off at the urging of former Nixon administration labor secretary George Shultz (then Reagan's secretary of state) and Samuel Pierce, the secretary of housing and urban development and the only African American in his cabinet. In his review of affirmative action policy—a review led by Christopher Edley, an African American White House staff assistant—President Clinton concluded that while some reforms might be appropriate, affirmative action programs were still necessary to assure equal opportunities for minorities and women. Thus, his formulation: "mend it, don't end it," via a 1995 policy directive—the most explicit statement on the policy to date—outlined specific criteria for affirmative action policy stating, "any program must be eliminated or reformed if it creates a quota, creates a preference for unqualified individuals, creates reverse discrimination, and continues even after its equal opportunity purposes have been achieved."[b]

Despite the policy directive, Republican congressional leaders were opposed to affirmative action; the 1996 Republican presidential nominee Bob Dole also opposed affirmative action; the Supreme Court in a series of cases has been edging away from the principle of affirmative action (led by African American Justice Clarence Thomas); and in 1996, the voters of California—by 56 to 44 percent— approved Proposition 209, the ballot initiative ending affirmative action in that state's education, employment, and contracting.[c] A leader of the California antiaffirmative action initiative was Ward Connerly, an African American.

In the George W. Bush administration, the Supreme Court took up the issue of affirmative action in university admissions for the first time since the *Bakke* case, involving two cases from the University of Michigan. Seeking to dismantle affirmative action, the Bush administration filed, to no avail, two *amicus curiae* briefs with the Supreme Court regarding the use of race in admissions in the two cases. Black appointees in the administration were divided on what position the administration brief to the Supreme Court should take. Three administration blacks—Ralph Boyd, the assistant attorney general for civil rights; Gerald Reynolds, the assistant secretary of education for civil rights; and Brian Jones, the general counsel in the Department of Education—all argued that *Bakke* should be reversed and any consideration of race in university admission should be unconstitutional.[d] African American Secretary of Education Rodney Paige, African American Deputy Attorney General Larry Thompson, and National Security Advisor Condoleezza Rice supported the position eventually adopted by Bush, which sidestepped the constitutional question but argued that the Michigan programs in question were racial quotas and therefore prohibited by *Bakke*. Rice, a former professor and Provost at Stanford, reportedly helped Bush to make the decision and write his speech on the cases.[e] Finally, Secretary of State Powell firmly and publicly opposed the president's position, saying he fully supported affirmative action in principle as well as the specific Michigan programs.[f]

[a] Quoted in Robert C. Smith, *We Have No Leaders: African Americans in the Post–Civil Rights Era* (Albany, NY: SUNY Press, 1996): 149–50. For a detailed analysis of the evolution of affirmative action from the Kennedy to the Nixon administrations, see Hugh Davis Graham, *The Civil Rights Era: Origins and Development of National Policy* (New York: Oxford, 1990): chaps. 10–13; on policy developments from the Nixon to the Bush administrations, see Smith, *We Have No Leaders*, chap. 5.
[b] See "Remarks by the President on Affirmative Action," The White House, Office of the Press Secretary, July 19, 1995. The Clinton administration's detailed review of affirmative action is *Affirmative Action Review: Report to President Clinton* (Washington, DC: Bureau of National Affairs, 1995). This report was prepared by White House advisors George Stephanopoulos and Christopher Edley, Jr.
[c] Several days after Proposition 209 was approved, Federal District Court judge Thelton Henderson suspended its implementation because he said it probably violated the Fourteenth Amendment's equal protection clause. Judge Henderson's order was later reversed by the Ninth Circuit Court of Appeals, and the proposition took effect in the late summer of 1997. See John Bourdeau, "Appeals Court Upholds Support for Prop. 209," *West County Times*, August 22, 1997, p. A1.
[d] "Black Lawyer Behind Bush's Affirmative Action Stance," *The Crisis* (March/April 2003), p. 9.
[e] Mike Allen and Charles Lane, "Rice Helped Shape Bush Decision on Admissions," *Washington Post*, January 17, 2003.
[f] Scott Lindlow, "Powell Backs Affirmative Action," *West County Times*, January 20, 2003.

affirmative action programs. Several Great Society programs were eliminated and the budgets for others were substantially cut. But Reagan also signed a 25-year extension of the Voting Rights Act, strengthened the Fair Housing Act, and (reluctantly) signed the Martin Luther King, Jr. holiday bill. He also refused to issue an executive order eliminating affirmative action, as he had implied he would during the 1980 campaign (see Box 11.3).

George H. W. Bush's administration was also characterized by ambivalence on civil rights. In 1990, he vetoed the Civil Rights Act (designed to overturn several Supreme Court decisions that made it difficult to enforce employment discrimination laws), calling it a "quota bill," but in 1991, he signed essentially the same bill he had vetoed a year earlier.[37] Bush also appointed the second black to the Supreme Court, but the appointee (Clarence Thomas) was a man described by most black leaders as an "Uncle Tom" and a "traitor to the race."[38] Justice Thomas was also accused by Anita Hill, a former black female employee, of sexual harassment. Additionally, Bush rejected proposals by his aides for new antipoverty programs, arguing that they were too expensive and too liberal.[39]

Bill Clinton was arguably the first authentically nonracist, non–white supremacist president in American history. American presidents are a product of the culture and socialization process of their time, and Bill Clinton was the first president to come of age in the nominally nonracist, non–white supremacist post–civil rights era. By all accounts, Clinton was as free of racist and white supremacist thinking as any white person can be.[40] Yet, to win the presidency, Clinton ran on a strategy of deliberately distancing himself from black voters in order to win over the so-called Reagan Democrats who had voted Republican because of the Democrats' close identification with African Americans.[41]

In his first term in office, Clinton appointed a large number of blacks to high-level positions in the administration (one-fourth of the cabinet) and to the courts. He also refused to support proposals to eliminate affirmative action (see Box 11.3) and was responsive to black concerns to use military force to restore the democratically elected president to office in Haiti (see Chapter 15) and became the first U.S. president to make state visits to several African countries. On material-based issues, Clinton proposed a complicated yet comprehensive plan to guarantee health care to all Americans. Clinton's major initiative on race during his second term was to propose a dialogue on race.[42]

However, if Clinton sought to universalize health care and establish it as a right for all citizens, he did the exact opposite with respect to welfare. During the 1992 election, Clinton campaigned on the pledge, "End Welfare as We Know It," by imposing a time limit on eligibility for Aid to Families with Dependent Children.

In addition, in spite of the opposition of the Black Caucus and most civil rights and civil liberties groups, Clinton signed a harshly punitive anticrime bill that included mandatory sentencing for a variety of crimes including first-time drug offenses, the punishment of juveniles as adults, life in prison for persons convicted of three felonies (the so-called "three strikes and you're out"), and expansion of the death penalty to cover more than 50 federal crimes. (The three-strikes law is widely viewed as responsible in part for the growing incarceration of young black men, discussed in Chapter 14.)

On the Clinton administration and race, Steven Shull concludes,

> Bill Clinton was the most rhetorical but also most symbolic and least supportive Democrat in his public statements. . . . Even such long-accepted remedies as affirmative action based on race alone were challenged, with Clinton suggesting that women and even economically disadvantaged white men should be eligible for government remedies.[43]

In spite of these policy differences between blacks and Clinton, when he left office and in his post–presidency, he remained extraordinarily popular among African American leaders and ordinary people. (Clinton located his post–presidential office in Harlem.) In a series of interviews with prominent blacks after Clinton left office, journalist Dewayne Wickham found that Clinton was viewed as among the best, if not the best, president in terms of African American interests.[44] Black public opinion was also highly favorable toward Clinton throughout his tenure, and especially during the investigations leading up to his impeachment, trial, and acquittal. By contrast, when Jimmy Carter, the last Democratic president, left office, his performance was approved of by only 30 percent of blacks compared to 70 percent approval of Clinton during his last year.

Since many of Clinton's policies were conservative, how can one account for his popularity among blacks? How did he capture the imagination of blacks, such that Nobel laureate Toni Morrison could call him the first black president and the Arkansas Black Hall of Fame could make him its first white member? Although scholars disagree on the sources of Clinton's popularity, many attribute it to the prosperous economy (which led to a substantial reduction in black unemployment), his appointments, various symbolic gestures, his obvious familiarity with and comfort among blacks, and to the fact that he became president after 12 years of Reagan and Bush, who were viewed as overtly hostile to black interests.

President George W. Bush entered the presidency with less support from African Americans than any president of the post–civil rights era, with black leaders and voters questioning the very legitimacy of his election. Partly as a result, Bush attempted to reach out to the black community with appointments, symbolic gestures, and substantive policies. Appointments are discussed below; among the symbolic gestures was a visit to several African countries. Among other symbolic gestures, Bush hung a portrait of Martin Luther King Jr. in the White House, laid a wreath at King's tomb, hosted Thomas Jefferson's black relatives at the White House, and signed legislation creating a National Museum of African American History and Culture.

In terms of policy, the Bush record, like Clinton's, is mixed. He issued broad guidelines prohibiting racial profiling by federal law enforcement agencies (except for cases involving terrorism and national security), proposed to Congress a program to increase low-income and home ownership for historically marginalized citizens, pushed through the No Child Left Behind Act designed to raise the performance of low-income and historically marginalized racial and ethnic students, and proposed the "Faith Based Initiative" to allow churches to provide social services to the poor. In foreign policy, he dispatched a special envoy to mediate the Sudanese civil war, sent a small U.S. peacekeeping force to Liberia, and proposed substantial increases in funds to combat AIDS in Africa. However, over the vigorous objections of the Congressional Black Caucus and other African American leaders, Bush brought about the removal of Jean Claude Aristide, the democratically elected president of Haiti. African American leaders also objected to the centerpiece of Bush's domestic policy agenda—his tax cuts—and of his foreign policy, the war on Iraq.

However, the most controversial race issue of the Bush administration was its decision on what kind of brief to file in the cases challenging the University of Michigan affirmative action programs. These two cases were the most important on the issue since the Supreme Court's landmark 1978 ruling in *Regents of University of California* v. *Bakke,* in which it banned quotas but held that race could be taken into consideration as a "plus factor" in university admissions in order to achieve diversity. The Bush administration was divided on what position it should argue before the Court (we discuss the Supreme Court's decision in the case in Chapter 12, and the role of black administration officials in the decision is discussed in Box 11.3). Conservatives in the administration led by the attorney general and the solicitor general argued that the administration should ask the Court to overrule *Bakke* and declare that the Fourteenth Amendment prohibited any consideration of race in university admissions. Moderates in the administration including Alberto Gonzalez, the president's Hispanic general counsel, urged President Bush to avoid the constitutional question of whether race could ever be used in admission decisions. Instead, they said the administration should simply ask the Court to declare the Michigan programs unconstitutional because they constituted racial quotas. Bush adopted the position of Gonzalez and the other moderates, saying that while he supported "diversity of all kinds," the Michigan programs were "fundamentally flawed" because they constituted "racial quotas," which are divisive, unfair, and impossible to square with the Constitution."[45]

Finally, the seeming indifference and the obvious incompetence of the administration's response to Hurricane Katrina, however, probably did more to damage the credibility of the administration among blacks than did any other single event. In one poll, Bush's approval rating after Katrina fell to a mere 2 percent, the lowest ever seen in presidential approval ratings.[46]

The Obama Administration

President Obama entered office at a time when the country faced serious problems. Abroad, the country was engaged in two wars plus a so-called war on terror. In addition, there was the ever-present fear of another 9/11-type catastrophic attack. At home, the country was in the midst of financial crises that led some to raise the specter of another Great Depression. At a minimum, the nation was in a deep recession with the unemployment rate at 7.7 percent, and rising. In this atmosphere, Obama was elected on a platform promising sweeping liberal reform at home and dramatic changes in the way the nation conducted its affairs in the world.

At home (we consider Obama's foreign policy in Chapter 15), Norman Ornstein, a political scientist at Washington's conservative American Enterprise Institute, writing at the end of Obama's first year, concluded that he "already has the most legislative success of any modern president—and that includes Ronald Reagan and Lyndon Johnson," and the *Congressional Quarterly* reported that Obama in his first year had the highest presidential success score with Congress since it began keeping records in 1953.[47] Obama had four legislative priorities—must pass bills—an economic recovery/stimulus program, financial regulatory reform, national health insurance, and climate/energy legislation. The Democratically controlled Congress (256 Democrats in the House to 179 Republicans; 60 Democratic senators) enacted some version of each of these priorities except energy/climate change legislation, which passed the House but never came up for a Senate vote. In addition, major reforms were enacted in the student loan program (providing for direct loans by the government), health information technology, children's health insurance, broadband and wireless Internet access, as well as a credit cardholders' bill of rights. The stimulus program included one of the largest tax cuts in history, increased funding for elementary and secondary education, home buying and college tuition, and tax credits for energy conservation and renewable "green" energy production.[48] These achievements are all the more remarkable because they were accomplished in spite of near-unified Republican opposition. Ornstein attributes these "astonishing" successes to Obama's "strategy—applying pressure quietly while letting congressional leaders find ways to build coalitions."[49]

Obama came to the presidency wishing to be a transformative, "reconstructive" president like Franklin D. Roosevelt and Ronald Reagan. He was committed to reversing the conservative reconstruction inaugurated by Reagan by raising taxes on the wealthy and increasing spending on programs to help ordinary Americans, especially on health and education. This was a politically risky and courageous effort (on health reform he acted against the advice of the vice president and virtually all of his senior staff) to create a more egalitarian society. Many of his egalitarian policies and programs were compromised during congressional consideration, but nevertheless taken as a whole they constitute the most ambitious and successful period of liberal reform since Lyndon Johnson's Great Society. Skocpol and Jacobs describe Obama's first two years as "reaching for a New Deal," with health reform enacting legislation "comparable to Social Security, Medicare and the Civil Rights Act of 1964."[50]

In previous editions of this text, we classified the first black president as a "neutral" on issues related specifically to race. This classification is not surprising as Smith demonstrates in *The Politics of Ethnic Incorporation and Avoidance: A Comparison of the Elections and Presidencies of John F. Kennedy and Barack Obama*.[51] As the first of their ethnic groups to reach the presidency, both Kennedy and Obama felt compelled to practice the "politics of ethnic avoidance" on issues relating to Catholics and African Americans. Of Kennedy's avoidance of Catholic issues, Garry Wills writes, "It is the old story: for 'one of your own' to get elected, he must go out of his way to prove he is not *just* one of your own. The first Catholic President had to be secular to the point (as we used to say in Catholic schools) of supererogation."[52] In Obama's case, unlike previous presidential administrations that routinely worked behind the scenes to "keep black grievances off the agenda,"[53] "supererogation" would require him—more so than Kennedy—to lean over backward so as not to appear to be doing anything "for his own people." As Bob Herbert, an African American columnist at the *New York Times*, put it, "President Obama would rather walk through hell than spend his time dealing with America's racial problems."[54]

As with Kennedy and the Catholics, African American intellectual and political leaders pressed the president to develop specific, race-targeted policies (mainly to address the double-digit unemployment rate of 16 percent among blacks),[55] and like Kennedy, Obama steadfastly refused (the main Catholic issue for Kennedy in the 1960s was federal aid to church schools). In December 2009, Obama told April Ryan of *American Urban Radio*, "The only thing I cannot do is, by law I can't pass laws that say I'm just helping black folks. I'm the President of the United States."[56] To this, some black intellectuals responded scornfully. For example, University of Michigan political scientist Vincent Hutchings wrote,

> Black America is in a depression. And we have a black president. Isn't that terrific. Well, it would be more terrific if he was doing something about it. And he doesn't appear to be doing so. I don't want to congratulate. I don't want to celebrate and I don't want to coronate a president black or otherwise who sits in office while African Americans are suffering at the level that we are throughout this country in terms of joblessness, in terms of health disparities, in terms of wealth disparities.[57]

At his 100th day in office press conference responding to a question from the correspondent for *BET,* raising concerns similar to those of Hutchings, the president said,

> So, my general approach is that if the economy is strong, that will lift all boats as long as it is supported by, for example, strategies around college affordability and job training; tax cuts for working families as opposed to the wealthiest, that level the playing field and ensure bottom-up growth. And I'm confident it will help the African American community live out the American dream at the same time it is helping communities all across the country.[58]

In this edition of the text, we reclassify Obama from a racial neutral to an "antiracist," because in his last two years in office, he became somewhat more outspoken in discussing institutional racism and proposed some modest policy initiatives to dismantle parts of the system of racial subordination. Obama and some scholars of his presidency, however, claim that he embraced antiracist policies and programs during his first term. Obama advances this claim, in particular, with respect to national health insurance. Since the end of the civil rights era, after full employment, national health insurance has been the priority item on the black agenda. President Obama claims that he understood the importance of health insurance to the black community, given the significant gaps and disparities in health and mortality between blacks and whites, and the fact that blacks were much more likely to be uninsured than whites (see Box 14.3). Thus, in responding to critics who accused him of avoiding the problems of blacks he said, "Spending on health care legislation [will] have a direct impact on African Americans who struggle to afford health insurance. People need to understand that one out of every five African Americans do not have health care. Nobody stands to gain more from this health care bill passing."[59]

Undoubtedly, as discussed in Chapter 14, the persistently high rate of poverty is the major problem confronting the post–civil rights era black community. As a result of the Great Recession, the already high rate of black poverty saw its highest single-year increase since the government began measuring poverty in 1959, increasing to 24.4 percent compared to 10.5 percent among whites. Yet Obama appeared to ignore the problem, rarely invoking the word poverty or discussing problems of poor people while constantly talking about the middle class, the middle class. As Obama was aware, in the "Dog Whistle" politics of the post–civil rights era middle class has been conflated with white identity, while poverty is conflated with blackness.[60] As Walters writes, this is a "subtle but nonetheless meaningful construction in which the middle class symbolizes whites."[61] Aware of this construction, part of Obama's politics of ethnic or race avoidance was to avoid the words poverty and poor people, yet work covertly to address the issue.

Consequently, as Michael Grunwald in *The New New Deal: The Hidden Story of Change in the Obama Era* asserts, Obama presided over the "biggest expansion of poverty initiatives since Lyndon Johnson."[62] Looking at the percentages Obama proposed to spend on poverty (in inflation-adjusted numbers) in his budgets, Mendelberg and Butler concur, writing that Obama proposed to spend more on "means tested," antipoverty programs than any first-term Democratic president since Johnson.[63] Spending on such programs constituted 8 percent of Carter's proposed budgets, 12 percent of Clinton's but 17 percent of Obama's.[64] Obama's first-term spending proposals per poor person was $13,731 compared to Clinton's $8,310 and Carter's $4,431 (in 2014 dollars).[65] Overall, they conclude that Obama's tax and transfer policies lowered the poverty rate in 2012 by 13 points compared to one point during the Johnson administration, adjusted for the larger number of poor as a result of the Great Recession.[66]

So, Mendelberg and Butler ask, "Why does he get so little credit?" They point to his rhetoric, writing "Listeners had to hunt for words like 'poor' in his speeches." Mendelberg and Butler compared words in the State of the Union addresses of Carter, Clinton, and Obama, finding the word poverty was used an average of 7 times by Obama, 9 by Carter, and 23 by Clinton.[67] Overall, the ratio of middle class to poverty words was 3:1. They conclude Obama "nearly gave up the 'bully pulpit,' but despite his 'pallid rhetoric' he has 'on the poor' been spending without saying."[68]

Rhetoric, of course, is an important part of presidential power, as the often-used "bully pulpit" phrase suggests. Presidents, with relatively few formal powers, have to persuade: persuade the Congress, the media, interest groups, and ultimately the American people. That Obama, a rhetorically gifted president, failed to employ this power on issues of race and poverty reflects his view of the imperative of the politics of ethnic avoidance. It may also reflect what Wilbur Rich refers to as "Depletion Theory," the view that "exposing the presidency to the conundrum of race relations could potentially squander a considerable amount of political capital with no assurance of results."[69] Thus, Obama, like his paradigmatic predecessor Lincoln and the few other presidents who have addressed the issue of race did so by "reassur[ing] whites that racial boundaries will remain intact and . . . that they have little to fear from conceding privileges to blacks or that racial progress will not take place at their expense. The rhetorical reassurances define racial etiquette and political correctness in discussions of the race problem."[70]

Most established black leaders—the Congressional Black Caucus and the heads of the major civil rights organizations—seemed to acquiesce or accept this notion of depletion theory as it related to Obama and race. For example, Wade Henderson, the head of the broad-based Leadership Conference on Civil and Human Rights, remarked, "I think the first half of Obama's tenure has many examples of significant civil rights accomplishments that are worth noting. I don't join those who criticize him for not talking about issues of race and poverty. I think that in the current atmosphere, those statements and well-intentioned efforts would be used against him in a highly politicized way."[71] The "current atmosphere" Henderson was referring to was the Republican conservatives and Tea Party campaign of all-out opposition to the Obama agenda, and the "otherization" of Obama in the conservative media (see Box 11.4).

As we indicated, in his last two years in office, Obama embraced several explicitly antiracist policies, and his rhetoric, while not embracing poverty and poor people, did become less racially condescending. Starting during the 2008 campaign, when Obama addressed a black audience he would usually simultaneously condemn racism and black people, arguing that while racism, historic and institutional, was a barrier to black progress so was black culture. Thus, he would inveigh in moral language against personal irresponsibility in terms of teenage pregnancy, fathers not taking responsibility for their children, drug

BOX 11.4

The "Otherized," Polarized Obama Presidency

During the 2008 campaign, some conservative elites attempted to "otherize" Obama, framing him as a radical, an Islamic extremist, and a socialist. George Edward concludes, "The polarization of the 2008 campaign and the nature of the opposition to Obama laid the groundwork for the intense aversion to Obama and his policies shortly after he took office."[a] Edwards also contends that Obama's race, his Ivy League education, his "somewhat detached manner," and his Islamic middle name caused many Republicans and conservatives not simply to oppose Obama but to "despise and fear" him.[b]

After Obama assumed office, what Skocpol and Jacobs call the "right wing noise and echo machine" "continued this otherization and polarization" with "wildly false ideas and information."[c] Indeed, there is what Gary Dorrien describes as a "paranoid literature on Obama."[d] In a series of very popular books among conservatives, writers like Jerome Corsi, Brad O'Leary, Aaron Klein, Jack Cashill, Michelle Malkin, and Dinesh D'Souza portray Obama as a native-born Kenyan (whose mother forged his birth certificate), "who imbibed socialism and anti-colonial, anti-western attitudes from his father."[e] This portrayal is manifestly false; however, it is believed by a substantial number of white Republicans and conservatives.

An April 2010 Gallup poll found that while 74 percent of whites believe Obama was born in the United States (a constitutional requirement to hold the presidential office), it was believed by only 57 percent of white Republicans and 56 percent of white conservatives (80 percent of blacks). An August 2010 Pew poll found 21 percent of whites believed Obama was a Muslim, including 31 percent of white Republicans (10 percent of white Democrats) and 34 percent of white conservatives compared to 6 percent of white liberals and 7 percent of blacks. An April 2010 *New York Times/CBS* news poll found that 62 percent of whites believed Obama's policies were "moving the country toward socialism" (35 percent of blacks) but this was believed by 85 and 86 percent of white Republicans and conservatives. These data suggest that Edwards is correct; among a large segment of the population, there is not just the normal partisan and ideological opposition to Obama but also fear and loathing.

The result is that the Obama presidency is the most politically, ideologically, and racially polarized in the history of modern polling. Polarization is measured by difference in Gallup approval ratings of a president between blacks and whites, white Democrats and Republicans, and white liberals and conservatives.[f] Obama's racial polarization score at the end of his third year was 45, which is five points higher than the score for Ronald Reagan, who previously held the record for a racially polarized presidency. Obama's partisan polarization score (the differences in approval between white Democrats and Republicans) was 69, which is eight points higher than George W. Bush's score of 61 for his eight years in office. Obama's ideological polarization score of 59 also exceeds George W. Bush's previous high of 50.

Why did the Obama presidency become so polarized so quickly? First, he entered office in an era of intense partisan, ideological, and racial polarization which started with the Reagan presidency.[g] Second, the systematic otherization of the president by the right-wing noise machine played a role. Third, while a pragmatic centrist well within the tradition of post–FDR liberalism,[h] Obama is a liberal— a northern liberal—the first elected since John F. Kennedy in 1960. Fourth, he was an ambitious liberal, determined to enact as much of the unfinished liberal agenda as the political time and his legislative majorities would allow. Finally, Obama is black. The first black elected to lead a country where historically race has been the great polarizer, where at the time of his election the country was still deeply divided by color, and where many whites felt uncomfortable with the idea of a black man "over me," as one southern white woman told the *New York Times.*[i]

[a] George Edwards, "Strategic Assessments: Evaluating Opportunities and Strategies in the Obama Presidency," in Bert Rockman, Andrew Rudalevige, and Colin Campbell, eds., *The Obama Presidency: Appraisals and Prospects* (Washington: CQ Press, 2012): 48.
[b] Ibid.
[c] Theda Skocpol and Lawrence Jacobs, *Reaching for a New Deal: Ambitious Governance, Economic Meltdown, and Polarized Politics in*

Obama's First Two Years (New York: Russell Sage Foundation, 2012): 29.
[d] Gary Dorrien, *The Obama Question: A Progressive Perspective* (Lanham, MD: Rowman & Littlefield, 2012): 208.
[e] Ibid.
[f] Robert C. Smith and Richard Seltzer, *Polarization and the Presidency from FDR to Obama* (Boulder, CO: Lynne Rienner, 2015).
[g] Pietro Nivola and David Brady, eds., *Red and Blue Nation: Characteristics and Causes of America's Polarized Politics, Vol. 1* (Washington, DC: Brookings Institution, 2006).
[h] Norman Ornstein, "Obama, A Pragmatic Moderate Faces the Socialist Smear," *Washington Post*, April 14, 2010.
[i] Adam Nossiter, "For South, A Waning Hold on National Politics," *New York Times*, November 10, 2008.

abuse, violence, and even how black boys needed to pull up their pants and speak correctly. Many blacks found this frequent litany by the president condescending and demeaning (Jesse Jackson was so offended that he was unknowingly recorded using crude language suggesting he wanted to castrate Obama for "talking down to black people"). Of this kind of rhetoric Walters in 2008 wrote:

> Barack Obama is running for president of the U.S., not the moral arbiter of the black community and rather than giving blacks an empowering message, he seems to be talking through blacks to someone else. Of course, we asked for it to some extent because black people are unique in America in that they conduct a public dialogue about their problems and invite everyone to give their views—on an equal footing with their own. On the other hand, you seldom hear whites commiserate about the people in jail, the poor or who has responsibility for these issues as culturally their own . . . even though this is the discussion we have on a regular basis in black barbershops, we should not legitimize this deflection of the way politicians come into our community and join in a community discussion rather than try to explain what they would do if they had the power to make the difference.[72]

In 2015 in speeches before black audiences this kind of rhetoric somewhat abated. As the *Christian Science Monitor* noted about his 2015 address at the NAACP, "Obama's rhetoric has also changed. In a fiery speech to the [NAACP] in July he made the case for societal racism without calling on 'brothers' to 'pull up their pants' or making other so-called personal responsibility arguments."[73]

Antiracist policies in the second term included proposals to address mass incarceration and suburban segregation in the housing market. In 2015, the

Department of Housing and Urban Development issued the final rules for "Affirmatively Furthering Fair Housing." This rule, long sought by civil rights and fair housing advocates and bitterly opposed by conservatives, requires cities to analyze housing patterns to identify institutional racism and then develop goals and timetables to reduce racial segregation or face a cutoff of federal funding. But perhaps the most aggressive antiracism proposals were in the area of criminal justice. Coming in the wake of several incidents of well-publicized killings of unarmed black men by the police and the protests by the Black Lives Matter Movement, Obama proposed several reforms to improve police–community relations including providing federal funds for police body cameras (refer to Chapter 6 for discussion on the Black Lives Matter Movement). He also urged Congress to change the mandatory minimums for drug crimes, pardoned a number of first-time drug offenders, prohibited in federal prisons the solitary confinement of juveniles, and ordered federal agencies to "Ban the Box" by not asking prospective job applicants about their criminal records at the initial application process (law enforcement, intelligence, and national security agencies were exempted). The president considered issuing an executive order requiring federal contractors to ban the box, but instead opted to send legislation to Congress. The administration established an experimental program to provide Pell Grants to inmates in federal and state prisons to pursue college degrees. Finally, to highlight his interest in the issue, in July 1915, Obama became the first sitting president to visit a federal prison to hold conversations with inmates. With funding from private sources, the president established "My Brother's Keeper," a program to provide assistance to young "boys of color" to improve their educational and employment opportunities so they might avoid the "school to prison" pipeline. (Obama pledged to continue this work in his post–presidency.) As a result of these initiatives, the *Christian Science Monitor* wrote the "Obama era may mark a turning point in the way the federal government approaches crime and incarceration" (see Chapter 14).[74]

Many in the black intellectual community viewed these policy initiatives and the change in presidential rhetoric as "too little, and too late." Meanwhile, the mainstream media celebrated these developments with headlines reading "The Black President Some Worried about Has Arrived" and "Obama Finds a Bolder Voice on Race Issues."[75] How, black scholars and political leaders ultimately will assess the record of the first black president on race is problematic. However, the verdict of the black public is clear. From the beginning of his tenure to the end of the second year of his second term, Obama has been phenomenally popular in the African American community. In no year during his first term did his Gallup approval rating among blacks fall below 86 percent (among whites his approval fell to 36 percent in 2011), averaging 90 percent for the first term compared to 42 percent among whites, and between 2012 and 2014 his approval among blacks averaged 88 percent compared to 37 percent among whites.[76] Obama's politics of ethnic avoidance does not appear to have undermined the widespread support he enjoyed in the black community, based on ties of ethnic kinship and solidarity.

Presidential Power and the Federal Bureaucracy

In previous editions, we discussed the federal bureaucracy in a separate chapter. However, given that one of the expressed powers granted by the Constitution to the president (see Article II, Sections 2 and 3) is to head the nation's bureaucracy, it perhaps necessarily should be included in this chapter on the presidency. Historically, presidents prefer to be seen as being forced to act on issues of race and civil rights.[77]

The Nature of the Federal Bureaucracy

In his classic studies, Max Weber defined *bureaucracy* as a form of power based on knowledge—rationally and hierarchically organized. In other words, a bureaucracy is the multiple bureaus and agencies that implement or carry out laws and policies on a routine, day-to-day basis, using hierarchy, standardized procedures, knowledge, and a specialization of duties.[78]

Figure 11.1 shows the structure, organization, and types of federal agencies and bureaucracies. Basically, the bureaucracy can be grouped into five major categories. First are the agencies within the *Executive Office of the President*, such as the Office of Management and Budget (OMB) and the National Security Council. Second are the 15 *cabinet departments*. There are also numerous *independent agencies* such as the Environmental Protection Agency, the National Aeronautics and Space Administration, and the Social Security Administration.

In addition to these administrative units, there are *government corporations*, which can function like private corporations. Examples are the United States Postal Service and Amtrak.

Finally, there are the *independent regulatory commissions*, which are supposed to be beyond direct presidential and congressional influence. Members of these commissions serve for fixed terms and therefore may not be fired by the president, so these commissions may in theory act in the public interest without political pressure. Figure 11.1 shows that only two of the numerous independent commissions and government corporations deal explicitly with issues of race or civil rights: the U.S. Commission on Civil Rights and the Equal Employment Opportunity Commission (EEOC). They represent 3.3 percent of the total commissions and corporations.

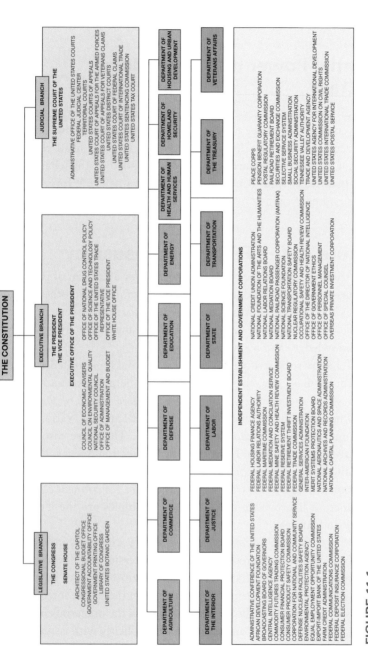

THE GOVERNMENT OF THE UNITED STATES

THE CONSTITUTION

LEGISLATIVE BRANCH

THE CONGRESS
SENATE   HOUSE

ARCHITECT OF THE CAPITOL
CONGRESSIONAL BUDGET OFFICE
GOVERNMENT ACCOUNTABILITY OFFICE
GOVERNMENT PRINTING OFFICE
LIBRARY OF CONGRESS
UNITED STATES BOTANIC GARDEN

EXECUTIVE BRANCH

THE PRESIDENT
THE VICE PRESIDENT

EXECUTIVE OFFICE OF THE PRESIDENT

COUNCIL OF ECONOMIC ADVISERS
COUNCIL ON ENVIRONMENTAL QUALITY
NATIONAL SECURITY COUNCIL
OFFICE OF ADMINISTRATION
OFFICE OF MANAGEMENT AND BUDGET

OFFICE OF NATIONAL DRUG CONTROL POLICY
OFFICE OF SCIENCE AND TECHNOLOGY POLICY
OFFICE OF THE UNITED STATES TRADE
REPRESENTATIVE
OFFICE OF THE VICE PRESIDENT
WHITE HOUSE OFFICE

JUDICIAL BRANCH

THE SUPREME COURT OF THE
UNITED STATES

ADMINISTRATIVE OFFICE OF THE UNITED STATES COURTS
FEDERAL JUDICIAL CENTER
TERRITORIAL COURTS
UNITED STATES COURTS OF APPEALS
UNITED STATES COURT OF APPEALS FOR THE ARMED FORCES
UNITED STATES COURT OF APPEALS FOR VETERANS CLAIMS
UNITED STATES DISTRICT COURTS
UNITED STATES COURT OF FEDERAL CLAIMS
UNITED STATES COURT OF INTERNATIONAL TRADE
UNITED STATES SENTENCING COMMISSION
UNITED STATES TAX COURT

DEPARTMENT OF
AGRICULTURE

DEPARTMENT OF
COMMERCE

DEPARTMENT OF
DEFENSE

DEPARTMENT OF
EDUCATION

DEPARTMENT OF
ENERGY

DEPARTMENT OF
HEALTH AND HUMAN
SERVICES

DEPARTMENT OF
HOMELAND
SECURITY

DEPARTMENT OF
HOUSING AND URBAN
DEVELOPMENT

DEPARTMENT OF
THE INTERIOR

DEPARTMENT OF
JUSTICE

DEPARTMENT OF
LABOR

DEPARTMENT OF
STATE

DEPARTMENT OF
TRANSPORTATION

DEPARTMENT OF
THE TREASURY

DEPARTMENT OF
VETERANS AFFAIRS

INDEPENDENT ESTABLISHMENT AND GOVERNMENT CORPORATIONS

ADMINISTRATIVE CONFERENCE OF THE UNITED STATES
AFRICAN DEVELOPMENT FOUNDATION
BROADCASTING BOARD OF GOVERNORS
CENTRAL INTELLIGENCE AGENCY
COMMODITY FUTURES TRADING COMMISSION
CONSUMER FINANCIAL PROTECTION BOARD
CONSUMER PRODUCT SAFETY COMMISSION
CORPORATION FOR NATIONAL AND COMMUNITY SERVICE
DEFENSE NUCLEAR FACILITIES SAFETY BOARD
ENVIRONMENTAL PROTECTION AGENCY
EQUAL EMPLOYMENT OPPORTUNITY COMMISSION
EXPORT-IMPORT BANK OF THE UNITED STATES
FARM CREDIT ADMINISTRATION
FEDERAL COMMUNICATIONS COMMISSION
FEDERAL DEPOSIT INSURANCE CORPORATION
FEDERAL ELECTION COMMISSION

FEDERAL HOUSING FINANCE AGENCY
FEDERAL LABOR RELATIONS AUTHORITY
FEDERAL MARITIME COMMISSION
FEDERAL MEDIATION AND CONCILIATION SERVICE
FEDERAL MINE SAFETY AND HEALTH REVIEW COMMISSION
FEDERAL RESERVE SYSTEM
FEDERAL RETIREMENT THRIFT INVESTMENT BOARD
FEDERAL TRADE COMMISSION
GENERAL SERVICES ADMINISTRATION
INTER-AMERICAN FOUNDATION
MERIT SYSTEMS PROTECTION BOARD
NATIONAL AERONAUTICS AND SPACE ADMINISTRATION
NATIONAL ARCHIVES AND RECORDS ADMINISTRATION
NATIONAL CAPITAL PLANNING COMMISSION

NATIONAL CREDIT UNION ADMINISTRATION
NATIONAL FOUNDATION OF THE ARTS AND THE HUMANITIES
NATIONAL LABOR RELATIONS BOARD
NATIONAL MEDIATION BOARD
NATIONAL RAILROAD PASSENGER CORPORATION (AMTRAK)
NATIONAL SCIENCE FOUNDATION
NATIONAL TRANSPORTATION SAFETY BOARD
NUCLEAR REGULATORY COMMISSION
OCCUPATIONAL SAFETY AND HEALTH REVIEW COMMISSION
OFFICE OF THE DIRECTOR OF NATIONAL INTELLIGENCE
OFFICE OF GOVERNMENT ETHICS
OFFICE OF PERSONNEL MANAGEMENT
OFFICE OF SPECIAL COUNSEL
OVERSEAS PRIVATE INVESTMENT CORPORATION

PEACE CORPS
PENSION BENEFIT GUARANTY CORPORATION
POSTAL REGULATORY COMMISSION
RAILROAD RETIREMENT BOARD
SECURITIES AND EXCHANGE COMMISSION
SELECTIVE SERVICE SYSTEM
SMALL BUSINESS ADMINISTRATION
SOCIAL SECURITY ADMINISTRATION
TENNESSEE VALLEY AUTHORITY
TRADE AND DEVELOPMENT AGENCY
UNITED STATES AGENCY FOR INTERNATIONAL DEVELOPMENT
UNITED STATES COMMISSION ON CIVIL RIGHTS
UNITED STATES INTERNATIONAL TRADE COMMISSION
UNITED STATES POSTAL SERVICE

FIGURE 11.1

Structure of the Federal Bureaucracy

Source: *The United States Government Manual 2013* (Washington, DC: U.S. Government Printing Office), p. 22. https://www.gpo.gov/fdsys/pkg/GOVMAN-2013-11-06/pdf/GOVMAN-2013-11-06.pdf.

Bureaucracies with Race Missions: A Brief History

In 1865, the Bureau of Refugees, Freedmen and Abandoned Lands, better known as the Freedmen's Bureau, was established. The Bureau was the first federal agency with a race mission. Its purposes were to address problems of the refugees displaced by the Civil War; to provide social, educational, and medical benefits to the newly freed slaves; to provide for the cultivation of abandoned lands; and to make sure the freed slaves received fair wages for their labor. However, because of the opposition of conservatives and white supremacists, Congress dissolved the Bureau in 1872.

In 1939, Attorney General Frank Murphy issued an order establishing a civil liberties unit within the Justice Department. The purpose of this unit was to put the federal government on the side of those fighting for civil liberties and civil rights, especially African Americans.

Then, in the 1957 Civil Rights Act, Congress created the Commission on Civil Rights—a fact-finding agency that makes recommendations to the president and Congress. In addition, this new law upgraded the civil liberties unit in the Justice Department to a full-fledged Civil Rights Division (CRD).

Congress followed up with the 1960 Civil Rights Act, which expanded the power of the CRD of the Justice Department. The Civil Rights Act of 1964 created three new race-oriented federal bureaucratic units, although with different structural arrangements. Title VI created inside all federal agencies, departments, and commissions an Office of Civil Rights Compliance (OCRC), which monitors state and local governments to ensure that they do not spend federal funds in a racially discriminatory fashion. The Office of Federal Contract Compliance (OFCC) was also created in the Department of Labor to assure nondiscrimination and affirmative action by employers with government contracts.

Title VII created the EEOC (Equal Employment Opportunity Commission) to ensure nondiscrimination in employment. In 1972, legislation sponsored by African American congressman Augustus Hawkins made the EEOC an independent commission.

Title X of the 1964 act created the Community Relations Agency, a federal office designed to improve race relations in communities having racial conflicts. The agency was empowered to use the carrot-and-stick approach: provide money and assistance and also use legal recourse to minimize racial conflict. Eventually, this agency was reduced in size and shifted to unit status within the Justice Department.

The 1965 Voting Rights Act created a unit inside the Justice Department's CRD to handle matters of racial discrimination in voter registration and voting, particularly in the southern states where efforts had been persistent in denying African Americans their voting rights.

BOX 11.5

The Bureaucracy at Work:
Dr. Martin Luther King Jr. and the FBI

The Federal Bureau of Investigation (FBI), a part of the Justice Department, is the nation's principal law enforcement and investigative agency, made famous in scores of television programs and movies. This agency, charged with enforcing the civil and constitutional rights of citizens, consistently failed to provide protection to civil rights workers in the South during the 1960s, claiming, in the words of its director, J. Edgar Hoover, that it was not a police force and therefore could not protect the civil rights of southern blacks. Yet the FBI and Hoover set about to systematically harass, discredit, and destroy America's preeminent civil rights leader.

From 1963 until Martin Luther King Jr.'s death in 1968, the FBI in its COINTELPRO program systematically attempted to destroy his effectiveness as the leader of the civil rights movement. According to the FBI agent in charge, "No holds were barred. We have used [similar] techniques against Soviet agents. [The same methods were] brought home against any organization which we targeted. We did not differentiate. This is a rough, tough business."[a] Among the many "rough, tough" tactics used against Dr. King were efforts to prove that he was a communist or that he was being manipulated by communists; wiretaps and microphone surveillance of his home, office, and hotel rooms; attempts to prove he had secret foreign bank accounts; attempts to prove that he had numerous affairs with women; and attempts to prevent him from publishing his books and from receiving the Nobel Peace Prize. Derogatory information about Dr. King's private life was given to members of Congress, the press, university and church leaders (including the Pope), and other leaders of the civil rights movement. Finally, in an act

of desperation, the FBI sent a letter to Dr. King urging him to commit suicide or face exposure as a "liar" and "pervert," leading Dr. King to exclaim that the FBI, the nation's chief law enforcement bureaucracy, was "out to break me."

To his eternal credit, Dr. King did not yield to the efforts of the FBI. However, for a time the FBI's dirty tricks caused deep distress for Dr. King, his family, and his associates. The FBI's attempt to destroy Dr. King is thoroughly documented in the Senate's investigation and in David Garrow's *The FBI and Martin Luther King, Jr.*[b] Many critics of the FBI's campaign against Dr. King contend that it was a product of J. Edgar Hoover's paranoia and a bureaucracy gone amok; however, Garrow, a political scientist, argues that this view is not correct. Granted, the FBI under Hoover had unprecedented power and autonomy; even so, the presidents and members of Congress in Hoover's time were mostly white men of narrow conservative views,[c] and Garrow contends that the FBI faithfully represented these same American values and was not an out-of-control bureaucracy. Garrow concludes, "The Bureau was not a renegade institution secretly operating outside the parameters of American values, but a virtually representative bureaucracy that loyally served 'to protect the established order against adversary challenges.'"[d]

[a] *Supplementary Detailed Staff Reports on Intelligence Activities and the Rights of Americans, Book III.* Final Report of the Select Committee to Study Government Operations with Respect to Intelligence Activities, United States Senate, 94th Congress, April 1976, p. 81.
[b] David Garrow, *The FBI and Martin Luther King, Jr.* (New York: Penguin Books, 1983).
[c] Ibid., pp. 224–25.
[d] Ibid., p. 213.

Last, in 1984 Congress created the Martin Luther King Jr., Federal Holiday Commission and eventually provided some small funding, empowering it to help in the celebration and promotion of the national holiday.

Overall, there are four federal bureaus devoted to an explicitly racial mission: (1) the Commission on Civil Rights, (2) the EEOC, (3) the Martin Luther King Jr., Federal Holiday Commission, and (4) the Civil Rights and Voting Rights units in the Justice Department. Each of these bodies is subject to political influences and pressures (as well as budgeting ones) that can reduce their enforcement effectiveness. Thus, the federal bureaucracy has not been a consistently useful tool in the African American quest for universal freedom, and occasionally it has been hostile to that quest (see Box 11.5).

Running the Bureaucracy: African American Political Appointees

When one analyzes and evaluates the federal bureaucracy, however, the entire story is not captured by focusing on federal agencies designed to deal with race and race relations. An important part was played by African Americans who obtained leadership roles in the federal bureaucracy in general.

During the New Deal, Mary McLeod Bethune announced, "My people will not be satisfied until they see some black faces in high places."[79] When she uttered these words, no African American had ever headed a federal agency or bureau.

More than three decades after her comment, there had still been no African American in such a capacity (although Roosevelt did appoint Bethune director of the Division of Negro Affairs of the National Youth Administration). Although President Eisenhower made a couple of token appointments, this situation would not change in a major way until the administration of President Kennedy in 1961. Thus, for the greater part of America's history, African Americans, though subject to the federal bureaucracy, were outside it. Therefore, the first quest of African Americans in terms of the bureaucracy was to make it representative of all the people.

President Grant began the initial process of appointing African American Republican leaders to minor federal posts in Washington, DC, and in the southern states, and to diplomatic posts in African and Caribbean nations. Posts such as custom collector and minister to foreign countries became the manner in which the Republican Party enhanced and enlarged its alliance with the African American electorate.

The first Democratic president to deal with black appointments was Grover Cleveland, who took office in 1885 and appointed blacks as ministers to Haiti and Liberia and a Recorder of Deeds in Washington, DC.[80]

But no matter whether the appointments were by the Democratic or the Republican parties, they were based on a single reality: "to identify and then latch onto a black leader who could coalesce a potentially powerful black vote."[81] As one white politician wrote President Grant, urging the appointment of an African American state leader to an ambassadorial post, "If [James Milton Turner] can go to Liberia for two years he will gain a national reputation which will make him the universally trusted leader of the colored men in the campaign of [18]72. . . . He can come back in '72 and take his place as the chosen leader of his race and whose [*sic*] claims to leadership will not be disputed."[82]

However, in the midst of such political appointments, white supremacists took over the southern governments and displaced most African American state and local appointive officials by violence, fraud, and corruption. These displaced officials then turned to Presidents Grant, Arthur, and Harrison as a source of federal appointments and patronage positions.[83] Thus, what started out as a trickle of federal jobs emerged into a full-fledged effort to find employment for black party loyalists.

In sum, the Republican Party's need for the black vote launched African Americans into the federal bureaucracy. Eventually this trend, coupled with the need for political jobs for the African American community, made federal patronage appointments all the more important and useful for the African American community. Thus, political patronage became a way in which blacks could gain access to the federal bureaucracy. These two links—the party's need

Mary MacLeod Bethune, the informal leader of Franklin D. Roosevelt's black cabinet.

Source: Gordon Parks/Getty Images

for votes and the community's need for employment—continued and expanded. The period of greatest expansion came in the New Deal Era, 1933–1945, as President Roosevelt appointed a significant number of African American advisors who became known informally as "the black cabinet."

The New Deal formalized the role of African American advisors to presidents, which had started with Frederick Douglass, who advised Presidents Lincoln and Grant, and continued with Booker T. Washington, who advised Cleveland, Harrison, Theodore Roosevelt, and Taft. These individuals, however, served in informal, nebulous, and unofficial positions. Roosevelt was the first to give his political appointees and advisors institutional positions in the bureaucracy.

Following the New Deal, the next great step came with Presidents Kennedy and Johnson, who appointed a number of blacks to high-level positions. In 1966, President Johnson became the first president to appoint an African American to cabinet rank, as Robert Weaver became secretary of the Housing and Urban Development (HUD) Department. President Gerald Ford appointed William Coleman secretary of Transportation. President Carter placed Patricia Harris first at HUD and then at Health, Education and Welfare (HEW) and appointed Andrew Young and later Donald McHenry as UN ambassadors; Reagan named Samuel Pierce secretary of HUD.

In 1993, President Clinton broke new ground. Usually African Americans were given one cabinet position, frequently at HUD or HEW (now Health and Human Services—HHS). Clinton placed four blacks in his cabinet—at Energy, Agriculture, Veterans Affairs, and Commerce—and named numerous others to subcabinet positions. Between 1966, when one black was appointed, and 1993, when four were appointed, Democratic presidents made the largest number of political appointments. Toward the end of his first term, Clinton named an African American—Franklin Raines—to head (with cabinet rank) the powerful OMB. Clinton also appointed blacks to head two important regulatory commissions: the National Labor Relations Board and the Federal Communications Commission.

President George W. Bush's record on the appointment of blacks and other minorities to high-level positions in the bureaucracy resembles more the record of his Democratic predecessors than it does his father's or Ronald Reagan's. As Table 11.2 on the appointment patterns of recent American presidents shows, about 10 percent of his appointments were black compared to 5 and 6 percent, respectively, for the Reagan and first Bush administrations. In the Clinton administration, 13 percent of the appointments were black. Not only did the second Bush appoint a relatively large number of blacks compared to prior Republican presidents, his overall appointments were the most ethnically diverse in history, including 6 percent Latino and 3 percent Asian American (compared to Clinton's 4 percent Latino and 1 percent Asian American). Like

Clinton, Bush appointed blacks to many high-visibility and powerful positions throughout the government, including three cabinet positions: secretary of state (the senior cabinet post), secretary of Education, and secretary of HUD. Condoleezza Rice, an African American political scientist, became the first woman and the second black (after Colin Powell in the Reagan administration) to serve as national security advisor. (The vice president, the secretaries of state and defense, the heads of the CIA, the Joint Chiefs of Staff, and the national security advisor constitute the principal national security decision makers in government. Thus, under Bush, blacks held one-third of these positions.) Bush also appointed blacks to the number-two positions in the departments of Health and Human Services, Justice, and HUD, as head of the CRD in the Justice Department, as vice chair of the Federal Reserve Board, as chair of the Federal Communications Commission (Michael Powell, the son of the secretary of state), and as assistant secretary of commerce in charge of postwar Iraqi reconstruction. In his second administration, Bush promoted Rice from national security advisor to secretary of state.

As of 2016, President Obama had appointed about the same percentage of blacks to senior positions in his administration as his immediate Democratic predecessors, 14 percent compared to 12 and 13 percent in the Carter and Clinton administrations (see Table 11.2). But in his first term he appointed only one black to the statutory cabinet (Eric Holder as attorney general), compared

TABLE 11.2 Percentage of African American Political Appointees from the Kennedy–Johnson Administrations to the Barack Obama Administration[a]

Administration	Percentage[b]
Kennedy–Johnson	2
Nixon–Ford	4
Carter	12
Reagan	5
Bush	6
Clinton	13
George W. Bush	10
Obama	14

[a] The Kennedy–Johnson administrations were treated as one for purposes of data collection, as were the Nixon–Ford administrations.
[b] Percentage is based on all presidential appointments, excluding judges and military officers.

Sources: The data on appointees from Kennedy–Johnson to Bush are from Robert C. Smith, *We Have No Leaders: African Americans in the Post-Civil Rights Era* (Albany, NY: SUNY Press, 1996): 131. The data on the George W. Bush and Obama administrations were collected by the authors.

to Clinton's four and George W. Bush's two in their first terms. Although he did grant his African American UN ambassador and special trade representative "cabinet rank," it is noteworthy that the first black president put fewer blacks in the cabinet than his white, conservative Republican predecessor. Further evidence of his first term practice of the politics of ethnic avoidance—he appointed three Latinos and two Asian Americans to the cabinet. Obama appointed a relatively larger number of blacks to the White House staff, including Valerie Jarrett as a senior advisor, and she was "one of the four or five people in the room with him when decisions get made."[84] However, in his second term, as perhaps evidence of his embracing blackness, Obama appointed three blacks to the cabinet as secretaries of Transportation, Homeland Security, and Education. He also named UN ambassador Susan Rice as National Security Advisor. It is also noteworthy that when Attorney General Holder resigned, he named another African American—Loretta Lynch—as his replacement.

Overall, the Obama administration's appointments were the most demographically diverse in history, with a majority of "top" appointments held by individuals from racial and ethnic backgrounds and women for the first time.[85] Of the 80 top positions in the executive branch, Professor Anne Cooper found that Obama's diversity appointments were 54 percent, compared to 26 percent for George W. Bush and 38 percent for Bill Clinton.[86] In addition, he appointed more than a dozen openly gay persons (including a gay secretary of the army and a transgender member of the White House staff).

Staffing the Bureaucracy: African American Civil Servants

African American political appointees cannot, in and of themselves, do the job alone.[87] All political appointees are transients. The average length of service is 22 months out of a four-year cycle. Thus, to influence and impact bureaucratic rule making and policy, any group needs a continuing presence and permanency inside the bureaucracy, a day-to-day involvement. This means African Americans had to become permanent bureaucrats through the civil service process. After a brief probationary period, individuals hired through this process—*civil servants*—may not be fired. They become part of the *permanent government*. (See Box 11.6.)

When political scientists treat the federal bureaucracy and the question of race, their focus is usually on African American employment in this permanent bureaucracy. Although black employees were appointed after the Civil War, by the time of the passage of the Pendleton Act (which created the civil service), there were only 620 black civil servants in the federal government. By 1893, the report of the Civil Service Commission indicated that the number had risen to 2,393, but this 74 percent increase was to run headlong into southern

BOX 11.6

The Bureaucracy and Your Race

In the United States—*and only in the United States*—a person of *any* known African ancestry is defined as black or African American. This peculiar definition of one's race was established early by the U.S. Bureau of the Census, which declared,

> A person of mixed white and Negro blood should be returned as a Negro, no matter how small the percentage of Negro blood. Both black and mulatto persons are to be returned as Negroes, without distinction. A person of mixed Indian and Negro blood should be returned as a Negro. . . . Mixtures of non-white races should be reported according to the race of the father, except that Negro Indian should be reported as Negro.[a]

At the founding of the Republic, the Census Bureau recognized three races: black, white, and red. However, as the nation became more ethnically diverse or multicultural, this definition became inadequate. Thus, in 1977 the bureaucracy changed the definition or meaning of race. The bureaucracy responsible for defining race is not the Census Bureau (an agency within the cabinet-level Department of Commerce) but the OMB, an agency within the Executive Office of the President, whose principal responsibility is to prepare the annual budget the president submits to Congress. In addition to its budget responsibilities, the OMB also has overall management or oversight responsibility for the federal bureaucracy. In this latter role, in 1977 it issued Statistical Policy Directive #15 defining the meaning of race for purposes of federal policy. According to this definition, there are four "races" in the United States: black, white, American Indian or Alaskan native, and Asian or Pacific Islander. To determine ethnic identification, black and white respondents are asked to check "Hispanic origin" or "not of Hispanic origin," in effect creating a fifth "race." The five categories are used by the Census Bureau and all other government

agencies that collect statistical data. Such data are used to determine the racial composition of the country, to redistrict the House and state and local legislative bodies, to monitor enforcement of civil rights and affirmative action laws, and for other purposes.

In recent years, however, this bureaucratic definition of race has been challenged by many Americans, especially the growing number of biracial or mixed-race couples. In 1967, the Supreme Court declared in *Loving* v. *Virginia* that a state was in violation of the Fourteenth Amendment's equal protection clause if it prohibited interracial or mixed marriages.[b] Since that time the number of mixed black–white marriages has increased dramatically—from 149,000 to 964,000.[c] Increasingly, some of these mixed couples, their offspring, and others are demanding that the OMB change its 1977 directive to include the category "mixed race" or "multiracial."[d] According to a 1995 *Newsweek* poll, 49 percent of blacks but only 36 percent of whites support adding this new category.[e] However, most African American leaders and civil rights organizations have opposed the change, arguing that the new category will result in a loss of black political power, undermine affirmative action, and lead to increased discrimination and stigmatization of African Americans.[f]

In 1993, the OMB agreed to consider adding the multiracial category in time for use in the 2000 census. However, a task force appointed to study the issue recommended that instead of a new multiracial category, people be allowed to check more than one race on the census questionnaire. The task force contended that a new multiracial category would "add to racial tensions and further fragmentation of our population."[g]

The 2000 census allowed individuals for the first time to check more than one race on the census questionnaire. Therefore, it included the traditional definition of who is black, as well as those persons who elected to select any other racial categories. Ninety-eight percent of Americans selected a single race and 2 percent—6.8 million persons—selected a second race, including 1.7 million blacks (about half the blacks who selected a second race reported they were white). This 1.7 million (25 percent of those who selected multiple categories) represents 4 percent of the "all-inclusive" black population or the population combining single- and mixed-race blacks. The all-inclusive figure is about 5 percent higher than the black figure, and adding the two together increases the black population percentage from 12.3 to 13.9 percent of the nation's population (from 34,658,190 to 36,419,434). The OMB decided that those blacks (and other racial and ethnic groups) who selected white would be assigned—following the practice of the first census—to the black category. However, it left ambiguous how those blacks who selected another racial and ethnic group would be categorized. Thus, the compromise on meaning of race for the 2000 census likely creates as many problems as it resolves and is likely to be revisited, especially as the number of mixed-race marriages or relationships increases and as the nation becomes more ethnically diverse. (According to the 2000 census, 3.1 percent of whites indicated they had a spouse of a different race, 5.7 percent of blacks, 16.3 percent of Asian Americans, and 16.3 percent of Latinos.) But one thing is clear—the meaning of race in America will continue to be determined more by bureaucracy than by biology.

a This definition from the first census is quoted in Langston Hughes and Milton Meltzer, *A Pictorial History of the Negro in America* (New York: Crown, 1964): 2. On the historical origins of America's definition of race, see F. James Davis, *Who Is Black: One Nation's Definition* (University Park: Pennsylvania State University Press, 1991). See also Melissa Nobles, *Shades of Citizenship: Race and the Census in Modern Politics* (Palo Alto, CA: Stanford University Press, 2000).
b 380 U.S. 1 (1967).
c See Michael Frisby, "Black, White or Other," *Emerge* (December/January 1996): 49.
d Jon Michael Spencer, *The New Colored People: The Mixed Race Movement in America* (New York: New York University Press, 1997).
e Tom Morganthau, "What Color Is Black?" *Newsweek,* February 13, 1995, p. 65.
f Frisby, "Black, White or Other," p. 51.
g Steven Holmes, "Panel Balks at a Multiracial Census Category," *New York Times,* July 9, 1997, p. A8.

opposition and the ideology of white supremacy and its emerging social and political context of segregation.[88]

Segregation occurred in federal government departments before 1913, but it was limited, received little White House consideration, depended largely on individual administrations, and did not prevent some black Americans from gaining promotions.[89] However, the rising federal acceptance of the southern system of segregation started slowly and gradually to have an impact in the federal bureaucracy despite the civil service merit system. For instance, the percentage of black employees fell from 6 percent in 1910 to 4.9 percent in 1918.[90] But the influence of the gradual and evolving southern forces of white supremacy and segregation coalesced into a tidal wave with the election of a Democratic Congress and a southern Democratic president, Woodrow Wilson, in 1913.[91]

Southern forces started to work on President Wilson from the first day of his administration. Thomas Dixon was the southern novelist who wrote the racist *The Clansman*, which became D. W. Griffith's racist film *The Birth of a Nation*. (President Woodrow Wilson saw this film at the White House and endorsed it, saying it was "history written with lightning.")[92] Dixon wrote President Wilson on his nomination of a black American to a post in the Treasury: "I am heartsick over the announcement that you have appointed a Negro to boss white girls as Register of the Treasury."[93] With these types of pleas pouring in, President Wilson permitted most federal bureaucracies in 1913 to segregate African Americans from whites; even the toilets and restrooms were segregated.

In May 1914, the U.S. Civil Service Commission, finding itself in a changed political context and environment, made photographs mandatory with all applications as means to further racial discrimination. With the president and the Commission supporting the segregation of the federal bureaucracy, in 1913 and 1914 Congress joined the process with calls for segregation of the workforce. Overall, the federal government's embrace of segregation outlasted the Wilson administration, since the succeeding Republican presidencies continued Wilson's policies.[94] Thus, the federal government's acceptance of the policies of white supremacy and segregation "determined the relationship between Black Americans and the federal government for the ensuing fifty years."[95] Desmond King concludes, "After 1913 Black American employees in Federal Agencies were disproportionately concentrated in custodial, menial and junior clerical positions and were frequently passed over for appointment at all."[96] The federal bureaucracy became a pillar of segregated race relations.

African Americans, through the NAACP and other African American groups, fought this trend; and while some of the worst features, such as photographs on applications, were removed in 1940, the final dismantling did not occur until the 1964 Civil Rights Act. Since the first appointment in 1881, African Americans have slowly risen in the staffing of the federal bureaucracy, but their presence has not yet made the federal bureaucracy representative of the nation's population,[97] at the current estimate of roughly 11 percent.[98]

For example, during Obama's presidency, the African American rates of federal employment slightly increased to 8.4 percent of senior-level positions, 8.3 percent of professional workers, 12.6 percent of technicians, 11.9 percent of sales workers, 11.3 percent of administrative support workers, 6.6 percent of craft workers, 13 percent of operatives, 10.7 percent of laborers and helpers, and 16.7 percent of service workers in the bureaucracy.[99] To improve this situation, in August 2011, the president issued Executive Order 13583, "Establishing a Coordinated Government-Wide initiative to Promote Diversity in the Federal Workforce." This order directs all federal agencies to develop specific plans to diversify the federal bureaucracy.

Civil Rights Enforcement in the Obama Administration

The George W. Bush administration was widely criticized for slowing down the enforcement of race-related civil rights law, cutting the budgets of the civil rights enforcement agencies, and using ideology rather than merit in hiring career civil servants.[100] One of the few race-specific pledges Obama made during the presidential campaign was to strengthen the enforcement of civil rights law, particularly in the areas of race discrimination in employment, housing, credit, and voting rights. In its first year under the leadership of the first African American attorney general, the administration took steps designed to keep the president's promise.[101] In its first budget, the administration proposed an 18 percent increase in the budget of the Justice Department's CRD.[102] It also proposed hiring additional staff, and in July 2009, CRD's acting head sent a memorandum to every federal agency "Urging more aggressive enforcement of regulations that forbid recipients of taxpayer money from policies that have a disparate impact on minorities."[103] The attorney general also urged Congress to eliminate the sentencing disparity between crack and powdered cocaine. In a 2013 speech before the American Bar Association, Holder announced that he was ordering federal prosecutors to stop seeking mandatory sentences for nonviolent drug offenders, and instead promote drug-treatment programs. Calling the racial disparities in sentencing between white and black males "unacceptable" and "shameful," Holder directed a panel of U.S. attorneys to study and suggest solutions to the problem. The Justice Department also sued Texas and North Carolina, charging that their newly enacted election laws would suppress the turnout of citizens of historically marginalized racial and ethnic backgrounds and low-income voters. In filing the suits, the attorney general emphasized that because of the Supreme Court's adverse ruling on Section 5 of the Voting Rights Act, he intended to vigorously use Section 2 to enforce the rights of minorities to vote. Overall, the Obama administration's civil rights record, even in the first term, reflected ethnic engagement rather than ethnic avoidance, reflecting to a considerable extent the aggressive and outspoken leadership of Attorney General Holder.

Faces and Voices in the Struggle for Universal Freedom
ARTHUR FLETCHER (1924–2005)

Arthur Fletcher's contribution to universal freedom and equality is controversial. In 1969 as an assistant secretary of labor in the Nixon administration, Fletcher was principally responsible for the design and implementation of affirmative action as the policy of the U.S. government. (Refer to Box 11.3.) As he told one of the authors of this text in a 1971 interview, "affirmative action was my baby." In fathering affirmative action, Fletcher used his position to advance the cause of racial equality more effectively than any other African American who has served in the bureaucracy. As one of the highest-ranking blacks in the bureaucracy during the Nixon administration, he was a leader in organizing other blacks in the administration to advocate for the interests of African Americans.

Born in Phoenix, Arizona, the son of a career military man, Fletcher was raised in Kansas. A star football player at Washburn University in Topeka, in 1954 he became the first African American player for the Baltimore Colts. After graduation, he became active in Kansas Republican politics and was one of the individuals who helped to finance the *Brown* v. *Board of Education* lawsuit. In the 1960s he moved to the West Coast, eventually settling in the state of Washington, where he ran successfully for lieutenant governor. Fletcher's Republican Party activism led to his appointment by Nixon, and

Arthur Fletcher.

Source: Michael Bryant/MCT/Newscom

subsequently, as one of the most visible black Republicans in the nation, he served as an advisor to Presidents Ford and Reagan, and under the first President Bush, he was named chairman of the U.S. Commission on Civil Rights. Although Fletcher considered himself a loyal Republican, he did not hesitate to criticize Republican presidents and policies, describing President Reagan, for example, as "the worst president for civil rights in the twentieth century."

As affirmative action became increasingly controversial after the Republican Party dropped its support for it in the 1980s, Fletcher briefly considered running for the party's presidential nomination in 1996 in order to defend "his baby." However, he ultimately declined to run, recognizing that as a liberal in a party that now stood strongly for conservatism, he would get little support in terms of money or votes.

Summary

In a historical review of American presidents, most have been white supremacists, and many have been racists. And of those who have been neither, they have generally been reluctant to act decisively against racism and in favor of universal freedom unless forced to do so during times of crisis. Abraham Lincoln established the pattern, the paradigm for how American presidents would deal with the African American freedom quest, when he said he would only grant blacks' freedom if it would help save the union—that is nation-maintaining. Otherwise, he said he would practice "benign neglect" and do nothing despite his personal antislavery convictions. Despite the great power and majesty vested in the office of the presidency, the 44 men who have held the office have been reluctant (with the exception of Lyndon Johnson) to use that power and majesty to further African American freedom, preferring "not to take the risk" of alienating white public opinion, jeopardizing other policy priorities, or damaging their chances for election and reelection. In this regard, even the first black president in his first term in office was no different than his predecessors.

Relatedly, the bureaucracy—the hundreds of departments, agencies, bureaus, and commissions that enforce the law and implement public policies—is integral to the African American quest for universal freedom and equality. Yet, the federal bureaucracy has not always been a consistently useful tool in the quest for universal freedom, and occasionally it has been hostile to it. That is, a law enacted by Congress or a decision by the Supreme Court is mere words on paper unless the bureaucracy acts to enforce or implement them. Although black inclusion in the bureaucracy started after the Civil War, effective representation did not begin to occur until the 1960s. Thus, bureaucratic rules and regulations to enforce and implement civil rights laws since the 1960s have depended on the policy priorities of the president.

Critical Thinking Questions

1. Why is Abraham Lincoln paradigmatic for how American presidents have dealt with issues of race in the United States?
2. Explain why American presidents have had to use executive orders to advance policies that promote racial equality and universal freedom. Be sure to discuss specific policies in your answer.
3. Discuss the concept of "ethnic avoidance" used to describe the behavior of President Obama as the first black president. How did his first and second terms differ? How did President Obama's cabinet appointments highlight his practice of politics? Give specific examples.
4. Discuss the role of African Americans in affirmative action policy making. What roles have specific presidential appointees played in shaping and enforcing affirmative action?
5. Discuss the history of the bureaucracy's definition of race in America. Do you believe that current racial classifications help or hinder the quest for universal freedom? How so? Give examples to support your claims.

Selected Bibliography

Altshuler, Alan, and Norman C. Thomas, eds. *The Politics of the Federal Bureaucracy.* New York: Harper & Row, 1977. A good collection of papers examining the structure and operation of the federal bureaucracy and its place in the political system.

Bennett, Lerone. *Forced into Glory: Abraham Lincoln's White Dream.* Chicago, IL: Johnson Publishing, 2000. A highly critical assessment of Lincoln, by one of the nation's leading African American historians.

Donald, David. *Lincoln.* New York: Simon & Schuster, 1995. One of the best biographies of the 16th president.

Fehrenbacher, Don. "Only His Stepchildren: Lincoln and the Negro." *Civil War History* 12 (1974): 293–309. A generally favorable analysis of the president's posture toward African Americans.

Fredrickson, George. "A Man Not a Brother: Abraham Lincoln and the Negro." *Journal of Southern History* 41 (1975): 39–58. A balanced assessment of the subject.

Harris, Fredrick. *The Price of the Ticket: Barack Obama and the Rise and Decline of Black Politics.* New York: Oxford, 2012. A cogent analysis of how the election of Obama contributed to a broader pattern of declining concern by black politicians with the problems of the black poor.

Hayes, L. J. *The Negro Federal Government Worker.* Washington, DC: Howard University Press, 1941. A pioneering work on the subject.

Kennedy, Randall. *The Persistence of the Color Line: Racial Politics and the Obama Presidency.* New York: Pantheon, 2011. An analysis of how the persistence of racism prevented Obama from dealing with the problems of African Americans.

King, Desmond. *Separate and Unequal: Black Americans and the U.S. Federal Government.* London: Oxford University Press, 1995. A historical account of African Americans in the federal bureaucracy.

Krislov, Samuel. *The Negro in Federal Employment: The Quest for Equal Opportunity.* Minneapolis: University of Minnesota Press, 1967. Generally considered the standard work on the subject.

Morgan, Ruth. *The President and Civil Rights: Policy Making by Executive Order.* New York: St. Martin's Press, 1970. A study of presidential use of executive orders to advance civil rights.

Naff, Katherine. *To Look Like America: Dismantling Barriers for Women and Minorities in Government.* Boulder, CO: Westview Press, 2001. An examination of the barriers to full inclusion of minorities and women in the bureaucracy.

O'Reilly, Kenneth. *Nixon's Piano: Presidents and Racial Politics from Washington to Clinton.* New York: Free Press, 1995. A useful study of the subject.

Osgood, Kenneth, and Derrick White, eds. *Winning while Losing: Civil Rights, the Conservative Movement and the Presidency from Nixon to Obama.* Gainesville: University Press of Florida, 2014. A collection of papers assessing the impact of the conservative movement on the presidency and the quest for universal freedom in the post–civil rights era.

Quarles, Benjamin. *Lincoln and the Negro.* New York: Oxford University Press, 1962. The definitive study of the subject.

Riley, Richard. *The Presidency and the Politics of Racial Inequality: Nation-Keeping from 1831 to 1965.* New York: Columbia University Press, 1999. The most recent book-length study of the subject.

Rossiter, Clinton. *The American Presidency*, rev. ed. New York: Harcourt Brace Jovanovich, 1960. The standard study of the role of the president and the presidency's central role in American politics.

Shull, Steven. *American Civil Rights Policy from Truman to Clinton.* Armonk, NY: M. E. Sharpe, 1999. A detailed empirical study, focusing mainly on the Reagan, George H. W. Bush, and Clinton administrations.

Sinkler, George. *The Racial Attitudes of American Presidents: From Abraham Lincoln to Theodore Roosevelt.* Garden City, NY: Doubleday, 1971. A comprehensive analysis of the subject.

Skocpol, Theda, and Lawrence Jacobs, eds. *Reaching for a New Deal: Ambitious Governance, Economic Meltdown, and Polarized Politics in Obama's First Two Years.* New York: Russell Sage, 2012. A collection of papers on Obama's progressive legislative agenda during his first two years, focusing on successes and failures.

Smith, Robert C. "Black Appointed Officials: A Neglected Category of Political Participation Research." *Journal of Black Studies* 14 (March 1984): 369–88. A study of African American presidential appointees from the Kennedy to the Carter administrations.

Smith, Robert C. "Blacks and Presidential Policy Making: Neglect, Policy Symbols and Cooptation." In Robert C. Smith, *We Have No Leaders: African Americans in the Post–Civil Rights Era* (chap. 5). Albany, NY: SUNY Press, 1996. A study of the policy-making roles of black presidential appointees from the Nixon to the first Bush administrations.

Smith, Robert C. *The Politics of Ethnic Incorporation and Avoidance: The Elections and Presidencies of John F. Kennedy and Barack Obama.* Albany, NY: SUNY Press, 2014. A comparison of the first two "ethnic" presidents.

Smith, Robert C., and Richard Seltzer. *Polarization and the Presidency from FDR to Obama.* Boulder, CO: Lynne Rienner, 2015. Includes an extended chapter on the hyperpolarized Obama presidency.

Walton, Hanes, Jr. *When the Marching Stopped: The Politics of Civil Rights Regulatory Agencies.* Albany, NY: SUNY Press, 1988. A comprehensive study of the ups and downs of the implementation of the 1964 Civil Rights Act, from the Johnson to the Reagan administrations.

Walton, Hanes, Jr. *African American Power and Politics: The Political Context Variable.* New York: Columbia University Press, 1996. A detailed study of how the Reagan and Bush presidencies changed the political context of discussions on race.

Notes

1 Letter to Horace Greeley, *Abraham Lincoln: Collected Works,* vol. V, pp. 388–89.
2 David Donald, *Lincoln* (New York: Simon & Schuster, 1995).
3 As quoted in George Sinkler, *The Racial Attitudes of American Presidents: From Abraham Lincoln to Theodore Roosevelt* (Garden City, NY: Doubleday, 1971): 11.
4 Alexis de Tocqueville, *Democracy in America,* edited by Phillips Bradley (Garden City, NY: Doubleday, 1848, 1969): 356.
5 Richard Riley, *The Presidency and the Politics of Racial Inequality: Nation-Keeping from 1831–1965* (New York: Columbia University Press, 1999): 18–19.
6 On Lincoln's racial attitudes, see Benjamin Quarles, *Lincoln and the Negro* (New York: Oxford University Press, 1962); George Fredrickson, "A Man Not a Brother: Lincoln and the Negro," *Journal of Southern History* 41 (1975): 39–58; and Don Fehrenbacher, "Only His Stepchildren: Lincoln and the Negro," *Civil War History* 12 (1974): 293–309.
7 Lincoln did not favor the abolition of slavery (frequently calling abolitionism "dangerous radical utopianism") but rather opposed its extension beyond the South to the Midwest and the West because he wanted these lands preserved for free (white) labor on free land. See Eric Foner, *Free Soil, Free Labor: The Ideology of the Republican Party Before the Civil War* (New York: Oxford University Press, 1970).
8 Fredrickson, "A Man Not a Brother," p. 46.

9 Quoted in ibid., p. 45.

10 Abraham Lincoln, "The Emancipation Proclamation," in K. Hall, W. Wiecek, and P. Finkelman, eds., *American Legal History: Cases and Materials* (New York: Oxford University Press, 1991): 224.

11 Ibid.

12 A standard study of the Emancipation Proclamation is John Hope Franklin, *The Emancipation Proclamation* (Garden City, NY: Doubleday, 1963).

13 The commander-in-chief clause was used by Franklin Roosevelt to incarcerate Japanese Americans as a World War II measure, which at the time was held to be constitutional by the Supreme Court although it was a clear violation of the Fifth Amendment prohibition on the deprivation of liberty without a trial.

14 Fredrickson, "A Man Not a Brother," p. 45.

15 Ibid., p. 48.

16 Fehrenbacher, "Only His Stepchildren," p. 307.

17 *The Life and Times of Frederick Douglass Written by Himself,* introduction by Rayford Logan (London: Collier Books, 1892, 1962): 489.

18 Wilbur Rich, "Presidential Leadership and the Politics of Race: Stereotypes, Symbols and Scholarship," in Rich, ed., *African American Perspectives on Political Science* (Philadelphia, PA: Temple University Press, 2007): 232.

19 Matthew Holden, Jr., "Race and Constitutional Change in the Twentieth Century: The Role of the Executive," in J. H. Franklin and G. R. MacNeil, eds., *African Americans and the Living Constitution* (Washington, DC: Smithsonian Institution Press, 1995): 117–43.

20 Arthur Schlesinger, Jr., "Rating the Presidents: From Washington to Clinton," *Political Science Quarterly* 112 (1997): 179–90.

21 Kenneth O'Reilly, *Nixon's Piano: Presidents and Racial Politics from Washington to Clinton* (New York: Free Press, 1995). O'Reilly argues that Andrew Jackson was the "first (and arguably the only) chief executive in American history not to consider slavery a moral evil," p. 31.

22 Ibid., chap. 1.

23 Quoted in William Freehling, "The Founding Fathers and Slavery," *American Historical Review* 77 (1972): 396.

24 O'Reilly, *Nixon's Piano*, p. 135.

25 Samuel Tilden, governor of New York, apparently won a majority of the vote for president, but the Republicans controlled enough southern electoral votes to give the presidency to Hayes in exchange for his promise to withdraw federal troops and leave the South alone with respect to the treatment of blacks. See C. Vann Woodward, *Reunion and Reaction: The Compromise of 1877 and the End of Reconstruction* (Garden City, NY: Doubleday, 1956).

26 Harrison's support for antilynching legislation came about not as a result of the lynching of blacks but rather after 11 Italian citizens were lynched in New Orleans. The Italian government filed a strong protest, and Harrison responded with his proposed legislation. See O'Reilly's *Nixon's Piano*, p. 59.

27 Ibid., p. 111. Roosevelt was even reluctant to send a written message to the annual NAACP convention.

28 Louis Ruchames, *Race, Jobs and Politics: The Story of FEPC* (New York: Columbia University Press, 1953).

29 See Mary Dudziak, "Desegregation as a Cold War Imperative," *Stanford Law Review* 41 (1988): 1147–75.

30 As Franklin Roosevelt had feared, Truman's support did cost him the support of white southern Democrats, who walked out of the 1948 convention, formed a third

party, and ran Strom Thurmond for president. Thurmond carried four southern states.

31 See John Ehrlichman, *Witness to Power* (New York: Auburn House, 1982): 222–23; and O'Reilly, *Nixon's Piano,* chap. 7.

32 Daniel P. Moynihan, *The Politics of a Guaranteed Income: The Nixon Administration and the Family Assistance Plan* (New York: Vintage Books, 1973).

33 O'Reilly, *Nixon's Piano*, chap. 7; and Hugh Davis Graham, *The Civil Rights Era: Origin and Development of National Policy* (New York: Oxford University Press, 1990): chaps. 12–14.

34 Robert C. Smith, "Black Appointed Officials: A Neglected Category of Political Participation Research," *Journal of Black Studies* 14 (March 1984): 369–88.

35 Eleanor Holmes Norton, "The Role of Black Presidential Appointees," *Urban League Review* 9 (Summer 1985): 108–9.

36 Harold Wolman and Astrid A. E. Merget, "The President and Policy Formulation: President Carter and Urban Policy," *Presidential Studies Quarterly* 10 (1980): 402–15; and Robert C. Smith, *We Have No Leaders: African Americans in the Post–Civil Rights Era* (Albany, NY: SUNY Press, 1996): 149–51.

37 On Bush's flip-flop on the 1990 and 1991 civil rights bills, see Smith's *We Have No Leaders,* pp. 170–82.

38 Arch Parsons, "Thomas Nomination Divides the Black Community," *West County Times,* July 28, 1991.

39 Robert Pear, "Administration Rejects Proposals for New Anti-Poverty Programs," *New York Times,* July 6, 1990.

40 O'Reilly, *Nixon's Piano,* chap. 9.

41 See O'Reilly, *Nixon's Piano*; and Smith, *We Have No Leaders,* chap. 9, for discussion of Clinton's electoral strategy.

42 Adolph Reed, Jr., "America Becoming—What Exactly?: Social Policy Research as the Fruit of Bill Clinton's Race Initiative" (Unpublished Manuscript, 2006); See also "President Clinton Journeys to Africa," *Jet,* April 20, 1998.

43 Steven Shull, *American Civil Rights Policy from Truman to Clinton* (Armonk, NY: M. E. Sharpe, 1999): 80, 93. On Clinton's relative conservative postures on race-related issues see also Robert C. Smith, "Civil Rights Policy Making in the Clinton Administration: In Reagan's Shadow," in Kenneth Osgood and Derrick White, eds., *Winning While Losing: Civil Rights, the Conservative Movement and the Presidency from Nixon to Obama* (Gainesville: University Press of Florida, 2014).

44 Dewayne Wickham, *Bill Clinton and Black America* (New York: Ballantine Books, 2002).

45 Amy Goldstein and Dana Milibank, "Bush Joins Admission Case Fight," *Washington Post,* January 16, 2003. See also Dana Milibank, "Bush Aides Split on Bias Case at U. Mich.," *Washington Post,* December 18, 2002.

46 Dan Froomking, "A Polling Free-Fall among Blacks," *Washington Post*, October 13, 2005.

47 Norman Ornstein, "A Very Productive Congress, Despite What the Approval Ratings Say," *Washington Post,* January 31, 2010; "2009 Was the Most Partisan Year Ever," *Congressional Quarterly Weekly Report,* January 11, 2010.

48 Ibid.

49 Ibid.

50 Theda Skocpol and Lawrence R. Jacobs, eds., *Reaching for a New Deal: Ambitious Governance, Economic Meltdown and Polarized Politics in Obama's First Two Years* (New York: Russell Sage, 2011): 8, 54.

51 Robert C. Smith, *The Politics of Ethnic Incorporation and Avoidance: The Elections and Presidencies of John F. Kennedy and Barack Obama* (Albany, NY: SUNY Press, 2013).

52 Gary Wills, *The Kennedy Imprisonment: A Meditation on Power* (New York: Pocket Books, 1982): 61.

53 Rich, "Presidential Leadership and the Politics of Race: Stereotypes, Symbols and Scholarship," p. 246.

54 Bob Herbert, "Anger Has Its Place," *New York Times*, August 1, 2009.

55 Michael Shear and Perry Bacon, "Black Lawmakers Call on Obama to Do More on Behalf of Blacks," *Washington Post*, December 9, 2009; and Steven Greenhouse "NAACP Prods Obama on Job Losses," *New York Times*, November 17, 2009.

56 Howard Kurz, "Color of Change," *Washington Post*, December 23, 2009.

57 Vincent Hutchings, "Obama's Report Card: One Year Later," *Black Enterprises*. www.blackenterprise.com/business/2010/01/20/obamas-report-card-one-year-later/pr.

58 Presidential Press Conference, "Transcript," *New York Times*, April 30, 2009.

59 Sheldon Alberts, "Obama Rejects Claim He Is Ignoring Black People," Canada.com. www.canada.com/business/story/html?id=2371848.

60 Ian Haney Lopez, *Dog Whistle Politics: How Coded Racial Appeals Have Reinvented Racism and Wrecked the Middle Class* (New York: Oxford, 2010): 71–74.

61 Ronald Walters, *White Nationalism, Black Interests: Conservative Public Policy and the Black Community* (Detroit, MI: Wayne State University Press, 2003): 61.

62 Michael Grunwald, *The New New Deal: The Hidden Story of Change in the Obama Era* (New York: Simon & Shuster, 2012): 11.

63 Tali Mendelberg and Bennett Butler, "Obama Cares: Look at the Numbers," *New York Times*, August 21, 2014.

64 Ibid.

65 Ibid.

66 Ibid.

67 Ibid.

68 Ibid.

69 Rich, "Presidential Leadership and the Politics of Race: Stereotypes, Symbols and Scholarship," p. 235.

70 Ibid., p. 233.

71 Quoted in Kenneth Cooper, "The President's Report Card: One Year Later," *The Crisis* (Fall 2012): 6.

72 Ronald Walters, "The Obama Message: Empowering?" in Walters, *Calling the Shots: Barack Obama and African American Politics from the Campaign to the First 100 Days* (unpublished manuscript, 2010): 41.

73 Linda Feldman, "Obama's Quest to Leave a Lasting Mark on Race," *Christian Science Monitor Weekly*, September 7, 2015, p. 29.

74 Harry Bruinius, "Criminal Justice: Obama's Push to Address Race, Quietly," *Christian Science Monitor*, November 3, 2015.

75 Janell Ross, "The Black President Some Worried about Has Arrived," *Washington Post*, July 15, 2015; and Peter Baker, "Obama Finds a Bolder Voice on Race Issues," *New York Times*, May 7, 2015.

76 Gallup News Service Polls, Roper Center.

77 Rich, "Presidential Leadership and the Politics of Race: Stereotypes, Symbols and Scholarship," p. 234.

78 See Max Weber, "Bureaucracy," in H. H. Gerth and C. W. Mills, eds., *From Max Weber: Essays in Sociology* (New York: Oxford University Press, 1969).

79 Quoted in Hanes Walton, Jr., *Invisible Politics* (Albany, NY: SUNY Press, 1985): 262. See also Mary McLeod Bethune, "Certain Unalienable Rights," in R. Logan, ed., *What the Negro Wants* (Chapel Hill: University of North Carolina Press, 1944): 248–58.

80 Lawrence Grossman, "Democrats and Blacks in the Gilded Age," in P. Kolver, ed., *Democrats and the American Idea* (Washington, DC: Center for National Policy Press, 1992): 149–61.

81 Gary Kremer, *James Milton Turner and the Promise of America: The Public Life of a Post–Civil War Black Leader* (Columbia: University of Missouri Press, 1991): 40.

82 Ibid., p. 53.

83 Ibid., p. 50.

84 Jodi Cantor, "An Old Hometown Mentor, Still at Obama's Side," *New York Times*, November 24, 2008.

85 Juliet Eilperin, "Obama Has Vastly Changed the Face of the Federal Bureaucracy," *Washington Post*, September 20, 2015.

86 Ibid.

87 For analysis of policy roles of black presidential appointees from the Nixon to the Bush administrations, see Robert C. Smith, *We Have No Leaders: African Americans in the Post–Civil Rights Era* (Albany, NY: SUNY Press, 1996): chap. 5.

88 John Hope Franklin and Alfred Moss, *From Slavery to Freedom: A History of Africans* (New York: Knopf, 2000): 336.

89 Ibid., p. 9.

90 Ibid., p. 49.

91 Ibid., p. 9.

92 Thomas Cripps, "The Reaction of the Negro to the Motion Picture, the Birth of a Nation," *Historian* 25 (May 1963): 224–62.

93 Desmond King, *Separate and Unequal: Black Americans and the U.S. Federal Government* (London: Oxford University Press, 1995): 5.

94 Ibid., pp. 20, 49.

95 Ibid., p. 20.

96 Ibid., p. 4.

97 See Katherine Naff, *To Look Like America: Dismantling Barriers for Women and Minorities in Government* (Boulder, CO: Westview Press, 2001).

98 U.S. Census Bureau, 2006–2010 American Community Survey (5-year ACS data)— Table Set 5, Federal Sector Jobs by Sex and Race/Ethnicity by Citizenship Status.

99 Ibid.

100 See *Associated Press,* "Enforcement of Civil Rights Law Declined since 1999, Study Finds," *New York Times*, November 11, 2004; Dan Eggen, "Civil Rights Enforcement Roils Staff," *Washington Post*, November 13, 2005; and Charlie Savage, "Civil Rights Hiring Shifted in Bush Era," *Boston Globe*, July 23, 2006.

101 Charlie Savage, "Justice Department to Recharge Enforcement of Civil Rights," *New York Times*, September 1, 2009.

102 Ibid.

103 Ibid.

CHAPTER 12

The Supreme Court and the African American Quest for Universal Freedom

LEARNING OBJECTIVE

Identify the time period in history when the Supreme Court was the most pro–universal freedom.

The question is simply this: can a Negro, whose ancestors were imported into this country, and sold as slaves, become a member of the political community formed and brought into existence by the Constitution of the United States, and as such become entitled to all the rights, and privileges, and immunities, granted by that instrument to the citizens. . . . We think they are not, and they are not included, were not intended to be included, under the word "citizen" in the Constitution, and can therefore claim none of the rights and privileges which that instrument provides for and secures to citizens of the United States. On the contrary, they were at that time [1787] considered as a subordinate and inferior class of beings, who had been subjugated by the dominant race, and, whether emancipated or not, yet remained subject to their authority, and had no rights or privileges but such as those who held the power and the government might choose to grant them.

—Chief Justice Roger B. Taney[1]

We begin this chapter with an excerpt from Chief Justice Taney's remarkable opinion in *Dred Scott* v. *Sanford* (1857). The *Dred Scott* decision is historically important because the case marks the first time in the then 70-year history of the Court that it squarely addressed the rights of the African people in the United States, holding that they had no rights—none whatsoever—except those that white people might choose to give them.[2] For the next 70 years of its history, the Court ignored the rights and freedoms of Africans, in spite of the adoption of the Civil War amendments to the Constitution, which granted citizenship to blacks and guaranteed universal rights and freedoms.[3] Then, beginning in the 1940s and lasting until the 1980s, the Supreme Court in a series of cases began slowly to enforce the Constitution's guarantees of universal rights and freedoms. Except for this remarkable 40-year period—1940s to 1980s—the Supreme Court historically has been a racist institution, refusing to support universal freedom for African Americans. On the contrary, as in the *Dred Scott* case, for much of its more than 200 years, the Court has taken the position that the rights of African Americans were not universal but rather existed only as whites might "choose to grant them." It now appears, in its third century, that the Court may once again be reverting to its racist past.[4]

The Supreme Court of the United States is a political institution. That is, unlike the courts in most nations, the courts in the United States are not simply legal institutions deciding questions of innocence or guilt in criminal cases or liability in civil cases. Rather, as Professor Robert Dahl writes, "To consider the Supreme Court of the United States strictly as a legal institution is to underestimate its significance in the American political system. For it is also a political institution, an institution, that is to say, for arriving at decisions on controversial questions of national policy."[5] In its decisions on controversial issues of national policy, the Court responds slowly but surely to public opinion and the fundamental currents of national election majorities. Thus, if the Supreme Court is reverting to racism, it may reflect its understanding of public opinion and the outcome of recent presidential elections, which were often won by candidates perceived by blacks as hostile to their quest for universal freedom. Or in the famous words of humorist Finley Peter Dunne's "Mr. Dooley," "The Supreme Court follows the election returns."

Judicial Appointments and African Americans

One hundred and thirteen persons have served as Supreme Court justices. Two have been African Americans. The first was Thurgood Marshall, the legendary chief lawyer for the NAACP and one of the greatest African American leaders of all time.[6] Appointed by President Johnson in 1967, Marshall's confirmation was held up for several months by racists and white supremacists, but he was eventually approved and went on to serve on the Court for more than two decades until he retired in 1991. When Marshall retired, President George H. W. Bush nominated Clarence Thomas, then a judge on the District of Columbia Court of Appeals, to replace him. Thomas was bitterly opposed by African American leaders because of his opposition to affirmative action and his conservative ideology generally. This opposition was reinforced by the last-minute allegations of sexual harassment by Anita Hill, an African American lawyer and former assistant to Thomas. Although black leaders opposed Thomas's nomination, he was supported by black public opinion, and this support continued after the Hill allegation.[7] However, in several southern states, this support was diminished to some extent, especially among black women.[8] And in an interesting example of how events can shape the socialization process, African Americans were more informed about the issue (particularly their senator's vote) than whites, closing the traditional gap in political information between the races.[9]

Justice Marshall in his years on the Court became one of the most liberal justices in the Court's history, forging a jurisprudence of activism in which the Court would seek to resolve racial and other social problems.[10] Thomas in his years on the Court has been its most conservative member, forging a jurisprudence of "strict constructionism," which rejects the idea that the Court should attempt to resolve societal problems.[11] Perhaps the most striking difference in their jurisprudence on race is affirmative action. Justice Marshall wrote some of the earliest opinions in favor of affirmative action while Justice Thomas is categorically opposed to any considerations of race in government allocative decisions.

President Franklin D. Roosevelt was the first president to appoint a black person to the federal courts, naming William Hastie as a judge in the Virgin Islands. President Kennedy appointed three black judges to the federal courts; President Johnson nominated 10 and named seven; and President Nixon, nominated six and named three. Generally, appointments to the courts are based on party and ideology. That is, American presidents and senators tend to select judges from their party, who share their ideology, whether liberal or conservative. For example, African Americans who tend to be liberal Democrats are more likely to receive judicial appointments from Democratic presidents. This trend is shown in Table 12.1. In the Carter administration, 14.2 percent of all judicial appointments were black, and in the Clinton administration the figure was 16.6 percent. In the Reagan administration, however, 1.9 percent of the appointees were black, while in the first Bush administration, the total was 5.8 and 7.4 percent in the second. The first African American president far exceeded the record of his predecessors, by appointing 18.8 percent of African American judges to federal courts. President Obama also appointed a record number of women and other underrepresented social groups—Hispanics, Asian Americans and gays and lesbians—to the bench.

TABLE 12.1	African American Appointees to the Federal Courts, from Carter to the Obama Administrations		
President	**Percentage of Black[a] Appointees**	**Total of Black Appointees**	**Total of All Appointments to Federal Courts**
Carter (1977–1981)	14.2	37	260
Reagan (1981–1989)	1.9	7	360
George H. W. Bush (1989–1993)	5.8	11	188
Clinton (1993–2000)	16.6	61	367
George W. Bush (2001–2009)	7.4	24	323
Obama (2009–2017)	18.8	60	318

[a] For detailed data on presidential appointments of African American judges to the federal courts by court type (circuit and district), race and sex, see Barry J. McMillion, *U.S. Circuit and District Court Judges: Profile of Select Characteristics*, Congressional Research Service Report, Series R43426 (Washington, DC: Government Printing Office, 2014): 14–24.
[b] Total number of African American judges on the federal courts = 213, see "Diversity of the Bench," www.fjc.gov/servlet/nDsearch?race=African+American (accessed March 8, 2016).

Source: "African American Judges on the Federal Courts," Federal Judicial Center, www.fjc.gov/history/home.nsf/page/judges_diversity.html (accessed March 8, 2016).

How Should the Constitution Be Interpreted? Judicial Restraint versus Judicial Activism and the Implications for Universal Freedom

Throughout the Court's history, but especially in the twentieth century, there has been a debate among scholars, politicians, and judges over how the Constitution should be interpreted. Conservative scholars and jurists tend to favor *judicial self-restraint*, or "strict constructionism." That is, they argue that justices and judges should look to the intent of the framers of the Constitution and precedents in interpreting the Constitution rather than applying their own political values or changing the Constitution to fit the needs of a changing society. By contrast, liberal scholars and jurists tend to favor *judicial activism*, or "loose constructionism." That is, they argue that the intent of the framers on many issues is vague and unclear and that the framers designed the Constitution as a "living" document to be interpreted broadly to fit the needs of a changing society.[12]

Although an important legal and political debate, it is in some ways misleading, since at times liberals have favored judicial restraint and conservatives have favored activism. For example, an important principle of conservative jurisprudence is that the courts should adhere to precedent (*stare decisis*) and not overturn the decisions of democratically elected legislative bodies unless they clearly violate the Constitution. Yet, the current conservative majority on the Supreme Court has in recent years been active in overturning precedents and congressional and state legislative acts in the areas of commerce, affirmative action, campaign finance, and voting rights. The liberal bloc led by Justice John Paul Stevens, on the other hand, in its dissents has called for restraint, adherence to precedents, and deference to legislative majorities. Thus, whether one is for "strict" or "loose" interpretation depends, as the saying goes, "on whose ox is gored."

Table 12.2 lists the number of federal and state laws declared unconstitutional from 1800 to 2014. The data in the table show that there have been two periods of sustained judicial activism: from 1910 to 1949, and from 1950 to 1999. In the first period, a conservative Supreme Court declared unconstitutional 34 federal laws and 350 state laws. This represents 19 percent of all the federal laws and 26 percent of all the state laws declared unconstitutional in the entire history of the Court. This spate of judicial activism involved a conservative Court overturning a series of progressive reforms regulating private property and the industrial economy. The second period of judicial activism involved a liberal Supreme Court overturning state and federal laws that restricted civil rights, liberties, and freedoms. In this period, 81 federal laws and 638 state laws were declared unconstitutional, representing more than 45 and 48 percent, respectively, of all federal and state laws declared unconstitutional by the Court.

For African Americans and their quest for universal freedom, the debate on how the Constitution should be interpreted depends on the context and the times. In the post–Reconstruction Era, when the Court ignored the intent of the framers of the Fourteenth and Fifteenth Amendments and declared unconstitutional several civil rights laws, black interests would have been served by judicial self-restraint. But in the 1960s and 1970s, black interests were served when the Court for the first time began to enforce the Fourteenth and Fifteenth Amendments by declaring state laws unconstitutional and upholding federal civil rights laws. In the current period of judicial activism (1990–until today), African American interests are adversely affected by the conservative Court's state-centered federalism, which limits the authority of the federal government to expand and extend universal rights and freedom (see Chapter 2).

As a result of the activism of the Court under Chief Justice Earl Warren's leadership, liberals and progressives came to view the Court as a defender of minority rights. Historically, however, the Warren Court is an anomaly since for much of the Court's history it has been a racist, antifreedom institution.

TABLE 12.2 Number of Federal, State, and Local Laws Declared Unconstitutional by the Supreme Court, 1800–2014

Years	Federal Laws	State and Local Laws
1800–1809	1	1
1810–1819	0	7
1820–1829	0	8
1830–1839	0	3
1840–1849	0	10
1850–1859	1	7
1860–1869	4	24
1870–1879	7	36
1880–1889	4	46
1890–1899	5	36
1900–1909	9	40
1910–1919[a]	6	119
1920–1929	15	139
1930–1939	13	92
1940–1949	2	61
1950–1959[a]	4	66
1960–1969	18	151
1970–1979	19	195
1980–1989	16	164
1990–1999	24	62
2000–2009	16	38
2010–2014	13	16
TOTAL	**177**	**1,321**

[a] Periods of judicial activism: 1910–1949 and 1950–1999.

Source: Lawrence Baum, *The Supreme Court*, 12th ed. (Washington, DC: Congressional Quarterly Press, 2001): 160. Data from 1990 to 2014 taken from Table 5-2 in Baum, who updated the data from the Congressional Research Service, *The Constitution of the United States of America: Analysis and Interpretation* (Washington, DC: Government Printing Office, 2014).

Legal scholar Girardeau Spann argues that this racist, antiminority stance of the Court is "structurally" inevitable. He writes,

> My argument is that, for structural reasons, the institutional role that the Court is destined to play within our constitutional scheme of government is the role of assuring the continued subordination of racial minority interests.

I believe that this subordination function is inevitable; that it will be served irrespective of the Court's composition at any particular point in time; and that it will persist irrespective of the conscious motives of the individual justices.[13]

The Supreme Court and African Americans: Rights- and Material-Based Cases

The Supreme Court was transformed into a liberal institution beginning with the New Deal. President Roosevelt appointed nine justices to the Court and his successor, President Truman, appointed four. Most of the Roosevelt and Truman appointees were more or less liberal, as were the four appointees made by President Eisenhower, including Chief Justice Warren. This liberal tendency of the Court was consolidated by the four appointments made by Presidents Kennedy and Johnson. Among the leading liberal jurists appointed to the Court from the 1930s to the 1960s were Hugo Black, William O. Douglas, William Brennan, Arthur Goldberg, Thurgood Marshall, and Abe Fortas. As a result, by the late 1940s the Court was in the process of shifting its jurisprudence from a focus on protecting property rights and business interests toward a concern with individual civil liberties and the civil rights of minorities.[14]

Simultaneous with this transformation of the Court, the NAACP transformed its approach to civil rights from lobbying to litigation. In 1939 the NAACP Legal Defense Fund was created, and under the leadership of Thurgood Marshall, it developed a systematic strategy of using the courts to achieve social change and racial justice, a strategy later employed by many other American groups (see Box 12.1). This strategy was enormously successful as, during the 1960s and early 1970s, the Court issued a number of landmark rulings expanding the rights of blacks, other ethnic minorities, women, atheists, communists, and persons accused of crimes.

These successes, however, brought reactions from conservative and racist forces (during the 1950s and 1960s there were billboards throughout the South reading "Impeach Earl Warren"), and conservative Republican presidents began to campaign against the Court's "liberal activism" and promise to appoint "strict constructionists" as justices. Between 1969 and 1991, Presidents Nixon, Ford, Reagan, and Bush one and two appointed 13 justices to the Court. By the late 1980s, as a result of these appointments, the Supreme Court had a narrow five-person conservative majority (see Table 12.3). Immediately, this majority, led by Chief Justice William Rehnquist, began to retreat from the civil rights reforms of the 1960s and 1970s. We examine this retreat on rights- and material-based cases in an analysis of the last three decades of Supreme Court decision making on school desegregation, voting rights, and affirmative action (for the Court's own record on affirmative action see Box 12.2). But first we examine President Obama's first two appointments to the Court.

BOX 12.1

Litigation and Social Change: The Legacy of *Brown*

In Chapter 6, we discussed how the African American civil rights and black power movements of the 1960s and 1970s sparked and served as a model for social movements among women, gays, and other minorities. The success of the NAACP Legal Defense Fund's litigation strategy in the *Brown* v. *Board of Education* case also led other groups in the United States to create organizations and develop strategies using litigation to bring about social change.[a]

Following the NAACP model, in the late 1960s scores of groups organized legal defense funds—women, Mexican Americans, Puerto Ricans, Asian Americans, gays and lesbians, and evangelical Christians. Once organized, these groups followed the strategy pioneered by Thurgood Marshall of bringing a series of well-researched, strategically selected "test cases" before the Court to force it to establish new rights and expand the idea of freedom.

Supreme Court justice Ruth Bader Ginsberg is sometimes referred to as the "Thurgood Marshall of the women's movement" for her work as an attorney on women's legal projects in the 1960s and 1970s; these were projects that led

to an expansion of women's rights and freedoms, including the critical right of a woman to choose an abortion. As a result of the litigation, new rights have been established for the elderly, the poor, language minorities, immigrants, environmentalists, and the handicapped.

The NAACP turned to the courts in the 1930s to pursue its civil rights agenda because its leaders felt relatively powerless in the ordinary politics of lobbying Congress and the president. Other groups, also feeling powerless and seeing the success of the NAACP in *Brown,* also turned to the Courts, and the process significantly expanded the idea of universal freedom.[b]

a See Clement Vose, "Litigation as a Form of Pressure Group Activity," *Annals of the American Academy of Social and Political Science* 319 (September 1958): 20–31; and Karen O'Connor, *Women's Organizations' Use of the Courts* (Lexington, MA: Lexington Books, 1980).
b In recent years, right-wing conservative and religious groups have also adopted the NAACP approach to litigation, filing strategic test cases, for example, on voting rights, affirmative action, and campaign finance.

Thurgood Marshall, George Hayes, and James Nabrit outside the Supreme Court after it announced its landmark decision in *Brown* v. *Board of Education.*

Source: Bettmann/Corbis

TABLE 12.3 Justices of the Supreme Court by Ideological Inclination, 1986–2016

Justice[a]	Year Born	Appointed By	Appointed	Ideological Inclination
Samuel Alito	1950	George W. Bush	2005	Strict Constructivism
John Roberts[b] (Chief Justice)	1955	George W. Bush	2005	Strict Constructivism
Antonin Scalia	1936–2016	Reagan	1986	Strict Constructivism
Clarence Thomas	1948	George H.W. Bush	1991	Strict Constructivism
Anthony Kennedy[c]	1936	Reagan	1988	Moderate to Strict Constructivism
Sonia Sotomayor	1954	Obama	2009	Liberal Activism[d]
Elena Kagan	1960	Obama	2010	Liberal Activism
Ruth Bader Ginsberg	1933	Clinton	1993	Liberal Activism
Stephen Breyer	1938	Clinton	1994	Liberal Activism

[a] The current appointees have all been federal judges with the exception of Justice Kagan, who served as solicitor general.

[b] Chief Justice Roberts is characterized as "strict constructivist," notwithstanding his decision on upholding the Patient Protection and Affordable Care Act of 2010 (see Box 12.3).

[c] Justice Anthony Kennedy is now considered the swing vote on the court after the retirement of Justice Sandra Day O'Connor.

[d] Liberal Activism is often associated with loose constructivism.

President Obama in the first two years in office had the opportunity to appoint two of the nine justices. Although African American leaders lauded Obama for his record number of appointees to the lower courts, some were critical because no blacks were among the half dozen or so names on the highly publicized short lists for the two Supreme Court appointments. To replace Justice David Souter, Obama appointed the first Latino to the Court, Third Circuit Court judge Sonia Sotomayor. For his second appointment, he named Elena Kagan, his solicitor general and the former dean of Harvard Law School. After the naming of Kagan, Melanie Campbell of the Black Women's Roundtable and Elsie Scott, the president of the Congressional Black Caucus Foundation, wrote

BOX 12.2

To Be Young, White, and Male: The Supreme Court Record on Equal Employment Opportunity

A principal responsibility of the Supreme Court in the post–civil rights era is to decide cases involving implementation of the 1964 Civil Rights Act's prohibition on employment discrimination. In its affirmative action jurisprudence, the Court has to deal with issues of "diversity"—the extent to which universities and employers may take race and gender into account in creating a workplace and university class that reflects the diverse racial and ethnic makeup of the nation.

Although the Supreme Court is the ultimate judge of equal employment and affirmative action for the nation, its own record on these matters is itself suspect. Indeed, under ordinary circumstances, the Court's record might lead to its being sued for violations of the Civil Rights Act and for failure to achieve a diverse workplace (the Court is, of course, exempt from such suits).

Each year, each of the nine justices is allowed to select up to four clerks to serve for a one-year term. These young persons—usually selected from among the best students at the nation's elite law schools—play an influential role in screening cases the Court will hear, in doing research, and in writing draft opinions for the justices. Thus, these clerks play powerful behind-the-scenes roles in shaping the kinds of cases the Court will hear and the legal rationales and scope of its opinions.[a]

In 1998, Tony Mauro and *USA Today* conducted the first-ever demographic study of Supreme Court law clerks.[b] (See Table 12.4.) The study found that this elite of the Court's workforce was largely composed of young white males. Specifically, the study found that of the 394 clerks hired during the tenure of the justices from 1972 to 1998, 1.8 percent

TABLE 12.4 Percentage of Whites Hired as Clerks by Justices of the Supreme Court (1972–1998)[a]

Justice[b]	Number of Clerks	Percentage White
Rehnquist	79	99
Stevens	58	86
O'Connor	68	91
Scalia	48	100
Kennedy	45	91
Souter	31	94
Thomas	29	86
Ginsberg	20	90
Breyer	16	80

[a] These data are reported in Tony Mauro, "Schools Urged to Press for Diversity in Court Clerkships," *USA Today,* May 8–10, 1998, p. 4A. Unfortunately, Mauro (2014) reports that there has been little measurable progress to date (see citation below).

[b] The justices are listed by length of service on the Court.

were black, 1 percent were Latino, and 4.5 percent were Asian Americans.[c] Four of the nine justices (including the chief justice, who had served on the Court for more than a quarter of a century) had never hired a black clerk.

In 2008, Mauro revisited the progress since 1998. Tracking the demographics for several more years, he found there were occasional spikes in the number of non-white law clerks, but not really a consistent trend. There were still years when the number of African American clerks was one or zero. Table 12.4 shows the percentage of white clerks appointed by the justices.

[a] The screening of cases is an especially important role. For example, typically more than 5,000 cases are appealed to the Court annually, but it usually hears fewer than a hundred.
[b] In 1996, as part of the research for this book, we tried unsuccessfully to obtain data on the racial composition of the Court's clerks. We were told by the Office of the Clerk of the Court that such information was not available either from the Clerk's office or the chambers of the individual justices. The results of the *USA Today* study are reported in Tony Mauro, "Court Faulted on Diversity," *USA Today,* May 8–10, 1998, p. A1. Data on clerks is still difficult to obtain; neither the Clerk nor the justices provide demographic data. However, since the Court publishes the names of each clerk annually, gender diversity often can be discerned. But for racial or ethnic groups, it is still very difficult to determine. Mauro continues to update his 1998 study. Preliminary findings since 2008 indicate that on the current Court the percentage of women increased from a quarter to about a third (because 57 percent of clerks were hired by the female justices). Data are not available for blacks but Mauro observes, "The number of racial and ethnic clerks, especially those who are not Asian heritage, still appears to be low." See Tony Mauro, "Diversity and Supreme Court Law Clerks," *Marquette Law Review,* 98 (2014): 361–66, http://scholarship.law.marquette.edu/mulr/vol98/iss1/17/.
[c] Seventy-five percent of the clerks during this period were men. On the role of the clerks, see Artemus Ward and David Weiden, *Sorcerers Apprentices: 100 Years of Law Clerks at the United States Supreme Court* (New York: New York University Press, 2006).

a letter to Obama expressing disappointment that African American women were not considered for the nomination. Obama's first two appointments did not alter the ideological makeup of the Court (see Table 12.3), since they replaced two of the four members of the Court's liberal bloc. In 2016, however, Justice Scalia, the long-serving leader of the Court's conservative bloc died, giving the president the opportunity to change the Court's ideological balance. The Republican Majority Leader of the Senate, however, indicated the Senate would not approve any nominee until a new president was elected. Apparently in an effort to get Senate approval, President Obama nominated Merrick Garland, a white, 63-year-old, moderate judge on the District of Columbia Appeals Court.

Rights-Based Cases

School Desegregation

In 1954 the Supreme Court, in a unanimous decision written by Chief Justice Warren, in effect overruled its decision in the 1896 *Plessy* v. *Ferguson* case by declaring that, at least in the area of public education, the principle of "separate but equal" violated the equal protection clause of the Fourteenth Amendment.[15] "Separate educational facilities," Chief Justice Warren wrote, are *"inherently unequal*" (emphasis added). The *Plessy* decision dealt with segregation on railroad cars, but thereafter it was applied to all areas of southern life, including public schools.

Although, according to the Court, separate was constitutionally permissible only if facilities for blacks and whites were equal, the equality part of the principle was never enforced. Three years after *Plessy*, in *Cummings* v. *Richmond County Board of Education*, the Court held that it was permissible to provide a high school for whites but not for blacks.[16] Thus, the doctrine of equality in *Plessy* was a lie. *African Americans in violation of the Court's own decision were relegated to separate and unequal schools and other facilities.* The initial strategy of the NAACP, therefore, was to attack not the practice of segregation itself but rather the absence of equality in the education of blacks.

This attack on unequal educational opportunities began at the graduate and professional levels. In 1938 in *Missouri ex rel. Gaines* v. *Canada,* the Court invalidated Missouri's policy of excluding blacks from its law school and instead offering to pay for their attendance at out-of-state law schools.[17] In *Sweatt* v. *Painter* (1950), the Court found that Texas's all-black law school was "inherently inferior" to its school for whites and ordered the admission of blacks to the white school.[18] In *McLaurin* v. *Oklahoma State Regents*, the Court ruled that Oklahoma State University's practice of segregating black students in its graduate school was unconstitutional.[19] After these victories at the graduate level, the NAACP, after extensive research and debate, changed its strategy and decided to launch a direct attack on the doctrine of separate but equal.[20] The result was the Court's 1954 *Brown* decision.

When the Court declared that segregated schools were unconstitutional, it did not order the schools to be integrated. Rather, a year later, in what is called *Brown II*, the Court ordered the states practicing segregation in public education to "desegregate" with "all deliberate speed."[21] In other words, the states were told to take their time—to desegregate the schools, but slowly. It was not until 1969 in *Alexander* v. *Holmes County Board of Education* that the Court ordered the states to desegregate the schools "at once."[22] Only after this decision—some 15 years after *Brown*—did most southern states begin to desegregate their separate and unequal schools. In addition to the Court's unequivocal order in this case, southern school districts began to rapidly desegregate because the Civil Rights Act of 1964 provided that districts practicing segregation could not receive federal financial aid. In 1969 the Nixon administration began to vigorously enforce this provision.

In 1971, in *Swann* v. *Charlotte Mecklenburg*, the Court ordered school districts to use busing to achieve racial balance or quotas so that "pupils of all grades are assigned in such a way that as nearly as practicable the various schools at various grade levels have about the same proportion of black and white students."[23] The principles of the *Swann* case were soon applied nationwide, leading to an enormous political controversy and eventually a decision by the Court to reverse its position and put an end to school busing.[24]

Busing for purposes of school desegregation was overwhelmingly opposed by white Americans (in the range of 75–80 percent); African American opinion was about equally divided, with polls showing about half supporting busing. In many cities, court-ordered busing led to mass protests by whites, boycotts, violence, and "white flight" to private or suburban schools.

In *Milliken* v. *Bradley,* the Supreme Court began the process of dismantling busing for purposes of desegregation. Specifically, the Court overturned a lower court order that required busing between largely black Detroit and the largely white surrounding suburbs. The Court majority agreed that Detroit's schools were unconstitutionally segregated but held that cross-district busing between city and suburbs was not required to comply with *Brown.*[25] In an angry dissenting opinion, Justice Thurgood Marshall accused his colleagues of bowing to political pressure and of being unwilling to enforce school busing because it was unpopular with the white majority. Since *Milliken,* the court has continued to retreat from busing as a device to desegregate the schools.

Because of white flight to the suburbs, America's urban school systems cannot be desegregated unless there is cross-district busing between city and suburbs. The Supreme Court, however, will not permit this. Thus, 50 years after *Brown*, most African American school children remain in schools that are separate and unequal—inequalities that are so great that one observer describes them as "savage."[26]

In 2004, there were numerous conferences, special classes, and seminars at colleges and universities, several books, and scores of newspaper articles and television stories commemorating the fiftieth anniversary of the May 17, 1954, *Brown* decision. Virtually all commentators celebrated the courage and skill of the individuals who brought the cases and the wisdom of the justices in their decision. *Brown* was also celebrated as the most important Court decision of the twentieth century, and one of the two or three most important in the history of the Court. The historical significance of the case, however, was not in terms of school integration but rather in terms of its symbolism—its symbolism in striking down the constitutional foundations and legitimacy of racism and white supremacy. In terms of school integration, most commentators agreed that *Brown* had been a failure. That is, 50 years after *Brown*, most black (and Latino) children in the North and South attend schools that are separate and unequal.[27] The separateness is a function of the segregated housing patterns that characterize most urban areas of the United States, where blacks live mostly in central city ghettos and whites mainly in affluent urban enclaves or suburbia. Thus, in 2000, 40 percent of all public schools were almost all African American, Hispanic, or both. The inequality flows from the fact that states generally rely on the local property tax to finance schools. This means that affluent, high-property value school districts are able to provide much more in per pupil spending than poor districts. And since whites live disproportionately in affluent districts and blacks disproportionately in poor districts, the effect is to create school systems throughout the nation that in some ways are as separate and unequal as they were prior to *Brown*.

Voting Rights and Racial Representation

Prior to the passage of the Voting Rights Act in 1965, very few African Americans were elected to office in the United States. In that year, approximately 280 blacks held elected offices in this country, including six members of Congress. Today there are more than 8,000 black elected officeholders, including 43 members of Congress.[28] Thus, blacks in the last 25 years have made considerable progress in their quest for public office; however, 8,000 offices constitute a minuscule 1.5 percent of the more than 500,000 elective offices in the United States. Even this tiny number of blacks holding elected office may be in jeopardy as a result of recent Supreme Court interpretations of the Voting Rights Act.

When the Voting Rights Act was passed, it was initially used to guarantee southern blacks the simple right to cast a vote. However, in the late 1960s, the Supreme Court issued a series of decisions interpreting various provisions of the act as guaranteeing not just the simple right to vote but also the right to cast an effective vote—a vote that would allow African Americans to choose candidates of their choice, presumably one of their own race.[29] The key case in this regard is *United Jewish Organizations* v. *Carey*.[30]

In 1972, the New York State Legislature redrew Brooklyn's state senate and assembly districts so that several would have black and Puerto Rican majorities ranging from 65 to 90 percent. In doing this, the Legislature divided a cohesive community of Hasidic Jews between separate assembly and senate districts in the Williamsburg section of Brooklyn, where previously they had been located within single districts. The Hasidic Jews alleged that the creation of the majority–minority districts was "reverse discrimination" against whites, and the United Jewish Organizations of Williamsburg filed suit, claiming that the New York Legislature's actions violated the Fourteenth Amendment's equal protection clause.

In a 7–1 decision, the Supreme Court rejected the claims of the Hasidic Jews, holding that deliberate creation of majority–minority legislative districts was not reverse discrimination and therefore did not violate the equal rights of Brooklyn's white voters. Writing for the majority, Justice White noted that whites made up 65 percent of Brooklyn's population and were majorities in 70 percent of its senate and assembly districts. Therefore, "as long as whites, as a group, were provided with fair representation, we cannot conclude that there was a cognizable discrimination against whites or an abridgment of their right to vote."[31] In 1993 in *Shaw* v. *Reno,* the Supreme Court in effect reversed its holding in *Carey*, deciding that the deliberate creation of majority black districts might indeed violate the equal protection rights of white voters.[32]

After the 1990 census, most of the southern states, following the precedent established in *Carey*, created new majority black congressional districts. These districts in turn elected 12 new black congresspersons. In several states (North Carolina, South Carolina, Florida, Alabama, and Virginia), this was the first time a black had been elected to Congress since Reconstruction. In North Carolina, several white voters sued, alleging, as did the Hasidic Jews in Brooklyn two decades earlier, that the creation of the black districts was "reverse discrimination" and a violation of the Fourteenth Amendment's equal protection clause.

In *Shaw*, a narrow 5–4 majority of the Court agreed with North Carolina's white voters. Writing for the majority, Justice O'Connor held that the North Carolina districts were unconstitutional because they were irregularly shaped. (The 12th district in North Carolina stretched approximately 160 miles along Interstate 85 and for much of its length is no wider than the I-85 corridor.) Justice O'Connor said the districts were "so extremely irregular on [their] face . . . that they rationally can be viewed as an effort to segregate the races for purposes of voting." Such segregation, Justice O'Connor wrote, "reinforces the perception that members of the same racial group—regardless of their age, education, economic status or the community in which they live—think alike, share the same political interests and will prefer the same candidate. We have rejected such perceptions elsewhere as impermissible racial stereotyping."[33]

In his dissent, Justice Stevens pointed out the irony and perversity of the situation in which the Fourteenth Amendment, which was enacted to protect the rights of African Americans, was being used in this case to deny them rights and representation. He wrote,

> If it is permissible to draw boundaries to provide adequate representation for rural voters, for union members, for Hasidic Jews, for Polish Americans or for Republicans, it necessarily follows that it is permissible to do the same thing for members of the very minority group whose history in the United States gave birth to the Equal Protection Clause. A contrary conclusion could only be described as perverse.[34]

After eight years of litigation and more than a dozen cases in several states, the Supreme Court in 2001 in *Easley* v. *Cromartie* to some extent clarified the principles of *Shaw* in a way that permits some use of race as a factor in legislative redistricting.[35] This case once again involved the drawing of the lines in North Carolina's 12th congressional district, which was the district in dispute in the original case. After the Court declared the majority black 12th district unconstitutional, the North Carolina legislature redrew the lines of the district to create a 41 percent majority black district. The three-judge federal district court in North Carolina ruled this new district unconstitutional because it had used race as the "predominant factor" in redrawing the lines. In *Easley* a 5–4 majority reversed the district court, holding that the district court's conclusion that race was the predominant factor in drawing the lines was "clearly erroneous." Rather, Justice Stephen Breyer, writing for the majority (which included Justice O'Connor), concluded that the district lines were based on party affiliation rather than race, and since there is a high correlation between race and party (95 percent of black voters in North Carolina typically vote for Democratic candidates), it was appropriate for the legislature to take race into account as a surrogate for party. Thus, Breyer concluded that race was not an illegitimate consideration in redistricting as long as it was not the "dominant and controlling" one. Justice Clarence Thomas, writing for himself and the other dissenting justices, argued that the majority should not have second-guessed the conclusions of the district court but that even if the majority was correct that party rather than race was the predominant factor, the lines were still unconstitutional because "it is not a defense that the Legislature merely may have drawn the district based on the stereotype that blacks are reliable Democratic voters." While the Court's narrow decision suggested to state legislatures that race could be used in the redistricting process, it still left the situation muddled in terms of the factual determination of when the use of race was "predominant," "dominant," or "controlling."

Gutting the Voting Rights Act: The Case of *Shelby County Alabama v. Holder*

In Chapter 9, we discussed the "amazingly effective devices" employed by the southern states after Reconstruction to keep African Americans from voting. We also discussed in the chapter a series of Supreme Court decisions and congressional laws culminating with the 1965 Voting Rights Act (VRA) that in an uneven and painfully slow process restored the African American vote in the South. Ultimately, the key to this restoration was the VRA, enacted after the brutal police attack on black citizens in Selma, Alabama, on "bloody Sunday" as they peacefully marched for the ballot. In Chapter 10, we discussed the renewal of the VRA in 2006, noting its overwhelming approval in both houses of Congress with the enthusiastic support of congressional leaders and President Bush. Yet, in spite of the widely recognized significance of the VRA in securing and protecting the right of southern blacks to vote and have their votes count, the Supreme Court's five-man conservative majority in 2013 in *Shelby County Alabama v. Holder* effectively rendered one of its most effective provisions null and void.

The Court accomplished this by declaring Section 4 of the Act unconstitutional. Section 4 establishes the formula for Section 5 "preclearance" (see Chapter 10 on Section 5 and preclearance). The formula, adopted initially in

1965, is based on (1) whether a state at that time used literacy or other tests to disqualify voters and (2) whether it had low voter registration and turnout. Writing for the majority in *Shelby County*, Chief Justice Roberts declared this formula was "Unconstitutional in light of current conditions":

> Coverage today is based on decades-old data and eradicated practices. The formula captures states by reference to literacy tests and low voter registration and turnout in the 1960s and 1970s. But such tests have been banned for over forty years. And voter registration and turnout in covered states have risen dramatically. In 1965, the states could be divided into those with a recent history of voting tests and low voter registration and turnout and those without those characteristics. Congress based its coverage formula on that distinction. Today the nation is no longer divided along those lines, yet the Voting Rights Act continues to treat it as if it were. . . . Congress—if it is to divide the states—must identify those jurisdictions to be singled out on a basis that makes sense in light of current conditions.[36]

In a lengthy and spirited dissent, Justice Ginsberg, writing for the four-person liberal minority, declared the Constitution gives Congress the authority to enforce the right to vote and,

> After exhaustive evidence-gathering and deliberative process, Congress reauthorized the VRA, including the coverage provision, with overwhelming bipartisan support. It was the judgment of Congress that 40 years has not been sufficient time to eliminate the vestiges of discrimination following nearly 100 years of disregard for the dictates of the 15th Amendment and to ensure that the right of citizens to vote is protected as guaranteed by the Constitution. That determination of the body empowered to enforce the Civil War Amendments "by appropriate legislation" merits this Court's utmost respect. In my judgment, the Court errs egregiously by overriding Congress' decision.[37]

Justice Ginsberg also cited evidence that racial discrimination in voting was still more pervasive in the South than elsewhere in the nation. For example, she wrote that while the covered (southern) states accounted for only 25 percent of the population, since 1982, 56 percent of the successful race discrimination cases in voting (under Section 2 of the VRA) were from the South, nearly four times more than from noncovered northern states.[38] Noting that during that time Alabama, after Mississippi, had the second highest number of such cases, Ginsberg wrote its "sorry history of Section 2 violations alone provides sufficient justification for Congress' determination in 2006 that it should remain under Section 5's preclearance."[39]

We should note that while Justice Thomas joined the majority opinion, he wrote separately to indicate he would have declared Section 5 itself unconstitutional.

As the Roberts opinion stands, Congress could update the Section 4 formula or apply Section 5 to all of the states. Neither is likely to happen (in 2006 congressional committees considered reworking the formula but could not come up with a workable alternative), which means blacks in Alabama and other parts of the South will likely have their voting rights manipulated and abridged until they can go into Court and prove racism after the fact. (After the fact, in egregious cases Section 3 of the VRA allows states to be temporally brought back under the preclearance requirement.) This is precisely the situation Section 5 was designed to prevent. As Justice Ginsberg put it, concerning black voting rights in the South "What's past is prologue."[40]

As to Justice Ginsberg's prologue, shortly after *Shelby* went into effect Alabama made it more difficult to obtain voter identifications by closing 31 Department of Motor Vehicle Offices (where the identifications are obtained), mostly in majority black counties. These are precisely the kinds of changes that likely would have been stopped by Section 5, since approximately 250,000 Alabama residents do not have driver's licenses or other acceptable forms of identification.

Material-Based Cases: Affirmative Action

Affirmative action, initiated in the late 1960s to early 1970s, consists of a broad collection of executive orders, bureaucratic decisions, court cases, and state legislation designed to eliminate unlawful discrimination of applicants and ensure access to educational programs, employment, and government contracts for one or more of the following reasons: (1) to remedy or compensate historically marginalized racial and ethnic groups for past discrimination; (2) to enforce or implement provisions of the 1964 Civil Rights Act; and (3) to create diversity in education, employment, and government contracting. These programs and policies were designed to assure universal freedom via access to material benefits or rights for protected classes in the areas of education, employment, and government contracts. Targeted legislation has expanded protections beyond underrepresented racial and ethnic groups in education and employment to include women, people of a certain age, people with disabilities, and veterans; yet, affirmative action is often portrayed or perceived by opponents as a policy for "blacks only," which distorts the policy directive.[41] As a result, these programs and policies are now under attack by black conservatives as well as conservative Republicans in Congress and at the state and local levels (see Box 11.3). Leading this attack is the Supreme Court's five-person conservative majority. Next, we review the history of Supreme Court decision making on affirmative action in cases dealing with education, employment, and government contracting.

Education

In 1978 in *Regents of the University of California* v. *Bakke*, the Supreme Court in a split decision upheld the constitutionality of affirmative action.[42] The case involved two issues: first, whether it was constitutionally permissible for a state to take race into account in allocating material benefits—in this specific case, access to medical school; second, if the use of race was deemed permissible, whether the state could use a numerical racial quota to allocate these benefits (in *Bakke* this involved setting aside 16 of 100 slots for students from racial and ethnic backgrounds only). In deciding the case, the Court was deeply divided, issuing six separate opinions. Four conservative justices led by Justice Rehnquist argued that the University of California program violated Title VII of the 1964 Civil Rights Act (which prohibits discrimination by institutions receiving federal funds) as well as the equal protection clause of the Fourteenth Amendment. In the view of these four justices, taking race into consideration in allocating material benefits was never permissible. Four liberal justices led by Justices Brennan and Marshall held that a state, in order to remedy past discrimination or create ethnic diversity, could take race into consideration in allocating benefits and could, if it wished, use a fixed quota. Justice Lewis Powell, the Court's only southerner, split the difference between his liberal and conservative colleagues by holding that a state could use race for purposes of diversity but that a fixed quota was illegal and unconstitutional.

In the 25 years since *Bakke*, the country and the courts became increasingly divided about affirmative action in higher education. Of the 12 circuit courts of appeal, four issued different opinions on the issue. The Fifth and Eleventh Circuits (covering six southern states) overruled *Bakke* and banned affirmative action, and the Sixth and Ninth Circuits (covering several Midwestern and nine western states) upheld *Bakke*. Because of these conflicts between the circuits (which meant the Constitution and the law had different meanings depending on what part of the country one lived in), the Supreme Court in 2003 decided to revisit *Bakke*.

The Court considered two cases from the University of Michigan. The first involved the university's undergraduate admissions program, in which African American, Hispanic, and Native American applicants were automatically awarded 20 points of the 100 needed to guarantee admission. The second dealt with the university's law school admission program, which was designed to achieve a "critical mass" of students from historically marginalized racial and ethnic backgrounds by requiring admission officials to consider all aspects of an applicant's record (including his or her ethnicity) in an "individualized assessment" of the extent to which the applicant contributed to the university's goal of a well-qualified and diverse law school class. Both programs were challenged by white applicants who had been denied admission. They alleged that the university's use of race as a factor in its admissions decisions violated the Civil Rights Act of 1964 and the equal protection clause of the Fourteenth Amendment. The Sixth Circuit rejected the challenge to the law school's program, and its decision on the undergraduate program was pending when the Supreme Court decided to take both cases. These two cases, *Gratz et al. v. Bollinger et al.* and *Grutter v. Bollinger et al.*, were argued before the Court on April 1 and decided on June 29, 2003.

In its decision, the Court upheld the law school program but declared the undergraduate program unconstitutional. Writing for a 5–4 majority in *Grutter*, Justice O'Connor reaffirmed *Bakke*, writing, "Today we endorse Justice Powell's view that student body diversity is a compelling state interest that can justify the use of race in university admissions."[43] The chief justice and Justices Kennedy, Thomas, and Scalia dissented, concluding that the law school admission program operated as a racial quota system. As Justice Scalia wrote, the program was little more than "a sham to cover a scheme of racially proportionate admissions."[44]

In *Gratz,* however, Justice O'Connor joined the other side, voting to strike down the undergraduate program with its automatic 20 points for minorities as a quota system. In his opinion for the majority, the chief justice held that the 20 points awarded to "every single 'underrepresented minority' applicant because of race was not narrowly tailored to achieve educational diversity."[45] In his concurring opinion, Justice Thomas went beyond the chief justice to declare that even if the program was narrowly tailored it would still be unconstitutional because the use of race in admissions decisions is "categorically prohibited by the Fourteenth Amendment."[46]

In her dissent, Justice Ginsberg suggested that affirmative action was a compelling interest of states not only to achieve diversity in their universities but also to remedy past and ongoing racism. She wrote, "The racial and ethnic groups to which the College accords special consideration (African Americans, Hispanics and Native Americans) historically have been relegated to inferior status by law and social practice; their members continue to face class based discrimination to this day."[47] She also suggested that Justice O'Connor was somewhat disingenuous in approving the law school program that indirectly took race into consideration, while disapproving the undergraduate program because it did so openly. She wrote, "If honesty is the best policy, surely Michigan's accurately described, fully disclosed college affirmative action program is preferable to achieving similar numbers through winks, nods and disguises."[48]

While the Court in *Grutter* narrowly upheld the use of race to achieve diversity in higher education, in 2008 in two related cases it held that race could not be used to achieve diversity in elementary and secondary education. The two cases, *Parents Involved in Community Schools* v. *Seattle School District* and *Meredith* v. *Jefferson County Board of Education*, involved the use of race as one factor in assigning students to schools in order to maintain diversity or racial integration. White parents sued claiming that the assignment of pupils by race violated the Fourteenth Amendment's equal protection clause. A bitterly divided Court, in a 5–4 decision, agreed. Writing for the majority, the chief justice invoked the famous *Brown* decision, declaring that the Constitution forbids the classification of students on the basis of race, whether for purposes of integration or segregation. In his dissent, Justice Breyer wrote that use of *Brown* in these cases was a "cruel distortion of history" because the "lesson of history is not that efforts to continue racial segregation is constitutionally indistinguishable from efforts to achieve racial integration." Although Justice Kennedy joined the majority, he was unwilling to conclude that the Constitution prevented any consideration of race in order to achieve racial integration. Describing the chief justice's opinion as "all-too unyielding" in its insistence that race can never be a factor in pupil assignments, Kennedy wrote that in some instances race might be used to reach *Brown*'s objective of ending "de facto re-segregation in schooling."

Meanwhile, in Michigan in 2006, the voters approved Proposition 2, prohibiting the use of racial preferences by any state agency including colleges and universities. The proposition was approved by a margin of 58 to 42 percent. While only 14 percent of blacks voted yes, the proposition was approved by 62 percent of whites, including 68 percent of white men and 57 percent of white women. In 2008, a similar proposition was defeated in Colorado and approved in Nebraska.

In 2007, the Sixth Circuit overturned Michigan's Proposition 2, ruling that banning the use of race in university admissions imposed an "impermissible burden on minorities."[49] However, in 2014 in *Schuette* v. *Coalition to Defend Affirmative Action* the Supreme Court reversed the Sixth Circuit and upheld the right of Michigan voters to ban affirmative action.

In December 2011, the Obama administration issued "Guidelines on the Voluntary Use of Race to Achieve Diversity in Post-Secondary Education." Issued jointly by the Departments of Education and Justice, the guidelines effectively revoked Bush administration guidelines which had discouraged universities from using race in admission decisions. Instead, the Obama guidelines declare that race can be used to achieve ethnic diversity, and in some cases "race can be the outcome determinative."[50] The Obama administration earlier (in July 2011) also announced the "White House Initiatives on Educational Excellence for African Americans." This initiative creates an office in the Department of Education, and a 25-person advisory commission "to expand educational opportunities and outcomes for blacks at all levels of education."[51]

This initiative, the guidelines on the use of race in university admissions, and the Executive Order on diversity in the bureaucracy, discussed in the last chapter, are further evidence, not widely publicized and little noted, of targeted, race-specific policies adopted by the Obama administration.

Meanwhile, in *Fisher* v. *University of Texas at Austin et al.*, the Court in a compromise 7–1 decision upheld *Grutter*, while directing the lower courts to more strictly examine ("strict scrutiny") whether the university's use of race was "narrowly tailored," and that there was no workable race–neutral alternatives to the use of race to achieve a diverse student body.[52] Justice Ginsberg dissented, reiterating her view that given the "lingering effects" of "centuries of law sanctioned inequality," it was constitutionally permissible for the university to openly and candidly use race in the admission process.[53] Again, Justice Thomas, while joining the majority, wrote separately a long concurring opinion to reiterate his long-held view that it was never permissible to use race in admissions decisions.[54]

In its 2016 reexamination of *Fisher* (*Fisher* v. *University of Texas*, #14-981) the eight-person court in a 4–3 vote (Justice Kagan recused herself because she had worked on the case while Solicitor General in the Obama administration) upheld the university's affirmative action program. Justice Kennedy, who voted in favor of affirmative action for the first time in his 28 years on the court, in his majority opinion reaffirmed *Grutter* v. *Michigan et al.*, holding that the Texas admission program was "narrowly tailored" in its use of race as one factor to achieve a diverse student body. Justice Thomas, Chief Justice Roberts, and Justice Alito dissented, with the latter declaring from the bench: "This is affirmative action gone berserk."[55]

Employment

The equivalent to the *Bakke* case in the area of employment is *Griggs et al.* v. *Duke Power Company*, decided in 1971.[56] In this case, a unanimous Supreme Court struck down educational and test requirements that had a discriminatory impact on blacks seeking employment, unless such requirements could be shown to be necessary to the performance of the job. In *Wards Cove* v. *Atonio*, decided in 1989, the Supreme Court by a 5–4 vote in effect overruled *Griggs*, holding that a business could engage in racially discriminatory hiring practices if they served "legitimate employment goals." Unlike the Court's decisions in the areas of affirmative action involving education and government contracts, which involved interpreting the Constitution, the employment cases involve interpreting a statute or law (specifically Title VII of the 1964 Civil Rights Act). Thus, the Congress could change the Court's decision by simply passing a new law. This it did in the 1991 Civil Rights Act. Specifically, with respect to *Wards Cove*, the Congress reinstated the principles of *Griggs* by requiring that employee qualifications be nondiscriminatory and "job related for the position in question and consistent with business necessity."[57]

In its 2009–2010 term, the Court rendered two decisions that appeared to undermine and then reinforce *Griggs*. In *Ricci* v. *DeStefano*, the Court ruled against the City of New Haven, Connecticut, for abandoning a 2003 fire department promotional examination that appeared to discriminate against blacks and Hispanics (no blacks scored high enough on the test to be promoted). Writing for the 5–4 majority, Justice Kennedy agreed that the test had a "disparate impact" on minorities but that the city's use of "express, race-based decision-making" to set aside the test results could not be used to remedy a "statistical disparity based on race" because it discriminated against those individual whites who scored well on the exam. In her dissent, Justice Ginsberg wrote that the majority's opinion broke the promise of *Griggs* "that group's long denied equal opportunity would not be held back by tests fair in form but discriminatory in action."[58] Later, however, the Court ruled unanimously in *Lewis* v. *City of Chicago* that black firefighters may sue the city if it uses tests that exclude disproportionate numbers of racial and ethnic groups.[59] *Ricci* and *Lewis* appear to create a catch-22 situation for employers—damned if you use discriminatory tests and damned if you don't.

Government Contracts

In 1977, to increase historically marginalized groups' access to government contracts, Congress added a provision to the Public Works Act requiring that at least 10 percent of federal funds granted for local projects be awarded to minority-owned businesses. White businesspeople challenged this 10 percent set-aside as an unconstitutional racial quota, but the Court in *Fullilove* v. *Klutznik* rejected their claims.[60] In *Fullilove*, the Court held that Congress, to remedy past discrimination, had the authority to establish the 10 percent set-aside as a reasonable method to assure historically marginalized groups' access to contracts. In 1989 in *Metro Broadcasting* v. *Federal Communications Commission*, the Court upheld similar minority set-aside programs in the allocation of broadcast licenses.[61] Both these decisions were overruled by the conservative Court majority.

In 1983, Richmond, Virginia, established a minority set-aside program for its contracts modeled on the plan passed by Congress and approved by the Supreme Court in *Fullilove*. In *J. A. Croson* v. *City of Richmond*, the Court in a 5–4 decision declared the Richmond plan unconstitutional.[62] Writing for the majority, Justice O'Connor declared that Congress as a coequal branch of government had the authority to establish such set-asides, but the states and localities were prohibited by the Fourteenth Amendment's equal protection clause from doing so unless the plans were "narrowly tailored" to meet identified discriminatory practices. In one of his many angry dissents during his last years on the Court, Justice Marshall described his colleagues' overturning of Richmond's set-aside program as a "deliberate and giant step backward in this Court's affirmative action jurisprudence" that assumes "racial discrimination is largely a phenomenon of the past, and that governmental bodies need no longer preoccupy themselves with rectifying racial injustice."[63]

In *Croson*, Justice O'Connor implied that Congress had the authority to do what the city of Richmond could not do in remedying racial discrimination. Six years later, in *Adarand Constructors* v. *Pena*, she rejected this view and ruled that Congress had to follow the same strict standards as the states.[64] In *Adarand*, the Court, again by 5–4, overturned the *Fullilove* and *Metro Broadcasting*

▒▒▒▒▒▒▒▒▒▒ BOX 12.3 ▒▒▒▒▒▒▒▒▒▒

Material-Based Rights: The Patient Protection and Affordable Care Act of 2010 (aka "Obamacare")

Although there was an overwhelming consensus among constitutional scholars that under precedents established during the New Deal, Congress clearly had the authority to enact Obama's health reforms pursuant to its power to regulate commerce, the five conservative justices on the Supreme Court rejected this consensus. However, Chief Justice Roberts broke with his conservative colleagues and joined with the liberals to uphold the requirement that individuals purchase health insurance or pay a penalty as a valid exercise of the Congress's power to tax. Although the Obama administration had argued that the penalty could be interpreted as a tax, its principal contention was that persons opting not to purchase insurance were engaged in and affecting the delivery of health care in interstate commerce. In using the taxing power rather than the commerce clause, the chief justice in *National Federation of Independent Business* v. *Sebelius* was adhering to the Rehnquist Court's precedents limiting the power of Congress to extend universal rights and freedoms (see Chapter 2). Further, Roberts joined with the conservatives and two of the liberal justices in striking down the provision in the Patient Protection and Affordable Care Act—the formal title of the Obama health reforms—requiring the states to expand coverage of their Medicaid program for low-income persons or lose all of their Medicaid funds. This too is consistent with the Rehnquist Court's emphasis on state-centered federalism rather than universal freedom.

Thus, although Obama's health reforms survived the most serious challenge to Congress's authority to enact universal rights and freedoms since the New Deal, the narrow basis of the chief justice's opinion suggests that the tide in American jurisprudence is toward limited rather than universal freedom. (In 2015 in *King* v. *Burwell* in a technical decision involving implementation the Court in a 6–3 decision reaffirmed the legality of the Affordable Care Act.)

precedents. As a result of the *Croson* decision, there was a dramatic decline in historically marginalized groups' access to contracts in Richmond and other states and localities.[65] A similar result may follow in the wake of *Adarand*. For example, after *Adarand*, President Clinton suspended most federal affirmative action programs that reserved contracts exclusively for minorities and women.[66]

Civil Rights without Remedies: Institutional Racism v. Individual Racism

In its 2000–2001 term, the Court went out of its way to take a case in civil rights law that dealt a death blow to the right of individuals to challenge practices of institutional racism by the states. In doing so, it overruled the decisions of 9 of the 12 circuit courts that had ruled on the issue in more than two decades of litigation.

Institutional racism (which the Court refers to as "disparate impact") deals with policies or programs that have a racially discriminatory impact or effect. By contrast, individual racism (which the Court refers to as "disparate treatment") deals with intentional acts of discrimination. Since the adoption of the Civil Rights Act of 1964, individuals have had the right to sue states for both types of discrimination. But in a 5–4 decision, the Court's conservatives in *Alexander* v. *Sandoval* (#99-1908, 2000) took away the individual right to sue states practicing institutional racism. The case involved a challenge to an Alabama law requiring all applicants to take the state's written driver's license examination in English. The suit alleged that in its impact or effect, the requirement discriminated on the basis of language or ethnic origin. The district court and the Eleventh Circuit agreed. But in *Sandoval*, the Court, without reaching the merits of the case as to whether the requirement was discriminatory, held that the Civil Rights Act of 1964 allowed individuals to sue only in disparate treatment cases. In another one of his unusually harsh dissents (parts of which he read, a step a justice takes to signal the importance or significance of a decision), Justice Stevens condemned his colleagues for reaching out to take the case when there was no conflict between the circuits and for overturning two decades of precedent and concluded that "it makes no sense" to distinguish between types of discrimination in terms of an individual's right to sue. *Sandoval* is a potentially far-reaching decision since disparate treatment cases are difficult to prove (it is not likely, for example, that the authorities in Alabama openly discussed their intent to use the English requirement as a means to discriminate on the basis of ethnic origins), which is why individuals in the post–civil rights era resorted to disparate impact suits in the first place.

In 2015, in *Texas Department of Housing and Community Development, et al.* v. *Inclusive Communities Project Inc. et al.*, the Court appeared to break with the *Sandoval* precedent. The 5–4 decision in this case held that individual or intentional racism was not necessary to establish proof of discrimination in housing cases. Rather, it was only necessary to show institutional racism—that the policies of the Department had a "disparate" negative or harmful effect on protected racial or ethnic groups. While the majority opinion did not directly address the issue raised in *Sandoval*, it limited its potential far-reaching consequences.

Faces and Voices in the Struggle for Universal Freedom
EARL WARREN (1891–1974)

As the 14th chief justice of the United States, Earl Warren did more to address the cause of equality and universal freedom than all of his predecessors combined.

Indeed, Chief Justice Warren is one of the best friends of freedom ever to hold a high position in the U.S. government.

Warren was appointed to the Court by President Eisenhower in 1953 as a political favor because as governor of California he had helped Eisenhower win the Republican nomination (Eisenhower later said Warren's appointment was one of the worst mistakes he made as president). Although a popular and progressive governor, Warren had no experience as a judge and his record had not shown any particular concern for civil rights or civil liberties. (For example, he had strongly supported the incarceration of Japanese Americans during World War II.) Once on the Court, however, he showed remarkable skills in leading the most pro–universal freedom court in the history of the United States.

Earl Warren.

Source: Collection of the Supreme Court of the United States

Warren is most famous for the *Brown* v. *Board of Education* school desegregation decision. Although his opinion in *Brown* was narrowly focused on education, Warren used it as a precedent to end segregation in all government-operated institutions. In 1967 in *Loving* v. *Virginia,* in the name of freedom and equality, the Court declared state bans on interracial marriage unconstitutional.

Although best known for *Brown* and related civil rights cases, the Warren Court extended universal freedom and equality to many other oppressed and stigmatized minorities, including persons accused of crimes, atheists, religious minorities, communists, and women. Warren said he was most proud of the Court's decision in *Baker* v. *Carr*, which established the principle of "one man, one vote." This decision was important, he said, because it helped to make democracy a reality for all Americans.[a]

---

[a] Bernard Schwarz, *Super Chief: Earl Warren and His Supreme Court* (New York: New York University Press, 1983).

Summary

For much of its history, the Supreme Court has been a racist institution. From its 1857 decision in *Dred Scott*, declaring that African Americans had no rights whatsoever, until the remarkable period of the Warren Court in the 1960s, the Court generally ruled against the freedom interests of blacks. In its decisions on race, as with most other cases, the Court tends to reflect the opinions of the white majority and to follow the ideological directions established by the electorate.

In his last year on the Court, Justice Thurgood Marshall in a 1989 speech characterized the Court's 1988–1989 term by stating, "It is difficult to characterize [the] last term's decisions as the product of anything other than a deliberate retrenching of the civil rights agenda. . . . [We have] put at risk not only the civil rights of minorities but the civil rights of *all* citizens. . . . We have come full circle." Marshall then suggested that in order to protect their rights and freedoms blacks should look to Congress, not the courts. Blacks did turn to the Congress after the 1988–1989 term, and the result was the Civil Rights Act of 1991. However, since 1989 other major civil rights laws have been targeted for review by the Court. Therefore, ultimately, the African American quest for freedom still can be profoundly shaped by five people.

Critical Thinking Questions

1. Explain why the "Warren Court" is viewed as the most pro–universal freedom Supreme Court in the history of the United States.
2. Explain the symbolic significance of the Supreme Court's famous *Brown* v. *Board of Education* decision. Discuss, giving examples, why most commentators consider it to be a substantive failure.
3. Discuss the concepts of judicial restraint and judicial activism in relation to African Americans and the quest of universal freedom. Which concept historically has proven to be more advantageous?
4. The conservative majority on the Supreme Court has tended in recent years to retrench in enforcement of civil rights in education, employment, and voting rights. Discuss a case from each of these areas that show this retrenchment.
5. Define institutional racism and individual racism. Discuss the difference between using "disparate impact" v. "disparate treatment" as the burden of proof in relation to African Americans and the quest for universal freedom. What are the effects on civil rights?

Selected Bibliography

Abraham, Henry. *The Judicial Process*, 4th ed. New York: Oxford University Press, 1980.
A general overview of the judicial process in the United States, including local, state, and federal courts.

Burns, James MacGregor. *Packing the Court: The Rise of Judicial Power and the Coming Crisis of the Supreme Court.* New York: Penguin, 2009. The renowned liberal historian argues that the current conservative court may precipitate a crisis of democratic legitimacy.

Dahl, Robert. "Decision Making in a Democracy: The Supreme Court as a National Policy Maker." *Journal of Public Law* 6 (Fall 1957): 257–88. A classic analysis of the Court's role in the political process.

Hall, Kermit, William Wiecek, and Paul Finkelman. *American Legal History: Cases and Materials.* New York: Oxford University Press, 1991. A nearly comprehensive collection of cases and commentary on the development of law in the United States, focusing on all areas of law including race and civil rights.

Howard, John R. *The Shifting Wind: The Supreme Court and Civil Rights from Reconstruction to Brown.* Albany, NY: SUNY Press, 1999. A sprightly and often moving analysis of the Court's role in pushing and subverting the African American quest for freedom. Especially valuable for its insights into the internal dynamics of Supreme Court decision making.

Leuchtenburg, William. *The Supreme Court Reborn: The Constitutional Revolution in the Age of Roosevelt.* New York: Oxford University Press, 1995. A lucid account of the transformation of the Supreme Court into a liberal reform institution beginning with the New Deal and ending with the Warren Court.

Rosenberg, Gerald. *The Hollow Hope: Can Courts Bring About Social Change?* Chicago, IL: University of Chicago Press, 1996. An analysis of the limited capacity of the courts to foster social change, including detailed study of school desegregation.

Spann, Girardeau. *Race against the Court: The Supreme Court and Minorities in America.* New York: New York University Press, 1993. An argument that the Supreme Court will enforce minority rights only to the extent that whites are not disadvantaged.

Vose, Clement. "Litigation as a Form of Pressure Group Activity." *Annals of the American Academy of Political and Social Science* 319 (September 1958): 20–31. The classic analysis of the use of litigation as a means of influencing the making of public policy.

Walton, Eugene. "Will the Supreme Court Revert to Racism?" *Black World* 21 (1972): 46–48. A cogent analysis of the racist history of the Court.

Notes

1 *Dred Scott* v. *Sanford*, 19 Howard, 60 U.S. 393 (1857), as cited in Kermit Hall, William Wiecek, and Paul Finkelman, eds., *American Legal History: Cases and Materials* (New York: Oxford University Press, 1991): 208.

2 Dred Scott was a slave residing in Illinois, a free state. When his owner returned to Missouri, a slave state, Scott argued that as a result of living in Illinois, he had become free and remained free even in Missouri. The Supreme Court of Missouri rejected Scott's claims, and he appealed to the Supreme Court of the United States, which upheld the decision of the Missouri court. Historians contend that this decision (described by Horace Greeley at the time as "wicked," "atrocious," "abominable," and "detestable hypocrisy") was one of the factors that helped to cause the Civil War. Greeley is quoted in Hall, Wiecek, and Finkelman, *American Legal History*, p. 213.

3 J. Morgan Kouser, *Dead End: The Development of Nineteenth Century Litigation on Racial Discrimination* (New York: Oxford University Press, 1986).

4 Eugene Walton, "Will the Supreme Court Revert to Racism?" *Black World* 21 (1972): 46–48.

5 Robert Dahl, "Decision Making in a Democracy: The Supreme Court as a National Policy-Maker," *Journal of Public Law* 6 (Fall 1957): 281. In his analysis of the Court, Dahl concluded that its main function is to confer legitimacy on decisions taken by the political branches.

6 Robert C. Smith, "Rating Black Leaders," *National Political Science Review* 8 (2001): 124–38. In a list of the 12 greatest African American leaders of all time selected by a panel of black political scientists Marshall ranked sixth.

7 See Robert C. Smith and Richard Seltzer, *Contemporary Controversies and the American Racial Divide* (Lanham, MD: Rowman & Littlefield, 2000): 68–72.

8 Vincent Hutchings, "Political Context, Issue Salience and Selective Attentiveness: Constituent Knowledge of the Clarence Thomas Confirmation Vote," *Journal of Politics* 63 (2002): 846–68.

9 Ibid.

10 See J. Clay Smith, Jr., *Supreme Justice: The Speeches and Writings of Thurgood Marshall* (Philadelphia: University of Pennsylvania Press, 2003).

11 Scott Gerber, *First Principles: The Jurisprudence of Clarence Thomas* (New York: New York University Press, 1999).

12 On this debate, see Edwin Meese (Reagan's attorney general, for the judicial self-restraint view), *The Great Debate: Interpreting Our Written Constitution* (Washington, DC: Federalist Society, 1986); and William Brennan (the former justice, for the activism view), *The Great Debate: Interpreting Our Written Constitution* (Washington, DC: Federalist Society, 1986).

13 Girardeau Spann, *Race against the Court: The Supreme Court and Minorities in Contemporary America* (New York: New York University Press, 1993).

14 William Leuchtenburg, *The Supreme Court Reborn: The Constitutional Revolution in the Age of Roosevelt* (New York: Oxford University Press, 1995).

15 *Brown* v. *Board of Education,* 347 U.S. 483 (1954).

16 175 U.S. 528 (1899).

17 305 U.S. 337 (1938).

18 339 U.S. 629 (1950).

19 339 U.S. 737 (1950).

20 For detailed analysis of this strategy shift, see Richard Kluger, *Simple Justice: The History of* Brown *v.* Board of Education (New York: Vintage Books, 1977).

21 *Brown* v. *Board of Education,* 349 U.S. 294 (1955).

22 392 U.S. 430 (1969).

23 402 U.S. 1 (1971).

24 See Nicholas Mills, ed., *The Great School Bus Controversy* (New York: Teachers' College Press, 1973).

25 *Milliken* v. *Bradley,* 418 U.S. 717 (1974).

26 Jonathan Kozol, *Savage Inequalities: Children in America's Schools* (New York: Crown, 1991).

27 See Charles Ogletree, *All Deliberate Speed: Reflections on the First Half Century of* Brown v. Board of Education (New York: W. W. Norton, 2004); and Sheryl Cashin, *The Failure of Integration: How Race and Class Are Undermining the American Dream* (New York: Public Affairs Press, 2004).

28 On the growth of black elected officials since the Voting Rights Act, see Theresa Chambliss, "The Growth and Significance of African American Elected Officials," in R. Gomes and L. Williams, eds., *From Exclusion to Inclusion* (Westport, CT: Praeger, 1992): 53–70.

29 For a review of these cases, see Robert C. Smith, "Liberal Jurisprudence and the Quest for Racial Representation," *Southern University Law Review* 15 (Spring 1988): 1–51.

30 430 U.S. 144 (1977).

31 Ibid.

32 *Shaw* v. *Reno*, 509 U.S. 690 (1993).

33 Ibid.

34 Ibid.

35 *Easley* v. *Cromartie* (#99-1864, 2001). The case was originally *Hunt* v. *Cromartie* (after James Hunt, the governor of the state at the time of the appeal); however, the Court renamed the case to reflect the name of the new governor, Michael Easley.

36 *Shelby County, Alabama* v. *Holder*, Attorney General et al. (slip opinion) #12-96 (2013).

37 Ibid.

38 Ibid.

39 Ibid.

40 Ibid.

41 See Sherri L. Wallace and Marcus D. Allen, "Affirmative Action Debates in American Government Introductory Textbooks," *Journal of Black Studies* 47 (7) (2016): 1–23.

42 438 U.S. 265 (1978).

43 *Grutter* v. *Bollinger et al.* (slip opinion) #0-241 (2003).

44 Ibid.

45 *Gratz et al.* v. *Bollinger et al.* (slip opinion) #02-516 (2003).

46 Ibid.

47 Ibid.

48 Ibid.

49 Tamar Lewin, "Court Overturns Michigan Affirmative Action Ban," *New York Times*, July 2, 2011.

50 Sam Dillon, "US Urges Creativity by Colleges to Gain Diversity," *New York Times*, December 3, 2011.

51 *The White House Initiative on Educational Excellence for African Americans* (Washington, DC: The White House, 2011).

52 *Fisher* v. *University of Texas at Austin et al.* (slip opinion) #11-345 (2013).

53 Ibid.

54 Ibid.

55 Quoted in Adam Liptak, "Supreme Court Upholds Affirmative Action at the University of Texas," *New York Times*, June 23, 2016.

56 401 U.S. 424 (1971).

57 "The Compromise on Civil Rights," *New York Times*, December 12, 1991.

58 Ricci v. DeStefano, 557–US.

59 *Lewis* v. *Chicago* (slip opinion) #08-974 (2010).

60 448 U.S. 448 (1980).

61 110 S.Ct. 2997 (1990).

62 488 U.S. 469 (1989).

63 Ibid.

64 (Slip opinion) 903-1841 (1995). This case involved a suit by white contractors challenging a minority set-aside in federal highway construction.

65 Augustus Jones and Clyde Brown, "State Responses to *Richmond* v. *Croson*: A Survey of Equal Employment Opportunity Officers," *National Political Science Review* 3 (1992): 40–61. See also W. Avon Drake and Robert Holsworth, *Affirmative Action and the Stalled Quest for Racial Progress* (Urbana: University of Illinois Press, 1996): chap. 7.

66 Steven Holmes, "White House to Suspend a Program for Minorities," *New York Times*, March 8, 1996, p. A1; and Steven Holmes, "Administration Cuts Affirmative Action While Defending It," *New York Times*, March 16, 1998, p. A17.

CHAPTER 13

State and Local Politics and the African American Quest for Universal Freedom

---

LEARNING OBJECTIVE

Explain devolution in the states and how it impacts political representation and policy responsiveness to the African American electorate.

Reconstruction: The Brief Era of Universal Freedom in State Politics

In Chapter 2, we showed that the brief Reconstruction era, 1863–1877, was the first period of national-centered power. This period also saw the first era of progressive, pro–universal freedom government in the United States, as many of the southern states were governed by minority–majority coalitions that adopted rights and material-based policies that expanded freedom for all Americans. W. E. B. Du Bois described the Reconstruction era state and local governments as "the finest efforts to achieve democracy for the working millions which this world had ever seen."[1] And, in a recent history of the era, Douglas Egerton calls it "the most progressive period" in American history.[2]

The most basic rights-based reforms initiated by the Reconstruction governments were the extension of the right to vote to all men, without regard to race, literacy, or property ownership. These voters then formed biracial

Republican minority–majority coalitions of blacks and whites that elected African Americans to state and local offices for the first time in U.S. history. Once in office, this Republican Party coalition enacted a series of social and economic reforms, including free public schools, asylums, property rights for married women, reductions in the number of crimes, legislation regulating private markets and insurance companies. At the local level, streets were paved, boards of health and sanitation were established and police forces and public transportation were integrated. These programs were financed by increased taxation, especially on the wealthy planters.[3]

These progressive, universal freedom governments within a decade were overthrown through terrorism and massacres by groups like the Ku Klux Klan; the most infamous of the massacres took place in Colfax, Louisiana, in 1873 when perhaps as many as 100 black men were slaughtered.[4] These terror campaigns were successful because northern whites agreed to withdraw the U.S. Army (which had provided security and protection to African Americans) from the southern states. Without the protection of the army, these progressive, democratic governments could not survive.

One of the reasons northern whites turned against the Reconstruction era governments was racism, but as Heather Cox Richardson shows it was more than racism. It was also because of their progressive tax and welfare policies. Wealthy and powerful whites, Cox writes, turned against Reconstruction because they

> increasingly perceived the mass of African Americans as adherents of a theory of political economy in which labor and capital were at odds and in which a growing government would be used to advance laborers at the expense of capitalists. For these northerners, the majority of ex-slaves became the face of "communism" or "socialism" as opponents dubbed their views. . . . Northerners turned against freed people after the Civil War because African Americans came to represent a concept of society and government that would destroy the "free labor world," that is a view that labor and capital had mutually compatible interests. Black citizens, it seemed threatened the core of American society.[5]

After the Reconstruction governments were overthrown, many of the progressive reforms were repealed but many were not and constitute a part of the legacy of progressivism in southern politics.

Constitutionalism and Federalism in the States

As we have discussed, the separation of powers and federalism were two major contributions of the framers of the Constitution to the art and practice of government. Both allowed coexisting sovereigns—national and the state governments—to share power and authority over their jurisdictions and citizens.

In Chapter 2, the impact of national-centered federalism was discussed. In this chapter, we focus on the impact of state-centered federalism.

The Tenth Amendment states, "The powers not delegated to the United States by the Constitution, nor prohibited by it to the states, are reserved to the states respectively, or to the people." These "reserved" powers include the power to make laws that promote and protect the health, safety, and morals of citizens, including creating and granting powers to local governments, counties, cities, and school districts. The powers of these local governments, indeed their very existence—unlike the states in the federal system—are determined by the states. The *complete* dependency of local governments on their states for their powers was unambiguously stated by Judge John Dillion in 1898 in the case of *City of Clinton* v. *Missouri R.R.* In what has come to be known as "Dillion's Rule," the judge said local governments "owe their origins to, and derive their powers and rights *wholly* from, the legislature. It breathes into them the breath of life, without which they cannot exist. *As it creates, it may destroy. . . .*[local governments] are, so to phrase it, the mere tenants at will of the legislature."[6]

Given their unique institutional structures, laws and regulations, political cultures, histories, demographics, economies, and geographies,[7] states and their local governments rely on their own capacities and utilize resources within their respective boundaries to respond to the challenges and choices facing their citizens.[8] The various ways by which states manage conflict over politics, policy, and public services determines "who gets what and how."[9] States vary in the powers given to governors, the structure of their legislatures, their judicial review and selection processes, the strength of the party system, the roles of interest groups and the media, and taxing and spending policies.[10] A state's level of social diversity—racial and ethnic composition—also shape its political processes and influence its policy tendencies.[11] Thus, generalizations are difficult; however, similarities emanate from the political histories and cultures that define the state.

The political culture of the southern states is defined by its historical association with the American institution of slavery, Jim Crow segregation, and racial discrimination. As W. E. B. Du Bois wrote, "freedom and citizenship were primarily a matter of state legislation."[12] Thus, "states' rights" was used by southern states to defend slavery, define rights and freedoms for their citizens, and, subsequently, impede universal freedom for racial and ethnic groups. Tensions over federalism and state autonomy and power came in direct response to the federal government and judicial protections for (and interventions on the behalf) of African American citizens,[13] particularly in the South where racial conflict has characterized much of its history.[14] Menifield and Shaffer surmise:

> V.O. Key (1949), in *Southern Politics in State and Nation*, demonstrated how white citizens employed their one-party Democratic monopoly to maintain white supremacy by disenfranchising African Americans through

numerous voting devices. Even as late as 1960s and 1970s, white legislators in states such as Mississippi employed multi-member districts to dilute the black vote in state legislative districts, and gerrymandered congressional districts to ensure white majorities in each district. . . . As white Southerners began to realize the futility of continued resistance to integration, and during the stagflation of the 1970s became more concerned over economic issues that united the races, biracial coalitions within Democratic parties emerged and usually fended off challenges from the increasingly strong Republican Party. . . . By the turn of the century, however, "white flight" among conservatives to the Republican Party yielded a Southern landscape where a very competitive, two-party system had finally been established. . . . With Southern legislatures polarized between liberal African American Democrats and [tea-party] Republicans.[15]

Thus, federal–state relations would become a tug-of-war known as "devolution," the process of taking power and responsibility away from the federal government and giving it to state and local governments.[16] By the early 1980s, King-Meadows and Schaller wrote "devolutionary sentiments had gained wider currency. National solutions were depicted as not merely infringing on state's rights, but as inadequate for dealing with the specific needs of individual states."[17] In this regard, federal legislation prevented states from experimenting in their "laboratories" to find innovative solutions suitable to particular programmatic preferences for their citizens. Although, devolution may, in part, have been initially intended by states' rights advocates to disenfranchise African Americans, it actually to some extent expanded opportunities for political participation for the African American electorate. African Americans could now elect, mobilize, and retain black state elected officials to actively promote and protect African American interests,[18] which led to a political backlash from majority Republican state legislatures.

Black Political Representation and Policy Responsiveness in State Legislatures

Many of the early studies on African American legislative behavior were limited, partly because of the absence of data but mostly due to the small numbers of African Americans serving in state legislatures.[19] The number of African American state lawmakers increased significantly after the passage of the Voting Rights Act in 1965 and the states' redrawing of state legislative and congressional districts in the 1970s. As a result, by the 1980s, southern legislative districts over 65 percent black population were electing African American legislators almost 90 percent of the time, with the greatest increase in black representation in states covered by the Section 5 preclearance provision of the Voting Rights Act, and in states shifting from multi-member to single-member districts.[20] In

Chapter 10, we used three criteria to measure representativeness of African Americans in Congress: descriptive, symbolic, and substantive. In this chapter, descriptive and substantive criteria are used to discuss the extent to which state legislatures represent African Americans.

Descriptive Representation in State Legislatures

Between 1971 and 2009, the percentage of African American state lawmakers rose from 2 percent to 9 percent. Likewise, the number of women state lawmakers jumped from 4 percent in 1971 to nearly 25 percent in 2009.[21] (Unfortunately, because of the lack of intersectionality in the recent data, it is difficult to determine the percentage of state lawmakers by race *and* gender.) Both increases had a significant impact on descriptive representation for the African American electorate. In general, state legislators, like their congressional counterparts, tend to be male, white, and well educated, often with business backgrounds. (See Box 13.1.)

BOX 13.1

Descriptive and Substantive Representation: Does Race *and* Gender Matter?

The few studies on intersectionality in state legislatures have proven the importance of examining the race *and* gender of state lawmakers with respect to descriptive and substantive representation. Early studies on African Americans and women state lawmakers revealed distinctive findings for the various subgroups: black men, black women, white men, and white women. For example, studies of African American state lawmakers found ambivalence among black women toward the women's liberation movement in the 1970s[a]; while later studies found that African American women tended to "prioritize one identification over the other," making race issues the primary concern.[b]

Edith Barrett found that African American and women legislators, all of whom tend to name education, health care reform, unemployment, and economic development as top issues, were more liberal than white male legislators, generally.[c] Yet, when asked to list their three greatest concerns, black women appeared to be the most united in their views that "states need to focus their attention on reforming education and the healthcare system, stimulating economic development, and reducing unemployment."[d] Also, African American women state lawmakers differed from their black male colleagues who are more likely to perceive racial gaps as more important than gender gaps and from white women who are more likely to perceive the opposite of this view.[e] Indeed, Bratton, Haynie, and Reingold found that the legislative activity of African American women is a "particularly interesting avenue through which to explore the intersections of race, gender and political representation" due to the findings that when controlling for partisanship and district demographics, African American women are more likely to focus on *both* women's interests and black interests, giving credence to Evelyn Simien's[f] finding that, in the mass public, racial identification enhances rather than detracts from gender identification.[g] Given that choices made by individual legislators are influenced by the institutional context in which they work, black women lawmakers will sponsor women's interests bills, as necessary, if there are relatively few women legislators; however, their decisions regarding the sponsorship of black interests measures "are impervious to the racial composition of the chamber."[h] Meaning, African American female state lawmakers use their affiliations with both the women's caucus and the black caucus to leverage their influence "by positioning themselves as a bridge" on issues that both caucuses consider important.[i]

Further, not only are African American women state lawmakers distinct from their black male and white female counterparts in their legislative activity, they also tend to be better educated than their colleagues, many coming from professional backgrounds. Their unity among themselves, with the support from African American males and white women peers, highlights their public visibility, and affords them some freedom to "hold a particular policy niche" less "beholden to white male constituents," while increasing the likelihood of their successfully pushing bills through the legislature.[j] Finally, Nadia Brown has discovered in her examination of how identity informs black women legislators' descriptive and substantive representation, that this group's unique experiences with racism and sexism influences their legislative decision-making and policy preferences, underscoring how

intersectionality enhances political representation as well.[k]

[a] Jewell Prestage, "Black Women State Legislators," In Marianne Githens and Jewell Prestage, eds., *A Portrait of Marginality: the Political Behavior of the American Women* (New York: David McKay, 1977).
[b] Robert Darcy and Charles D. Hadley, "Black Women in Politics: The Puzzle of Success," *Social Science Quarterly* 69(30) (1988): 629–45.
[c] Edith J. Barrett, "The Policy Priorities of African American Women in State Legislatures," *Legislative Studies Quarterly* 20(2) (1995): 242.
[d] Ibid., p. 242.
[e] Quoted in Kathleen A. Bratton, Kerry L. Haynie, and Beth Reingold, "Agenda Setting and African American Women in State Legislatures," *Journal of Women, Politics & Policy* 28(3–4) (2006): 74. See also, Edith J. Barrett, "Gender and Race in the State House: The Legislative Power," *Social Science Journal* 34(2) (1997): 131–44.
[f] Ibid., p. 73. See also, Evelyn Simien, "Race, Gender, and Linked Fate," *Journal of Black Studies* 35(5) (2005): 529–50.
[g] Ibid., p. 91.
[h] Ibid., p. 91.
[i] See Wendy Smooth, "A Case of Access Denied? Gender, Race and Legislative Influence," National Symposium Series: Women in Politics: Seeking Office and Making Policy (Institute of Governmental Studies, UC Berkeley, 2006).
[j] Barrett, "The Policy Priorities of African American Women in State Legislatures," p. 243.
[k] See Nadia E. Brown, *Sisters in the Statehouse: Black Women and Legislative Decision Making* (New York: Oxford University Press, 2014).

Like their counterparts in Congress, blacks in state legislatures are elected from majority black places or majority–minority districts where most of the voters are Democrats.[22] Based on the latest data available in 2009, Table 13.1 shows there are roughly 7,382 state elected officials; African American state lawmakers constitute 628 or 9 percent. Of the total 1,971 seats in state Senates, African Americans hold 161 or 8 percent, and 467 or 9 percent of the total 5,411 seats in state Houses. The five states with the largest black delegations are located in the South: Georgia, with 53 legislators; Mississippi, with 50; Maryland, 43; South Carolina, 37; and Alabama with 35. There are nine states—Hawaii, Idaho, Iowa, Maine, Montana, North Dakota, South Dakota, Utah, and Wisconsin—with no African American state legislators.[23]

TABLE 13.1 Total Numbers and Percentage of African Americans in State Legislatures

State	Total Legislative Seats	% of African Americans in State	Total African American State Legislators	% of Total Seats	Total State Senate Seats	Total African American Senators	% of Senate Seats	Total State House Seats	Total African American House Members	% of House Seats	Under/Over Represented in State Legislatures
Alabama	140	26.5%	35	25%	35	8	23%	105	27	26%	-1.5%
Alaska	60	4.1%	1	2%	20	1	5%	40	0	0%	-2.5%
Arizona	90	4.0%	2	2%	30	1	3%	60	1	2%	-1.8%
Arkansas	135	15.8%	14	10%	35	4	11%	100	10	10%	-5.4%
California	120	6.7%	13	11%	40	6	5%	80	7	9%	4.1%
Colorado	100	4.2%	2	2%	35	1	3%	65	1	2%	-2.2%
Connecticut	187	10.3%	15	8%	36	4	8%	151	11	7%	-2.3%
Delaware	62	20.9%	5	8%	21	1	5%	41	4	10%	-12.8%
Florida	160	15.9%	26	16%	40	7	18%	120	19	16%	0.4%
Georgia	236	30.0%	53	22%	56	12	21%	180	41	23%	-7.6%
Hawaii	76	2.9%	0	0%	25	0	0%	51	0	0%	-2.9%
Idaho	105	0.9%	0	0%	35	0	0%	70	0	0%	-.9%
Illinois	177	15.0%	31	18%	59	10	17%	118	21	18%	2.5%
Indiana	150	9.0%	12	8%	50	4	8%	100	8	8%	-1.0%
Iowa	150	2.6%	0	0%	50	0	0%	100	0	0%	-2.6%
Kansas	165	6.1%	7	4%	40	2	5%	125	5	4%	-1.8%
Kentucky	138	7.7%	7	5%	38	1	3%	100	6	6%	-2.6%
Louisiana	144	31.9%	26	18%	39	6	23%	105	20	19%	-13.8%
Maine	186	1.0%	0	0%	35	0	0%	151	0	0%	-1.0%
Maryland	188	29.5%	43	23%	47	10	17%	141	33	23%	-6.6%
Massachusetts	200	6.9%	9	5%	40	0	3%	160	9	6%	-2.4%
Michigan	148	14.3%	22	15%	38	5	11%	110	17	15%	0.5%
Minnesota	201	4.5%	2	1%	67	0	0%	134	2	1%	-3.5%
Mississippi	174	37.2%	50	29%	52	13	21%	122	37	30%	-8.5%

State										
Missouri	197	11.5%	19	34	10%	3	9%	163	16	10%	-1.9%
Montana	150	0.6%	0	50	0%	0	0%	100	0	0%	-0.6%
Nebraska	49	4.4%	2	49	4.1%	2	4.1	0	0	0.0	-0.3%
Nevada	63	8.0%	7	21	11%	3	14%	42	4	10%	3.2%
New Hampshire	424	1.2%	1	24	0%	0	0%	400	1	0%	-1.0%
New Jersey	120	14.5%	15	40	13%	5	5%	80	10	13%	-2.0%
New Mexico	112	2.8%	2	42	2%	0	0%	70	2	3%	-1.1%
New York	212	17.3%	34	62	16%	10	18%	150	24	16%	-1.3%
North Carolina	170	21.7%	32	50	19%	9	14%	120	23	19%	-2.9%
North Dakota	141	1.0%	0	47	0%	0	0%	94	0	0%	-1.0%
Ohio	132	12.0%	19	33	14%	5	15%	99	14	14%	2.4%
Oklahoma	149	7.9%	6	48	4%	2	2%	101	4	4%	-3.9%
Oregon	90	2.0%	2	30	2%	2	10%	60	0	0%	0.3%
Pennsylvania	253	10.8%	19	50	8%	3	8%	203	16	8%	-3.3%
Rhode Island	113	6.3%	3	38	3%	1	0%	75	2	3%	-3.7%
South Carolina	170	28.7%	37	46	22%	8	17%	124	29	23%	-7.0%
South Dakota	105	1.1%	0	35	0%	0	0%	70	0	0%	-1.1%
Tennessee	132	16.9%	18	33	14%	3	6%	99	15	15%	-3.2%
Texas	181	12.0%	16	31	9%	2	3%	150	14	9%	-3.1%
Utah	104	1.2%	0	29	0%	0	0%	75	0	0%	-1.2%
Vermont	180	0.8%	1	30	1%	1	0%	150	0	0%	-0.3%
Virginia	140	19.9%	14	40	10%	5	13%	100	9	9%	-9.9%
Washington	147	3.6%	2	49	1%	1	2%	98	1	1%	-2.3%
West Virginia	134	3.5%	3	34	2%	0	0%	100	3	3%	-1.3%
Wisconsin	132	6.0%	0	33	0%	0	6%	99	0	0%	-6.0%
Wyoming	90	1.2%	1	30	1%	0	0%	60	1	2%	-0.1%
Total	**7,382**	**12.9%**	**628**	**1,971**	**9%**	**161**	**8%**	**5,411**	**467**	**9%**	**-4.3%**

Sources: National Black Caucus of State Legislatures and the National Conference of State Legislatures, "African-American Legislators 2009," www.ncsl.org/research/about-state-legislatures/african-american-legislators-in-2009.aspx. Percentage of African Americans in the state and percentage of over/underrepresentation taken from https://allotherpersons.wordpress.com/2009/04/16/factoid-black-state-legislators-in-2009/.

Research on state legislatures has shown the importance of seniority and holding leadership positions as committee chairs and party leaders in successfully getting bills or amendments introduced and enacted for any lawmaker, whatever their race or party membership.[24] In 2009, the year Barack Obama first took the oath of office as President, Colorado—where African Americans comprise only 4.2 percent of the state population—became the first state with an African American president (or presiding officer) of the Senate and Speaker of the House, simultaneously. The same year, New York had its first African American president of the Senate, and Nevada had its first African American Senate majority leader.[25] In both states, the population percentage of African Americans constitutes roughly 17.3 and 8 percent, respectively.

With regards to committee assignments, black legislators were over-represented on "black interests" committees—where black interests is defined as health, education, welfare, economic redistribution, and civil rights issues—yet had increased their representation on "prestige" committees (e.g. Rules, Budget, Appropriations) the longer they served, suggesting a broadening of their influence.[26] Kerry Haynie concluded, "The presence and growth of African American representation in government has indeed had noticeable and meaningful policy consequences."[27] Thus, the racial and ethnic composition of state legislatures is a difference that makes a difference.[28]

Table 13.1 shows the states for which the African American population percentage exceeds the legislature's African American percentage causing African Americans to be "underrepresented" are primarily located in the South or black-belt region: Louisiana, Delaware, Virginia, Mississippi, Georgia, and South Carolina. The states for which the legislature's African American percentage exceeds the state's African American population percentage causing African Americans to be "overrepresented" are located in the western and Midwest regions: California, Nevada, Illinois, and Ohio.[29] The underrepresentation of African American lawmakers in the southern state legislatures indicates challenges remain in the South in terms of African Americans getting descriptive representation in state legislatures.

Substantive Representation in State Legislatures

In the summer of 2000, the *Journal of Black Studies* released a special issue devoted to examining African American politics at the state level.[30] All studies in the volume supported the notion that African American state lawmakers served as "the primary mouthpiece for African American citizens in the respective states and were the most likely to pursue legislation that would have direct benefits to African Americans."[31] The findings from the collective studies also concluded, "On questions of public policy, ideology, and candidate choice, African Americans have been the most cohesive and consistent policy subgroup in United States politics."[32]

As a group, African American legislators are more likely to sponsor bills (independently or jointly) that address black interests,[33] particularly when the percentage of registered voters in a district is majority African American.[34] Studies have found, by contrast, white legislators almost never introduce such legislation.[35] In fact, King-Meadows and Schaller found that, as discretionary power and decisions about issues important to the black electorate devolved from the federal level to the states, African Americans were the most cohesive among groups in the states, often using political strategies—from group caucus to biracial coalitions—to secure legislation beneficial to their African American constituents. Indeed, "cohesiveness [among black state legislators] facilitates the effective and strategic allocation of resources dedicated toward building biracial coalitions."[36] It also allows African American lawmakers to be responsive to black interests, despite the states' varied political cultures and devolutionary sentiments.[37]

However, the protection and promotion of black state interests are conditioned not only by what ideas and policies black state lawmakers represent, but their degree of political incorporation and the legislative environment within which they attempt to advance those interests.[38] In the era of devolution, the danger for African American lawmakers is that it presents a "constituency–institutional" dilemma. On one hand, African American state legislators risk repudiation from entrenched, state-level (increasingly Republican) conservatives, who prefer to retain policy control for themselves. On the other hand, African American state lawmakers risk condemnation from national and local liberal interest groups that favor national-centered federalism as the primary mechanism to protect minority and underserved interests. Consequently, African American proponents of increased discretionary power may lose campaign contributions, endorsements, face media attacks, and suffer political scorn from political allies. Yet, always seeking national intervention may only strengthen perceptions that black interests are synonymous with increased federal oversight of state practices and support the perception that black state legislators are "mere proxies for federal elites."[39] Nevertheless, effective representation of black interests may require that African American citizens and black state officials recognize and exploit their newfound power to give voice to underrepresented interests,[40] even as conservative Republicans take control of state legislatures, seeking to repeal laws that promoted universal freedom (more discussion below).

African American Representation in Statewide Offices: Challenges and Opportunities

In the history of the nation, very few African Americans have been elected to statewide offices or the United States Senate. At the state level, only two African Americans—Douglas Wilder of Virginia in 1979 and Deval Patrick of

Massachusetts in 2006—have been elected as governors. In 1873, Pinckney Benton Stewart (P.B.S.) Pinchback, the African American Lieutenant Governor of Louisiana, served as acting governor for 43 days, but was never elected. In 2008, Basil Patterson, New York's Lieutenant Governor, succeeded to the governorship after Elliot Spitzer resigned due to a sex scandal, but did not run for election. Legally blind, he was also the nation's first disabled person to serve as governor. There are few data on African Americans who have been elected to other executive positions. As of 2016, only four African Americans were elected at the executive level: Secretary of State, Jesse White (D-IL), elected in 1999; State Treasurer, Denise L. Nappier (D-CT), elected in 1999; Attorney General, Kamala Harris (D-CA), elected in 2011; and Lieutenant Governor, Jenean Hampton (R-KY), elected in 2016. Interestingly, these executive-level officials were elected in states, save Illinois, where the percentage of the African American population is less than the national average at 13 percent. If the numbers of statewide officeholders were in line with this percentage, there would be at least 12 African American senators and six governors.

Since the people began to directly elect U.S. senators in 1914, only five African Americans have been elected: Edward Brooke (R-MA), Carol Mosley Braun (D-IL), Barack Obama (D-IL), Cory Booker (D-NJ), and Kamala Harris (D-CA). Two African Americans have been appointed: Roland Burris (D-IL) to replace Obama; and Tim Scott (R-SC) to fill the seat vacated by Jim DeMint (R-SC). Scott later won the senate seat in a special election. With the exception of Massachusetts, these senators emerged from just two states—Illinois and South Carolina—where the percentage of the African American population is greater than the national average at 15 percent and 29 percent, respectively. These states have significant local black majorities; however, this alone is not enough to win statewide offices. In general, enough white voters have been unwilling to vote for an African American candidate—whatever his or her ideology or qualifications—to make such candidacies politically realistic. Racism or subconscious bias is part of the explanation for this unwillingness, as is the perception among some whites that African Americans are too liberal for their moderate, independent, or conservative ideological inclinations.

Given this political reality, only two African American members of the Congress have left the House to seek statewide office, which is frequently the career path of White House members. Alan Gerber summarizes the situation as follows:

> African American members of Congress rarely seek higher office. Prospects for winning statewide are discouraging. No African American has moved from the House to the Senate or to the governor's mansion. The liberal voting record that African American representatives typically compile does not provide a strong foundation for winning statewide elections and there remains some resistance to voting for African Americans for higher office.[41]

Recent studies have identified other explanations. Despite the significant gains made for other political offices, including city councils, mayors, state legislatures, and various statewide offices that provide "professional training" and serve as "stepping stones" to higher office, African Americans face a glass ceiling in winning U.S. Senate seats due to structural and contextual hurdles such as state size and lack of sufficient campaign funds.[42] We know that majority–minority districts, coupled with the Supreme Court protection against unfavorable gerrymandering, significantly improved prospects for African Americans, allowing these state lawmakers and congressional representatives to overcome the competitive electoral disadvantages locally and district-wide.[43] However, given that African American state lawmakers and house members typically represent disproportionately less-affluent, majority–minority districts in larger states, raising initial funds for expensive statewide campaigns is more difficult because they are less likely to be recruited as candidates by party agents and more likely to be encouraged to run by people from their churches, their neighborhoods and families.[44] As Carol Mosely Braun, the first African American woman elected to the Senate surmised, "If a person does not have access to very deep pockets, they really don't have a chance."[45] Relatedly, the geographic concentration of majority–minority districts—shaped by historic housing patterns—limits "name recognition" for African Americans among a larger pool of competitors in the statewide electorate of Senate seats. Interestingly, because the few black Republicans in Congress usually represent largely white districts, their political ideologies are viewed as more "mainstream" and less liberal than black Democrats. This affords them access to important donors and party activists, and opportunities to increase their name recognition in the state while building their reputation in the Republican Party. However, it also raises the question of which is most important: racial diversity in the overall political system or effective representation of minority interests? Historically, African American lawmakers who represent white constituencies have little history of supporting policies that promote universal freedom for African Americans.[46]

Racism alone isn't the barrier, rather it's the "accumulated effects of long-term racial discrimination—the limitations associated with representing heavily black House districts or leading majority black cities—that block further advancement" to statewide position.[47] Nevertheless, the success of Obama, Governor Patrick in Massachusetts and Senator Booker in New Jersey (the former mayor of heavily black Newark), suggests that a new structure of ambition is emerging in black politics, where a new generation of politicians perceive that the white electorate in the twenty-first century is willing to vote for an ideologically and culturally mainstream African American candidate for any office.[48]

State Courts: Who Judges?

State courts handle more than 90 percent of the criminal and civil cases in the United States. In most cases, if one obtains justice, one does so in the trial and appellate courts of the states, since very few of these cases are successfully appealed in the federal courts. Thus, the racial, ethnic, and gender composition of the state courts is important in the African American quest for a universal freedom and social justice.

In 2016 the American Constitution Society for Law and Policy developed for the first time a database of more than 10,000 judges on state trial and appeals courts, and compared the racial, ethnic, and gender composition of the courts with state populations. The results are stated simply: "We find the courts are not representative of the people they serve. That is, a gap exists between the bench and the citizens."[49] Table 13.2 displays the results.

While white women do not have proportionate representation, they are much better represented than women and men of color on state benches. There is little regional variation in the representation of white women, but the South and West have less representation of racial and ethnic groups than the Northeast and Midwest.[50] States vary in the methods of selecting judges; appointment by governors and legislatures, merit selection (requiring the governor to select from a merit selected panel), and partisan and nonpartisan elections. No data are available on the impact of these different selection methods on the representation of people of color and white women.

The underrepresentation of blacks on state courts, the report concludes, may have an impact on judicial outcomes: "For example, while African Americans

TABLE 13.2 Racial, Ethnic, and Gender Representation on State Courts, 2016

State Judges by Category	Percentage on Trial Courts	Percentage on Appeals Courts
Women[a] of color	8	8
Men[b] of color	9	12
White men	57	58
White women	26	22

[a] Women of color constitute 20 percent of state populations and white women 31 percent.
[b] Men of color constitute 19 percent of state populations and white men 30 percent.

Source: Tracy George and Albert Yoon, *The Gavel Gap: Who Sits in Judgment on State Courts?* (Washington, DC: American Constitution Society for Law and Policy, 2016).

constitute 44 percent of defendants in criminal cases, only 7 percent of the persons who judge them are black."[51]

The Republican Dominance of State Politics in the Obama Era

It is well known that the Democratic Party suffered what President Obama in 2010 called a "Shellacking" in congressional elections during his terms in office, losing control of both the House and Senate. Under Obama the Democrats lost a net 13 Senate and 69 House seats, more than any other two-term president since Eisenhower.[52] What is less discussed is the shellacking the Democrats suffered in state politics, losing 30 state legislative chambers, near 1,000 net legislative seats, and 11 governorships.[53] As a result, at the end of Obama's presidency, Republicans held 32 governors offices, majorities in both houses of 30 of the 50 state legislatures and at least one house in eight other states.

Control by conservative Republicans of state governments impacts both rights- and material-based freedoms. In terms of rights-based freedoms, in 2011 the gerrymandering of state legislative and congressional districts decreased the opportunities for African Americans, Latinos, and liberal whites sympathetic to minority interests to win office. These gerrymanders also helped Republicans to win legislative majorities without winning majorities of the votes of the people. For example, in 2012 Democrats won 1.4 million more votes in the congressional elections, but in part because of gerrymandering the Republicans won a 33-seat majority in the House.

Another rights-based freedom impacted by Republican control of state governments is the right to vote. In 2008 when Obama was elected, no state required photo identification (Voter ID) in order to vote. Since then, 19 states, all controlled in whole or part by Republicans, have passed some kind of photo ID law as a requisite to vote. The conclusion of the most comprehensive study of the effects of these laws on voting is unambiguous: "Requiring identification of any sort appears to have real effects on who votes and who does not. These laws hurt the minority community and help to give whites an oversized voice in American politics."[54]

The most consequential effect of Republican dominance of state politics on material-based rights of African Americans is in the area of health insurance. In its decision upholding President Obama's health insurance law, the Supreme Court invoked principles of states' rights and declared the provision of the law requiring the states to expand their Medicaid program to cover more of the uninsured unconstitutional. As a result of this decision, two-thirds of poor blacks and single mothers, and more than half of all low-wage workers without health insurance are denied coverage, because their state governments, largely controlled by Republicans, refused to expand Medicaid.[55]

States have also used their "Dillion's Rule" prerogatives to prohibit their city governments, which tend to have African American or liberal minority–majority coalition governments, from enacting material-based reforms, such as increasing the minimum wage, affordable housing, tenant rights, or mass transit projects that improve the life chances of the poor and working class.[56]

Republican dominance of state politics is not by chance; to the contrary it is partly the result of a deliberate, well-financed campaign by the American Legislative Exchange and other conservative organizations linked to the billionaire, ultra-conservative Koch brothers—Charles and David—who fund a variety of conservative candidates, causes, and movements.[57] Belatedly, recognizing the impact of these conservative groups on state politics, liberals and progressives in 2014 created the "State Innovation Exchange" (SIX), formerly American Legislative and Issue Campaign (ALICE), to counteract the influence of the conservative "American Legislative Exchange Council" (ALEC) and its allied groups.[58]

Local Representation: "Black Regime" Cities and "Black-Belt" Counties

Carl Stokes in Cleveland, Ohio, and Richard Hatcher in Gary, Indiana, became the first blacks to be elected mayors of major cities in 1967. By 2014, African Americans were mayors of more than 700 cities and towns across the nation, including and increasingly majority white, large cities like Chicago, Los Angeles, New York, and Philadelphia. By 2006, African Americans had been elected to an estimated 5,446 positions nationwide as county officials, municipal officials, and school board officials.[59]

Chapter 2 briefly highlights the major exodus of blacks leaving the South. Many of the major cities that would become the "receiving stations of the Great Migration,"[60] also became the most economically, politically, and racially segregated—due to government-sanctioned, discriminatory housing policies—by the time the migration reached its conclusion in the late 1970s (see Chapter 14). Consequently, these cities and local communities that would eventually result in black majority-rule often shared a similar characteristic—poverty—that yields a "hollow prize" for the black electorate.

Poverty among African Americans is especially concentrated in what political scientists refer to as "black regime" cities, cities with majority or near-majority black populations and where blacks control the government—the mayor's office, the city council, the school board, and most of the senior positions in the bureaucracy.[61] By the late 1970s, there were nine such cities: Atlanta; Baltimore; Detroit; Gary, Indiana; Newark, New Jersey; Richmond, Virginia; Washington, DC; Birmingham, Alabama; and New Orleans. At the time of the election of the black regimes, the poverty rate in these cities averaged 16 percent, ranging from 12.3 percent in Gary to 22 percent in New Orleans. By 1990, the average poverty rate had increased to 28 percent, ranging from 16.9 percent in Washington to 32.4 percent in Detroit (New Orleans had the second highest poverty rate at 31.6 percent).[62] A 2015 study by the Brookings Institute identified the cities with greatest "levels of inequality," defined as the measure by a "95/20 ratio," where the figure represents the income at which a household earns more than 95 percent of all other households, divided by the income at which a household earns more than 20 percent of all other households; simply, the distance between the richest and poorest households.[63] Although 31 of the 50 largest U.S. cities exhibited a higher level of income inequality than the national average, among those characterized as "black regime" cities, high extreme levels of inequality were more frequent. For example, in Atlanta, the richest 5 percent of households earned more than $280,000, while the poorest 20 percent earned less than $15,000. In two other black regime cities, Washington, DC, and Baltimore, the 95/20 ratio was exceeded by 12,[64] despite evidence, according to the 2016 *State of Black America Report* by the National Urban League, that the Washington–Arlington–Alexandria, DC–VA–MD–WV area had the highest median household income for both blacks ($66,151) and whites ($109,460).[65]

A similar situation exists in the rural South where high rates of concentrated poverty and social isolation pervade black-belt counties given "their large populations of disproportionately poor, uneducated, unemployed, and politically powerless residents."[66] In fact, the states with the most black mayors have been in the black-belt or "plantation counties," characterized as a southern area with a sizable African American population in parts of Virginia, North and South Carolina, Georgia, Florida, Alabama, Mississippi, Louisiana, Texas, Arkansas, and Tennessee.[67] Although empirical studies of the rural South are limited, Sharon Wright Austin writes, "In rural towns and counties and to some extent urban cities, African American politicians have found it impossible to reduce economic disparities among the privileged and the powerful. . . . The poverty rates in all the Delta's predominantly African American communities, however, including those with high amounts of black political power, usually doubled and tripled state and national averages."[68] The problem of concentrated, racialized poverty—whether urban or rural—is beyond the resources and legal authority of local governments to address.[69] And, as power has devolved from the federal government to the states, cities and towns have had to cope using the limited resources available.

Faces and Voices in the Struggle for Universal Freedom
UNITA BLACKWELL (1933–)

Unita Blackwell is the first African American woman elected mayor of a Mississippi town. Moreover, she was more than mayor of Mayersville; as a civil rights activist, she was also principally responsible for organizing the struggle that in 1976 established Mayersville as an incorporated, legally recognized town. Before incorporation in Mayersville, Blackwell said "There wasn't no nothing, no city hall, there wasn't no telephone, no nothing."[a] As a result of her leadership, the desperately poor town of 500, not only built a "city" hall but obtained federal funds to pave streets, establish police and fire services, a clean water system, and public housing.

Blackwell was born in 1933 to a family of poor tenant farmers. In the eighth grade, she dropped out of school to work in the fields hoeing and picking cotton. In 1964, she tried to register to vote; she and her husband were fired. This changed her life because, as a result, she became a full-time worker in the civil rights movement. Like Fannie Lou Hamer (see Box 8.2), Blackwell was a leader of the Mississippi Freedom Democratic Party, serving as one of its delegates to the 1964 Democratic Convention in Atlantic City. In 1980, she was elected cochair of the Party and later a member of the Democratic National Committee. From 1990 to 1992, she was elected president of the National Conference of Black Mayors and was cofounder and president of the Women's Conference of Black Mayors in 1991.

In addition to her work as a civil rights activist, party leader, and mayor, for many years she was president of the U.S.–China Friendship Association, traveling to China on numerous occasions promoting cultural exchanges. Although she

The Honorable
Unita Blackwell.

Source: Undated Photo "Mayor Unita Blackwell" Retrieved 4 October 2016 from www.fannielouhamer.info/blackwell.html

had only an eighth-grade education, the University of Massachusetts, Amherst, admitted her on the basis of life experiences, and in 1982 she earned a master's degree in regional planning.

In 1992, Blackwell was awarded a MacArthur Foundation "Genius" grant; in 2016 she published her memoir, *Barefootin: Life and Lessons on the Road to Freedom*. The political scientist, Minion K. C. Morrison, describes Blackwell as the "Heroine of Mayersville" for "she was the spark of a major transformation in the thinking and behavior of blacks in Mayersville and the surrounding area."[b]

a Minion K. C. Morrison, *Black Political Mobilization: Leadership, Power and Mass Society* (Albany, NY: SUNY Press, 1987): 110.

b Ibid., p.108.

See also Unita Blackwell with JoAnne Prichard Morris, *Barefootin: Life and Lessons on the Road to Freedom* (Portland, OR: Powell's Books, 1992).

Summary

The first era of progressive, pro–universal freedom government in the United States was the Reconstruction era, when many southern states were governed by minority–majority coalitions that adopted rights- and material-based policies that expanded freedom for all Americans. The political culture of the southern states—strong advocates of states' rights under the Tenth Amendment—is defined by its historical association with the institution of slavery, Jim Crow segregation, and racial discrimination that impeded universal freedom for African Americans for centuries. The recent era of devolution may, in part, have been initially intended by states' rights advocates to disenfranchise African Americans, but it actually, to some extent, expanded opportunities for political participation for the African American electorate, resulting in an increase in the numbers of black and women state lawmakers.

Nevertheless, African American state lawmakers are still underrepresented in the southern state legislatures. As a result, these lawmakers rely on political strategies—from group caucus to biracial coalitions—to secure legislation beneficial to their African American constituents. In terms of winning statewide offices, racism alone isn't the barrier; rather it's the accumulated effects of long-term racial discrimination that block further advancement. Finally, evidence from the limited research available on black regime cities and black-belt counties reveals a similar characteristic—poverty—that yields a "hollow prize" for the black electorate, generally.

Critical Thinking Questions

1. Discuss the brief period of universal freedom during the Reconstruction era. What were some of the rights gained and lost for all Americans?

Give examples of universal rights lost to African Americans that were not regained until after the Civil Rights era.

2. Discuss the Tenth Amendment and Dillion's Rule. What impact does the Tenth Amendment have on specific local government ordinances? Using a modern example, how might universal freedom for citizens at the local level be subject to state government?

3. Discuss the Tenth Amendment, Devolution, and the southern state governments. How does the Tenth Amendment legally empower southern states to limit the freedom of African Americans? How has the period of devolution aided the limiting of freedom of African Americans?

4. Compare descriptive and substantive representation of African Americans in state legislatures and Congress. What are some similarities and differences? What impact has devolution had on representation of the black electorate? Give examples to support your argument.

5. Discuss the challenges to winning statewide offices for African Americans. What would you propose as a plausible solution? Give specific examples to support your argument.

Selected Bibliography

Austin, Sharon Wright. *The Transformation of Plantation Politics: Black Politics, Concentrated Poverty, and Social Capital in the Mississippi Delta.* Albany, NY: SUNY Press, 2006. A study that examines the political and economic changes of recent decades in the Mississippi Delta.

Brown, Nadia. *Sisters in the Statehouse: Black Women and Legislative Decision Making.* New York: Oxford University Press, 2014. A study on the connection between descriptive and substantive representation of black women legislators.

Du Bois, W. E. B. *Black Reconstruction: An Essay toward a History of the Part which Black Folk Played in the Attempt to Reconstruct Democracy in America.* New York: Athenaeum, 1935, 1969. A classic, in-depth study of the role of black Americans during the period after the Civil War known as Reconstruction.

Egerton, Douglas. *Wars of Reconstruction: The Brief, Violent History of America's Most Progressive Era.* New York: Bloomsbury Press, 2014. A study on Reconstruction that places emphasis on the active role that African Americans played in this crucial period.

Foner, Eric. *Reconstruction: America's Unfinished Revolution, 1886–1877.* New York: Harper & Row, 1988. A classic study on the post–Civil War period that shaped modern America, and the evolution of racial attitudes and patterns of race relations.

Haynie, Kerry L. *African American Legislators in the American States.* New York: Columbia University Press, 2001. One of the first studies to analyze the behavior of African American state legislators in multiple legislative sessions across five states to reveal the dynamics and effectiveness of black participation in the legislative process.

Hero, Rodney. *Faces of Inequality: Social Diversity in American Politics.* New York: Oxford University Press, 2000. A study of the ways in which a state's racial and ethnic composition, as much as any other factor, shapes its political processes and policies.

Keith, Lee Anna. *The Colfax Massacre: The Untold Story of Black Power, White Terror and the Death of Reconstruction.* New York: Oxford University Press, 2009. An in-depth study on the most deadly incident of racial violence of the Reconstruction era—the Colfax Massacre—that unleashed a reign of terror that all but extinguished the campaign for racial equality in 1873.

King-Meadows, Tyson, and Thomas F. Schaller. *Devolution and Black State Legislators: Challenges and Choices in the Twenty-first Century*. Albany, NY: SUNY Press, 2006. A comprehensive study of the position of black state legislative politics.

Menifield, Charles E., and Stephen D. Shaffer. *Politics in the New South: Representation of African Americans in Southern State Legislatures*. Albany, NY: SUNY Press, 2005. A collection of empirical studies that document political advances made by African Americans in the South over the last 25 years.

Morrison, Minion K. C. *Black Political Mobilization: Leadership, Power and Mass Society*. Albany: SUNY Press, 1987. A detailed study on the political success of African Americans in the South from the political activism of the 1960s to the 1980s.

Richardson, Heather Cox. *The Death of Reconstruction: Race, Labor and Politics in the Post-Civil War North*. Cambridge, MA: Harvard University Press, 2001. A unique investigation of how class, along with race, was critical to Reconstruction's end, particularly among the northern elite.

Notes

1 W. E. B. Du Bois, *Black Reconstruction: An Essay toward a History of the Part which Black Folk Played in the Attempt to Reconstruct Democracy in America* (New York: Athenaeum, 1935, 1969): 14.

2 Douglas Egerton, *Wars of Reconstruction: The Brief, Violent History of America's Most Progressive Era* (New York: Bloomsbury Press, 2014).

3 Eric Foner, *Reconstruction: America's Unfinished Revolution, 1863–1877* (New York: Harper & Row, 1988): 305.

4 LeeAnna Keith, *The Colfax Massacre: The Untold Story of Black Power, White Terror and the Death of Reconstruction* (New York: Oxford, 2009).

5 Heather Cox Richardson, *The Death of Reconstruction: Race, Labor and Politics in the Post–Civil War North* (Cambridge, MA: Harvard, 2001): 244–45.

6 Quoted in Anwar Hussain Syed, *The Political Theory of American Local Government* (New York: Random House, 1969): 68.

7 Kevin B. Smith and Alan Greenblatt, *Governing States and Localities*, 5th ed. (Washington, DC: CQ Press): xxii.

8 Ann O'M. Bowman and Richard C. Kearney, *State and Local Government*, 10th ed. (Boston, MA: Cengage, 2017): xi.

9 Thomas R. Dye and Susan A. MacManus, *Politics in States and Communities*, 14th ed. (Upper Saddle River, NJ: Pearson, 2012): xiii.

10 David Magleby, Paul C. Light, and Christine L. Nemacheck, *State and Local Government by the People*, 16th ed. (Upper Saddle River, NJ: Pearson, 2014): viii.

11 Rodney Hero, *Faces of Inequality: Social Diversity in American Politics* (Oxford: Oxford University Press, 2000).

12 W. E. B. Du Bois, *The Gift of Black Folk: The Negroes in the Making of America* (New York: Square One Publishers, 2009): 109.

13 Tyson King-Meadows and Thomas F. Schaller, *Devolution and Black State Legislators: Challenges and Choices in the Twenty-first Century* (Albany, NY: SUNY Press, 2006): 219.

14 Charles E. Menifield and Stephen D. Shaffer, *Politics in the New South: Representation of African Americans in Southern State Legislatures* (Albany, NY: SUNY Press, 2005): 1.

15 Ibid., pp. 1–2.
16 Smith and Greenblatt, *Governing States and Localities,* p. 18.
17 King-Meadows and Schaller, *Devolution,* p. 219.
18 Ibid.
19 Menifield and Schaffer, *Politics in the New South*, p. 1.
20 Ibid.
21 Karl Kurtz, "Who We Elect: The Demographics of State Legislatures," National Council of State Legislatures and the Pew Charitable Trusts, Report (December 2015): 21, www.ncsl.org/research/about-state-legislatures/who-we-elect.aspx.
22 David Bositis, "Blacks & The 2008 Democratic National Convention," Washington, DC: Joint Center for Political and Economic Studies Report (2008): 7, http://joint center.org/sites/default/files/Dem%20guide.pdf.
23 Blog posted by "AllOtherPersons," "Factoid: Black Legislators in 2009," April 16, 2009, https://allotherpersons.wordpress.com/2009/04/16/factoid-black-state-legisla tors-in-2009/. This report is based on a reexamination of the National Black Caucus of State Legislatures and the National Conference of State Legislatures, "African-American Legislators 2009," www.ncsl.org/research/about-state-legislatures/african-american-legislators-in-2009.aspx.
24 Menifield and Schaffer, *Politics in the New South*, p. 10.
25 Smith and Greenblatt, *Governing States and Localities,* pp. 222–23.
26 Menifield and Schaffer, *Politics in the New South*, p. 13.
27 Kerry L. Haynie, *African American Legislators in the American States* (New York: Columbia University Press, 2001): 107.
28 Ibid., Rodney Hero, *Faces of Inequality: Social Diversity in American Politics.*
29 Ibid., "AllOtherPersons" Report.
30 Menifield and Schaffer, *Politics in the New South*, p. 12.
31 Ibid., p.12.
32 Haynie, *African American Legislators in the American States*, p. 19.
33 Ibid., p. 25.
34 Ibid., Menifield and Schaffer, *Politics in the New South*, p. 10.
35 Ibid.
36 King-Meadows and Schaller, *Devolution,* p. 182.
37 Menifield and Schaffer, *Politics in the New South*, p. 10.
38 King-Meadows and Schaller, *Devolution,* p. 218.
39 Ibid., p. 220.
40 Ibid., p. 222.
41 Alan Gerber, "African Americans' Congressional Careers and the Democratic House Delegation," *Journal of Politics* 58 (1996): 831–45.
42 Gbemende Johnson, Bruce I. Oppenheimer, and Jennifer L. Selin, "The House as a Stepping Stone to the Senate: Why Do So Few African American House Members Run?" (Manuscript, Vanderbilt University, Nashville, TN, 2009): 26.
43 Gary Copeland and Cynthia Opheim, "Multi-Level Political Careers in the USA: The Cases of African Americans and Women," *Regional and Federal Studies* 21(2) (2011): 141–64.
44 Ibid., Copeland and Opheim, p. 150.
45 Jamelle Bouie, "The Other Glass Ceiling," *American Prospect*, March 14, 2012.
46 Jamelle Bouie, "What about Black Republicans?" *American Prospect*, March 15, 2012.
47 Ibid., Jamelle Bouie, "The Other Glass Ceiling."
48 Andra Gillespie, *The New Black Politician: Cory Booker, Newark and Post–racial America* (New York: NYU Press, 2012).

49 Tracy George and Albert Yoon, *The Gavel Gap: Who Sits in Judgment on State Courts?* (American Constitution Society for Law and Policy, 2016): 3, http://gavelgap.org/pdf/gavel-gap-report.pdf.

50 Ibid.

51 Ibid., p. 12.

52 Chris Cillizza, "The 2015 Election Tightened the Republican Stranglehold on State Government," *Washington Post*, November 4, 2015.

53 Ibid.

54 Zultan Hajnal, Nazita Laijevardi, and Lindsay Nelson, "Voter Identification Laws and the Suppression of Minority Votes" (Manuscript, Department of Political Science, University of California, San Diego, 2016): 25.

55 Sabrina Tavernise and Robert Gebeloff, "Millions of Poor are Left Uncovered by Health Law," *New York Times*, October 2, 2013.

56 Ben Adler, "State Legislatures are Undercutting Their Liberal Cities—and Unlikely to Stop," *Washington Post*, March 30, 2016.

57 Alexander Hertel-Fernandez and Theda Skocpol, "How the Right Trounced Liberals in the States," *Democracy* 39 (Winter) 2016.

58 David Lieb, "Partisans Set Sights on State Legislative Races," *West County Times*, November 8, 2015.

59 The Gender and Multi-Cultural Leadership Project, 2006, http://gmcl.org/maps/national/state.htm.

60 Isabel Washington, *The Warmth of Other Suns: The Epic Story of America's Great Migration* (New York: Vintage, 2011): 398.

61 Adolph Reed, "The Black Urban Regime: Structural Origins and Constraint," in P. Orleans, ed., *Power, Community and the City: Comparative Urban Research* (New Brunswick, NJ: Transaction, 1988).

62 Robert C. Smith, "Urban Politics," *Encyclopedia of African American Politics* (New York: Facts on File, 2003): 360–63.

63 Alan Berube, "All Cities Are Not Created Equal," Brookings Report: Metropolitan Opportunity Series, February 20, 2014.

64 Ibid.

65 For more discussion and to see the full list of Black–White 2016 Metro Income Inequality Index rankings, see the National Urban League, "Locked Out: Education, Jobs & Justice," *2016 State of Black America Report* (New York, 2016): 10, http://soba.iamempowered.com/.

66 Sharon D. Wright Austin, Sekou M. Franklin, and Angela K. Lewis, "The Effects of Concentrated Poverty on Black and White Participation in the Southern Black Belt," *National Political Science Review*, 15 (2013): 57–69.

67 Ibid., p. 57.

68 Sharon Wright Austin, *The Transformation of Plantation Politics: Black Politics, Concentrated Poverty, and Social Capital in the Mississippi Delta* (Albany, NY: SUNY Press, 2006): 173.

69 Paul Peterson, *City Limits* (Chicago, IL: University of Chicago Press, 1981).

PART V

Public Policy

CHAPTER 14

Domestic Policy and the African American Quest for Social and Economic Justice

---

LEARNING OBJECTIVE

Explain why material-based rights are central to domestic policy concerns for African Americans.

"The only time we had full employment was during slavery." The tragic irony of this often-heard lament among African Americans reflects the centrality of the problem of unemployment and underemployment in explaining the social and economic problems confronting African American communities. In their struggle for freedom, African Americans had to secure their basic civil rights (i.e., rights-based policies) before pursuing material-based policies that would improve their quality of life. As we know, the history of white supremacy and institutional racism targeted at African Americans banned them from full labor market participation and marginalized them in the housing market, leading to the high levels of racial segregation in housing, its consequent social ills, and a widening wealth gap. Economic and racial segregation resulting from historic, persistent, chronic, long-term unemployment and underemployment, coupled with decades of discrimination, are primary explanations for the severe conditions of concentrated, racialized poverty, low-performing schools, low-income and single-parent households, crime and mass incarceration, ill-health,

351

substance abuse, and low homeownership that disproportionately impact African American communities nationwide.

In 1984 Harvey Brenner, a sociologist, prepared a report for the Joint Economic Committee of Congress. In it, he showed that for every 1 percent increase in the rate of unemployment there is an associated increase of 5.7 percent in murders, 4.1 percent in suicides, 1.9 percent in mortality, 3.3 percent in mental institutionalization, and a 4.7 percent increase in divorce and separation.[1] A similar study found correlations between increases in unemployment and increases in child abuse, alcoholism, wife battering, and other individual and community pathologies.[2] Multiply Brenner's 1 percent increase by a factor of 10 over multiple generations to get a sense of the damaging consequences of long-term unemployment and underemployment on African American citizens, which impacts the less educated to even college graduates.[3]

It was because of the centrality of unemployment among the multifaceted issues in the black community that Dr. Martin Luther King Jr. made full employment the focus of his work in his last years, and why black leaders have made full employment (a job for all willing and able to work) the number one priority on the black agenda (see Chapters 7 and 10). This chapter will focus on domestic policies that can address and improve the economic well-being of African Americans. The problem is treated here as one of race and racism; however, it could also be treated as a problem of class in a capitalist economy. As Ralph Bunche wrote during the New Deal era:

> there is an economic system, as well as a race problem in America and that when a Negro is unemployed, it is not just because he is a Negro, but more seriously, because of the defective operation of the economy under which we live—an economy that finds it impossible to provide an adequate number of jobs and economic security for the population.[4]

In other words, in the U.S. political economy, the race problem is invariably and inextricably a class problem. Before discussing the significance of broad material-based domestic policies, it is important to offer a brief explanation for describing the material basis for black politics.

In his early critique of the historical colonial model—where blacks are viewed as a racially segregated, spatially separated underclass of workers not integral to or within the U.S. capitalist system—economist Donald Harris countered that African Americans—despite being spatially separated and racially segregated in U.S. society—are and "have always been, organically linked with American capitalism from [the] very beginning,"[5] and their persistence in unequal status and condition is explained by understanding how the basic structure of the American political economy and the essential laws of American capitalist development are conditioned by the ideology of white supremacy to determine the position of blacks in the economy. In addition to the structure, laws, and role of white supremacy, the enduring unequal economic conditions of African Americans also are affected by the American economy's division into two distinct sectors: the corporate capitalist class (i.e., the upper-middle class to the top 1 percent) and the petty capitalist class (i.e., working poor to lower-middle class). In addition there is a fluctuating number of potential workers (surplus of labor), who are unable to find work in either sector. The unequal distribution of African American workers within these sectors, particularly the disproportionate clustering of blacks in the least rewarding petty capitalist sector of the economy, is said to be the result of the laws of American economic development conditioned by racism. Racism—institutional and individual—ensures that African Americans remain in "subordinate" positions. Harris posits that educational, social, political, and cultural institutions evolve as part of a social whole that routinely recreates and sustains conditions that ensure whites' access to favored positions and relegates African Americans to the least desired ones.[6]

Given this logic, long-term unemployment and underemployment, particularly for African Americans, are best understood as systemic conditions the economy produces and reproduces. Thus, socioeconomic justice for African Americans is best achieved by the implementation of race-specific or targeted material-based policies.

Black Unemployment and Underemployment in Historical and Systemic Context

In the Jim Crow South after the end of slavery, black workers were in general relegated to joblessness or menial, low-paid work, mainly as field workers and domestics. This is well known. Less well known is that these same processes took place in cities of the North as well. Modern historical research, however, amply documents this manufacturing of black joblessness and subsequent economic dislocation in the North.[7] In a longitudinal study that is a model of historically informed social science research, Theodore Hershberg and his colleagues at the Philadelphia Social History Project at the University of Pennsylvania innovatively demonstrate the role of racism historically in creating black unemployment. Whites often ask if the Irish, the Italians, Jews, and Poles were able to work their way up out of poverty, why have not the blacks? Hershberg's study provides an answer by analyzing the experiences of separate waves of immigrants to Philadelphia during three historical periods[8]—first, the Irish and Germans who settled in the "industrializing city" at the turn of the nineteenth century; then the Poles, Italians, and Russian Jews who settled in Philadelphia at the turn of the twentieth century; and African Americans who, although present throughout, arrived in their greatest numbers in the "post–industrial city" after World War II. In both the industrializing and the industrial city, immigrant whites found employment in the manufacturing sector throughout the occupational hierarchy, laying the foundation for the upwardly mobile status of their grandchildren and children after World War II. African Americans, however, were virtually excluded from these jobs, relegated instead, as in the South, to the low-paying domestic and laborer jobs at the bottom of the occupational hierarchy.

Of the industrial city, Hershberg and his colleagues write, "Although 80 percent of the blacks lived in the city within one mile of 5,000 industrial jobs, less than 13 percent of the black workforce found gainful employment in manufacturing."[9] Earlier in the industrializing city, "blacks were not only excluded from the new and well-paying positions, they were uprooted as well from many of their traditional unskilled jobs, denied apprenticeship for their sons and prevented from practicing the skills they already possessed."[10]

This situation did not begin to change in a major way in Philadelphia and elsewhere in the country until the Civil Rights Act of 1964 was passed and affirmative action was implemented. Yet at almost the same time as employment became somewhat free of overt, blatant racism, manufacturing jobs in and around America's cities began to disappear. (Between 1930 and 1970, Philadelphia lost 75,000 manufacturing jobs; and of every 10 jobs in the three-mile ring around the city in 1930, there were only 4 in 1970.) In other words, when blacks began to be allowed to equally compete for the good manufacturing work, the work disappeared.[11] As a result, in nineteenth-century Philadelphia, Hershberg and his colleagues write, "Blacks occupied the worst housing in the . . . slums and suffered from the greatest degree of impoverishment. Their mortality rate was roughly twice that of whites, and the death of black men early in their adult lives was the major reason that blacks were forced to raise their children in fatherless families."[12] Unfortunately, in the new millennium, this historic and systemic relationship between high unemployment and community well-being persists.

Understanding Unemployment and Underemployment in Post–Industrial America

In perfect market competition with perfectly rational players, virtually all economists assume that some level of unemployment (anywhere from 4 to 6 percent) is necessary for the proper functioning of capitalism in the United States. If this necessary level of unemployment is distributed on the basis of race, then high rates of black unemployment (as compared to other social groups) are a necessary, logical result. Market forces do not account for racism, the preference for the use of ethnic networks, the impact of undocumented workers on wages and employment,[13] and other factors that can affect who gets hired for jobs that results in the disproportionate higher levels of unemployment for African Americans (on the contemporary role of racism in manufacturing black unemployment, see Box 14.1).

BOX 14.1

Race, Racism, and African American Unemployment and Underemployment

Until the passage of the Civil Rights Act of 1964, it was perfectly legal for white employers to post signs or simply say to black job seekers, "We don't hire coloreds." Since the passage and implementation of the 1964 act and the development of affirmative action policies, racism has declined in the employment of blacks. However, studies still show continuing discrimination as African Americans seek work.

In 1991, the Urban Institute conducted a "hiring audit" to determine the degree of racial discrimination in entry-level employment in Washington, DC, and Chicago. The research used selected black and white "job testers" carefully matched in age, physical size, education (all were college educated), and experience, as well as such intangible factors as poise, openness, and articulateness. They were then sent to apply for entry-level jobs advertised in Washington and Chicago area newspapers. The study found what the authors call "entrenched and widespread" discrimination at every step in the hiring process, with whites three times as likely to advance to the point of being offered a job.[a]

Similarly, a study by Kirschenman and Neckerman, titled "We'd Love to Hire Them But, ... " found that Chicago area white employers were extremely reluctant to hire blacks, especially black men. Speaking of potential black workers, these employers told the researchers, "They are lazy; they steal; they lack motivation; they don't have a work ethic." Or, "I need someone who will fit in"; "my customers are 95 percent white . . . I wouldn't last very long if I had a black"; and "my guys don't want to work with blacks."[b]

In an experimental study of racism in employment between 2001 and 2002, researchers sent 5,000 applications to prospective employers in Boston and Chicago. The applications were identical except one group had names identified

with African Americans, the other whites. The names were randomly assigned so that applicants with black and white identified names applied for the same set of jobs with the same résumés. Applicants with white-sounding names were 50 percent more likely to be called for interviews than those with black-sounding names.[c] In a similar experiment, Dorvah Pager, a graduate student at the University of Wisconsin, found that a white man with a criminal record had a better chance to get a job than an identically qualified black man without a record. For her dissertation research, Pager sent teams of black and white young men—well groomed, well spoken, college educated, and with identical résumés—to seek entry-level jobs. The only difference was that some indicated they had an 18-month prison sentence for cocaine possession. She found that the employer call-back rate for a black with this criminal record was 5 percent and 14 percent without a record. But for whites the rate was 17 percent with the record and 34 percent without the record.[d]

More recently, in yet another example of the apparent pervasiveness of racism by employers, a 2015 study found that a degree from an elite university (e.g., Harvard, Stanford, or Duke) does result in more job opportunities for both black and white job applicants. But black graduates from elite universities did only as well as white applicants from nonelite state universities.[e] Moreover "race results in a double penalty: when employers respond to black candidates from elite institutions, it is for jobs with lower salaries and lower prestige than those of their white peers,"[f] supporting evidence that college-educated blacks are more likely to be underemployed. In fact, a Georgetown University Study reported that the 2015 underemployment rates for college-educated blacks was 9 percentage points higher at 16.8 percent compared to 7.9 percent for whites.[g]

a Margery Turner, M. Fix, and R. Struyk, *Opportunities Denied, Opportunities Diminished: Discrimination in Hiring* (Washington, DC: Urban Institute, 1991).

b Joleen Kirschenman and Kathryn Neckerman, "We'd Love to Hire Them But . . . The Meaning of Race for Employers," in C. Jencks and P. Peterson, eds., *The Urban Underclass* (Washington, DC: Urban Institute, 1991).

c M. Bertrand and S. Mullainathan, "Are Emily and Brendan More Employable than Lakisha and Jamal?: A Field Experiment on Labor Market Discrimination," http://gsb.uchicago.edu/pdf/bertrand.pdf (November 8, 2002).

d Brooke Koreger, "When a Dissertation Makes a Difference," *New York Times*, April 20, 2004.

e S. Michael Gaddis, "Discrimination in the Credential Society: An Audit Study of Race and College Selectivity in the Job Market," *Social Forces* 93 (2015): 1445–479.

f Ibid., p. 1476.

g Anthony P. Carnevale and Nicole Smith, "Sharp Declines in Underemployment for College Graduates," Georgetown University Center on Education and the Workforce (analysis of U.S. Census Bureau, American Community Survey micro data, 2010–2014) Report, November 2015, https://cew.georgetown.edu/wp-content/uploads/Underemployment-Declines.pdf.

Since the 1970s, globalization has resulted in the deindustrialization of the economy, as good manufacturing jobs are increasingly "outsourced" to other parts of the world.[14] Related to this, an inevitable result of globalization of the economy is the loss of U.S. economic hegemony and the rise of competitive economies in China, India, and Brazil. These processes of globalization and deindustrialization have been facilitated by the adoption of neoliberal trade policies such as the North American Free Trade Agreement (NAFTA) and the General Agreement on Tariffs and Trade.

These global processes have created two interrelated problems that disproportionately impact African Americans seeking work. The first is the "skills mismatch," where the available jobs require increasing levels of education and skills that African Americans disproportionately tend not to possess when compared to whites. Second is the "spatial mismatch," where because of racial residential segregation, the available entry-level jobs tend to be located outside the largely black-concentrated central city despite studies that reveal a trend in job growth and business expansion in central cities, particularly for the higher-skilled, higher-paying jobs while entry-level to working-class jobs largely remain in the suburbs.[15] Thus, the result of these two "mismatches" is the kind of concentrated, racialized poverty that leads to isolation from positive social networks, and continues to impact the economic well-being of black communities during times of both economic growth and recession.

Economic Well-Being in the African American Community: Material-Based Challenges

In their quest for universal freedom, African Americans have made significant social and economic progress since the passage of seminal civil rights legislation of the 1960s. However, as a recent report on the economic well-being in all

50 states by United States Congress Joint Economic Committee (JEC) reveals, by most important measures of economic well-being, they continue to lag behind white Americans in rates of unemployment, poverty, incarceration, education, and wealth (Table 14.1). At the release of the report, the Congressional Black Caucus (CBC) Chairman, Representative G. K. Butterfield and JEC ranking Democrat Representative Carolyn B. Maloney wrote in a joint statement, "We'll never eliminate economic disparities based on race if Congress continues to ignore the issues facing the black community."[16]

African Americans and Unemployment

As indicated previously, unemployment, as expected on the basis of historical and systemic patterns, was more devastating in the black community as a result of the Great Recession. In January 2007, when the recession started, the unemployment rate in the black community was 7.9 percent compared to 4.2 percent among whites (interestingly, the smallest difference on record at 3.4 percentage points). By January 2009, as President Obama was taking office, it had climbed to 12.7 percent among blacks, while among whites it climbed to 7.1 percent. At its peak in the black community in August 2011, the unemployment rate was 16.8 percent; at its peak among whites in October 2009, it was 9.3 percent, which is the largest gap since 1986.[17] Blacks also remained unemployed longer than whites, with a median duration of 27 weeks compared to 19 for whites.[18] In response, the Obama administration implemented the

TABLE 14.1 The Black–White Divide: Measures of Economic Well-Being, 2016

Economic Index	Blacks	Whites
U.S. Population Total	*13%*	*64%*
Unemployment	8.8%	4.3%
Poverty	26.2%	12.7%
Incarceration[a]	40%	39%
Education[b]	22%	36%
Median Net Worth	$11,000	$141,900

[a] This percentage is for total U.S. prison and jail population by race. See Peter Wagner and Bernadette Rabuy, "Mass Incarceration: The Whole Pie 2016," March 14, 2016.
[b] This percentage is for African Americans and white college graduates who are at least 25 years old with a Bachelor's degree or higher.

Source: United States Department of Labor, Bureau of Labor Statistics Report, February 2016 (Seasonally adjusted data). The United States Congress Joint Economic Committee (JEC) and the Congressional Black Caucus (CBC), "The American Dream on Hold: Economic Challenges in the African American Community", National Fact Sheet (2016).

broad, material-based American Recovery and Reinvestment Act of 2009 (ARRA), commonly referred to as "the stimulus," which was expected to save and create jobs by providing job training and infrastructure improvement. The ARRA was successful in stimulating the economy and increasing access to capital for business, but fell short in creating more economic opportunities for African Americans due to the large volume of those who lost jobs or remained unemployed due to the recession.

By 2015 during the economic recovery, evidence revealed that the underemployment rate for African Americans still far exceeded whites[19] (see discussion below). In 2016, rates declined further; however, the rate of unemployment for African Americans at 8.8 percent is more than twice the rate of white Americans at 4.3 percent (see Table 14.1).

African Americans and Concentrated Poverty: Economic and Environmental Effects

The historic and systemic consequences of unemployment on the African American family have been nearly disastrous. As noted in Chapter 11, during the Obama administration's first year, the persistently high poverty rate among blacks saw its highest single-year increase since the government began measuring poverty in 1959.[20] Using the government's official definition of poverty—about $21,000 for a family of four—roughly a quarter of the African American community is poor. Only about 11 percent of all Americans fit this definition. While there are more poor whites than blacks (about 12.7 percent or 20 million whites compared to 26.2 percent or 9 million blacks), poverty has a more devastating impact on the African American *community* than on the white (see Table 14.1). For example, according to the 2014 U.S. Census Bureau American Community Statistics (ACS), 38 percent of black children live in poverty compared to 22 percent of all children in America. Poverty rates for African American families vary based on the family type. While 23 percent of all black families live below the poverty level, only 8 percent of black families with married couples live in poverty. This is considerably lower than the 23 percent of black families headed by single men and 37 percent of black families headed by single women, who live below the poverty line. The highest poverty rates (46 percent) are for African American families with children headed by single women, which constitutes about 56.3 percent of all African American families. Despite the economic recovery, the poverty rate of African American families has remained relatively unchanged from 2010 to 2014 (dropping slightly from 24.1 percent to 22.9 percent).[21]

Persistently high unemployment is one significant contributing factor to the high rate of divorce, separation, and children born to single mothers in the black community, who rely on some form of public assistance. Evidence that the decision by President Clinton and the Congress to abolish the Aid to Families with Dependent Children (AFDC) federal benefit and replace it with the Temporary Assistance to Needy Families (TANF) shows that former AFDC recipients could find and keep jobs.[22] For example, the average monthly participation rates of African Americans who received public assistance varied greatly by benefit type, with 42 percent of African Americans—largely children— who participated in at least one program receiving the most aid for Supplemental Nutrition Assistance Program (SNAP) food assistance (30 percent), Medicaid health insurance (29 percent), Section 8 housing assistance (14.5 percent), Supplemental Security (7 percent) to the least for TANF cash assistance (2.5 percent).[23] More importantly, the type of benefits received support findings that show poverty in black families is not only affected by black male joblessness, but is heavily impacted by the disparities in wages earned by African American women.

On average, women who work full-time, year round in the United States are paid roughly 79 cents for every dollar paid to men. For African American women, the average is only about 60 cents for every dollar paid to white men, which negatively impacts their economic security, their families and their communities. Pay for black women working full-time, year round can range from 48 to 69 cents depending on the industry and state. Black women, nationally, are more likely to be employed in the lowest-paying occupations and live in the South where wages are lower.[24] The first legislation signed by President Obama was the Lilly Ledbetter Fair Pay Act of 2009, which was designed to narrow the gender gap in wages by extending the time to file discrimination claims. In addition, elected officials and policy advocates continue to push for specific material-based policy, such as the adoption of the Paycheck Fairness Act to combat wage discrimination and strengthening the Equal Pay Act 1993 as well as for a higher national minimum wage and paid family leave.[25] Closing the pay gap for African American women is fundamental to the economic stability of black communities.

Finally, concentrated poverty among African Americans is not only the result of high unemployment, underemployment, and the female wage gap, but also is due to decades of discriminatory practices in unbalanced, postwar suburban development—white flight and urban blight—that has perpetuated inequality via entrenched residential segregation.[26] As a result, low-income African American communities are afflicted by "environmental racism"—defined as the existence of racial and socioeconomic disparities in the distribution of a wide variety of pollution and environmental hazards—that negatively impact health in these communities (see Box 14.2). An example is the 2016 public health crisis due to contaminated water in Flint, Michigan, where large numbers of children (majority African American) were exposed to high levels of lead poisoning that will cause neurological damage for the rest of their lives. The health effects caused by placement of the majority of hazardous sites, municipal landfills, incinerators, and other facilities disproportionally in poor, black

BOX 14.2

African American Health, Mortality, and Voting Power

Since the 1970s, national health insurance has, after full employment, been the priority on the black policy agenda. This is because African Americans face not only individual but also social determinants of health—shaped by political, social, and economic forces—that influence their quality of care. A key social determinant of health is the level of poverty. However, a growing body of epidemiological evidence shows strong associations between self-reported racism and poor health outcomes across diverse racial and ethnic groups in developed countries,[a] resulting in the current public health initiatives by the U.S. Department of Health and Human Services (DHHS) aimed at reducing racial and ethnic health care disparities and accelerating health equity "from the cradle to the grave."[b] Two measures frequently serve as summary measures of a people's health—the infant mortality rate and life expectancy. The black infant mortality rate (the number of deaths per 1,000 live births before a child reaches 1 year of age) is 11.0, nearly twice that of whites, which is 5.1. The black life expectancy rate is 74.6 compared to 78.9 for whites.[c] Why this enormous gap between the races in health? The most basic explanation is the lack of quality care and health insurance among African Americans stemming from historic and systemic disadvantage in accessing medical care.

As discussed in Chapter 12, the Patient Protection and Affordable Care Act (ACA) ("Obamacare") has helped millions of Americans—especially African Americans—gain access to affordable, high quality health care coverage.[d] Between 2013 and 2014, under the ACA the percentage of uninsured blacks dropped from 24.1 percent to 16.1 percent. In 2015, as a result of "Obamacare," nearly 6.8 million of African Americans have become eligible for health coverage. The DHHS estimates if all the states would expand Medicaid, as the law allows, 95 percent of eligible blacks would

qualify for some form of coverage. In addition, the ACA has increased funding for community health centers (about $11 billion) that serve nearly 25 percent of African American patients. More importantly, with an infant mortality rate at 2.3 times higher and a life expectancy rate lower than whites, having access to preventive care at no additional costs, under the ACA, will help to reduce these disparities.[e]

Historic and systemic ill-health and mortality of African Americans has political consequences. It is estimated that the mortality rate significantly reduces voting power. Specifically, Javier Rodriquez and his colleagues estimate that "excess" black deaths between 1970 and 2004 totaled 2.7 million, at which 1.7 million would have been voting age and 1 million would have voted in 2004. Calculating these deaths along with felon disenfranchisement, they concluded 15 percent of blacks who otherwise would have voted did not have the opportunity to do so in 2004. While this would not likely have affected the outcome of the 2004 presidential election, they estimate between 1970 and 2004 the Democrats would have won seven additional Senate seats and eleven additional governors.[f]

Thus, the Affordable Health Care Act, if fully implemented, may not only improve the health and mortality of African Americans, it will also improve their power at the ballot box.

[a] Y. Paradies, N. Priest, J. Ben, M. Truong, A. Gupta, A. Pieterse, et al., "Racism as a Determinant of Health: A Protocol for Conducting A Systemic Review and Meta-Analysis," PubMed.gov Systemic Reviews, September 23, 2013, www.ncbi.nlm.nih.gov/*pubmed*/24059279. See also, "Closing the Gap in a Generation: Health Equity through Action on the Social Determinants of Health," World Health Organization, Commission on Social Determinants of Health (2008): 3, http://apps.who.int/iris/bitstream/10665/43943/1/9789241563703_eng.pdf.

b U.S. Department of Health and Human
Services, Office of the Secretary, Office of the
Assistant Secretary for Planning and Evaluation,
and Office of Minority Health. HHS Action Plan
to Reduce Racial and Ethnic Health Disparities:
Implementation Progress Report. Washington,
DC: Office of the Assistant Secretary for
Planning and Evaluation, 2015.
http://minorityhealth.hhs.gov/assets/pdf/FINAL_H
HS_Action_Plan_Progress_Report_11_2_2015.pd
f. See also Dayna Matthew, *Just Medicine: A
Cure for Racial Inequality in American Health
Care* (New York: New York University Press,
2016). Matthew estimates that 84,000 non-
whites die annually due to racism in health
delivery systems.
c T. J. Matthews, Marian F. MacDorman, and
Marie E. Thomas, "Infant Mortality Statistics
from the 2013 Period: Linked Birth/Infant Death
Data Set," National Vital Statistics Reports 64 (9)
(August 6, 2015): 1–30. www.cdc.gov/nchs/
data/nvsr/nvsr64/nvsr64_09.pdf.

d Emmanuel Hurtado, "5 Key Facts about the
Affordable Care Act for African Americans,"
Center for American Progress, January 20,
2015.
https://www.americanprogress.org/issues/race/n
ews/2015/01/20/104494/5-key-facts-about-the-
affordable-care-act-for-african-americans/. See
also, "The Affordable Care Act is Working for
the African American Community," Department
of Health and Human Services, September,
2015.
e Ibid.
f Javier Rodriquez, Arline Geronmus, John
Bound, and Danny Darling, "Black Lives Matter,
Black Mortality and Elections: Differential
Mortality and the Racial Composition of the U.S.
Electorate, 1970–2004," *Social Science and
Medicine*, www.stieredirect.com/science/
article/pic/5027795361/5002439.

communities dates from W. E. B. Du Bois's pioneering study on "The Philadelphia Negro" (1899) to the environmental justice research by Robert Bullard that well documents the links between concentrated poverty and racial and ethnic disparities in health.[27]

African Americans and the Criminal Justice System

In her widely discussed 2010 book *The New Jim Crow: Mass Incarceration in the Age of Colorblindness*, Michelle Alexander describes the relationship of blacks to the criminal justice system as a twenty-first-century version of the old South system of Jim Crow segregation and exploitation.[28] The U.S. criminal justice system holds more than 2.3 million people. There is a historic and systemic pattern embedded in the system. African Americans at 13 percent of the U.S. population are overrepresented at 40 percent; while whites at 64 percent of total population are underrepresented at 39 percent (see Table 14.1). Although white females comprise 49 percent of the prison population compared to 22 percent for black females, the rate of imprisonment for black females (113 per 100,000) is twice the rate of white females (51 per 100,000).[29] Comprising only 16 percent of the U.S. youth population, African American youth have higher rates of juvenile arrests (28 percent), incarceration (37 percent), residential treatment (38 percent), and are more likely to be sentenced to adult prison (58 percent).[30] Relatedly, African American students are 3.5 times more likely to face harsher discipline in school-related suspensions, arrests, or referrals to law enforcement compared to their white peers which places them in contact with the juvenile justice system at an earlier age.[31]

A partial explanation of this disproportionately high rate of black incarceration is the relationship between employment and crime. We know that poor and unemployed people tend to commit more crime, and young blacks who are poor tend to reside in concentrated, racialized neighborhoods that are "over policed" (see Chapter 6, "#BlackLivesMatter" discussion). Given the disproportionate number of encounters with law enforcement, a report by the Department of Justice concluded that one in three black men can expect to go to prison in their lifetime[32] due in part to race bias or "racial profiling" (the practice by police of stopping drivers of certain racial groups because they believe these groups are more likely to commit certain types of crimes).

Another explanation of the racial and ethnic disparity in the criminal justice system is unfairness in the enforcement of drug laws. This has been shown in numerous studies on the use of illegal drugs and the war on drugs. Although African Americans are no more likely to use or sell illegal drugs than whites, they receive higher rates of arrests for these offenses.[33] Relatedly, black offenders receive longer sentences, about 10 percent longer compared to white offenders, and African Americans are more likely to receive a mandatory-minimum sentence and are sent to prison at a rate of 20 percent higher than whites.[34] Disparities in the criminal justice system also result in disparities in voting (see Box 2.2). There is also evidence that spending time incarcerated affects wage trajectories which disproportionately impacts African Americans, resulting in wage growth at a 21 percent slower rate for black former inmates as compared to whites.[35] Finally, these post–incarceration consequences significantly impact the access to other material benefits that can enhance economic well-being.

African Americans and Education

Unemployment and underemployment are strongly associated with education. As Table 14.1 shows, among Americans at least 25 years old, African Americans are significantly less likely than whites to have a Bachelor's degree or higher (22 percent versus 36 percent). Similarly, about 22 percent of African Americans ages 25–29 have a Bachelor's degree or higher compared to the nearly 41 percent of whites of the same age. In the same age group, black women earned their Bachelor's degree at twice the rate of black men (21 percent versus 12 percent).[36] Although unemployment and underemployment levels are lower for those with more education—with underemployment levels on the decline for all college graduates—the rate for African Americans remain consistently higher than whites (16.8 percent versus 7.9 percent).[37] In addition, African Americans gaining a college degree tend to be concentrated in low-paying majors.

A recent study revealed two key findings about African American college majors and earnings. The first is that black college students are concentrated in open-access four-year institutions that offer limited choices for majors. The second, and perhaps most critical, is that black college students are under-represented in the number of degree holders associated with the fastest-growing, highest-paying occupations—in science, technology, engineering, and mathematics (STEM), health and business—and overrepresented in low-earning majors such as health and medical administration services (21 percent), human services and community organization (20 percent), and social work (19 percent), with median earnings of $46,000, $39,000, and $41,000 respectively. Holding a college degree is crucial to avoiding debt, unemployment and underemployment; however, economic success is also closely associated with college majors and earnings, and translates into greater lifetime wealth.[38]

African Americans and Median Net Worth

Although the Great Recession had a devastating impact on the economic well-being of all Americans, its impact on the African American community was worse, particularly on the black middle class, wiping out decades of accumulated wealth.

In 2004, aggregate black wealth or median net worth (assets minus liabilities) was already miniscule in relationship to the median wealth of whites, $13,450 for blacks compared to $134,280 for whites. During the Great Recession from 2007 to 2010, the median net worth of all American families decreased by 39.4 percent, from $135,000 to $82,300. In the economic recovery between 2010 and 2013, the median wealth of white households increased by 2.4 percent, from $138,600 to $141,900. In the same period, the median wealth of black households fell 33.7 percent, from $16,600 to $11,000, resulting in the median household wealth of white households being 13 times higher than the median wealth of black households (see Table 14.1). In an Institute on Assets and Social Policy (IASP) study tracing the household wealth between white and African American families over 25 years, researchers determined the biggest drivers of the growing racial wealth gap were explained by years of homeownership, household income, unemployment, college education, and inheritance. For reasons stated above, blacks are much more likely to be single and less likely to be married compared to other race or ethnic groups,[39] when measuring the impact of marriage, the study revealed that marriage among African Americans—which typically combines two comparatively low-level wealth portfolios—did not significantly elevate the family's wealth.[40] The relative decline in black wealth is due to what has been called the "Black Tax"—the inflated property assessments and predatory tax-liens targeted at black homeowners[41]—coupled with the recent collapse of the housing market and the disproportionate rate of foreclosures in the African American community.

Of African Americans who bought homes between 2005 and 2008, 8 percent lost them in foreclosures compared to 4.5 percent of whites.[42] This higher rate of foreclosures is partly due to "reverse redlining" as black neighborhoods are often the target of subprime lenders; while African American borrowers face "subtle" racial bias in mortgage lending.[43] For example, "in neighborhoods where at least 80 percent of the population is black, those obtaining refinance loans were 2.2 times more likely to get a subprime loan than the national average. More striking is the fact that upper income borrowers living in predominantly black communities received subprime loans at twice the rate of low income white borrowers."[44] Another study found that black borrowers are rejected for mortgage loans at a substantially higher rate than whites, mainly due to racial characteristics more so than income or creditworthiness.[45] Housing is the primary means by which Americans build their wealth. The material benefits earned from homeownership is the basis for political, social, and economic power and stability within the community.

In 2013, with substantial evidence on the stark differences and outcomes in the housing market, the Obama administration codified the legal standard of "disparate impact" (see Chapter 12) to enforce fair housing laws and hold banks accountable for their role in the foreclosure crisis. With the disparate impact standard, the United States Department of Housing and Urban Development (HUD) was able to argue that "disproportionate harm to communities of color put predatory lenders in violation of the Fair Housing Act and Equal Credit Opportunity Act." Seven cases against major lenders resulted in settlements of nearly $594 million.[46] In the appeal of the cases, the Supreme Court, in a 5–4 ruling, upheld the disparate impact approach. Justice Anthony Kennedy wrote for the majority that "Recognition of disparate impact claims is consistent with FHA's [Federal Housing Administration] central purpose, [which was] enacted to eradicate discriminatory practices within a sector of our nation's economy."[47]

African Americans and Affluence

Crucial to the African American quest for universal freedom is addressing wealth inequality. During its protests, the Occupy Wall Street movement called attention to the inequality between the wealthiest 1 percent of Americans and the 99 percent of the rest of the population, with the largest growth in America's income and wealth flowing to the top one-tenth (0.1) of the richest 1 percent.[48] Relatively few African Americans participated in the occupy protests on Wall Street or elsewhere in the country. Doing so would have been consistent with their material conditions since virtually all blacks are 99 percenters. African American total wealth accounts for only 2.5 percent of the total wealth of American households.[49]

A recent study observed that "the level of U.S. wealth inequality has grown so lopsided that our classic wealth distributional pyramid now more resembles the shape of Seattle's iconic Space Needle,"[50] The top one-thousandth of the U.S. population (about 115,000 households) have a net worth starting at $20 million and owns more than 20 percent of U.S. household wealth. The small cohort who made the *Forbes 400* all possess fortunes worth at least $1.7 billion, which is more than 61 percent of the total U.S. population wealth.

Persistent racial and ethnic wealth divides result from multigenerational discrimination that stymied asset building for African Americans, which affect both economic stability and social mobility. As a result, a 2015 Brookings Institute report observed that about half of African Americans born poor remain poor, and that there is a downward intergenerational social mobility for black middle-class children due to the Great Recession and subsequent loss of household wealth.[51] To eliminate this social and economic racial inequality, the *Forbes 400* study argues that it is necessary to close "wealth escape routes" that allow wealthy individuals and companies to shift wealth into offshore tax havens or bury it in private trusts to avoid taxation.[52]

President Obama posited that legal loopholes in the tax code "come at the expense of middle class families," meaning "we're not investing as much as we should in schools, in making college more affordable, in putting people back to work, in rebuilding our roads, our bridges, our infrastructure, creating more opportunities for our children."[53] This proposed broad, universal material-based tax reform policy, designed to increase benefits to all Americans, will also specifically help African Americans.

Faces and Voices in the Struggle for Universal Freedom
JOHNNIE TILLMON (1926–1995)

Johnnie Tillmon contributed to universal freedom and equality by attempting to make the welfare of *all* children a universally accepted right in the United States. In contrast to the United States, where welfare polices stigmatize children born out of wedlock and are used to encourage marriage, in much of Western Europe welfare policies are designed to support all children equally, whatever the marital status of their parents. As founding chair and later executive director of the National Welfare Rights Organization (NWRO), Tillmon worked to achieve these kinds of reforms for American children. Born in Scott, Arkansas, to impoverished sharecroppers, Tillmon moved to Los Angeles to escape Jim Crow segregation and poverty. The mother of six children, she was disabled as a result of diabetes and other illnesses and began to receive welfare assistance. While living in a Los Angeles housing project, Tillmon—after a series of degrading encounters with welfare officials in 1962—organized Aid to Needy Children and Mothers Anonymously. This support network for women on welfare eventually led to her leadership of NWRO, the first national organization in African American politics devoted exclusively to the interests of poor black women and their children.

Between 1967 and 1975 (when NWRO ceased operations), NWRO under Tillmon's leadership mobilized a national grassroots network of over 100 local chapters and more than 10,000 members who filed lawsuits and engaged in numerous protest demonstrations at welfare offices, state legislatures, and in Washington. Although NWRO did not achieve its ultimate objective of transforming welfare policies in the United States, it was effective in increasing the number of children receiving assistance and in expanding benefits. It also enhanced the image of welfare mothers among themselves and was responsible for helping to establish a right of privacy for welfare recipients. NWRO also helped to eliminate state residency requirements and establish due process procedures for the termination of benefits. Ironically, perhaps its greatest achievement was its role in the defeat of the Nixon administration's Family Assistance Plan, which would have established universal assistance for all children. NWRO opposed the plan because it believed the benefit levels were too low and the work requirements for mothers too harsh and punitive.

Johnnie Tillmon, Welfare Rights Advocate.

Source: 1972 Photo "Johnnie Tillmon," *Ms.* Magazine. California State University Long Beach University Library, Digital Repository. Retrieved 4 October 2016 from http://symposia.library.csulb.edu/iii/cpro/Collecti onViewPage.external;jsessionid=02D6733D0B0 C07699931838383D1C94E?lang=&sp=1000076 &suite=def

Although Tillmon had little formal education, her 1972 *Ms.* magazine essay "Welfare Is a Women's Issue" is a sharp analysis of the intersection between gender, race, and poverty in the United States and is widely read in women's studies courses.

Summary

In the U.S. political economy, the race problem is invariably and inextricably a class problem. Since the federal government assumed responsibility for management of the economy, to assure economic growth, employment, and price stability, full employment has been the top priority of African Americans and their leaders. It appears, however, that the American economy cannot be made to operate at full employment (without risking high inflation). Rather, today most economists seem to assume that an unemployment rate of 5–5.5 percent is the "natural rate" of unemployment. Long-term unemployment and underemployment, particularly for African Americans, are best understood a pattern of historic, systemic conditions—based on a socioeconomic system that locks in the racial inequality—that the economy produces and reproduces. Generations of recession-level unemployment and underemployment at 10 percent or more have had devastating consequences for the African American family and community, resulting in a racial wealth divide related to concentrated poverty, disparities in health, inequalities in criminal justice and education and wealth asset-building.

This chapter has focused on the African American quest for universal freedom in terms of access to material-based benefits. This quest has met with limited success. African Americans are not likely to be satisfied with this limited success. Policy aimed at ending racial inequality while promoting wealth equity is crucial to the future of the African American freedom struggle. It will require minority–majority coalitions and broad material-based policies that address entrenched racial disparities. This, too, is a matter of universal freedom.

Critical Thinking Questions

1. Why has full employment been the priority item on the black agenda since the end of the civil rights movement?
2. Discuss the multiple consequences of historic, long-term, persistent unemployment on the African American community and its overall economic well-being.
3. Discuss the differential impact of the "Great Recession" on the African American community.
4. Discuss how material-based policies are necessary to end the black–white economic divide. Which material-based policies would you propose?
5. Why have Congress and the president been more likely to enact rights-based than material-based reforms?

Selected Bibliography

Alexander, Michelle. *The New Jim Crow: Mass Incarceration in the Age of Colorblindness*. New York: New Press, 2012. A study of how the largely drug-driven mass incarceration of blacks is impacting the African American community.

Bullard, Robert. *Dumping in Dixie: Race, Class and Environmental Quality*. Boulder, CO: Westview Press, 2000. The standard empirical study on environmental racism in the field.

Cole, David. *No Equal Justice: Race and Class in the American Criminal Justice System*. New York: Free Press, 1999. A study documenting the systematic nature of racism in the criminal justice system.

Du Bois, W. E. B. *The Philadelphia Negro: A Social Study*. New York: Schocken Books, 1967. Originally published 1899. Historic empirical research—analyzing social and economic conditions of African Americans in Philadelphia—that challenged prevailing assumptions about inherent racial differences to reveal the systemic relationship between racism and class.

Edelman, Peter. "Clinton's Worst Mistake." *Atlantic Monthly* (May 1997). An incisive critique of the welfare reform bill signed by President Clinton.

Hancock, Lynneil. *Hands to Work: The Stories of Three Families Facing the Welfare Clock.* New York: William Morrow, 2002. A fascinating ethnographic study of how the reform of welfare impacts the lives of poor women and their children.

Harvey, Phillip. *Securing the Right to Employment: Social Welfare Policy and the Unemployed in the United States.* Princeton, NJ: Princeton University Press, 1989. An analysis with recommendations on how to achieve full employment.

Hershberg, Theodore. "A Tale of Three Cities: Blacks and Immigrants in Philadelphia, 1850–1880, 1930 and 1970."*Annals of the American Academy of Political and Social Science* 441 (1979): 55–81. An innovative, multidisciplinary historical case study of how racism in housing and employment created what is today referred to as the black underclass.

Kirshernman, J., and K. Neckerman. "We'd Love to Hire Them But . . . The Meaning of Race for Employers." In C. Jencks, ed., *The Urban Underclass.* Washington, DC: Brookings Institution, 1992. A study of the role of race and racism in the employment decisions of white employers.

Shapiro, Thomas. *The Hidden Cost of Being African American: How Wealth Perpetuates Inequality.* New York: Oxford, 2004. A study of how the lack of wealth—inheritance, saving accounts, stocks, bonds, home equity—sustains racial inequality in the U.S.

Sugure, Thomas. *Sweet Land of Liberty: The Forgotten Struggle for Civil Rights in the North.* New York: Random House, 2008. The fight against Jim Crow in the North, focusing especially on housing and employment.

Williams, Linda. *The Constraint of Race: Legacies of White Skin Privilege and Politics of American Social Policy.* College Park: Pennsylvania State University Press, 2003. An illuminating study of racism's impact on the development of social welfare policies from Reconstruction to the Clinton administration.

Wilson, William J. *When Work Disappears: The World of the New Urban Poor.* New York: Vintage, 1997. The nation's leading authority on race and poverty discusses the impact of deindustrialization and globalization on the work prospects of the urban poor.

Wilson, William. *The Truly Disadvantaged: The Inner City, the Underclass and Public Policy.* Chicago, IL: University of Chicago Press, 1987. A very influential study that focuses on the loss of industrial jobs as the key factor in the rise and growth of the underclass.

Notes

1 Harvey M. Brenner, "Estimating the Effects of Economic Change on National Health and Social Well Being," Paper prepared for the Subcommittee on Economic Goals and Intergovernmental Policy, Joint Economic Committee, July 15, 1984.

2 Jeanne Prial Gordus and Sean McAliden, "Economic Change, Physical Illness and Social Deviance," Paper prepared for the Subcommittee on Economic Goals and Intergovernmental Relations, Joint Economic Committee, July 14, 1984.

3 Anthony P. Carnevale and Nicole Smith, "Sharp Declines in Underemployment for College Graduates," Georgetown University Center on Education and the Workforce (analysis of U.S. Census Bureau, American Community Survey micro data, 2010–2014) Report, November 2015, https://cew.georgetown.edu/wp-content/uploads/Underemployment-Declines.pdf.

4 Ralph Bunche, "The Programs of Organizations Devoted to the Improvement of the Negro," *Journal of Negro Education* 8 (1939): 542–43. Bunche developed this point more extensively in his "Critique of New Deal Planning as it Affects the Negro," *Journal of Negro Education* 5 (1936): 59–65. See more generally Stanley Greenberg, *Race and State in Capitalist Development* (New Haven, CT: Yale University Press, 1980).

5 Donald Harris, "The Black Ghetto as Colony: A Theoretical Critique and Alternative Formulation," *Review of Black Political Economy* (Summer 1972): 30.

6 Ibid.

7 Thomas Sugure, *Sweet Land of Liberty: The Forgotten Struggle for Civil Rights in the North* (New York: Random House, 2008); and Matthew Countryman, *Up South: Civil Rights and Black Power in Philadelphia* (College Park: Pennsylvania State University Press, 2005).

8 Theodore Hershberg et al., "A Tale of Three Cities: Blacks and Immigrants in Philadelphia, 1850–1880, 1930 and 1970," *Annals of the American Academy of Political and Social Science* 441 (1979): 55–81.

9 Ibid., p. 75.

10 Ibid., p. 66.

11 William J. Wilson, *When Work Disappears: The World of the New Urban Poor* (New York: Vintage, 1997).

12 F. F. Furstenberg, T. Hershberg, and J. Model, "The Origins of Female-Headed Households: The Impact of the Urban Experience," *Journal of Interdisciplinary History* 6 (1975): 65–78. See also W. E. B. Du Bois, *The Philadelphia Negro: A Social Study* (New York: Schocken, 1899, 1965).

13 Gerald Reynolds, "The Impact of Illegal Immigration on the Wages and Employment Opportunities of Black Workers," Briefing Report to the United States Commission on Civil Rights (2010), https://www.law.umaryland.edu/marshall/usccr/documents/cr12im2010.pdf.

14 Barry Bluestone and Bennett Harrison, *The Deindustrialization of America: Plant Closings, Community Abandonment, and the Dismantling of Basic Industry* (New York: Basic Books, 1982).

15 Joe Cortright, "Surging City Center Job Growth," City Observatory Report, February 2015: 1–39, http://cityobservatory.org/wp-content/uploads/2015/02/Surging-City-Center-Jobs.pdf. See also, Claire Cain Miller, "More New Jobs Are in City Centers, While Employment Growth Shrinks in the Suburbs," *New York Times*, February 24, 2015, www.nytimes.com/2015/02/24/upshot/more-new-jobs-are-in-city-centers-while-employment-growth-shrinks-in-the-suburbs.html.

16 The United States Congress Joint Economic Committee (JEC) and the Congressional Black Caucus (CBC), "The American Dream on Hold: Economic Challenges in the African American Community," National Fact Sheet (2016), www.jec.senate.gov/public/_cache/files/18a8f306-f6ff-4d2c-9814-73151731926b/national-fact-sheet.pdf. Also for a similar perspective over the last 40 years (1976–2016), see the National Urban League, "Locked Out: Education, Jobs & Justice," *2016 State of Black America Report* (New York, 2016): 10, http://soba.iamempowered.com/.

17 "The African-American Labor Force in the Recovery," Department of Labor, Special Reports, www.dol.gov/_sec/media/reports/blacklaborforce/.

18 Ibid.

19 Carnevale and Smith, "Sharp Declines in Underemployment for College Graduates," Report.

20 Hope Yen and Liz Sidoti, "Figures Expected to Show Record Rise in U.S. Poverty," *Contra Costra Times*, September 12, 2010.

21 U.S. Census Bureau, Survey of Income and Program Participation (SIPP) and "Dynamics of Economic Well-Being: Participation in Government Programs, 2009–2012: Who Gets Assistance?" http://blackdemographics.com/households/poverty/.

22 Elizabeth Shogren, "New Welfare System Seen As Recession Proof," *Los Angeles Times*, April 24, 2003.

23 U.S. Census Bureau, "Who Gets Assistance?" Report.

24 African American Women and the Wage Gap Fact Sheet, The National Partnership for Women & Families (December 2015), www.nationalpartnership.org/research-library/workplace-fairness/fair-pay/african-american-women-wage-gap.pdf.

25 Ibid.

26 Leif Frederickson, "The Surprising Link between Postwar Suburban Development and Today's Inner-City Lead Poisoning," *The Conversation*, February 25, 2016, https://theconversation.com/the-surprising-link-between-postwar-suburban-development-and-todays-inner-city-lead-poisoning-54453.

27 Ibid.

28 Michelle Alexander, *The New Jim Crow: Mass Incarceration in the Age of Colorblindness* (New York: New Press, 2012).

29 E. Ann Carson, "Prisoners in 2013," U.S. Department of Justice, Bureau of Justice Statistics, September 2014, NCJ 247282, www.bjs.gov/content/pub/pdf/p13.pdf.

30 "Criminal Justice Primer: Policy Priorities for the 111th Congress," The Sentencing Project, 2009, www.sentencingproject.org/doc/publications/cjprimer2009.pdf.

31 Caralee J. Adams, Erik W. Robelen, and Nirvi Shah, "Civil Rights Data Show Retention Disparities," *Education Week*, March 6, 2012; see also Sophia Kerby, "The Top 10 Most Startling Facts about People of Color and Criminal Justice in the United States: A Look at the Racial Disparities Inherent in our Nation's Criminal-Justice System," March 13, 2012, https://www.americanprogress.org/issues/race/news/2012/03/13/11351/the-top-10-most-startling-facts-about-people-of-color-and-criminal-justice-in-the-united-states/.

32 Christopher Lyons and Becky Pettit, "Compounded Disadvantage: Race, Incarceration and Wage Growth," *Social Problems*, 58 (2) (May 2011): 257–80.

33 "U.S.: Drug Arrests Skewed by Race: National Data on 1980–2007 Cases Show Huge Disparities," *Human Rights Watch*, March 2, 2009, https://www.hrw.org/news/2009/03/02/us-drug-arrests-skewed-race.

34 Kerby, "The Top 10 Most Startling Facts about People of Color and Criminal Justice in the United States."

35 Lyons and Pettit, "Compounded Disadvantage: Race, Incarceration and Wage Growth."

36 Bureau of Labor Statistics, U.S. Department of Labor, "Labor Market Activity, Education, and Partner Status among America's Young Adults at 29: Results from a Longitudinal Study," Report USDL-16-0700, Washington, DC, 2016: 2, www.bls.gov/news.release/pdf/nlsyth.pdf.

37 Anthony P. Carnevale, Megan L. Fasules, Andrea Porter, and Jennifer Landis-Santos, "African Americans: College Majors and Earnings," Georgetown University Center on Education and the Workforce (analysis of U.S. Census Bureau, American Community Survey micro data, 2010–2014) Fact Sheet, 2016. https://cew.georgetown.edu/cew-reports/african-american-majors/.

38 Ibid.

39 See Bureau of Labor Statistics, U.S. Department of Labor, "Labor Market Activity, Education, and Partner Status among America's Young Adults at 29: Results from a Longitudinal Study," p. 6. This recent study revealed that partner status varied

greatly by race and ethnicity. Blacks were much more likely to be single than whites. At 29 years of age, 60 percent of blacks were single compared to 34 percent of whites. Blacks were also significantly less likely to be married than whites (22 percent versus 46 percent).

40 Thomas Shapiro, Tatjana Meschede, and Sam Osoro, "The Roots of the Widening Racial Wealth Gap: Explaining the Black–White Economic Divide," Institute on Assets and Social Policy, Research and Policy Brief, February 2013, p. 6.
41 Kriston Capps, "How the 'Black Tax' Destroyed African American Homeownership in Chicago," *The Atlantic*: City Lab, June 11, 2015, www.citylab.com/housing/2015/06/how-the-black-tax-destroyed-african-american-homeownership-in-chicago/395426/; see also Ta-Nehisi Coates, "The Case for Reparations," *The Atlantic*, June 2014, www.theatlantic.com/magazine/archive/2014/06/the-case-for-reparations/361631/.
42 Jesse Washington, "Blacks' Economic Gains Wiped Out in Downtown: A Generation That Played by the Rules and Saw Progress Falls Out of the Middle Class," *NBCNews.com*, AP, July 12, 2011, accessed at www.nbcnews.com/id/43645168/ns/business-eye_on_the_economy/t/blacks-economic-gains-wiped-out-downturn/#.V_Z-18nXAUc.
43 Peter Eavis, "Study Strongly Links Baltimore Mortgage Denials to Race," *New York Times*, November 16, 2015, www.nytimes.com/2015/11/17/business/dealbook/study-strongly-links-baltimore-mortgage-denials-to-race.html.
44 Ruby Mendenhall, "The Political Economy of Black Housing: From the Housing Crisis of the Great Migration to the Subprime Mortgage Crisis," *Black Scholar* 40 (2010): 31.
45 Eavis, "Study Strongly Links Baltimore Mortgage Denials to Race."
46 Christie Thompson, "Disparate Impact and Fair Housing: Seven Cases You Should Know," *ProPublica*, February 12, 2013, https://www.propublica.org/article/disparate-impact-and-fair-housing-seven-cases-you-should-know.
47 Greg Stohr and David McLaughlin, "Supreme Court Backs Housing Discrimination Lawsuits," *Bloomberg,* June 25, 2015, www.bloomberg.com/news/articles/2015-06-25/housing-discrimination-lawsuits-backed-by-u-s-supreme-court.
48 Chuck Collins and Josh Hoxie, "Billionaire Bonanza Report: The Forbes 400 and the Rest of Us," Institute of Policy Studies, Table 2, December 2015, p. 2, www.ips-dc.org/wp-content/uploads/2015/12/Billionaire-Bonanza-The-Forbes-400-and-the-Rest-of-Us-Dec1.pdf.
49 Ibid., p. 6.
50 Ibid., p. 2.
51 Richard V. Reeves and Edward Rodrigue, "Five Bleak Facts on Black Opportunity," Brookings Social Mobility Memo, January 15, 2015, www.brookings.edu/blogs/social-mobility-memos/posts/2015/01/15-mlk-black-opportunity-reeves.
52 Ibid., p. 1.
53 Michael J. de la Merced and Leslie Picker, "Pfizer and Allergan Are Said to End Merger as Tax Rules Tighten," *New York Times*, April 5, 2016, www.nytimes.com/2016/04/06/business/dealbook/tax-inversion-obama-treasury.html?_r=0.

CHAPTER 15

The African American Quest for Universal Freedom and U.S. Foreign Policy

---

LEARNING OBJECTIVE

Identify the various roles African Americans have assumed in their efforts to influence U.S. foreign policy.

In the 1940s, Edith Sampson, Chicago attorney, was appointed by President Truman as a delegate to the United Nations General Assembly. Over the years she has been followed by Pearl Bailey, Zelma George, Marian Anderson, Coretta Scott King, and a host of others. Sampson became the first African American, male or female, to represent the United States at the United Nations.[1]

African Americans have served as consuls, ministers, and ambassadors to foreign capitals as well as to the United Nations. African Americans have been employed as foreign service officers and career officials at the Department of State. Outside the bureaucracy, African Americans have served the nation in an ad hoc fashion. For example, in 1889, upon learning that historian–lawyer George Washington Williams would be making a visit to the Congo, President Benjamin Harrison asked him to gather information and submit a report on his return, which could be used in determining the nation's policy toward the Congo.[2] President Jimmy Carter sent Muhammad Ali on a goodwill tour of Africa, and President Clinton, during his first term, sent Jesse Jackson as a special representative to Nigeria and William Gray, a former congressman, as special envoy to Haiti. In addition to performing these brief diplomatic functions, African Americans have been selected to serve and represent the nation on international commissions and tribunals. Fisk University president and sociologist Charles S. Johnson was appointed by President Herbert Hoover in 1929 to serve on the International Commission to Investigate Slavery and Forced Labor in Liberia.[3]

Although they have played numerous roles in implementing and managing American foreign policies, African Americans have also served as *creators* in foreign matters, particularly as America's policy has related to the Third World and Africa. In their role as creators, African Americans have been critics, as was the NAACP after its investigation of the U.S. Marine occupation of Haiti (1915–1934). African Americans have been innovators, as were Sylvester Williams and W. E. B. Du Bois in organizing the Pan-African Congresses; or William Monroe Trotter and Du Bois at the Paris Peace Conference in 1919; or Mary McCleod Bethune, Walter White, and Du Bois at the founding conference of the United Nations. William Patterson and Malcolm X presented petitions to the United Nations on human rights.

Thus, in their quest for universal freedom, African Americans, who were born in foreign affairs through African slavery and the slave trade, have turned to America's foreign policy to support ideals of human rights and humanitarianism. Any appreciation of the universal freedom thrust of African American politics must include an understanding of African Americans' role in foreign affairs.

African Americans as Foreign Policy Implementers/Managers: The Search for "Black Nationality"

In his study of African Americans in the foreign policy apparatus, Jake Miller made the following comments: "When one considers the input of Blacks into the foreign policy-making machinery, the State Department immediately becomes the major part of the focus, since it is in this governmental department that foreign policy is traditionally formulated."[4] But looking at the State Department as late as 1998, only 2.7 percent of the entire Foreign Service Corps was African American. In 2005, the figure was 6.5 percent and by 2008, of the approximately 11,471 members of the U.S. Foreign Service, African Americans comprised some 5.6 percent, including 36 African American women serving as U.S. Ambassador to date.[5] In recent years, African Americans have held the top foreign policy posts of National Security Advisor and Secretary of State; however these posts did not alter the minor role of blacks in the overall conduct of foreign policy.

Given this basic reality, Miller concluded that decision-making powers in the State Department reside in a very limited number of officers, relatively few of whom are blacks.[6] African Americans have not had the key positions in the bureaucracy, yet as an interest group they have had a recognizable and continuing role throughout their sojourn in America. And they have had to fashion this role inside the bureaucracy in a different manner from that used by other pressure groups.

Inside the bureaucracy, African Americans had to fashion their role from positions as ministers and ambassadors to small African nations. Elliot P. Skinner, African American scholar, former ambassador to the Republic of Upper Volta, and student of these early African American diplomats, notes that this collective role could be encapsulated in the concept of *black nationality*.[7] Skinner writes, "Diplomats such as J. Milton Turner, Henry H. Smyth and Ernest Lyon were openly confrontational with the State Department to achieve their objectives. They endeavored to prove that they could serve faithfully as American foreign service officers even while protecting the black nationality."[8] Many of these African American implementers of American foreign policy believed that by helping to create a strong and developed Africa, they would contribute to the solution of its people's problems the world over. They would also be helping to preserve the already existing nation-states of Liberia and Haiti. This was their expression of "black nationality," which is understood as an effort to advance the idea of universal freedom for all African peoples. Black nationality is an expression of the idea of Pan Africanism: the historical, cultural, and political movement that asserts common bonds—a black nationality—that unites all peoples of African descent. At a minimum these Pan African bonds require Africans everywhere to resist racism, racial subordination, and the ideology of white supremacy.

An example of black nationality or Pan African consciousness began with Abraham Lincoln's annual message to Congress in December 1861. President Lincoln announced, "If any good reason exists why we should persevere longer in withholding our recognition of the independence and sovereignty of Haiti and Liberia, I am unable to discern it."[9] At a National Convention meeting in Syracuse, New York, African Americans passed a resolution praising Congress for honoring Lincoln's request.[10] Senator Charles Summer of Massachusetts introduced the bill, which authorized the president to appoint diplomatic representatives to Haiti and Liberia. The bill was attacked but eventually passed by 32 to 7 in the Senate and 86 to 37 in the House. For decades southerners had blocked the formal recognition of Haiti and Liberia, but even with this action the United States was the last Western nation to open normal diplomatic relations with Haiti and Liberia.[11]

After recognition of the two countries, the first African American diplomats to these nations began to use their influence in the State Department on their behalf. Miller writes that an analysis of the diplomatic correspondence of the black ministers accredited to Port-au-Prince revealed that no issue tended to be more dominant than those involving the granting of asylum to Haitians and the protection of Americans and their interests in the "black republic."[12] Clearly related to this issue was the question of political instability in the country.[13]

In Liberia, black ministers were preoccupied with the attempts by European powers to encroach on the territorial sovereignty of the young black republic. Their notes to the State Department reflected their concern with such matters as Liberian border frictions with England and France.

In pressing the concerns of Haiti and Liberia, diplomats in both these nations found themselves in conflictual and confrontational stances with the State Department. Here is an example of bureaucrats opposing their own bureaucracy. As Miller writes, "The structural challenge for African Americans chosen as envoys (diplomats) was that they also had to serve a nation that denigrated them and Africa itself."[14] The first African American diplomat to Liberia, J. Milton Turner (1871–1878), realized that these black diplomats had to use "extreme prudence"; he designed his dispatches "as much . . . to educate the officials in the State Department about the realities of Liberia as to enlist the help of his government for the Liberians."[15]

However, not all the black diplomats took such a frontal and conflictual approach with the State Department. Some moved in fugitive, back-channel, and secretive manners, acting on their own beyond the normal diplomatic channels. Of this tactic, Miller writes that while most black ministers participated in the drive for greater Liberian security in a noncontroversial manner, the State Department has felt compelled to chastise some for overstepping guidelines.

An example was diplomat Ernest Lyon. Lyon, a protégé of Booker T. Washington, became adept at "back-channel" manipulation, establishing important contacts outside the State Department in order to affect policy. Lyon knew how to exploit Booker T. Washington's strong support among both northern and southern African Americans and his accommodationist attitude toward the white power structure to accomplish his goals.[16] To achieve their aims and objectives, these back-channel diplomats used symbolic structures as a means of seeking to influence U.S. policy toward Africa and its people. These "symbolic structures" were conferences and hortatory rhetoric, newspaper coverage, lectures, letters, and contact with interested and powerful white individuals and groups.[17] Symbolic structures were devices to mobilize public opinion and mass interest in both African American and white communities.

In sum, African American ministers, envoys, and ambassadors found in their own individual manner three discernible ways to articulate their concern for universal freedom and respect. First, they could be conflictual and confrontational with the State Department. This tactic was an effort to move the department toward a more positive policy in maintaining and enhancing the independence of these new black republics. The second technique was individual initiatives. Here, they took matters in their own hands, devising solutions independent of the State Department. The third and final tactic was the back-channel technique. Here insiders passed vital information to elites inside the black community. This procedure, unlike the others, forged a link between the diplomats and the African American community, as well as with key individuals in the white community.

These strategies may not have been influential, but they perpetuated a legacy for the future. For instance, when African Americans served as delegates to the United Nations General Assembly, they continued the tradition taken by the early diplomats. In 1960, alternate delegate Zelma George displayed contempt for the position taken by the United States when she stood and joined African and Asian representatives in applauding the adoption of the resolution calling for an end of colonialism—a resolution on which the United States had abstained.[18]

In 1971, UN delegate Congressman Charles Diggs of Michigan sent a telegram to Secretary of State William Rogers expressing his opposition to the U.S. position on apartheid and resigned from the delegation.

African Americans as Foreign Policy Dissenters

Black diplomats were not solely concerned with black nations. Because of their posting to these nations, they could speak to only this one aspect. But the limitations of federal bureaucrats are not the limitations of the entire black community. Elites, organizations, and institutions inside the community also helped shape responses to a wider array of issues and concerns.

Paul Cuffe began an aspect of black nationality when in 1815 he took 38 blacks to Africa at a personal expense of $3,000 or $4,000.[19] His African colonization plan was a critique of the possibilities of African American universal freedom in the United States. His critique was a harbinger of a new American policy of colonization, as well as an African American policy of emigration.

Cuffe's initial articulation through activism was taken up by Martin Delany and Robert Campbell when they launched a trip to explore the Niger River area as a site for emigration. On their return to America, Delany and Campbell had to face the reality that it was not easy for African Americans to go to Africa.[20] After the Berlin Conference of 1884–1885, colonialism arrived in full force in Africa, and the visions created by Cuffe, Delany, and Campbell went sour under the terror brought on by some of the colonial powers. At the 1884–1885 Berlin Conference, the Congo was "given" to King Leopold of Belgium, and he "instituted one of the harshest, cruelest and most violent systems of colonialism in Africa."[21] American foreign policy stood silent as the atrocities of King Leopold occurred on a daily basis.[22] George Washington Williams—historian, politician, and Ohio legislator—bitterly criticized King Leopold's policies in the Congo.[23] African American dissenters to American foreign policy now began to fashion a role in line with specific events and places. The actions by Williams were more specific and more focused than had been the work of Cuffe, Delany, and Campbell.

Many African American leaders were vigorous opponents of the Mexican–American War. Frederick Douglass, for example, was scathing in his criticism, writing in his newspaper the *North Star* that the U.S. government had

> succeeded in robbing Mexico of her territory, and are rejoicing over their success under the hypocritical pretense of a regard for peace. Had they not succeeded in robbing Mexico of the most important and most valuable of her territory, many of those now loudest in their professions of favor for peace would be loudest and wildest for war.[24]

Following in the path blazed by Williams and Douglass was Bishop Alexander Walters of the National African American Council, who was strongly critical when the United States annexed the Philippines during the Spanish–American War.[25] There, in the cause of white supremacy, the United States turned from a policy of cooperating with Tagalog insurgents against the Spanish colonial authorities to one of joining with the defeated Spaniards against the Filipinos.[26] Therefore, as a foreign policy dissenter, Walters noted that "had the Filipino been white and fought as brave as they have, the war would have been ended and their independence granted a long time ago."[27]

In the Boer War, where the British fought the white South Africans, American foreign policy was one of solidarity with the British. African Americans spoke out, denouncing the war as aggression.[28] At first blacks viewed the struggle as between whites with little interest to them. As they learned more of the racism in Afrikaner society, they became increasingly hostile to the Boers.[29]

With the coming of World War I, African American socialists A. Philip Randolph and Chandler Owens demanded a change in America's foreign policy. They published a newspaper, *The Messenger,* in New York, and because of an article they wrote, "Pro-Germanism among Negroes," Randolph and Owens were sentenced to jail, and their second-class mailing privileges were revoked.[30]

The Paris Peace Conference, the Treaty of Versailles, and the founding of the League of Nations all gave African American leaders an opportunity to further express their foreign policy concerns. Both W. E. B. Du Bois and William Monroe Trotter attended the Paris Peace Conference. While Du Bois was able to influence the creation of the League of Nations mandate system for the colonial-held Third World nations,[31] Trotter found that the State Department denied him a passport and thereby an official presence at the Conference.[32] Yet Trotter attended and wrote his critical observations in his newspaper, the *Boston Guardian.*[33]

The Italian invasion of Ethiopia mobilized the African American community to action on foreign policy like no other event. Mussolini had come to power in Italy in 1922, and, by 1935, he was seeking to restore the Roman Empire by overrunning Ethiopia. In the face of such naked imperialism, it could be expected that a few lonely voices and organizations might have spoken out. However, Franklin and Moss write, "When Italy invaded Ethiopia African Americans protested with all the means at their command. Almost overnight even the most provincial among black Americans became international-minded. Ethiopia was a black nation, and its destruction would symbolize the final victory of white over blacks."[34] In opposition, African Americans held pro-Ethiopian demonstrations, sent money and medical supplies to Ethiopia, and boycotted Italian-made goods. Ethiopia was also a major concern of the black press in the 1930s, with most of the black media criticizing the Italian invasion of Ethiopia.[35] The *Pittsburgh Courier* assigned J. A. Rogers as a war correspondent to send the news on the war front back to the United States; and there were pleas made both to the U.S. government and the League of Nations. For instance, the NAACP telegraphed the League of Nations on behalf of 12,000,000 American Negroes, demanding action to restrain Mussolini.[36]

All this frenzied lobbying set the African Americans against outspoken Italian American groups that, as a matter of ethnic pride, supported their ancestral homeland. In some eastern cities where Italian and black neighborhoods adjoined, riots erupted.[37] In this intense and rising competition between the two groups to affect policy toward the war, the African Americans were more successful than the Italian Americans because the Roosevelt administration imposed an arms embargo on Italy.[38] The intensity as well as the strength of the African American reaction to the Italian invasion helped considerably in arousing a general American sympathy for Ethiopia.[39] This time the outcry came from all quarters and sectors of African American society. Indeed, the demand for help for Ethiopia was so systematic and comprehensive this time that in the midst of the conflict, in January 1937, African American leaders founded the Council on African Affairs, a national organization to lobby for Africa—a forerunner of Trans Africa.

During World War II, the global nature of the struggle and the indeterminate post–world war realities forced African Americans to wage a "Double V" campaign, victory at home as well as abroad.[40] In World War II, African Americans were willing to do their part and to make necessary sacrifice to ensure victory, but they constantly reminded the people of the United States that they resented all forms of racism.[41] In addition to the Double V, the African American press simultaneously called for a new and more progressive approach to colonialism and the problems of Third World nations.[42]

African American leaders supported an independent Israel but, after the 1973 Yom Kippur War, increasing numbers of African Americans began to speak for the cause of Palestinian independence as well.

During 1946–1947, leading black newspapers were opposed to the cold war policies of the United States. At the same time, these papers reminded Americans that the best defense against communism was universal freedom, at home and abroad.[43]

One of the crisis events of the cold war that U.S. policy makers had to cope with was the Nigerian civil war, better known as the Biafran secession, which emerged during the Nixon administration. President Nixon supported the Biafran secession, a position that put him at odds with the African American community.[44] From the outset, African Americans put their support behind the Nigerian federal government. Thus, when the Biafran secessionists surrendered in January 1970, the Nigerians expressed gratitude toward African Americans who helped to keep Washington committed to the one-Nigeria policy.[45] Like the situation in Ethiopia some three-and-a-half decades earlier, blacks had helped to shape events in Nigeria in a way supportive of African nationality.

The Student Nonviolent Coordinating Committee (SNCC) was among the first national organizations to oppose the Vietnam War. Muhammad Ali, Martin Luther King Jr., and many other prominent blacks also voiced opposition to the Vietnam War. When Martin Luther King Jr. dissented from the rising American consensus about the war, it divided the civil rights movement and angered liberals and President Johnson. Several African American leaders, notably Whitney Young of the Urban League, denounced King and supported President Johnson. But King's prestige made him a major voice in the antiwar movement.[46] Inside the military, African American troops spoke out against both the racial epithets and some of the inhumane policies of American troops fighting in Vietnam.[47]

When President Reagan ordered an invasion of the Caribbean island nation of Grenada in October 1984, five members of the Congressional Black Caucus moved to impeach the president, and the entire Caucus condemned the invasion as being nurtured essentially by white racism. African Americans also opposed George H. W. Bush's Persian Gulf War[48] and his son's invasion of Iraq.

African Americans have not had a commanding influence in American foreign policy, but they have had a continuing presence. On several occasions, that presence has had a decided impact on the outcome of American foreign policy, such as the Ethiopian War. African Americans were successful in changing the Nixon administration policy during the Nigerian civil war and in pressuring President Clinton to intervene in the Haitian conflict on the side of the democracy. These are *direct* linkages between the expressed desires of black Americans and American foreign policy. However, there is a very important indirect link. For example, King's outspoken stance against the Vietnam War led to a larger, much more powerful, and vocal antiwar and peace movement.

African American opposition to America's wars comes as no surprise to students of U.S. foreign policy. In some ways, it is as old as black opposition to the 1848 Mexican–American War and the 1890s war against the Filipino insurgency. Since Vietnam this opposition has come earlier and been more intense and widespread. Scholars trace the sources of this antiwar sentiment in black

America to a kind of Third World solidarity with the world's people of color; what one scholar calls an "Afro-Centric" foreign policy perspective.[49] Also, many blacks feel that racism and poverty force many young blacks into the military because they cannot find educational and economic opportunities in the civilian economy. Thus, it is argued that blacks will suffer disproportionate casualties in what some refer to as the "white man's wars."

Trans Africa: African Americans as Foreign Policy Lobbyists

Figure 15.1 reveals the rise, fall, and evolution of African American organized interest and pressure group activity up to the founding of Trans Africa. In 1976 Congressmen Charles Diggs of Michigan (chair of the House Foreign Affairs Subcommittee on Africa) and Andrew Young convened 30 black leaders to challenge the Ford administration policy toward white-ruled Rhodesia. But, little changed during the Ford administration. The incoming Carter administration, however, was concerned with human rights, and its leaders were willing to listen to Congressman and later UN Ambassador Young. As a result, the political context changed significantly. In May 1978, Young and his colleagues organized Trans Africa, the first mass-based African American lobby.

To carry out its lobbying, Trans Africa—the "Black American Lobby for Africa and the Caribbean"—sends out "Issue Briefs" and a newsletter to alert its membership and individuals in the Congress to matters on which its leaders want action. It holds news conferences, public demonstrations, and annual dinners and symposiums to keep its constituency informed. To involve as well as mobilize people, Trans Africa has engaged in boycotts, marches, mass demonstrations, letter writing, and a hunger strike by its former director Randall Robinson. Out of these different tactics and strategies, the organization has met with considerable success.

Outstanding among its efforts was its protests against South Africa, which began on Thanksgiving eve, 1984, as a sit-in at the South African Embassy in Washington. These protests eventually led to the Comprehensive Anti-Apartheid Act. Introduced by Congressman William Gray of Pennsylvania, this act passed both houses of Congress but was vetoed by President Reagan. However, the veto was overridden when Republicans joined with African Americans and Democrats to impose sanctions on the South African regime.

During the Clinton administration, Trans Africa's executive director, Randall Robinson, used a hunger strike to force the president to change his policy toward Haiti.[50] Initially, Clinton had essentially followed the Bush immigration policy limiting Haitian immigration, and had successfully defended that policy in the Supreme Court. Trans Africa, under Robinson's leadership, helped to reverse the policy.

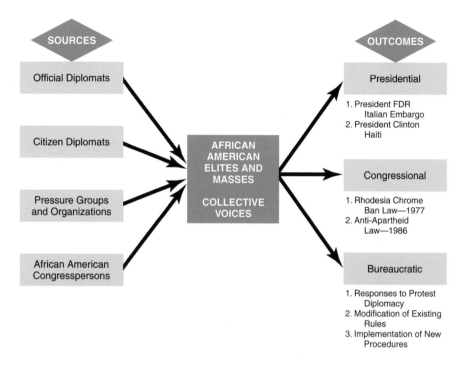

FIGURE 15.1

Sources and Outcomes of African American Foreign Policy-Making Initiatives

Sources: Adapted from Hanes Walton, Jr., ed., "African American Foreign Policy: From Decolonization to Democracy," in *African American Power and Politics: The Political Context Variable* (New York: Columbia University Press, 1997), chap. 18; and Jake Miller, *The Black Presence in American Foreign Affairs* (Washington, DC: University Press of America, 1978).

Trans Africa has also embarked on a program of action designed to influence some of the African and other Third World dictatorships (especially Nigeria) to pursue, with America's help, democratic elections and governance.[51] With colonialism as a political system disappearing from African and Third World countries, this new course helped to achieve democracy in some African countries.

Thus, this organizational presence of African Americans, through interest group lobbying, like its counterparts in other parts of the foreign policy process, has had some successes in changing America's foreign policies toward Africa and the Third World.

African Americans and Citizen Diplomacy: Historical Background and Context

African American foreign policy leaders have a long history of creating new strategies and tactics to influence and shift the State Department's direction of foreign policy.[52] One of these strategies for articulating the African American position is *citizen diplomacy.*

Professor Karin Stanford has defined citizen diplomacy "as the diplomatic efforts of private citizens in the international arena for the purpose of achieving a specific objective or accomplishing constituency goals."[53] This particular technique for influencing foreign policy arose when George Logan, a white private citizen, decided on his own to intervene when the United States ratified the Jay Treaty with Great Britain in 1798. The French responded negatively, and, with military force, seized U.S. ships on the high seas. Logan went to Paris and asked the French to avoid a military crisis and defuse the situation by releasing the hostages and expressing goodwill. The U.S. government responded to Logan's efforts by passing the Logan Act on January 30, 1799, an act that prohibited individual citizens from trying to conduct official diplomatic endeavors.[54] But the government did not prosecute Logan then, and it has never prosecuted anyone for violating this law. Throughout America's history, numerous individuals have engaged in citizen diplomacy. During the Vietnam War, scores of individual citizens journeyed to Hanoi to participate and engage in citizen diplomacy. Among them were former attorney general Ramsey Clark, movie stars Jane Fonda and Clint Eastwood, and the 1996 Reform Party presidential candidate H. Ross Perot.

African American Citizen Diplomats

From the time of slavery, African Americans have consistently engaged in citizen diplomacy; for example, Frederick Douglass and many others traveled to Europe in efforts to universalize the struggle against slavery.

As mentioned earlier, in the post–Reconstruction Era, there were forays by George Washington Williams and Booker T. Washington into the Congo.[55] At the start of the twentieth century, Sylvester Williams and W. E. B. Du Bois launched the Pan-African Congresses to call attention to the global oppression of African peoples. The NAACP sent an observer to Haiti when American occupation began. Black journalist George Schuyler went to Liberia in 1931 for three months to investigate slavery there, and on his return, he used the data he had amassed on forced labor and slavery to write a novel, *Slaves Today: A Story of Liberia.*[56] In the preface to the novel he stated his objective:

> If this novel can help arouse enlightened world opinion against this brutalizing of the native population in a Negro republic, perhaps the conscience of civilized people will stop similar atrocities in native lands ruled by proud white nations that boast of their superior culture.[57]

The 1930s were a period of great activity. Colonel Hubert Julian, a fighter pilot, fought for Ethiopia in that conflict and tried to serve as a diplomatic negotiator,[58] while numerous African Americans did the same in the Spanish civil war.[59]

There were also African Americans who advocated the Soviet point of view about the communist system and its vision of universal freedom and global peace. Chief among them were W. E. B. Du Bois and entertainer-scholar Paul Robeson in the 1950s and early 1960s.[60]

Malcolm X made numerous pilgrimages to Africa and the Middle East, where he met with the heads of state of such nations as Egypt, Ghana, and Tanzania. The purpose of these missions was to universalize the African freedom struggle by developing linkages between the African and African American leadership communities. At the time of his murder, Malcolm X was attempting to develop support among African and other Third World nations for a UN resolution condemning the United States for violating the human rights of its African American citizens. Another example of a citizen diplomat was Reverend Leon Sullivan and his articulation of the Sullivan principles (requiring equality in employment and working conditions) in regard to American corporations doing business in South Africa.

Reverend Jesse Jackson was continuing the long history of African American citizen diplomats when he went to Syria to secure the release of Lieutenant Robert O. Goodman, Jr., an African American pilot who had been shot down in an air raid over Syria earlier in the month.[61] Out of this history of black citizen diplomats, there is a fairly discernible model and pattern.

On the whole, African American citizen diplomats have been (1) well-known domestic leaders, (2) spokespersons for a specific issue, (3) persons wanting to activate world public opinion, and (4) citizens who want to reshape

Reverend Jesse Jackson on one of his many exercises in citizen diplomacy. Here he is with Cuban leader Fidel Castro. On this mission, Jackson secured the release of scores of political prisoners.

Source: Jacques M. Chenet/Corbis

American foreign policy. However, the Jackson forays departed significantly from the models of the past. They differed from past efforts because Jackson was an announced Democratic presidential candidate in the midst of the presidential primary season and had a long history of international human rights missions. Jackson also had significant personal relations and friendships with many world leaders. These domestic and global characteristics significantly distance the Jackson model of citizen diplomat from many of his African American predecessors. Jackson's model was different because of his credentials—personal and political.

The Foreign Policy of the First African American President

President Obama during the campaign promised to change the style and substance of U.S. foreign policy, to move away from the Bush administration's unilateralism and reliance on military power. He also pledged to engage the rest of the world, including Iran and other nations defined as America's adversaries. With the notable exception of Israel, his election was greeted globally with enthusiasm. To the leaders, nations, and peoples of the world, Obama—the talented, charismatic, and multicultural son of an African—was the embodiment of hope and change—hope for change in America's relations with the world. Not since John F. Kennedy had an American president inspired such sentiments. The Nobel Committee, in recognition of this hope and in order to encourage it, awarded Obama its peace prize after he was only several weeks in office.

In speeches in Europe, Asia, Africa, and the Middle East, Obama espoused a less confrontational, more cooperative foreign policy. The administration's official "National Security Strategy" document issued in the spring of 2010 explicitly repudiated his predecessor's emphasis on unilateralism and the right to wage preemptive war, while emphasizing international alliances and institutions.[62] The strategy document also emphasized the reduction and eventual elimination of nuclear weapons, and strategies to fight global poverty and climate change. On nuclear weapons, the president hosted a global summit and successfully completed negotiation of a nuclear arms reduction treaty with Russia. The president also established diplomatic relations with Cuba, ending the 50-year-old policy of nonrecognition and isolation of Fidel Castro's communist government; negotiated with other major powers an agreement with Iran to delay, if not stop, its development of nuclear weapons; orchestrated the Paris Climate Agreement to curb the global growth of greenhouse gases and meliorate global warming; and concluded the Trans Pacific Partnership trade agreement.

In Iraq, President Obama withdrew all U.S. combat forces by the end of 2011. In Afghanistan, in his first term he dispatched 30,000 additional troops but near the end of his second term the number of U.S. troops had declined to a small

President Obama meeting with Raul Castro, President of Cuba.

Source: "President Obama and Cuban leader Raul Castro shake hands during a bilateral meeting at the United Nations Headquarters on Sept. 29, 2015, in New York City." 22 February 2016. Retrieved 4 October 2016 from https://www.studentnewsdaily.com/wp-content/uploads/2016/02/RaulCastro-Obama-820x512.png

residual force. The president's war policies are also characterized by what he did not do. Going against the advice of most of his military and security advisors, he refused to intervene militarily in the Syrian civil war; refused to send arms to the Ukraine in its conflict with Russian-backed rebels; and refused to send combat troops to combat ISIL (Islamic State of Iraq and the Levant), the brutal Middle East terrorist group. These decisions by Obama to rely on diplomacy rather than war were sharply criticized by conservatives in Congress and the media, who accused the president of weakening the U.S. position in global politics and emboldening the nation's adversaries including China, Russia, and Iran.

While Obama's reluctance to pursue war was controversial, in general it accorded with the African American perspective in foreign policy which shows greater reluctance toward the pursuit of war as compared to white Americans. It should be clear, however, that Obama's reluctance to use military force was relative. His administration, for example, was far more aggressive than the Bush administration in waging the so-called war on terror, making extensive use of drones to pursue targeted killings in Yemen, Pakistan, and East Africa. The most important example of this aggressiveness was the May 2011 killing in Pakistan of Osama bin-Laden, the mastermind of the 9/11 attacks.[63]

The first U.S. president of African descent did not advance any new Africa policy initiatives; as one scholar wrote "Lots of Hope, Not Much Change."[64] Obama visited the continent on several occasions (including a visit to his ancestral homeland, Kenya) and hosted in August 2014 a summit in Washington of 50 African leaders to discuss issues of trade, development, and security. But in general Africa for the first African American president was not, as it was not for all of his predecessors, a major concern of Obama's foreign policy.

Overall while Obama embraced diplomacy and multilateralism more than his predecessors and to some extent changed the style and tone of U.S. foreign policy, fundamentally the "Obama Doctrine" did not depart from the policy priorities of his post–cold war predecessors.[65]

Faces and Voices in the Struggle for Universal Freedom
RALPH BUNCHE (1904–1971)

Ralph Bunche contributed to the idea of universal freedom in international politics through his work as a founding diplomat at the United Nations. The first African American to be awarded the Nobel Peace Prize (in 1950 for his work in negotiating peace between Arabs and Israelis in 1948), Bunche viewed the UN as indispensable in the maintenance of world peace and the establishment of a rule of law that would respect the human rights and aspirations for freedom of all the world's peoples. Although President Truman in 1949 offered him an appointment that would have made him the first African American assistant secretary of state, Bunche declined, preferring to work as an international rather than an American diplomat. In 1954 he was named UN under-secretary general for political affairs, a position he held until his death.

Dr. Ralph Johnson Bunche.

Source: Biography of Ralph Johnson Bunche, UN Ambassador and Recipient of the Nobel Peace Prize 1950. Retrieved 4 October 2016 from www.nobelprize.org/nobel_prizes/peace/laureates/1950/bunche-bio.html

Born in Detroit, the son of a barber, Bunche was graduated *summa cum laude* from UCLA and in 1934 became the first African American to earn a Ph.D. in political science from Harvard. While a professor at Howard University, he wrote a series of monographs on black politics and leadership for the landmark work *An American Dilemma. The Negro Problem and Modern Democracy*. While at the UN, he advocated for civil rights in the United States and marched with Martin Luther King Jr. in the famous Selma-to-Montgomery voting rights protest. Throughout, however, he remained committed to the UN as humankind's last best hope for peace, freedom, and equality.[a]

[a] Charles Henry, *Ralph Bunche: Model Negro or American Other* (New York: New York University Press, 1999).

Summary

As with most areas of American life, African Americans have had to struggle to become participants in the making of U.S. foreign policy. But since historically foreign policy in the United States has been the almost exclusive preserve of the white Anglo-Saxon establishment, the black struggle for inclusion here has required innovative and creative strategies as diplomats and consuls in official positions, as foreign policy dissenters (from the Mexican–American War to the Vietnam War to the Iraq War), as lobbyists through interest groups such as Trans Africa, and as "citizen-diplomats." In all of these strategies and approaches, African Americans have consistently pursued universal freedom, opposing the international slave trade, imperialist wars, colonialism, and wars of aggression—whether by Italy in Ethiopia or the United States in Vietnam. And in their efforts to influence and shape U.S. foreign policy, the African American minority—sometimes alone and sometimes in coalitions with whites—has produced results that occasionally have directed and reshaped the nation's foreign policy in the direction of its ideal of freedom, universal freedom.

Critical Thinking Questions

1. Define "black nationality" as it relates to the African diaspora and foreign policy. Are there similarities with black nationalism within the United States? Explain by giving examples to support your argument.
2. Discuss the various roles African Americans have played in shaping U.S. foreign policy.
3. From the Mexican–American War to the Iraq War, African American leaders have been in the forefront of opposition. Explain this tradition of antiwar dissent in African American politics.

4. Explain how African Americans used their position as U.S. diplomats to advance "black nationality."
5. Discuss some techniques or strategies used by African Americans to influence foreign policy and advance universal freedom globally.

Selected Bibliography

Clemons, Michael, ed. *African Americans in Global Affairs: Contemporary Perspectives.* Boston, MA: Northeastern University Press, 1991. A collection of essays examining the role of African Americans in foreign policy, focusing on the role of interest groups, black policy makers, and the Congressional Black Caucus.

DeConde, Alexander. *Ethnicity, Race and American Foreign Policy: A History.* Boston, MA: Northeastern University Press, 1992. An excellent comparative history, covering all major ethnic groups over the course of American history.

Dudziak, Mary. *Cold War Civil Rights.* Princeton, NJ: Princeton University Press, 2000. A study of how the international struggle against communism influenced the domestic struggle for civil rights.

Goldberg, Jeffrey. "The Obama Doctrine: How He Has Shaped the World." *Atlantic,* April, 2016. A long article based on multiple interviews with the President over several years in which Obama articulates his foreign policy worldview and the limits of military power.

Henderson, Errol. *Afrocentrism and World Politics: Toward a New Paradigm.* Westport, CT: Praeger, 1995. An important work that suggests and details a new "Afrocentric" approach to U.S. foreign policy.

Kegley, Charles, and Eugene Wittkopf. *American Foreign Policy: Pattern and Process,* 3rd ed. New York: St. Martin's Press, 1987. A good introduction to the structures and processes of U.S. foreign policy making.

Krenn, Michael. *Black Diplomacy: African Americans and the State Department, 1945–1969.* Amonk, NY: M. E. Sharpe, 1998. A study of the integration of the State Department after 1945 and the appointment of black ambassadors to Africa and other Third World nations.

Krenn, Michael, ed. *The African American Voice in U.S. Foreign Policy since World War II.* New York: Garland Publishing, 1999. A collection of articles that demonstrates how the fight for civil rights in the United States spilled over into concerns about the cold war and race and foreign policy.

Lusanne, Clarence. *Colin Powell and Condoleezza Rice: Foreign Policy, Race and the New American Century.* Westport, CT: Praeger, 2006. This first book-length study of the role of Powell and Rice in the formulation of U.S. foreign policy is critical of the two diplomats for their failure to embrace their racial identities and stress global equality.

Miller, Jake. *The Black Presence in American Foreign Affairs.* Washington, DC: Howard University Press, 1978. The standard work on the subject, with an excellent summary and overview from a historical perspective.

Skinner, Elliot. *African Americans and U.S. Policy toward Africa, 1850–1924: In Defense of Black Nationality.* Washington, DC: Howard University Press, 1992. The definitive work by the African American historian and diplomat, with detailed and comprehensive treatment through 1924. Unsurpassed as a source.

Skinner, Elliot, and Pearl Robinson, eds. *Transformation and Resiliency on Africa.* Washington, DC: Howard University Press, 1983. A good collection of case studies and a wonderful essay on the African American intelligentsia and Africa.

Stanford, Karin. *Beyond the Boundaries: Reverend Jesse Jackson in International Affairs.* Albany, NY: SUNY Press, 1997. A pioneering exploration of the concept of citizen diplomacy, African American citizen diplomats, and Jesse Jackson's role in foreign affairs.

Tillery, Alvin. *Between Homeland and Motherland: Africa, U.S. Foreign Policy and Black Leadership.* Ithaca, NY: Cornell University Press, 2011. A history of black elite engagement with U.S. Africa policy, focusing on how it relates to domestic policy concerns.

Notes

1 Hanes Walton, Jr., *Black Women at the United Nations* (Irvine, CA: Borgo Press, 1995): chap. 2.

2 John Hope Franklin and Alfred Moss, Jr., *From Slavery to Freedom,* 7th ed. (New York: McGraw-Hill, 1994): 391.

3 John Stanfield, II, "Preface," in C. Johnson, ed., *Bitter Canaan: The Story of the Negro Republic* (New Brunswick, NJ: Transaction Books, 1987): vii.

4 Jake Miller, *The Black Presence in American Foreign Affairs* (Washington, DC: University Press of America, 1978): 1.

5 See "Distinguished African Americans at the Department of State," U.S. Department of State, FY 2008 Financial Report, Bureau of Resource Management, www.state.gov/s/d/rm/rls/perfrpt/2008/html/112148.htm (accessed March 10, 2016).

6 Ibid.

7 Elliott Skinner, African Americans and U.S. Foreign Policy toward Africa, 1850–1924: In Defense of Black Nationality (Washington, DC: Howard University Press): 515.

8 Ibid., p. 517.

9 Quoted in Skinner, *African Americans and U.S. Policy toward Africa,* p. 53.

10 Ibid.

11 Alexander DeConde, *Ethnicity, Race and American Foreign Policy: A History* (Boston, MA: Northeastern University Press, 1992): 39.

12 Miller, *The Black Presence in American Foreign Affairs,* p. 18.

13 Ibid., pp. 23–32. See also Norma Brown, ed., *A Black Diplomat in Haiti: The Diplomatic Correspondence of U.S. Minister Frederick Douglass from Haiti, 1889–1891* (Salisbury, NC: Documentary Publications, 1977).

14 Ibid., p. 32.

15 Skinner, *African Americans and U.S. Policy toward Africa,* p. 519.

16 Ibid., p. 517.

17 Ibid., pp. 520–21.

18 Miller, *The Black Presence in American Foreign Affairs,* p. 99.

19 Franklin and Moss, *From Slavery to Freedom,* p. 98. See also Lamont Thomas, *Rise to Be a People: A Biography of Paul Cuffe* (Urbana: University of Illinois Press, 1986).

20 Skinner, *African Americans and U.S. Policy toward Africa,* p. 52.

21 Booker T. Washington, "Cruelty in the Congo Country," *Outlook* 78 (October 8, 1904): 375–77.

22 Ibid.

23 Franklin and Moss, *From Slavery to Freedom,* p. 296. See also John Hope Franklin, *George Washington Williams* (Chicago, IL: University of Chicago Press, 1985).

24 "Frederick Douglass on the Mexican American War," in H. Aptheker, ed., *A Documentary History of the Negro People,* vol. 1 (New York: Citadel Press, 1967): 267.

25 DeConde, *Ethnicity, Race and American Foreign Policy*, p. 64.

26 Ibid., p. 63.

27 Ibid., p. 65.

28 Ibid., p. 66. See also Willard B. Gatewood, Jr., "Black Americans and the Boer War, 1899–1902," *South Atlanta Quarterly* 75 (Spring 1976): 234.

29 Ibid.

30 Franklin and Moss, *From Slavery to Freedom*, p. 345.

31 Hanes Walton, Jr., "The Southwest Africa Mandate," *Faculty Research Bulletin* 26 (December 1972): 94.

32 William Monroe Trotter, "How I Managed to Reach the Peace Conference," in P. Foner, ed., *The Voice of Black America* (New York: Simon & Schuster, 1972): 740–42.

33 See Stephen Fox, *Guardian of Boston: William Monroe Trotter* (New York: Atheneum, 1971); George Padmore, "Review of the Paris Peace Conference," *Crisis* (November 1946): 331–33, 347–48; and George Padmore, "Trusteeship: The New Imperialism," *Crisis* (October 1946): 302–9.

34 Ibid.

35 Miller, *The Black Presence in American Foreign Affairs*, p. 235. See also J. R. Hooker, "The Negro American Press and Africa in the 1930s," *Canadian Journal of African Studies* (March 1967): 43–50; and W. E. B. Du Bois, "Interracial Implications of the Ethiopian Crisis," *Foreign Affairs* 14 (October 1935): 1982–92.

36 DeConde, *Ethnicity, Race and American Foreign Policy*, p. 107.

37 Ibid.

38 Ibid.

39 Ibid., p. 108.

40 Franklin and Moss, *From Slavery to Freedom*, p. 454.

41 Ibid., p. 453.

42 Ibid., p. 236.

43 Ibid., p. 237. See also Mark Solomon, "Black Critics of Colonialism and the Cold War," in T. Patterson, ed., *Cold War Critics* (Chicago, IL: Quadrangle Books, 1971): 205–39. For a comprehensive study of the relationship between the international struggle against communism and the struggle for civil rights, see Mary Dudziak, *Cold War Civil Rights* (Princeton, NJ: Princeton University Press, 2000).

44 Deconde, *Ethnicity, Race and American Foreign Policy*, p. 148.

45 Ibid.

46 For a discussion of King's anti-Vietnam remarks, see Martin Luther King Jr., *The Trumpet of Conscience* (New York: Harper & Row, 1968).

47 Wallace Terry, *Bloods: An Oral History of the Vietnam War* (New York: Random House, 1984): xvi.

48 Lynne Duke, "Emerging Black Anti-War Movement Rooted in Domestic Issues," *Washington Post* (February 8, 1991).

49 Errol Henderson, *Afrocentrism and World Politics: Toward a New Paradigm* (Westport, CT: Praeger, 1995).

50 Hanes Walton, Jr., "African American Foreign Policy: From Decolonization to Democracy," in Walton, *African American Power and Politics: The Political Context Variable* (New York: Columbia University Press, 1997): chap. 18.

51 Ibid.

52 Miller, *The Black Presence in American Foreign Affairs*, pp. 127–242.

53 Karen Stanford, *Beyond the Boundaries: Reverend Jesse Jackson in International Affairs* (Albany, NY: SUNY Press, 1997): 9.

54 Ibid., p. 19.

55 Elliott P. Skinner, "Booker T. Washington: Diplomatic Initiatives," in Skinner, *African Americans and U.S. Policy*, pp. 291–348.

56 George Schuyler, *Slaves Today: A Story of Liberia* (Baltimore, MA: McGrath, 1931): 5.

57 Ibid., p. 6.

58 Robin Kelley, "This Ain't Ethiopia but It'll Do: African Americans and the Spanish Civil War," in Kelley, *Race Rebels* (New York: Free Press, 1994): 130.

59 Ibid., pp. 123–60.

60 See Gerald Horne, *Black and Red: W. E. B. Du Bois and the Afro-American Response to the Cold War* (Albany, NY: SUNY Press, 1986).

61 For a short account of that rescue mission, see Wyatt Tee Walker, *The Road to Damascus* (New York: Martin Luther King Jr. Fellows Press, 1985).

62 "National Security Strategy," www.whitehouse.gov/site/default/files/rss-viewer/national-security-strategy.pdf.

63 Peter Bergen, "Warrior in Chief," *New York Times*, April 28, 2012; and David Sanger, *Confront and Conceal: Obama's Secret Wars and Surprising Use of American Power* (New York: Random House, 2012).

64 Nicolas Van De Walle, "Obama and Africa: Lots of Hope, Not Much Change," *Foreign Affairs* 94 (2015), www.foreignaffairs.com/articles/obama-and-africa.

65 For a balanced overview of Obama's foreign policy from liberal and conservative perspectives see the special issue of *Foreign Affairs*, "Obama's World: Judging His Record" 94 (2015), www.foreignaffairs.com/press/2015-08-19/obama-5-world-leading-experts-assess-president-5foreign-policy-record-thusfar-new. For a black perspective see Clarence Lusane, "We Must Lead the World: The Obama Doctrine and the Re-Branding of U.S. Hegemony," in Charles Henry and Robert Allen, eds., *The Obama Phenomena: Toward A Multiracial Democracy* (Urbana: University of Illinois Press, 2014).

APPENDIX

Parts of the Constitution Relating to the Presence of Africans in America

Article I

Section 2   Representatives and direct Taxes shall be apportioned among the several States which may be included within this Union, according to their respective Numbers which shall be determined by adding to the whole Number of free Persons, including those bound to Service for a Term of Years, and excluding Indians not taxed, three fifths of all other Persons.

Section 9   The Migration or Importation of such Persons as any of the States now existing shall think proper to admit, shall not be prohibited by the Congress prior to the Year one thousand eight hundred and eight, but a Tax or duty may be imposed on such Importation, not exceeding ten dollars for each Person.

Article IV

Section 2   No Person held to Service or Labour in one State under the Laws thereof, escaping into another, shall, in Consequence of any Law or Regulation therein, be discharged from such Service or Labour, but shall be delivered up on Claim of the Party to whom such Service or Labour may be due.

Article V

Provided that no Amendment which may be made prior to the Year One thousand eight hundred and eight shall in any Manner affect the first and fourth Clauses in the Ninth Section of the first Article;

Amendment XIII

[Ratified on December 6, 1865]

Section 1 Neither slavery nor involuntary servitude, except as a punishment for crime whereof the party shall have been duly convicted, shall exist within the United States, or any place subject to their jurisdiction.

Section 2 Congress shall have power to enforce this article by appropriate legislation.

Amendment XIV

[Ratified on July 9, 1868]

Section 1 All persons born or naturalized in the United States, and subject to the jurisdiction thereof, are citizens of the United States and of the State wherein they reside. No State shall make or enforce any law which shall abridge the privileges or immunities of citizens of the United States; nor shall any State deprive any person of life, liberty, or property, without due process of law; nor deny to any person within its jurisdiction the equal protection of the laws.

Section 2 Representatives shall be apportioned among the several States according to their respective numbers, counting the whole number of persons in each State, excluding Indians not taxed. But when the right to vote at any election for the choice of electors for President and Vice President of the United States, Representatives in Congress, the Executive and Judicial officers of a State, or the members of the Legislature thereof is denied to any of the male inhabitants of such State, being twenty-one years of age, and citizens of the United States or in any way abridged, except for participation in rebellion, or other crime, the basis of representation therein shall be reduced in the proportion which the number of such male citizens shall bear to the whole number of male citizens twenty-one years of age in such State.

Section 3 No person shall be a Senator or Representative in Congress, or elector of President and Vice President, or hold any office, civil or military, under the United States, or under any State, who, having previously taken an oath, as a member of Congress, or as an officer of the United States, or as a member of any State legislature, or as an executive or judicial officer of any State, to support the Constitution of the United States, shall have engaged in insurrection or rebellion against the same, or given aid or comfort to the enemies thereof. But Congress may by a vote of two-thirds of each House remove such disability.

Section 4 The validity of the public debt of the United States, authorized by law, including debts incurred for payment of pensions and bounties for services in suppressing insurrection or rebellion, shall not be questioned. But neither the United States nor any State shall assume or pay any debt or obligation incurred in aid of insurrection or rebellion against the United States, or any claim for the loss or emancipation of any slave, but all such debts, obligations and claims shall be held illegal and void.

Section 5   The Congress shall have power to enforce, by appropriate legislation, the provisions of this article.

Amendment XV

[Ratified on February 3, 1870]

Section 1   The right of citizens of the United States to vote shall not be denied or abridged by the United States or by any State on account of race, color, or previous condition of servitude.

Section 2   The Congress shall have power to enforce this article by appropriate legislation.

CREDITS

Chapter 1:
p. 12 (image 1.1), The White House Historical Association
p. 22 (image 1.2), "Black Patriots During the Revolution," Varsity Tutors. Retrieved October 4, 2016 from https://www.google.com/search?q=jame+forten&source=lnms&tbm=isch&sa=X&ved=0ahUKEwi3pIqbysHPAhXq7YMKHRfyDGsQ_AUICCgB&biw=1280&bih=900#tbm=isch&q=jame+forten%2C+black+and+white%2C+image&imgrc=W9KJUBu0nsFW9M%3A

Chapter 2:
p. 30 (image 2.1) Elliot Erwitt/Magnum Photos
p. 44 (image 2.2) AP Images
p. 49 (image 2.3) "AP Photo #693150408 695." *AP Images*. 9 December 2014. Associate Press. Web 4 October 2016.

Chapter 3:
p. 63 (image 3.1) Bettmann/Corbis
p. 66 (image 3.2) "Obama Calls for Racial Understanding, Unity as Thousands Mourn S. C. Pastor," *Washington Post*. 26 June 2015. Retrieved 4 October 2016 from https://www.washingtonpost.com/politics/thousands-gather-to-mourn-the-rev-clementa-pinckney-in-charleston/2015/06/26/af01aaae-1c0c-11e5-ab92-c75ae6ab94b5_story.html
p. 68 (image 3.3) "Harry Belafonte #ZZZ003917-PP-RC1" Wolfgang's Vault. Retrieved 4 October 2016 from http://images.wolfgangsvault.com/images/catalog/detail/ZZZ003917-PP.jpg

Chapter 4:
p. 86 (image 4.1) Edney, Hazel Trice. "Dr. Ron Walters: 'Scholarly Grant,'" *Los Angeles Sentinel*. 17 September 2010. Retrieved 4 October 2016 from https://lasentinel.net/dr-ron-walters-scholarly-grant.html

Chapter 5:
p. 99 (image 5.1) "Melissa Harris-Perry on MSNBC" Retrieved 4 October 2016 from www.msnbc.com/sites/msnbc/files/styles/headshot—260tall/public/field_headshot_small/melissaharris-perry_s.png?itok=EBYtvLMu
p. 99 (image 5.2) "Dorian Warren at the Roosevelt Institute" Retrieved 4 October 2016 from http://rooseveltinstitute.org/dorian-warren/
p. 102 (image 5.3) "Legend: Ida B. Wells-Barnett, Journalist and Anti-Lynching Crusader" National Women's History Museum. Retrieved 4 October 2016 from https://www.nwhm.org/html/support/events/depizan/ida.html

Chapter 6:
p. 126 (image 6.1) Schomburg Center/Art Resource, NY
p. 133 (image 6.2) S.F. Examiner/AP Images
p. 140 (image 6.3) "John Brown, 1800–1859" The West, *PBS*. Retrieved 4 October 2016 from www.pbs.org/weta/thewest/people/a_c/brown.htm

Chapter 7:
p. 155 (image 7.1) Malet, Jeff. "Inside the D.C. Statehood Senate Hearings," *The Georgetowner*. 17 September 2014. Retrieved 4 October 2016 from www.georgetowner.com/articles/2014/sep/17/inside-dc-statehood-senate-hearing-photos/
p. 162 (image 7.2) Eve Arnold/Magnum Photos
p. 164 (image 7.3) Zeilinger, Julie. "Maria W. Stewart." *Identities.Mic*. 3 March 2015. Retrieved 4 October 2016 from https://images.mic.com/qhcestoueglge8

xiosoiud9tz6weiwycnpn9no98io8f0f7xzb4
8wbl2ztgnybfh.jpg

Chapter 8:
p. 175 (image 8.1) Bettmann/Corbis
p. 176 (image 8.2) Bettmann/Corbis
p. 187 (image 8.3) Photo retrieved 4 October
2016 from www.marketsmithinc.com/wp-
content/uploads/2013/02/Chisholm.gif

Chapter 9:
p. 214 (image 9.1) Brady, Mathew. "John
Mercer Langston." Library of Congress
Prints and Photographs Division. Brady-
Handy Photograph Collection. Retrieved 4
October 2016 from http://hdl.loc.gov

Chapter 10:
p. 234 (image 10.1) Getty Images/CQ Roll
Call/Meredith Dake
p. 241 (image 10.2) AP Photo/Ric Feld

Chapter 11:
p. 260 (image 11.1) Cecil Stoughton/LBJ
Library Collection
p. 280 (image 11.2) Gordon Parks/Getty
Images
p. 288 (image 11.3) Michael Bryant/MCT/
Newscom

Chapter 12:
p. 303 (image 12.1) Bettmann/Corbis
p. 321 (image 12.2) Collection of the
Supreme Court of the United States

Chapter 13:
p. 342 (image 13.1) Undated Photo "Mayor
Unita Blackwell" Retrieved 4 October
2016 from www.fannielouhamer.info/
blackwell.html

Chapter 14:
p. 366 (image 14.1) 1972 Photo "Johnnie
Tillmon," *Ms.* Magazine. California State
University Long Beach University Library,
Digital Repository. Retrieved 4 October
2016 from http://symposia.library.csulb.
edu/iii/cpro/CollectionViewPage.external;
jsessionid=02D6733D0B0C07699931838
383D1C94E?lang=&sp=1000076&suite
=def

Chapter 15:
p. 383 (image 15.1) Jacques M. Chenet/
Corbis
p. 385 (image 15.2) "President Obama and
Cuban leader Raul Castro shake hands
during a bilateral meeting at the United
Nations Headquarters on Sept. 29, 2015,
in New York City." 22 February 2016.
Retrieved 4 October 2016 from https://
www.studentnewsdaily.com/wp-content/
uploads/2016/02/RaulCastro-Obama-
820x512.png
p. 386 (image 15.3) Biography of Ralph
Johnson Bunche, UN Ambassador and
Recipient of the Nobel Peace Prize 1950.
Retrieved 4 October 2016 from www.
nobelprize.org/nobel_prizes/peace/laureates
/1950/bunche-bio.html

INDEX

Note: Page numbers followed by 'b', 'f', 'I' and 't' refer to boxes, figures, illustrations and tables respectively.